YPSILANTI PUBLIC LIBRARY

DEMCO
FOR REFERENCE
Do Not Take From This Room

A Dictionary of Slavic Word Families

YPSILANTI PUBLIC LIBRARY

A Dictionary of Slavic Word Families

Compiled and edited by
Louis Jay Herman

Ref
491.8
H

Columbia University Press
New York and London 1975

c. 1

Louis Jay Herman is senior translator in the English-language Translation Service, United Nations Secretariat.

Library of Congress Cataloging in Publication Data

Herman, Louis Jay.
A dictionary of Slavic word families.

Russian, Polish, Czech, and Serbo-Croatian entries appearing in that order in 4 parallel columns.
1. Slavic languages—Word formation. 2. Slavic languages—Dictionaries. 3. Dictionaries, Polyglot.
I. Title.
PG305.H4 491.8 74-13341
ISBN 0-231-03927-1

Copyright © 1975 Columbia University Press
Printed in the United States of America

A Dictionary of Slavic Word Families

Preface

A characteristic of the Slavic languages which impresses itself with particular forcefulness upon the English-speaking student is that they are, in the fullest sense of the term, vernacular tongues. Unlike English, which owing to historical circumstance has turned to foreign sources for most of its literary and specialized vocabulary, the Slavic languages have evolved from their basic store of native word-roots a vocabulary suited to all levels of discourse and capable of expressing abstractions and technical concepts in every field of human endeavor. This process of word-formation has, of course, been very largely a conscious one; many Slavic words are deliberate copies---loan-translations or "calques"---of Latin, Greek or German equivalents. Nevertheless, the result has been to endow the Slavic languages with a unity and coherence which English, with its successive overlays of French, Latin, Greek and other foreign words, does not have. Unless he is at least an amateur Latinist, the English speaker who uses an abstraction like the word coincide can make no associations between it and the concrete words of everyday speech; the meaning seems to have been assigned quite arbitrarily and must be accepted, as it were, on faith. To even a linguistically untrained and unobservant Russian, on the other hand, the equivalent word совпада́ть is immediately recognizable as a combination of three familiar words expressing the notion of "falling in together."

In compiling the present dictionary, the author has sought to afford a broad view of the vocabulary structure of the four major Slavic languages, Russian, Polish, Czech and Serbo-Croatian, by assembling all the significant words derived from 200 of the more productive roots occurring in those languages. The work is addressed, in the first instance, to students of the Slavic languages who wish to enlarge their vocabulary in the language or languages with which they are familiar or to take up the study of another. At the same time, it is the author's hope that Slavic specialists, and perhaps students of other languages as well, will derive pleasure and profit from contemplation of the extraordinary richness and diversity of the vocabulary which has evolved from these relatively few, for the most part monosyllabic, roots.

The basic scheme of the dictionary is a comparative one. The words in each root-group are set out in four parallel columns, the Russian, Polish, Czech and Serbo-Croatian entries appearing in that order. Words in the various languages which are morphologically identical, or virtually so, appear on the same line, regardless of meaning. (Under root ДЕРЖ [etc.], for example, Rus. держáва "power [sovereign state, country]," Pol. dzierżawa "lease," Cz. država "domain, possession" and S-C država "state [political entity]" are entered on the same line, since all are formed from the root by means of the same suffix.) Thus, by looking down the column the reader can view the entire range of derivatives formed from the root in the given language, while by looking across the line he can note any semantic differences that have arisen in the various languages in words which are morphologically the same. The order of words in the column is, generally speaking, as follows: primary root-word, derivatives formed by suffixation, compounds formed by union with other roots, derivatives formed by prefixation.

The semantic link between a given Slavic word and its root is sometimes so obvious as to require no explanation and at other times exceedingly tenuous and obscure. Since the meaning of a derivative formed purely by the addition of a suffix is generally not far removed from that of the root (see, for example, Cz. chodba "corridor; passageway," chodník "pavement," chodidlo "sole of the foot" < root CHOD "to go, walk"), it has not seemed necessary to present and define the vast array of suffixes in the four languages in tabular form. On the other hand, since prefixation normally produces a clearly defined change in meaning, a table of prefixes, indicating the various functions which each performs in combining with roots, is appended to this preface. The semantic basis of compounds, which are listed under both component roots (unless, of course, one of the roots is not included in this dictionary), can usually be clarified by determining the other root from the index of root-forms (or, where necessary, the partial index of words) in the back of the book. The primary purpose of the notes accompanying each root-group is to solve those problems relating to individual words which cannot be solved by reference to the meaning of the root, the table of prefixes and the indexes. The notes also identify and define the second root in compounds whenever it is not among those included in this dictionary. Finally, both in order to clarify the semantic basis of the words to which they refer and in order to place the over-all process of Slavic word-formation in broader perspective, they call attention to comparable instances of word-formation in other languages. A further auxiliary feature is the table at the end of this preface showing the consonant changes evident in the various forms assumed by the roots in the four languages.

Several principles have governed the selection of words for the dictionary. It was obviously neither possible nor desirable to include every word derived from a given root in the four languages. The fundamental aim has been, rather, to present all those words which are significant in themselves and/or illustrate a significant development in the meaning of the root. Words composed of prefix + root have, for example, been excluded if the meaning of the derivative reflects nothing more than the combined meanings of the two component parts (e.g. Rus. увозить, Pol. uwozić "to carry away" < у- [u-] "away" + root ВОЗ [WOZ] "to carry"). In the case of related nouns, adjectives, adverbs and verbs which are differentiated only by their functions as parts of speech (e.g. Rus. забáва "amusement," забáвный "amusing," забáвно "amusingly," забавлять "to amuse"), an effort has been made to select the particular word which (1) most clearly illustrates the semantic use made of the root, (2) constitutes the primary derivative, and (3) is most frequently used. (Needless to say, it has not always been possible to realize all three of these desiderata. In many cases, the most graphic and least cumbersome method of presentation has seemed that of omitting a primary verbal derivative with a multiplicity of meanings---e.g. S-C izdati "to publish; to betray; to spend; etc."---and illustrating its various meanings through the nouns and adjectives formed from it: izdanje "edition; publication," izdaja "treason, betrayal," izdatak "expenditure," izdašan "abundant.") Both aspects of verbs are given (the perfective and imperfective forms appearing in that order) if the differentiation of aspect is achieved by lengthening or otherwise altering the stem; where the perfective is formed by means of a prefix, only the imperfective form is shown. (Perfective forms which lack a corresponding imperfective or are listed separately for technical reasons are denoted by an asterisk [*], while verbs which are both perfective and imperfective take a double asterisk [**]. In the case of imperfective verbs which have a durative and an iterative form, the two appear in that order and are preceded by a dagger [†], as are those iteratives which are listed separately. Alternate forms of verbs are given in parentheses. Notes introduced by the perfective or durative verb of a perfective-imperfective or durative-iterative combination can be taken to refer to both forms unless the context indicates otherwise.) The vocabulary presented is, of course, essentially that of contemporary Russian, Polish, Czech and Serbo-Croatian; words that have wholly passed from use have been excluded, regardless of interest. At the same time, a place has been given to those archaic words and meanings which, chiefly because of their occurrence in the literary classics, continue to appear in standard dictionaries and may be presumed to be familiar to the educated native speaker of the language. Dialectal and most purely colloquial words and meanings have been omitted. Like all principles and rules, those outlined in this paragraph are subject to occasional violation. For the most part, such departures have been made in order to preserve the comparative feature of the dictionary; wherever a word in one language is listed for its intrinsic interest, its analogues in the other three languages are given as well for purposes of comparison, even though they may have no other claim to inclusion.

The root-groups are arranged in Latin alphabetical order, although the vagaries of phonetic development in the four languages make a completely consistent scheme impossible and a particular group can therefore be located most readily by referring to the index of root-forms. References in the notes are keyed to the first Russian root-form in the given group.

Serbo-Croatian words are given in the Latin "Zagreb" orthography.

TABLE OF PREFIXES

The table indicates the various forms which the prefixes assume in the four languages together with their more readily identifiable meanings. It should be borne in mind that in many words the prefix has lost its original force or performs such purely grammatical functions as transforming nouns and adjectives into verbs, forming perfective and transitive verbs, etc.

R	P	Cz	S-C	
без, бес	bez	bez	be(z), bes	without, -less
до	do	do, dů	do	to, toward; up to; before, prior (to); ---often expresses striving; reaching, attainment; addition; completion
из(о), ис	z, s	z	i(z)(a), is	out, ex-, e-; ---sometimes expresses exhaustion, deterioration; extraction, acquisition, obtaining
на	na	na, ná	na	on, onto; to; at, near; ---often expresses accumulation, amassing
над	nad	nad	na(d), nat	over, above, super-, sur-; up to; ---often expresses superiority; (act of) exceeding, surpassing
не	nie	ne	ne	not, un-, in-; ---negative, sometimes pejorative
об(о), оби, о	ob(e), obo, o	ob(e), o, ů	ob(a), op, o	around, about; all over; ---expresses surrounding, covering; sometimes error, failure, adverse effect
от(о)	od(e), ot	od(e), ot(e)	o(d)(a), ot	off, away; back, re-; ---expresses separation; undoing; opening; rejection, refusal; negation; return; reply, response

R	P	Cz	S-C	
по, па	po, pa	po, pů, pa	po, pa	all over; along; after; (sometimes in S-C) back, re-; ---expresses covering; distribution; imitation; inferior quality; adverse effect; inception; limited duration
под(о)	pod(e)	pod(e)	po(d)(a), pot	under, sub-; toward; ---sometimes expresses substitution or falsification
пра	pra	pra	pra	proto-, first
пере, пре*	prze	pře	pre, prije	over, across, trans-; super-, sur-; athwart; through; over, again, re-; ---often expresses transition, transfer, transformation; extreme degree, intensity; superiority; (act of) exceeding, surpassing; interruption, interference; alternation, reciprocity; error, failure
пред*, преди*	przed	před(e)	pre(d), prijed, pret	before, in front; before, prior (to); fore-, pre-
при	przy	při, pří	pri	to, toward; at, near; ---often expresses addition, attachment; adjustment; application (to); agreement, consent; incomplete, limited action
про	pro, prze	pro, prů	pro	through; by, past; forth, forward; before, prior (to); proto-, first; for (in some prepositional compounds); ---often expresses completion; thoroughness; loss; error, failure
против(о)	przeciw	proti	protiv(u), protu	against, anti-, contra-

*Of Church Slavic origin.

R	P	Cz	S-C	
раз(о)*, рас*, роз, рос	roz(e)	roz(e)	ra(z)(a), ras, raš	away, apart, in pieces; un-, dis-, di-; ---expresses separation, division; dissolution; undoing; spreading; distribution, arrangement; intensity
с(о), су	z(e), s(e), ś, są, su	s(e), z, sou	s(a), z, su	with, together, co-, con-
с(о)	z(e), s, ś	s(e), z(e)	s	off, away; down
у, ю*	u	u, ú	u	off, away; ---sometimes expresses negation; distribution, arrangement
в(о)	w(e), wą	v(e), u, ú	u, va*	in, into
вы	wy	vy, vý		out, ex-, e-; ---sometimes expresses exhaustion, deterioration; extraction, acquisition, obtaining
вз, вс, воз*, вос*	wz, ws, wś, wsz, wez, wes	vz(e)	uz, us, vaz**, vas**	up; upon; back, again, re-; ---sometimes expresses sudden inception, emergence
за	za	za, zá	za	(in) back, behind, beyond; ---often expresses motion up to a certain point, within a certain range; halting, detaining; blocking, closing; replacement; inception; (sometimes in S-C) error, failure

*Of Church Slavic origin.

**Of Church Slavic or Russian origin.

TABLE OF CONSONANT CHANGES

Russian

б is sometimes lost before н

в " " " after б

г alternates with ж and з

  is sometimes lost before н

д alternates with ж and жд

  is normally lost before л

  " sometimes " " н

з alternates with ж

  sometimes > с before т

к alternates with ч and ц

  is normally lost between с and н

с alternates with ш

  > з before д

ск alternates with щ

ст " " щ

т " " ч and щ

  is normally lost between с and л

  " sometimes " " р " н

х alternates with ш

ц " " ч

Polish

b is sometimes lost before n

c alternates with cz

ch " " sz and s

d " " dz " dź

  is sometimes lost between r and c

  " " " before ł

  > t before ch

g alternates with ż

  > k before k

k alternates with cz

  is sometimes lost between s and ł

  " " " " s " n

r alternates with rz

s " " ś and sz

st " " śc, ść and szcz

t " " c and ć

  is normally lost between s (ś) and ł (l)

  " " " between s (ś) and n

w " sometimes " after b

z alternates with ź and ż

ż is normally lost before st

zd alternates with ździ and żdż

Czech

b is sometimes lost before n

c alternates with č

d " " z

  is sometimes lost before l

h alternates with ž and z

ch " " š " s

k " " č " c

r " " ř

s " " š

š > ž before d

sk alternates with št

t " " c

v is sometimes lost after b

z alternates with ž

Serbo-Croatian

b is sometimes lost before *n*

  〉 *p* before *s*

č 〉 *dž* " *b*

ć alternates with *št*

d " " *đ*

  is sometimes lost between *r* and *c* or *č*

  " normally " before *l* or *o* (〈*l*)

  " sometimes " " *n*

  〉 *t* before *k*

g alternates with *ž* and *z*

  is normally lost before *k*

  〉 *k* before *č* or *š*

h alternates with *š* and *s*

k " " *č* " *c*

  is normally lost between *s* and *n*

l (when final in a word or syllable) often 〉 *o*

n 〉 *m* before *b*

s alternates with *š*

  〉 *z* before *b* or *d*

sk alternates with *št*

t " " *ć* and *št*

  is normally lost between *s* and *l*

  " " " " *š* " *m*

  " sometimes " " *r* " *n*

  " normally " " *s* " *n*

  " sometimes " before *st*

v " " " after *b*

z alternates with *ž*

  〉 *s* before *k* or *t*

ž 〉 *š* " *k* " *t*

ABBREVIATIONS

a.	adjective
acc.	accusative
act.	active
adv.	adverb
anat.	anatomy
arch.	archaic
astr.	astronomy
attr.	attributive use
av.	aviation
biol.	biology
bot.	botany
cap.	initial capital
Ch. Sl.	Church Slavic
chem.	chemistry
coll.	colloquial
comm.	commerce
conj.	conjunction
Cz.	Czech
Dan.	Danish
dat.	dative
dim.	diminutive
dir. obj.	direct object
Du.	Dutch
econ.	economics
elec.	electricity
Eng.	English
esp.	especially
_et al_.	indicates all words following the given word on the same line
(etc.)	indicates all other forms of the given root
fem.	feminine
fig.	figurative use
Fin.	Finnish
Fr.	French
gen.	genitive
geog.	geography
geol.	geology
Ger.	German
Goth.	Gothic
Gr.	(ancient) Greek
gram.	grammar
Heb.	Hebrew
hort.	horticulture
Hung.	Hungarian
impers.	impersonal construction
inst.	instrumental
intr.	intransitive
It.	Italian
Lat.	Latin
ling.	linguistics
lit.	chiefly literary usage
Lith.	Lithuanian
loc.	locative
log.	logic
masc.	masculine
math.	mathematics
med.	medicine
mil.	military
MLat.	Medieval Latin
mus.	music
n.	noun
naut.	nautical
NLat.	New Latin
nom.	nominative
Nor.	Norwegian
O	(before the name of a language) Old
obs.	obsolete
opp.	opposite
orig.	original(ly)
o.s.	oneself
part.	participle
pass.	passive
perf.	perfective
phil.	philosophy
phon.	phonetics
phot.	photography
phys.	physics
pl.	plural
pol.	politics
Pol.	Polish
Port.	Portuguese
pred.	predicate; predicative use
prep.	preposition; prepositional
pres.	present tense
prob.	probably
pron.	pronoun
punc.	punctuation
refl.	reflexive
rel.	religion
Rum.	Rumanian
Rus.	Russian
Sansk.	Sanskrit
sc.	scilicet (=following word understood)
S-C	Serbo-Croatian
sg.	singular
s.o.	someone
Sp.	Spanish
s.th.	something
Sw.	Swedish
tech.	technical
tr.	transitive
ult.	ultimately
usu.	usually
v.	verb
VLat.	Vulgar Latin
zool.	zoology
1	first person
3	third person
=	equals
>	becomes, develops into; source of
<	derived from
* (in the notes)	hypothetical form
* (in the word listings)	See Preface
**	See Preface
†	See Preface

БД, БОД, БУД, БУЖД, БЛЮ(Д)	BUD(Z)	BD, BED, BOD, BUD, BUZ, BOUZ	BD, BOD, BUD, BUĐ
бдеть (arch.): to be awake		bdíti: to be awake; to see (to), attend (to)	bdjeti: to be awake; to see (to), attend (to)
бди́тельный: vigilant		bdělý: vigilant	
бо́дрый: cheerful, spirited, lively		bodrý: genial, good-natured	bodar: cheerful, spirited, lively
бо́дрствовать (lit.): to be awake			
		bedlivý: careful, thorough; mindful	
буди́ть: to awaken (tr.); to arouse, stimulate	budzić: to awaken (tr.); to arouse, stimulate	buditi: to awaken (tr.); to arouse, stimulate	buditi: to awaken (tr.); to arouse, stimulate
			budan: awake; vigilant
буди́льник: alarm-clock	budzik: alarm-clock	budík, budíček: alarm-clock; (mil.) reveille	budilica, budilnik: alarm-clock
			budnica: (mil.) reveille
блюсти́ (lit.): to keep (order), observe (a law)			
[R]	[P]	[Cz]	[S-C]

наблюда́ть: to observe, watch; (за + inst.) to supervise			
побуди́ть, побужда́ть: to impel, prompt, induce	pobudzić, pobudzać: to arouse, stimulate; to impel, prompt, induce	povzbuditi, povzbuzovati: to encourage; to promote, foster	pobuditi, pobuđivati: to arouse, stimulate; to impel, prompt, induce
побу́дка: (mil.) reveille	pobudka: motive; (mil.) reveille		pobuda: motive; stimulus
соблюсти́, соблюда́ть: to keep (order), observe (a law)			
возбуди́ть, возбужда́ть: to arouse, stimulate; to excite; to incite; to raise (a question), present (a petition), institute (legal proceedings)	wzbudzić, wzbudzać: to arouse, stimulate	vzbuditi, vzbouzeti (vzbuzovati): to awaken (tr.; vzbuditi and vzbouzeti only); to arouse, stimulate	uzbuditi, uzbuđivati: to excite
[R]	[P]	[Cz]	[S-C]

NOTES

Basic meaning of root: to be awake

The Russian root-form БУЖД is of Church Slavic origin.

бдеть et al.: The corresponding Polish word has not survived.

bodrý-bodar: <Rus. бо́дрый.

буди́ть et al.: the causative form of бдеть et al.

блюсти́: The 1 sg. form is блюду́.

БЕГ, БЕЖ	BIE(G), BIEŻ	BĚH, BÍH, BĚŽ	BIJEG, BJE(G), BJEŽ
†бежа́ть, бе́гать: to run	†biec (biegnąć), biegać: to run	†běžeti, běhati: to run	bježati: to flee
бег: run, running; race	bieg: run, running; race; course (of time, events)	běh: run, running; race; course (of time, events)	bijeg: flight, escape
[R]	[P]	[Cz]	[S-C]

[R]	[P]	[Cz]	[S-C]
бéгство: flight, escape			
беглéц: fugitive			bjegunac: fugitive; refugee; deserter
бéженец: refugee		běženec: refugee	
	bieżący: current (a.)	běžný: current (a.); common, ordinary, usual	
бéглый: fluent; cursory, superficial; brief, fleeting; fugitive (a.)	biegły: fluent; skilful, expert		
бегýн: runner	biegun: trotter (horse); rocker (of a chair, etc.); (phys., geog.) pole	běhoun: trotter (horse); (carpet-, table-) runner	
	biegunka: diarrhea		
центробéжный: centrifugal			
	krwiobieg: circulation of the blood		
	obieżyświat: globetrotter		
		rovnoběžný: parallel (a.)	
		různoběžník: (math.) trapezoid	
			sredobježan: centrifugal
		světoběžník: globetrotter	
	współubiegać się: to compete		
избéгнуть (избежáть), избегáть: to avoid, evade			izbjegnuti (izbjeći), izbjegavati: to avoid, evade; to escape
			izbjeglica: fugitive; refugee
набéг: raid, incursion	nabieg (arch.): raid, incursion	náběh: start, approach (to a problem, etc.); assault	
	nabiegły: swollen	naběhlý: swollen	

[R]	[P]	[Cz]	[S-C]
		nadbíhavý: fawning, servile	
	obieg: circulation (of blood, currency)	oběh: circulation (of blood, currency)	
		oběživo: currency (money)	
		oběžnice: planet	
		oběžník: circular (letter)	
побéг: flight, escape; shoot, sprout			
		poběhlík: vagabond	
	pobieżny: cursory, superficial		
перебéжчик: deserter; turncoat		přeběhlík: deserter; turncoat	prebjeg, prebjeglica: deserter; turncoat
		předběžný: preliminary; temporary, provisional	predbježan: preliminary; temporary, provisional
		příběh: event, occurrence	
прибéжище: refuge; recourse, resort			pribježište: refuge
пробéг: run, running; race	przebieg: course (of events)	průběh: course (of time, events)	
	przebiegły: sly, cunning		
	rozbieżny: divergent	rozbíhavý: divergent	
		sběh: crowd, throng; concurrence, coincidence	
	zbieg: fugitive; deserter; concurrence, coincidence; confluence; crossroads	zběh: fugitive; deserter	zbjeg: refugee camp; refugees (collectively)
	zbiegowisko: crowd, throng		
			zbježište: refuge
		zběhlost: skill, experience	

[R]	[P]	[Cz]	[S-C]
		zběžný: cursory, superficial	
	zbieżny: convergent	sbíhavý: convergent	
		souběžný: parallel (a.)	
	ubiegać się: to strive, contend (for); to run (for public office)	*uběhati se: to become tired from running	
	ubiegły: past, last (year, etc.)		
убéжище: refuge; (air-raid, etc.) shelter			ubježište: refuge
	wybieg: subterfuge, evasion	výběh: pasture	
		výběžek: projection, protuberance	
забéг: heat (in a race)	zabieg: (medical) procedure, treatment, operation	záběh: trial run (of a vehicle or machine)	
	zabiegi (pl.): steps, measures; efforts		
	zapobiec, zapobiegać: to prevent, avert		
	zapobiegliwy: provident; thrifty		

NOTES

Basic meaning of root: to run

A number of the derivatives have semantic parallels among those listed under root TE(K) (etc.).

bieg-běh, bieżący-běžný: See note on Rus. ток et al., течéние and текýщий, S-C tečaj and tekući; regarding the second meaning of běžný, see note on Pol. potoczny.

бéглый-biegły: The various meanings reflect three basic ideas: "quick, speedy" (>"fluent, cursory, fleeting"), "running" (>"fugitive") and "widely traveled, experienced" (>"skilful, expert"); compare Eng. cursory (ult. <Lat. currere "to run"), Ger. geläufig "fluent" (<laufen "to run"),

bewandert "experienced, skilled" (<*wandern* "to wander") and *erfahren* "experienced, skilled" (<*fahren* "to go, travel"). See also *przebiegły* below.

biegun: orig. also "pivot"; the meaning "pole" represents semantic borrowing from Gr. *πόλος* "pivot; pole," whence Eng. *pole*. Compare Cz. *točna*.

biegunka: Compare colloquial Eng. *the runs*.

центробéжный: The first element is from *центр* "center"; see note on *sredobježan*.

krwiobieg: The first element is from *krew* "blood."

rovnoběžný: Compare Ger. *gleichlaufend* "parallel" (<*gleich* "even, level" + *laufen* "to run").

různoběžník: The first element is from *různý* "different."

sredobježan: See note under root СЕРД (etc.).

współubiegać się: See *ubiegać się* and note on S-C *stečaj*.

набéг et al.: Compare Eng. *incursion* (ult. <Lat. *in* "in, on" + *currere* "to run"), Ger. *Anlauf* "start; assault" (<*an* "on, at, to" + *laufen* "to run"), Cz. *útok*, *zteč*.

nabiegły-naběhlý: Compare Ger. *angelaufen* "swollen" (<*an* "on, at, to" + *laufen* "to run").

nadbíhavý: The underlying notion is that of eagerly running to meet someone in order to ingratiate oneself with him.

oběživo: Compare Eng. *currency* (ult. <Lat. *currere* "to run").

oběžnice: See note on S-C *ophodnica*.

pobieżny: See note on *бéглый-biegły*.

předběžný-predbježan: ="running (*i.e.* coming) before the final decision or action"; the word is modeled on Ger. *vorläufig* "preliminary; temporary, provisional" (<*vor* "before" + *laufen* "to run").

příběh: that which "runs to meet" a person, is encountered, comes to pass; compare Eng. *occurrence* (ult. <Lat. *occurrere* "to run to meet" <*currere* "to run").

прибéжище: Compare Eng. *recourse* (ult. <Lat. *re-* "back" + *currere* "to run"), Cz. *útočiště*, S-C *utočište*.

przebieg-průběh: See note on Rus. *ток et al.*, *течéние* and *текýщий*, S-C *tečaj* and *tekući*.

przebiegły: See note on Rus. *пройдóха*.

sběh, *zbieg*, *zbiegowisko*: Compare Eng. *concourse* in the archaic sense of "crowd" and *concurrence* (both ult. <Lat. *cum* "with, together" + *currere* "to run"), Rus. *стечéние et al.*; in Pol. *zbieg*, the prefix shows the contrasting meanings "off, away" and "with, together."

zběhlost, *zběžný*: See note on *бéглый-biegły*.

wybieg: Compare Ger. *Ausflucht* "subterfuge, evasion" (<*aus* "out" + *fliehen* "to flee").

výběh: Compare Rus. *вы́гон et al.*

výběžek: Compare Ger. *Auslauf* "projection, protuberance" (<*aus* "out" + *laufen* "to run").

zabieg, zabiegi, zapobiec: Implicit in all three words is the idea of action directed toward some end; compare ubiegać się.

zapobiegliwy: =given to planning ahead and taking timely action; see zapobiec.

БИ, БОЙ, БО(И,-Е)	BI, BÓJ, BO(I)	BI, BÍ, BOJ	BI, BOJ
бить: to beat, strike	bić: to beat, strike	bíti: to beat, strike	biti: to beat, strike
бич: whip	bicz: whip	bič: whip	bič: whip
би́вень: tusk			
			bilo: pulse; mountain ridge
	bitny: warlike; brave		
	bitka: fight, scuffle; trick (in cards)	bitka: fight, scuffle; skirmish	bitka: battle
би́тва, бой: battle	bitwa, bój: battle	bitva, boj: battle	boj: battle
	boisko: threshing-floor; athletic field		
бо́йня: slaughterhouse; slaughter, carnage			
бо́йкий: clever; brisk, lively			
боеви́к: hit (movie, etc.)			
братоуби́йство: fratricide	bratobójstwo: fratricide		bratoubistvo: fratricide
	bydłobójnia: slaughterhouse		
челоби́тчик (arch.): petitioner, supplicant	czołobitny: humble, servile		
			dvoboj: duel
	ludobójstwo: genocide		
матереуби́йство: matricide	matkobójstwo: matricide		
	mężobójstwo: homicide		
[R]	[P]	[Cz]	[S-C]

[R]	[P]	[Cz]	[S-C]
отцеуби́йство: patricide	ojcobójstwo: patricide		ocoubistvo, oceubistvo: patricide
			probisvijet: vagabond
самоуби́йство: suicide	samobójstwo: suicide		samoubistvo: suicide
доби́ться, добива́ться: to gain, achieve; (добива́ться only) to strive (for)	dobić się, dobijać się: to gain, achieve; (dobijać się only) to strive (for)		
	dobitny: clear, distinct; emphatic		
изби́тый: hackneyed, trite			
			izbojak: protuberance
наби́ть, набива́ть: to stuff, fill; to print (textiles)	nabić, nabijać: to stuff, fill; to load (a gun); (elec.) to charge	nabíti, nabíjeti: to stuff, fill; to load (a gun); (elec.) to charge	nabiti, nabijati: to stuff, fill; to load (a gun)
	nabój: cartridge; powder charge; electric charge	náboj: cartridge; powder charge; electric charge	naboj: cartridge; powder charge
			nabojit: compact, dense
			nadbiti, nadbijati: to defeat, vanquish; to surpass, outdo
	niedobitki (pl.): remnants (of an army)		
оби́вка: upholstery	obicie: upholstery; wall-paper; beating, thrashing		
			obijač: burglar, housebreaker
обо́и (pl.): wall-paper			
отби́ть, отбива́ть: to hit back (a ball); to beat off, repel; to beat (time)	odbić, odbijać: to hit back (a ball); to beat off, repel; to reflect; to print; to cast off, shove off (from shore)	odbíti, odbíjeti: to hit back (a ball); to strike, sound the hours; (arch.) to beat off, repel	odbiti, odbijati: to hit back (a ball); to beat off, repel; (math.) to subtract; to deduct; to reject, refuse;

			to reflect; to strike, sound the hours; to cast off, shove off (from shore); to disgust, repel
		odbíjená: volleyball	odbojka: volleyball
отбо́й: (mil.) signal to retreat		odboj: revolt, rebellion; resistance	odboj: rebound, ricochet
		odbojný: rebellious	odbojan: repulsive, disgusting
подби́вка: lining	podbitka: lining		
	podbój: conquest		podboj: floor of a stable
перебо́й: interruption			preboj, prijeboj: partition (wall)
прибо́й: surf		příboj: surf	
пробо́й: staple for padlock	przebój: hit (movie, etc.)		proboj: breach; (mil.) breakthrough
		průbojný: vigorous, energetic; (mil.) armor-piercing	probojan: piercing, penetrating; penetrable
разбо́й: robbery, banditry	rozbój: robbery, banditry		razboj: loom; parallel bars (for gymnastics); battlefield
разбо́йник: robber, bandit	rozbójnik: robber, bandit		razbojnik: robber, bandit
сби́вчивый: confused, inconsistent (reply, etc.)			
		souboj: duel	saboj: crowd, throng
уби́йство: murder			ubistvo: murder
	wybitny: outstanding, prominent		
вы́боина: dent; pothole (in road)	wybój: pothole (in road)	výboj: attack; aggression; (elec.) discharge	
	zbicie: refutation		
[R]	[P]	[Cz]	[S-C]

[R]	[P]	[Cz]	[S-C]
	zbój, zbójca: robber, bandit zabójstwo: murder	zbojník: robber, bandit	

NOTES

Basic meaning of root: to beat, strike

Many of the derivatives show the secondary meanings "to fight" and "to kill."

bilo: Compare Eng. pulse (ult. ‹Lat. pellere "to beat, strike"). The second meaning arose from the fancied resemblance of a mountain ridge to a wooden beam, the meaning "beam, log" (now obsolete) reflecting the notion of "an instrument for beating or clubbing."

bitka, би́тва et al.: Compare Eng. battle (ult. ‹Fr. battre "to beat, strike").

бо́йня: Compare Eng. slaughter (akin to Ger. schlagen "to beat, strike").

бо́йкий: orig. "pugnacious, combative."

боеви́к: Compare Eng. hit, Ger. Schlager "hit" (‹schlagen "to beat, strike").

братоуби́йство et al.: The first element is from брат-brat "brother"; compare Eng. fratricide (ult. ‹Lat. frater "brother" + caedere "to kill").

bydłobójnia: See note on бо́йня.

челоби́тчик-czołobitny: The first element is from чело́-czoło "forehead"; see Rus. бить чело́м "to beat one's forehead (by bowing to the ground)," an old expression suggesting submission or humble entreaty. The Polish word is borrowed from Russian.

dvoboj: Compare Ger. Zweikampf "duel" (‹zwei "two" + Kampf "fight").

ludobójstwo: Compare Eng. genocide (ult. ‹Gr. γένος "race, nation" + Lat. caedere "to kill").

матереуби́йство-matkobójstwo: The first element is from мать-matka "mother"; compare Eng. matricide (ult. ‹Lat. mater "mother" + caedere "to kill").

mężobójstwo: The first element is from mąż "man"; compare Eng. homicide (ult. ‹Lat. homo "man" + caedere "to kill").

отцеуби́йство et al.: The first element is from оте́ц-ojciec-otac "father"; compare Eng. patricide (ult. ‹Lat. pater "father" + caedere "to kill").

probisvijet: The first element is from probiti "to strike or break through; to wander, roam."

самоубийство et al.: Compare Eng. suicide (ult. ‹Lat. sui "of oneself" + caedere "to kill").

добиться-dobić się: ="to fight one's way (to s.th.)."

dobitny: orig. "final, decisive" (said of a mortal blow, etc.).

nabojit: See nabiti.

niedobitki: ="those not finished off, killed off."

обивка-obicie, обои: Compare Ger. Beschlag "covering, mounting, lining" (‹be- "[here =] around, over" + schlagen "to beat, strike").

odbić (third meaning)-odbiti (sixth meaning): Compare Rus. отразить, Cz.-S-C odraziti.

odbiti (fourth meaning): Compare Eng. rebate (‹Fr. rabattre "to knock down") and to knock (a certain sum) off the price, Ger. Abschlag "discount, rebate" (‹ab "off" + schlagen "to beat, strike"), Cz. odraziti and srážka.

odbiti (last meaning), odbojan: See note on Cz. odpudivý.

отбой: orig. "drum-beat."

подбивка-podbitka: See note on обивка-obicie, обои.

перебой et al.: In both cases, the underlying idea is that of "striking across," hence breaking, dividing.

przebój: See note on боевик.

razboj: In its first meaning, the word is descriptive of the manner in which the threads of the woof are brought together to form a fabric after being shot across the warp threads by the shuttle; the second meaning is an outgrowth of the first.

сбивчивый: ‹ сбиться "to be knocked down; to go astray, become confused."

saboj: ‹sabiti "to pound, push together."

убийство-ubistvo: Compare Eng. slay (akin to Ger. schlagen "to beat, strike").

wybitny: ="striking out, pushing forward."

výboj (third meaning): Compare náboj.

zabójstwo: See note on убийство-ubistvo.

БЛАГ, БЛАЖ	BŁOG, BŁAG, BŁAŻ	BLAH, BLAŽ	BLAG, BLAŽ
благой (arch.): good благо: welfare, weal, good	błogi: blissful; pleasant; beneficial błagać: to implore	blahý: blissful; pleasant blaho: welfare, weal, good; bliss	blag: gentle, mild blago: treasure; wealth; cattle
[R]	[P]	[Cz]	[S-C]

[R]	[P]	[Cz]	[S-C]
			blagovati: to eat; to live opulently
		blažiti: to gratify, gladden	blažiti: to soothe, allay; to moderate, mitigate; to dilute (wine)
			blagajnik: cashier
блаже́нство: bliss		blaženost: bliss	blaženstvo: bliss
		blahobyt: well-being, prosperity	
благочести́вый (arch.): pious, devout			blagočastiv (arch.): pious, devout
			blagdan: holiday
благодари́ть: to thank			blagodariti: to thank
благода́рный: grateful		blahodárný: beneficial	blagodaran: grateful
благода́тный: beneficial; abundant			blagodatan: beneficial
благоде́яние: good deed, benefaction			blagodejanje (arch.): scholarship (student's allowance)
благоде́тель: benefactor			
благоде́тельный (lit.): beneficial			blagodjetan: abundant
благоде́нствие (arch.): well-being, prosperity			
благоду́шный: placid, contented			blagodušan: good-natured
			blagoglasan: euphonious, melodious
благоле́пие (arch.): splendor, grandeur			
			blagonaklon: gracious, kindly disposed

[R]	[P]	[Cz]	[S-C]
благообра́зный: handsome			
благополу́чие: well-being, prosperity			
		blahopřáti: to congratulate	
благоприя́тный: favorable, propitious			
		blahořečiti: to be grateful (to); to praise	
благоро́дный: noble (a.); (arch.) of noble birth		blahorodý: honorable (title)	blagorodan: honorable (title); of noble birth
благоскло́нный (lit.): gracious, kindly disposed		blahosklonný: gracious, kindly disposed	
благослови́ть, благословля́ть: to bless	błogosławić: to bless	blahoslaviti: to praise	blagosloviti, blagosiljati (blagoslivljati): to bless
благосостоя́ние: well-being, prosperity	błogostan: bliss		blagostanje: well-being, prosperity
благотво́рный (lit.): beneficial			blagotvoran: beneficial
благотвори́тельный: charitable, philanthropic			
бла́говест (arch.): ringing of church bells			Blagovijest: (rel.) Annunciation
Благове́щение: (rel.) Annunciation			
			blagovjesnik: apostle; evangelist, preacher of the gospel
благови́дный: seemly; specious			
благоволи́ть (arch.): to show benevol-			blagovoljeti: to show benevolence, good

[R]	[P]	[Cz]	[S-C]
ence, good will; to deign, condescend			will; to deign, condescend
		blahovolný: benevolent	
благозву́чный: euphonious, melodious			blagozvučan: euphonious, melodious
благожела́тельный (lit.): benevolent			
	pobłażliwy: indulgent, forbearing		
ублажи́ть, ублажа́ть (coll.): to humor, indulge			ublažiti, ublažavati (ublaživati): to soothe, allay; to moderate, mitigate

NOTES

Basic meaning of root: good

The secondary meanings "blissful" and "gentle" are apparent in a number of derivatives. The root occurs in numerous abstract compounds as a prefix meaning "good" or "well" and often corresponding to Eng. bene- (<Lat. bene "well") and eu- (<Gr. εὖ "well"). (Compare the similar derivatives under root ДОБР [etc.] and the antonyms under root ЗЛ [etc.].)

The Russian root-forms and most of the individual words are of Church Slavic origin, as are many of the Serbo-Croatian compounds. (The native Russian root-form is found in ORus. бологo [=бла́го].) The Polish forms BŁAG and BŁAŻ are generally attributed to borrowing from Czech.

blago: The development of the notion of "goods, property, wealth" from that of "good" is found in many languages, e.g. Eng. goods, Fr. biens "goods" (<bien "well"), Ger. Güter "goods" (<gut "good"), Hung. javak "goods" (<jó "good"); see also Rus. добро́, Pol. dobra, S-C dobro. The meaning "cattle" represents specialization of the broader notion of wealth or property. The fact that cattle was one of the principal forms of wealth in early societies is widely attested linguistically, the semantic shift usually being "wealth" > "cattle" but occasionally proceeding from the particular to the general. See, for example, Eng. fee (related to Ger. Vieh "cattle," which retains the older meaning), pecuniary (ult. <Lat. pecus "cattle"), chattel and cattle (both ult. <Lat. capitale "property"), Sp. ganado "cattle," orig. "property" (<ganar "to gain, acquire"), Rum.

marfă "goods" (<Hung. marha "cattle"), Rus. скот "cattle" (related, either primitively or through borrowing, to Goth. skatts "money," Ger. Schatz "treasure"); compare also Pol. bydło and dobytek, Cz. dobytek, S-C stoka.

błagać: orig. "to soothe"; compare S-C blažiti.

blagovati (first meaning): orig. (and sometimes still) "to eat well, feast"; compare the second meaning.

blagajnik: <blagajna "cash-box"; see blago.

благочести́вый-blagočastiv: modeled on Gr. εὐσεβής "pious, devout" (<εὖ "well" + σέβειν "to honor, worship").

благодари́ть-blagodariti, благода́рный et al.: modeled on Gr. εὐχαριστεῖν "to thank," εὐχάριστος "grateful" (<εὖ "well" + χαρίζεσθαι "to give freely"); Cz. blahodárný is borrowed from Russian.

благодея́ние-blagodejanje, благоде́тель, благоде́тельный-blagodjetan: modeled on Gr. εὐεργεσία "good deed," εὐεργέτης "doer of good; doing good" (<εὖ "well" + ἔργον "work, deed"); compare also Eng. benefaction, benefactor and beneficial (all ult. <Lat. bene "well" + facere "to do"), благотво́рный-blagotvoran below, Pol. dobrodziej et al., S-C dobročinstvo.

благоде́нствие: modeled on Gr. εὐημερία "prosperity" (<εὖ "well" + ἡμέρα "day").

blagoglasan: See note on благозву́чный-blagozvučan.

благоле́пие: The second element is related to obsolete ле́пый "beautiful."

благополу́чие: modeled on Gr. εὐτυχία "prosperity" (<εὖ "well" + τύχη "luck, fortune").

blahopřáti: The second element is from přáti "to wish"; see note on S-C čestitati.

blahořečiti: orig. "to bless"; the word is modeled on Lat. benedicere "to praise; to bless" (<bene "well" + dicere "to say"), whence Eng. benediction. Compare Cz. dobrořečiti, which is formed on the same Latin model, and see note on благослови́ть et al.

благоро́дный et al.: ="well-born"; the words are modeled on Gr. εὐγενής "noble" (<εὖ "well" + the root of γίγνεσθαι "to be born"), whence Eng. eugenic. The use of the Czech and Serbo-Croatian words as a term of address follows the similar use of Ger. Wohlgeboren (<wohl "well" + geboren "born"). Cz. blahorodý is borrowed from Russian.

благослови́ть et al.: See note under root СЛЫ (etc.).

благотво́рный-blagotvoran: See note on благодея́ние-blagodejanje, благоде́тель, благоде́тельный-blagodjetan.

бла́говест-Blagovijest, Благове́щение, blagovjesnik: Blagovijest has also been attested in the meaning "gospel"; the words are modeled on Gr. εὐαγγέλιον "glad tidings; gospel," εὐαγγελισμός "Annunciation" and εὐαγγελιστής "bearer of glad tidings; evangelist" (<εὖ "well" + ἀγγέλλειν "to report, bring news"), whence Eng. evangel, evangelist.

благови́дный: See note under root ВИД (etc.).

blahovolný: See note under root $ВЕЛ_2$ (etc.).

благозву́чный-blagozvučan: The second element is from звук-zvuk "sound"; compare Eng. euphonious (ult. ‹Gr. εὖ "well" + φωνή "voice; sound"), blagoglasan above, Cz. libozvučný, S-C miloglasan, milozvučan.

благожела́тельный: The second element is from жела́ть "to wish"; see note on blahovolný.

БО(Г), БОЖ	BÓG, BOG, BÓ(Ż), BOŻ, BOSZ	BŮH, BOH, BŮŽ, BOŽ	BOG, BOŽ, BOŠ
Бог: God	Bóg: God	Bůh: God	Bog: God
божо́к: idol	bożek, bożyszcze: idol	bůžek: idol	
			Božić: Christmas
божество́: deity	bóstwo: deity	božstvo: deity	božanstvo: deity
божни́ца: icon-case	bóżnica: house of worship; synagogue		
бога́тый: rich	bogaty: rich	bohatý: rich	bogat: rich
			bogac: beggar; pauper; cripple
			bogočašće: worship; religious service
богаде́льня (arch.): almshouse, poorhouse			
Богоявле́ние: (rel.) Epiphany			Bogojavljenje: (rel.) Epiphany
			bogomolja: house of worship; synagogue
Богоро́дица: the Virgin Mary	Bogarodzica: the Virgin Mary	Bohorodička: the Virgin Mary	Bogorodica: the Virgin Mary
богосло́вие: theology		bohosloví: theology	bogoslovlje: theology
			bogoštovlje: worship; religious service
боготвори́ть: to idolize, adore			
		bohovláda: theocracy	
единобо́жие: monotheism	jednobóstwo: monotheism	jednobožství: monotheism	jednoboštvo: monotheism
[R]	[P]	[Cz]	[S-C]

многобо́жие: polytheism		mnohobožství: polytheism	mnogoboštvo: polytheism
		nazdařbůh: at random	
		neznaboh: atheist	neznabožac: heathen, pagan (n.)
спаси́бо: thank you			
	wielobóstwo: polytheism		
безбо́жие: atheism	bezbożność: atheism	bezbožství: atheism	bezboštvo: atheism
на́божный: pious, devout	nabożny: pious, devout	nábožný: pious, devout	nabožan: pious, devout
	nabożeństwo: religious service; piety	náboženství: religion	
	niebogi: miserable, wretched	nebohý: miserable, wretched	nebog: poor; miserable, wretched
	nieboszczyk: deceased person	nebožtík: deceased person	
	pobożny: pious, devout	pobožný: pious, devout	pobožan: pious, devout
убо́гий: wretched, shabby, paltry	ubogi: poor	ubohý: miserable, wretched; wretched, shabby, paltry	ubog: poor; miserable, wretched; wretched, shabby, paltry
	zboże: grain	zboží: goods, merchandise	
	zbożny: pious, devout	zbožný: pious, devout	
[R]	[P]	[Cz]	[S-C]

NOTES

Basic meaning of root: God; rich

Бог et al. is thought to have meant first "wealth, happiness, one's earthly portion" and then "he who distributes wealth and happiness, i.e. lord, master" (cognate Sansk. bhágas means both), whence ultimately the meaning "supreme being, God." The original notion of wealth is still apparent in the words бога́тый et al., zboże-zboží and (with the meaning transformed by negative prefixes) niebogi et al. and убо́гий et al.

Božić: a diminutive form of Bog; the literal meaning is "young god," i.e. (festival of the) Christ child.

bóstwo: for earlier bożstwo.

bogac: for ubogac; see ubog.

богаде́льня: See note under root ДЕ (etc.).

Богоявле́ние-Bogojavljenje: See note under root ЯВ (etc.).

bogomolja: The second element is from moliti "to pray."

Богоро́дица et al.: ="She who gives birth to God, i.e. Mother of God"; the word is modeled on Gr. ϑεοτόκος (<ϑεός "god" + τίκτειν "to bear, give birth to") and Lat. deipara (<deus "god" + parere "to bear, give birth to").

богосло́вие et al.: See note under root СЛЫ (etc.).

боготвори́ть: Compare Eng. deify (ult. <Lat. deus "god" + facere "to make").

bohovláda: See note under root ВОЛО (etc.).

единобо́жие et al.: Compare Eng. monotheism (ult. <Gr. μόνος "only, single" + ϑεός "god").

многобо́жие et al.: The first element is from мно́го-mnoho-mnogo "much, many"; compare Eng. polytheism (ult. <Gr. πολύς "much, many" + ϑεός "god").

nazdařbůh: See note under root ДА (etc.).

спаси́бо: See note under root ПАС (etc.).

wielobóstwo: See note on многобо́жие et al.

безбо́жие et al.: Compare Eng. atheism (ult. <Gr. ἀ-, negative prefix + ϑεός "god").

niebogi et al.: orig. "poor"; see introductory note above.

nieboszczyk-nebožtík: <niebogi-nebohý; Pol. nieboszczyk is for earlier niebożczyk.

убо́гий et al.: orig. "poor"; see introductory note above.

zboże-zboží: The root-meaning "wealth" is strengthened here by an infrequently occurring prefix meaning "good" (compare Rus. сдо́ба and сча́стье et al., Pol. zdobić and śliczny, Cz. zdobiti and sličný).

zbożny-zbožný: <zboże-zboží, but now assimilated in meaning to nabożny-nábožný, pobożny-pobožný; the word meant "happy" in earlier Polish usage, "rich" in Old Czech.

БОК, БОЧ	BOK, BOCZ, BACZ	BOK, BOČ	BOK, BOČ
бок: side	bok: side boczyć się (na + acc.): to shun, avoid; to be sulky (with), look askance (at) czworobok: quadrangle, square	bok: side	bok: side bočiti se: to quarrel
[R]	[P]	[Cz]	[S-C]

[R]	[P]	[Cz]	[S-C]
		levoboček: illegitimate child	
	wielobok: polygon		
			*izbočiti se: to project, protrude
	obok: near, beside		
	oboczny: adjacent		
		odbočka: branch office; branch line (of a railroad); digression	
побочный: secondary, accessory, collateral; (arch.) illegitimate (child)	poboczny: secondary, accessory, collateral; adjacent; illegitimate (child)	poboční, pobočný: side (attr.), lateral; secondary, accessory, collateral	pobočan: side (attr.), lateral
		pobočka: branch office; tributary (of a river)	
		pobočník: adjutant	pobočnik: adjutant
	ubocze: secluded spot; (arch.) slope, hillside	úbočí: slope, hillside	
	uboczny: secondary, accessory, collateral		
		vybočiti, vybočovati: to swerve, turn aside; to deviate; to digress	
	zboczyć, zbaczać: to swerve, turn aside; to deviate; to digress		
	zboczeniec: deviate, pervert		
		zabočiti, zabočovati: to swerve, turn aside; to digress	

NOTES

Basic meaning of root: side

boczyć się: Compare Pol. stronić, Rus. сторони́ться, Cz. straniti se.

czworobok: The first element is a combining form of cztery "four."

levoboček: The first element is from levý "left (opp. of right)." The term was originally applied chiefly to the illegitimate children of noblemen; for the meaning, see Eng. bar sinister (=bar + Lat. sinister "left"), a heraldic marking commonly (but erroneously) thought to denote illegitimate descent.

pobočnik: <Cz. pobočník.

ubocze: Compare Pol. ustronie et al.

vybočiti, zboczyć, zabočiti: Compare S-C zastraniti.

БОР, БР, (БОРОН), (БРАН)	BOR, (BRON), (BROŃ), (BRAN), (BRAM)	BR, BOR, (BRAN), (BRÁN), (BRAŇ)	BOR, (BRAN)
боро́ться: to struggle, fight; to wrestle	borykać się: to struggle, fight		boriti se: to struggle, fight
борьба́: struggle; wrestling			borba: struggle; battle
боре́ц: champion (of a cause); wrestler		borec: wrestler; athlete	borac: fighter, warrior
брань: abusive language; (arch.) warfare, battle	broń: weapon		
бра́нный: abusive (language); (arch.) warlike, martial		branný: military	
брани́ть: to scold, upbraid	bronić: to defend; to forbid	brániti: to defend; to prevent	braniti: to defend; to prevent; to forbid
	brama: gate	brána: gate	brana: flood-gate, dam
			branik: bulwark, rampart; bumper (on an automobile)
			branjevina: (forest, game, etc.) preserve
[R]	[P]	[Cz]	[S-C]

		domobrana (arch.): militia, home guard	domobranstvo: militia, home guard
			kišobran: umbrella
			padobran: parachute
		zeměbrana (arch.): militia, home guard	
оборо́на: defense	obrona: defense	obrana: defense	obrana, odbrana: defense
*поборо́ть: to defeat, vanquish; to overcome, surmount			
побо́рник: champion (of a cause)			pobornik: champion (of a cause)
возбрани́ть, возбраня́ть (arch.): to forbid	wzbronić, wzbraniać: to forbid	zbraňovati: to prevent; to forbid	
		zbraň: weapon	
забра́ло: visor (on a helmet)		zábradlí: railing; banisters	
	zabronić, zabraniać: to forbid	zabrániti, zabraňovati: to prevent	zabraniti, zabranjivati: to forbid
			zabran: (forest, game, etc.) preserve
[R]	[P]	[Cz]	[S-C]

NOTES

Basic meaning of root: to fight

The addition of a suffix to the basic root-form produced брань (and ORus. боронь "battle; obstacle"), broń, OCz. braň "weapon; defense" and OS-C bran "battle; defense" together with their derivatives, most of which show a secondary root-meaning, "to defend." (The further semantic development from "defend" to "forbid" parallels that of Fr. défendre, which also has both meanings.)

The Russian forms БР and БРАН are of Church Slavic origin.

borykać się: a Ukrainian loan-word which supplanted native bróć się (=боро́ться).

boriti se: formed from the root of earlier brati se (1 sg.: borem se), which is cognate with боро́ться.

borec: ‹Rus. боре́ц.

brama: a loan-word from Cz. brána which supplanted native brona.

branjevina: ="forbidden area"; see also zabran and compare Rus. запове́дник, зака́зник.

domobrana-domobranstvo: The first element is from dům-dom "house, home."

kišobran: The first element is from kiša "rain"; compare Fr. parapluie "umbrella" (‹It. parare "to protect, shield" + Fr. pluie "rain"), Ger. Regenschirm "umbrella" (‹Regen "rain" + Schirm "shield").

padobran: See note under root ПА(Д) (etc.).

pobornik: ‹Rus. побо́рник.

zbraňovati: prefix z- for orig. vz-.

zbraň: for earlier braň; the prefix in the modern word resulted from the influence of zbroj "armor; weapons" or (*zbrániti-)zbraňovati.

забра́ло-zábradlí: The basic idea in both words is that of defense, protection.

zabran: See note on branjevina.

БР, БИР, БОР, БЕР	BR, BIER, BIÓR, BIOR, BÓR, BOR, BRZ	BR, BÍR, BER, BĚR, BĚŘ, BOR, BŘ	BR, BIR, BOR
брать: to take	brać: to take	bráti: to take	brati: to pick, pluck; to gather, harvest
			birati: to choose; to elect
	braniec (arch.): prisoner of war	branec: recruit	
	branka: recruitment; (arch.) female prisoner of war		
брак: marriage			brak: marriage
	bierny: passive; (gram.) passive	berný: good, acceptable (as applied to money)	
		berně (arch.): tax	
	biernik: (gram.) accusative case		
			bora: fold, pleat; wrinkle
бре́мя: burden	brzemię: burden	břemeno, (lit.) břímě: burden	breme: burden
[R]	[P]	[Cz]	[S-C]

бере́менная: pregnant	brzemienna: pregnant		bremenita: pregnant
		březí: pregnant (said of animals)	bređa: pregnant (said of animals)
			brakolom, brakolomstvo: adultery
двоебра́чие: bigamy			
	gwiazdozbiór: constellation		
единобра́чие: monogamy			
	księgozbiór: library		
многобра́чие: polygamy			
новобра́нец: recruit			
	wodozbiór: reservoir		
безбра́чие: celibacy			
	dobór: choice, selection		
	doborowy: choice, select		
избра́ть, избира́ть: to choose; to elect			izabrati, izabirati; izbrati, izbirati: to choose; to elect
			izbirljiv: fastidious, choosy
			izbirak: scraps, refuse
избира́тель: voter			
			izbor: choice, selection; election
набра́ть, набира́ть: to gather, collect; to recruit; to set (type)	nabrać, nabierać: to scoop; to gain, acquire	nabrati, nabírati: to scoop; to gain, acquire; to gather into folds	nabrati, nabirati: to gather, collect; to gather into folds; to wrinkle (tr.)
[R]	[P]	[Cz]	[S-C]

БР

[R]	[P]	[Cz]	[S-C]
набо́р: recruitment; typesetting; composed type; set (of tools, etc.)		nábor: recruitment	nabor: fold, pleat; wrinkle
		naběračka: ladle	
недобо́р: shortage; arrears	niedobór: shortage; deficit		
	nieprzebrany: inexhaustible	nepřeberný: inexhaustible	
	obierać się: to suppurate, fester	obírati se: to occupy, concern o.s. (with)	
	obiór: election		
			odbirak: scraps, refuse
	odbiór: receipt (act of receiving); (radio) reception	odběr: consumption (of fuel, etc.); subscription (to a newspaper)	
	odbiorca: recipient; customer	odběratel: customer; subscriber (to a newspaper)	
	odbiornik: radio (receiving) set		
отбо́р: choice, selection		odbor: section, department	odbor: committee
		odbory (pl.): trade union, labor union	
отбо́рный: choice, select		odborný: specialized, technical	
		odborník: specialist	odbornik: committeeman
	pobrać się, pobierać się: to marry		
	pobór: collection (of taxes); recruitment		
побо́ры (pl., arch.): exactions, extortionate taxes	pobory (pl.): salary		

[R]	[P]	[Cz]	[S-C]
подобра́ться, подбира́ться: to approach stealthily		podebrati se, podbírati (podebírati) se: to suppurate, fester	
подбо́р: choice, selection			
	przedsiębrać: to undertake		
	przedsiębiorczy: enterprising, venturesome		
	przedsiębiorstwo: (business) enterprise, concern		
	przedsiębiorca: entrepreneur, businessman		
прибра́ть, прибира́ть: to tidy, put in order; to put away	przybrać, przybierać: to take more (of s.th.); to assume (a name, appearance, etc.); to adopt (a child); to adorn; to gain weight; to rise (water level)	přibrati, přibírati: to take more (of s.th.); to assume (a name, appearance, etc.); to call upon (for help); to gain weight	pribrati, pribirati: to gather, collect
прибо́р: instrument, appliance, device; (tea) service, (toilet, desk) set, (table) setting	przybór: instrument, appliance, device; (tea) service; rise in water level	příbor: (tea) service, (table) setting	pribor: (tea) service, (toilet, desk) set, (table) setting, (hunting) gear
пробо́р: part (in hair)			
разбо́р: (act of) sorting out; disassembly; analysis; trial, hearing; discrimination, fastidiousness; quality, grade (of goods)	rozbiór: analysis; partition, dismemberment (of a country)	rozbor: analysis	razbor: good sense, judgment
разбо́рчивый: legible; discriminating, fastidious			
разбира́тельство: trial, hearing			

собрáть, собирáть: to gather, collect; to gather into folds; to assemble (machinery); to equip (s.o. for a journey)	zebrać, zbierać: to gather, collect	sebrati, sbírati: to gather, collect	sabrati, sabirati; zbrati, zbirati: to gather, collect; to gather into folds; (math.) to add
собрáние: collection; meeting, gathering; (legislative) assembly	zebranie: meeting, gathering; (legislative) assembly		
	zbiór: (act of) gathering, collecting; collection; collection, anthology; harvest	sběr: (act of) gathering, collecting	zbir: sum, total
		sběř, sebranka: rabble, riffraff	
сбор: (act of) gathering, collecting; (financial) receipts, (crop) yield; duty, tax; (mil.) assembly, muster	zbór: (Protestant) church; (arch.) church council, synod	sbor: (diplomatic) corps, (teaching) staff, (fire) brigade; (Protestant) church; choir; (mil.) corps	zbor: meeting, gathering; (teaching) staff; choir; (mil.) corps; (mil.) assembly, muster; fair, bazaar
сбóры (pl.): preparations (for a journey)			
сбóрка: (act of) assembling (machinery); fold, pleat	zbiórka: collection, fund-raising; (mil.) assembly, muster	sbírka: collection; collection, anthology	zbirka: collection; collection, anthology
сбóрник: collection, anthology	zbiornik: reservoir; tank; receptacle	sborník: collection, anthology	zbornik: collection, anthology
собóр: cathedral; church council, synod	sobór: cathedral; church council, synod	soubor: collection; ensemble, troupe	sabor: (legislative) assembly; church council, synod
убрáнство: decoration; furniture; (arch.) clothing	ubranie: clothing; decoration		
[R]	[P]	[Cz]	[S-C]

[R]	[P]	[Cz]	[S-C]
убо́р (arch.): clothing	ubiór: clothing	úbor: clothing	
убо́рная: lavatory, toilet; (actor's) dressing-room			
убо́рщица: cleaning woman			
убо́ристый: close-set (type, handwriting)			
вы́брать, выбира́ть: to take out; to choose; to elect	wybrać, wybierać: to take out; to levy (e.g. taxes); to choose; to elect	vybrati, vybírati: to take out; to levy (e.g. taxes); to choose	
	wybierki (pl.), wybiórki (pl.): scraps, refuse		
		výběr: choice, selection	
		vyběravý: fastidious, choosy	
вы́бор: choice, selection	wybór: choice, selection; election	výbor: committee; collection, anthology	
	wyborowy: choice, select	výběrový: selective; choice, select	
вы́борный: elective (office); electoral	wyborny: excellent	výborný: excellent	
	zabór: conquest; annexation; annexed territory	zábor: occupation (of territory); annexation	

NOTES

Basic meaning of root: to take

Two widely occurring secondary meanings are "to gather, collect" and "to choose."

The original Indo-European meaning of the root, "to bear, carry," is preserved in бре́мя et al., бере́менная et al., březí-bređa. Compare cognate Eng. bear, Lat. ferre "to bear, carry" (>Eng. fertile, defer, offer, suffer, transfer), Gr. φέρειν "to bear, carry" (>Eng. euphoria, metaphor, periphery).

<u>брать</u>-<u>brać</u>-<u>bráti</u>: used as the imperfective forms of <u>взять</u>-<u>wziąć</u>-<u>vzíti</u> (<u>q.v.</u>).

<u>birati</u>: orig. an iterative form of <u>brati</u>.

<u>брак</u>-<u>brak</u>: ="a taking" (as husband or wife); compare <u>pobrać się</u> below. Both words are borrowed from Church Slavic.

<u>bierny</u>, <u>biernik</u>: The basic idea is that of "taking" (<u>i.e</u>. receiving, enduring) action instead of performing it.

<u>bora</u>: Compare <u>nabor</u> and <u>nabrati</u>.

<u>бре́мя</u>: a Church Slavic borrowing which has replaced the obsolete native form <u>бере́мя</u>.

<u>бере́менная</u> <u>et al</u>.: formed respectively from obsolete <u>бере́мя</u> "burden" (see preceding note) and from <u>brzemię</u>-<u>breme</u>.

<u>brakolom</u>, <u>brakolomstvo</u>: See <u>brak</u> and compare Ger. <u>Ehebruch</u> "adultery" (<<u>Ehe</u> "marriage" + <u>brechen</u> "to break").

<u>двоебра́чие</u>: See <u>брак</u> and compare Eng. <u>bigamy</u> (ult. <Lat. <u>bis</u> "twice" + Gr. <u>γάμος</u> "marriage").

<u>gwiazdozbiór</u>: See <u>zbiór</u>; the first element is from <u>gwiazda</u> "star."

<u>единобра́чие</u>: See <u>брак</u> and compare Eng. <u>monogamy</u> (ult. <Gr. <u>μόνος</u> "only, single" + <u>γάμος</u> "marriage").

<u>księgozbiór</u>: See <u>zbiór</u>; the first element is from <u>księga</u> "book."

<u>многобра́чие</u>: The first element is from <u>мно́го</u> "much, many"; see <u>брак</u> and compare Eng. <u>polygamy</u> (ult. <Gr. <u>πολύς</u> "much, many" + <u>γάμος</u> "marriage").

<u>новобра́нец</u>: The first element is from <u>но́вый</u> "new."

<u>wodozbiór</u>: See <u>zbiór</u>.

<u>безбра́чие</u>: See <u>брак</u>.

<u>izbirak</u>: Here the process of "taking out" is seen as one of discarding what is not wanted rather than---as in many other derivatives---one of selecting what is wanted.

<u>nábor</u>: <Rus. <u>набо́р</u>.

<u>недобо́р</u>-<u>niedobór</u>: ="that which has not been fully taken, collected"; compare Rus. <u>недои́мка</u>.

<u>nieprzebrany</u>-<u>nepřeberný</u>: <<u>przebrać</u>-<u>přebrati</u> in the archaic sense "to take all of (s.th.), exhaust, deplete."

<u>obierać się</u>: ="to gather, come to a head."

<u>obírati se</u>: orig. "to pick at (a bone, etc.)"; compare S-C <u>brati</u>.

<u>odbirak</u>: See note on <u>izbirak</u>.

<u>odbor</u> (Cz.), <u>odbory</u>, <u>odborný</u>, <u>odborník</u>: The original meaning of <u>odbor</u> was "field of activity"; the notion of specialization underlying the various meanings appears to be an outgrowth of that of "choice, selection."

<u>odbor</u> (S-C): ="a group of selected persons."

<u>pobrać się</u>: ="to take each other"; compare <u>брак</u>-<u>brak</u>.

<u>podebrati se</u>: See note on <u>obierać się</u>.

<u>przedsiębrać</u>, <u>przedsiębiorczy</u>, <u>przedsiębiorstwo</u>, <u>przedsiębiorca</u>: See note on Rus. <u>предприня́ть</u>, <u>предприи́мчивый</u> <u>et al</u>., <u>предприя́тие</u> and <u>предприним-</u>

áтель et al., S-C preduzeti and preduzeće.

прибрáть-przybrać-přibrati: The Polish and Czech words show semantic parallels with Ger. annehmen "to assume (a name, appearance, etc.); to adopt (a child)" (<an "to, on" + nehmen "to take") and zunehmen "to gain weight" (<zu "to" + nehmen). Regarding the meanings "to tidy" and "to adorn," see note on убрáнство-ubranie, убóр et al., убóрная, убóрщица, убóристый.

прибóр et al.: Regarding the last meaning of przybór, see przybrać. Otherwise, the basic meaning of the various words is "collection, set (of things used for some purpose)," whence the later application to one of the pieces comprising such a set; compare набóр above. The Czech and Serbo-Croatian words are borrowed from Russian.

пробóр: <пробрáть "to pierce, penetrate"; see note on Rus. пронять et al., проём and прóйма, Cz. průjem.

разбóр et al., разбóрчивый, разбирáтельство: Common to the various meanings is the notion of "taking apart," either literally (whence the meanings "sorting out," "disassembly," "dismemberment") or in the figurative sense of logically dissecting, scrutinizing, distinguishing (whence the meanings "analysis," "trial," "discrimination," "judgment"); the meaning "quality, grade" can be explained as "a distinction, differentiation," the meaning "legible" as "distinguishable." Compare Eng. analysis (ult. <Gr. λύειν "to loosen, dissolve, break up"), Cz. rozjímavý.

sběř, sebranka: ="collection"; see note on Rus. свóлочь.

сбóры: ="(act of) gathering oneself together"; see the last meaning of собрáть.

собóр-sobór: The Russian word is a Church Slavic borrowing modeled on Gr. συναγωγή "assembly; place of assembly; synagogue" (<σύν "with, together" + ἄγειν "to lead, bring"); the Polish word is borrowed from Russian.

убрáнство-ubranie, убóр et al., убóрная, убóрщица, убóристый: The various meanings result from the semantic progression "to take (i.e. put) away" > "to put in order, make tidy" > "to decorate, adorn" > "to clothe"; the original meaning of убóрная was "dressing-room." Cz. úbor is borrowed from Russian or Polish.

wybierki, wybiórki: See note on izbirak.

výbor (first meaning): See note on S-C odbor.

wyborny-výborný: orig. "choice, select."

БЫ, БУД, БАВ	BY, BĄDŹ, BUD, BAW	BY, BÝ, BUD, BUĎ, BAV	BI, BUD, BAV
†быть, бывáть: to be; (бывáть only) to happen	†być, bywać: to be; (bywać only) to happen	†býti, bývati: to be; (bývati only) to happen	†biti, bivati: to be; (bivati only) to happen
	bawić: to stay, sojourn; to amuse, entertain	baviti: to amuse, entertain	
	bawić się: to amuse o.s.; to play	baviti se: to amuse o.s.; to converse	baviti se: to stay, sojourn; to occupy o.s. (with), engage (in)
бытиé (lit.): existence	bycie: existence	bytí: existence	biće: creature, being; existence
бытьё (arch.): mode of life			
быт: mode of life	byt: existence	byt: dwelling, living quarters	bit: essence
бы́тность (arch.): stay, sojourn	bytność: stay, sojourn		bitnost: essence
		bytost: essence; creature, being	
	bydło: cattle	bydlo: livelihood, living; (arch.) dwelling, living quarters	
		bydliště: residence, domicile	
		bytelný (arch.): sturdy, robust	
былóй: past, bygone	były: former, erstwhile		
бывáлый: experienced	bywały: experienced	bývalý: former, erstwhile	
бы́вший: former, erstwhile			bivši: former, erstwhile
быль: fact; true story			
были́на: Russian folk epic	bylina: perennial plant	bylina: plant, herb	biljka, bilina: plant, herb
были́нка: blade of grass	bylinka: blade of grass	bylinka: small plant or herb	
			biljarstvo: botany
[R]	[P]	[Cz]	[S-C]

[R]	[P]	[Cz]	[S-C]
	bądź ... bądź: either ... or	buď ... buď: either ... or	
бу́дто: as if; that (conj. implying doubt concerning the statement that follows)		buďto (... [a]nebo): either (... or)	
бу́дущее, бу́дущность: future (n.)		budoucnost, budoucno: future (n.)	budućnost: future (n.)
	bawialnia: parlor		
	bawidełko: toy		
		blahobyt: well-being, prosperity	
	bydłobójnia: slaughterhouse		
		býložravý: herbivorous	biljožder, biljojed: herbivorous
	dobrobyt: well-being, prosperity		dobrobit: well-being, prosperity; welfare, weal, good
местопребыва́ние: residence, domicile			
			možebitan: possible
первобы́тный: primitive		prvobytný (arch.): primitive	prvobitan: primitive; original, initial
самобы́тный: original, distinctive	samobytny: independent	samobytný (arch.): original, distinctive; independent	samobitan: original, distinctive
	tubylec: native (n.)		
добы́ть, добыва́ть: to get, obtain; to mine	dobyć, dobywać: to extract; (arch.) to conquer	dobýti, dobývati: to extract; to mine; to get, obtain; to conquer	dobiti, dobivati (dobijati): to get, obtain; to conquer
	dobytek: property; cattle	dobytek: cattle	dobit, dobitak: profit, gain; advantage
доба́вить, добавля́ть: to add			dobaviti, dobavljati: to supply; to gain, acquire; to purchase

избы́ть, избыва́ть (arch.): to get rid of	zbyć, zbywać: to get rid of; to sell, market; to be left over, remain; to be lacking	zbýti, zbývati: to be left over, remain	izbivati: to be absent
		*zbýti se: to get rid (of)	
избы́ток: surplus; excess; abundance	zbytek: excess; luxury	zbytek: remainder	
	zbyt: too, excessively		
	zbytnik: scamp, rogue		
изба́вить, избавля́ть: to rescue, deliver; to rid, relieve (of)	zbawić, zbawiać: to rescue, deliver	zbaviti, zbavovati: to deprive; to rid, relieve (of)	izbaviti, izbavljati: to rescue, deliver; to rid, relieve (of)
	zbawienny: salutary, beneficial		
	nabyć, nabywać: to gain, acquire; to purchase	nabýti, nabývati: to gain, acquire	
	nabytek: acquisition; purchase	nábytek: furniture	
наба́вить, набавля́ть: to add; to increase (tr.)	nabawić, nabawiać: to inflict		nabaviti, nabavljati: to supply; to gain, acquire; to purchase
		nadbytek: surplus; excess; abundance	
	niebytność: absence		
	niebyły: null and void		
небыва́лый: unprecedented	niebywały: unprecedented	nebývalý: unprecedented	
небыли́ца: tall story, concoction			
		nezbytný: necessary	
		neodbytný: importunate, persistent	
[R]	[P]	[Cz]	[S-C]

[R]	[P]	[Cz]	[S-C]
незабу́дка: (bot.) forget-me-not	niezabudka: (bot.) forget-me-not	nezabudka (arch.): (bot.) forget-me-not	
	obyć się, obywać się: to manage, do (without); to content o.s. (with); to familiarize o.s., become conversant (with)		
	obycie (się): good manners, breeding		
		obydlí: dwelling, living quarters	
обыва́тель: Philistine; (arch.) inhabitant	obywatel: citizen	obyvatel: inhabitant; tenant, lodger	
обыва́тельский: Philistine (attr.), narrow-minded	obywatelski: civil; civic		
			ozbiljan: serious, earnest; serious, grave (situation, etc.)
отбы́ть, отбыва́ть: to serve (a prison sentence); to depart	odbyć, odbywać: to discharge (an obligation), serve (a prison sentence), complete (one's studies), hold (a meeting)	odbýti, odbývati: to discharge (an obligation), serve (a prison sentence), complete (one's studies), (lit.) hold (a meeting); to snub, spurn; to botch, do hastily; to sell, market	
	odbyć się, odbywać się: to take place	odbýti se, odbývati se: to take place; to content o.s. (with)	
	odbyt: demand, market (for goods); (anat.) anus	odbyt: demand, market (for goods)	
	odbytnica: (anat.) rectum		

отбáвить, отбавля́ть: to take away part of		odbaviti, odbavovati: to send, ship, dispatch; to attend to (a matter)	
	pobyt: stay, sojourn	pobyt: stay, sojourn	
	pozbyć się, pozbywać się: to get rid (of)	pozbýti, pozbývati: to lose	
	pozbawić, pozbawiać: to deprive		
пребывáние: stay, sojourn	przebywanie: stay, sojourn	přebývání (lit.): stay, sojourn	prebivanje: stay, sojourn
		přebytek: surplus; excess	
прибы́ть, прибывáть: to arrive; to increase (intr.)	przybyć, przybywać: to arrive; to increase (intr.)	přibýti, přibývati: to arrive; to increase (intr.)	pribivati: to attend, be present
	przybytek: increase; temple, sanctuary	příbytek: dwelling, living quarters; (arch.) increase	
при́быль: profit, gain; increase			
прибáвить, прибавля́ть: to add; to increase (tr.)			pribaviti, pribavljati: to supply; to gain, acquire
			probit, probitak: profit, gain; advantage
			probava: digestion
разбáвить, разбавля́ть: to dilute	rozbawić, rozbawiać: to amuse, entertain		
сбыть, сбывáть: to get rid of; to sell, market; to recede (said of water)			
сбы́ться, сбывáться: to come true, materialize			zbiti se, zbivati se: to happen
			zbilja: reality; seriousness, gravity (of a situation, etc.)
[R]	[P]	[Cz]	[S-C]

[R]	[P]	[Cz]	[S-C]
собы́тие: event			
сба́вить, сбавля́ть: to reduce, diminish			
убы́ть, убыва́ть: to diminish, decrease (intr.); to recede (said of water); to go away (on leave)	ubyć, ubywać: to diminish, decrease (intr.)	ubýti, ubývati: to diminish, decrease (intr.); to recede (said of water)	
убы́ток: loss	ubytek: loss; diminution, decrease	úbytek: diminution, decrease	
уба́вить, убавля́ть: to reduce, diminish	*ubawić: to amuse, entertain		
	wybawić, wybawiać: to rescue, deliver	vybaviti, vybavovati: to equip, furnish	
		zbytnění: (med.) hypertrophy	
	zdobyć, zdobywać: to gain, acquire; to conquer		
забы́ть, забыва́ть: to forget			
забы́ться, забыва́ться: to doze; to forget o.s. (in one's behavior)		zabývati se: to occupy o.s. (with), engage (in)	
			zabit: solitude, seclusion; solitary, secluded place
	zabytek: historical monument, relic		
забавля́ть: to amuse, entertain	zabawić, zabawiać: to stay, sojourn; to amuse, entertain	zabaviti, zabavovati: to amuse, entertain; to confiscate	zabaviti, zabavljati: to amuse, entertain; to detain
	zabawka: toy		

NOTES

Basic meaning of root: to be

A widespread secondary meaning is "to live, dwell." The original Indo-European meaning of the root, "to grow" (see reference to cognate Gr. φῦναι below), is preserved in bylina et al., былйнка et al.

The derivatives containing root-forms БАВ-BAW-BAV are causatives reflecting the basic meaning "to cause to be," whence the further semantic progression "to cause to remain, i.e. to detain" > "to occupy (with a task)" > "to occupy (with something pleasant), amuse, entertain." (The effect of the reflexive pronoun in S-C baviti se "to stay, sojourn" is to bring the meaning approximately back to that of intransitive biti; in the first meaning of Pol. [za]bawić, the causative force of the word has been lost.)

The primary verb быть et al. often acquires the sense of "to go, move" in compound formations. In combination with prefixes expressing the notion of movement toward (or, by extension, the idea of addition or acquisition), it forms derivatives with such meanings as "to arrive," "to increase (intr.)" and "to get, obtain, acquire" (whence also "to mine," "to conquer"); on the other hand, union with prefixes expressing the notions of movement away or deprivation produces such meanings as "to depart," "to recede," "to decrease (intr.)," "to get rid of" (whence "to sell") and "to lose." The corresponding causatives tend to show comparable semantic development; prefixes of the first type serve to form derivatives meaning "to increase (tr.)," "to add," "to supply, furnish," etc., while those of the second type give rise to such meanings as "to dispatch," "to reduce," "to rid, deprive" and "to rescue." (In a few instances, compounds of быть et al. are themselves causative in meaning; see notes on various individual words below.)

The present-tense forms of the primary verb are supplied by root ЕС (etc.).

The Slavic root is related to Eng. be, Ger. bin "am," Lat. fui "I have been" and futurus "about to be" (>Eng. future), Gr. φῦναι "to grow" (>Eng. physics, phylum, phytology, neophyte).

bawić-baviti, bawić się et al.: Rus. бáвить(ся) is obsolete or dialectal; the modern Czech verb is not primary but a recent formation resulting from loss of the prefix in zabaviti.

bit, bitnost, bytost: See note on Rus. суть.

bydło: The semantic development has been "dwelling" > "property" > "cattle"; see note on S-C blago.

bytelný: orig. "living, dwelling," then "lasting, enduring," finally "sturdy, robust."

bądź-buď, будто-buďto: from the imperative (the element то-to = "that, it"); regarding the meaning "either ... or," compare Fr. soit ... soit "either ... or" (literally, "be it ... be it"). The root-form is the same as that in бýдущее et al.

бýдущее et al.: formed from a present active participle which expresses future meaning; the origin of the root-form, which contains an original nasal vowel and a d-formant, has been variously explained.

bydłobójnia: See bydło and note under root БИ (etc.).

býložravý et al.: See bylina et al.

moźebitan: See note under root МО(Г) (etc.).

первобы́тный et al.: The first element is from пéрвый-prvý-prvi "first."

tubylec: The first element is from tu "here."

dobiti: The imperfective form dobijati arose as a result of confusion with the compounds of biti "to beat, strike" (q.v.).

dobytek (Pol.-Cz.): The original meaning in both languages was "something obtained or acquired," hence "property"; see dobyć-dobýti and note on S-C blago.

dobaviti: The sense of the word is "to cause (s.th.) to go"---either to another person ("to supply") or to oneself ("to gain, acquire").

избы́ть et al., избы́ток et al., zbyt: In these words, prefix and root have combined to produce both the transitive meaning "to get rid of" (see introductory note above) and the intransitive notion of "being out, away," whence the seemingly contradictory meanings "to be left over, in excess" and "to be lacking, absent." The Russian words are of Church Slavic origin. Regarding S-C izbivati, see note on Rus. отсýтствие and присýтствие et al., S-C odsustvo and odsutnost.

zbýti se: In this reflexive construction, zbýti acts as a causative verb, i.e. is synonymous with zbaviti.

zbytnik: orig. "a profligate, one given to luxurious living"; see zbytek.

избáвить: borrowed from Church Slavic.

zbawienny: ="bringing salvation and deliverance"; see zbawić and compare Eng. salutary (ult. from the same Latin root as save and salvation).

nábytek: The meaning was originally the same as that of Pol. nabytek; see nabýti.

nabawić: orig. also "to bestow, confer" but today always pejorative; compare the first meaning of S-C nabaviti.

nabaviti: See note on dobaviti.

niebytność: See note on Rus. отсýтствие and присýтствие et al., S-C odsustvo and odsutnost.

небыли́ца: Compare быль.

nezbytný: ="not left over or in excess, hence essential"; see zbýti.

neodbytný: See the second meaning of odbýti.

незабýдка et al.: See забы́ть; the Polish and Czech words are borrowed from Russian. Regarding the root-form, see note on бýдущее et al.

obyć się: ="to be (i.e. live, get along) with or without s.th."

obycie (się): ="knowledge of the world, savoir-vivre"; see the last meaning of obyć się.

обыва́тель: The semantic link between the original meaning and the present one is "(local) inhabitant, townsman" > "person with a limited outlook, Philistine."

obywatel: orig. "inhabitant"; the word is borrowed from Cz. obyvatel.

obywatelski: See obywatel and note on S-C građanin and građanski, Rus. граждани́н and гражда́нский.

ozbiljan: <zbilja.

отбы́ть et al., odbyć się-odbýti se, odbyt (Pol.-Cz.), odbytnica: Underlying some of the meanings is the idea of "being" (present in a place, engaged in an activity) for a given period of time. At the same time, the notion of carrying on an activity is difficult to separate from the causative meaning "to dispatch, dismiss, dispose of, send on its (or his) way" (compare the two meanings of odbaviti) which explains much of the semantic development of this group of words. The meaning "to take place" (="to be done, carried out") clearly shows odbyć-odbýti acting as a causative in a reflexive construction. Similarly, "to content o.s. (with)" (in effect, ="to treat o.s. in summary fashion, deny o.s. satisfaction") can be construed as the reflexive counterpart of "to snub, spurn."

odbaviti: Regarding the relationship between the two meanings, see preceding note and compare Rus. отпра́вить, Pol. odprawić, S-C otpraviti.

pozbyć się: See pozbawić and note on zbýti se.

pribivati: See note on Rus. отсу́тствие and прису́тствие et al., S-C odsustvo and odsutnost.

przybytek-příbytek: the product, in both languages, of the fusion of two originally separate words. The meaning "increase" derives from that of przybyć-přibýti, while the meanings "temple, sanctuary" (orig. "dwelling") and "dwelling, living quarters" reflect the replacement of earlier prze- by przy- in the Polish word and of OCz. přie- (=pře-) by pří- in the Czech word; compare przebywanie-přebývání.

pribaviti: See note on dobaviti.

probava: a process by which food is "passed through" the stomach.

разба́вить: See note on Rus. раствори́ть et al.

zbilja: <zbiti se.

vybaviti: The prefix here has the force of Eng. out in to fit out.

zbytnění: <archaic bytný, orig. "essential" (<byt in the earlier meaning "essence"; compare S-C bit), then "substantial, solid."

забы́ть: ="to go beyond, i.e. cease to have (in one's mind)"; compare Eng. get and forget (in which for- is a negative prefix), Pol. zapomnieć, Cz. zapomenouti.

zabývati se: variously explained as reflecting the notion of "forgetting oneself" in what one is doing (see Rus. забы́ться) or as a construction in which zabývati is causative, i.e. roughly synonymous with zabavovati (first meaning).

zabit: orig. "forgetfulness, oblivion"; see Rus. забы́ть.

zabytek: a survival or reminder of a bygone way of life; see byt.

zabaviti (Cz., second meaning): Compare the second meaning of S-C zabaviti.

ХОД, ХОЖ, ХАЖ, ХОЖД, Ш(Е)(Д)	CHOD(Z), CHÓD, CHODŹ, CHADZ, SZ	CHOD, CHŮD, CHOZ, CHŮZ, CHÁZ, Š	HO(D), Š(A)
†ходи́ть: to go, walk	†chodzić: to go, walk	†choditi: to go, walk	hoditi (hodati): to walk, go on foot
ход: motion; course (of events); entrance (place of entry); passageway; move (e.g. in chess)	chód: gait, pace; motion	chod: gait, pace; motion; dish, course	hod: gait, pace; motion
ходьба́: (act of) walking		chodba: corridor; passageway	
		chůze: (act of) walking; gait, pace	
	chodnik: pavement	chodník: pavement	hodnik: corridor; passageway
		chodidlo: sole of the foot	
ходу́ли (pl.): stilts		chůdy (pl.): stilts	hodulje (pl.): stilts
ходу́льный: stilted, high-flown			
хода́тай (arch.): agent, legal representative			
хода́тайство: application, petition			
			hodočasnik: pilgrim
хо́дкий: salable, selling well; fast (boat, etc.)	chodliwy: salable, selling well		
ше́ствие: procession			
[R]	[P]	[Cz]	[S-C]

			dobrodošao: welcome (a.)
йноходь: amble (horse's gait)	jednochoda, jednochód: amble (horse's gait)	jinochod: amble (horse's gait)	
местонахожде́ние: location, whereabouts			
		mimochod: amble (horse's gait)	mimohod: march-past, military review
мимохо́дом: while passing by; incidentally, en passant	mimochodem: incidentally, en passant	mimochodem: incidentally, en passant	
мореходство (arch.): navigation; seafaring			
парохо́д: steamboat			
путеше́ствие: journey			
самохо́д: self-propelled machine, gun, etc.	samochód: automobile		
снисходи́тельный: lenient, forbearing; condescending			snishodljiv: lenient, forbearing; condescending
судохо́дство: navigation			
сумасше́дший: mad, insane; madman			
безвы́ходный: hopeless, desperate (situation, etc.)	bezwyjściowy: hopeless, desperate (situation, etc.)	bezvýchodný: hopeless, desperate (situation, etc.)	
дохо́д: income	dochód: income	důchod: income; pension	dohodak: income
	dochodzenie: investigation		
дохо́дчивый: intelligible, easy to understand			
			došljak: newcomer
[R]	[P]	[Cz]	[S-C]

[R]	[P]	[Cz]	[S-C]
исхо́д: result, outcome; end (e.g. of the day)			ishod: exit, (act of) going out; exit, egress, way out; result, outcome; rise, rising (esp. of the sun); (arch.) east
			iznahoditi: to invent; to discover
находи́ть: to find	nachodzić: to invade; to importune	nacházeti: to find	nahoditi: to find
нахо́дчивый: resourceful, clever			
			nahoče, nahod: foundling
наше́ствие (lit.): invasion	najście: invasion		
			našastar: inventory
		nedochůdče: prematurely born child; puny, stunted creature	
необходи́мый: necessary			neophodan: urgent, indispensable
обходи́ться: to manage, make do (with); to manage, do (without); to cost; (с + inst.) to treat, behave (toward)	obchodzić się: to manage, make do (with); to manage, do (without); (z + inst.) to treat, behave (toward); (z + inst.) to handle (e.g. a tool)		ophoditi se (s + inst.): to treat, behave (toward)
обходи́тельный: courteous, affable			ophodljiv: courteous, affable
обхо́д: round (postman's, sentry's, etc.); circuitous route; evasion	obchód: round (postman's, sentry's, etc.); celebration, observance	obchod: trade, commerce, business; store, shop	ophod: procession
обихо́д: general use, currency			

[R]	[P]	[Cz]	[S-C]
		obchodnice: merchant woman, businesswoman	ophodnica: planet
отхо́ды (pl.): (industrial) waste materials	odchody (pl.): excrement		
отхо́дная: prayer for the dying			
отше́льник: hermit			
похо́д: march; campaign; hike	pochód: march; procession	pochod: march; procession; process	pohod: visit; march; campaign; raid, incursion
похо́дка: gait, pace		pochůzka: errand	
похожде́ние: adventure	pochodzenie: origin		
	pochodnia: torch	pochodeň: torch	
похо́жий: like, resembling			
по́шлый: commonplace, banal		pošlý: dead (said of animals)	
по́шлина: (customs, etc.) duty			pošalina: typhus
			pošast: epidemic
		poschodí: floor, story	
подхо́д: approach (to a place; to a problem)	podchód: (military) approach route; deerstalking	podchod: underpass	
подходя́щий: proper, suitable			
	podejście: approach (to a place; to a problem); trick, stratagem, deceit		
перехо́дный: transitional; (gram.) transitive	przechodni: connecting (rooms, etc.); (gram.) transitive	přechodný: transitory, temporary; transitional; (gram.) transitive	

[R]	[P]	[Cz]	[S-C]
преходя́щий: transient, ephemeral	przejściowy: transitional; transitory, temporary		
превосходи́ть: to surpass, exceed			
превосхо́дный: excellent; (gram.) superlative			prevashodan: excellent
Превосходи́тельство: Excellency (title)			
		předcházející, (lit.) předchozí: previous, preceding	prethodan: previous, preceding; preliminary
		předchůdce: predecessor; forerunner, precursor	prethodnik: predecessor; forerunner, precursor
		předešlý: previous, preceding	
предше́ственник: predecessor; forerunner, precursor			predšasnik: predecessor; forerunner, precursor
приходи́ться: to fit; to fall (on a certain day); to be necessary; to fall to (s.o.'s) lot; to be related, kin			
прихо́д: arrival; (monetary) receipts; parish	przychód: (monetary) receipts	příchod: arrival	prihod: income
	przychodzień: newcomer	příchozí: newcomer	
	przychodnia: clinic, dispensary		
прише́ствие: Advent, Coming (of Christ); (arch.) arrival	przyjście: arrival		
прише́лец: newcomer			
	przyszłość: future (n.)		

[R]	[P]	[Cz]	[S-C]
		příští: next; future (a.); (arch.) future (n.)	
			pridošlica: newcomer
прохо́жий: passerby	przechodzień: passerby		
проходи́мец (coll.): scoundrel			
			prođa: sale
	przeszło: more than, over		
про́шлое, проше́дшее: past (n.)	przeszłość: past (n.)		prošlost: past (n.)
происхожде́ние: origin			
происше́ствие: event, occurrence			
		protichůdný: antagonistic, conflicting	
расхо́д: expense, expenditure	rozchód: expense, expenditure	rozchod: separation, parting; gauge (distance be-tween rails)	rashod, rashodak: expense, expenditure
расхожде́ние: divergence (of opinion, etc.)			
		schůze: meeting, gathering	
схо́дка (arch.): meeting, gathering	schadzka: meeting, appointment, rendezvous	schůzka: meeting, appointment, rendezvous	
		schodek: deficit	
			shodište: (social, etc.) club
схо́дни (pl.): gangway, gangplank	schodnie (pl.): gangway, gangplank		
схо́дный: simi-lar; (coll.) reasonable (e.g. price)			shodan: proper, suitable; reasonable (e.g. price)

	zeszły: last, past (week, etc.)	sešlý: decrepit; shabby	
уха́живать (за + inst.): to nurse; to tend, look (after); to woo, court			
		ucházeti se (o + acc.): to compete (for); to apply (for a job, etc.); to woo, court	
	uchodźca: refugee		
вход: entrance, entry (act of entering); entrance (place of entry)	wchód: entrance, entry (act of entering); entrance (place of entry)	vchod: entrance, entry (act of entering); entrance (place of entry)	
	wejście: entrance, entry (act of entering); entrance (place of entry)		
			uhoda: spy
вы́ход: exit, (act of) going out; exit, egress, way out; way out, escape (from a situation); output	wychód: exit, (act of) going out; exit, egress, way out	východ: east; rise, rising (esp. of the sun); exit, (act of) going out; exit, egress, way out	
	wychodek: lavatory, toilet		
вы́ходка: trick, prank			
вы́ходец: immigrant; one who has changed from one social class to another	wychodźca: emigrant		
	wyjście: exit, (act of) going out; exit, egress, way out; way out, escape (from a situation)		
[R]	[P]	[Cz]	[S-C]

[R]	[P]	[Cz]	[S-C]
восхóд: rise, rising (esp. of the sun)	wschód: east; rise, rising (esp. of the sun)		
всхóды (pl.): shoots, sprouts	schody (pl.): stairs, staircase	schody (pl.): stairs, staircase	
захóд: setting (of the sun); stop, call, visit	zachód: west; setting (of the sun); trouble, bother, effort	záchod: lavatory, toilet	zahod: setting (of the sun); lavatory, toilet
	zajście: incident; stop, call, visit	zášť, (lit.) zášti: hatred	

NOTES

Basic meaning of root: to go, walk

Except in the case of S-C hoditi (hodati), the verbs formed from this root serve to translate Eng. go where the goer is on foot. (Compare root ЕХ [etc.].) The root supplies the imperfective counterparts of Russian, Polish and Czech compound verbs derived from root И(Д) (etc.); in Serbo-Croatian that function has been taken over by root ЛЕЗ (etc.), although many of the old imperfectives in HOD still exist.

The Common Slavic root-form *ŠЬD, showing palatalization of the initial consonant, has produced various suppletive forms of the verbs from И(Д) (etc.): (1) the past tense (e.g. 3 sg. masc. шёл, szedł, šel, [je] išao) and the participial derivatives below in ШЕЛ-ШЛ---SZŁ---ŠL---ŠAO-ŠAL-ŠL (<*ŠЬDLЪ); (2) the past active participle exemplified by Rus. прошéдшее and сумасшéдший; (3) verbal nouns (and derivatives from them) containing the forms ШЕСТ---JŚC---ŠT---ŠAS(T) (<*ŠЬDT).

The Russian root-form ХОЖД is of Church Slavic origin.

A non-Slavic cognate is Gr. ὁδός "way, path" (>Eng. episode, exodus, method, period, synod).

ходúть-chodzić-choditi: See note on Rus. идтú et al.

ходáтай: ="one who walks (on behalf of his client)"; the word is borrowed from Church Slavic.

hodočasnik: a back-formation from obsolete hodočastvo "travel," which was formed with the aid of the suffix -stvo from a word meaning "walker"; the present meaning of hodočasnik resulted from the mistaken belief that it contained čast "honor" (q.v.) as its second element and therefore properly referred to one who made a journey for reasons of religious piety.

шéствие: borrowed from Church Slavic.

dobrodošao: Compare Eng. welcome (in which the first element is, however, derived from *will* "wish, desire" although influenced by the word *well*), Fr. *bienvenu* "welcome" (<*bien* "well" + *venu* "come").

и́ноходь et al.: The literal meaning is "single gait," which characterizes the manner in which an ambling horse raises first both of its left feet, then both of its right feet off the ground. (Compare Eng. *single-foot*, an alternative term for *amble*.) The Russian and Czech words (and obsolete Pol. *inochoda*) show the original meaning of root ИН (etc.), *i.e*. "one." (The Czech word is, however, a relatively recent borrowing from Russian and Polish; see note on *mimochod*.)

местонахожде́ние: See *находи́ться* "to be found, be (in a given place)."

mimochod: corrupted, through popular association with the word *mimo* "past, by" (*q.v*.), from presumed earlier **jinochod*; see note on *и́ноходь et al*.

мореxо́дство: The first element is from *мо́ре* "sea."

парохо́д: The first element is from *пар* "steam."

снисходи́тельный- *snishodljiv*: (*с*)*нис*-, (*s*)*nis*- = "down"; in the case of the Slavic words as in that of Eng. *condescending*, the notion of "descending" to another person's level, *i.e*. showing forbearance and understanding, ultimately acquired overtones of haughty, patronizing behavior.

судохо́дство: The first element is from *су́дно* "ship."

сумасше́дший: See note under root УМ (etc.).

безвы́ходный et al.: See the third meaning of *вы́ход* and *wyjście*; in its present meaning (as distinct from the original meaning, "having no exit"), the Czech word shows semantic borrowing from Russian.

dochodzenie: See note on Pol. *dociekanie*.

дохо́дчивый: The underlying idea is that something which is readily comprehensible "reaches, gets to" a person.

ishod: See note on *wschód*.

iznahoditi: See *nahoditi* and compare Eng. *invent* (ult. <Lat. *invenire* "to find"), Ger. *erfinden* "to invent" (<*er*- "out" + *finden* "to find"), Rus. *изобрести́*.

находи́ть-*nacházeti*-*nahoditi*: ="to come upon"; compare Lat. *invenire* "to find" (<*in* "in, on" + *venire* "to come") and see notes on *iznahoditi* and *našastar*.

нахо́дчивый: Compare Ger. *findig* "resourceful, clever" (<*finden* "to find").

nahoče: <**nahodče*.

našastar: ="a list of things found"; the word is modeled on Lat. *inventarium* "inventory" (<*invenire* "to find").

nedochůdče: ="a child which has not gone all the way"; compare Rus. *недоно́сок et al*.

необходи́мый- *neophodan*: ="not to be gone around, *i.e*. avoided"; the words are modeled on Ger. *unumgänglich* "indispensable" (<*un*- "un-, not" + *um* "around" + *Gang* "[act of] going").

обходи́ться et al., обходи́тельный-ophodljiv: In these words the basic notion of "going around" has undergone considerable semantic elaboration. The meaning "to manage with, without" (whence, by extension, "to cost," i.e. "to be manageable, feasible for a price") has a parallel in the similar use of Eng. to get along. Underlying the meanings "to treat, behave toward," "courteous, affable" and "to handle (a tool)" is the general notion of "dealing with (s.o. or s.th.)"; comparable development is shown by Ger. umgehen mit "to associate, have dealings with; to treat, behave toward; to handle (a tool)" (<um "around" + gehen "to go" + mit "with"), umgänglich "sociable" (<um + Gang "[act of] going"). See also Rus. обраща́ться.

obchód (second meaning): from the earlier meaning "procession."

obchod: The original reference was to a peddler's house-to-house rounds.

обихо́д: orig. "intercourse, dealings; household; property"; see note on обходи́ться et al., обходи́тельный-ophodljiv.

ophodnica: Compare Eng. planet (ult. <Gr. πλανᾶσθαι "to wander"), Ger. Wandelstern "planet" (<wandeln "to wander" + Stern "star"), Cz. oběžnice.

похожде́ние: orig. "wandering, travel."

pochodzenie: See note on происхожде́ние.

pochodnia-pochodeň: orig. "light carried in a nocturnal procession."

похо́жий: <походи́ть (на + acc.) "to resemble"; compare Eng. to take after (one's father, etc.), in which take is an intransitive verb with the meaning "to go," and see Pol. wdać się.

по́шлый: orig. "having come down (from antiquity), i.e. traditional," then "customary, usual," finally "commonplace" in a pejorative sense.

pošlý: ="gone, vanished."

по́шлина: orig. "ancient custom," then "customary tax"; compare Eng. customs and see note on по́шлый.

pošalina, pošast: a disease which is "going" (i.e. prevalent, widespread) in a given area; compare Hung. járvány "epidemic" (<járni "to go").

подходя́щий: ="approaching, coming close," hence "suited (to a purpose), fitting."

перехо́дный et al., преходя́щий-przejściowy: Underlying the various meanings is the idea of "going across, passing"; thus, "transitional" = "pertaining to a passage from one state or condition to another," "transitive" = "expressing verbal action which 'passes' from a subject to an object," "transitory, transient" = "passing away, not enduring." Compare Eng. transi(tional, -tive, -tory, -ent) (ult. <Lat. trans "over, across" + ire "to go"), S-C prelazan, prijelazan, prolazan.

превосходи́ть: Compare Eng. surpass (<Fr. surpasser < sur "over" + passer "to pass"), exceed (ult. <Lat. ex "out; [here=] beyond" + cedere "to go").

prevashodan: <Rus. превосхо́дный.

predšasnik: <Rus. предше́ственник.

приходи́ться: The underlying meaning is "to come, happen," hence "to come at the right time, be opportune, fitting, proper"; regarding the further semantic progression to the notion of necessity, compare It. occorrere "to be necessary" (<Lat. occurrere "to meet, come up to; to occur, happen").

прихо́д (third meaning): orig. "a coming together, meeting."

przychodnia: ="a place to which one comes, which one visits."

przyszłość, příští: Compare Fr. avenir "future (n.)" (<à "to" + venir "to come"), Ger. Zukunft "future (n.)" (<zu "to" + kommen "to come").

проходи́мец: See note on Rus. пройдо́ха.

prođa: <earlier prohođa < prohoditi "to go by, pass; to sell (intr.) well."

происхожде́ние: Compare Eng. provenance (ult. <Lat. pro- "forth" + venire "to come"), Ger. Herkunft "origin" (<her "hither" + kommen "to come").

происше́ствие: Compare Eng. event (ult. <Lat. e "out" + venire "to come"), Ger. Vorkommnis "event, occurrence" (<vor "forth" + kommen "to come").

schodek: that which "goes off, away," i.e. falls short, is missing.

shodište: ="meeting-place."

схо́дный-shodan: ="going together"; the Serbo-Croatian word originally meant "conforming, corresponding." Regarding the shift in meaning, see the introductory note on root ЛИК (etc.).

sešlý: The underlying idea is that of going down, declining.

уха́живать, ucházeti se: ="to go after, go for (s.th. or s.o.)."

uhoda: ="one who enters, hence explores, pries."

východ: See note on wschód.

wychodek: See note on Pol. ustęp.

вы́ходка: The basic notion of "coming forth (from a group)" gave rise to the semantic progression "solo performance in choral singing" > "distinctive behavior of any kind" > "improper behavior, trick, prank."

wschód: The word for "east" originated in most languages as a designation of the direction in which the sun rises; compare Eng. east (akin to Lat. aurora "dawn"), Orient (ult. <Lat. oriri "to rise"), Levant (<Fr. levant "east" < se lever "to rise") and Anatolia (ult. <Gr. ἀνατολή "east" < ἀνατέλλειν [sc. ἑαυτόν] "to rise"), Ger. Morgenland "Orient" (<Morgen "morning" + Land "land"), Hung. kelet "east" (<kelni "to rise"), Rus. восто́к, Cz. východ, S-C ishod and istok. A similar association is commonly found between words for "west" and the setting of the sun; compare Eng. Occident (ult. <Lat. occidere "to go down, set"), Fr. couchant "west" (<se coucher "to go down, set"), Sp. poniente "west" (<ponerse "to go down, set"), Ger. Abendland "Occident" (<Abend "evening" + Land), Gr. δύσις "west" (<δύνειν "to go down, set"), Hung. nyugat "west" (<the root of

lenyugodni "to go down, set"), Rus. за́пад, Pol. zachód, Cz. západ, S-C zapad. See also note on Rus. по́лдень, Pol. południe, Cz. poledne.

schody (Pol.-Cz.): for earlier wschody-vzchody.

zachód: See note on wschód; regarding the third meaning, compare Rus. уха́живать, Cz. ucházeti se.

záchod-zahod: See note on Pol. ustęp.

zajście (first meaning): See note on происше́ствие.

zášť, záští: See zacházeti in the earlier sense of "to get into, become embroiled in (a quarrel, etc.)."

ХОТ	CHC, CHOT, CHOC, CHOĆ, CHĘT, CHĘC, CHĘĆ, CHUĆ	CHT, CHO(T), CHUT, CHOUT, CHUŤ, CHUC	HT, HOT
хоте́ть: to want, wish	chcieć: to want, wish	chtíti: to want, wish	htjeti (hotjeti): to want, wish; will, shall (auxiliary verb used to form future tense)
	chciwy: greedy	chtivý: greedy	
		chtíč: lust	
			hotimice: intentionally
хоть, хотя́: although; at least, if only	choć, chociaż: although; at least, if only		
	chęć: wish, desire	chuť: taste; appetite; wish, desire	
	chętny: willing; friendly, kindly disposed	chutný: tasty	
		choutka: whim	
	chuć: lust		
доброхо́тный (arch.): voluntary			dobrohotan: benevolent
		vědychtivý: curious, inquisitive	
охо́та: wish, desire; hunting	ochota: wish, desire	ochota: willingness; obligingness	
[R]	[P]	[Cz]	[S-C]

охóтник: hunter; volunteer; (sports-, book-, etc.) lover	ochotnik: volunteer	ochotník: amateur	
		ochočiti, ochočovati: to tame	
пóхоть: lust			pohota: lust; greed
прúхоть: whim			
		vychutnati, vychutnávati: to enjoy	
	zniechęcić, zniechęcać: to discourage; to disincline	znechutiti, znechucovati: to disgust; to disincline	
	zachcianka: whim		zahtjev: request; demand
	zachęcić, zachęcać: to encourage		
[R]	[P]	[Cz]	[S-C]

NOTES

Basic meaning of root: to want, wish

The forms CHĘT-CHĘC-CHĘĆ and CHUT-CHOUT-CHUŤ-CHUC go back to a secondary root-form in Common Slavic in which the vowel was nasalized.

htjeti (second meaning): The transition to an auxiliary verb in future constructions parallels that of Eng. will, which originally expressed desire, then intention, finally futurity. (See Ger. ich will "I want.") Further parallels are the use of a vrea "to want" to form the future tense in Rumanian and the use of the particle ϑά (<ϑέλω "I want" + the conjunction ἵνα) as an invariable future auxiliary in modern Greek.

хоть et al.: probably from an old participial form; the underlying meaning is, roughly, "if you will, if you like," with concessive force. Compare Pol. lubo.

chuć: <Cz. chuť or from Ukrainian.

dobrohotan: See note on Cz. blahovolný.

vědychtivý: See chtivý and note under root ВЕД$_1$ (etc.).

охóта (second meaning): in this sense, originally a taboo-word; compare Lat. venari "to hunt" (whence ult. Eng. venery "hunting" and venison), which is generally linked to Venus "Goddess of Love" and Sansk. vanati "he desires." See also Pol. myśliwy et al.

ochotník: Compare Eng. amateur (<Fr. amateur <Lat. amator "lover"), Rus. любитель; an amateur engages in an activity out of love rather than

professionally.

ochočiti: for earlier *ochotčiti*; the underlying meaning is "to cause to become willing, tractable" (see *ochota*).

znechutiti: See *chuť* and compare Eng. *disgust* (ult. <Lat. *dis-* "off, away" + *gustus* "taste").

ХОРОН, ХРАН	CHRON, CHRAN	CHRÁN, CHRAŇ	HRAN, HRAM
хорони́ть: to bury	*chronić*: to guard, protect	*chrániti*: to guard, protect	*hraniti*: to feed
храни́ть: to keep, preserve			
			hrana: food
		chráněnec: protégé; ward, charge	*hranjenik*: foster-child
храни́лище: storehouse			
	spadochron: parachute		
водохрани́лище: reservoir			
охрани́ть, *охраня́ть*: to guard, protect	*ochronić*, *ochraniać*: to guard, protect	*ochrániti*, *ochraňovati*: to guard, protect	
	ochronka (arch.): orphanage; day nursery		
			prehrambina: alimony
предохрани́тель: safety device (on machinery, etc.)			
	**schronić*: to shelter	*schrániti*, *schraňovati* (lit.): to save, amass	**shraniti*: to keep, preserve
сохрани́ть, *сохраня́ть*: to keep, preserve			*sahraniti*, *sahranjivati*: to bury; to keep, preserve
		schránka: box, receptacle	
		zachrániti, *zachraňovati*: to save, rescue	
[R]	[P]	[Cz]	[S-C]

NOTES

Basic meaning of root: to keep, preserve

The Russian root-form ХРАН is of Church Slavic origin.

hranjenik: The same idea underlies Eng. foster-child, the first element in which originally meant "food" and is etymologically related to the word food.

spadochron: See note under root ПА(Д) (etc.).

prehrambina: Compare Eng. alimony (ult. <Lat. alere "to feed, nourish"), Cz. výživné.

ХИТ, ХИЩ, ХВАТ	CHWYT, CHWYC, CHYT	CHYT, CHVAT, CHVÁT, CHVAC	HIT, HIĆ, HVAT, HVAĆ
	chwycić, chwytać: to grasp, seize	chytiti (chytnouti), chytati: to grasp, seize; to catch; to catch fire	hitnuti (hititi), hitati: to throw; (hitati only) to hurry (intr.)
			hitjeti: to hurry (intr.)
*хвати́ть: to suffice; (coll.) to grasp, seize; (coll.) to hit, strike			*hvatiti: to grasp, seize
хвата́ть: to grasp, seize; to suffice		chvátati: to hurry (intr.)	hvatati: to grasp, seize; to catch
	chwytny: prehensile		hitan: urgent
		chvat: haste	hvat: fathom; cord (of wood)
хи́щный: predatory			
хи́трый: sly, cunning; intricate, complicated	chytry: sly, cunning; greedy	chytrý: clever, smart	hitar: quick; agile
			dohvat: extent, scope; range
обхвати́ть, обхва́тывать: to clasp, embrace		obchvátiti, obchvacovati: (mil.) to outflank	obuhvatiti, obuhvatati (obuhvaćati): to clasp, embrace; to embrace,
[R]	[P]	[Cz]	[S-C]

[R]	[P]	[Cz]	[S-C]
			comprise, include; to contain
охвати́ть, охва́тывать: to clasp, embrace; to seize (e.g. with fear); to envelop (in flames); to grasp, comprehend; to embrace, comprise, include; (mil.) to outflank			
похити́тель: thief; kidnaper			
			poduhvat, pothvat: undertaking, venture
перехвати́ть, перехва́тывать: to intercept	przechwycić, przechwytywać: to intercept		
предвосхи́тить, предвосхища́ть: to anticipate			
			prihvat: acceptance
			shvaćanje: grasp, comprehension
схва́тка: skirmish, clash			
схва́тки (pl.): cramp, spasm			
		uchvatitel: aggressor, invader; usurper	
	uchwytny: palpable, tangible	uchvacující, úchvatný: delightful, ravishing	
восхище́ние: rapture, delight			ushit, ushićenje: rapture, delight
захва́т: seizure, capture	zachwyt: rapture, delight	záchvat: (med.) seizure, fit, attack; fit (of anger, etc.)	zahvat: grasp, grip

захва́тчик: aggressor, invader захва́тывающий: gripping, exciting; keen (interest, etc.)	zachwycający: delightful, ravishing		
[R]	[P]	[Cz]	[S-C]

NOTES

Basic meaning of root: to grasp, seize

The secondary meaning "to hurry" occurs in Czech and Serbo-Croatian.

The derivatives reflect the existence of two distinct vowel grades in Common Slavic, one of them represented in modern Russian, Czech and Serbo-Croatian by forms ХИТ-ХИЩ---CHYT---HIT-HIĆ and the other by forms ХВАТ---CHVAT-CHVÁT-CHVAC---HVAT-HVAĆ. (See note below referring to Pol. chwycić, chwytać.) Russian root-form ХИЩ is of Church Slavic origin.

chwycić et al.: The primary verb appears in Old Russian as хытати but not in the modern language. Pol. chwycić, chwytać resulted from confusion between the two original verbs (see OPol. chycić, chytać and chwacić, chwatać); an earlier root-form survives in chytry. Regarding the shift in meaning to "to throw" in Serbo-Croatian, see note on Rus. ти́снуть et al.

hitjeti: originally a variant of hititi, but now imperfective.

хвати́ть-hvatiti, хвата́ть et al.: Cz. chvátiti "to grasp, seize; to hurry" is obsolete; see also note on chwycić et al. Regarding the meaning "to suffice" in Russian, see note on S-C stignuti, stizati.

hvat: See note on Pol. sąg, Cz. sáh, Rus. са́же́нь et al.

охвати́ть (fourth meaning): See note on Rus. поня́ть et al. and поня́тие, Pol. pojęcie, Cz. ponětí, pojetí and pojem, S-C pojam.

предвосхи́тить: See note on Cz. předejmouti.

shvaćanje: See note on Rus. поня́ть et al. and поня́тие, Pol. pojęcie, Cz. ponětí, pojetí and pojem, S-C pojam.

uchvacující, úchvatný, восхище́ние et al., zachwyt, zachwycający: A person overcome by intense emotion, enthusiasm, joy, etc. is often conceived of as being seized and carried or pulled along as though by some external force. This idea is apparent in the English expressions to be carried away by emotion and to be in transports of joy and in the words ravishing and rapture (both ult. <Lat. rapere "to seize, carry away"). Compare also Ger. Entzückung "delight" (<zücken "to pull"), Du. verrukking "delight" (<rukken "to pull"), Rus. восто́рг and увлече́ние, Pol. porywający and uniesienie, Cz. vytržení, S-C zanos and zanesenost.

ЧА, ЧИН, КОН, КАН	CZĄ, CZYN, KON, KOŃ	ČÍ, ČÁ, ČIN, ČÍN, KON	ČE, ČIN, KON
	konać: to be dying, at death's door	konati: to do, perform	
коне́ц: end	koniec: end	konec: end	konac: end; thread
ко́нчить, конча́ть: to finish	kończyć: to finish	končiti: to finish	končati: to stitch
коне́чный: final; finite	konieczny: necessary	konečný: final; finite	konačan: final; finite
коне́чно: of course	koniecznie: absolutely, without fail; necessarily	konečně: finally, at last	konačno: finally, at last
коне́чность: limb, extremity; finiteness	konieczność: necessity	konečnost: finality; finiteness	konačnost: finality; finiteness
кончи́на: death, decease	kończyna: limb, extremity	končina: region	
		končetina: limb, extremity	
		konečník: (anat.) rectum	
первонача́льный: original, initial		prvopočáteční (lit.): original, initial	
законода́тельство: legislation		zákonodárství: legislation	zakonodavstvo: legislation
безнача́лие: anarchy			
			*dočeti (arch.): to finish
			dočetak: (gram.) suffix
доконáть, докáнывать (coll.): to finish, ruin, be the end of (s.o.)	dokonać, dokonywać: to complete; to accomplish	dokonati, dokonávati: to complete; to die	*dokonati: to complete; to decide
	dokonany: (gram.) perfective (aspect of Slavic verb); completed, finished	dokonavý: (gram.) perfective (aspect of Slavic verb)	
доскона́льный: thorough, detailed	doskonały: perfect; excellent	dokonalý: perfect; excellent; complete, total	
[R]	[P]	[Cz]	[S-C]

[R]	[P]	[Cz]	[S-C]
искóнный (lit.): primeval, primordial			iskonski: primeval, primordial
начáть, начинáть: to begin		načíti, načínati: to broach, tap; to cut into (a loaf)	načeti, načinjati: to broach, tap; to cut into (a loaf)
начáло: beginning; principle			načelo: principle
начáльник: chief, director			načelnik: chief, director
начáтки (pl.): rudiments			
			nakon: after
	napocząć, napoczynać: to broach, tap; to cut into (a loaf)		
			napokon: finally, at last
окончáтельный: final, definite, conclusive			
		okončetina: limb, extremity	
почáть, починáть (arch.): to begin; to broach, tap	począć, poczynać: to begin; to conceive (a child)	počíti, počínati: to begin; to conceive (a child)	početi, počinjati: to begin
почáток: ear (of corn, etc.); cop (thread wound on a spindle)	początek: beginning	počátek: beginning	početak: beginning
			počelo: element, basic component
почи́н: initiative		počin (lit.): act, action; initiative	
	pokonać, pokonywać: to conquer, defeat; to overcome, surmount		
	przekonać, przekonywać: to convince	překonati, překonávati: to conquer, defeat; to overcome, surmount; to surpass, outdo	

	rozpocząć, rozpoczynać: to begin		
	skon: death, decease	skon: death, decease	
			skončina: death, decease
		úkon: act, action; function	
	wykonać, wykonywać: to execute, carry out	vykonati, vykonávati: to execute, carry out	
	wykonawczy: executive (a.)	výkonný: executive (a.); efficient, productive	
	wszcząć, wszczynać: to begin		
*зача́ть (arch.): to conceive (a child)	*zacząć: to begin; to broach, tap; to cut into (a loaf)	*začíti: to begin	*začeti: to begin; to conceive (a child)
зачина́ть (lit.): to begin	zaczynać: to begin; to broach, tap; to cut into (a loaf)	začínati: to begin	začinjati: to begin; to conceive (a child)
зача́ток (lit.): embryo; fetus; rudimentary organ	zaczątek: beginning	začátek: beginning	začetak: beginning; embryo; fetus; rudimentary organ; (gram.) prefix
зача́тки (pl.): beginnings			
зако́н: law, statute	zakon: monastic order; knightly order; testament (of the Bible); (arch.) law, statute	zákon: law, statute; testament (of the Bible)	zakon: law, statute; testament (of the Bible); (arch.) religion
зако́нник (coll.): man versed in the law; strictly law-abiding man	zakonnik: monk	zákoník: code (of laws); (Biblical) scribe	zakonik: code (of laws)
зако́нница (coll.): woman versed in the law; strictly law-abiding woman	zakonnica: nun		
		započíti, započínati: to begin	započeti, započinjati: to begin
[R]	[P]	[Cz]	[S-C]

NOTES

Basic meaning of root: beginning; end

The dual meaning of this root appears less paradoxical if the beginning and end of a given line, span of time, etc. are conceived as its two extremities and hence essentially interchangeable. Obsolete Rus. кон and S-C kon could mean either "beginning" or "end" (the Serbo-Croatian word survives in the phrase od kona do kona "from beginning to end"). In the modern languages, the root-form КОН-KON normally expresses the meaning "end" (иско́нный-iskonski is an exception), while Rus. ЧА-ЧИН and their analogues, showing palatalization of the initial consonant, express the meaning "beginning" (see, however, S-C dočeti). The primary verb survives only in compounds, e.g. нача́ть et al.

From the meaning "to finish, bring to completion" have evolved in some derivatives the meaning "to perform, accomplish, carry out" and, hence, the idea of "perfection, excellence." (See introductory notes on roots ПОЛН [etc.] and ВЕРХ [etc.].)

konać-konati: orig. "to finish." The Polish and Czech verbs and dialectal Rus. кона́ть "to finish" are denominatives formed from кон (see introductory note above) and its equivalents; the corresponding Serbo-Croatian word is unattested.

konac (second meaning): The progression in meaning was apparently from an "end," i.e. bit, of thread (compare Eng. odds and ends and the use of Fr. bout "end" to mean "bit, piece") to the thread itself.

ко́нчить et al.: <коне́ц et al.

končati: orig. "to finish"; see the second meaning of konac.

konieczny: orig. "final"; the notion of finality gradually gave way to that of inevitability and, at length, necessity.

коне́чно: The semantic development here was from "finally" to "definitely" to "of course, naturally."

končina: The word originally referred to distant regions, i.e. "the ends of the earth."

первонача́льный-prvopočáteční: See нача́ло and počátek; the first element is from пе́рвый-prvý "first."

законода́тельство et al.: See зако́н-zákon-zakon and note under root ДА (etc.).

безнача́лие: The word reflects the earlier use of нача́ло in the meaning "power" (to translate Gr. ἀρχή "beginning; power") and is a loan-translation of Gr. ἀναρχία (<ἀν-, negative prefix + ἀρχή), whence Eng. anarchy. Compare Rus. безвла́стие, Cz. bezvládí, S-C bezvlađe.

dokonati (S-C, second meaning): The underlying idea is that of "coming to a conclusion"; compare Ger. entschliessen "to decide" (<schliessen "to close; to end").

dokonany-dokonavý, doskonały-dokonalý: Compare Eng. perfect and perfective (ult. <Lat. perficere "to finish, complete"), Rus. совершённый, S-C savršen and svršen; the perfective aspect of the verb expresses completed action.

доскона́льный: <Pol. doskonały.

иско́нный-iskonski: ="(existing) from the beginning"; the Russian word is of Church Slavic origin.

нача́ло-načelo: The Serbo-Croatian word originally meant "beginning." The meaning "principle" represents semantic borrowing from Ger. Prinzip or Fr. principe (<Lat. principium "beginning; first principle, element"); compare Gr. ἀρχή "beginning; first principle, element," Du. beginsel "principle" (<beginnen "to begin").

нача́льник-načelnik: The Russian word, a Church Slavic borrowing, reflects the earlier use of нача́ло in the meaning "power" (see note on безнача́лие); the Serbo-Croatian word, which originally meant "initiator," owes its present meaning to false association with čelo "forehead; front" (and perhaps to Russian influence). (Pol. naczelnik and Cz. náčelník, although identical in meaning with нача́льник and načelnik, are derived from czoło-čelo "forehead; front.")

поча́ток: orig. "beginning."

pokonać, przekonać-překonati: The meaning "to conquer, overcome" is presumably an extension of the notion of completing or accomplishing; regarding the further semantic shift to "to convince" in the case of przekonać (orig. "to conquer, overcome"), compare Eng. convince (ult. <Lat. vincere "to conquer, overcome"), Rus. победи́ть "to conquer, overcome" and убеди́ть "to convince."

skon (Pol.): See note on Pol. zgon.

úkon: Compare konati.

зако́н et al.: The original meaning in all four languages was "law"; the underlying idea is probably "a thing established and in existence since the beginning."

ЧАС	CZAS, CZES	ČAS	ČAS
час: hour часы́ (pl.): clock, watch часово́й: hourly, hour-long; clock,	czas: time; weather; (gram.) tense czasowy: temporary; temporal	čas: time; weather; (gram.) tense časový: temporal (pertaining to	čas: hour; moment, instant časovit: momentary, fleeting
[R]	[P]	[Cz]	[S-C]

watch (attr.); sentry, sentinel	(pertaining to time)	time); topical	
		časný: early; temporal (of this world)	
	czasownik: (gram.) verb		časovnik: clock, watch
		časovati: (gram.) to conjugate	
			časiti: to linger, hesitate
часо́вня: chapel			
	czasomierz: chronometer	časoměr: chronometer	
		časomíra: meter (of verse)	
	czasopismo: magazine, periodical	časopis: magazine, periodical	časopis: magazine, periodical
часосло́в: prayer-book, breviary			časoslov: prayer-book, breviary
			dugočasan: boring, tedious
	jednoczesny: simultaneous		
	międzyczas: interval of time		
	nowoczesny: modern		
	równoczesny: simultaneous		
сейча́с: now; very soon			
то́тчас: immediately			
	tymczasowy: temporary		
	współczesny: contemporary; modern		
	doczesny: temporal (of this world)	dočasný: temporary	
		nečas: bad weather	
		občasný: occasional	
		počasí: weather	
[R]	[P]	[Cz]	[S-C]

[R]	[P]	[Cz]	[S-C]
подчác: sometimes	podczas: during		
	przedwczesny: premature	předčasný: premature	
		současný: simultaneous; contemporary; modern	
	wczasy (pl.): rest, leisure		
	wczesny: early; (arch.) timely	včasný: timely	

NOTES

Basic meaning of root: time

The root has acquired specialized meanings in Russian and Serbo-Croatian, although the original notion of time in general is still apparent in some of the derivatives. (Compare root ВРЕМЯ [etc.].)

czas-čas (Cz.): The two notions of "time" and "weather" are expressed by the same word in many languages; compare Fr. temps, Sp. tiempo, It. tempo, Rum. timp and vreme, Hung. idő, modern Gr. καιρός, S-C vrijeme.

czasowy-časový, časný: Compare Eng. temporary and temporal (both ult. ‹Lat. tempus "time"), Rus. временный, S-C vremenit and privremen.

czasownik, časovati: A verb is situated in time rather than space and is characterized by time distinctions or "tenses" (Eng. tense ult. ‹Lat. tempus "time"); a conjugation comprises the various inflectional forms appropriate to each tense. Compare Ger. Zeitwort "verb" (‹Zeit "time" + Wort "word").

часóвня: properly speaking, a place for saying prayers at the canonical hours.

czasomierz-časoměr: See note under root $МЕР_1$ (etc.).

czasopismo et al.: modeled on Ger. Zeitschrift "magazine, periodical" (‹Zeit "time" + Schrift "writing").

часослóв-časoslov: a book of prayers to be said at the canonical hours; the word is modeled on Gr. ὡρολόγιον "prayer-book" (‹ὥρα "hour" + λόγος "saying, telling").

dugočasan: See note under root ДЛ (etc.).

nowoczesny: The first element is from nowy "new"; compare Ger. neuzeitlich "modern" (‹neu "new" + Zeit "time"), Cz. novodobý.

równoczesny: Compare Ger. gleichzeitig "simultaneous" (‹gleich "same; equal" + Zeit "time"), S-C istodoban, istovremen.

сейчáс, тóтчас: The first elements are, respectively, from сей "this" and тот "that."

tymczasowy: ⟨tymczasem "in the meantime" (literally, "during this time"); see note on czasowy-časový, časný.

współczesny: Compare Eng. contemporary (ult. ⟨Lat. cum "with, together" + tempus "time"), současný below, Rus. совреме́нный et al., Cz. soudobý.

doczesny-dočasný: See note on czasowy-časový, časný.

nečas, počasí: See čas.

současný: See note on współczesny.

wczasy: orig. "comforts, conveniences," i.e. things provided in a timely manner and when needed; see the second meaning of wczesny.

ЧАСТ	CZĘŚĆ, CZĘŚC, CZEST	ČÁST, ČAST, ČEST	ČES(T), ČEŠĆ
часть: part; (mil.) unit	część: part	část: part	čest: part; (arch.) destiny, fate, lot; (arch.) happiness; (arch.) (good) luck
			čestit: happy; honest, honorable; good, sound, proper
			čestitati: to congratulate
ча́стный: private; particular			
ча́стность: detail			
ча́стное: (math.) quotient			
безуча́стный: indifferent, apathetic			
прича́стие: (gram.) participle; (rel.) Eucharist, Communion		příčestí: (gram.) participle	pričest, pričešće: (rel.) Eucharist, Communion
сча́стье: happiness; (good) luck	szczęście: happiness; (good) luck	štěstí: happiness; (good) luck	
соуча́стие: complicity			saučešće: sympathy; condolence
у́часть: destiny, fate, lot		účast: participation; sympathy	
[R]	[P]	[Cz]	[S-C]

[R]	[P]	[Cz]	[S-C]
участие: participation; sympathy	uczestnictwo: participation	účastenství: sympathy	učešće: participation; učesništvo: participation
участок: lot, plot (of land); section, sector; district; (arch.) police station			

NOTES

Basic meaning of root: part

čest: The semantic evolution from "part, share" to "appointed share in life, destiny" is a fairly common one; compare the use of Eng. portion in such phrases as bitter portion, счáстье et al. and ýчасть below, Rus. удéл, Pol. udział, Cz. úděl. The third and fourth meanings illustrate the equally widespread tendency of words denoting "luck, fortune" in general to take on positive overtones. Thus, to have luck really means to have good luck, the words lucky and fortunate have come to refer exclusively to good luck and good fortune, and happy has shifted completely away from the neutral notion of "that which befalls" still apparent in hap, happen and perhaps. Similarly, Ger. Glück (cognate with Eng. luck) normally means "happiness, good luck," and Fr. heureux "happy" is descended from OFr. eür "destiny" (<Lat. augurium "augury"). Compare also Rus. лýчший, S-C sreća.

čestit: The progression in meaning has been, roughly, "enjoying good fortune" > "enjoying good repute, well thought of" > "good, worthy." Despite its second meaning, the word is unrelated to Rus. честь et al.

čestitati: ="to wish s.o. happiness"; compare Eng. felicitate (ult. <Lat. felix "happy"), Ger. beglückwünschen "to congratulate" (<Glück "happiness" + wünschen "to wish"), Cz. blahopřáti.

чáстный: Both meanings reflect the idea of a part in relation to the whole---in one case, the private (i.e. what pertains to the individual) in relation to the public (i.e. what pertains to the community); in the other, the particular in relation to the general. Compare Eng. particular (ult. <Lat. pars "part"); Fr. particulier means both "private" and "particular."

чáстность: <чáстный (see preceding note); compare Eng. particular (n.) "detail."

чáстное: ="part of a whole obtained through division."

безучáстный: ="without involvement or sympathy"; see учáстие.

причáстие et al.: In the meaning "participle," the word is a loan-translation of Lat. participium (<particeps "taking part"), which expresses

the idea that a participle partakes of the nature of both verb and adjective; in the meaning "Eucharist," the reference is to the act of partaking of the consecrated bread and wine.

счáстье et al.: The prefix is a sparsely represented one meaning "good" (see Rus. сдóба, Pol. zboże, zdobić and śliczny, Cz. zboží, zdobiti and sličný). For the development of the meaning, see note on čest above. Štěstí is from OCz. ščěstie.

соучáстие-saučešće, účast, учáстие-učešće, uczestnictwo et al.: The semantic link between the notion of "taking part, participating" and that of "sympathy" is also apparent in Ger. Teilnahme "participation; sympathy" (<Teil "part" + nehmen "to take"); uczestnictwo is for earlier uczęstnictwo.

ýчасть: See note on čest.

ЧИ, КОЙ, КО(И), КА(И)	CZĄ, CZY, KÓJ, KO(I), KAJ	ČI, ČÍ, KOJ, KÁJ	ČI, KOJ
	koić: to soothe, allay	kojiti: to suckle, breast-feed	
беспокóить: to disturb; to worry, perturb			
	niepokoić: to disturb; to worry, perturb		
*обеспокóить (arch.): to disturb; to worry, perturb			obespokojiti, obespokojavati: to worry, perturb
*опочúть (arch.): to fall asleep; to pass away, die			
опочивáльня (arch.): bed-chamber			
	odpocząć, odpoczywać: to rest (intr.)	odpočinouti si, odpočívati: to rest (intr.)	otpočinuti, otpočivati: to rest (intr.)
		odpočivné: pension	
*почúть (arch.): to fall asleep; to pass away, die			*počinuti: to rest (intr.)
почивáть (arch.): to sleep			počivati: to rest (intr.)
[R]	[P]	[Cz]	[S-C]

[R]	[P]	[Cz]	[S-C]
поко́й: peace, quiet; (arch.) room, chamber	pokój: peace, quiet; peace (absence of war); room, chamber	pokoj: peace, quiet; room, chamber	pokoj: peace, quiet
поко́йник: deceased person			pokojnik: deceased person
	spocząć, spoczywać: to rest (intr.)	spočinouti, spočívati: to rest (intr.); (spočívati only) to consist, reside (in)	
споко́йствие: peace, quiet	spokój: peace, quiet		spokojstvo: peace, quiet
	*ukoić: to soothe, allay	ukojiti, ukájeti (ukojovati): to quench (thirst), appease (hunger)	
		upokojiti, upokojovati: to calm, pacify	*upokojiti: to retire (tr.), pension off
		upokojiti se, upokojovati se: to grow calm	*upokojiti se: to pass away, die
успоко́ить, успока́ивать: to calm, pacify; to soothe, allay	uspokoić, uspokajać: to calm, pacify; to soothe, allay	uspokojiti, uspokojovati: to satisfy	*uspokojiti (lit.): to calm, pacify; to soothe, allay
	wypocząć, wypoczywać: to rest (intr.)		
		znepokojiti, znepokojovati: to disturb; to worry, perturb	
	zaspokoić, zaspokajać: to satisfy		
[R]	[P]	[Cz]	[S-C]

NOTES

Basic meaning of root: to rest; to quiet

This root appears almost invariably in combination with the prefix по-, po-. The forms represented by Russian ЧИ, showing palatalization of the initial consonant, retain the original root-meaning, "to rest." КОЙ and its equivalents in the other languages are causative forms with the meaning, "to cause to rest, to quiet." The Polish perfective form CZĄ arose through confusion with unrelated root ЧА (etc.). (See OPol. perfective odpoczynąć, spoczynąć, etc.)

The Slavic root is cognate with Eng. (*a*) *while* "period of time" (=Dan.-Nor. *hvile* "rest"), Lat. *quies* "rest" (>Eng. *quiet*).

koić-*kojiti*: No equivalent form has survived in Russian, while S-C *kojiti* "to nurse" is dialectal. Cz. *kojiti* is a relatively new formation resulting from loss of the two prefixes in *upokojiti*; with regard to the meaning, compare Ger. *stillen* "to suckle" (<*still* "still, quiet").

odpočivné: Compare Ger. *Ruhestand* "retirement" (<*Ruhe* "rest" + *Stand* "state, condition") and *Ruhegehalt* "pension" (<*Ruhe* + *Gehalt* "pay"), S-C *upokojiti* and *mirovina*.

поко́й-*pokój*-*pokoj* (Cz.): The underlying notion in the meaning "room, chamber" is "place where one rests, takes one's ease." This secondary meaning probably shows the influence of Ger. *Gemach* "room," which originally meant "rest, comfort" (hence Ger. *gemächlich* "comfortable").

ukojiti: the result of loss of the prefix *po*- in *upokojiti*; compare *kojiti*.

upokojiti (S-C): See note on *odpočivné*.

uspokojiti (Cz.), *zaspokoić*: Compare Ger. *befriedigen* "to satisfy" (<*Friede* "peace").

ЧИН	CZYN, CZYŃ	ČIN, ČIŇ	ČIN, ČIM
чин: rank, grade; (arch.) rite, ceremony	*czyn*: deed, act	*čin*: deed, act	*čin*: deed, act; act (of a play); rank, grade
			čini (pl.): magic, sorcery
чини́ть: to mend, repair; to sharpen (e.g. a pencil); to cause (trouble), create (obstacles)	*czynić*: to do, make	*činiti*: to do, make	*činiti*: to do, make; to dress (leather)
		činiti se: to strive, exert o.s.	*činiti se*: to seem; to pretend, feign
чи́нный: decorous, sedate	*czynny*: active; (gram.) active	*činný*: active; (gram.) active	
чино́вник: official, functionary		*činovník*: official, functionary	*činovnik*: official, functionary
	czynnik: factor; (math.) factor	*činitel*: factor; (math.) factor; figure (political, public, etc.)	*činilac*, *činitelj*: factor; doer, maker
[R]	[P]	[Cz]	[S-C]

			čimbenik: factor
			činjenica: fact
		činohra: drama	
		činorodý: active	
	dobroczynność: charity, philanthropy	dobročinnost: charity, philanthropy	dobročinstvo: good deed, benefaction
	iloczyn: (math.) product		
			preljubočinac: adulterer
	rękoczyn: blow, slap; (arch.) (surgical) operation		
самочи́нный: arbitrary, high-handed	samoczynny: automatic	samočinný: automatic	
	zadośćuczynienie, zadosyćuczynienie: satisfaction (redress for an injury)	zadostiučinění: satisfaction (redress for an injury)	
	złoczyństwo (arch.): crime	zločin: crime	zločin, zločinstvo: crime
бесчи́нство: rowdyism			
начини́ть, начиня́ть: to stuff (meat, etc.)			načiniti, načinjati: to do, make
			način: way, mode, manner; (gram.) mood
	naczynie: vessel, utensil (for kitchen); (anat.) vessel	náčiní: implements, equipment; kitchenware	
		náčinek: poultice, compress	
	odczynić, odczyniać: to undo (what has been done); to break (a magic spell)	odčiniti, odčiňovati: to atone, make amends for	*očiniti: to break (a magic spell)
	odczyn: (chem.) reaction		
			pačiniti, pačinjati: to falsify, counterfeit
[R]	[P]	[Cz]	[S-C]

подчини́ть, подчиня́ть: to subordinate		podčiniti, podčiňovati (arch.): to subordinate	podčiniti, podčinjavati: to subordinate; to subjugate, subdue
		přečin: misdemeanor	
причини́ть, причиня́ть: to cause	przyczynić, przyczyniać: to add; to cause	přičiniti, přičiňovati (lit.): to add	pričiniti, pričinjavati: to cause
	przyczynić się, przyczyniać się: to contribute	přičiniti se, přičiňovati se: to strive, exert o.s.	pričiniti se, pričinjavati se: to seem; to pretend, feign
причи́на: cause, reason	przyczyna: cause, reason	příčina: cause, reason	
	rozczynić, rozczyniać: to leaven; to dilute		raščiniti, raščinjati: to dilute; (chem.) to decompose, analyze
сочине́ние: (act of) writing, composing; literary work, composition			sačinjavanje: (act of) writing, composing; (act of) making, creating
		součin: (math.) product	
		součinnost: cooperation	
	uczynek: deed, act	účinek: effect	učinak: effect
	uczynny: obliging, helpful	účinný: effective	
		účinlivý: obliging, helpful	
	wyczynić, wyczyniać: to clean (grain); (coll.) to do (s.th. foolish or objectionable)	vyčiniti, vyčiňovati: to dress (leather); (coll.) to scold, upbraid	
	wyczyn: feat, exploit		
	zaczynić, zaczyniać: to leaven		začiniti, začinjati (začinjavati): to season, flavor
[R]	[P]	[Cz]	[S-C]

NOTES

Basic meaning of root: order, arrangement

The original notion of "putting in order, arranging" has given rise to the neutral meaning "to do, make" (which has become, in effect, the basic root-meaning in the modern languages) and to a host of derivatives referring to various specialized activities (mending, sharpening a pencil, dressing leather, stuffing meat, cleaning grain, leavening dough, seasoning food); the concept of "good or due order" is apparent in the meanings "rank" and "ceremony." Further semantic development is reflected in words meaning "mode, manner" (="how a thing is done") and "utensil, implement" (="the means by which a thing is done").

Somewhat comparable development of the basic meaning is shown by root РЯД (etc.).

A non-Slavic cognate is Gr. ποιεῖν "to do, make" (>Eng. poem, onomatopoeia).

čin (S-C): The meaning "rank, grade" has been taken over from Rus. чин.

čini: See činiti in the earlier meaning "to bewitch" and compare Ger. antun "to do (s.th.) to (s.o.); to bewitch" (<an "to" + tun "to do").

чини́ть et al.: a denominative verb from чин et al.; the Russian word meant "to do, make" in earlier usage.

činiti se (S-C): See note on Rus. притво́рство, S-C pritvorstvo.

чи́нный: ="observing established order, custom, etc."

чино́вник et al.: See the first meaning of чин; the Czech and Serbo-Croatian words are borrowed from Russian.

czynnik et al., čimbenik: A factor is a "doer," i.e. a thing or circumstance which helps to produce a given effect (or one of the mathematical elements which, when multiplied together, form a product); compare Eng. factor (ult. <Lat. facere "to do, make").

činjenica: ="that which has been done"; compare Eng. fact (ult. <Lat. facere "to do, make"), Hung. tény "fact" (<tenni "to do, make").

činohra: The second element is from hra "play"; compare Eng. drama (ult. <Gr. δρᾶν "to do").

činorodý: See note under root РОД (etc.).

dobročinstvo: See note on Rus. благодея́ние, благоде́тель and благоде́тельный, S-C blagodejanje and blagodjetan.

iloczyn: The first element is from ile "how much, how many"; compare czynnik.

rękoczyn: See note under root РУК (etc.).

zadośćuczynienie et al.: The second element is from dość (dosyć)-dost(i) "enough"; see note on Rus. удовлетвори́ть.

złoczyństwo et al.: See note under root ЗЛ (etc.).

бесчи́нство: ="disorder, breach of propriety"; compare чи́нный.

način: Compare the English grammatical term mood (ult. ‹Lat. modus "mode, manner"), Cz. způsob.

odczynić et al.: The original meaning in all three cases was "to undo"; S-C očiniti is from earlier odčiniti.

odczyn: Compare Eng. reaction (ult. ‹Lat. re- "back" + agere "to do, act").

pačiniti: See note on S-C patvoriti, Pol. potwora et al. and potwarz.

подчини́ть et al.: See note on Pol. podporządkować et al. and podrzędny, Cz. podřadný; the Serbo-Croatian word is borrowed from Russian.

přečin: a formation influenced by the word přestupek "offense" (see přestupník).

przyczynić-přičiniti: The notion of "adding" reflects the action of the prefix.

pričiniti se: See note on Rus. притво́рство, S-C pritvorstvo.

rozczynić-raščiniti: See note on Rus. раствори́ть et al.

сочине́ние-sačinjavanje: Compare Eng. poem (referred to in the introductory note above).

součin: Compare činitel.

uczynny, účinlivý: ="active."

wyczyn: Compare Eng. feat (ult. ‹Lat. facere "to do, make").

ЧТ, ЧИ(Т), ЧЕ(Т)	CZT, CZC, CZYT, CZE(T), CZĘ, C	ČT, ČIT, ČÍ(T), ČE(T), ČA, C	ČT, ŠT, ČI(T), ČA(T)
чита́ть: to read	czytać: to read	†čísti, čítati: to read; (čítati only) to count; (čítati only; arch.) to consider, deem, regard (as)	čitati: to read
честь: honor	cześć: honor	čest: honor	čast: honor; feast, banquet
чтить (lit.): to honor, revere	czcić: to honor, revere; to worship	ctíti: to honor, revere	
			štiti (arch.): to read
			štovati: to honor, revere
че́стный: honest, honorable	cny (arch.): honest, honorable; respectable, estimable	ctný (arch.): honest, honorable; respectable, estimable	častan: honest, honorable; respectable, estimable
		čestný: honest, honorable; honorary	
[R]	[P]	[Cz]	[S-C]

[R]	[P]	[Cz]	[S-C]
	cnota: virtue	ctnost: virtue	
че́ствовать: to hold a celebration in honor of (s.o.)	częstować: to treat, regale, entertain	častovati: to treat, regale, entertain	častiti: to honor, revere; to treat, regale, entertain
число́: number		číslo: number	čislo: rosary; (arch.) number
		číselník: clock-dial, watch-dial	
числи́тель: (math.) numerator			
чита́тель: reader		čitatel: (math.) numerator	čitatelj: reader
	czesne: school fees, tuition		
	cześnik (arch.): royal cup-bearer		časnik: (military) officer; official
чётки (pl.): rosary			
	czcionka: letter, type (in printing)		
чте́ние: reading; reading matter		čtení: reading; reading matter	
чёткий: legible; clear, precise			čitak: readable, interesting; legible
		četný: numerous	
благочести́вый (arch.): pious, devout			blagočastiv (arch.): pious, devout
			bogočašće, bogoštovlje: worship; religious service
честолю́бие: ambition			častoljublje: ambition
	czcigodny: respectable, estimable	ctihodný: respectable, estimable	
		ctižádost: ambition	
счетово́д: bookkeeper, accountant			
звездочёт (arch.): astrologer			zvjezdočatac (arch.): astrologer

[R]	[P]	[Cz]	[S-C]
		nadpočet: surplus, excess	
нечести́вый (arch.): impious, godless			nečastivi: the Devil
недочёт: deficit; shortcoming, defect			
		odečtení: deduction (of a sum of money)	
	odczytanie: reading	odčítání: (math.) subtraction	
отчёт: account, report	odczyt: lecture		
отчётливый: clear, distinct			
отчётность: bookkeeping, accounting; books, accounts			
почёт: respect, esteem	poczet: list; train, retinue; (arch.) number	počet: number	
		počty (pl.): arithmetic	
почти́: almost			
	poczytalny: (legally) responsible, of sound mind		
по́тчевать: to treat, regale, entertain			
	poczesne (arch.): gift; fee; tip, gratuity		
предпоче́сть, предпочита́ть: to prefer			
причита́ние: lamentation		přičítání: attribution, imputation	
причт: clergy of a single parish			
		příčetný: (legally) responsible, of sound mind	
расчёт: calculation; dismissal, discharge; gun-crew			

[R]	[P]	[Cz]	[S-C]
<u>расчётливый</u>: calculating, prudent; thrifty, economical			
		<u>rozpočet</u>: budget; estimate	
<u>счесть</u>, <u>считáть</u>: to count; to consider, deem, regard (as)		<u>sečísti</u>, <u>sčítati</u> (<u>sečítati</u>): to add	
<u>счёт</u>: calculation; (financial) account; bill, invoice; score		<u>součet</u>: total, sum	
<u>счёты</u> (pl.): abacus			
<u>учёт</u>: stock-taking, taking of inventory; registration; discounting (of a bill); consideration, regard		<u>účet</u>: (financial) account; bill, invoice	
		<u>účetní</u>: bookkeeper, accountant	
<u>учтúвый</u>: polite	<u>uczciwy</u>: honest, honorable	<u>uctivý</u>: respectful; polite	<u>učtiv</u>: polite
	<u>uczta</u>: feast, banquet	<u>úcta</u>: respect, esteem	
		<u>včetně</u>: including (adv.)	
<u>вычитáние</u>: (math.) subtraction			
<u>вы́чет</u>: deduction (of a sum of money)		<u>výčet</u>: enumeration	
		<u>výčitka</u>: reproach	
		<u>vypočítavý</u>: calculating, self-seeking	

NOTES

Basic meaning of root: to read; to count; to honor

The unifying idea underlying the various root-meanings is apparent in cognate Sansk. *cétati* "he notices, pays attention." From the general notion of attentiveness evolved that of scrutinizing letters ("reading") and numbers ("counting"). The semantic leap from "notice, attention" to "honor" was a short one; compare Eng. *respect* (ult. <Lat. *specere* "to look"). The development of the meaning "to consider, deem" from "to count," apparent in several derivatives, has parallels in English in such expressions as *I count it an honor* and in the similar use of *reckon*.

The forms ЧЕСТ---CZEŚ-CZES---ČEST---ČAS(T)-ČAŠĆ are derived from *честь et al*. (See note.)

чита́ть et al.: The original primary verb survives only in Cz. *číst* (1 sg.: *čtu*) as an independent word; obsolete Rus. *честь* "to read; to count; to consider, deem" (1 sg.: *чту*) occurs only in perfective compound verbs in the modern language, while earlier Pol. *czyść* "to read" (1 sg.: *cztę*) and S-C *čisti* "to read; to honor" (1 sg.: *čtem*) have vanished completely. The form represented by Rus. *чита́ть* was originally iterative in all four languages, as it still is in Czech.

честь et al.: <Common Slavic **čьstь*.

чтить et al.: contracted denominative formations from *честь-cześć-čest*; compare the Old Czech form *čstíti*.

štiti: for earlier *čtiti* "to read; to honor"; the word is regarded by some authorities as identical with *чтить et al*. and by others as a secondary formation from the root of the primary verb (see note on *чита́ть et al*.).

štovati: for earlier *čtovati*; compare *štiti*.

cny-ctný: <*cześć-čest*; compare the Old Polish forms *czestny*, *czesny*, *czsny* and OCz. *čstný*. Modern Cz. *čestný* is a new formation.

čestný: See preceding note.

cnota-ctnost: <*cny-ctný*.

częstować-častovati: for earlier *czestować-čestovati* <*cześć-čest*; the irregular vowel has been attributed to the influence of *część* "part" (*i.e.* to the notion of sharing one's bounty with another) in the case of the Polish word and to the influence of *častý* "frequent" (hence, to the notion of frequently playing host) or *šťastný* "happy" in the case of the Czech word.

число́ et al.: <Common Slavic **čitslo*; regarding the first meaning of the Serbo-Croatian word, see note on *чётки*.

числи́тель, *čitatel*: Compare Eng. *numerator* (ult. <Lat. *numerus* "number"), Ger. *Zähler* "numerator" (<*zählen* "to count") and see note on Cz. *jmenovatel et al*.

czesne: <OPol. *czesny* (see note on *cny-ctný*); the word is modeled on Lat. *honorarium* (*donum*) "a present made on being admitted to a post of

honor," whence Eng. honorarium.

cześnik: orig. "dignitary, official"; the present meaning reflects the influence of czasza "cup."

časnik: Compare Hung. tisztelet "honor" and tiszt "(military) officer."

чётки: a string of beads used for counting prayers.

благочести́вый-blagočastiv: See note under root БЛАГ (etc.).

bogoštovlje: See štovati.

честолю́бие-častoljublje: Compare Ger. Ehrgeiz "ambition" (<Ehre "honor" + Geiz "greed"), Gr. φιλοτιμία and φιλοδοξία "ambition" (<φίλος "loving" + τιμή "honor," δόξα "glory"), Hung. becsvágy "ambition" (<becs "esteem" + vágy "desire"), Fin. kunnianhimo "ambition" (<kunnia "honor" + himo "desire"), Cz. ctižádost below, S-C slavoljublje.

czcigodny-ctihodný, ctižádost: Czci and cti are the genitive forms of cześć and čest. The second element in ctižádost is from žádost "desire"; see preceding note.

звездочёт-zvjezdočatac: ="one who reads the stars"; the first element is from звезда́-zvijezda "star."

nadpočet: See počet.

отчётливый: See отчёт; the original meaning was "giving an accurate account of s.th."

poczet: The first two meanings are an outgrowth of the third.

почти́: an old imperative; the meaning is, roughly, "You can count it, estimate it."

poczytalny: <poczytać in the archaic sense "to attribute, impute"; see note on příčetný.

по́тчевать: a corrupted formation from по + чтить.

poczesne: See note on czesne.

предпоче́сть: Compare Gr. προτιμᾶν "to prefer" (<πρό "before" + τιμᾶν "to honor"); the word is borrowed from Church Slavic.

причита́ние: originally a reading or counting of the virtues of a departed person.

přičítání: Compare Eng. imputation (ult. <Lat. in "in, on" + putare "to think, reckon, count").

причт: See ORus. причитати "to count together; to join, unite."

příčetný: said of someone "to whom a thing may be imputed," i.e. who can be held accountable for his actions; see přičítání and compare Ger. zurechnungsfähig "(legally) responsible, of sound mind" (<zurechnen "to attribute, impute" [<zu "to" + rechnen "to reckon, count"] + fähig "capable"), Pol. poczytalny above.

расчёт (second and third meanings): ="settling of accounts" and "group of soldiers who have been 'counted off,' i.e. assigned to a detail."

учти́вый et al., uczta-ú́cta: <чтить et al.; the Serbo-Croatian word is borrowed from Russian.

včetně: ="counting in."

výčitka: The idea is that of "lecturing" someone (about his faults, etc.).

чу	CZU	ČI, ČÍ	ČU
	czuć: to feel; to smell, reek; to smell, scent	cíti: to feel; to smell, scent	**čuti: to hear
чу́ять: to smell, scent; to sense, be aware of			
	czuwać: to watch (over); to attend (to)		čuvati: to keep; to guard, protect; to save, store
			čuvaran: economical, thrifty
чу́вство: feeling; sense (sight, hearing, etc.)		čivstvo (arch.): nervous system	čuvstvo: feeling
чу́вствовать: to feel			čuvstvovati: to feel
чуть: hardly, barely			
чу!: hark! listen!			
	czujny: vigilant		čujan: audible
чу́ткий: keen (e.g. sense of hearing); sensitive; tactful, considerate			
			čuven: famous
		čidlo: sensory organ	čulo: sense (sight, hearing, etc.)
	czuły: affectionate; sensitive		čulan: sensual; sensory
	czułki (pl.): feelers, antennae; tentacles		
чу́вственный: sensual; sensory			čuvstven: affectionate; emotional
[R]	[P]	[Cz]	[S-C]

[R]	[P]	[Cz]	[S-C]
чувстви́тельный: sensitive; perceptible; sentimental			
	współczucie: sympathy		
			pričuva: reserve, stock, supply; (mil.) reserve
сочу́вствие: sympathy			
	znieczulenie: anesthesia		

NOTES

Basic meaning of root: to feel

The various derivatives of this root tend to fluctuate in meaning between sensory perception in general, i.e. feeling, and the particular sensations of smelling and hearing. (Compare Fr. sentir "to feel; to smell," It. sentire "to feel; to hear; to smell.") The further notion of watching or guarding is apparent in the words czuwać-čuvati, czujny, čuvaran and pričuva.

ORus. чути "to feel; to hear," corresponding to czuć et al., has not survived in the modern language. (See, however, notes on чуть and чу.) Чу́вствовать is a relatively recent formation from чу́вство.

The Slavic root is cognate with Lat. cavere "to beware" (>Eng. caution, caveat).

čuvstvovati: <Rus. чу́вствовать.

чуть: orig. an infinitive; in Old Russian, чути есть meant "it is (barely) perceptible." (See introductory note above.)

чу: an aorist or imperative form of ORus. чути. (See introductory note above.)

čuven: The underlying idea is "heard far and wide."

współczucie, сочу́вствие: Compare Ger. Mitgefühl "sympathy" (<mit "with" + fühlen "to feel"), Cz. soucit "sympathy" (<sou- + cítiti "to feel"), S-C sućut "sympathy" (<su- + ćutjeti "to feel"); see also Rus. сострада́ние, Cz. soustrast.

znieczulenie: formed from czuły (second meaning); compare Eng. anesthesia (ult. <Gr. ἀν- "un-" + αἰσθάνεσθαι "to feel").

ДА	DA	DA, DÁ	D(A)
дать, дава́ть: to give	dać, dawać: to give	dáti, dávati: to give; to put	dati, davati: to give
дань: tribute	dań, danina: tax; tribute	daň: tax; tribute	danak: tax; tribute
	datek: alms; donation		
	dawka: dose	dávka: tax; dose; portion, helping	
да́ча: (act of) giving; villa, country house; woodland tract			daća: tax; funeral feast; (arch.) good fortune
			dažbina: tax
да́нные (pl.): data	dane (pl.): data		
да́тельный: (gram.) dative			
дар: gift, present; gift, talent	dar: gift, present; gift, talent	dar: gift, present; gift, talent	dar: gift, present; gift, talent
дари́ть: to bestow, present	darzyć: to bestow, present	dařiti (arch.): to bestow, present	
	darzyć się: to go well, successfully	dařiti se: to go well, successfully	
**дарова́ть (arch.): to bestow, present	**darować: to bestow, present; to forgive	**darovati: to bestow, present; to forgive	darovati, darivati: to bestow, present
дарови́тый: gifted, talented			darovit: gifted, talented
			darežljiv: generous
да́ром: free of charge; in vain	darmo: free of charge; in vain	darmo: in vain; (arch.) free of charge	
		dareba, darebák: scoundrel	
благодари́ть: to thank			blagodariti: to thank
благода́рный: grateful		blahodárný: beneficial	blagodaran: grateful
благода́тный: beneficial; abundant			blagodatan: beneficial
дармое́д: parasite, sponger	darmozjad: parasite, sponger	darmožrout: parasite, sponger	
[R]	[P]	[Cz]	[S-C]

[R]	[P]	[Cz]	[S-C]
	jadłodajnia: restaurant		
	miarodajny: authoritative, decisive		mjerodavan: authoritative, decisive
		milodar: alms; donation	milodar: alms; donation
		nazdařbůh: at random	
	prawodawstwo: legislation		
		směrodatný: authoritative, decisive	
	sprawozdawca: reporter; reviewer, critic		
	ustawodawstwo: legislation		
			vjerodajnica: credentials
		zpravodaj: reporter	
законода́тельство: legislation		zákonodárství: legislation	zakonodavstvo: legislation
		dodávka: delivery, supply	
	dodatek: addition; supplement	dodatek: addition; supplement	dodatak: addition; supplement
	dodatni: positive, favorable; (math., phys.) positive		
изда́ние: edition; publication (act of publishing; published work)			izdanje: edition; publication (act of publishing; published work); delivery; issuance
изда́тельство: publishing house			
			izdaja: treason, betrayal
			izdatak: expenditure
			izdašan: abundant; productive; fertile; generous
[R]	[P]	[Cz]	[S-C]

	nadać się, nadawać się: to be suitable, fit		
		nadaný: gifted, talented	
	nadajnik: radio transmitter		
		nadávka: insult, term of abuse	
		nadace: foundation, endowment	
	nadarzyć się, nadarzać się: to arise, present itself (opportunity, etc.)		
			nadaren: gifted, talented
			nadarbina: ecclesiastical benefice, prebend
	naddatek: surplus; addition		
			nedaća: misfortune, adversity
	niezdarny: clumsy	nezdárný: naughty, badly behaved	
		nezadatelný: inalienable	
одарённый: gifted, talented			obdaren: gifted, talented
озада́чить, озада́чивать: to puzzle, perplex			
		oddavky (pl.): wedding	
	oddany: devoted, faithful; addicted, given (to)	oddaný: devoted, faithful	odan: devoted, faithful; addicted, given (to)
		odevzdaný: resigned (e.g. to one's fate); devoted, faithful	
подая́ние (arch.): alms	podanie: (act of) giving, presenting;	podání: (act of) giving, presenting;	
[R]	[P]	[Cz]	[S-C]

	petition, application; tradition, legend	petition, application; (auction) bid; tradition, legend	
подáрок: gift, present	podarek, podarunek: gift, present		podarak: gift, present
пóдать (arch.): tax	podatek: tax		podatak: datum, piece of information
	podaż: (econ.) supply		
		podávky (pl.): pitchfork	
			podašan: generous
	podatny: receptive, susceptible		podatan: pliable, soft
подáтливый: pliable, soft; compliant, tractable			podatljiv: compliant, tractable; generous
поддáться, поддавáться: to yield, submit	poddać się, poddawać się: to yield, submit; to surrender, capitulate; to be subjected (to), undergo	poddati se, poddávati se: to yield, submit; to surrender, capitulate	podati se, podavati se: to yield, submit; to be addicted, given (to)
пóдданный: subject (of a sovereign)	poddany: subject (of a sovereign); serf	poddaný: subject (of a sovereign); serf	podanik: subject (of a sovereign)
		poddajný: pliable, soft; compliant, tractable	
передáть, передавáть: to hand over; to transfer; to transmit; to communicate		předati, předávati: to hand over; to transfer; to transmit	predati, predavati: to hand over; to deliver; to surrender (tr.); (predavati only) to teach, lecture (at a university)
передáтчик: radio transmitter			
предáние: tradition, legend; (act of) handing over (to justice), committing (to		předání: (act of) handing over; transfer; transmittal	predanje: tradition, legend
[R]	[P]	[Cz]	[S-C]

[R]	[P]	[Cz]	[S-C]
the flames), consigning (to oblivion), etc.			
пре́данный: devoted, faithful			predan: devoted, faithful; handed over; delivered; surrendered
преда́тель: traitor			predatelj: deliverer, one who delivers
преподава́тель: teacher			
прида́ное: dowry; trousseau; layette			
прида́ток: addition; appendage	przydatek: addition; appendage	přídavek: addition	pridavak: addition
	przydatny: suitable, fit		
			prid, prida: premium, agio
		přídavné (jméno): (gram.) adjective	
	przydarzyć się, przydarzać się: to happen		
прода́ть, продава́ть: to sell		prodati, prodávati: to sell	prodati, prodavati: to sell
		protidávka: antidote	
сда́ться, сдава́ться: to surrender, capitulate; (coll.) to seem	zdać się, zdawać się: to seem; to rely (on); to be suitable, fit		
	zdanie: opinion; (gram.) sentence, clause		
	zdatny: suitable, fit	zdatný: efficient, able	
	sprzedać, sprzedawać: to sell		
		údaje (pl.): data	
		udavač: informer, tale-bearer	
	udany: successful; feigned, sham		

[R]	[P]	[Cz]	[S-C]
удало́й, уда́лый: bold, daring	udały: successful		
уда́чный: successful	udatny: successful	udatný: brave, courageous	
	udaremnić, udaremniać: to frustrate, thwart		
вда́ться, вдава́ться: to jut out, cut (into); to go (to extremes, into detail)	wdać się, wdawać się: to intervene, interfere; to engage (in); to go (into detail); (w + acc.) to take after, resemble	vdáti se, vdávati se: to marry, take a husband	udati se, udavati se: to marry, take a husband
	wydanie: edition; publication (act of publishing); delivery; issuance; extradition	vydání: edition; publication (act of publishing); delivery; issuance; extradition; expenditure	
	wydawnictwo: publication (act of publishing; published work); publishing house	vydavatelství: publishing house	
вы́дача: delivery; issuance; extradition	wydatek: expenditure	výdaj: expenditure	
	wydajny: productive; fertile		
	wydatny: prominent, protruding; prominent, outstanding	vydatný: substantial (meal), heavy (rain)	
выдаю́щийся: prominent, protruding; prominent, outstanding			
	wydarzyć się, wydarzać się: to happen	*vydařiti se: to go well, successfully	
		vzdáti se, vzdávati se: to surrender, capitulate; to renounce, give up	uzdati se: to rely (on)
[R]	[P]	[Cz]	[S-C]

[R]	[P]	[Cz]	[S-C]
воздая́ние (arch.): recompense; retribution			
	zdarzenie: event, occurrence		
	zdarzony: successful	zdařilý: successful	
		zdárný: successful; well-behaved	
зада́ние: task	zadanie: task; (math.) problem		
зада́ча: task; (math.) problem			zadaća: task
зада́ток: deposit, advance (payment)	zadatek: deposit, advance (payment)	závdavek: deposit, advance (payment)	zadatak: task; (math.) problem
зада́тки (pl.): inclination, bent, tendency	zadatki (pl.): inclination, bent, tendency		
[R]	[P]	[Cz]	[S-C]

NOTES

Basic meaning of root: to give

Apparent in a number of derivatives is the notion of persons, things or circumstances "giving (i.e. lending) themselves" to some purpose, whence the meanings "to be suitable, fit" and "to go well, successfully" (or, simply, "to happen"). Another recurring idea is that of "giving" in the sense of "giving way, yielding."

The meaning "to put" (whence, reflexively, "to put oneself" > "to go, proceed"), explicit in the Czech primary verb and evident in some derivatives in the other languages, is partly attributable to semantic confusion with root ДЕ (etc.).

An extensive sub-group of largely verbal and postverbal formations has grown out of the noun дар et al. (Pol. darzyć się, Cz. dařiti se and their derivatives are, however, thought by some to be unrelated to this root.)

Non-Slavic cognates are Lat. dare "to give" (various English derivatives of which are mentioned in notes on individual words below), donum "gift" (>Eng. donation) and dos "dowry" (>Eng. dowry, endow), Gr. διδόναι "to give" (>Eng. dose).

да́ча: The last two meanings reflect the practice of the Russian feudal nobility of making gifts in the form of tracts of land.

да́нные-dane: ="things given"; compare Eng. data (ult. <Lat. dare "to give"), Ger. Angaben "data" (<geben "to give"), Hung. adatok "data" (<adni "to give").

да́тельный: modeled on Lat. *dativus* (<*dare* "to give") and Gr. *δοτική* (<*διδόναι* "to give"); the dative relationship, normally expressed in English by the prepositions *to* and *for*, was seen by the early grammarians as essentially one of "giving."

darować-*darovati* (Cz.): Regarding the second meaning, compare Eng. *forgive* (<*give*), *pardon* and *condone* (the last two ult. <Lat. *donum* "gift").

да́ром *et al*.: Compare Ger. *vergebens* "in vain" (<*vergeben* "to give away").

dareba, *darebák*: back-formations from *darebný* "wicked" (orig. "worthless, good for nothing") < earlier *daremný* < *darmo*.

благодари́ть-*blagodariti*, *благода́рный* *et al*.: See note under root БЛАГ (etc.).

дармое́д *et al*.: See *darmo*; the first element in the Russian word is from unattested **дармо* (=*да́ром*).

miarodajny-*mjerodavan*: See note under root МЕР$_1$ (etc.).

nazdařbůh: <*na* + *zdařbůh*! "Godspeed! God keep you!" (see *zdařilý*); the meaning is thus: "left to God's good graces, to the fates."

prawodawstwo: See note on *законода́тельство* *et al*.

směrodatný: See note under root МЕР$_1$ (etc.).

ustawodawstwo: See note on *законода́тельство* *et al*.

vjerodajnica: See note under root ВЕР$_1$ (etc.).

законода́тельство *et al*.: Compare Ger. *Gesetzgebung* "legislation" (<*Gesetz* "law" + *geben* "to give"), Dan.-Nor. *lovgivning* "legislation" (<*lov* "law" + Dan. *give*, Nor. *gi* "to give"), Pol. *prawodawstwo* and *ustawodawstwo* above.

dodatek-*dodatak*: Compare Ger. *Zugabe* "addition" (<*zu* "to" + *geben* "to give").

dodatni: The basic idea is that of adding (as in *znak dodatni* "plus sign"); compare *dodatek* and see note on Pol. *ujemny*.

изда́ние-*izdanje*, *изда́тельство*: Compare Eng. *edition* (ult. <Lat. *e* "out" + *dare* "to give"), Ger. *Ausgabe* "edition" and *Herausgabe* "publication" (<[*her*]*aus* "out" + *geben* "to give").

izdaja: Compare Eng. *treason* and -*tray* in *betray* (both ult. <Lat. *tradere* "to hand over" < *trans* "over, across" + *dare* "to give").

izdatak: Compare Ger. *Ausgabe* "expenditure" (<*aus* "out" + *geben* "to give").

izdašan: Compare Ger. *ausgiebig*, *ergiebig* "abundant; productive; fertile" (<*aus*, *er*- "out" + *geben* "to give").

nadávka: The word originated from such expressions as *dáti komu jméno lumpů* "to give s.o. the name of a scoundrel."

nadace: The non-Slavic abstract ending -*ce* reflects the influence of the Latin-derived words *donace* "foundation, endowment" and *dotace* "subsidy."

nedaća: See *daća*.

niezdarny: < dialectal *zdarny* "successful; skilful"; compare *zdarzony*.

nezdárný: See zdárný.

nezadatelný: ‹zadati "to give up, forfeit."

озадачить: ="to confront (s.o.) with a problem"; see задача.

oddavky: See note on vdáti se-udati se.

oddany et al., odevzdaný: Compare Ger. ergeben "devoted; addicted; resigned" (‹geben "to give"); S-C odan is from *oddan.

podanie-podání: Compare Ger. Eingabe "petition, application" (‹eingeben "to hand in" ‹ ein- "in" + geben "to give") and see note on предание-predanje.

podatak: See note on данные-dane.

podati se: from original podati se and poddati se.

подданный et al.: Compare Ger. Untergebene(r) "underling, subordinate" (‹unter "under" + geben "to give"); the Russian word is borrowed from Polish, the Serbo-Croatian word from the earlier Russian form подданник.

предание-predanje: Compare Eng. to hand down (from generation to generation) and tradition (ult. ‹Lat. tradere "to hand over" ‹ trans "over, across" + dare "to give").

преданный-predan: See note on oddany et al., odevzdaný; the first meaning of the Serbo-Croatian word represents semantic borrowing from Russian.

предатель: Compare Eng. traitor (ult. ‹Lat. tradere "to hand over" ‹ trans "over, across" + dare "to give").

придаток et al., prid, prida: See note on dodatek-dodatak.

přídavné (jméno): ‹přidati "to add" (compare přídavek); see notes on Pol. przymiot, przymiotnik and on Rus. имя, Pol. imię, Cz. jméno.

protidávka: See dávka and compare Eng. antidote (ult. ‹Gr. ἀντί "against" + διδόναι "to give").

сдаться-zdać się: The meaning "to seem" = "to present itself (to the mind, eye, etc.)"; regarding the second meaning of the Polish word, see note on Pol. spodziewać się.

zdanie: An opinion is "the way it seems" to a person; see zdać się and compare Sp. parecer "opinion" (‹parecer "to seem"). In its second meaning, the word is a loan-translation of Lat. sententia "opinion, thought; thought expressed in words, sentence."

údaje: See note on данные-dane.

udavač: ="one who gives information"; see údaje and compare Ger. Angeber "informer" (‹geben "to give").

udany (second meaning): =falsely "given out," i.e. misrepresented.

удалой, удалый, udatný: presumed to have meant originally "successful, capable," then "self-confident, bold."

udaremnić: ‹daremny "vain, futile" ‹darmo; compare Ger. vereiteln "to frustrate, thwart" (‹eitel "vain, futile").

вдаться-wdać się: ="to go in" (see introductory note above); regarding the last meaning of the Polish word, see note on Rus. похожий.

vdáti se-udati se: ="to be given in marriage."

wydanie-vydání, wydawnictwo-vydavatelství, вы́дача et al.: See notes on издáние-izdanje, издáтельство and on izdatak and compare Eng. extradition (ult. ‹Lat. ex "out" + tradere "to hand over" ‹ trans "over, across" + dare "to give").

wydajny, vydatný: See note on izdašan.

wydatny, выдаю́щийся: ="going (i.e. standing, jutting) out" (see introductory note above).

uzdati se: See note on Pol. spodziewać się.

задáние-zadanie, задáча-zadaća, zadatak: ="something given, i.e. assigned"; compare Ger. Aufgabe "task" (‹geben "to give"), Hung. feladat "task" (‹adni "to give"). S-C zadaća is borrowed from Russian.

задáтки-zadatki: The meaning is a figurative extension of that of singular задáток-zadatek.

ДЕ, (ДЕЛ)	DZIE, DZIA, (DZIAŁ), (DZIEŁ), (DZIEL)	DÍ, DI, DĚ, DÁ, (DÍL), (DĚL)	DJE, DIJE, DE, D, Đ, (DJEL), (DJEO)
деть, девáть: to put			djenuti (djesti, djeti), djevati: to put
дéться, девáться: to disappear, be hidden		díti se: to happen; (lit.) to disappear, be hidden	djenuti (djesti, djeti) se, djevati se: to disappear, be hidden
	dziać: to knit		
дéяться (coll.): to happen	dziać się: to happen		
		**díti (arch.): to say	
де (coll.), дéскать (coll.): he says, they say, etc. (used for attribution of a statement)			
деяние (lit.): act, deed		děj: event, occurrence; plot (of a novel, etc.)	
		dějiště: scene (of action)	
	dzieje (pl.): history	dějiny (pl.): history	
[R]	[P]	[Cz]	[S-C]

[R]	[P]	[Cz]	[S-C]
де́ятель: figure (political, public, etc.)			
де́ятельность: activity			
де́йствие: act, deed; action, operation; effect; act (part of a play)		dějství: act (part of a play)	dejstvo: action, operation; effect
де́йствовать: to act; to operate, function; (на + acc.) to affect, have an effect (on)			dejstvovati: to act; to operate, function; (na + acc.) to affect, have an effect (on)
де́йственный: effective			
действи́тельный: real, actual; effective; valid, good (ticket, etc.); (gram.) active			
де́ло: affair, matter, business; cause (e.g. cause of peace, just cause); (judicial) case; act, deed	dzieło: act, deed; work (activity); work (of art, etc.)	dílo: act, deed; work (activity); work (of art, etc.)	djelo: act, deed; work (activity); work (of art, etc.)
	działo: cannon	dělo: cannon	
де́лать: to do, make	działać: to act; to operate, function; (na + acc.) to affect, have an effect (on)	dělati: to do, make; to work	djelati: to do, make; to work; to act; (na + acc.) to affect, have an effect (on)
			djelovati: to act; to operate, function; (na + acc.) to affect, have an effect (on)
де́льный: businesslike, efficient; sensible, serious	dzielny: energetic; brave	dělný (lit.): hard-working, industrious; working (e.g. working people, working class)	
		dělník: worker	
		dílna: workshop	

[R]	[P]	[Cz]	[S-C]
делови́тый: businesslike, efficient			
делово́й: businesslike, efficient; business (attr.)			djelovan: active
деле́ц: shrewd businessman, sharp dealer	działacz: figure (political, public, etc.)		
	działalność: activity		djelatnost: activity
благодея́ние: good deed, benefaction			blagodejanje (arch.): scholarship (student's allowance)
благоде́тель: benefactor			
благоде́тельный (lit.): beneficial			blagodjetan: abundant
богаде́льня (arch.): almshouse, poorhouse			
чароде́й (arch.): sorcerer	czarodziej: sorcerer	čaroděj, čarodějník: sorcerer	
	dziejopisarz: historian	dějepisec: historian	
			djelokrug: sphere of activity; sphere of authority, jurisdiction
			djelotvoran: active; efficient
	dobrodziej: benefactor	dobrodinec, (arch.) dobroděj: benefactor	
доброде́тель: virtue			
			drvodjelja: carpenter
	kaznodzieja: preacher		
лицеде́й (arch.): actor			

лиходе́й (arch.): scoundrel			
			poljodjelstvo: agriculture
прелюбоде́й (arch.): adulterer			
рукоде́лие: needlework; needlework product	rękodzieło: handicraft; handicraft product		rukodjelstvo: handicraft
самоде́льный: home-made	samodzielny: independent		
		veledílo: masterpiece	
	współdziałać: to cooperate		
земледе́лие: agriculture		zemědělství: agriculture	zemljodjelstvo: agriculture
злодея́ние (lit.), злоде́йство (lit.): crime	złodziejstwo: theft, thievery	zlodějství: theft, thievery	zlodjelo: misdeed
безде́лица: trifle			
безде́льник: idler			
издева́ться (над + inst.): to mock, ridicule			
изде́лие: manufacture, make; manufactured article			
	znienacka: suddenly, unexpectedly	znenadání: suddenly, unexpectedly	iznenada: suddenly, unexpectedly
			iznenaditi, iznenađivati: to surprise
наде́ть, надева́ть: to don, put on	nadziać, nadziewać: to stuff (meat, etc.); to don, put on	nadíti, nadívati: to stuff (meat, etc.)	nadjenuti (nadjesti, nadjeti), nadijevati: to stuff (meat, etc.); to give (a nickname)
			nadjevak: nickname
наде́жда: hope	nadzieja: hope	naděje: hope	nada, (lit.) nadežda: hope
надёжный: reliable			
[R]	[P]	[Cz]	[S-C]

[R]	[P]	[Cz]	[S-C]
неде́ля: week	niedziela: Sunday	neděle: Sunday; week	nedjelja: Sunday; week
оде́ть, одева́ть: to clothe, dress	odziać, odziewać: to clothe, dress	odíti, odívati (lit.): to clothe, dress; to don, put on	odjenuti (odjesti, odjeti), odijevati: to clothe, dress
одея́ло: blanket			
обде́лать, обде́лывать: to dress (leather); to set (a precious stone)		obdělati, obdělávati: to cultivate, till	obdjelati, obdjelavati: to process, treat, work (metal, wood, etc.); to cultivate, till
отде́лать, отде́лывать: to finish (goods, etc.); to trim, decorate	oddziałać, oddziaływać (na + acc.): to affect, have an effect (on)	oddělati, oddělávati: to remove; to work off (a debt)	
		**padělati: to falsify, counterfeit	
	podziać, podziewać: to put		**podijevati: to squander
	podziać się, podziewać się: to disappear, be hidden	*podíti se: to disappear, be hidden	**podijevati se: to disappear, be hidden
понеде́льник: Monday	poniedziałek: Monday	pondělí, pondělek: Monday	ponedjeljak, ponedjeljnik, ponedjeonik: Monday
подде́лать, подде́лывать: to falsify, counterfeit			
		přezdívka: nickname	
			pridjenuti (pridjesti, pridjeti), pridijevati: to fasten, attach; to add
			pridjev: (gram.) adjective
			pridjevak: nickname
приде́лать, приде́лывать: to fasten, attach		přidělati, přidělávati: to fasten, attach; to add	
проде́лка: trick; prank		prodělek: loss	

[R]	[P]	[Cz]	[S-C]
**соде́йствовать: to help, assist; to promote, further			*sadejstvovati: to cooperate
сде́лка: transaction, deal			
сде́льщик: piece-worker			
			sudjelovati: to participate; to cooperate
	spodziewać się: to expect; to hope		
		událost: event, occurrence	
вы́делать, выде́лывать: to make, manufacture; to dress (leather)		vydělati, vydělávati: to earn (money); to dress (leather)	
возде́ть, воздева́ть (arch.): to raise			
возде́лать, возде́лывать: to cultivate, till		vzdělati, vzdělávati: to educate; (arch.) to cultivate, till	
		zdáti se: to seem; to appear in a dream	
		zdání: (outward) appearance; notion, idea	
заде́ть, задева́ть: to touch; to offend			zadjenuti (zadjesti, zadjeti), zadijevati: to stick, poke (into); to tease, taunt; to pick (a quarrel)
			zadjevica: quarrel
	zapodziać, zapodziewać: to lose, mislay		zapodjenuti (zapodjesti, zapodjeti), zapodijevati: to pick (a quarrel), start (a conversation)

NOTES

Basic meaning of root: to do, make; to put

A number of derivatives show semantic elaboration in the form of such meanings as "to happen" (="to be done"), "to disappear" (="to be put away") and "to don, put on" (or, with a shift in the point of reference, "to clothe, dress"). The notion of "doing" often tends to shade into that of "working," whence such specialized meanings as "to till the soil," "to dress leather" and "to knit." A distinctive secondary root-meaning, "to say," is apparent in Rus. дé(скать) and издевáться, Cz. díti (see note below) and přezdívka (the same view of speech as constituting in itself a form of action may account for the meaning of Pol. prawić, Cz. praviti [q.v.]); S-C nadjevak, pridjevak express the idea of "putting on" or "attaching" a name (see nadjenuti, pridjenuti) but may also reflect a degree of semantic crossing with the meaning "to say."

The various derivatives go back to two primary verb forms, today largely defunct, in which the two root-meanings tended to overlap: (1) Common Slavic *děti, whence Rus. деть (orig. also "to do"), OPol. dzieć "to do; to put," obsolete Cz. díti "to do; to put," S-C djeti (djenuti and djesti are new infinitive forms modeled on other verb classes); (2) Common Slavic *dějati, whence obsolete Rus. дéять "to do," Pol. dziać (<earlier dziejać; the original meaning was "to do; to put"), assumed OCz. *ďáti "to do; to put" (whence, through contamination by dáti "to give," a number of modern derivatives with root-form DÁ), obsolete S-C djejati "to do" (probably a Church Slavic loan-word). In the modern languages, the root-meaning "to do, make" has been largely taken over by the denominative verb дéлать et al. (<дéло et al.), which also shows the meaning "to put" in some derivatives (Rus. обдéлать and придéлать, Cz. oddělati and přidělati).

The alternation in meaning characteristic of the Slavic root can also be seen in kindred Indo-European words, e.g. Eng. do (in which the meaning "to put" survives in don "to put on" [<do on] and doff "to put off, take off" [<do off]), Ger. tun and Du. doen (both generally "to do" but sometimes "to put"), Lat. facere "to do, make" (>Eng. fact, affect, effect, efficient) and (in compounds) -dere "to put"; cognate Gr. τιθέναι (>Eng. theme, thesis, antithesis, synthesis) has the one meaning "to put." Compare also Hung. tenni "to do, make; to put."

díti: differentiated by the 1 sg. form (dím) from obsolete díti "to do; to put" (1 sg.: ději).

де, дéскать: Де is derived from the 3 sg. of ORus. дѣти "to say"; regarding the second element in дéскать, see note under root КАЗ (etc.).

дéйствие et al.: The Russian and Serbo-Croatian words are borrowed from Church Slavic, the Czech word from Russian.

działo-dělo: variant forms of dzieło-dílo showing specialization of meaning; regarding the semantic development, compare Eng. works in the sense of "fortifications."

благодея́ние-blagodejanje, благоде́тель, благоде́тельный-blagodjetan: See note under root БЛАГ (etc.).

богаде́льня: ⟨ORus. Бога дѣля "for the sake of God"; the postposition дѣля is related to modern де́ло.

чароде́й et al.: The first element is from ORus. чаръ (in modern Rus., only pl. ча́ры), Pol. czar, Cz. čár (usu. pl. čáry) "charm, spell."

dobrodziej et al.: See note on благодея́ние-blagodejanje, благоде́тель, благоде́тельный-blagodjetan.

drvodjelja: The first element is from drva "wood."

kaznodzieja: The first element is from kaźń "punishment," which here retains its earlier meaning "commandment."

лицеде́й: ="one who makes (i.e. assumes) the face of another."

poljodjelstvo: The first element is from polje "field."

злодея́ние et al.: See note under root ЗЛ (etc.).

znienacka et al.: See nadzieja-naděje-nada; the Polish word is from earlier znienadzka.

наде́жда et al., надёжный: See note on spodziewać się. Наде́жда and nadežda are Church Slavic loan-words; nada contains the zero-grade of the root, D, plus a suffix.

неде́ля et al.: ="(day of) inactivity, rest." "Sunday" was the original meaning of the word in all four languages; the secondary meaning "week" can be traced to the fact that Gr. τὰ σάββατα commonly referred not only to the Sabbath day but also to the new week whose beginning it marked.

одея́ло: Compare оде́ть.

обде́лать (second meaning), oddělati (first meaning): See introductory note above.

padělati: See note on S-C patvoriti, Pol. potwora et al. and potwarz.

podijevati: ="to put away, i.e. scatter, disperse"; compare Ger. vertun "to squander" (⟨tun "to do; to put").

понеде́льник et al.: ="the day which follows Sunday"; see note on неде́ля et al.

подде́лать: See note on Rus. подки́дыш.

pridjenuti, přidělati: Compare Eng. add (ult. ⟨Lat. ad "to" + -dere "to put"), Rus. доложи́ть (докла́дывать) et al. and приложи́ть (прикла́дывать) et al., S-C dometak.

pridjev: See pridjenuti and note on Pol. przymiot, przymiotnik.

проде́лка: ⟨проде́лать "to do, perform (e.g. a trick)."

prodělek: The meaning results from the action of the prefix.

sadejstvovati: ⟨Rus. соде́йствовать.

сде́лка: ="something done, concluded."

spodziewać się: ="to put, set o.s. (i.e. lean, rest, rely) on s.o. or s.th."; compare наде́жда et al. and надёжный above, Rus. положи́ться, Pol.

polegać and zdać się, Cz. spolehnouti (se), S-C uzdati se.

vzdělati: The first meaning is an outgrowth of the second; compare the similar literal and figurative use of Eng. cultivate.

zdáti se: The original notion was that of something happening (in one's sleep).

задéть-zadjenuti: The semantic progression has been roughly the following: "to put" 〉 "to touch, poke" 〉 "to taunt, offend."

zapodjenuti: The prefix here has inceptive force.

ДЕЛ	DZIAŁ, DZIEL	DÍL, DĚL	DIJEL, DJEL, DIO
	dział: part; share; section, department	díl: part; share	dijel, dio: part; share
делúть: to divide; to share	dzielić: to divide; to share	děliti: to divide	dijeliti: to divide
делáнка: plot of land	działka: plot of land; scale (of map, etc.)		
	dzielnica: quarter (of town); region; (arch.) principality		dionica: share of stock
	spółdzielnia: cooperative (n.)		
водораздéл: watershed			vododijelnica: watershed
			dodijeliti, dodjeljivati: to allot; to assign
наделúть, наделáть: to allot; to endow		naděliti, nadělovati (nadíleti): to bestow, present	*nadijeliti: to bestow, present
	niedziałka (arch.): atom		
оделúть, оделáть: to bestow, present			
отделúть, отделáть: to separate (tr.)	oddzielić, oddzielać: to separate (tr.)	odděliti, oddělovati: to separate (tr.)	odijeliti, odjeljivati: to separate (tr.)
отдéл: part, section; section, department	oddział: section, department; branch office; (military) detachment	oddíl: part, section; (military) detachment	odjel, odio: section, department; (military) detachment;
[R]	[P]	[Cz]	[S-C]

[R]	[P]	[Cz]	[S-C]
			class (in school); (train) compartment
отделе́ние: separation; section, department; compartment; (mil.) squad	oddzielenie: separation	oddělení: separation; section, department; (train) compartment	odjeljenje: section, department; (military) detachment; (train) compartment
определи́ть, определя́ть: to define; to determine; to fix, set, specify; (arch.) to appoint (to office, etc.)			opredijeliti, opredjeljivati: to determine; to fix, set, specify
	podziałka: scale (of map, etc.)		
преде́л: boundary; limit	przedział: part (in the hair); (train) compartment	předěl: boundary; dividing line	predjel, predio: region; landscape
	przydzielić, przydzielać: to allot; to assign	přiděliti, přidělovati: to allot; to assign	pridijeliti, pridjeljivati: to allot; to assign
		přidělenec: attaché	
разде́л: division (act of dividing); section (of a book, etc.)	rozdział: distribution; separation; chapter	rozdíl: difference	razdjel, razdio: section, department
			razdjeljak: part (in the hair)
распредели́ть, распределя́ть: to distribute			raspodijeliti, raspodjeljivati: to distribute
		sděliti, sdělovati: to communicate, impart	
удели́ть, уделя́ть: to spare (time), pay (attention), appropriate (funds)	udzielić, udzielać: to pay (attention), impart (information), grant (permission), render (assist-	uděliti, udělovati (udíleti): to bestow, present; to impart (information), grant (a pardon),	udijeliti, udjeljivati: to bestow, present; to pay (attention)
[R]	[P]	[Cz]	[S-C]

[R]	[P]	[Cz]	[S-C]
	ance), administer (a sacrament)	confer (a rank), administer (a sacrament), issue (an order)	
удéл: destiny, fate, lot; (arch.) feudal domain, appanage; (arch.) principality	udział: share; participation; destiny, fate, lot; (arch.) principality	úděl: destiny, fate, lot; (arch.) feudal domain, appanage; (arch.) principality	udjel, udio: share; participation
вы́делить, выделять: to allot; to single out; to distinguish, honor; to exude; (med.) to secrete	wydzielić, wydzielać: to allot; to single out; to exude; (med.) to secrete		
	wydział: section, department; faculty (of a university)		

NOTES

Basic meaning of root: part; to divide

The root is related to Eng. deal (n. and v.; note such expressions as a great deal, to deal the cards) and dole, Ger. Teil "part" and teilen "to divide; to share."

dział et al., дели́ть et al.: The verb is denominative. Rus. дел "division" survives only in dialect.

водоразде́л-vododijelnica: See note under root ВОД (etc.).

niedziałka: ="indivisible particle"; the word is modeled on Gr. ἄτομος (<ἀ- "un-, not" + τέμνειν "to cut"), whence Eng. atom.

odijeliti, odjel, odio, odjeljenje: <oddijeliti, etc.

определи́ть-opredijeliti: See преде́л; the underlying notion is that of setting a boundary or limit, demarcating. Compare Eng. define (ult. <Lat. finis "boundary; end") and determine (ult. <Lat. terminus "boundary; end"), Pol. określić "to define; to determine" (<kres "boundary; end"), Hung. meghatározni "to define; to determine" (<határ "boundary"), Cz. vymeziti. S-C opredijeliti is borrowed from Russian.

преде́л-předěl-predjel, predio: Rus. преде́л is a Church Slavic loan-word from which the Czech and Serbo-Croatian words are in turn borrowed.

přidělenec: See the second meaning of přiděliti.

sděliti: ="to share"; compare Eng. impart and part, Ger. mitteilen "to communicate, impart" (<mit "with" + teilen "to share").

уде́л-udział-úděl: Regarding the meaning "destiny," see note on S-C čest; the Czech word is borrowed from Russian.

вы́делить-wydzielić (last meaning): ="to separate (from the body)"; compare Eng. secrete (ult. <Lat. secernere "to separate"), Ger. ausscheiden "to secrete" (<aus "out" + scheiden "to separate"), Cz. výměšek and výměsek, S-C lučiti and izlučiti.

ДЕН, ДН	DZI(EŃ), DZIEN, DN	DEN, DN	DAN, DN
день: day	dzień: day	den: day	dan: day
	dziś, dzisiaj: today	dnes: today	danas: today
	dnieć: to dawn	dníti se: to dawn	daniti se: to dawn
дневни́к: diary; journal	dziennik: newspaper; diary; journal	deník: daily newspaper; diary; journal	dnevnik: daily newspaper; diary; journal
	dziennikarz: journalist		
			bjelodan: obvious
			blagdan: holiday
благоде́нствие (arch.): well-being, prosperity			
			danguba: idler; idleness
долгоде́нствие (arch.): longevity			dugodnevica: summer solstice
			kratkodnevica: winter solstice
			objelodaniti, objelodanjivati: to publish; to disclose
по́лдень: noon; (arch.) south	południe: noon; south	poledne: noon; (arch.) south	podne, poldan: noon
по́лдник: light afternoon meal	południk: meridian	poledník: meridian	podnevak, podnevnik: meridian
повседне́вный: daily, everyday; everyday, commonplace	powszedni: daily, everyday; everyday, commonplace; venial		
равноде́нствие: equinox		rovnodennost: equinox	ravnodnevica: equinox
сего́дня: today			
	tydzień: week	týden: week	tjedan: week
[R]	[P]	[Cz]	[S-C]

злободнéвный: topical, burning (issue, etc.) обы́денный: everyday, commonplace		všední: daily, everyday; everyday, commonplace	
[R]	[P]	[Cz]	[S-C]

NOTES

Basic meaning of root: day

The Slavic root is related to Lat. dies "day."

dziś et al.: The suffix is the remnant of an old demonstrative (see, e.g., archaic Rus. сей "this"); thus, the meaning is "this day." The Polish words are from earlier dzińsia.

dnieć et al.: Compare Eng. dawn (from the root of day).

дневни́к et al.: Compare Eng. diary (ult. ‹Lat. dies "day"), journal (‹Fr. journal ‹jour "day").

bjelodan: The first element is from bijel "white"; thus, the meaning is "white (or bright) as day."

благодéнствие: See note under root БЛАГ (etc.).

danguba: ="loser (or loss) of a day."

dugodnevica, kratkodnevica: respectively the longest and shortest days of the year.

objelodaniti: See bjelodan.

пóлдень-południe-poledne: See note under root ПОЛ (etc.).

południk et al.: See note under root ПОЛ (etc.).

равнодéнствие et al.: the time of year when day and night are of equal length; compare Eng. equinox (ult. ‹Lat. aequus "equal" + nox "night"), Gr. ἰσημέριον "equinox" (‹ἴσος "equal" + ἡμέρα "day"), Ger. Tag- und Nachtgleiche "equinox" (="day and night equality"), Pol. równonoc.

сегóдня: the genitive of сей день "this day"; compare dziś et al.

tydzień et al.: The first element is an old demonstrative (see modern Pol.-Cz. ten, S-C taj "this"); the word arose as a reference to the lapse of time before the recurrence of "this (same) day," i.e. any given day.

злободнéвный: ="pertaining to the evil of the day"; the word is a recent formation from the passage in the gospel: Довлеетъ дневи злоба его "Sufficient unto the day is the evil thereof."

обы́денный: The origin of the letter ы after the prefix is disputed.

ДЛ, ДОЛ, ДОЛГ, ДОЛЖ	DL, DŁUG, DŁUŻ	DL, DÉL, DLOUH, DLOUŽ, DLUŽ	DUL, DUG, DUŽ
		dle (lit.): along; near, beside; according to	
длина́: length		délka: length; longitude	duljina: length
длить (arch.): to prolong		dlíti (lit.): to linger; to dwell	duljiti: to lengthen; to prolong; to delay
дли́ться: to last			duljiti se: to drag on (e.g. time)
до́лгий: long	długi: long	dlouhý: long	dug: long
долгота́: length; longitude	długość: length; longitude		dužina: length; longitude
			dugočasan: boring, tedious
долгоде́нствие (arch.): longevity			dugodnevica: summer solstice
	długorąk: gibbon		
долгове́чность: longevity	długowieczność: longevity	dlouhověkost: longevity	dugovječnost: longevity
			odugovlačiti: to delay
		obdélný: oblong	
по́дле: near, beside	podle: near, beside	podle: along; near, beside; according to	
		podélný: longitudinal, lengthwise	
по́длинный: genuine; original (text, etc.)			
	podług: according to		
	podłużny, podługowaty: oblong; longitudinal, lengthwise	podlouhlý: oblong	
продо́льный: longitudinal, lengthwise			
продолгова́тый: oblong			
[R]	[P]	[Cz]	[S-C]

[R]	[P]	[Cz]	[S-C]
продо́лжить, продолжа́ть: to continue (tr.); to prolong	przedłużyć, przedłużać: to lengthen; to prolong	prodloužiti, prodlužovati: to lengthen; to prolong	produžiti, produživati: to continue (tr.); to prolong
			uzdužan: longitudinal, lengthwise
	wedle: near, beside; according to	vedle: near, beside; besides	
	według: according to		
		zdlouhavý: slow, sluggish	

NOTES

Basic meaning of root: long

The root appears both in its simple form (ДЛ-ДОЛ---DL---DL-DÉL---DUL) and with a suffix (ДОЛГ-ДОЛЖ---DŁUG-DŁUŻ---DLOUH-DLOUŽ-DLUŽ---DUG-DUŽ).

dle: The basic idea is "along"; regarding the transition to the meaning "according to," compare Rus. по and Cz.-S-C po "along; according to."

dlíti: Compare Eng. linger (from the root of long).

dugočasan: ="lasting a long time"; compare Ger. langweilig "boring" (<lang "long" + Weile "(a) while, period of time"). See also Pol. krotochwilny, Cz. kratochvilný.

dugodnevica: See note under root ДЕН (etc.).

долгове́чность et al.: The second element is from век-wiek-věk-vijek "age"; compare Eng. longevity (ult. <Lat. longus "long" + aevum "age").

odugovlačiti: See note on Pol. odwlec.

по́дле et al., podług: See note on dle.

по́длинный: The word is generally thought to hark back to the early Russian practice of beating prisoners with long sticks (по́длинники) during interrogation; the facts thus elicited were presumed to be authentic. Rus. подного́тная "secrets, ins and outs (of a matter)" (<под "under" + но́готь "fingernail") is similarly traceable to an early method of establishing the truth.

wedle-vedle, według: See note on dle.

ДО(Б)	DOB	DOB	DOB, DAB
	doba: day (twenty-four hours); time, period	doba: time, period	doba: time, period
			dob: age (time of life)
до́блесть: bravery, valor			
			istodoban: simultaneous; contemporary
			malodoban: minor, under age
		mezidobí: interval of time	
		novodobý: modern	
подобостра́стие: servility, obsequiousness			
правдоподо́бный: probable, likely	prawdopodobny: probable, likely	pravděpodobný: probable, likely	
		nádoba: vessel (kitchenware, etc.)	
на́добный (arch.): necessary	nadobny: handsome, attractive		
на́до: it is necessary, one must			
		napodobiti, napodobovati: to imitate	
			nedoba: inopportune time
			nepodoba: monster
		obdoba: analogy; analogue	
		období: time, period; season	
подо́бие: similarity, resemblance	podoba: model, pattern	podoba: similarity, resemblance; shape, form	
	podobizna: likeness; photograph; facsimile	podobizna: likeness; portrait; photograph	
подо́бный: similar	podobny: similar	podobný: similar	podoban: able, capable
[R]	[P]	[Cz]	[S-C]

[R]	[P]	[Cz]	[S-C]
подоба́ть: to be fitting, proper	**podobać się: to please	podobati se: to resemble; (arch.) to please; (arch.) to seem	
преподо́бный: reverend (title)			prepodoban: reverend (title)
			prispodobiti, prispodabljati: to compare
			razdoblje: time, period
сдо́ба: enriching ingredient added to dough; fancy bread			
	zdobić: to decorate, adorn	zdobiti: to decorate, adorn	
		soudobý: simultaneous; contemporary; modern	
сна́добье (coll.): drug, medicine			
		spodoba: (phon.) assimilation	spodoba: shape, form
			spodoban: similar
		údobí: time, period	
удо́бный: comfortable; convenient			udoban: comfortable; convenient
[R]	[P]	[Cz]	[S-C]

NOTES

Basic meaning of root: good, suitable

The meaning "time" is reflected in many of the derivatives. (See note on doba below.)

The notion of "similarity, resemblance" (whence the further meaning "to seem") is an outgrowth of that of "suitability." A similar semantic shift (proceeding, however, inversely) is apparent in Eng. to seem and seemly, like (="similar") and to like (orig. ="to please," as in the archaic phrase it likes me not) and in S-C sviđanje (q.v.). Note also the comparable relationship among many of the words listed under root ЛИК (etc.), and see S-C goditi se.

The root is related to root ДОБР (etc.).

doba: The word referred originally to a suitable, opportune time (compare S-C nedoba), then to any given period of time. (Russian дóба "time" is dialectal.) A similar shift in meaning is discussed in the introductory note on root ГОД (etc.).

дóблесть: borrowed from Church Slavic. The general notion of goodness is not infrequently associated with the more specific attribute of physical bravery; compare Fr. brave "good; brave," Eng. valor (ult. ‹Late Lat. valor "value").

istodoban: See note on Pol. równoczesny.

malodoban: See note on Rus. малолéтний et al.

novodobý: The first element is from nový "new"; see note on Pol. nowoczesny.

подобострáстие: See note under root СТРА(Д) (etc.).

правдоподóбный et al.: ="resembling the truth, seeming true." The word is a loan-translation; compare Eng. verisimilar (ult. ‹Lat. verus "true" + similis "similar"), Fr. vraisemblable "probable" (‹vrai "true" + semblable "similar"), Ger. wahrscheinlich "probable" (‹wahr "true" + scheinen "to seem").

nádoba: orig. "useful, attractive object."

нáдобный: orig. "suitable, useful."

нáдо: shortened from an oblique form of ORus. надоба "necessity"; compare нáдобный.

nepodoba: orig. "something unseemly, indecent."

obdoba: a relatively new word; compare podobný.

преподóбный-prepodoban: borrowed from Church Slavic, in which подобьнъ meant "worthy, seemly"; the prefix has intensive force.

сдóба, zdobić-zdobiti: The root-meaning is reinforced here by a prefix meaning "good" (compare Rus. счáстье et al., Pol. zboże and śliczny, Cz. zboží and sličný).

soudobý: See note on Pol. współczesny.

снáдобье: orig. "seasoning for food"; compare сдóба.

spodoba (Cz.): Compare Eng. assimilation (ult. ‹Lat. ad "to" + similis "similar").

ДОБР, ДАБР	DOBR	DOBR, DOBŘ	DOBAR, DOBR
дóбрый: good; kind добрó: welfare, weal, good; property, goods	dobry: good dobro: welfare, weal, good	dobrý: good; kind dobro: welfare, weal, good	dobar: good; kind dobro: welfare, weal, good; property, goods; estate, landed property
[R]	[P]	[Cz]	[S-C]

[R]	[P]	[Cz]	[S-C]
	dobra (pl.): property, goods; estate, landed property		
	dobrobyt: well-being, prosperity		dobrobit: well-being, prosperity; welfare, weal, good
доброхо́тный (arch.): voluntary			dobrohotan: benevolent
	dobroczynność: charity, philanthropy	dobročinnost: charity, philanthropy	dobročinstvo: good deed, benefaction
	dobrodziej: benefactor	dobrodinec, (arch.) dobroděj: benefactor	
доброде́тель: virtue			
			dobrodošao: welcome (a.)
		dobrodruh: adventurer	
доброду́шный: good-natured	dobroduszny: good-natured	dobrodušný, dobromyslný: good-natured	dobrodušan: good-natured
		dobrořečiti (lit.): to be grateful (to); to praise	
			dobrostanje: well-being, prosperity
			dobrotvoran: charitable, philanthropic
доброво́льный: voluntary	dobrowolny: voluntary	dobrovolný: voluntary	dobrovoljan: voluntary; good-humored
доброжела́тельный: benevolent			
одо́брить, одобря́ть: to approve			odobriti, odobravati: to approve
сдо́брить, сда́бривать: to flavor, spice			
удо́брить, удобря́ть: to fertilize, manure		udobřiti, udobřovati: to conciliate, appease	udobriti, udobravati: to conciliate, appease
задо́брить, зада́бривать: to coax, cajole			

NOTES

Basic meaning of root: good

The root is, properly speaking, an expanded form of root ДО(Б) (etc.). It occurs as a prefix meaning "good" or "well" in numerous abstract compounds. (See introductory note on root БЛАГ [etc.].)

добро́-dobro (S-C), dobra: See note on S-C blago.

dobrohotan: See note on Cz. blahovolný.

dobročinstvo, dobrodziej et al.: See note on Rus. благодея́ние, благоде́тель and благоде́тельный, S-C blagodejanje and blagodjetan.

доброде́тель: borrowed from Church Slavic.

dobrodošao: See note under root ХОД (etc.).

dobrodruh: See note under root ДРУГ (etc.).

dobrořečiti: orig. "to bless"; see note on Cz. blahořečiti.

доброжела́тельный: The second element is from жела́ть "to wish"; see note on Cz. blahovolný.

odobriti: ‹Rus. одо́брить.

сдо́брить, удо́брить: ="to improve"; compare Sp. abono "fertilizer, manure" (ult. ‹Lat. bonus "good").

ДР, ДИР, ДОР	DRZ, DZIER(Z), DAR	DR, DŘ, DĚR, DOR	DR, DER, DIR, DOR
драть (coll.): to tear; to flay, skin		dráti: to tear; to flay, skin	derati (drati): to tear; to flay, skin
	drzeć: to tear; to flay, skin	dříti: to rub, chafe; to flay, skin	drijeti: to tear; to flay, skin
дра́ка: fight, brawl			
			derač: fang; flayer, skinner
		dravý: rapacious; swift	
		dravec: beast of prey	
			dirnuti, dirati: to touch
			dirljiv: touching, pathetic
			neboder: skyscraper
			oblakoder: skyscraper
[R]	[P]	[Cz]	[S-C]

[R]	[P]	[Cz]	[S-C]
		nádor: tumor; abscess	
		navzdor, navzdory: in spite (of)	
			odora: (military, etc.) uniform
	obdartus: ragamuffin		
			poderanac: ragamuffin
придирчивый: captious, carping			
			prodoran: piercing, penetrating
раздóр: discord, dissension			razdor: discord, dissension
	wedrzeć się, wdzierać się: to intrude; to encroach		
	wydzierca: robber	vyděrač: blackmailer, extortionist	
вздор: nonsense		vzdor: defiance; obstinacy; (prep.) in spite (of)	
	zadzierzysty: quarrelsome		
			zadrtost: obstinacy
задóр: fervor, enthusiasm			
			zadorica: quarrel

NOTES

Basic meaning of root: to tear

Драть et al. and drzeć et al. are two parallel imperfective derivatives of the root. (OPol. drać no longer exists; the Russian verb corresponding to drzeć et al. is not attested.) S-C dirnuti, dirati is a variant form which has acquired a distinct meaning.

The root tends to form abstract derivatives expressing vehement feeling of various kinds. (Compare Eng. to be torn by emotion, Ger. Zorn "anger" [<zerren "to pull, tear"].)

Non-Slavic cognates are Eng. tear, Ger. zerren, Gr. δέρειν "to flay, skin," whence δέρμα "skin" (>Eng. dermatology, epidermis).

драка: Compare Cz. rváti se, S-C rvati se.

neboder: The first element is from nebo "sky."

oblakoder: See note under root ВОЛОК (etc.).

nádor: orig. a bruise caused by a blow.

navzdor, navzdory: See note on vzdor.

odora: <odrijeti "to flay, skin; to strip"; the word originally referred to the clothing and equipment of which a defeated enemy was "stripped" and eventually became restricted to its present meaning. Eng. robe (ultimately derived from an earlier form of Ger. Raub "robbery, plunder, booty") offers an exact semantic parallel.

vyděrač: Compare Eng. extort (ult. <Lat. ex "out" + torquere "to twist").

вздор: An earlier meaning, "quarrel," tallies with that of other derivatives of this root, but the word has also been explained as meaning originally "scraps of bark left over from the cleaning of a tree," then "rubbish, nonsense."

vzdor: Compare Eng. spite and in spite of, Ger. Trotz "defiance" and trotz "in spite (of)."

ДРУГ, ДРУЖ	DRUG, DRUH, DRUŻ	DRUH, DRUŽ	DRUG, DRUK, DRUŽ, DRUŠ
друг: friend	druh: friend	druh: kind, sort; species; (lit.) friend	drug: companion, comrade, colleague
другóй: other	drugi: second; other	druhý: second; other	drugi: second; other
дрýжка: best man at wedding	drużka: bridesmaid; (arch.) female friend	družka: female friend	
		družice: (astr.) satellite; (lit.) bridesmaid	družica: female companion, comrade, colleague
		družička: bridesmaid	
	druhna: bridesmaid		
дрýжба: friendship	drużba: friendship; best man at wedding	družba: friendship; best man at wedding	družba: society (organization); set, coterie; gang; comradeship
дружúна: detachment, brigade; (arch.) prince's bodyguard	drużyna: team; detachment, brigade	družina: suite, retinue	družina: domestic servants; troupe; team; set, coterie
[R]	[P]	[Cz]	[S-C]

ДРУГ

[R]	[P]	[Cz]	[S-C]
		družstvo: society (organization); cooperative; team; (mil.) squad	društvo: society (organization); society (the company of others); society (social entity, order); company, firm; set, coterie
		druhotný: secondary	drugotan: secondary; second-rate
			drugačije, drugojačije, drukčije: otherwise
		druhdy (lit.): formerly, at one time	drugda: at another time
			drugdje: elsewhere, at another place
			drugamo, drugud: elsewhere, to another place
		dobrodruh: adventurer	
		druhopis: duplicate, copy	
	drugorzędny: secondary; second-rate	druhořadý: secondary; second-rate	drugoredan: secondary; second-rate
		půldruhého: one and a half	podrug, poldrug: one and a half
nédруг: enemy			
		podruh: farm-hand	
			predrugojačiti, predrugojačavati: to alter
		přidružiti, přidružovati: to join, unite (tr.)	pridružiti, pridruživati: to join, unite (tr.)
			udružiti, udruživati: to join, unite (tr.)
вдруг: suddenly			
			zadruga: cooperative (n.)

NOTES

Basic meaning of root: friend, comrade

The meaning "other" represents an extension of the original root-meaning. The further semantic development to "second" (i.e. "the other of two") has parallels in non-Slavic languages. Thus, Eng. other originally had the additional meaning "second" (and still does in the expression every other day), as did Ger. ander "other"; Dan. anden, Nor. annen and Swed. annan have retained both meanings. Similarly, Fin. toinen can mean either "other" or "second," while Hung. második "second" is derived from más "other."

The basic root-meaning is reflected in numerous derivatives expressing, in one form or another, the general notion of association.

druh (Pol.): a borrowed word (from Ukrainian, Byelorussian or Czech) which has supplanted OPol. drug.

druh (Cz.): The meaning "kind, sort" (and, in specialized usage, "species") arose from the former use of the word in the sense of "mate, matching piece" in such expressions as toho druh "(a thing which is) the mate of (i.e. of the same kind as) that one"; owing to misunderstanding of the construction, druh came to appear in the genitive (toho druhu) and was therefore taken to mean "kind."

dobrodruh: ‹OCz. dobrý (q.v.) druh "brave comrade."

půldruhého et al.: See note under root ПОЛ (etc.).

не́друг: Similar formations are Rus. неприя́тель, Pol. nieprzyjaciel, Cz. nepřítel, S-C neprijatelj "enemy" (all from the negative prefix + a word meaning "friend") and Eng. enemy (ult. ‹Lat. inimicus "enemy" ‹ in- "un-, not" + amicus "friend").

predrugojačiti: Compare drugojačije.

вдруг: The sense of the word is, roughly, "the next moment, from one moment to another."

ДЕРЖ	DZIERŻ	DRŽ	DRŽ
держа́ть: to hold	dzierżyć (arch.): to hold; to own, possess	držeti: to hold	držati: to hold
держа́ва: power (i.e. sovereign state, country)	dzierżawa: lease; leased property	država: domain, possession	država: state (political entity)
			državljanin: citizen
[R]	[P]	[Cz]	[S-C]

[R]	[P]	[Cz]	[S-C]
			državnik: statesman
	dzierżawczy: (gram.) possessive		
			državoslovlje: political science
		místodržící, místodržitel: governor	
самодéржец: autocrat	samodzierżca: autocrat		samodržac: autocrat
издержáть, издéрживать: to spend (money)	*zdzierżyć (arch.): to bear, endure		izdržati, izdržavati: to bear, endure; to maintain, support (as a financial dependent)
		nádrž, nádržka: reservoir; tank	
одержáть, одéрживать: to gain, win			održati, održavati: to maintain, keep up; to gain, win; to keep (a promise); to hold (a meeting)
одержúмый: possessed, obsessed			
		obdržeti, obdržovati: to receive	obdržati, obdržavati: to celebrate, observe
подéржанный: second-hand, used			
поддержáть, поддéрживать: to support, uphold, sustain; to maintain, keep up			podržati, podržavati: to support, uphold, sustain; to maintain, keep up
сдержáть, сдéрживать: to restrain; (сдержáть only) to keep (a promise)		zdržeti, zdržovati: to detain; to delay; to restrain	
содержáние: maintenance, upkeep; maintenance, support (of a			sadržaj: content, substance, matter; contents (of a book); summary

financial dependent); salary, wages; content (chemical, etc.); content, substance, matter; contents (of a book)			
содержи́мое: contents (of a receptacle)			sadržina: content, substance, matter; contents (of a receptacle); content (chemical, etc.)
		soudržný: compact; cohesive	
удержа́ть, уде́рживать: to keep, retain; to restrain; to deduct		udržeti, udržovati: to keep, retain; to maintain, keep up; (udržovati only) to maintain, keep in good repair	
*вы́держать: to bear, endure; to contain, restrain o.s.; to pass (an examination); to season (wood, tobacco, etc.)		*vydržeti: to bear, endure	
выде́рживать: to bear, endure; to contain, restrain o.s.; to pass (an examination); to season (wood, tobacco, etc.)		vydržovati: to maintain, support (as a financial dependent)	
вы́держка: endurance; self-restraint; (phot.) exposure; excerpt, extract			
воздержа́ться, возде́рживаться: to refrain, abstain (from)			uzdržati se, uzdržavati se: to refrain, abstain (from); to contain, restrain o.s.
[R]	[P]	[Cz]	[S-C]

задержáть, задéрживать: to check, hold back; to detain; to delay; to arrest, apprehend [R]	[P]	zadržeti, zadržovati: to check, hold back; to restrain; to arrest, apprehend; to attach (property) [Cz]	zadržati, zadržavati: to check, hold back; to detain; to delay; to keep, retain [S-C]

NOTES

Basic meaning of root: to hold

Pol. dzierżyć has been displaced in modern usage by trzymać (q.v.), which has united with prefixes to form compound verbs with roughly the same range of meanings as the derivatives formed from this root in the other three languages.

Many of the Slavic derivatives listed here have semantic parallels in English words containing the stem -tain or -ten(t) (ult. <Lat. tenere "to hold").

državoslovlje: See note under root СЛЫ (etc.).

místodržící, místodržitel: See note under root МЕСТ (etc.).

самодéржец et al.: See note under root САМ (etc.).

издержáть: Держáть here retains an earlier meaning, "to have," while из serves as a negative prefix; thus, the underlying meaning of the word is, roughly, "not to have, to cease to have."

zdzierżyć-izdržati: Compare Eng. to hold out in the sense of "to endure," Ger. aushalten "to endure" (<aus "out" + halten "to hold"), Pol. wytrzymać.

podržati: <poddržati.

содержáние-sadržaj, содержи́мое-sadržina: Compare Ger. Gehalt "salary; content(s)," Inhalt "content(s)," enthalten "to contain" (all <halten "to hold").

вы́держать-vydržeti, выдéрживать, вы́держка: See note on zdzierżyć-izdržati.

вы́держка (fourth meaning): ="s.th. held (i.e. taken) out."

ДВА, ДВУ, ДВОЙ, ДВО(Е,-И,-Ю,-Я)	DWA, DWU, DWÓJ, DWOJ, DWO(I), DWAJ	DVA, DVOJ	DVA, DVO, DVOJ, DVAJ
два: two	dwa: two	dva: two	dva: two
двоя́кий: double	dwojaki: double	dvojaký: non-committal; two-faced, insincere	dvojak: double
дво́йственный: (gram.) dual; non-committal; two-faced, insincere	dwoisty: double; non-committal; two-faced, insincere	dvojí, dvojitý: double	
двойно́й: double		dvojný: double; (gram.) dual	dvojan: double
			dvojina: (gram.) dual number
двойни́к: double (person perfectly resembling another)		dvojník: double (person perfectly resembling another)	dvojnik: double (person perfectly resembling another)
дво́йня: twins	dwojaki (pl.), dwojaczki (pl.): twins	dvojčata (pl.): twins	dvojci (pl.): twins
			dvojba: doubt
			dvoboj: duel
двоебра́чие: bigamy			
двоеду́шие (arch.): duplicity, insincerity			
двугла́сный: (phon.) diphthong	dwugłoska: (phon.) diphthong	dvojhláska: (phon.) diphthong	dvoglas, dvoglasnik: (phon.) diphthong
			dvogled: binoculars
			dvogub: twofold, double
	dwukropek: (punc.) colon		
двули́чный: two-faced, insincere	dwulicowy: two-faced, insincere		dvoličan: two-faced, insincere
			dvopek: biscuit
двою́родный (брат), двою́родная (сестра́): (male, female) first cousin			
[R]	[P]	[Cz]	[S-C]

[R]	[P]	[Cz]	[S-C]
двурушник: double-dealer			
двусмысленный: ambiguous		dvojsmyslný: ambiguous	dvosmislen: ambiguous
	dwuśpiew: duet	dvojzpěv: duet	dvopjev: duet
двоеточие: (punc.) colon		dvojtečka: (punc.) colon	dvotočka: (punc.) colon
			dvoumica: doubt
двузначный: (math.) consisting of two digits	dwuznaczny: ambiguous	dvojznačný: ambiguous	
двоежёнство: bigamy	dwużeństwo: bigamy	dvojženství: bigamy	dvoženstvo: bigamy
			dvoživac: amphibian (n.)
			izdvojiti, izdvajati: to separate; to isolate
			odvojiti, odvajati: to separate
	podwójny: double; (gram.) dual	podvojný: double	
раздвоить, раздваивать: to divide in two	rozdwoić, rozdwajać: to divide	rozdvojiti, rozdvojovati: to divide in two; to disunite, set at variance	razdvojiti, razdvajati: to separate; to divide
			zdvojnost: despair
[R]	[P]	[Cz]	[S-C]

NOTES

Basic meaning of root: two

The root is cognate with Eng. two, Ger. zwei, Lat. duo (>Eng. dual, duet), Gr. δύο.

двойня et al.: Compare Eng. twin (related to two), Ger. Zwilling "twin" (related to zwei "two").

dvojba: To be in doubt is to be "of two minds"; compare Eng. doubt (ult. <Lat. duo "two"), Ger. Zweifel "doubt" (<zwei "two"), Gr. δοιή "doubt" (<δύο "two"), Hung. kétség "doubt" (<két "two").

dvoboj: See note under root БИ (etc.).

двоебрачие: See note under root БР (etc.).

двугласный et al.: See note under root ГОЛОС (etc.).

dvogub: See note under root ГИБ (etc.).

dwukropek: The second element is from kropka "point, dot."

dvopek: See note under root ПЕ(К) (etc.).

двою́родный (брат), двою́родная (сестра́): See note under root РОД (etc.).

двуру́шник: See note under root РУК (etc.).

двусмы́сленный et al.: Compare Ger. doppelsinnig "ambiguous" (⟨doppel- "double" + Sinn "sense, meaning"), dwuznaczny-dvojznačný below.

dwuśpiew et al.: The second element is from śpiew-zpěv-pjev "song."

dvoumica: See note on dvojba.

dwuznaczny-dvojznačný: See note on двусмы́сленный et al.

двоежёнство et al.: The second element is from жена́-żona-žena "woman; wife."

dvoživac: See note on Cz. obojživelník.

odvojiti: ⟨oddvojiti.

zdvojnost: the ultimate extreme of doubt; see dvojba and compare Ger. Verzweiflung "despair" (⟨Zweifel "doubt").

ДВИ(Г), ДВИЖ, ДВИЗ	DŹWIG	DVIH, DVÍH, DVIŽ	DI(G), DVIG, DIZ
дви́нуть, дви́гать: to move (tr.)	dźwignąć, dźwigać: to raise, lift; (dźwigać only) to carry (a burden)		dignuti (dići), dizati: to raise, lift
движе́ние: movement, motion; movement (political, etc.); traffic			
	dźwig: elevator; crane, derrick		dizalo, dizalica: elevator; crane, derrick
	dźwignia: lever		
дви́гатель: motor, engine			
недви́жимость: real estate, immovable property			
подвиза́ться (lit.): to be active (in some field of endeavor)			
по́двиг: feat, exploit			podvig: feat, exploit
[R]	[P]	[Cz]	[S-C]

[R]	[P]	[Cz]	[S-C]
		pozdvižení: excitement, commotion; (lit.) uprising, rebellion	
сдвиг: shift; improvement			
вы́двинуть, выдвига́ть: to move out (tr.); to advance (a theory, proposal), raise (a question), make (an accusation); to promote (to a higher position)	wydźwignąć, wydźwigać: to lift out		
воздви́гнуть, воздвига́ть: to erect, build		zdvihnouti, zdvíhati: to raise, lift	uzdignuti (uzdići), uzdizati: to raise, lift
		zdviž: elevator	
задви́жка: bolt (on door, etc.)			

NOTES

Basic meaning of root: to move; to raise, lift

The simple verb has not survived in Czech, where it has been replaced by zdvihnouti (see note below).

Regarding the variation in the root-meaning, see note on Rus. ти́снуть et al.

дви́гатель: ="mover"; compare Eng. motor (ult. ‹Lat. movere "to move"), Cz. hýbadlo.

podvig: ‹Rus. по́двиг.

вы́двинуть (third meaning): Compare Eng. promote (ult. ‹Lat. pro- "forward" + movere "to move").

zdvihnouti: prefix z- for orig. vz-.

ДЫХ, ДЫШ, ДОХ, ДУХ, ДУШ	DYCH, DYSZ, DECH, TCH, DUCH, DUSZ, DUS	DYCH, DÝCH, DYŠ, DECH, DŠ, DUCH, DUŠ, DUS	DIH, DIS, DAH, DUH, DUŠ
дыша́ть: to breathe	dyszeć (dychać): to pant	dýchati: to breathe	disati (dihati): to breathe
*дохну́ть: to breathe	**tchnąć: to breathe	*dýchnouti (dechnouti): to breathe	*dahnuti: to breathe
до́хнуть: to die (said of animals)			
		dychtiti: to aspire, yearn	dahtati: to pant
души́ть: to stifle, choke, smother; to scent, perfume	dusić: to stifle, choke, smother; to stew	dusiti: to stifle, choke, smother; to stew	dušiti: to stifle, choke, smother
	dech: breath	dech: breath	dah: breath
дух: spirit; breath	duch: spirit	duch: spirit; mind	duh: spirit; mind
духи́ (pl.): perfume			
душа́: soul	dusza: soul	duše: soul	duša: soul
духота́: closeness, sultriness			
ду́шный: close, sultry	duszny: close, sultry	dusný: close, sultry	
душни́к: air-hole, vent			dušnik: (anat.) windpipe
			dušnice (pl.): (anat.) bronchi
	tchawica: (anat.) windpipe		
	dychawica: asthma	dýchavičnost: shortness of breath	
дохля́тина (coll.): carrion			
		dusík: nitrogen	dušik: nitrogen
			duhovit: witty
душе́вный: mental; cordial		duševní: mental	duševan: mental; cordial
духове́нство: clergy	duchowieństwo: clergy	duchovenstvo: clergy	duhovništvo: clergy
		Dušičky (pl.): All Souls' Day	
[R]	[P]	[Cz]	[S-C]

[R]	[P]	[Cz]	[S-C]
		dušovati se: to swear, vow	
благоду́шный: placid, contented			blagodušan: good-natured
доброду́шный: good-natured	dobroduszny: good-natured	dobrodušný: good-natured	dobrodušan: good-natured
		duchaplný: witty	
		dušesloví (arch.), duševěda (arch.), dušezpyt (arch.): psychology	
двоеду́шие (arch.): duplicity, insincerity			
единоду́шный: unanimous		jednoduchý: simple, plain	jednodušan: unanimous
криводу́шие (arch.): duplicity, insincerity			
малоду́шный: pusillanimous, faint-hearted	małoduszny: pusillanimous, faint-hearted	maloduchý, malodušný: pusillanimous, faint-hearted	malodušan: pusillanimous, faint-hearted
раду́шный: cordial			
равноду́шный: indifferent, apathetic			ravnodušan: indifferent, apathetic
тщеду́шный: feeble, frail			
		veleduch: genius	
великоду́шный: magnanimous	wielkoduszny: magnanimous	velkodušný: magnanimous	veledušan, velikodušan: magnanimous
		vzducholoď: dirigible, airship	
воздухопла́вание: aeronautics		vzduchoplavectví, vzduchoplavba: aeronautics	vazduhoplovstvo: aeronautics
издо́хнуть, издыха́ть: to die (said of animals)	zdechnąć, zdychać: to die (said of animals)	*zdechnouti: to die (said of animals)	izdahnuti, izdisati: to exhale; to die, expire, breathe one's last
	zdechlizna (coll.): carrion	zdechlina: carrion	
		nádech: tinge, tint, shade	

	natchnienie: inspiration	nadšení: enthusiasm	nadahnuće: inspiration
		neprodyšný: airtight	neprodušan: airtight
одушевле́ние (lit.): animation		oduševnění, oduševnělost: animation	oduševljenje: enthusiasm
		ovzduší: atmosphere	
отдохну́ть, отдыха́ть: to rest	odetchnąć, oddychać: to breathe	oddechnouti (oddychnouti) (si), oddechovati (oddychovati) (si): to take a breath	*odahnuti: to recover one's breath
отду́шина, отду́шник: air-hole, vent			oduška: air-hole, vent
про́дух: air-hole, vent		průduch: air-hole, vent	
проду́шина: air-hole, vent		průdušnice: (anat.) windpipe	
		průdušky (pl.): (anat.) bronchi	
вдохнове́ние: inspiration			
воодушевле́ние: enthusiasm			
	wytchnienie: respite		
вздохну́ть, вздыха́ть: to breathe; to sigh	westchnąć, wzdychać: to sigh	vzdychnouti (vzdechnouti), vzdychati: to sigh	uzdahnuti, uzdisati: to sigh
во́здух: air		vzduch: air	uzduh, vazduh: air
			zdušan: conscientious, scrupulous
			zadah: stench
	zaduch: stuffy, fetid air	záducha: asthma	zaduha: shortness of breath
	Zaduszki (pl.): All Souls' Day		Zadušnice (pl.): All Souls' Day
[R]	[P]	[Cz]	[S-C]

NOTES

Basic meaning of root: to breathe

A number of derivatives reflect the notion of "breathing with difficulty," whence such meanings as "to pant," "to stifle" (expressed by the causative verb *души́ть et al*.), "close, sultry," "asthma" and "to die" (see *до́хнуть*; however, the idea of "breathing out," *i.e*. breathing one's last, is also apparent in *издо́хнуть et al*.).

As in many other languages, the abstract concept of a spirit or soul tends to be linked with the physical phenomenon of breathing; compare Eng. *spirit* (ult. <Lat. *spirare* "to breathe"), Lat. *anima* "breath; soul," Gr. *ψυχή* "breath; spirit; soul" (>Eng. *psyche*) and *πνεῦμα* "wind, air; breath; spirit" (>Eng. *pneumatic*), Dan.-Nor. *ånd* "spirit" (<*ånde* "to breathe"), Ger. *atmen* "to breathe" and cognate Sansk. *ātman* "soul" (>Gandhi's title *mahatma* "great-souled"). The notions "spirit" and "soul" (and often, by extension, "mind") underlie the meanings of many of the derivatives, although it is not always possible to make a clear-cut distinction between them.

The Slavic words *дух et al*. are cognate with Eng. *deer* (orig. "animal"; compare Eng. *animal* <Lat. *anima*), Ger. *Tier* "animal."

dychtiti: Compare Eng. *aspire* (ult. <Lat. *ad* "to, toward" + *spirare* "to breathe").

души́ть (second meaning): See *духи́*.

dusík-dušik: a "stifling" element which is incapable of supporting life; see *dusiti-dušiti* and compare Ger. *Stickstoff* "nitrogen" (<the root of *ersticken* "to stifle" + *Stoff* "matter, substance"). The same idea is reflected in Rus. *азо́т*, Pol.-S-C *azot*, Fr. (and archaic Eng.) *azote* "nitrogen" (all ult. <Gr. *ἀ-* "un-, not" + *ζωή* "life").

duhovit: See note on *duchaplný*.

духове́нство et al.: Compare Ger. *Geistlichkeit* "clergy" (<*geistlich* "spiritual, religious" <*Geist* "spirit").

dušovati se: from the oath *na mou duši* "upon my soul."

duchaplný: Compare Ger. *geistvoll* and *geistreich* "witty" (<*Geist* "spirit; mind" + *voll* "full," *reich* "rich"), S-C *duhovit* above.

dušesloví et al.: See respective notes under roots СЛЫ (etc.), ВЕЛ$_1$ (etc.) and ПЫТ (etc.).

единоду́шный-jednodušan: See note under root ОДИН (etc.).

малоду́шный et al.: See note under root МАЛ (etc.).

раду́шный: <**радодушный*, in which the first element is from *рад* "glad."

равноду́шный-ravnodušan: See note under root РОВ (etc.).

тщеду́шный: The first element is from the root of *то́щий* "empty; emaciated."

великоду́шный et al.: See note under root ВЕЛ$_1$ (etc.).

vzducholoď, *воздухопла́вание et al*.: See *во́здух-vzduch-vazduh*; the second element in vzducholoď is from loď "ship."

издо́хнуть et al.: Compare Eng. expire (ult. ‹Lat. ex "out" + spirare "to breathe").

natchnienie et al., одушевле́ние et al.: Compare Eng. inspiration (ult. ‹Lat. in "in, on" + spirare "to breathe") and animation (ult. ‹Lat. anima "soul"), Ger. Begeisterung "enthusiasm" (‹Geist "spirit"); S-C oduševljenje is borrowed from Russian.

ovzduší: ‹vzduch.

odahnuti, oduška: for oddahnuti, *odduška.

вдохнове́ние, воодушевле́ние: See note on natchnienie et al., одушевле́ние et al.; вдохнове́ние is borrowed from Church Slavic.

во́здух et al.: The Russian word is borrowed from Church Slavic, the Czech word from Russian; the two Serbo-Croatian words are of Church Slavic or Russian origin, although the variant uzduh contains the native form of the prefix.

zdušan: See duša.

Г(ИБ), ГУБ	G(I)(B), GUB	H(B), HY(B), HÝB, HEB, HUB, HOUB	G(I)(B), GA, GUB
гнуть: to bend (tr.)	giąć: to bend (tr.)	hnouti, hýbati: to move (tr.)	ganuti, gibati: to move (tr.); (ganuti only) to move, touch (emotionally)
ги́бнуть: to perish	ginąć: to perish; to disappear	hynouti: to perish	ginuti: to perish
губи́ть: to destroy, ruin	gubić: to lose; to destroy, ruin	hubiti: to destroy, ruin	gubiti: to lose; to execute, put to death
		hnutí: movement, motion; movement (political, etc.); emotion	ganuće: emotion
ги́бкий: flexible	gibki, giętki: flexible	hebký: soft, delicate	gibak: flexible
		hybný: lively; mobile; motive (force, etc.)	giban: eager, avid
			gibljiv: mobile; flexible
			gibanj: spring (elastic device)
		hbitý: agile; alert	
[R]	[P]	[Cz]	[S-C]

[R]	[P]	[Cz]	[S-C]
		hýbadlo (arch.): motor	
ги́бель: ruin, destruction			
		hubený: thin, lean	
			gubilište: scaffold, place of execution
			danguba: idler; idleness
			dvogub, trogub, četverogub, etc.: twofold, double; threefold, triple; fourfold, quadruple; etc.
нагну́ть, нагиба́ть: to bend (tr.)	nagiąć, naginać: to bend (tr.)	nahnouti, nahýbati: to bend (tr.)	nagnuti, nagibati: to bend (tr.)
		nevyhnutelný: inevitable, unavoidable	
		ohebný: flexible	
		pohnutí: movement, motion; emotion	
		pohnutka: motive (n.)	
поги́бель (arch.): ruin, destruction			pogibao, pogibelj: danger
			pogibija: ruin, destruction
па́губный: pernicious, ruinous			poguban: pernicious, ruinous
	przegięcie: bend		pregnuće: energy, assiduity
	przegub: wrist; (anat., tech.) joint		
пригну́ть, пригиба́ть: to bend (tr.)	przygiąć, przyginać: to bend (tr.)	přihnouti, přihýbati: to bend (tr.)	prignuti, prigibati: to bend (tr.)
сугу́бый: special, particular, extremely great; (arch.) twofold, double			sugub: twofold, double
		vyhýbavý: evasive	

[R]	[P]	[Cz]	[S-C]
		výhybka: railroad switch	
	zgubny: pernicious, ruinous	zhoubný: pernicious, ruinous; (med.) malignant	

NOTES

Basic meaning of root: to bend

The Czech and Serbo-Croatian simple verbs have lost their original meaning, although it survives in the prefixed verbs and in a number of other derivatives. (See note on Rus. ти́снуть et al.) A second pair of verbs, ги́бнуть et al. and губи́ть et al., show figurative development of the root-meaning: "to be bent" 〉 "to perish" and "to bend" 〉 "to destroy."

гнуть et al.: An original b was lost before n in гнуть and its counterparts (compare Czech root-form HB in hbitý); Pol. giąć is for earlier gnąć. ORus. гыбати "to bend," corresponding to hýbati-gibati, does not survive in the modern language; Pol. gibać "to rock, sway" is dialectal.

губи́ть et al.: See introductory note on root ТРАТ (etc.).

hnutí-ganuće: Compare Eng. motion and emotion, Pol. wzruszenie et al.

giban: ="bent, leaning, inclined (toward)."

hýbadlo: See note on Rus. двигатель.

hubený: originally a past participle of hubiti; the meaning of the word in Old Czech was "poor."

danguba: See note under root ДЕН (etc.).

dvogub et al.: Compare similarly formed Eng. twofold, threefold, fourfold and double, triple, quadruple (the last three ult. 〈Lat. duo "two," tres "three," quattuor "four" + the root of plicare "to fold").

naginać: for earlier nagibać.

pohnutí: See note on hnutí-ganuće.

pohnutka: Compare Eng. motive (ult. 〈Lat. movere "to move"), Ger. Beweggrund "motive" (〈bewegen "to move" + Grund "reason").

pregnuće: Regarding the meaning, compare the English expression to bend every effort.

przyginać: for earlier przygibać.

сугу́бый-sugub: ="bent or folded together," i.e. in two; the Russian word is a Church Slavic borrowing.

ГЛЯД	GLĄD, GLĘD(Z)	HLED, HLÍD	GLED
глядéть: to look		hleděti: to look; to try	
		hledati: to seek	gledati: to look; to try
		hlídati: to watch, guard	
			gledalac: spectator
		hledisko: point of view	
		hlediště: auditorium	gledište: point of view
			gledalište: auditorium
		hledí: visor; sight (of a gun)	
		dalekohled: telescope	
		drobnohled: microscope	
			dvogled: binoculars
	światopogląd: ideology, Weltanschauung		
		škarohlíd: pessimist	
		vůčihledě (lit.): obviously	očigledan: obvious
	bezwzględny: absolute; ruthless	bezohledný: ruthless; rude, tactless	
	dogląd: supervision	dohled: field of vision; supervision	dogled: field of vision; binoculars
			izgled: view, vista; prospect, outlook; (outward) appearance
		náhled: opinion, view	
нагля́дный: graphic, clear			
			nadgledanje: supervision
			negled: imprudence, rashness
[R]	[P]	[Cz]	[S-C]

[R]	[P]	[Cz]	[S-C]
		nehledě, nehledíc (k + dat., na + acc.): in spite (of)	
		nedohledný: vast, boundless; remote	nedogledan: vast, boundless; remote
неогля́дный (lit.): vast, boundless	nieoględny: imprudent, rash		
		nepřehledný: vast, boundless; unclear, badly arranged	nepregledan: vast, boundless; unclear, badly arranged
непригля́дный: unsightly, unattractive			
непрогля́дный: pitch-dark, impenetrable		neprůhledný: opaque	
		ohled: consideration, regard (for s.o. or s.th.); regard, respect (e.g. s ohledem na: with regard, respect to; v tomto ohledu: in this regard, respect)	ogled: inspection, examination; sample, specimen; experiment, test
	oględny: cautious, circumspect		ogledan: experimental; sample, specimen (attr.)
	oględziny (pl.): inspection, examination	obhlídka: inspection, examination; reconnaissance	
			ogledalo: mirror
	pogląd: opinion, view	pohled: look, glance; view, vista; picture post-card	pogled: look, glance; view, vista; regard, respect (e.g. u pogledu na: with regard, respect to; u tom pogledu: in this regard, respect)
		pohlednice: picture post-card	

[R]	[P]	[Cz]	[S-C]
	przegląd: inspection, examination; survey; magazine, periodical	přehled: survey; summary; wide knowledge	pregled, prijegled: inspection, examination; survey; summary
		přehlídka: parade, review	
		prohlídka: inspection, examination	
		průhledný: transparent	
		rozhled: field of vision; mental horizon, outlook	razgled: inspection, examination; view, vista
			razglednica: picture post-card
соглядáтай (arch.): spy			
	spoglądać: to look		
			ugled: prestige, reputation; model; example
		úhledný: good-looking, attractive	ugledan: eminent, distinguished; exemplary, model
	wygląd: (outward) appearance	výhled: view, vista; prospect, outlook	
взгляд: look, glance; opinion, view	wzgląd: consideration, regard (for s.o. or s.th.); regard, respect (e.g. względem: with regard, respect [to]; pod tym względem: in this regard, respect)	vzhled: (outward) appearance	
	względny: relative, comparative; considerate, thoughtful (of others)	vzhledný: good-looking, attractive	

NOTES

Basic meaning of root: to look

The original primary verb is represented by Rus. глядéть and Cz. hleděti (as well as by OPol. ględzieć); the semantically differentiated Czech doublets hledati and hlídati and S-C gledati were originally iterative forms (as were ORus. глядати and OPol. glądać). In modern Polish, the root appears only in combination with prefixes.

Many of the derivatives have semantic parallels under roots МОТР (etc.), PATR(Z) (etc.), ВИД (etc.) and ЗР (etc.). (See the introductory note on root ВИД [etc.].)

dalekohled: The first element is from daleký "distant"; compare Eng. telescope (ult. ‹Gr. τῆλε "distant" + σκοπεῖν "to look"), Pol. dalekowidz, S-C dalekozor.

drobnohled: The first element is from drobný "small"; compare Eng. microscope (ult. ‹Gr. μικρός "small" + σκοπεῖν "to look"), Pol. drobnowidz, S-C sitnozor.

światopogląd: See pogląd and note on Rus. мировоззрéние.

škarohlíd: The first element is from škaredý "bad, ugly"; compare Eng. pessimist (ult. ‹Lat. pessimus "worst").

vůčihledě-očigledan: See note under root ОК (etc.).

bezwzględny-bezohledný: In its first meaning, bezwzględny is the antonym of względny in the latter's first meaning (see note). Regarding the second meaning of bezwzględny and the two meanings of bezohledný, see the first meanings of wzgląd and ohled and the second meaning of względny; compare Ger. rücksichtslos "ruthless" (‹Rücksicht "consideration, regard" + -los "-less, without").

нагля́дный: Compare Ger. anschaulich "graphic, clear" (‹an "at" + schauen "to look"), Cz. názorný.

nehledě, nehledíc: ="not looking (at), taking no notice (of)"; compare Rus. несмотря́, невзира́я.

nedohledný-nedogledan, неогля́дный, nepřehledný (first meaning)-nepregledan (first meaning): ="not capable of being looked across, around, etc."; compare Ger. unabsehbar "vast" (‹un- "un-, not" + ab "off, away" + sehen "to see, look") and unübersehbar "vast" (‹un- + über "over, across" + sehen), Rus. необозри́мый et al.

nepřehledný (second meaning)-nepregledan (second meaning): ="not easily inspected, looked over"; see přehled et al. and compare Ger. unübersichtlich "unclear, badly arranged" (‹un- "un-, not" + über "over, across" + Sicht "sight").

ohled (second meaning): ="a manner of looking at s.th."; compare Eng. regard (‹Fr. regarder "to look") and respect (ult. ‹Lat. specere "to look"), Ger. (in dieser) Hinsicht "(in this) regard, respect" (‹hin "toward" + Sicht "sight"), S-C obzir and pogled, wzgląd below.

ogled (second meaning): See note on Pol. wzór et al. and wzorzec, Cz. vzorec.

oględny: Compare Eng. circumspect (ult. ⟨Lat. circum "around" + specere "to look"), Ger. umsichtig "circumspect" (⟨um "around" + Sicht "sight"), Rus. осмотрительный, Pol. opatrzny, Cz. opatrný and obezřelý et al., S-C smotren.

ogledalo: See note on Rus. зеркало et al.

pogled (third meaning): See note on ohled.

průhledný: See note on Pol. przejrzysty, S-C proziran, Rus. прозрачный et al.

ugled: Compare Ger. Ansehen "prestige, reputation" (⟨an "at" + sehen "to see, look") and see note on Pol. wzór et al. and wzorzec, Cz. vzorec.

wzgląd (second meaning): See note on ohled.

względny (first meaning): ±"viewed with respect to something else rather than in absolute terms"; compare wzgląd and bezwzględny.

ГОЛОС, ГЛАС, ГЛАШ	GŁOS, GŁOŚ, GŁASZ	HLAS, HLÁS, HLAŠ, HLÁŠ	GLAS, GLAZ, GLAŠ
го́лос: voice; vote	głos: voice; vote	hlas: voice; vote	glas: voice; sound, noise; news; reputation; vote
глас (arch.): voice			
голоси́ть: to wail, lament	głosić: to proclaim; to preach	hlásiti: to announce; to report	glasiti: to read, be worded (said of a text)
гласи́ть: to read, be worded (said of a text)			
		hlásati: to proclaim; to preach	glasati: to vote
**голосова́ть: to vote	**głosować: to vote	hlasovati: to vote	glasovati: to vote
гла́сный: public (a.); (phon.) vowel	głośny: loud; famous	hlasný (lit.): loud	glasan: loud
		hlasitý: loud	glasovit, (arch.) glasit: famous
			glazba: music
[R]	[P]	[Cz]	[S-C]

	głoska: (phon.) sound; letter, character	hláska: (phon.) sound; watch-tower	
		hláskovati: to articulate; to spell	
	głośnik: loudspeaker, megaphone	hlásník: herald	glasnik: herald; messenger
		hlásnice: loudspeaker, megaphone; watch-tower	glasnica: female herald, messenger; (anat.) glottis
			glasilo: official organ, newspaper (of a political party, etc.)
			glasina: rumor; stentorian voice
	głośnia: (anat.) glottis	hlasivky (pl.): (anat.) vocal cords	
	głosownia: phonetics, phonology		
глаша́тай (arch.): town-crier			
			blagoglasan: euphonious, melodious
двугла́сный: (phon.) diphthong	dwugłoska: (phon.) diphthong	dvojhláska: (phon.) diphthong	dvoglas, dvoglasnik: (phon.) diphthong
			glasonoša: herald; messenger
		hláskosloví: phonetics, phonology	
единогла́сный: unanimous	jednogłośny: unanimous	jednohlasný: unanimous	jednoglasan: unanimous
			miloglasan: euphonious, melodious
разногла́сие: disagreement; discrepancy			
	samogłoska: (phon.) vowel	samohláska: (phon.) vowel	samoglasnik: (phon.) vowel
[R]	[P]	[Cz]	[S-C]

	spółgłoska: (phon.) consonant		
			zloglasnost: disrepute
			naglasak: accent, stress; emphasis
огласи́ть, оглаша́ть: to announce; to fill with sound	ogłosić, ogłaszać: to proclaim; to announce; to publish; to advertise	ohlásiti, ohlašovati: to announce; to report	oglasiti, oglašivati (oglašavati): to announce; to advertise
		ohlas: echo; response	oglas: announcement; advertisement
		ohlášky (pl.): marriage banns	
отголо́сок: echo	odgłos: echo; sound, noise		
	pogłoska: rumor		
пригласи́ть, приглаша́ть: to invite		přihlásiti, přihlašovati: to register (tr.)	*priglasiti: to summon
провозгласи́ть, провозглаша́ть: to proclaim		prohlásiti, prohlašovati: to proclaim; to declare	proglasiti, proglašivati (proglašavati): to proclaim
разгласи́ть, разглаша́ть: to divulge, publicize	rozgłosić, rozgłaszać: to divulge, publicize	rozhlásiti, rozhlašovati: to divulge, publicize	razglasiti, razglašivati (razglašavati): to divulge, publicize
	rozgłos: renown	rozhlas: radio broadcasting	
	rozgłośnia: radio station		
согласи́ть, соглаша́ть (lit.): to reconcile, adjust		souhlasiti: to agree, consent; to agree, concur	
согласи́ться, соглаша́ться: to agree, consent; to agree, concur			saglasiti se, saglašivati (saglašavati) se; suglasiti se, suglašavati se: to agree, consent; to agree, concur
согласова́ть, согласо́вывать: to coordinate			
[R]	[P]	[Cz]	[S-C]

согла́сный: (phon.) consonant		souhláska: (phon.) consonant	suglasnik: (phon.) consonant
	zgłosić, zgłaszać: to file (a claim, application), report (a crime)		
	zgłosić się, zgłaszać się: to report (for duty), apply (for a position)		
	zgłoska: syllable		
	wygłosić, wygłaszać: to utter, express; to deliver (a speech)	vyhlásiti, vyhlašovati: to proclaim; to declare (war)	
во́зглас: exclamation			
[R]	[P]	[Cz]	[S-C]

NOTES

Basic meaning of root: voice

The Russian root-forms ГЛАС and ГЛАШ are of Church Slavic origin.

го́лос et al.: The meaning "vote" represents semantic borrowing from Fr. voix and Ger. Stimme, both of which mean "vote" as well as "voice."

гла́сный (second meaning): modeled on Gr. φωνῆεν (<φωνή "voice; sound") and Lat. vocalis (<vox "voice; sound"), from the latter of which is ultimately derived Eng. vowel. The basic meaning of the Greek and Latin words is "sounding, resounding"; a vowel, in contrast to a consonant, is characterized essentially by resonance rather than by constriction or closure of the breath channel. See notes on samogłoska et al. and согла́сный et al.

głoska: The word refers both to the sound and to its written representation.

hláskovati: Compare the two meanings of Pol. głoska.

głosownia: Compare Eng. phonetics (ult. <Gr. φωνή "voice; sound").

blagoglasan: See note on Rus. благозву́чный, S-C blagozvučan.

двугла́сный et al.: Compare Eng. diphthong (ult. <Gr. δίς "twice, double" + φθόγγος "voice; sound").

hláskosloví: See note under root СЛЫ (etc.).

единогла́сный et al.: modeled on Ger. einstimmig "unanimous" (<ein "one" + Stimme "voice").

miloglasan: See note on Rus. благозву́чный, S-C blagozvučan.

разногла́сие: The first element is from ра́зный "different."

samogłoska et al.: modeled on Ger. *Selbstlaut* "vowel" (<*selbst* "self" + *Laut* "sound"); the underlying idea is that a vowel sound is one which can be uttered independently (in contrast to a consonant, which requires an accompanying vowel in order to be pronounced). See notes on *гла́сный* and *согла́сный et al*.

spółgłoska: See note on *согла́сный et al*.

zloglasnost: See the fourth meaning of *glas*.

priglasiti: <Rus. *пригласи́ть*.

согласи́ть-souhlasiti, *согласи́ться et al.*, *согласова́ть*: The Russian words are modeled on Gr. *συμφωνεῖν* "to agree" (<*σύν* "with" + *φωνή* "voice; sound"); the Serbo-Croatian words are borrowed from Russian. Compare also Eng. *consonance* (ult. <Lat. *cum* "with" + *sonare* "to sound"), Ger. *beistimme* and *übereinstimmen* "to agree" (<*bei* "at, by," *überein* "in accordance" + *stimmen* "to be in tune" <*Stimme* "voice").

согла́сный et al.: ="sounding together (with a vowel)" (see note on *samogłoska et al.*). The Russian word translates Gr. *σύμφωνον* (<*σύν* "with" + *φωνή* "voice; sound") and Lat. *consonans* (<*cum* "with" + *sonare* "to sound"); the Czech and Serbo-Croatian words (and Pol. *spółgłoska*) are probably modeled on Ger. *Mitlaut* "consonant" (<*mit* "with" + *Laut* "sound").

zgłoska: The underlying idea is that of "several letters taken togethe to form a sound"; see the second meaning of *głoska* and compare Eng. *syllabl* (ult. <Gr. *συλλαμβάνειν* "to take together, gather").

ГОЛОВ, ГЛАВ	GŁOW, GŁÓW	HLAV	GLAV
голова́: head; (arch.) head, chief	*głowa*: head; head, chief	*hlava*: head; head, chief; chapter	*glava*: head; head, chief; chapter
глава́: head, chief; chapter; (arch.) head			
головно́й: head (attr.); (mil.) leading, advance (detachment, etc.)	*główny*: principal, chief (a.)	*hlavní*: principal, chief (a.)	*glavan*: principal, chief (a.)
гла́вный: principal, chief (a.)			
главе́нство: supremacy, domination			
			glavnica: capital, stock
[R]	[P]	[Cz]	[S-C]

[R]	[P]	[Cz]	[S-C]
			glavarina: poll-tax, head-tax
головáстик: tadpole			
головокружéние: dizziness, giddiness			
головолóмка: puzzle, riddle	łamigłówka: puzzle, riddle	hlavolam: puzzle, riddle	
			punoglavac: tadpole
		svéhlavý: obstinate; wilful	svojeglav: obstinate; wilful
			vrtoglavica: dizziness, giddiness
изголóвье: head of the bed			
	nagłówek: heading, title		
		nadhlavník: zenith	
оглавлéние: table of contents			
поголóвье: head (of cattle)	pogłowie: head (of cattle); number (of people)	pohlaví: sex	poglavlje: chapter
			poglavit: principal, chief (a.); honorable (title)
уголóвный: criminal, penal		úhlavní: sworn, mortal (enemy)	
			uglaviti, uglavljivati: to fix, fasten, fit in place; to fix, set, stipulate
	wezgłowie: pillow; head of the bed		uzglavlje: pillow; head of the bed
			zglavak: (anat.) joint
			zglavan: clever
заглáвие: heading, title		záhlaví: back of the head; heading, title	zaglavlje: epilogue; heading, title

NOTES

Basic meaning of root: head

The Russian root-form ГЛАВ is of Church Slavic origin.

голова́ et al., глава́: The Church Slavic derivative enables Russian to use separate words to differentiate between the literal and figurative meanings of "head." Compare Eng. head and chief (<OFr. chief "head" <Lat. caput "head"), Fr. tête "head" and chef "chief" (orig. "head"), Ger. Kopf "head" and Haupt "chief" (orig. "head"). Regarding the second meaning of глава́ and the third meaning of hlava and glava, compare Eng. chapter (ult. <Lat. caput), Du. hoofdstuk "chapter" (<hoofd "head" + stuk "piece"), Hung. fejezet "chapter" (<fej "head").

glavnica: Compare Eng. capital as used in this sense (ult. <Lat. caput "head" in its secondary meaning of "principal sum, capital, stock").

голова́стик: so called because of its large head; see punoglavac. Compare also Eng. tadpole (from an obsolete form of toad + poll "head"), Fr. têtard "tadpole" (<tête "head").

punoglavac: a corruption of earlier puloglavac, the first part of which is related to Cz. pulec "tadpole"; the modern form of the word is presumably influenced by pun "full." See preceding note.

svéhlavý-svojeglav: Compare Eng. headstrong, Fr. têtu "obstinate" (<tête "head").

vrtoglavica: See note under root ВЕРТ (etc.).

оглавле́ние: See the second meaning of глава́.

pohlaví: The word expresses the collective notion of "so many head (of males and females)." Compare поголо́вье and pogłowie, the latter of which could also mean "sex" in earlier usage.

poglavlje: See note on голова́ et al., глава́.

уголо́вный-úhlavní: The underlying sense in both cases is that of "threatening someone's head, i.e. life." Compare the use of Lat. capitalis (<caput "head") to mean "capital (in the case of a crime), mortal (in the case of an enemy)," whence the English expressions capital offense, capital punishment.

uglaviti: u- here = "in"; hence, the meaning is to "head," i.e. wedge or fit, in. From this developed the figurative meaning "to stipulate," as in the case of Eng. fix.

zglavak: ="something fitted together"; for the development of the meaning (modified here by the prefix z- "together"), see preceding note.

ГН, ГОН	GN, GON, GOŃ, GAN	HN, HON, HÁN, HÁŇ	GN, GON, GAN
гнать: to chase, drive; to distill	gnać: to chase, drive; to rush, dash	hnáti: to chase, drive	gnati (arch.): to chase, drive
†гоня́ть: to chase, drive	gonić (ganiać): to chase, drive; to rush, dash	†honiti: to chase, drive; to hunt	goniti (ganjati): to chase, drive
гоне́ц (arch.): courier	goniec: courier; cattle-drover; bishop (chess piece)	honec: cattle-drover; beater (in hunting)	
	gonitwa: race; tournament		
самого́н: home-brewed liquor	samogon: home-brewed liquor		
изгна́ние: exile, banishment			izgnanje, izgnanstvo: exile, banishment
			nagon: impulse; instinct
	ogon: tail	ohon, oháňka: tail	
пого́ня: pursuit	pogoń: pursuit	pohon: propulsion, motive force; gear, drive, transmission	pogon: propulsion, motive force; operation, functioning
		půhon (arch.): summons, subpoena	
		přehánění: exaggeration	pregonjenje: exaggeration
			prognanstvo, progonstvo: exile, banishment
прого́ны (pl., arch.): traveling allowance			
		prohnaný: cunning, crafty	
	zgon: death, decease; waters in which last casting of fishnets is made; (arch.) pen, enclosure	shon: bustle, commotion; hunt, search	
		úhona: flaw, fault, blemish	
[R]	[P]	[Cz]	[S-C]

	wygnanie: exile, banishment	vyhnanství: exile, banishment	
выгон: pasture	wygon: pasture	výhon: pasture; shoot, sprout	
загóн: pen, enclosure; (act of) driving (into s.th.)	zagon: strip of farmland; raid, incursion	záhon: (flower-, etc.) bed	zagon (arch.): attack
[R]	[P]	[Cz]	[S-C]

NOTES

Basic meaning of root: to chase, drive

Many of the words in this group show semantic development similar to that of the derivatives of root PĘD(Z) (etc.).

гнать (second meaning): The reference is to the driving off of gas or vapor in the distillation process; compare Pol. pędzić.

goniec (third meaning): Compare Ger. Läufer "runner; bishop (chess piece)" (<laufen "to run").

самогóн-samogon: See the second meaning of гнать; the Polish word is borrowed from Russian.

nagon: Compare Eng. impulse (ult. <Lat. in "in, on" + pellere "to drive"), Ger. Antrieb "impulse" (<an "on" + treiben "to drive") and Trieb "impulse; instinct" (<treiben), Pol. popęd, Cz. pud and popud.

ogon et al.: The reference is to the animal's use of its tail to drive away insects.

pohon (second meaning): Compare Pol. napęd.

pogon: Compare Ger. Betrieb "operation, functioning" (<treiben "to drive").

půhon: a legal instrument for "driving" someone into court.

přehánění-pregonjenje: modeled on Ger. Übertreibung "exaggeration" (<über "over" + treiben "to drive"); compare also S-C pretjerivanje "exaggeration" (<pre- + tjerati "to drive").

прогóны: The word originally referred to the payment made for fresh horses at relay stations (гóны).

prohnaný: modeled on Ger. durchtrieben, past part. of durchtreiben "to drive through." The semantic development of durchtrieben carried it from its literal meaning, "driven through," to "shot through (with), pervaded (by)," then "versed, skilled (in)" and finally---the pejorative meaning it possesses today---"cunning, crafty." The Czech loan-translation also meant "versed, skilled" in somewhat earlier usage.

zgon: The first meaning arose from the second as a figure of speech referring to the fisherman's final casting from which there was no escape;

the semantic development was, however, influenced by the unrelated word skon (q.v.).

úhona: ⟨uhnati si "to catch (a disease); to bring (shame) upon o.s."

výhon (second meaning): Compare Pol. pęd.

zagon (Pol., first meaning), záhon: The semantic development is not clear; the Czech word is discussed by Machek and by Holub and Kopečný (see Bibliography).

ГОД, ГОЖД	GOD(Z), GÓD, HOD, GADZ	HOD, HŮZ, HAZ, HÁZ	GOD, GOĐ, GAĐ
год: year		hod: principal religious holiday (Christmas, Easter, etc.); throw	god: anniversary; birthday; festival, holiday; annual ring (of a tree)
	gody (pl.): feast, banquet	hody (pl.): feast, banquet	
годи́на: time, era; (arch.) year	godzina: hour	hodina: hour	godina: year
		hodiny (pl.): clock	
	godzinki (pl.): the hours (prayers)	hodinky (pl.): watch	
годовщи́на: anniversary			godišnjica: anniversary
	godzić: to reconcile; to hire; to aim	*hoditi: to throw	goditi: to please; to decide
		házeti: to throw	gađati: to aim; to throw; to shoot
годи́ться: to be suitable	godzić się: to be suitable; to agree; to reconcile o.s. (to); to hire o.s. out, accept employment	hoditi se: to be suitable	goditi se: to please; to seem; to agree
го́дный: suitable, fit; valid, good (ticket, etc.)	godny: worthy, deserving	hodný: worthy, deserving; good, kind; (coll.) substantial, sizable	
		hodnota: value, worth	
[R]	[P]	[Cz]	[S-C]

[R]	[P]	[Cz]	[S-C]
	godność: dignity; high rank, position; surname	hodnost: rank, title	
		hodnostář: dignitary	
	godziwy: fair, just; permissible		
	godło: symbol, emblem		
	godować (arch.): to feast	hodovati: to feast	godovati: to celebrate a holiday
	hodować: to raise (vegetables, cattle); to rear, raise (a child)		
чревоугóдник (arch.): glutton			
	czcigodny: respectable, estimable	ctihodný: respectable, estimable	
		hodnověrný: trustworthy; authentic	
	jednozgodny: unanimous		
		pamětihodný: memorable	
		pozoruhodnosti (pl.): sights (e.g. of a city)	
	wiarogodny: trustworthy; authentic	věrohodný: trustworthy; authentic	
	dogodzić, dogadzać: to gratify, oblige	dohoditi, dohazovati: to throw (as far as); to negotiate, arrange, procure	dogoditi se, događati se: to happen
	dogodny: convenient		
		dohoda: agreement	
		dohodce: broker	
			dogod: until
			nagađati: to guess
		náhoda: chance, accident	nagodba: agreement

[R]	[P]	[Cz]	[S-C]
		nehoda: accident, mishap	
негодяй: scoundrel	niegodziwiec: scoundrel		
негодование: indignation			negodovanje: indignation
непогода: bad weather	niepogoda: bad weather	nepohoda: bad weather	nepogoda: bad weather
невзгода: misfortune	niezgoda: disagreement	neshoda: disagreement	nezgoda: accident, mishap; trouble, difficulty
		odhoditi (odházeti), odhazovati: to throw off, away	odgoditi, odgađati: to postpone, delay
*погодить (coll.): to wait a moment	*pogodzić: to reconcile	pohoditi (poházeti), pohazovati: to strew, scatter; (pohoditi and pohazovati only) to toss (one's head)	pogoditi, pogađati: to hit, strike; to guess; to agree on, stipulate
			pogodba: condition, stipulation, proviso; agreement
			pogodben: (gram.) conditional
погода: weather	pogoda: weather; good weather; cheerful mood	pohoda: good weather; cheerful mood	
погодный: weather (attr.)	pogodny: fair, clear (sky, day, etc.); cheerful	pohodlný: comfortable; lazy	pogodan: favorable, propitious
		předhůzka: reproach	
	przygoda: adventure	příhoda: event, occurrence	prigoda: opportunity; occasion
пригодный: suitable, fit	przygodny: chance, accidental; occasional	příhodný: favorable, propitious; convenient	prigodan: occasional; for a special occasion
		rozhoditi (rozházeti), rozhazovati: to strew, scatter; (rozházeti and rozhazovati only) to squander	razgoditi, razgađati: to postpone, delay; to separate; to punctuate

[R]	[P]	[Cz]	[S-C]
		rozhazovač: spendthrift	
		rozhodnouti, rozhodovati: to decide	
		rozhodčí: arbitrator; referee, umpire	
	zgoda: agreement; harmony; consent	shoda: agreement; harmony; concurrence, coincidence	zgoda: opportunity; occasion; event, occurrence
угоди́ть, угожда́ть: to gratify, oblige; (угоди́ть only; coll.) to fall (into), get (into); (угоди́ть only; coll.) to hit, strike	ugodzić, ugadzać: to hit, strike; to hire	*uhoditi: to hit, strike; to set in (said of weather, etc.)	ugoditi, ugađati: to gratify, oblige; to agree on, stipulate; to tune (a musical instrument)
	ugoda: agreement		
уго́дный: agreeable (to), to one's liking			ugodan: pleasant; comfortable; convenient
уго́дливый: obsequious			ugodljiv: obliging, accommodating
		vhodný: convenient; suitable	
вы́года: advantage, benefit	wygoda: comfort; convenience	výhoda: advantage, benefit	
	wygódka: toilet		
			zagođe: opportunity
[R]	[P]	[Cz]	[S-C]

NOTES

Basic meaning of root: good, suitable

From a semantic standpoint, the derivatives can be divided into three broad groups:

(1) The basic meaning is apparent in a wide variety of words expressin such notions as suitability, worthiness, convenience, advantage, pleasure and agreement (the last of these giving rise to the meanings "to hire," "to negotiate" and "to decide") or, with the addition of a negative prefix, suc ideas as misfortune, displeasure and disagreement.

(2) The widespread secondary meaning "time" reflects a semantic shift

rom the notion of "suitable time" (still apparent in "festival, holiday," feast," "opportunity") to that of "time in general" (>"time, era," "year," hour," "occasion," "to wait," "to postpone," "until"); it is implicit in he meanings "to happen," "event" and "chance, accident." (A similar proression in meaning is discussed in the note on Pol.-Cz.-S-C doba.)

(3) The verbal derivatives, in a reversal of the normal process of emantic development from the concrete to the abstract, have undergone sucessive changes in meaning from "to be suitable, pleasing" to "to aim," "to hrow" and, finally, "to hit" (whence, further, "to get (into)" and "to uess").

Non-Slavic cognates include Eng. good and (reflecting the original ndo-European meaning of the root, "fitting, belonging together") gather, ogether.

hod: In the meaning "throw," the word is a relatively recent postverbal ormation from hoditi.

goditi se: Regarding the relationship between the first two meanings, ee the introductory note on root ДО(Б) (etc.).

hodný (third meaning): See note on Cz. slušeti (se) and slušný, Pol. łuszny.

godność: See godny and compare Eng. dignity (ult. <Lat. dignus "worhy"), Ger. Würde "dignity" (<wert "worthy"), Rus. досто́инство et al., Pol. ostojność, Cz. důstojnost; regarding the third meaning, see note on Rus. еличáть.

godło: ="something agreed upon," hence a conventional sign.

hodować: orig. "to regale, entertain"; the word is a doublet of godwać, the initial h presumably reflecting the influence of Czech.

чревоугóдник: ="one who gratifies his belly"; the first element is from рéво "belly."

czcigodny-ctihodný: See godny-hodný.

hodnověrný: See hodný and note on Rus. достовéрный.

jednozgodny: See zgoda.

pamětihodný: See hodný.

pozoruhodnosti: See hodný and note under root ЗР (etc.).

wiarogodny-věrohodný: See godny-hodný and note on Rus. достовéрный.

негодовáние-negodovanje: The Russian word is borrowed from Church lavic, the Serbo-Croatian word from Russian.

непогóда et al.: See погóда et al.

погóда: orig. "good weather"; compare the corresponding Polish and zech words.

předhůzka: modeled on Ger. Vorwurf "reproach" (<vor "before, in front of" + werfen "to throw"); the same idea is reflected in Eng. to throw something up to someone. Compare also Eng. objection (ult. <Lat. ob "before, in ront of" + jacere "to throw"), Hung. ellenvetés "objection" (<ellen "against" + vetni "to throw"), Pol. wyrzut and zarzut, Cz. námitka.

угоди́ть: The root-form ГОЖД is of Church Slavic origin.
wygódka: ‹wygoda.

ГОР, ГАР, ГР, ЖАР	GOR(Z), GÓR, GAR, GRZ, ŻAR(Z)	HOR, HOŘ, KOŘ, HÁR, HŘ, HR, ŽÁR	GOR, GAR, GR, ŽAR, ŽER
горе́ть: to burn (intr.)	gorzeć (goreć): to burn (intr.)	hořeti: to burn (intr.)	gorjeti: to burn (tr. and intr.)
		hárati (lit.): to blaze	
греть: to warm, heat	grzać: to warm, heat	hřáti: to warm, heat	grijati (grejati): to warm, heat
горя́чий: hot	gorący: hot	horoucí: passionate	
горя́чка: fever	gorączka: fever	horečka: fever	
го́рький: bitter	gorzki: bitter	hořký: bitter	gorak, grk: bitter
		horký: hot	
	gorliwy: ardent, zealous	horlivý: ardent, zealous	gorljiv: ardent, zealous
	gorszy: worse (a.)	horší: worse (a.)	gori: worse (a.)
	gorszyć: to shock, scandalize	horšiti: to make worse	goršati: to make worse; to become worse
гарь: anything burnt or burning			gar: soot
горю́чее: fuel			gorivo: fuel
гори́лка: brandy	gorzałka: brandy	kořalka: brandy	
	gorzelnia: distillery		
горчи́ца: mustard	gorczyca: mustard	hořčice: mustard	gorušica: mustard
		hořčík: magnesium	
го́ре: sorrow, grief		hoře (lit.): sorrow, grief	
горн: furnace			
горшо́к: pot	garnek: pot	hrnek: pot	
га́рнец: unit of measure equivalent to about a gallon	garniec: unit of measure equivalent to about a gallon	hrnec: pot	grnac: pot
жар: heat; fever; embers	żar: heat; embers	žár: heat	žar: heat; embers
жара́: heat			žara: nettle
жа́рить: to fry, roast, broil (tr.)	żarzyć: to heat to a glow		žariti: to heat to a glow
[R]	[P]	[Cz]	[S-C]

жáркий: hot			žarki: hot; glowing
	żarliwy: ardent, zealous	žárlivý: jealous	
			žarište: focus; center (of activity), seat (of a disease)
	żarówka: electric light-bulb	žárovka: electric light-bulb	žarulja: electric light-bulb
			žeravica: embers
огорчи́ть, огорчáть: to grieve, distress			ogorčiti, ogorčivati (ogorčavati): to make bitter; to irritate, exasperate
		pohoršlivý: shocking, scandalous	
пожáр: fire	pożar: fire	požár: fire	požar: fire
разгáр: height (of the season, of a battle, etc.)			
		rozháraný: disorganized, disorderly	
		rozhořčení, rozhořčenost: irritation, exasperation; indignation	
угáр: carbon monoxide; carbon-monoxide poisoning; intoxication; waste materials	ugór: (state of lying) fallow; fallow land	úhor: (state of lying) fallow; fallow land	ugar: (state of lying) fallow; fallow land
	zgorzel: gangrene		
	zagorzalec: fanatic		
[R]	[P]	[Cz]	[S-C]

NOTES

Basic meaning of root: hot

The root is represented by two primary verbs, горéть et al. and греть et al. (from the former of which have come numerous deverbatives, e.g. горя́чий et al., гóрький et al., gorliwy et al.), and by such distinctive formations as гарь-gar, гóре-hoře, горн, жар et al. and žeravica. (The root-forms ЖАР-ŻAR-ŽÁR-ŽAR and ŽER show palatalization of the initial consonant before an original front vowel.)

Kindred non-Slavic words are Eng. warm, Lat. fornax "furnace" (>Eng. furnace), Gr. θερμός "hot" (>Eng. thermal, thermos, thermometer).

hárati: originally an iterative form of hořeti; ORus. гарати and OPol gorać have not survived.

го́рький et al.: ="burning."

horký: originally a doublet of hořký.

gorliwy et al.: Compare Eng. ardent (ult. <Lat. ardere "to burn").

gorszy et al.: ="more bitter."

gorszyć: orig. "to make worse." The notion of "badness" tends to be associated with that of "anger, displeasure, irritation"; compare Ger. ärgern "to anger, irritate" (<ärger "worse") and see the introductory note on root ЗЛ (etc.).

горю́чее-gorivo: Compare Eng. fuel (ult. <Lat. focus "fireplace; [in Late Latin] fire"), Ger. Brennstoff "fuel" (<brennen "to burn" + Stoff "substance, material"), Pol. paliwo "fuel" (<palić "to burn"), Cz. palivo "fuel" (<páliti "to burn").

гори́лка et al.: The Russian word is borrowed from Ukrainian, the Czech word from Polish. Compare Eng. brandy (<brandywine <Du. brandewijn "brandy" <branden "to burn; to distill" + wijn "wine"), Cz. pálenka "brandy" (<páliti "to burn; to distill"), S-C peći. Pol. gorzeć, as an intransitive verb, does not have the meaning "to distill"; gorzałka and gorzelnia (q.v.) are formed from an assumed participle *gorzały "burnt."

gorzelnia: See preceding note and note on S-C pecara.

горчи́ца et al.: The Serbo-Croatian word is formed from gorjeti, the other three from го́рький et al.

hořčík: so called because magnesium, when it burns, produces a dazzlingly bright light.

го́ре-hoře: ="that which burns"; see the introductory note on root ПЕ(К (etc.).

горшо́к et al., га́рнец et al.: diminutives of words represented today only by Rus. горн. Pol. garniec was originally synonymous with garnek; Rus. га́рнец is borrowed from Polish.

жа́рить et al.: denominatives formed from жар et al.

żarliwy-žárlivý: See note on gorliwy et al.; regarding the shift in meaning apparent in the Czech word, compare Eng. zealous and jealous (both ult. <Gr. ζῆλος "zeal; jealousy"), Ger. Eifer "zeal" and Eifersucht "jealousy" (Sucht = "sickness"), Rus. ре́вностный "zealous" and ревни́вый "jealous

žarište: Compare Eng. focus (<Lat. focus "fireplace; [in Late Latin] fire"), Ger. Brennpunkt "focus" (<brennen "to burn" + Punkt "point"), Pol. ognisko "focus" (<ogień "fire"), Cz. ohnisko "focus" (<oheň "fire").

огорчи́ть-ogorčiti: <го́рький-gorak.

pohoršlivý: See horšiti and note on gorszyć.

разга́р: ="white heat, fever pitch."

rozháraný: ‹*hárati*; orig. "ablaze, aflame," then "chaotic."

rozhořčení, *rozhořčenost*: ‹*hořký*.

ugór et al.: It has been suggested that the word was applied first to woodland which was reclaimed for cultivation by burning away the trees and then, in an extension of the meaning, to any field which at a given time was not under cultivation.

zgorzel: Compare Ger. *Brand* "blight; gangrene" (‹*brennen* "to burn").

zagorzalec: Compare *gorliwy*.

ГОВОР, ГОВАР	GAWORZ, GWAR(Z)	HOVOR, HOVOŘ	GOVOR, GOVAR
говори́ть: to speak; to say, tell	*gaworzyć*: to chat; to babble	*hovořiti*: to chat	*govoriti*: to speak
го́вор: talk; dialect; pronunciation		*hovor*: talk; conversation	*govor*: talk; (power of) speech; speech, address; dialect
	gwarzyć: to chat		
	gwar: sound of voices		
	gwara: dialect; slang		
			govorništvo: oratory; eloquence
громкоговори́тель: loudspeaker (in radio)			
до́гово́р: treaty; contract			*dogovor*: agreement
			izgovor: pronunciation; pretext, excuse
наговóр: slander; (arch.) charm, spell			*nagovor*: persuasion
оговóр: slander			*ogovor*: slander
оговóрка: condition, stipulation, proviso; slip of the tongue			
отговори́ть, *отговáривать*: to dissuade			*odgovoriti*, *odgovarati*: to answer; (*odgo-*
[R]	[P]	[Cz]	[S-C]

[R]	[P]	[Cz]	[S-C]
			varati only) to correspond, conform
			odgovoran: responsible
			odgovarajući: corresponding; suitable, appropriate
отговóрка: pretext, excuse			
	pogwar: sound of voices	pohovor: chat	pogovor: epilogue; rejoinder, retort
поговóрка: proverb	pogwarka: chat		
подговори́ть, подгова́ривать: to incite			podgovoriti, podgovarati: to incite
переговóры (pl.): negotiations			pregovori (pl.): negotiations
			predgovor: preface, foreword
приговóр: sentence, verdict			prigovor: reproach; objection
разговóр: conversation	rozgwar: uproar, hubbub	rozhovor: conversation	razgovor: conversation
сгóвор: agreement; (arch.) betrothal			
сговóрчивый: compliant, tractable			
уговóр: persuasion; agreement			ugovor: treaty; contract
вы́говор: pronunciation; rebuke, reprimand			
зáговор: conspiracy; charm, spell			zagovor: intercession, plea

NOTES

Basic meaning of root: to speak

The basic notion of speech readily gives rise to such semantic elaborations as "a thing fixed or established by speech, i.e. an agreement" (reflected variously in the derivatives by such further meanings as "treaty," "contract," "stipulation," "betrothal" and "conspiracy"), "an effect produced by the cunning use of speech, i.e. a charm or spell" and, in some cases, "evil speech," i.e. "slander," "reproach," "rebuke." In Polish and Czech, where this root is relatively unproductive, many parallel derivatives have been formed from root МОЛВ (etc.). See also the listings under roots РЕК (etc.) and ВЕТ (etc.).

Polish GWAR(Z) is a secondary root-form which does not occur in the other three languages.

говори́ть et al.: denominatives formed from го́вор et al. (Pol. gaworzyć and earlier goworzyć are from obsolete gawor, gowor.) In its second meaning, the Russian word serves as the imperfective aspect of сказа́ть (q.v.).

gwarzyć: a denominative formed from gwar.

громкоговори́тель: The first element is from гро́мкий "loud."

izgovor: In its first meaning, the word is paralleled by Ger. Aussprache "pronunciation" (<aus "out" + sprechen "to speak"), Pol. wymowa, Cz. vysloviti; regarding the second meaning, compare Eng. to talk (one's way) out (of s.th.), Ger. Ausrede "pretext, excuse" (<aus + reden "to talk"), Pol. wymówka, Cz. výmluva.

огово́рка: Regarding the first meaning, compare Rus. усло́вие, S-C uslov and uvjet; regarding the second meaning, see note on S-C omaška.

odgovoriti: The prefix here has the force of "off, back, against"; compare Eng. answer (ult. <OEng. and- "against" + swerian "to swear" [from a root meaning "to speak"]), Ger. Antwort "answer" (<ant- "against" + Wort "word"), Rus. отве́тить and о́тповедь, Pol. odpowiedź, odpowiedzieć and odrzec, Cz. odpověď, odpověděti and odvětiti. Regarding the second meaning of odgovarati, compare Eng. correspond and respond as well as answer in such phrases as to answer the purpose, Ger. entsprechen "to correspond" (orig. "to answer") (<ent- "away, against" + sprechen "to speak"), Rus. соотве́тствовать, Pol. odpowiedzieć, Cz. odpovídati.

odgovoran: Compare Eng. answerable and answer, responsible and respond, Ger. verantwortlich "responsible" (<Antwort "answer"), Rus. отве́тственный, Pol. odpowiedzialny, Cz. odpovědný.

odgovarajući: The second meaning is an outgrowth of the first; compare Rus. соотве́тствующий, Pol. odpowiedni.

отгово́рка: See note on izgovor.

pogovor (first meaning): po- here = "after."

pregovori: <Rus. перегово́ры.

сгово́рчивый: See сго́вор.

вы́говор (first meaning): See note on izgovor.

zagovor: Compare Ger. Fürsprache "intercession" (⟨für "for" + sprechen "to speak").

ГОРОД, ГОРОЖ, ГОРАЖ, ГРАД, ГРАЖД	GRÓD, GROD(Z), GRADZ	HRAD, HRÁD, HRAZ, HRÁZ	GRAD, GRAĐ
го́род, (arch.) град: city, town	gród: castle; fortress; (arch.) city, town	hrad: castle; fortress	grad: city, town; castle; fortress
	grodzić: to fence, enclose	hraditi: to fence, enclose; to fortify	graditi: to build
горожа́нин: city-dweller			građanin: citizen; city-dweller; civilian
граждани́н: citizen			
гражда́нский: civil; civic; civilian			građanski: civil; civic; civilian
	grodza: dam	hráz: dam; dike	građa, gradivo: material
			graditeljstvo: architecture
	grodzień: compartment (of a ship)		
огороди́ть, огора́живать: to fence, enclose	ogrodzić, ogradzać: to fence, enclose	ohraditi, ohrazovati: to fence, enclose	ograditi, ograđivati: to fence, enclose
огради́ть, огражда́ть: to guard, protect; (arch.) to fence, enclose			
		ohraditi se, ohrazovati se: to protest	ograditi se, ograđivati se: to protest
огоро́д: kitchen-garden, market-garden	ogród: garden		
прегра́да: barrier	przegroda: partition (wall); compartment	přehrada: partition (wall); barrier; dam	pregrada: partition (wall); compartment; barrier
[R]	[P]	[Cz]	[S-C]

перегоро́дка: partition (wall)	*przegródka*: pigeonhole		
при́город: suburb			*predgrađe*: suburb
		příhrada: compartment	
		přihrádka: pigeonhole; shelf	
вы́городить, *выгора́живать*: to fence off		*vyhraditi*, *vyhrazovati*: to reserve (a right, a room, etc.)	
		výhrada: condition, reservation, proviso	
		výhradní: exclusive	
			zgrada: building, edifice
	zagroda: enclosure; farm	*zahrada*: garden	*zagrada*: fence; (punc.) parentheses, brackets
[R]	[P]	[Cz]	[S-C]

NOTES

Basic meaning of root: enclosure

The basic meaning is reflected in a wide range of derivatives denoting either an enclosed place of some kind (town, castle, garden, farm) or a means of enclosing (fence, dam, partition). The same semantic process can be seen at work in Eng. *town*, Du. *tuin* "garden," Ger. *Zaun* "fence"---all descended from a Germanic root with the basic meaning "enclosure." The Slavic root-meaning is also apparent in such non-Slavic cognates as Eng. *yard*, Ger. *Garten* "garden" (>Eng. *garden* by way of French), Lat. *hortus* "garden."

The Russian root-forms ГРАД and ГРАЖД are of Church Slavic origin.

građanin, *граждани́н*, *гражда́нский*-*građanski*: A "citizen" was originally one who lived in a city and enjoyed certain rights and freedoms by virtue of that fact; compare Eng. *citizen* and *city*, Ger. *Bürger* "citizen" (<*Burg* "castle," in earlier German also "city"). The basic meaning of Eng. *civil*, *civic* and *civilian* (all ult. <Lat. *civis* "citizen") is "pertaining to a citizen"; compare Ger. *bürgerlich* "civil; civic; civilian" (<*Bürger*), Pol. *obywatelski*, Cz. *občanský*.

građa, *gradivo*: The meaning reflects that of *graditi*; the words originally referred only to building materials, then to "material" in all senses.

Građa, which is etymologically identical with grodza and hráz, retains the meaning "fence" in dialectal use.

ohraditi se-ograditi se: The underlying idea is that of defending oneself, raising barriers against something.

výhrada, výhradní: ‹vyhraditi.

И(Д), ЫД, Й(Д)	I, J(D)	JÍ	I(D)
идти́: to go, walk	iść: to go, walk	jíti: to go, walk	ići: to go, walk; to go, ride
			*iznaći: to invent; to discover
*найти́: to find	*najść: to invade; to importune	*najíti: to find	*naći: to find
на́йтие: inspiration, intuitive thought			
найдёныш (arch.): foundling			
*обойти́сь: to manage, make do (with); to manage, do (without); to cost; (с + inst.) to treat, behave (toward)	*obejść się: to manage, make do (with); to manage, do (without); (z + inst.) to treat, behave (toward); (z + inst.) to handle (e.g. a tool)	*obejíti se: to manage, do (without)	
*превзойти́: to surpass, exceed			*prevazići: to surpass, exceed
предыду́щий: previous, preceding			predidući: previous, preceding
*прийти́сь: to fit; to fall (on a certain day); to be necessary; to fall to (s.o.'s) lot			
пройдо́ха (coll.): sly, cunning person			
[R]	[P]	[Cz]	[S-C]

	znajdować (znajdywać): to find znajda, znajdek: foundling wynajdować (wynajdywać): to invent; to discover	*vynajíti: to invent; to discover	*pronaći: to invent; to discover *snaći: to befall (misfortune, etc.)
[R]	[P]	[Cz]	[S-C]

NOTES

Basic meaning of root: to go, walk

In Russian, Polish and Czech, the verbs formed from this root serve to translate Eng. go only in cases where the goer is on foot; the Serbo-Croatian verb also applies to travel in a vehicle. (Compare root ЕХ [etc.].) The root supplies the perfective counterparts of Russian, Polish and Czech compound verbs derived from root ХОД (etc.) (see, however, notes below on znajdować and wynajdować) and of Serbo-Croatian compounds formed from ЛЕЗ (etc.). Regarding the formation of the past tense, see the introductory note on ХОД (etc.). In Serbo-Croatian, the initial letter i in the simple verb is generally lost after a prefix ending in a vowel.

Non-Slavic cognates are Lat. ire "to go" (>Eng. exit, initial, transit), Gr. ἰέναι "to go."

идти́ et al.: The first three are durative verbs whose iterative counterparts are ходи́ть-chodzić-choditi (q.v.); the Serbo-Croatian word performs both durative and iterative functions. The present tense---e.g. 1 sg. иду́, idę, jdu, idem---shows an expanded root-form ending in d. The original form of the infinitive survives only in Czech; Rus. идти́ (<ORus. ити) has been altered to conform to the present tense, while Pol. iść (<OPol. ić) shows the influence of verbs like wieść whose stem ends in d and S-C ići (<earlier iti) is influenced by such verbs as moći.

iznaći: See naći and note on S-C iznahoditi.

найти́-najíti-naći: See note on Rus. находи́ть, Cz. nacházeti, S-C nahoditi.

на́итие: that which "comes upon" a person; the word is borrowed from Church Slavic.

обойти́сь et al.: See note on Rus. обходи́ться et al. and обходи́тельный, S-C ophodljiv.

превзойти́-prevazići: See note on Rus. превосходи́ть; the Serbo-Croatian word is borrowed from Church Slavic.

прийти́сь: See note on Rus. приходи́ться.

пройдо́ха: one who has "been through it," who knows the ins and outs; compare Rus. проходи́мец and прола́за, Pol. przebiegły.

pronaći: See naći and note on S-C iznahoditi.

znajdować-snaći: See note on Rus. находи́ть, Cz. nacházeti, S-C nahoditi; the progression in the meaning of the Serbo-Croatian word has been "to find" > "to attack" > "to befall." Pol. znajdować serves as the imperfective form of znaleźć (q.v.); the original perfective and imperfective verbs, znajść and znachodzić, are obsolete.

wynajdować-vynajíti: See najść (orig. = "to find")-najíti and note on S-C iznahoditi. Pol. wynajdować serves as the imperfective form of wynaleźć (q.v.); the original perfective and imperfective verbs, wynajść and wynachodzić, are obsolete.

ИМЯ, ИМЕН	IM(IĘ), IMIE(N)	JMEN, JMÉN	IME(N)
и́мя: name; (gram.) (существи́тельное) noun, substantive; (gram.) (прилага́тельное) adjective	imię: name; (gram.) noun, substantive	jméno: name; (gram.) (podstatné) noun, substantive; (gram.) (přídavné) adjective	ime: name
			imenica: (gram.) noun, substantive
и́менно: namely, to wit; just, exactly	imiennie: by (one's) name		
		jmenovitě: especially	
имени́тый (arch.): eminent, distinguished			imenit: eminent, distinguished
имени́тельный: (gram.) nominative			
		jmenovatel: (math.) denominator	imenilac, imenitelj: (math.) denominator
	imiesłów: (gram.) participle		
местоиме́ние: (gram.) pronoun			
	przedimek: (gram.) article		
	przyimek: (gram.) preposition		
[R]	[P]	[Cz]	[S-C]

[R]	[P]	[Cz]	[S-C]
	zaimek: (gram.) pronoun	zejména: especially zájmeno: (gram.) pronoun	

NOTES

Basic meaning of root: name

The Slavic root is related to Eng. name, Lat. nomen "name" (>Eng. nominate, nominal), Gr. ὄνομα "name" (>Eng. synonym, homonym, onomatopoeia).

и́мя-imię-jméno: As grammatical terms, the words represent a loan-translation of Lat. nomen (>Eng. noun) and Gr. ὄνομα; Russian and Czech usage reflects the older grammarians' practice of applying the word nomen to both nouns and adjectives (hence, in earlier English usage, the terms noun substantive and noun adjective). See notes on Rus. существи́тельное and прилага́тельное, Cz. podstatné and přídavné.

imenica: See preceding note.

jmenovitě: Compare Ger. namentlich "especially" (<Name "name").

имени́тый-imenit: Compare Eng. renowned (ult. <Lat. nomen "name"), Ger. namhaft "eminent" (<Name "name").

имени́тельный: modeled on Lat. nominativus (<nomen "name") and Gr. ὀνομαστική (<ὄνομα "name"); the nominative, as distinct from the oblique cases, is used when one wishes simply to name a thing. Compare Pol. mianownik "nominative case" (<miano "name").

jmenovatel et al.: Compare Eng. denominator (ult. <Lat. nomen "name"), Ger. Nenner "denominator" (<nennen "to name"), Pol. mianownik "denominator" (<miano "name"), S-C nazivnik; the denominator "denominates" or names the parts into which the unit is divided, while the numerator indicates the number which are taken. See also Rus. знамена́тель and числи́тель, Cz. čitatel.

imiesłów: formed from imię, in its earlier application to adjectives as well as nouns (see note above on и́мя-imię-jméno), and słowo "verb" (q.v.); a participle is a verbal adjective.

местоиме́ние: Ме́сто here = "instead of"; the word is modeled on Gr. ἀντωνυμία (<ἀντί "instead of" + ὄνομα "name; noun"). See note below on zaimek-zájmeno.

przedimek: ="a word which precedes a noun."

przyimek: ="a word which accompanies a noun."

zejména: See note on jmenovitě.

zaimek-zájmeno: modeled on Lat. pronomen (<pro "for" + nomen "name; noun"); compare Ger. Fürwort "pronoun" (<für "for" + Wort "word"), Cz. náměstka, S-C zamjenica and see note above on местоиме́ние.

ИН	IN	JIN	IN
ино́й: other; some	inny: other	jiný: other	ini (arch.): other
ина́че: otherwise	inaczej: otherwise	jinak, (arch.) jináče: otherwise	inače, inako: otherwise
			inačica: variant (n.)
		jinačiti: to alter	
иногда́: sometimes		jindy: at another time	
		jinde: elsewhere, at another place	
		jinam: elsewhere, to another place	
			inoča: concubine
и́нок (arch.): monk			inok (arch.): monk
			inokosan: solitary
и́ноходь: amble (horse's gait)		jinochod: amble (horse's gait)	
иносказа́ние: allegory			
иностра́нец: foreigner			inostranac: foreigner
		jinotaj: allegory	
инозе́мец (arch.): foreigner	innoziemiec: foreigner	jinozemec (arch.): foreigner	inozemac: foreigner
переина́чить, переина́чивать (coll.): to alter; to distort	przeinaczyć, przeinaczać: to alter; to distort	přejinačiti, přejinačovati (arch.): to alter	preinačiti, preinačivati (preinačavati): to alter
[R]	[P]	[Cz]	[S-C]

NOTES

Basic meaning of root: one; some; other

The original meaning, "one" (compare cognate Eng. one, Lat. unus "one" appears in only a few derivatives (и́нок-inok, inokosan, и́ноходь-jinochod) and as the second element in root ОДИН (etc.). The further semantic development was presumably: "one" 〉 "some (one)" (still apparent in the use of Rus ино́й in such phrases as ино́й раз "sometimes" and in Rus. иногда́) 〉 "(some) other (one)"; "other" is today the normal meaning in all four languages.

inoča: ="other wife"; the word was originally applied to the three wives a Moslem is permitted to take in addition to his first.

и́нок-inok: ="one who lives alone" (a reflection of the original meaning of the root); the word is a loan-translation of Gr. μοναχός "monk" (<μόνος "alone"), whence Eng. monk.

inokosan: from earlier inokost "solitude" (<inok).

и́ноходь-jinochod: See note under root ХОД (etc.).

иносказа́ние: ="that which implies other than what is said"; the word is a loan-translation of Gr. ἀλληγορία (<ἄλλος "other" + ἀγορεύειν "to speak"), whence Eng. allegory.

jinotaj: presumably a somewhat free loan-translation (in which the second element is from tajiti "to conceal"); see preceding note.

ИСК, ЫСК, ИЩ, ЫЩ	ISK, YSK	ISK, ÍSK, IŠT	ISK
иска́ть: to seek	iskać: to delouse		iskati: to request; to demand
иск: lawsuit			
ище́йка: bloodhound, police dog			
изыска́ть, изы́скивать: to find; (изы́скивать only) to seek; (изы́скивать only; geol.) to prospect	zyskać, zyskiwać: to gain, acquire	získati, získávati: to gain, acquire	iziskati, iziskivati: to demand; (iziskati only) to obtain; (iziskivati only) to require
изы́сканный (lit.): elegant, refined			
	zysk: profit, gain	zisk: profit, gain	
		zištný: mercenary, self-seeking	
при́иск: (gold-, etc.) mine			
про́иски (pl.): intrigues, machinations			
ро́зыск: investigation			
сниска́ть, сни́скивать (arch.): to gain, acquire			
соиска́ние: competition			
[R]	[P]	[Cz]	[S-C]

ИСТ

сыщик: detective взыскáть, взыскивать: to exact, recover (a sum of money); (с + gen.) to punish зайскивать: to fawn, curry favor	wyzyskać, wyzyskiwać: to exploit		*uziskati: to request; to demand *zaiskati: to request; to demand
[R]	[P]	[Cz]	[S-C]

NOTES

Basic meaning of root: to seek

The simple verb has not survived in Czech.

A non-Slavic cognate is Eng. ask.

iskać: an instance of semantic specialization.

изысканный: ="sought out," i.e. "choice, select"; the word is a loan-translation of Fr. recherché "elegant" (<chercher "to seek"). Compare Eng. exquisite (ult. <Lat. ex "out" + quaerere "to seek"), Ger. ausgesucht "exquisite" (<aus "out" + suchen "to seek").

прииск: orig. "a find," now specialized in meaning.

прóиски: The sense of the word is, roughly, "underhanded efforts to attain some end."

снискáть: The prefix is from ORus. сън "with, together" (=modern Rus. с). See introductory note on root Я (etc.); compare also снедáть et al., снедь.

соискáние: Compare Eng. competition (ult. <Lat. cum "with, together" + petere "to seek").

ИСТ	IST, IŚC, ISZCZ	JIST, JIŠŤ	IST
йстый (lit.): real	istny: real istnieć: to exist	jistý: certain, sure; safe, secure; a certain, particular (one)	isti: same
[R]	[P]	[Cz]	[S-C]

[R]	[P]	[Cz]	[S-C]
		jistiti (arch.): to assert, affirm	
	istota: essence; creature, being	jistota: certainty; security, bail	
и́стина: truth		jistina: capital, funds	istina: truth
исте́ц: plaintiff			
			istovetan: identical
и́стовый (arch.): earnest, zealous			
			istodoban: simultaneous; contemporary
			istorodan: homogeneous; similar
			istosmjeran: parallel (a.)
			istovremen: simultaneous; contemporary
	samoistny: independent		
неи́стовый: furious, raging, violent			
		pojistka: insurance; insurance policy; safety-catch; (elec.) fuse	
	przeistoczyć, przeistaczać: to transform		
	uiścić, uiszczać: to pay (a debt)	ujistiti, ujišťovati: to assure, give (verbal) assurance to	
	ziścić, ziszczać: to accomplish, realize, fulfil	zjistiti, zjišťovati: to ascertain, determine, establish	
		zajistiti, zajišťovati: to guarantee, insure, assure; to safeguard, secure; to take into custody	

NOTES

Basic meaning of root: real, true; certain

и́стый et al.: OPol. ist, isty has been replaced by istny in the modern language. The meaning "same" (which the Russian, Polish and Czech words also possessed at one time) arises from the notion of "the true one (i.e. not some other one)." Compare the use of Eng. very (<OFr. verai "true") in the phrase the very (same) one.

istnieć: ="to be real."

jistina: ="something real, secure"; ORus. истина could also mean "capital."

исте́ц: The original meaning (and that of OPol. iściec, OCz. jistec) was "true, rightful owner"; the present meaning is influenced by иска́ть "to seek," иск "lawsuit" (q.v.).

istovetan: an augmentative form of isti.

и́стовый: orig. "real; good, righteous."

istodoban: See note on Pol. równoczesny.

istorodan: See note under root РОД (etc.).

istovremen: See note on Pol. równoczesny.

samoistny: ="existing by itself"; compare istnieć.

неи́стовый: orig. "unreal, untrue"; the semantic development is not clear.

przeistoczyć: formed from prze- + istota.

uiścić, ziścić: formed from OPol. iścić; in both cases, the underlying meaning is "to make real, certain."

Я, ИМ, ЫМ, ЙМ, ЕМ, М	JĄ, JĘ, IĄ, IĘ, JE(N), IM, JM, JEM, M	Í, JA, A, Á, JE, Ě, E, JIM, JÍM, ÍM, JM, JEM, ĚM, M	E, JA, A, IM, JM, JAM, JEM, M
	jąć, imać (arch.): to grasp; (jąć only) to begin jąć się, imać się: to set about (a task) imadło: vise jeniec: prisoner of war	jmouti, jímati (lit.): to grasp *jmouti se (lit.): to begin	jemati: to gather grapes jamac, jemac: guarantor
[R]	[P]	[Cz]	[S-C]

			jamčiti (jemčiti) (za + acc.): to guarantee, vouch (for) jamačno: surely, undoubtedly
		jímavý (lit.): touching, moving (emotionally) jemný: delicate, fine; thin; soft, gentle	
ёмкий: capacious ёмкость: volume, capacity			
име́ть: to have	mieć: to have	míti: to have	imati: to have
име́ние: estate, manor; (arch.) property	mienie: property	jmění: property; wealth, fortune	imanje: property; estate, manor imovina: property
иму́щество: property	majątek: property; wealth, fortune; estate, manor	majetek: property; wealth, fortune	imetak, imutak: property; wealth, fortune
иму́щий (lit.): wealthy	majętny: wealthy	majetný: wealthy	imućan, (arch.) imatan: wealthy
		majitel, (arch.) majetník: owner	
благоприя́тный: favorable, propitious лицеприя́тие (arch.): partiality, bias мероприя́тие: measure, action, step (urgent measure, etc.)			
		Nanebevzetí: (rel.) Assumption	
неимове́рный: incredible, extraordinary, very great			
	obojętny: indifferent, apathetic; (chem.) neutral	obojetný: ambiguous, non-committal; two-faced, insincere; hermaphroditic	
[R]	[P]	[Cz]	[S-C]

[R]	[P]	[Cz]	[S-C]
рукоя́ть, рукоя́тка: handle, haft	rękojeść: handle, haft	rukojeť: handle, haft; (arch.) handbook, manual	
	rękojmia: guarantee	rukojmí: guarantor; hostage	
		rukověť: handbook, manual; (arch.) handle, haft	rukovet: handful, bunch
вероя́тный: probable, likely			vjerojatan, vjerovatan: probable, likely
	Wniebowzięcie: (rel.) Assumption		
водоём: reservoir		vodojem: reservoir	
доня́ть, донима́ть: to harass, annoy	dojąć, dojmować: to harass, annoy; to offend, cut to the quick	dojmouti, dojímati: to touch, move (emotionally)	
		dojem: impression	dojam: impression
изъя́тие (lit.): withdrawal, removal; exception			iznimka, izuzetak: exception
изя́щный: elegant, refined			
наня́ть, нанима́ть: to hire, rent	nająć, najmować: to hire, rent	najmouti, najímati: to hire, rent	najmiti, naimati: to hire, rent
наёмник, наймит: hireling	najemnik: hireling	nájemník: tenant	najamnik, najemnik: hireling; tenant
неиме́ние: lack, absence			neimanje, neimaština, nemaština: poverty
недоимка: arrears			
необъя́тный: vast, boundless	nieobjęty: vast, boundless		
неотъе́млемый: inalienable			
неуёмный (lit.): indefatigable; incessant			
обня́ть, обнима́ть: to clasp, embrace; to embrace, comprise, include	objąć, obejmować: to clasp, embrace; to embrace, comprise, include;	obejmouti, objímati: to clasp, embrace	*obujmiti: to clasp, embrace

[R]	[P]	[Cz]	[S-C]
	to take, assume (office, command, possession, etc.)		
*объя́ть (arch.): to seize (e.g. with fear); to envelop (in flames)			
	objętość: volume, capacity		
объём: volume, capacity; size, quantity, bulk		objem: volume, capacity; size, quantity, bulk	obim, objam, obujam: volume, capacity; size, quantity, bulk; circumference
			obuzeti, obuzimati: to seize, grip; to seize (e.g. with fear)
отня́ть, отнима́ть: to take away; to amputate	odjąć, odejmować: to take away; to amputate; (math.) to subtract	odejmouti (odníti), odnímati: to take away; to amputate	oteti, otimati: to seize, carry off; to abduct
			oduzeti, oduzimati: to take away; (math.) to subtract
	odwzajemnić się, odwzajemniać się: to repay, requite, reciprocate		
поня́ть, понима́ть: to understand	pojąć, pojmować: to understand; to take (in marriage)	pojmouti, pojímati (lit.): to understand; to take; to take (in marriage); to include; to accommodate, have room for; to seize (e.g. with fear); to conceive (e.g. a plan)	pojmiti, poimati: to understand
поня́тие: concept; notion, idea		pojetí: notion, idea	
	pojęcie: concept; notion, idea	pojetí: conception (of a problem, etc.)	
		pojem: concept; notion, idea	pojam: concept; notion, idea
[R]	[P]	[Cz]	[S-C]

[R]	[P]	[Cz]	[S-C]
*поймáть: to catch	*pojmać: to apprehend, arrest		
пóйма: floodlands			
поёмный: subject to spring flooding	pojemny: capacious		
	pojemność: volume, capacity		
	pojemnik: container		
подня́ть, поднимáть (подымáть): to raise	podjąć, podejmować: to raise; to undertake; (podejmować only) to entertain, play host to		
подня́ться, поднимáться (подымáться): to rise	podjąć się, podejmować się: to undertake	podejmouti se, podjímati se (lit.): to undertake	*podnimiti se: to rest one's head on one's arms
подъём: (act of) raising; rise; progress, advance; enthusiasm; instep; (mil.) reveille			
подъёмник: elevator			
			poduzeti, poduzimati: to undertake
			poduzetan, poduzimljiv: enterprising, venturesome
			poduzeće: undertaking, venture; (business) enterprise, concern
			poduzetnik, poduzimač: entrepreneur, businessman
перени́ть, перенимáть: to take over, adopt		přejmouti, přejímati: to take; to accept; to take over, adopt	
преéмник: successor			

[R]	[P]	[Cz]	[S-C]
преиму́щество: advantage; privilege			preimućstvo: advantage; privilege
преиму́щественно: mainly, for the most part			
			preuzetan: arrogant, presumptuous
		předejmouti, předjímati: to anticipate	
		předpojatý: preconceived; biased, prejudiced	
предприня́ть, предпринима́ть: to undertake			preduzeti, preduzimati: to undertake
предприи́мчивый: enterprising, venturesome			preduzetan, preduzimljiv: enterprising, venturesome
предприя́тие: undertaking, venture; (business) enterprise, concern			preduzeće: undertaking, venture; (business) enterprise, concern
предпринима́тель: entrepreneur, businessman			preduzetnik, preduzimač: entrepreneur, businessman
предвзя́тый: preconceived; biased, prejudiced			
	*przedsięwziąć: to undertake	*předsevzíti (arch.): to undertake	
		*předsevzíti si: to decide, resolve	
приня́ть, принима́ть: to take; to accept; to receive (guests)	przyjąć, przyjmować: to accept; to receive (guests)	přijmouti, přijímati: to take; to accept; to receive	primiti, primati: to take; to accept; to receive
приня́ться, принима́ться: to begin; (за + acc.) to set about (a task); to take root	przyjąć się, przyjmować się: to take root		primiti se, primati se: to set about (a task); to take root

[R]	[P]	[Cz]	[S-C]
приня́тие: (act of) taking; acceptance	przyjęcie: acceptance; reception, welcome; reception (in s.o.'s honor, etc.)	přijetí: acceptance; reception, welcome	
		přijímání: acceptance; (rel.) Eucharist, Communion	primanje: acceptance; receipt (act of receiving); reception (in s.o.'s honor, etc.)
			primalja: midwife
прия́тный: pleasant			prijatan: pleasant
приём: acceptance; reception, welcome; reception (in s.o.'s honor, etc.); dose; method		příjem: receipt (act of receiving); income	prijam, prijem: acceptance; receipt (act of receiving); reception, welcome
приёмный: reception, calling (hours); entrance (examination); foster-(parent, child)	przyjemny: pleasant	příjemný: pleasant	prijamni, prijemni: entrance (examination); (radio) receiving (set)
приёмник: radio (receiving) set		přijímač: radio (receiving) set	prijemnik: radio (receiving) set
		*přiměti: to force, compel	
проня́ть, пронима́ть (coll.): to pierce, penetrate (e.g. cold); to seize (e.g. with fear)	przejąć, przejmować: to pierce, penetrate (e.g. cold); to seize (e.g. with fear); to intercept; to take over, adopt	projmouti, projímati: to pierce, penetrate (e.g. cold); to take in (a piece of clothing); (projímati only) to act as a laxative	
проём: window opening or doorway		průjem: diarrhea	
про́йма: armhole (in garment)			
		rozjímavý: meditative, contemplative	

[R]	[P]	[Cz]	[S-C]
	rozejm: truce, armistice		
	rozjemca: arbitrator		
сня́тие: (act of) taking off, taking away, taking down, removing; (act of) renting; (act of) photographing	zdjęcie: (act of) taking off, taking away, taking down, removing; photograph		
сни́мок: photograph		snímek: photograph; (sound) recording, record	snimak, snimka: photograph; copy
сонм, со́нмище (arch.): crowd, multitude	sejm: parliament	sněm: parliament; assembly	sajam: fair, market
		sňatek: wedding, marriage	
уня́ть, унима́ть: to calm, pacify; to soothe, allay	ująć, ujmować: to grasp; to seize, apprehend; to grasp, comprehend; to couch, formulate; to captivate, win over; to belittle, detract (from)	ujmouti, ujímati: to reduce, decrease	ujmiti, uimati: to reduce, decrease
уня́ться, унима́ться: to grow calm, quiet; to abate	ująć się, ujmować się: to intercede, plead (for)	ujmouti se, ujímati se: to set about (a task); to take charge, care (of s.th. or s.o.); to intercede, plead (for); to take root	ujmiti se, uimati se: to decline, decrease
		ujímání: reduction, decrease; (med.) colic	
у́йма (coll.): plenty, a lot	ujma: harm, detriment	újma: harm, detriment	
	ujemny: negative, unfavorable; (math., phys.) negative		
внима́ние: attention		vnímání: perception	
вня́тный: audible			
		vjem: perception	

[R]	[P]	[Cz]	[S-C]
взаимный: mutual, reciprocal	wzajemny: mutual, reciprocal	vzájemný: mutual, reciprocal	uzajaman: mutual, reciprocal
	wyjątek: exception; extract, excerpt	výňatek: extract, excerpt	
вы́емка: (act of) taking out; seizure (of property during search of premises); excavation; groove, hollow	wyimek: extract, excerpt	výjimka: exception	
	wywzajemnić się, wywzajemniać się: to repay, requite, reciprocate		
*взять: to take	*wziąć: to take	*vzíti: to take	*uzeti: to take; to begin
взима́ть: to levy, collect			uzimati: to take
взя́тка: bribe; trick (in card-playing)	wziątek, wziątka: trick (in card-playing)		
	wziętość: popularity; demand (for a product)		uzetost, uzma: paralysis
	zacny: honest, honorable	vzácný: precious; rare	
*возыме́ть (lit.): to conceive (a desire, etc.); to have, produce (an effect)			
восприня́ть, воспринима́ть: to grasp, comprehend			
восприе́мник (arch.): godfather			
заня́ть, занима́ть: to occupy (space, time, a country, etc.); to interest; to amuse, entertain; to borrow	zająć, zajmować: to occupy (space, time, a country, etc.); to interest; to seize, confiscate	zajmouti, zajímati: to capture, take prisoner; (zajímati only) to interest	zajmiti, zaimati: to borrow; to lend

[R]	[P]	[Cz]	[S-C]
			zanimati: to interest; to amuse, entertain
заня́ться, занима́ться: to occupy o.s. (with), engage (in); to catch fire	zająć się, zajmować się: to occupy o.s. (with), engage (in); to catch fire	zajímati se: to be interested, take an interest	zanimati se: to occupy o.s. (with), engage (in); to be interested, take an interest; to amuse o.s.
		zajatec: prisoner, captive	
заём: loan		zájem: interest	zajam: loan
заимствовать: to borrow			
		zaujatý: biased, prejudiced; absorbed, engrossed	
			zauzeti, zauzimati: to occupy (space, a country, etc.); to conquer
завзя́тый (coll.): inveterate, confirmed, habitual	zawzięty: bitter, unrelenting		zauzet: occupied; conquered

NOTES

Basic meaning of root: to take

This root, moribund or extinct in all four languages in its primary verbal form, is nevertheless highly productive as a source of compound formations showing broad semantic development. The secondary meaning "to have" (whence, further, such meanings as "property," "wealth" and "owner") reflects a semantic shift from the act of taking to the resulting state of possession.

The letter n preceding the root in various Russian, Czech and Serbo-Croatian derivatives occurred originally in words formed from the Common Slavic prefixes *sъn and *vъn (=modern s and v), as exemplified by Rus. сня́тие and внима́ние below, and ultimately spread to other words by analogy. (Compare Rus. снеда́ть et al., снедь, сниска́ть.)

Cz. jmouti, which serves to form most of the perfective compounds, is a new infinitive constructed from 1 sg. jmu; the original form represented by OCz. jieti survives only in odníti and vzíti in modern usage. Of the original Serbo-Croatian perfectives in -(j)eti, only oteti and uzeti remain;

the newer forms in *-jmiti* (*-imiti*) are in some instances denominative (*najmiti* < *najam* "hire, rent," *zajmiti* < *zajam*) and in others of uncertain origin. A new set of perfective and imperfective compounds has also been created from *uzeti*, *uzimati* in Serbo-Croatian. The old Polish imperfective form *-jmać* has given way to *-jmować* throughout. (See also note below on *jąć et al.*)

The Slavic root is cognate with Lat. *emere* "to buy; (in early usage) to take" (>Eng. *exempt*, *pre-empt*, *redeem*), which combines with *sub* "under" to form *sumere* "to take" (>Eng. *assume*, *consume*, *presume*, *resume*).

jąć et al.: Rus. *ять*, *имáть* and S-C *jeti* "to take" are obsolete. S-C *jemati* (orig. "to take") is a reconstituted infinitive based on 1 sg. *jemam* (*jemljem*); unattested **imati* survives in imperfective compounds. (See also introductory note above.)

jąć (second meaning), *jmouti se*: ="to take (or catch) hold"; compare Eng. *inception* (ult. <Lat. *capere* "to take"), Ger. *anfangen* "to begin" (<*fangen* "to catch").

jeniec: <OPol. *jęciec* < *jęty*, past pass. part. of *jąć*.

jamac, *jemac*: The original sense has been explained as "one who takes the word of another."

jamčiti (*jemčiti*), *jamačno*: <*jamac*, *jemac*.

jemný: orig. "pleasant"; see note on *приятный-prijatan*, *przyjemny-příjemný*.

ёмкий, *ёмкость*: Compare Eng. *capacious*, *capacity* (both ult. <Lat. *capere* "to take").

mieć-míti: <OPol. *imieć*, OCz. *jmieti*.

imati: The original form, *imjeti*, is obsolete.

благоприятный: See *приятный*.

лицеприятие: See note under root ЛИК (etc.).

мероприятие: See note under root MEP$_1$ (etc.).

Nanebevzetí: The second element is from *nebe* "sky; heaven."

неимовéрный: from the Old Russian words for "I take (*i.e.* have) no faith (=I do not believe)"; compare *вероятный et al.*

obojętny-obojetný: ="capable of being taken from either side or in either of two ways"; the first element is from *oba* "both."

rękojeść: for earlier *rękojęć*.

rukověť-rukovet: The intrusive *v* arose as a result of hiatus.

вероятный et al.: A probable thing is one in which one can "take (*i.e.* have) faith"; compare *неимовéрный*. Regarding the Serbo-Croatian form *vjerovatan*, see preceding note.

Wniebowzięcie: The second element is from *niebo* "sky; heaven."

донять et al.: The underlying meaning is "to grasp for, get at."

dojem-dojam: See *dojmouti*; the Serbo-Croatian word is borrowed from Czech.

изъя́тие et al.: Compare Eng. *exception* (ult. < Lat. *ex* "out" + *capere* "to take"), Ger. *Ausnahme* "exception" (< *aus* "out" + *nehmen* "to take"), Hung. *kivétel* "exception" (< *ki* "out" + *venni* "to take").

изя́щный: ="taken out," *i.e.* "choice, select"; the word is borrowed from Church Slavic.

неиме́ние et al.: < *име́ть-imati*.

недои́мка: See note on Rus. *недобо́р*, Pol. *niedobór*.

необъя́тный-nieobjęty: ="so large that it cannot be embraced, encompassed"; see *обня́ть-objąć*.

неотъе́млемый: See *отня́ть*.

неуёмный: See *уня́ться*.

objętość, *объём et al.*: See note on *ёмкий*, *ёмкость* and compare Ger. *Umfang* "volume; size; extent, scope; circumference" (< *um* "around" + *fangen* "to catch"), Cz. *obsah*, S-C *opseg*; S-C *objam* is borrowed from Czech.

odwzajemnić się: See *wzajemny*.

поня́ть et al., *поня́тие-pojetí*, *pojęcie-pojetí*, *pojem-pojam*: Understanding is commonly conceived of as a process of "taking" or "grasping" with the mind; compare Eng. *comprehend* (ult. < Lat. *prehendere* "to grasp, seize"), Eng. *conceive* and *concept(ion)* (ult. < Lat. *capere* "to take"), Ger. *begreifen* "to understand" and *Begriff* "concept" (< *greifen* "to grasp, seize"), Ger. *Vernunft* "sense, reason, intelligence" (< *nehmen* "to take"), Rus. *охвати́ть* and *пости́гнуть*, Cz. *obsáhnouti*, *postihnouti* and *vystihnouti*, S-C *shvaćanje*. S-C *pojam* is borrowed from Czech.

по́йма, *поёмный*: < *поня́ть* in the earlier meaning "to take, seize; to occupy, fill (with water)."

pojemny, *pojemność*: See note on *ёмкий*, *ёмкость*.

подня́ть-podjąć: The meaning "to raise" reflects the idea of grasping a thing underneath in order to lift it; compare Pol. *podnieść*. The third meaning of *podejmować* resulted from the semantic progression "to raise" > "to prop, support" > "to support, maintain (a dependent)" > "to entertain."

podnimiti se: < obsolete *podnimiti* "to prop, support."

poduzeti, *poduzetan*, *poduzimljiv*, *poduzeće*, *poduzetnik*, *poduzimač*: See note on *предприня́ть-preduzeti*, *предприи́мчивый et al.*, *предприя́тие-preduzeće*, *предпринима́тель et al.*

прее́мник: one who takes over another's position, office, etc.; see *переня́ть*. The word is a Church Slavic borrowing.

преиму́щество-preimućstvo: something which one person has "over," before or in preference to another; see *име́ть-imati*. The Serbo-Croatian word is borrowed from Russian.

preuzetan: modeled on Lat. *praesumptuosus* "presumptuous" (< *praesumere* "to presume, anticipate, take for granted" < *prae* "before" + *sumere* "to take"); *pre-* here is the Latin rather than the Slavic prefix.

předejmouti: Compare Eng. *anticipate* (ult. < Lat. *ante* "before" + *capere* "to take"), Rus. *предвосхи́тить*.

předpojatý: Compare Ger. (vor)eingenommen "biased, prejudiced" (<vor "before" + einnehmen "to bias, prejudice" < nehmen "to take").

предприня́ть-preduzeti, предприи́мчивый et al., предприя́тие-preduzeće, предпринима́тель et al.: Compare Eng. enterprise, enterprising and entrepreneur (all ult. <Fr. entreprendre "to undertake" < prendre "to take"), Ger. unternehmen "to undertake" (<nehmen "to take"), unternehmend "enterprising," Unternehmen "(business) enterprise" and Unternehmer "entrepreneur," Pol. przedsiębrać, przedsiębiorczy, przedsiębiorstwo and przedsiębiorca, Cz. podniknouti, podnikavý, podnik and podnikatel.

предвзя́тый: See note on předpojatý.

приня́ться: See note on jąć, jmouti se.

primalja: a woman who "receives" the newborn child after its birth.

приятный-prijatan, przyjemny-příjemný: ="acceptable"; compare Ger. angenehm "pleasant" (<annehmen "to accept" < nehmen "to take").

приём (last meaning): See the second meaning of приня́ться.

přiměti: <míti; compare the similar use of Eng. have in such sentences as I had him come.

проня́ть et al., проём-průjem, про́йма: Most of the meanings reflect the notion of "seizing (=cutting, going) through, i.e. piercing" (compare Rus. пробо́р); in its last two meanings, however, Pol. przejąć is etymologically identical with переня́ть-přejmouti.

rozjímavý: See note on Rus. разбо́р et al., разбо́рчивый, разбира́тельство

rozejm, rozjemca: The underlying idea is that of "taking apart, separating," hence "deciding, resolving (an issue)"; see note on S-C odlučiti, odluka.

сня́тие-zdjęcie, сни́мок et al.: A photograph, recording or copy is conceived as being "taken" or "picked up" from its subject or from the original; compare Ger. Aufnahme "photograph; recording" (<auf "up" + nehmen "to take"), Hung. felvétel "photograph; recording" (<fel "up" + venni "to take"). The intrusive d in the Polish word has been attributed to the influence of odjąć (q.v.).

сонм et al., sňatek: The basic meaning of all these words is "a taking together, i.e. assembly, gathering"; Rus. сонм and со́нмище are borrowed from Church Slavic.

уня́ть et al.: The Russian, Czech and Serbo-Croatian words and the last meaning of the Polish word reflect the idea of "taking away," hence "making (s.th.) less." Regarding the third meaning of ująć, see note on поня́ть et al., поня́тие-ponětí, pojęcie-pojetí, pojem-pojam; the meaning "to couch, formulate" (="to grasp in words, in a verbal framework") shows semantic parallelism with Ger. abfassen "to couch, formulate" (<fassen "to grasp, seize").

ująć się-ujmouti se: Compare Ger. sich annehmen "to take charge, care (of s.th. or s.o.)" (<sich, refl. pron. + an "to" + nehmen "to take").

ujímání (second meaning): a pain which "grips, grasps"; compare Eng.

grip and the variant form gripe "to afflict with abdominal pain."

ýйма: ="all one can grasp."

ujma-újma: ="a taking away, reduction"; roughly the same idea is expressed by Eng. detriment (ult. <Lat. deterere "to rub, wear away"), Ger. Abbruch "harm, detriment" (<abbrechen "to break off").

ujemny: The basic idea is that of taking away (as in znak ujemny "minus sign"); see note on Pol. dodatni.

внимáние-vnímání, внятный, vjem: Reflected in all these words is the notion of "taking in" with the senses; compare Eng. perception (ult. <Lat. capere "to take"), Ger. vernehmen "to hear" (<nehmen "to take"). Cz. vnímání is borrowed from Russian.

взаимный et al.: <заём-zajam and obsolete Pol. zajem "loan"; the same association of ideas is apparent in Eng. mutual (ult. <Lat. mutuus "borrowed, lent"), Hung. kölcsön "loan" and kölcsönös "mutual, reciprocal." The Czech word is borrowed from Polish.

wyjątek, výjimka: See note on изъятие et al.

wywzajemnić się: See wzajemny.

взять-wziąć-vzíti: used as the perfective forms of брать-brać-bráti (q.v.).

uzeti: See note on jąć, jmouti se.

uzetost, uzma: Compare Eng. seizure in the medical sense, numb (orig. ="taken, seized"; see OEng. niman "to take"), epilepsy (ult. <Gr. λαμβάνειν "to take").

zacny: borrowed from Cz. vzácný; the meaning is influenced by that of unrelated cny (q.v.).

vzácný: ="worth taking," i.e. "of value."

возымéть: <имéть.

воспринять: See note on понять et al., понятие-ponětí, pojęcie-pojetí, pojem-pojam.

восприéмник: so called because the godfather takes the newly baptized child in his arms to indicate that he is standing sponsor to it.

zajmiti: See note on S-C posuditi.

zanimati: <Rus. занимáть.

zaujatý: See note on předpojatý.

завзятый-zawzięty: See Pol. zawziąć się "to be obstinate" (orig. "to set about [a task], be bent upon [a purpose]"); the Russian word is borrowed from Polish.

ЯВ	JAW	JEV	JAV
явь: reality	jawa: wakefulness, waking state; reality		java: wakefulness, waking state; reality
яви́ть, явля́ть (lit.): to show, manifest		jeviti (lit.): to show, manifest	javiti, javljati: to announce
яви́ться, явля́ться: to report, present o.s.; to be		jeviti se: to be evident, manifest itself; (lit.) to seem, appear	javiti se, javljati se: to report, present o.s.
		jev: phenomenon	
явле́ние: phenomenon; occurrence; scene (part of a play)			
		jeviště: stage (in a theater); scene (of action)	
я́вный: obvious	jawny: public (a.); overt, avowed		javan: public (a.)
я́вственный: clear, distinct			
Богоявле́ние: (rel.) Epiphany			Bogojavljenje: (rel.) Epiphany
			brzojav: telegram
			dojaviti, dojavljivati: to inform
изъявле́ние: expression (of an opinion or sentiment)		zjevení: specter, apparition; (divine) revelation	
	zjawienie się: appearance, (act of) appearing		
	zjawa: specter, apparition	zjev: phenomenon	izjava: declaration, statement; expression (of an opinion or sentiment)
	zjawisko: phenomenon; fact		
		zjevný: obvious	
изъяви́тельный: (gram.) indicative			
[R]	[P]	[Cz]	[S-C]

[R]	[P]	[Cz]	[S-C]
наяву́: in a waking state	na jawie: in a waking state	najevě (arch.): obvious (pred.)	na javi: in a waking state
			*najaviti: to announce
объяви́ть, объявля́ть: to announce; to declare (war)	objawić, objawiać: to disclose, reveal; to show, manifest	objeviti, objevovati: to discover	objaviti, objavljivati: to announce; to publish; to declare (war)
	objawić się, objawiać się: to appear, make an appearance	objeviti se, objevovati se: to appear, make an appearance	
	objaw: symptom; sign, manifestation	objev: discovery	objava: announcement; declaration (of war); publication (act of publishing)
отъя́вленный: arrant, thorough (scoundrel, etc.)			
появи́ться, появля́ться: to appear, make an appearance	pojawić się, pojawiać się: to appear, make an appearance		pojaviti se, pojavljivati se: to appear, make an appearance
			pojava: phenomenon; occurrence; appearance, (act of) appearing; scene (part of a play)
предъяви́ть, предъявля́ть: to produce (documents), present (a claim), bring (suit)			
			prijaviti, prijavljivati: to announce; to denounce, inform against
прояви́ть, проявля́ть: to show, manifest; to develop (film)	przejawić, przejawiać: to show, manifest	projeviti, projevovati: to show, manifest; to express	
вы́явить, выявля́ть: to disclose, reveal	wyjawić, wyjawiać: to disclose, reveal	vyjeviti, vyjevovati: to disclose, reveal	
[R]	[P]	[Cz]	[S-C]

заяви́ть, заявля́ть: to declare, state [R]	[P]	výjev: scene (part of a play) [Cz]	[S-C]

NOTES

Basic meaning of root: wakefulness

From the notion of wakefulness as distinct from sleep have evolved the secondary meanings "to show, make known" and (in reflexive verbs) "to show oneself, appear." The present-day noun, verbal and adjectival forms are probably derived from a vanished primary adverb meaning "in a waking state. (See, however, note on Cz. jev.)

jev: a relatively recent postverbal form; regarding the meaning, compare Eng. phenomenon (ult. ‹Gr. φαίνεσθαι "to appear" ‹ φαίνειν "to show") Ger. Erscheinung "phenomenon" (‹erscheinen "to appear"), Cz. úkaz.

явле́ние (first meaning): See preceding note.

Богоявле́ние-Bogojavljenje: ="manifestation or appearance of God"; the word is modeled on Gr. Θεοφάνεια (‹θεός "god" + φαίνειν "to show"). Compare also Eng. Epiphany (ult. ‹Gr. ἐπιφάνεια "manifestation, appearance" ‹ φαίνειν).

brzojav: The first element is from brz "swift"; compare javiti.

zjevení, zjawa: Compare Eng. apparition (ult. ‹Lat. apparere "to appear"), S-C prikaza.

zjev, zjawisko (first meaning): See note on jev.

отъя́вленный: ‹archaic отъяви́ть "to proclaim publicly (e.g. as a criminal)."

pojava (first meaning): See note on jev.

EX, ЕЗД	JECH, JAZD, JEŹDZ, JEŻDŻ	JE(ZD), JÍZD	JAH, JEZD
†е́хать, е́здить: to go, ride езда́: ride, riding [R]	†jechać, jeździć: to go, ride jazda: ride, riding; trip, journey; cavalry [P]	†jeti, jezditi: to go, ride jízda: ride, riding; trip, journey; cavalry [Cz]	jahati (jezditi) to ride on horseback [S-C]

		jezdectvo: cavalry	
		jízdárna: riding-school	
			jahaliště: riding-school
наéзд: sudden visit; (arch.) raid, incursion	najazd: raid, incursion; invasion	nájezd: raid, incursion	najezda: raid, incursion; invasion
		nadjezd: viaduct	
пóезд: (railroad) train	pojazd: coach, carriage; vehicle		
поéздка: trip, journey			
съезд: congress; arrival (of many persons); slope; descent	zjazd: congress; arrival (of many persons); descent	sjezd: congress; slope; descent	
уéзд: district		újezd: district	
	ujeżdżalnia: riding-school		
заéзд: stop, call, visit; heat (in a race)	zajazd: stop, call, visit; inn; (arch.) raid, incursion	zájezd: trip, journey; (arch.) raid, incursion	
[R]	[P]	[Cz]	[S-C]

NOTES

Basic meaning of root: to go, ride

Except in Serbo-Croatian, the verbs formed from this root serve to translate Eng. go in all cases where some means of conveyance is used; compare roots ХОД (etc.) and И(Д) (etc.).

The original verbal root survives only in Cz. jeti, the equivalent Russian, Polish and Serbo-Croatian infinitives representing an expanded root-form. An expanded form ending in d appears in the present tense of these verbs in Russian, Polish and Czech (e.g. in 1 sg. éду, jadę, jedu); the Serbo-Croatian present tense (e.g. 1 sg. jašem) is formed from jahati. Rus. éздить and its equivalents in the other languages are probably denominatives deriving from the Common Slavic ancestor of éздá et al., which contain the original root + a suffix.

съезд et al.: The various meanings reflect both meanings of the prefix, i.e. "together" and "off, down." Regarding the first meaning of the words, compare Eng. congress (ult. ‹Lat. cum "together" + gradi "to step; to go"), convention (ult. ‹Lat. cum + venire "to come").

уéзд-újezd: orig. a piece of land which was "ridden around" for the purpose of placing and maintaining boundary markers.

Е(Д), Я(Д)	JA(D), IAD, JE	JÍ(D), ÍD, JE(D), ĚD	JE(D), JA
есть: to eat	ˈjeść, jadać: to eat	ˈjísti, jídati: to eat	jesti: to eat
еда́: food; meal	jadło: food	jídlo: food; meal	jelo: food; meal
	jadalnia: dining-room	jídelna: dining-room; restaurant	
		jídelníček: menu	jelovnik: menu
я́ства (pl., arch.): food			jestiva (pl.): food
			jestvenik: menu
			jednjak: esophagus
		jícen: esophagus; crater (of a volcano); muzzle (of a gun)	
я́сли (pl.): manger; nursery, crèche	jasła (pl.): manger	jesle (pl.): manger; nursery, crèche	jasle (pl.): manger; nursery, crèche
е́дкий: caustic, corrosive (substance); caustic, biting (remark); acrid			
			biljojed: herbivorous
чужея́дный: (biol.) parasitic			
дармое́д: parasite, sponger	darmozjad: parasite, sponger		
	jadłodajnia: restaurant		
	jadłospis: menu		
костое́да: (med.) caries			kostojed, kostojedica: (med.) caries
людое́д: cannibal	ludojad: cannibal	lidojed: cannibal	
плотоя́дный: carnivorous			mesojed: carnivorous
травоя́дный: herbivorous			travojed: herbivorous
тунея́дец: parasite, sponger			
[R]	[P]	[Cz]	[S-C]

[R]	[P]	[Cz]	[S-C]
всеядный: omnivorous			
изъесть, изъедать: to corrode, eat away			izjesti, izjedati: to corrode, eat away; to devour
			izjelica: glutton
надоесть, надоедать: to bore, weary; to importune, harass			
недоедание: malnutrition			
обед: dinner	obiad: dinner	oběd: dinner	objed: dinner
обедня: (rel.) Mass			
разъесть, разъедать: to corrode, eat away; to erode			razjesti, razjedati: to corrode, eat away; to erode
снедать: to consume (with remorse, envy, etc.)	śniadać: to eat breakfast	snídati: to eat breakfast	
снедь (arch.): food			
заядлый (coll.): inveterate, confirmed, habitual	zajadły: fierce, bitter		
[R]	[P]	[Cz]	[S-C]

NOTES

Basic meaning of root: to eat

Many of the words in this group have semantic counterparts among the derivatives of root ЖР (etc.).

The letter d in the root changed to s before t through dissimilation (see есть and its analogues, яства-jestiva, jestvenik, jícen [in which c < st]) and was lost before s (see ясли et al.) in Common Slavic; d was lost before l in Serbo-Croatian (see jelo, jelovnik, izjelica).

The Slavic root is cognate with Eng. eat, Lat. edere "to eat" (>Eng. edible).

есть et al.: The root of the primary verb is apparent in, for example, the 3 pl. forms: respectively, едят, jedzą, jedí, jedu.

ясли et al.: Compare Eng. manger (related to Fr. manger "to eat").

<u>е́дкий</u>: See note on <u>разъе́сть-razjesti</u>. (S-C <u>jedak</u> "angry; caustic, corrosive; caustic, biting; acrid" is from <u>jed</u> "bile; poison; anger," whose relationship to this root is uncertain; some of the meanings of <u>jedak</u> are probably influenced by the Russian word.)

<u>чужея́дный</u>: The first element is from <u>чужо́й</u> "alien, foreign"; compare Cz. <u>cizopasník</u>.

<u>костое́да</u> <u>et al</u>.: The first element is from <u>кость-kost</u> "bone."

<u>плотоя́дный-mesojed</u>: The first elements are from, respectively, <u>плоть</u> "flesh" and <u>meso</u> "flesh; meat."

<u>травоя́дный-travojed</u>: The first element is from <u>трава́-trava</u> "grass."

<u>тунея́дец</u>: The first element can be seen in archaic <u>вту́не</u> "in vain, to no purpose"; compare <u>дармое́д-darmozjad</u>.

<u>изъе́сть-izjesti</u>: See note on <u>разъе́сть-razjesti</u>.

<u>надое́сть</u>: <<u>дое́сть</u> "to finish eating"; for the development of the meaning, compare the English expression <u>fed up</u>.

<u>обе́дня</u>: =the Lord's Supper, <u>i.e</u>. Holy Communion.

<u>разъе́сть-razjesti</u>: Compare Eng. <u>corrode</u>, <u>erode</u> (both ult. <Lat. <u>rodere</u> "to gnaw").

<u>снеда́ть</u> <u>et al</u>., <u>снедь</u>: The prefix represents an earlier form of modern Rus. <u>с</u> and its analogues in the other languages. See the introductory note on root Я (etc.); compare also Rus. <u>сниска́ть</u>.

<u>зая́длый-zajadły</u>: For the underlying meaning of the Polish word, see <u>zajeść się</u> "to eat heartily, with abandon" and compare Pol. <u>zażarty</u>, Cz. <u>zažraný</u>; <u>зая́длый</u> is borrowed from Polish.

ОДИН, ОДН, ЕДИН	JEDEN, JEDYN, JEDN, JEN, ODYN	JEDEN, JEDIN, JEDN, JEN	JEDAN, JEDIN, JEDN
<u>оди́н</u>: one	<u>jeden</u>: one	<u>jeden</u>: one	<u>jedan</u>: one
	<u>jednać</u>: to reconcile	<u>jednati</u>: to act; to negotiate; to hire; to deal (with a subject)	
		<u>jednatel</u>: secretary; agent	
<u>еди́ный</u>: united; single	<u>jedyny</u>: only, sole; unique	<u>jediný</u>: only, sole	<u>jedini</u>: only, sole
			<u>jediniti</u>: to unite (tr.)
	<u>jedynak</u>: only son	<u>jedináček</u>: only child	
		<u>jedinec</u>: individual (n.)	<u>jedinac</u>: only son
<u>едини́чный</u>: single		<u>jedinečný</u>: unique	
[R]	[P]	[Cz]	[S-C]

[R]	[P]	[Cz]	[S-C]
едини́ца: unit; individual (n.)			jedinica: unit; only daughter
еди́нство: unity			jedinstvo: unity
еди́нственный: only, sole; unique; (gram.) singular			jedinstven: only, sole; united; unique
	jedność: unity	jednota: unity; union, association	
	jednoczyć: to unite (tr.)	jednotiti: to unite (tr.)	
	jednostka: unit; individual (n.)	jednotka: unit	
		jednotný: uniform (a.); (gram.) singular	
	jednotliwy: (gram.) semelfactive (aspect of Slavic verb)	jednotlivý: single; separate	
		jednotlivec: individual (n.)	
		jednotlivost: detail	
	jednaki: identical, equal		jednak: identical, equal
одина́ковый: identical, equal	jednakowy: identical, equal		
одна́ко: however	jednak: however	jednak ... jednak: on the one hand ... on the other hand	jednako: equally; constantly
			jednačina, jednadžba: (math.) equation
одино́кий: solitary; lonely; single, unmarried			
			jednina: (gram.) singular number
одна́жды: once		jednou: once	jednom: once
	jeno (arch.): only (adv.)	jen, jenom: only (adv.)	
	odyniec: wild boar		
единобо́жие: monotheism	jednobóstwo: monotheism	jednobožství: monotheism	jednoboštvo: monotheism
единобра́чие: monogamy			

[R]	[P]	[Cz]	[S-C]
	jednochoda, jednochód: amble (horse's gait)		
	jednoczesny: simultaneous		
единоду́шный: unanimous		jednoduchý: simple	jednodušan: unanimous
единогла́сный: unanimous	jednogłośny: unanimous	jednohlasný: unanimous	jednoglasan: unanimous
			jednoličan, jednolik: monotonous; uniform
	jednolity: uniform, homogeneous; unitary	jednolitý: solid, compact	
	jednomyślny: unanimous	jednomyslný: unanimous	
однообра́зный: monotonous			jednoobrazan: uniform (a.)
единообра́зный: uniform (a.)			
одноро́дный: homogeneous	jednorodny: homogeneous		jednorodan: homogeneous
единоро́г: unicorn	jednorożec: unicorn	jednorožec: unicorn	jednorog: unicorn
	jednostajny: monotonous; uniform	jednostejný (arch.): monotonous	jednostavan: simple
		jednotvárný: monotonous	
единовла́стие: autocracy	jednowładztwo, jedynowładztwo: autocracy		
одновре́ме́нный: simultaneous			jednovremen: simultaneous; contemporary
	jednozgodny: unanimous		
однозна́чный: synonymous; (math.) simple (consisting of one digit)	jednoznaczny: synonymous	jednoznačný: synonymous; unambiguous	
	jednożeństwo: monogamy	jednoženství: monogamy	jednoženstvo: monogamy
неоднокра́тно: repeatedly, more than once	niejednokrotnie: repeatedly, more than once		

[R]	[P]	[Cz]	[S-C]
		najednou: suddenly, all at once; together, at once	najednom: suddenly, all at once
		objednati, objednávati: to order (merchandise)	
объедини́ть, объединя́ть: to unite (tr.)			
			odjednom: suddenly, all at once
	pojednanie: reconciliation	pojednání: treatise	
поеди́нок: duel	pojedynek: duel		
			pojedinac: individual (n.)
	pojedynczy: single; (gram.) singular		pojedinačan: individual (a.)
			pojedinost: detail
	przejednać, przejednywać: to conciliate, propitiate	projednati, projednávati: to discuss; to hear, try (a case)	
		sjednati, sjednávati: to arrange, agree upon; to conclude (a treaty, etc.)	
соедини́ть, соединя́ть: to unite (tr.)		sjednotiti, sjednocovati: to unite (tr.)	sjediniti, sjedinjavati (sjedinjivati): to unite (tr.)
уедини́ть, уединя́ть: to seclude, isolate			ujediniti, ujedinjavati (ujedinjivati): to unite (tr.)
			zajednica: union, association; community (of interests, etc.)
			zajednički: common; joint

NOTES

Basic meaning of root: one

The root is actually a compound dating back to Common Slavic; see the introductory note on root ИН (etc.). The Russian root-form ЕДИН is of Churc Slavic origin.

Many of the derivatives have English equivalents derived from Lat. unu "one" (e.g. union, unique, unit, unite, unity).

jednać-jednati: The underlying notion is "to make one, bring to agreement," whence the meanings "to reconcile," "to negotiate" and "to hire." Th Czech meanings "to act" and "to deal (with)" are a fairly recent generaliza tion of the original sense of the word.

jednatel: ‹jednati.

jedyny et al., еди́нственный-jedinstven: Compare Eng. only (‹one), Ger. einzig "only" (a.) (‹ein "one").

jednotliwy: a verbal aspect expressing an action that occurs only once

jednotlivost: ‹jednotlivý; compare Ger. Einzelheit "detail" (‹einzeln "single; separate" ‹ein "one").

одна́ко-jednak: See jednaki and compare Eng. all the same in the sense of "however, nevertheless," Gr. ὅμως "however" (‹ὁμός "same").

jednačina, jednadžba: ‹jednak; see note on Cz. rovnice, Pol. równanie.

одино́кий: Compare Eng. lonely (‹alone ‹ all + one), Ger. einsam "lonely" (‹ein "one").

jeno et al.: for earlier Pol. jedno and Cz. jedno, *jednom; see note o jedyny et al., еди́нственный-jedinstven.

odyniec: ‹obsolete Rus. одине́ц "solitary person; wild boar."

единобо́жие et al.: See note under root БО(Г) (etc.).

единобра́чие: See note under root БР (etc.).

jednochoda, jednochód: See note on Rus. и́ноходь et al.

единоду́шный-jednodušan: Compare Eng. unanimous (ult. ‹Lat. unus "one" animus "mind, mood"), Ger. einmütig "unanimous" (‹ein "one" + Mut "[arch. o in compounds] mind, mood; [otherwise] courage"), Pol. jednomyślny and Cz. jednomyslný below.

единогла́сный et al.: See note under root ГОЛОС (etc.).

jednoličan, jednolik: Compare Eng. uniform (ult. ‹Lat. unus "one" + forma "shape, form").

jednolity-jednolitý: See note under root ЛИ (etc.).

jednomyślny-jednomyslný: See note on единоду́шный-jednodušan.

jednoobrazan, единообра́зный: See note on jednoličan, jednolik.

одноро́дный et al.: See note under root РОД (etc.).

единоро́г et al.: a loan-translation of Lat. unicornis (‹unus "one" + cornu "horn"); the second element is from рог-róg-roh-rog "horn."

jednostajny et al.: See note under root СТА (etc.).

jednotvárný: orig. "uniform"; see note on jednoličan, jednolik.

единовла́стие et al.: Compare Ger. Alleinherrscher "autocrat" (<allein "alone" + Herrscher "ruler").

jednożeństwo et al.: The second element is from żona-žena "woman; wife."

неоднокра́тно-niejednokrotnie: ="not once"; the last element is from the root of archaic Rus. кра́та, Pol. -kroć "(one, two, three, etc.) time(s)."

objednati: See the second and third meanings of jednati.

pojednání: See the fourth meaning of jednati and compare Eng. treatise and to treat (of a subject).

поеди́нок-pojedynek: ="single combat"; the Russian word is borrowed from Polish.

pojedinost: See note on jednotlivost.

projednati: See the second and fourth meanings of jednati.

sjednati: See the second meaning of jednati.

едини́ть: ="to cause to be one" (i.e. alone, separate).

EC, C, (СУТ), (СУЩ)	JES, S	JE(S), JS, (JSOUC)	JE(S), S, (SU[T]), (SUŠ[T])
есть: there is, there are; (lit.) is; суть (arch.): (they) are	jestem: am; jesteś: (you) are; jest: is; jesteśmy: (we) are; jesteście: (you) are; są: (they) are	jsem: am; jsi: (you) are; je, (lit.) jest: is; jsme: (we) are; jste: (you) are; jsou: (they) are (also used as auxiliary verb in first and second persons to form past tense)	jesam, sam: am; jesi, si: (you) are; jest, je: is; jesmo, smo: (we) are; jeste, ste: (you) are; jesu, su: (they) are (short forms also used as auxiliary verb to form perfect tense)
естество́: (lit.) nature, character; (arch.) nature (the physical world)	jestestwo: creature, being; existence		jestastvo (arch.): nature (the physical world); nature, character
есте́ственный: natural			jestastven (arch.): natural
			jestastvenica (arch.): natural science
суть: essence			
су́щий: real; downright, utter, sheer			sušti: real; downright, utter, sheer
[R]	[P]	[Cz]	[S-C]

сýщность: essence существó: creature, being; essence существовáть: to exist (и́мя) существи́тельное: (gram.) noun, substantive естествознáние, (arch.) естествовéдение: natural science насýщный: urgent, vital осуществи́ть, осуществля́ть: to bring about, effect, accomplish отсýтствие: absence присýтствие: presence; (arch.) official business, functions; (arch.) office, agency присýщий: inherent (in), peculiar (to)		jsoucnost: existence	suština, suštastvo: essence nasušan: urgent, vital odsustvo: absence; leave, holiday odsutnost: absence prisustvo, prisutnost: presence
[R]	[P]	[Cz]	[S-C]

NOTES

Basic meaning of root: to be

This root supplies only the present-tense forms of "to be." The remaining tenses and the infinitive are formed from root БЫ (etc.).

The Russian forms СУТ and СУЩ (but not the word суть) and the Serbo-Croatian form SUŠ(T) are derived from the Church Slavic present participle.

The Slavic present-tense forms are related to the English present tense and to the corresponding forms in Latin (sum, es, est, sumus, estis, sunt) and Greek (εἰμί, εἶ, ἐστί, ἐσμέν, ἐστέ, εἰσί).

есть et al.: The remaining Russian forms (есмь "am"; еси́ "[you] are"; есм "[we] are"; éсте "[you] are") are no longer in use. Pol. jestem, jesteś, jesteśmy, jesteście, reconstructed forms based on jest, have taken the place of OPol. jeśm, jeś, jeśmy, jeście.

естество́ et al., есте́ственный-jestastven: an abstract formation based on the 3 sg.; all these words are ultimately derived from Church Slavic---Pol. jestestwo probably by way of Russian.

суть: a relatively recent substantive use of the 3 pl.; compare Eng. essence (ult. <Lat. esse "to be"), S-C bit and bitnost, Cz. bytost.

су́щий-sušti: ="being, existing" (see the introductory note above). The same semantic development is apparent in Germanic cognates: Eng. sooth "true; truth" (as in forsooth, soothsayer), Dan. sand "true," Nor.-Swed. sann "true" (all derived from an old pres. part. of "to be").

jsoucnost: from pres. part. jsoucí.

(имя) существи́тельное: modeled on Gr. οὐσιαστικόν (ὄνομα) (<οὐσία "being, essence"); see note on Rus. и́мя, Pol. imię, Cz. jméno.

насу́щный-nasušan: orig. "daily," especially in the phrase "daily bread" in the Lord's Prayer, whence the present meaning. The Church Slavic source of the Russian and Serbo-Croatian words is a loan-translation of Gr. ἐπιούσιος "daily, sufficient for the day" (<ἐπὶ τὴν οὖσαν ἡμέραν "for the existing [=current] day").

осуществи́ть: ="to bring into being."

отсу́тствие-odsustvo, odsutnost, прису́тствие et al.: Compare Eng. absence and presence (ult. <Lat. ab "away," prae "before, in front" + esse "to be"), S-C izbivati and pribivati, Pol. niebytność; the Serbo-Croatian words are borrowed, in modified form, from Russian.

КАЗ	KAZ, KAŹ	KAZ, KÁZ	KAZ, KAS
	**kazać: to order, command; (arch.) to preach	kázati: to preach; (lit.) to order, command	**kazati: to say, tell
			kazivati: to tell, report, relate
каза́ться: to seem			
	kazalnica: pulpit	kazatelna: pulpit	
			kazalo: table of contents; index; hand (of a watch or clock); indicator, pointer (in a machine, etc.)
[R]	[P]	[Cz]	[S-C]

			kazaljka: hand (of a watch or clock)
			kazalište: theater
де́скать (coll.): he says, they say, etc. (used for attribution of a statement)			
			igrokaz: drama, play
иносказа́ние: allegory			
доказа́ть, дока́зывать: to prove	dokazać, dokazywać: to accomplish; to prove; (dokazywać only) to frolic, play pranks	dokázati, dokazovati: to accomplish; to prove	dokazati, dokazivati: to prove
			iskazati, iskazivati: to express, utter; to state, declare; to testify
			iskaz: list, schedule; report, statement; testimony, deposition
			iskaznica: identity card
наказа́ть, нака́зывать: to punish; (arch.) to order, command	nakazać, nakazywać: to order, command	nakázati, nakazovati: to order, command	
оказа́ть, ока́зывать: to render (e.g. assistance); to exert (e.g. influence); (arch.) to show	okazać, okazywać: to render (e.g. assistance); to produce (e.g. a document); to show	okázati, okazovati (arch.): to show	
оказа́ться, ока́зываться: to find o.s. (in a place, situation, etc.); to prove, turn out (to be)	okazać się, okazywać się: to prove, turn out (to be)		
	okaz: sample, specimen		
[R]	[P]	[Cz]	[S-C]

[R]	[P]	[Cz]	[S-C]
	okazały: magnificent, stately	okázalý: showy, ostentatious	
отказáть, откáзывать: to refuse, deny (s.th. to s.o.); (arch.) to bequeath		odkázati, odkazovati: to bequeath; to refer (s.o. for information, etc.)	otkazati, otkazivati: to give notice (to employee, landlord, etc.); to cancel (an order); to refuse, deny (s.th. to s.o.)
отказáться, откáзываться: to refuse (to do s.th.); (от + gen.) to renounce, give up; (от + gen.) to repudiate, disown			
показáть, покáзывать: to show; to testify	pokazać, pokazywać: to show		pokazati, pokazivati: to show
показнóй: showy, ostentatious	pokaźny: substantial, considerable; handsome		pokazni: (gram.) demonstrative
показáтель: (statistical) index number; (math.) exponent			pokazatelj, pokazivač: (statistical) index number
		poukázati, poukazovati: to refer, allude (to); to remit (money)	
		poukázka: draft, money-order	
			potkazati, potkazivati: to denounce, inform against
подсказáть, подскáзывать: to prompt			
	przekazać, przekazywać: to transmit; to transfer; to remit (money)		
	przekaz: draft, money-order		

[R]	[P]	[Cz]	[S-C]
предсказа́ть, предска́зывать: to predict			predskazati, predskazivati: to predict
приказа́ть, прика́зывать: to order, command	przykazać, przykazywać (arch.): to order, command	přikázati, přikazovati: to order, command; to assign	prikazati, prikazivati: to show; to depict, describe; to report
			prikaza: specter, apparition
		prokázati, prokazovati: to reveal, manifest; to prove; to render (e.g. assistance)	prokazati, prokazivati: to denounce, inform against
	rozkazać, rozkazywać: to order, command	rozkázati, rozkazovati: to order, command	
	rozkazujący: imperious, peremptory; (gram.) imperative	rozkazovací: imperious, peremptory; (gram.) imperative	
расска́з: story; account, recital			
*сказа́ть: to say, tell	skazać, skazywać: to condemn, sentence		
сказа́ться, ска́зываться: to tell, have an effect (on); to report o.s. (sick, etc.)			
ска́зка: story		zkazka (lit.): legend	skaska: story
сказу́емое: (gram.) predicate			
указа́ть, ука́зывать: to point out; to indicate	ukazać, ukazywać: to show	ukázati, ukazovati: to show; to point out	ukazati, ukazivati: to point out; to indicate; to render (e.g. assistance)
ука́з: decree, edict, ukase	ukaz: decree, edict, ukase	úkaz: phenomenon	ukaz: decree, edict, ukase
указа́тель: indicator, pointer (in a machine, etc.); road-sign;		ukazatel: indicator, pointer (in a machine, etc.); road-sign;	

[R]	[P]	[Cz]	[S-C]
guide, directory; index		guide, directory; index; (statistical) index number	
		ukazováček, ukazovák: index finger	
	wykaz: list, schedule; report, statement	výkaz: report, statement	
вы́сказать, выска́зывать: to express, utter			
	wskazać, wskazywać: to point out; to indicate	vzkázati, vzkazovati: to inform, notify; to send (for s.o.)	
	wskaźnik: index; (statistical) index number; indicator, pointer (in a machine, etc.)		
	wskazówka: hand (of a watch or clock); instruction, direction		
заказа́ть, зака́зывать: to order (merchandise); (arch.) to forbid	zakazać, zakazywać: to forbid	zakázati, zakazovati: to forbid; (arch.) to order (merchandise)	zakazati, zakazivati: to fix, set (a time, date)
зака́зник: (forest, game, etc.) preserve		zákazník: customer, client	
зака́зчик: customer, client			
[R]	[P]	[Cz]	[S-C]

NOTES

Basic meaning of root: to show; to say

The original root-meaning (no longer apparent in the primary verbs) was "to show," whence the secondary meaning "to say," i.e. "to show by means of words." (Compare Lat. dicere "to say" and cognate Gr. δεικνύναι "to show.") The widespread meaning "to order, command" is an extension of the notion of saying.

kazać et al.: Rus. казáть "to show" is obsolete; both of the basic root-meanings are attested in older Polish and Serbo-Croatian, the meaning "to show" in Old Czech. The Russian and Old Czech words show further semantic development to "to teach" and "to punish" (see Rus. наказáть). Pol. kazać is both perfective and imperfective in the first meaning, always imperfective in the second.

казáться: ="to show itself or oneself (to be)."

kazalište: ="a place for showing."

дéскать: formed from two different words for "to say." -скать is contracted from сказáть; regarding the first element, see note under root ДЕ (etc.). Compare Rus. мол, Cz. prý.

igrokaz: The first element is from igra "play, game."

иносказáние: See note under root ИН (etc.).

dokazać-dokázati: Regarding the first meaning, compare Eng. to show progress, to show improvement, etc.; the third meaning of the Polish word can be construed as "to show off."

iskazati (third meaning): Compare Ger. aussagen "to testify" (‹aus "out" + sagen "to say"), Cz. vypověděti.

iskaz, iskaznica: The two basic root-meanings are variously reflected in these words. Semantic borrowing from Ger. Ausweis "report, statement; identity card" (‹aus "out" + weisen "to show") is apparent in the second meaning of iskaz and in iskaznica; regarding the third meaning of iskaz, compare Ger. Aussage "testimony, deposition" (‹aus + sagen "to say").

наказáть (first meaning): See note on kazać et al.

okaz: ="something shown"; compare Ger. Muster "sample, specimen" (ult. ‹Lat. monstrare "to show").

okazały-okázalý: Compare Eng. showy, ostentatious (ult. ‹Lat. ostentar "to show, display").

отказáть et al., отказáться: In most of the senses of these words, the root-meaning is "to say" and the prefix has negative force. The meaning "to bequeath" shows a parallel with Eng. bequeath (akin to archaic quoth "said" regarding the second meaning of the Czech word, compare Ger. verweisen "to refer" (‹weisen "to show").

показнóй-pokaźny: See note on okazały-okázalý.

poukázati, poukázka, przekazać, przekaz: Compare Ger. hinweisen "to re fer, allude," anweisen "to remit," Anweisung "draft, money-order," überweis en "to transmit, transfer, remit" (respectively ‹hin "toward," an "to," übe "over, across" + weisen "to show").

predskazati: ‹Rus. предсказáть; S-C skazati "to say" is obsolete.

prikaza: ="that which shows itself, appears"; see note on Cz. zjevení, Pol. zjawa.

rozkazujący-rozkazovací: Compare Eng. imperious (ult. ‹Lat. imperium "order, command") and imperative (ult. ‹Lat. imperare "to order, command"), Rus. повелúтельный, S-C zapovjedni.

сказáть: serves as the perfective aspect of говорúть (q.v.).

skazać: orig. "to say."

zkazka-skaska: ⟨Rus. скáзка.

сказýемое: ="that which is said (about the subject of a sentence)"; compare Eng. predicate (ult. ⟨Lat. praedicare "to say, declare"), Ger. Aussage "predicate" (⟨aus "out" + sagen "to say"), Pol. orzeczenie, Cz. výrok, S-C prirok.

ukaz (Pol.-S-C): ⟨Rus. укáз.

úkaz: ="that which shows itself, appears"; see note on Cz. jev.

wykaz-výkaz: See note on iskaz, iskaznica.

заказáть-zakazać-zakázati: Similar formation and a comparable alternation between positive and negative meanings are shown by Rus. зáповедь, Cz. zápověď, S-C zapovijed, Pol. zamówienie.

закáзник: See the second meaning of заказáть and note on S-C branjevina.

КИ(Д)		KYD	KI(D)
кúнуть, кидáть: to throw		kydati: to clear away (dung from a stable, etc.); to heap (insults, etc. upon s.o.)	kidnuti, kidati: to tear (kidati only); to break (kidati only); to throw out (rubbish, etc.) (kidati only); to decamp, take to one's heels
			dokinuti, dokidati: to cancel, annul, abrogate
накúдка: cloak, cape; pillow-cover			
покúнуть, покидáть: to leave, abandon			*pokidati: to tear; to break
подкúдыш: foundling, abandoned child			
перекúнуть, перекúдывать: to throw over, across			prekinuti, prekidati: to interrupt
			prekidač: (elec.) switch
[R]		[Cz]	[S-C]

<u>скидка</u>: discount, rebate <u>выкидыш</u>: miscarriage [R]		[Cz]	<u>raskid</u>: break, tear; abrogation; (med.) rupture, hernia <u>ukinuti</u>, <u>ukid-ati</u>: to cancel, annul, abrogate [S-C]

NOTES

<u>Basic meaning of root</u>: to throw

<u>ки́нуть</u> <u>et al</u>.: Pol. <u>kinąć</u>, <u>kidać</u> "to throw" survives only as a provincialism. Regarding the shift in meaning in Serbo-Croatian, see note on Rus. <u>ти́снуть</u> <u>et al</u>.

<u>наки́дка</u>: See note on Pol. <u>narzutka</u>.

<u>поки́нуть</u>: Compare Pol. <u>porzucić</u>, <u>rzucić</u>.

<u>подки́дыш</u>: The effect of the prefix here is to suggest something "palme off," stealthily foisted upon someone or wrongfully substituted for something else; compare Pol. <u>podrzutek</u>, S-C <u>podmeče</u>. Lat. <u>sub</u> "under" has much the same force in <u>supponere</u> "to falsify; to substitute fraudulently" (<<u>sub</u> + <u>ponere</u> "to put"), whence Eng. <u>supposititious</u> in the expression <u>supposititious child</u> (=a child fraudulently passed off as a legitimate heir). Compar also Ger. <u>unterschieben</u> (<<u>unter</u> "under" + <u>schieben</u> "to push"), Gr. <u>ὑποβάλλεσθαι</u> (<<u>ὑπό</u> "under" + <u>βάλλειν</u> "to throw"), both of which mean "to falsify; to substitute fraudulently (<u>e.g</u>. one child for another)." A similar notion of falsification appears in Rus. <u>подде́лать</u> and <u>подло́г</u>, Pol. <u>podrobić</u>, Cz. <u>podvrhnouti</u>, S-C <u>podvala</u>.

<u>prekinuti</u>: Compare Eng. <u>interrupt</u> (ult. <Lat. <u>rumpere</u> "to break, tear" Rus. <u>переры́в</u>, Pol. <u>przerwa</u>.

<u>ски́дка</u>: ="something thrown off."

<u>вы́кидыш</u>: The reference is to the premature expulsion of the fetus; com pare synonymous Pol. <u>poronienie</u> (<<u>ronić</u> "to drop"), S-C <u>pobačaj</u> (<<u>baciti</u> "t throw") and <u>pometnuće</u>, Hung. <u>elvetélés</u> (<<u>el</u>- "off, away" + <u>vetni</u> "to throw"

КЛА(Д)	KŁA(D)	KLAD, KLÁ(D)	KLA(D)
класть: to lay, put; to lay (eggs)	kłaść: to lay, put	klásti: to lay, put	klasti (arch.): to lay, put
клад: buried or hidden treasure		klad: thesis, proposition; affirmation; positive quality, asset	
		kladný: positive, favorable; (math., phys.) positive; affirmative (reply, etc.)	
кладь: load			
кладовáя: pantry; storeroom			
клáдбище: cemetery			
			kladiti se: to bet
доклáдывать: to add; to report, make a report	dokładać: to add; to exert (efforts)	dokládati: to add; to prove, substantiate	
доклáд: report; lecture		doklad: proof; document	
докладнóй: containing, or having the form of, a report	dokładny: accurate, precise; detailed	důkladný: thorough; solid, substantial	
	nakład: expense; circulation (of a newspaper); printing, edition; publication (act of publishing)	náklad: load; freight; expense; circulation (of a newspaper); printing, edition; publication (act of publishing)	naklada: printing, edition; publication (act of publishing)
	nakładca: publisher	nakladatel: publisher	nakladnik: publisher
накладнóй: plated (silver, etc.); false (hair, beard); overhead (expenses)		nákladný: expensive	
накладнáя: invoice, way-bill			
обклáдывать: to circle, surround (with);	okładać (obkładać): to circle, surround (with);	obkládati: to circle, surround (with);	
[R]	[P]	[Cz]	[S-C]

to cover; to line, face, panel; to besiege	to cover; to impose (tax, fine, etc.) upon	to cover; to line, face, panel	
окла́д: rate (of pay, taxation)	okład: poultice, compress	obklad: poultice, compress; lining, facing, paneling	oklada, opklada: bet
окла́дистый: broad and thick (said of a beard)			
откла́дывать: to put aside; to put off, postpone, delay	odkładać: to put aside; to put off, postpone, delay	odkládati: to put aside; to doff, take off; to put off, postpone, delay	
	pokładać: to lay, put	pokládati: to lay, put; (za + acc.) to consider, deem, regard (as)	
	pokład: layer, stratum; mineral deposit; deck (of a ship)	poklad: treasure	
		pokladna: safe, strong-box; ticket-office, box-office; treasury	
			Poklade (pl.): Shrovetide, carnival
покла́дистый: complaisant, obliging			
	podkład: base, foundation; railroad tie	podklad: base, foundation; basis	
подкла́дка: lining	podkładka: prop, stay; pad; washer (for screw, etc.)		
	przekład: translation	překlad: translation	
	przedkładać: to submit, present	předkládati: to lay, put before (s.o.); to submit, present; to serve (food)	
		předpokládati: to assume, postulate	
[R]	[P]	[Cz]	[S-C]

[R]	[P]	[Cz]	[S-C]
прикла́дывать: to add; to apply (a plaster to a wound), set (one's hand to a task), affix (one's signature)	przykładać: to add; to apply (a plaster to a wound), set (one's hand to a task), affix (one's signature), attach (importance to s.th.)	přikládati: to add; to append, annex, enclose; to apply (a plaster to a wound), set (one's hand to a task), affix (one's signature), attach (importance to s.th.)	
прикла́д: butt (of a gun); trimmings (for clothing and footwear)	przykład: example; butt (of a gun)	příklad: example	
прикладно́й: applied (science, etc.)	przykładny: exemplary, model	příkladný: exemplary, model	prikladan: suitable, fit
		protiklad: opposite, antithesis; conflict, contradiction	
	rozkład: disintegration, dissolution; decomposition, decay; (chem.) decomposition, analysis; arrangement, disposition, distribution; schedule, time-table	rozklad: disintegration, dissolution; decomposition, decay; (chem.) decomposition, analysis; explanation, analysis; protest, remonstrance	
скла́дываться: to pool money, take a collection; to take shape	składać się: to consist, be composed (of); to pool money, take a collection; to fold (intr.); to turn out, work out (well, badly, etc.)	skládati se: to consist, be composed (of); to pool money, take a collection	
склад: warehouse, storehouse; stock, supply; character, cast of mind	skład: composition, structure, make-up; staff, personnel; type-setting, composition; warehouse, storehouse; stock, supply	sklad: warehouse, storehouse; stock, supply; (lit.) composition, structure, make-up; (lit.) harmony, accord	sklad: harmony, accord; conformity

[R]	[P]	[Cz]	[S-C]
скла́дный (coll.): harmonious; coherent; handsome, well-formed	składny: harmonious; handsome, well-formed	skladný: spacious, roomy; easy to store, not bulky	skladan: harmonious; handsome, well-formed
склады́ (pl., arch.): syllables			
скла́дка: fold, pleat	składka: pool, collection; dues	skládka: (act of) dumping; dump	
		skladba: (musical) composition; composition, structure, make-up; (gram.) syntax	skladba: (musical) composition
	składnia: (gram.) syntax		
	składnik: component, constituent (n.)	skladník: warehouseman	
		skladiště: warehouse, storehouse	skladište: warehouse, storehouse
укла́д: (social, political) order, structure	układ: system; arrangement, disposition, distribution; agreement; (arch.) manners, behavior		
	układy (pl.): negotiations	úklady (pl.): intrigue, machinations	
	układny: gracious, well-mannered	úkladný: insidious, crafty; premeditated	
вклад: investment; deposit (of funds); contribution	wkład: investment; deposit (of funds); contribution	vklad: investment; deposit (of funds)	
выкла́дывать: to lay out; to line, face, panel	wykładać: to lay out; to display; to expound, set forth, explain; to teach; to disburse; to line, face, panel	vykládati: to lay out; to display; to unload; to expound, set forth, explain; to interpret; to line, face, panel	

	wykład: explanation, exposition; lecture	výklad: explanation, exposition; interpretation; display-window	
	wykładnik: (math.) exponent		
		vynakládati: to spend (money); to exert (efforts)	
заклáд: pledge, pawn; mortgage; (arch.) bet	zakład: institution, establishment; pledge, pawn; bet	základ: base, foundation; basis	zaklad (arch.): pledge, pawn; mortgage; valuable object
			zaklada: endowment, fund
	zakładnik: hostage		zakladnik: one who establishes an endowment or fund
		základna: (military) base; basis	
[R]	[P]	[Cz]	[S-C]

NOTES

Basic meaning of root: to lay, put

In Polish, Czech and, in some instances, Russian, this root supplies the imperfective counterparts of compound verbs derived from the causative form of root ЛЕГ$_1$ (etc.).

Kindred non-Slavic words are Eng. lade, Ger. laden "to load."

класть et al.: The Russian, Polish and Czech words serve as imperfective forms of положи́ть-położyć-položiti (q.v.) (see also note on pokładać-pokládati below); the respective 1 sg. forms are кладу́, kładę, kladu, kladem.

klad: The first two meanings reflect the notion of "something laid down, i.e. stated, asserted"; compare Eng. thesis (ult. ⟨Gr. τιθέναι "to put"), Ger. Satz "thesis, proposition" (⟨setzen "to set, put"), Rus. положе́ние, Pol. założenie, S-C postavka. Regarding the third meaning, see next note.

kladný: a loan-translation of Lat. positivus "laid down, set in place; positive" (⟨ponere "to put"); compare Rus. положи́тельный.

кладова́я: ⟨клад.

кла́дбище: ="a place where one is laid away"; compare Ger. beisetzen "to bury" (⟨bei "at, by" + setzen "to set, put").

kladiti se: a denominative formation from unattested *klad "something which has been laid down." The notion of "placing a bet," "putting money on something," etc. is common to most languages; in this instance, the reflexive verb conveys the idea that the bettor is "staking himself" on the outcome, offering himself as a pledge. Compare Ger. Satz "stake (in gambling)" (⟨setzen "to set, put"), Fr. mise "stake" (⟨mettre "to put"), Rus. закла́д and ста́вка, Pol. zakład and stawka, Cz. saditi (se) and sázeti, S-C oklada, opklada and oblog.

докла́дывать et al.: See note on Rus. доложи́ть et al.

dokładny: The basic idea is that of application, of "putting onself to the job at hand; see the second meaning of dokładać.

důkladný: orig. "well documented, fully substantiated"; see doklad and the second meaning of dokládati.

nakład et al., nakładca et al.: The meaning "expense" reflects the notion of "putting (i.e. applying)" money to some purpose; compare Ger. Anlag "investment" (⟨an "to" + legen "to lay, put"). The meaning "circulation; printing, edition," originally a reference to the number of sheets of paper "laid on" the press, was acquired by semantic borrowing from Ger. Auflage (⟨auf "on" + legen). The further application of these words to the general activity of publishing arose from the publisher's role as an entrepreneur who assumes the expense of publication, but the persistence of this usage i probably due in part to the association with the idea of printing; compare Ger. verlegen "(in the present-day language) to publish; (originally) to la out money, assume the expense of a business venture" (⟨legen). S-C naklada is borrowed from Czech.

накладно́й: ="laid on, i.e. added, superimposed."

накладна́я: See dialectal на́кладь "load, freight."

обкла́дывать et al., okład-obklad: See note on Rus. обложи́ть et al., S-C oblog, Pol. obłoga et al.

окла́д: originally used only with reference to taxation; see the fourth meaning of Rus. обложи́ть.

oklada, opklada: See note on kladiti se.

окла́дистый: ⟨окла́д in the obsolete meaning "contour," hence ="framing the face"; see обкла́дывать.

pokładać-pokládati: alternate imperfective forms of położyć-položiti (see note on класть et al.); regarding the second meaning of the Czech word see note on Rus. полага́ть.

pokład: ="something laid down, spread out"; compare Eng. layer (⟨lay) and deposit (ult. ⟨Lat. de "down" + ponere "to put"), Rus. отложи́ть, Pol. złóg and złoże.

poklad: originally synonymous with Rus. клад.

Poklade: a time when meat is "laid aside."

покла́дистый: ⟨dialectal покла́д "agreement"; compare Pol. układ below.

przekład-překlad: Compare Ger. Übersetzung "translation" (⟨über "over, across" + setzen "to set, put") and see note on Rus. перево́д, S-C prevod an prijevod.

předpokládati: See note on Rus. предположи́ть.

прикла́дывать et al.: See note on Rus. приложи́ть et al., Cz. příloha, S-C prilog.

прикла́д et al.: The butt is the part of a gun which is laid against the shoulder when the weapon is fired; trimmings are "something added," extras, accessories (see прикла́дывать); an example is a specific application of a general rule or principle (compare Rus. прикладно́й).

прикладно́й: ="put, directed (to some practical use)."

prikladan: ="put or brought close (to)," i.e. adapted, adjusted (to); compare Eng. apposite (ult. ‹Lat. ad "to" + ponere "to put").

protiklad: Compare Eng. opposite (ult. ‹Lat. ob "against" + ponere "to put") and antithesis (ult. ‹Gr. ἀντί "against" + τιθέναι "to put"), Ger. Gegensatz "opposite, antithesis; conflict, contradiction" (‹gegen "against" + setzen "to set, put"), Rus. противополо́жный.

rozkład-rozklad: See note on Rus. разложе́ние et al. and расположе́ние et al., S-C razlog, razložan, razložit and raspolaganje.

скла́дываться et al., склад et al., скла́дный et al., склады́, скла́дка et al., skladba, składnia, składnik-skladník, skladiště-skladište: See note on Rus. сложи́ться et al., слага́ться, сложе́ние, сложённый et al., слог and сло́жный, Cz. složení, sloh, sloha, složka and složitý, S-C slagati se, slog, sloga, složan, slagar and slagalište.

укла́д-układ, układy-úklady, układny-úkladný: The basic idea is that of "laying out, arranging, putting in order," whence the figurative notions of "making arrangements with some end in view" (="negotiating, concluding an agreement, intriguing") and "ordering one's actions along certain lines" (="behaving").

вклад et al.: See note on Rus. вложе́ние, S-C ulaganje and ulog.

выкла́дывать et al., wykład-výklad: Compare Eng. expound, exposition (both ult. ‹Lat. ex "out" + ponere "to put") and outlay, Ger. auslegen "to lay out; to line, face, panel; to display; to expound; to interpret; to disburse" (‹aus "out" + legen "to lay, put"), Rus. изложи́ть and вы́ставка, Pol. wystawa, Cz. výloha, S-C izložiti and izlog.

wykładnik: so called because it "sets forth" the power to which a number is raised; see wykładać and compare Eng. exponent (ult. ‹Lat. ex "out" + ponere "to put"), S-C izložitelj.

vynakládati: See note on nakład et al., nakładca et al.

закла́д et al., zaklada, zakładnik-zakladnik, základna: See notes on kladiti se above, on Rus. зало́г and зало́жник, S-C zalog and zaloga and on Pol. założenie, Cz. založení.

КЛОН, КЛАН	KŁON, KŁAN	KLON, KLOŇ, KLAN, KLÁN	KLON, KLAN
клони́ть: to bend, incline (tr.)	kłonić: to bend, incline (tr.)	kloniti: to bend, incline (tr.)	
клони́ться: to bend down; (к + dat.) to approach	kłonić się: to bend down	kloniti se: to bend down; (k + dat.) to approach	kloniti se: to avoid
			klanjati: to make a bow; to pray (said of Moslems)
кла́няться: to bow, greet	kłaniać się: to bow, greet	klaněti se: to bow, greet; to worship	klanjati se: to bow, greet; to worship
			*klonuti: to languish, collapse; to despond
благоскло́нный (lit.): gracious, kindly disposed		blahosklonný: gracious, kindly disposed	blagonaklon: gracious, kindly disposed
накло́н: slope, incline			naklon: slope, incline; bow, greeting
накло́нность: inclination, tendency, leaning		náklonnost: inclination, tendency, leaning; favor, good will, liking	naklonost: inclination, tendency, leaning; favor, good will, liking
наклоне́ние: (gram.) mood			
непрекло́нный (lit.): inflexible, adamant			
неукло́нный (lit.): steady, continuous; steadfast			
отклони́ть, отклоня́ть: to deflect; to reject, decline, refuse		odkloniti, odkláněti (odkloňovati): to turn away (tr.); to deflect	otkloniti, otklanjati: to reject, decline, refuse; to avert, ward off
покло́нник: admirer, worshipper			poklonik: pilgrim
прекло́нный: advanced, extreme (age)			
[R]	[P]	[Cz]	[S-C]

[R]	[P]	[Cz]	[S-C]
		příklonný: (gram.) enclitic (a.)	
склон: slope, incline; end, decline (of life, etc.)	skłon: bend; firmament	sklon: slope, incline; (astr.) declination; inclination, tendency, leaning sklonek: end, decline (of life, etc.)	
скло́нность: inclination, tendency, leaning	skłonność: inclination, tendency, leaning		sklonost: inclination, tendency, leaning; favor, good will, liking
склоне́ние: (gram.) declension; (astr.) declination		sklonování: (gram.) declension	
			sklonidba: (gram.) declension sklonište: refuge; shelter ukloniti, uklanjati: to remove
укло́н: slope, incline; tendency, trend; political deviation укло́нчивый: evasive	ukłon: bow, greeting	úklon, úklona: bow, greeting	
			zaklon, zaklonište: refuge; shelter
[R]	[P]	[Cz]	[S-C]

NOTES

Basic meaning of root: to bend, incline

Many of the derivatives of this root have acquired figurative meanings comparable to those of such English words as leaning and (<Lat. clinare "to bend, incline") inclination, decline.

The Slavic root is probably unrelated etymologically to Lat. clinare, Gr. κλίνειν "to bend, incline."

kloniti se (S-C): ="to bend away."

klonuti: Compare Eng. decline (ult. ‹Lat. de "off, down" + clinare "to bend").

благосклóнный et al.: Compare наклóнность et al., склóнность et al.

наклонéние: The notion expressed here is that of "bending" verb forms in various directions. Gr. ἔγκλισις (‹ἐν "in" + κλίνειν "to bend"), on which the Russian word is modeled, refers to the inflection of verbs, more particularly modal inflection. Compare Eng. inflection (ult. ‹Lat. in "in" + flectere "to bend"), Ger. beugen "to bend; (gram.) to inflect." See also note on склонéние-skloňování, sklonidba below.

непреклóнный, неуклóнный: ="unbending."

отклони́ть-otkloniti: Compare Eng. decline (ult. ‹Lat. de "off, away" + clinare "to bend"), Ger. ablehnen "to reject, decline, refuse" (‹ab "off, away" + lehnen "to lean, incline").

поклóнник-poklonik: Compare кла́няться et al.

преклóнный: Compare the English expression declining years and Rus. склон (second meaning), Cz. sklonek.

příklonný: modeled on Gr. ἐγκλιτικός (‹ἐν "in" + κλίνειν "to bend"), whence Eng. enclitic; an enclitic word "leans against" the preceding word, which bears the accent.

skłon (second meaning): The reference is to the apparent curvature of the sky, the "vault of heaven."

склонéние (first meaning)-skloňování, sklonidba: modeled on Lat. declinatio (‹de "off, away" + clinare "to bend"), whence Eng. declension; the Latin word was applied to all types of grammatical inflection or "bending" by the early grammarians. See note on наклонéние.

sklonište, zaklon, zaklonište: Compare kloniti se.

КЛЮК, КЛЮЧ	KLUK, KLUCZ	KLIK, KLIČ, KLÍČ	KLJUK, KLJUČ
клюка́: crutch	kluka: hook	klika: handle	kljuka: hook; handle
ключ: key	klucz: key	klíč: key	ključ: key
клю́чник (arch.): steward, housekeeper	klucznik: turnkey; (arch.) steward, housekeeper	klíčník: turnkey; (arch.) steward, housekeeper	
ключа́рь: sacristan			ključar: steward housekeeper; turnkey; locksmith
			ključanica: lock; keyhole
[R]	[P]	[Cz]	[S-C]

[R]	[P]	[Cz]	[S-C]
ключи́ца: (anat.) collar-bone, clavicle			ključica, ključnjača: (anat.) collar-bone, clavicle
злоключе́ние (arch.): mishap			
исключи́ть, исключа́ть: to exclude; to expel			isključiti, isključivati: to exclude; to expel; to switch off (current, etc.)
исключе́ние: exception; exclusion; expulsion			isključenje: exclusion; expulsion
		obklíčiti, obkličovati: to surround, encircle	
переключи́ть, переключа́ть: to switch (current, conversation, production, etc.)			
приключе́ние: adventure; (act of) connecting up (with an electric circuit, etc.)			priključenje: (act of) joining, connecting; (act of) connecting up (with an electric circuit, etc.)
включи́ть, включа́ть: to include; to switch on (current, etc.)	wkluczyć, wkluczać: to include		uključiti, uključivati: to include; to switch on (current, etc.)
вы́ключить, выключа́ть: to exclude; to switch off (current, etc.)	wykluczyć, wykluczać: to exclude		
заключи́ть, заключа́ть: to conclude, end (tr.); to conclude, infer, deduce; to conclude (an agreement, etc.); to confine, imprison; to enclose;			zaključiti, zaključivati: to conclude, end (tr.); to conclude, infer, deduce; to conclude (an agreement, etc.); to decide

(заключа́ть only; в себе́) to contain [R]	[P]	[Cz]	zakljućati, zakljućavati: to lock [S-C]

NOTES

Basic meaning of root: hook; key; to close

The original root-meaning, "hook," is preserved in клюка́ et al. The words ключ et al. show a semantic extension to "hook-like device for opening and closing a door." The verbal derivatives, all of which contain the underlying meanings "to close" and "to connect," are formed from the nouns. A similar relationship exists between Lat. clavis "key" and claudere "to close," which are cognate with the corresponding Slavic words.

клю́чник et al., ключа́рь-ključar: Underlying all these words is the meaning "keeper of the keys."

ключи́ца et al.: modeled on Lat. clavicula (dim. of clavis "key"), whence Eng. clavicle; see also Ger. Schlüsselbein "clavicle" (<Schlüssel "key" + Bein "bone; [more commonly] leg"). The clavicle is so called because of its shape.

злоключе́ние: See ORus. ключитися "to happen," the underlying meaning of which was "to hook together, fit together," and compare приключе́ние.

исключи́ть-isključiti: Compare Eng. exclude (ult. <Lat. ex "out" + claudere "to close"), Ger. ausschliessen "to exclude" (<aus "out" + schliessen "to close").

obklíčiti: Compare the fourth and fifth meanings of заключи́ть.

приключе́ние: The first meaning reflects that of ORus. ключитися "to happen"; see note on злоключе́ние.

включи́ть et al.: Compare Eng. include (ult. <Lat. in "in" + claudere "to close"), Ger. einschliessen "to include" (<ein- "in" + schliessen "to close").

вы́ключить-wykluczyć: See note on исключи́ть-isključiti.

заключи́ть-zaključiti: The first three meanings coincide with those of Eng. conclude (ult. <Lat. cum "together" + claudere "to close") and of Ger. schliessen "to close," which can mean "to conclude" in each of these senses. Compare also Pol. zawrzeć, Cz. uzavříti, závěr.

КОЛ	KOŁ, KÓŁ, KOL, KÓL, KAL	KOL	KO(L)
	koło: wheel; circle	kolo: wheel; circle	kolo: wheel; circle
колесó: wheel		koleso (lit.): wheel	
			kola (pl.): wagon; carriage; railroad car; automobile
коля́ска: carriage	kolasa, kolaska: carriage	koleska, (arch.) kolesa: carriage	
колея́: rut; track, rails	kolej: rut; railroad; turn (in alternation); vicissitude	kolej: rut; track, rails	
	kolejny: alternate, successive		
кольцó: ring	kolce: ring; link (in a chain)		kolut: ring
	kołować: to whirl, go in circles	kolovati: to circulate	kolati: to circulate; to rotate
	koło: around; near; about, approximately	kolem, (lit.) kol: around; past, by; about, approximately	
			kolosijek: rut; track, rails
			kolotečina: rut
			kolovoz: August; rut
			okovratnik: collar; necktie
	bezokolicznik: (gram.) infinitive		
	dokoła: around	dokola: around	
	naokoło: around		naokolo: around
			oko: military camp
óколо: around; near; about, approximately	około: around; near; about, approximately	okolo: around; past, by; about, approximately	oko, okolo: around; near; about, approximately
	okolić, okalać: to surround		opkoliti, opkoljavati: to surround
[R]	[P]	[Cz]	[S-C]

	okole: surroundings	okolí: environs, vicinity; environment	
			okolina: environs, vicinity; environment
окóлица: boundary of a village; circuitous route	okolica: environs, vicinity; region		okolica: environs, vicinity
околи́чность (arch.): circumlocution	okoliczność: circumstance	okolnost: circumstance	okolnost: circumstance
окóлыш: cap-band			okoliš: environs vicinity
			okolišiti, okolišati: to be evasive, hedge
	okólnik: circular (letter)		
		okolky (pl.): fuss, ado, ceremony	
	wkoło, wokoło, wokół: around	vůkol (lit.): around	
[R]	[P]	[Cz]	[S-C]

NOTES

Basic meaning of root: wheel; circle

The root originally referred only to the wheel itself, then also to it shape.

A non-Slavic cognate is Eng. wheel.

kolo (n.) et al.: ORus. коло has been replaced by колесó in the modern language (see following note).

колесó-koleso: a new nominative singular modeled on the oblique singular forms and plural of the original declension (see, e.g., ORus. nom. sg. коло, nom. pl. колеса).

коля́ска et al.: orig. a neuter plural (="wheels"); the Russian word is borrowed from Polish, the Polish words possibly from Czech. Compare S-C kol

kolej (Pol., third meaning): Compare the similar use of Eng. rotation (ult. <Lat. rota "wheel").

kolotečina: ="track worn by the rolling of wheels."

kolovoz (first meaning): ="wagon-carrying"; the word denotes the month in which the harvest is brought in.

okovratnik: See oko "around" and note under root ВЕРТ (etc.).

bezokolicznik: See *okoliczność*; the infinitive is a form of the verb which does not indicate "circumstances," *i.e*. tense, number and person.

oko (n.): orig. "circle," later "enclosure, encampment for soldiers."

okoliczność et al.: See note on Rus. *обстоя́тельство*; the Serbo-Croatian word is borrowed from Czech.

KOP, KAP	KOR(Z), KÓR, KAR	KOR, KOŘ, KÁR	KOR, KAR
кори́ть (coll.): to reproach			*koriti*: to reproach
	korzyć się: to humble o.s., submit	*kořiti se*: to humble o.s., submit; to worship	
	korny: humble, submissive		
кара́ть: to punish	*karać*: to punish	*kárati*: to reproach	*karati*: to scold, upbraid; to punish
кара́тельный: punitive	*karny*: disciplined; disciplinary; punitive; criminal, penal (statute, etc.)	*kárný*: disciplinary; punitive	*karni* (arch.): disciplinary
		káranec: convict	
напереко́р: in defiance (of), contrary (to)	*na przekór*: in defiance (of), contrary (to)		
покори́ть, *покоря́ть*: to subjugate, subdue		*pokořiti*, *pokořovati*: to subjugate, subdue; to humble, humiliate	*pokoriti*, *pokoravati*: to subjugate, subdue
поко́рный: humble, submissive	*pokorny*: humble, submissive	*pokorný*: humble, submissive	*pokoran*: humble, submissive
			prijekor: reproach
	przekorny: obstinate, refractory		*prekoran*, *prijekoran*: reproachful; deserving of reproach
		příkoří: wrong, injury	
уко́р, *укори́зна*: reproach		*úkor*: harm, detriment	*ukor*: reprimand
[R]	[P]	[Cz]	[S-C]

NOTES

Basic meaning of root: to scold; to punish

The root probably referred originally to verbal abuse and later acquired the other meanings which are reflected in its derivatives.

КРЕП	KRZEP	KŘEP	KREP, KRIJEP
кре́пкий: strong, vigorous; firm	krzepki: strong, vigorous	křepký: nimble, quick	krepak: strong, vigorous
кре́пость: stronghold, fortress; strength; (arch.) deed (of sale)			krepost: virtue, chastity; strength; validity (of a contract, etc.)
крепостно́й: serf			
кре́пнуть: to become strong	krzepnąć: to coagulate; to curdle		
подкрепи́ть, подкрепля́ть: to strengthen; to confirm, corroborate; to refresh (with food and drink); (mil.) to reinforce			potkrijepiti, potkrepljivati: to strengthen; to confirm, corroborate
прикрепи́ть, прикрепля́ть: to fasten, attach			
закрепи́ть, закрепля́ть: to fasten, attach; to consolidate, secure; (phot.) to fix; to allot, assign			
[R]	[P]	[Cz]	[S-C]

NOTES

Basic meaning of root: strong

кре́пость: Regarding the first meaning, compare Eng. stronghold and fortress (ult. ‹Lat. fortis "strong"), Ger. Festung "fortress" (‹fest "firm, fast"); regarding the third meaning, compare Eng. farm (‹OFr. ferme "lease," ult. ‹Lat. firmus "firm, strong").

крепостно́й: from кре́пость in the former sense of "oath"; compare the third meaning given here for кре́пость.

подкрепи́ть-potkrijepiti: Compare Eng. confirm and firm, Eng. corroborate (ult. from the root of Lat. robur "strength," robustus "strong, robust").

прикрепи́ть, закрепи́ть: Compare Eng. fasten (<fast in the sense of "firm"), Ger. befestigen "to fasten" (<fest "firm, fast"), Pol. przymocować and umocować.

КРИВ	KRZYW	KŘIV	KRIV
криво́й: crooked, twisted; curved	krzywy: crooked, twisted; curved	křivý: crooked, twisted; curved; wrong, false	kriv: crooked, twisted; curved; wrong, false; guilty
кри́вда (arch.): falsehood	krzywda: wrong, injury	křivda: wrong, injury	krivda: falsehood; injustice
криви́ть: to bend, twist	krzywić: to bend, twist	křiviti: to bend, twist	kriviti: to accuse; to bend, twist
	krzywica: rickets	křivice: rickets	krivica, krivnja: fault, guilt; crime
		křivule: (chem.) retort	krivulja: curve
криводу́шие (arch.): duplicity, insincerity			
			krivokletstvo: perjury
	krzywoprzysięstwo: perjury	křivopřísežnictví: perjury	
			**krivotvoriti: to falsify, counterfeit
			krivovjerac: heretic
[R]	[P]	[Cz]	[S-C]

NOTES

Basic meaning of root: crooked, twisted

Many of the derivatives show a semantic shift to the notion of "wrongness, falsity" which has parallels in other languages, e.g. Eng. crooked in the sense of "dishonest," Eng. wrong (related to wring), Eng. tort (=a wrongful act subject to a civil suit) and Fr. tort "error, fault" (both ult. <Lat. tortus "twisted"). (Regarding the comparable relationship between the

notions of "straightness" and "rightness," see the introductory note on ro[ot] ПРАВ [etc.].)

The Slavic root is cognate with Lat. *curvus* "crooked; curved."

křivule: so called because of its shape; compare Eng. *retort* (ult. ‹Lat. *tortus* "twisted").

krivokletstvo: The second element is from *kleti se* "to take an oath."

КРО(И), КРАЙ, КРА(И)	KRO(I), KRÓJ, KRA(J)	KROJ, KRAJ, KRÁJ, KREJ	KROJ, KRAJ
кройть: to cut	*kroić*: to cut	*krojiti* (arch.): to cut	*krojiti*: to cut
	[1]*krajać*: to cut	*krájeti*: to cut	
	krój: cut, style (of clothes)	*kroj*: costume	*kroj*: cut, style (of clothes)
	krawiec: tailor	*krejčí*: tailor	*krojač*: tailor
край: region; edge	*kraj*: country (national entity); edge	*kraj*: region; edge	*kraj*: region; end; edge
			kraj: at, by, near; despite
		krajina: region; landscape	*krajina*: borderland
	krajowiec: native (n.)		
		krajan: fellow-countryman, compatriot	
кра́йний: extreme; last, final		*krajní*: extreme; last, final	*krajan*, *krajnji*: extreme; last, final
			krajnik: (anat.) tonsil
	krajka: selvage	*krajka*: lace (fabric)	
		cizokrajný: foreign; exotic	
	krajobraz: landscape		*krajobraz*, *krajolik*: landscape
	obcokrajowy: foreign		
		stejnokroj: (military, etc.) uniform	
окра́ина: outskirts; borderland			
[R]	[P]	[Cz]	[S-C]

	skraj: edge skrajny: extreme		pokraj: at, by, near; despite pokrajina: province skrajan, skrajnji: extreme; last, final
[R]	[P]	[Cz]	[S-C]

NOTES

Basic meaning of root: to cut

The semantic development of this group of words has parallels in some of the derivatives of root РУБ (etc.).

krawiec et al.: Compare Eng. tailor (ult. ‹OFr. taillier "to cut"), Ger. Schneider "tailor" (‹schneiden "to cut").

край et al.: These words and their numerous derivatives mark various stages in what has been the following semantic progression: "cut" › "edge, border" (sometimes = "end") › "borderland, distant region" › "region (in general)." See note on Cz. končina.

kraj (prep.): ‹kraj "edge"; regarding the shift from the notion of juxtaposition ("near") to that of opposition or contrast ("despite"), compare archaic Eng. withal "nevertheless" (‹with + all), S-C pored.

крáйний et al.: ‹край et al. in the sense "edge; end."

krajnik: probably so called because the tonsils are situated at the "edge" of the throat.

cizokrajný: The first element is from cizí "alien, foreign."

pokraj: See note on kraj.

skrajny et al.: See note on крáйний et al.

КОРОТ, КРАТ, КРАЩ	KROT, KRÓT, KRÓC	KRAT, KRÁT, KRÁC	KRAT, KRAĆ
корóткий, крáткий: short, brief	krótki: short, brief	krátký: short, brief	kratak: short, brief
			kratica: abbreviation
	krotochwilny: jocular, facetious	kratochvilný (arch.): amusing	
[R]	[P]	[Cz]	[S-C]

			kratkodnevica: winter solstice kratkorijek: curt, laconic
прекратить, прекращать: to stop, cease (tr.)			prekratiti, prekraćivati: to shorten; to reduce
сокращение: (act of) shortening, abbreviating; reduction; abbreviation	skrócenie: (act of) shortening, abbreviating; abridged version	zkrácení: (act of) shortening, abbreviating	skraćenje: (act of) shortening, abbreviating
	skrót: abbreviation; abridged version	zkrat: short circuit	
		zkrácenina, zkratka: abbreviation	skraćenica: abbreviation
			uskratiti, uskraćivati; zakratiti, zakraćivati: to forbid; to refuse, deny
[R]	[P]	[Cz]	[S-C]

NOTES

Basic meaning of root: short

The Russian root-forms КРАТ and КРАЩ are of Church Slavic origin.

The Slavic root is probably cognate with Lat. curtus "shortened, mutilated" (>Eng. curt).

krotochwilny-kratochvilný: The second element is from chwila-chvíle "(a) while, period of time"; hence, the meaning is "serving to make time short." The words are modeled on Ger. kurzweilig "amusing" (<kurz "short" + Weile "[a] while"). (Pol. chwila and Cz. chvíle were borrowed from Old High Ger. hwīla [=modern Ger. Weile].) Compare S-C dugočasan.

kratkodnevica: See note under root ДЕН (etc.).

КРУГ, КРУЖ	KRĄG, KRĘG, KRĄŻ	KRUH, KRUŽ	KRUG, KRUŽ
круг: circle	krąg: circle	kruh: circle	krug: circle
	kręg: vertebra		
		kružnice: circumference	kružnica: circle
	krążownik: cruiser (warship)		
кругóм: around			
			djelokrug: sphere of activity; sphere of authority, jurisdiction
	domokrążca: peddler		
головокружéние: dizziness, giddiness			
круговорóт: rotation (of the seasons), succession (of events)			
кругозóр: field of vision; mental horizon, outlook			
	ostrokrąg: (math.) cone		
	widnokrąg: horizon		vidokrug: horizon
		zvěrokruh: zodiac	
			naokrug: around
окружи́ть, окружáть: to surround	okrążyć, okrążać: to surround; to circle around (tr.)		okružiti, okruživati: to surround
óкруг: district	okrąg, okręg: district; circumference	okruh: circle; sphere (of authority, activity, etc.); radius, range; district	okrug, okružje: district
окрýжность: circumference			
	okrążnica: (anat.) colon		okružnica: circular (letter)
вокрýг: around	wokrąg: around		uokrug: around
[R]	[P]	[Cz]	[S-C]

NOTES

Basic meaning of root: circle

The Slavic root is cognate with Eng. ring.

kręg: a new nominative singular, specialized in meaning, which arose through the use of kręgi (nom. pl. of krąg) in the sense of "vertebrae."

domokrążca: The first element is from dom "house."

кругозóр: Compare Ger. Gesichtskreis "horizon" (<Gesicht "sight" + Kreis "circle"), widnokrąg-vidokrug below.

ostrokrąg: The first element is from ostry "sharp."

widnokrąg-vidokrug: See note on кругозóр.

zvěrokruh: The first element is from zvíře "animal"; compare Eng. zodiac (ult. <Gr. ζωδιακός "of animals" [sc. κύκλος "circle"]), Ger. Tierkreis "zodiac" (<Tier "animal" + Kreis "circle").

óкруг et al.: Compare Ger. Kreis "circle; district," Bezirk "district" (ult. <Lat. circus "circle").

КРУТ	KRĘT, KRĘC, KRUT, KRZĄT, KRZĘT	KROUT, KRUT	KRUT, KRE(T)
крутúть: to twist (tr.); to twirl (tr.)	kręcić: to twist (tr.); to twirl (tr.); to cheat, prevaricate	kroutiti: to twist (tr.); to twirl (tr.)	krutiti: to harden, stiffen (tr.); to starch
			krenuti, kretati: to move (tr.); to start out, set out
	krzątać się: to fuss, bustle about		krenuti se, kretati se: to move (intr.); to start out, set out
крутóй: steep; sudden, abrupt; stern, severe; hard-boiled (egg)	kręty: winding, tortuous	krutý: cruel; severe (e.g. pain, winter)	krut: hard, stiff; cruel; severe (e.g. pain, winter)
	krętacz: swindler, double-dealer		
			krutilo: starch
		krutovláda: tyranny	
			nekretnina, nepokretnina: real estate, immovable property
[R]	[P]	[Cz]	[S-C]

[R]	[P]	[Cz]	[S-C]
	okręt: ship		
	okrutny: cruel		*okrutan*: cruel
			okrenuti, *okretati*: to turn (tr.); to revolve (tr.)
			okretan: nimble, agile
			pokret: movement, motion; movement (political, etc.)
			prekretnica: crisis, turning-point
			preokret: revolution, upheaval
	skrzętny: industrious, diligent		
			skretnica: railroad switch
		ukrutný: cruel	
	wykręt: subterfuge, dodge	*výkrut*: subterfuge, dodge; (av.) barrel roll	

NOTES

Basic meaning of root: to twist

Rus. *крути́ть*, Pol. *kręcić*, Cz. *kroutiti* and their derivatives reflect the original root-meaning as well as the further notion of "twisting" in a figurative sense, *i.e*. cheating and resorting to subterfuge. (See, however, note on S-C *krutiti*.) A more general idea of movement is apparent in Pol. *krzątać się*, S-C *krenuti* (*se*) and their derivatives. See also note on *крутой et al*.

krutiti: not a primary verb but a denominative formed from *krut*---hence the meaning.

krzątać się-krenuti (*se*): Rus. *кря́нуть*, *кря́тать* "to move" survives only in dialectal use, while Cz. *křátati* "to walk clumsily" is obsolete.

крутой et al.: The original meaning is still evident in Pol. *kręty*; from the further meaning "tightly twisted, taut" evolved the notions of hardness, steepness, severity, etc.

okręt: orig. "a twisted (*i.e*. woven, plaited) receptacle or vessel";

obsolete S-C okrut retains the original meaning of the Polish word.

okrutny-okrutan: Compare крутой et al.; the Polish word may be borrowed from Cz. ukrutný.

skrzętny: Compare krzątać się.

ukrutný: Compare крутой et al.

КРЫ, КРОВ	KRY	KRÝ, KROV	KRI, KROV
крыть: to cover	kryć: to hide (tr.); to cover	krýti: to cover; to shield, protect	kriti: to hide (tr.)
	kryjomy: secret (a.)		kriomice: secretly
			krijumčar: smuggler
крыша: roof			
			krišom: secretly
кров: shelter		krov: rafters, beams; roofing	krov: roof
открыть, открывать: to open; to disclose; to discover	odkryć, odkrywać: to uncover; to disclose; to discover	odkrýti, odkrývati: to uncover; to disclose; to discover	otkriti, otkrivati: to uncover; to disclose; to discover
открытка: post-card	odkrytka (arch.): post-card		
откровение: revelation			
откровенный: frank, candid			
покрыть, покрывать: to cover	pokryć, pokrywać: to cover	pokrýti, pokrývati: to cover	pokriti, pokrivati: to cover
покровитель: patron, protector			pokrovitelj: patron, protector
скрыть, скрывать; (arch.) *сокрыть: to hide (tr.)	skryć, skrywać: to hide (tr.)	skrýti, skrývati: to hide (tr.)	skriti, skrivati; sakriti, sakrivati: to hide (tr.)
сокровенный: secret; intimate, innermost (thoughts, etc.)			skrovan, skrovit: secret; secluded
сокровище: treasure			skrovište: hiding-place; refuge
[R]	[P]	[Cz]	[S-C]

закры́ть, закрыва́ть: to shut, close; to cover	wykryć, wykrywać: to disclose; to discover zakryć, zakrywać: to cover; to hide (tr.)	zakrýti, zakrývati: to cover; to hide (tr.)	zakriti, zakrivati: to cover
[R]	[P]	[Cz]	[S-C]

NOTES

Basic meaning of root: to cover

A secondary meaning, "to hide," is apparent in many of the derivatives. The addition of a negative prefix produces such meanings as "to open," "to disclose," "to discover."

The Slavic root is cognate with Gr. κρύπτειν "to hide" (>Eng. crypt, cryptic).

откры́тка-odkrytka: ="an open, unsealed message"; the Polish word is borrowed from Russian.

открове́ние, открове́нный: borrowed from Church Slavic.

pokrovitelj: ‹Rus. покрови́тель.

сокрове́нный, сокро́вище: borrowed from Church Slavic.

КУС, КУШ	KUS, KUSZ	KUS, KUŠ, KOUŠ	KUS, KUŠ
	kusić: to tempt kusić się (o + acc.): to try, attempt		
ку́шать: to eat			kušati: to taste; to test; to try, attempt; to tempt
искуси́ть (arch.), искуша́ть: to tempt	*skusić: to tempt	zkusiti, zkoušeti: to test; to try, attempt; to undergo, suffer; (zkoušeti only) to examine, give an examination to (students)	*iskusiti: to experience
			iskušati, iskušavati: to tempt; to test; to experience
[R]	[P]	[Cz]	[S-C]

[R]	[P]	[Cz]	[S-C]
искушённый: experienced		zkušený: experienced	
			iskušenik: (rel.) novice
и́скус (lit.): trial, test; (rel.) novitiate			iskus: trial, test
иску́сный: skilful			iskusan: skilful; experienced
иску́сство: art; skill			iskustvo: experience
иску́сственный: artificial			iskustven: experimental, empirical
			okus: taste, flavor
покуше́ние: attempt (esp. on s.o.'s life); encroachment	pokuszenie: temptation	pokušení: temptation	
	pokusa: temptation	pokus: attempt; trial, test; experiment	pokus: trial, test; experiment
			pokušaj: attempt; trial, test
вкус: taste, flavor; taste (in art, clothes, etc.)		vkus: taste (in art, clothes, etc.)	ukus: taste, flavor; taste (in art, clothes, etc.)
		zakusiti, zakoušeti: to undergo, suffer	

NOTES

Basic meaning of root: to taste

This root has produced a wide range of derivatives expressing such notions as testing, trying, experience, temptation, etc. The semantic links between the various words are evident from parallels in other languages, e.g. Eng. try in its dual meaning "to attempt" and "to test," Eng. tempt and attempt (both ult. ‹Lat. tentare [temptare] "to touch; to test; to attempt; to tempt"), Eng. experiment and experience (both ult. ‹Lat. experiri "to test; to experience," whence also Fr. expérience "experience; experiment" and expérimenté "experienced"), Ger. versuchen in its dual meaning "to tempt" and "to attempt." Compare also Pol. doświadczenie and the largely comparable derivatives of root ПЫТ (etc.).

The Slavic root is an early borrowing from Goth. kausjan "to taste," which is related to Eng. choose, Lat. gustare "to taste" (⟩Eng. gusto, disgust). Rus. кусáть, Pol. kąsać and Cz. kousati "to bite" and S-C kusati "to eat greedily" are not related.

All the Russian words with the exception of кýшать are of Church Slavic origin.

kusić: ORus. кусити "to taste" has not survived in the modern language, while S-C kusiti "to taste" is obsolete. The unprefixed verb is not attested in Czech.

iskustvo: ⟨Rus. искýсство.

искýсственный: ⟨искýсство, hence ="made by art (rather than by nature)"; compare Eng. artificial and art, Ger. künstlich "artificial" (⟨Kunst "art"), Pol. sztuczny "artificial" (⟨sztuka "art"), Cz. umělý, S-C umjetan and vještački.

pokus (S-C): ⟨obsolete Rus. покýс "trial, test" or Cz. pokus.

vkus-ukus: ⟨Rus. вкус.

ЛЕ(Г)$_1$, ЛЯГ, ЛЕЖ, ЛОГ, ЛОЖ, ЛАГ	LE(G), LEŻ, ŁÓG, ŁOG, ŁOŻ, ŁÓŻ, LĄ(G), LĘG	LEH, LÉH, LEŽ, LOH, LOŽ, LŮŽ, LÍH	LE(G), LIJEG, LEŽ, LOG, LOŽ, LOZ, LAG
лежáть: to lie, recline	leżeć: to lie, recline	ležeti: to lie, recline	ležati: to lie, recline
*лечь: to lie down	*lec (legnąć) (lit.): to fall (in battle), perish; to lie down	lehnouti (si), lehati (si): to lie down	lèći (legnuti), lijegati: to lie down
	lęgnąć (ląc) (arch.): to hatch (tr.)	líhnouti (arch.): to hatch (tr.)	léći: to hatch (tr.)
	łożyć: to spend (money)	**ložiti: to load	ložiti: to stoke, fuel; to heat
ложúться: to lie down			
	leże (pl.): military quarters, billets		ležaj: bed; bearing (mechanical part); layer, stratum
		ležení: military camp	
			ležište: bearing (mechanical part); mineral deposit
			legalo: lair, den; bed
[R]	[P]	[Cz]	[S-C]

ЛЕГ$_1$

[R]	[P]	[Cz]	[S-C]
	legowisko: lair, den		
		lehátko: couch; beach-chair	
лежáк: beach-chair	leżak: chaise longue; lager beer	ležák: lager beer; idler; idle stock (non-selling goods)	ležak: idler
легáвая, лягáвая (собáка): pointer, setter	legawiec, (pies) legawy: pointer, setter		
лежáлый: stale, old			
		ležatý: slanting; italic (type)	
лог, ложбúна: ravine			log: lair, den
лóгово, лóговище: lair, den			
лóже: river-bed; (arch.) bed	łoże: bed; stock (of a gun); gun-carriage	lože: lair, den; mineral deposit; (lit.) bed	
лóжа: stock (of a gun)			
	łóżko: bed	lůžko: bed; (anat.) placenta	
	łożysko: river-bed; bearing (mechanical part); (anat.) placenta	ložisko: mineral deposit; bearing (mechanical part)	
			leglo: litter, brood; lair, den; hotbed, breeding ground
		líheň: incubator	
	cudzołożnik, cudzołóżca: adulterer	cizoložník: adulterer	
	dziwoląg: monster		
мужелóжство (lit.): sodomy			
низложúть, низлагáть (lit.): to depose, dethrone			
		polohopis (arch.): topography	
	równoległy: parallel (a.)		

рукоположéние: ordination (of a priest), laying on of hands			rukopolaganje: ordination (of a priest), laying on of hands
		důležitý: important	
	dolegliwy: painful		
*доложи́ть: to add; to report, make a report	*dołożyć: to add; to exert (efforts)	*doložiti: to add; to prove, substantiate	
изложи́ть, излага́ть: to expound, set forth, explain			izložiti, izlagati: to lay out; to display; to expound, set forth, explain; to expose (e.g. to danger)
			izlog: display-window
			izložba: exhibition, exposition
			izložitelj: (math.) exponent
	należeć: to belong; (impers.) (one) should, ought to	náležeti: to belong; (impers.; arch.) (one) should, ought to	
	należny: fitting, proper; due, owing (to s.o.)		
	należyty: fitting, proper	náležitý: fitting, proper	
нале́чь, налега́ть: to lean (against)	nalegać: to urge, insist	nalehnouti, naléhati: to lean (against); (naléhati only) to urge, insist	naleći (nalegnuti) (se), nalijegati (se): to lean (against); to gather, assemble (intr.)
		naléhavý: urgent, vital; insistent	
			naloga: crowd, throng
нало́г: tax	nałóg: vice, bad habit		nalog: order, command; decree; warrant
[R]	[P]	[Cz]	[S-C]

[R]	[P]	[Cz]	[S-C]
		nálož: powder charge	
налóжница: concubine, paramour	nałożnica: concubine, paramour		naložnica: concubine, paramour
			naslaga: layer, stratum; sediment, deposit; heap, pile
надлежáщий: fitting, proper			nadležan: competent, authorized
	niepodległy: independent		
непрелóжный: immutable, unalterable; indisputable			
	niezależny: independent		
облéчь, облегáть: to cover; to fit closely	oblec, oblegać: to besiege	oblehnouti, obléhati: to besiege	
	obłożny: serious (said of an illness)		
обложи́ть, облагáть: to impose (tax, fine, etc.) upon; (обложи́ть only) to circle, surround (with); (обложи́ть only) to cover; (обложи́ть only) to line, face, panel; (обложи́ть only) to besiege	*obłożyć: to circle, surround (with); to cover; to impose (tax, fine, etc.) upon	*obložiti: to circle, surround (with); to cover; to line, face, panel	obložiti, oblagati: to circle, surround (with); to cover; to line, face, panel
			oblog: poultice, compress; (arch.) bet
	obłoga: covering, coating	obloha: sky	obloga: poultice, compress; lining, facing, paneling
			odlijegati se: to resound
	odległość: distance; remoteness	odlehlost: remoteness	
	odleżyna: bedsore		

[R]	[P]	[Cz]	[S-C]
	odłóg: (state of lying) fallow; fallow land		
отлóгий: sloping			
отложи́ть, отлага́ть: to put aside (отложи́ть only); to put off, postpone, delay; (geol.) to deposit	*odłożyć: to put aside; to put off, postpone, delay	*odložiti: to put aside; to doff, take off; to put off, postpone, delay	odložiti, odlagati: to put aside; to doff, take off; to put off, postpone, delay
	polegać: to rely (on); to consist (in)		
полóгий: sloping			položit: sloping
*положи́ть: to lay, put	*położyć: to lay, put	*položiti: to lay, put	*položiti: to lay, put
полага́ть: to think, suppose			polagati: to lay, put
положи́ться, полага́ться: to rely (on); (полага́ться only) to be permissible, acceptable	*położyć się: to lie down	*položiti se: to lie down	
	połóg: childbirth, confinement		polog: pledge, pawn; deposit, security; nest egg
	położna: midwife		
		poloha: position, location	
положе́ние: position, location; position, posture; position, standing (in society, etc.); situation; thesis, proposition; provision (of a law, etc.)	położenie: position, location; situation	položení (arch.): position, location	
			položaj: position, location; position, posture; position, standing (in society, etc.); posi-

			tion, post, job; (mil.) position; situation
		položka: item; (bookkeeping) entry	
положи́тельный: positive, favorable; (math., phys.) positive; affirmative (reply, etc.)			
подлежа́ть: to be subject, liable (to)			podležati: to be subject, liable (to)
	podlec, podlegać: to be subject, liable (to); to be subordinate (to)	podlehnouti, podléhati: to be subject, liable (to) (podléhati only); to be subjected (to), undergo; to be subordinate (to) (podléhati only); to yield, submit; to succumb	podleći (podlegnuti), podlijegati: to be subject, liable (to) (podlijegati only); to yield, submit; to succumb
подлежа́щее: (gram.) subject			
подло́г: forgery			
		podloha (arch.): base, foundation; basis; pad	podloga: base, foundation; basis; pad
	podłoże: base, foundation	podložka: pad; washer (for screw, etc.)	
перело́г: fallow land			prijelog: fallow land
предложи́ть, предлага́ть: to offer; to propose, suggest	*przedłożyć: to submit, present	*předložiti: to lay, put before (s.o.); to submit, present; to serve (food)	predložiti, predlagati: to propose, suggest
предложе́ние: offer; proposal, suggestion; (econ.) supply; (gram.) sentence, clause	przedłożenie: submission, presentation	předložení: (act of) laying, putting before (s.o.); submission, presentation; serving (of food)	
[R]	[P]	[Cz]	[S-C]

предло́г: pretext; (gram.) preposition			predlog, prijedlog: proposal, suggestion; (gram.) preposition
		předloha: bill (proposed law); model, pattern	
		předložka: bedside rug; (gram.) preposition	predložak: model, pattern
предположи́ть, предполага́ть: to assume, postulate; (предполага́ть only) to intend			
приле́жный: diligent, industrious			priležan: diligent, industrious
прилега́ющий: close-fitting, clinging; adjacent	przyległy: adjacent	přilehlý: adjacent	
		přiléhavý: close-fitting, clinging; fitting, apt	
		příležitost: opportunity; occasion	
			priležnica: concubine, paramour
приложи́ть, прилага́ть: to add; to append, annex, enclose; to exert (efforts); (приложи́ть only) to apply (a plaster to a wound), set (one's hand to a task), affix (one's signature)	*przyłożyć: to add; to apply (a plaster to a wound), set (one's hand to a task), affix (one's signature), attach (importance to s.th.)	*přiložiti: to add; to append, annex, enclose; to apply (a plaster to a wound), set (one's hand to a task), affix (one's signature), attach (importance to s.th.)	priložiti, prilagati: to add; to append, annex, enclose; to contribute
		příloha: supplement (to a newspaper), annex (to a document), enclosure (in	prilog: supplement (to a newspaper), annex (to a document), enclosure (in
[R]	[P]	[Cz]	[S-C]

[R]	[P]	[Cz]	[S-C]
		a letter); vegetables (as an addition to a meat course)	a letter); contribution; benefit, advantage; (gram.) adverb
(и́мя) прилага́тельное: (gram.) adjective			
принадлежа́ть: to belong	przynależeć (arch.): to belong	přináležeti (lit.): to belong	prinadležati: to be within (s.o.'s) jurisdiction, sphere of competence
про́лежень: bedsore		proleženina: bedsore	
	przełożony: chief, superior (n.)		
противополо́жный: opposite, facing; opposite, contrary	przeciwległy: opposite, facing	protilehlý: opposite, facing; (arch.) opposite, contrary	
*разле́чься: to sprawl	rozlec się, rozlegać się: to resound	rozlehnouti se, rozléhati se: to resound	razleći se, razlijegati se: to resound
	rozległy: extensive	rozlehlý: extensive	
разложе́ние: disintegration, dissolution; decomposition, decay; (chem.) decomposition, analysis; demoralization	rozłożenie: arrangement, disposition, distribution	rozložení: arrangement, disposition, distribution	razlaganje: explanation, analysis; (chem.) decomposition, analysis
	rozłóg: tract, expanse		razlog: cause, reason
	rozłoga: runner (of a plant)	rozloha: area, space	
	rozłożysty: spreading, branchy	rozložitý: spreading, branchy; broad-shouldered	razložan, razložit: reasonable, sensible
расположе́ние: arrangement, disposition, distribution; location; liking, inclination, favor; inclination, disposition, tendency; mood, frame of mind		rozpoložení: mood, frame of mind	raspoloženje: liking, inclination, favor; inclination, disposition, tendency; mood frame of mind; good mood; disposition, (act of) disposing (of property, etc.); (na
[R]	[P]	[Cz]	[S-C]

[R]	[P]	[Cz]	[S-C]
			nečijemu: at s.o.'s) disposal
			raspolaganje: disposition, (act of) disposing (of property, etc.); (na nečijemu: at s.o.'s) disposal
		slehnouti se, sléhati se: to settle (ground, building, etc.)	sleći (slegnuti) se, slijegati se: to settle (ground, building, sediment, etc.); to crowd together (intr.)
		slehnutí: childbirth, confinement	
		souložnice: concubine, paramour	suložnica: concubine, paramour
*сложи́ться: to pool money, take a collection; to take shape	*złożyć się: to pool money, take a collection; to fold (intr.); to turn out, work out (well, badly, etc.)	*složiti se: to pool money, take a collection	*složiti se: to agree, concur; to agree, consent
слага́ться: to consist, be composed (of)			slagati se: to agree, concur; to agree, consent
сложе́ние: physique, build; (math.) addition		složení: composition, structure, make-up; physique, build; set of millstones	
сложённый: (well-, etc.) formed, built (said of the body)	złożony: complex, composite; complicated; (gram.) compound	složený: complex, composite; (gram.) compound	složen: complex, composite; complicated; compound (interest); (gram.) compound
слог: syllable; (literary) style	złóg: sediment, deposit; (med.) stone, concretion	sloh: (literary, architectural) style	slog: syllable; (literary, architectural) style; typesetting, composition

[R]	[P]	[Cz]	[S-C]
		sloha: folder, portfolio	sloga: harmony, accord
	złoże: mineral deposit		
		složka: component, constituent (n.); (military) unit; quire (of paper)	
		složenka: draft, money-order	
сло́жный: complex, composite; complicated; compound (interest); (gram.) compound			složan: harmonious, in agreement
		složitý: complicated; compound (interest)	
			slagar: compositor, typesetter
			slagalište: warehouse, storehouse
		spolehnouti (se), spoléhati (se): to rely (on)	
сослага́тельный: (gram.) subjunctive			
	ulec, ulegać: to yield, submit; to be subjected (to), undergo; (ulegać only) to be subject, liable (to)	ulehnouti, uléhati: to lie down	
уложе́ние: code (of laws)	ułożenie: arrangement, disposition, distribution; manners, behavior		
		úloha: task; (math.) problem; role	uloga: role
вложе́ние: (act of) putting in, inserting; investment; enclosure (in a letter)	włożenie: (act of) putting in, inserting	vložení: (act of) putting in, inserting	ulaganje: investment; deposit (of funds)

[R]	[P]	[Cz]	[S-C]
			ulog: investment; deposit (of funds); contribution; dues; stake (in gambling)
		vlohy (pl.): talent, ability	ulozi (pl.): (med.) gout
влага́лище: (anat.) vagina			
	wylęgarnia, wylęgarka: incubator		
*вы́ложить: to lay out; to line, face, panel	*wyłożyć: to lay out; to display; to expound, set forth, explain; to disburse; to line, face, panel	*vyložiti: to lay out; to display; to unload; to expound, set forth, explain; to interpret; to line, face, panel	
	wyłogi (pl.): facings (on uniform); lapels	výloha: expenditure, outlay; display-window	
		výložky (pl.): facings (on uniform); lapels	
		*vynaložiti: to spend (money); to exert (efforts)	
возложи́ть, возлага́ть: to lay, put; to impose (an obligation), entrust (a task), place (one's hopes), lay (blame)			
	zależeć: to depend; to matter, be important (to s.o.)	záležeti: to depend; to matter, be important (to s.o.); to consist (in)	
		záležitost: affair, matter, business	
за́лежь: mineral deposit; long-fallow land; idle stock (non-selling goods)		zálež (coll.): compost	

залóг: pledge, pawn; mortgage; deposit, security; (gram.) voice залóжник: hostage	załegłość: arrears założenie: founding, establishment; premise, assumption załoga: crew; garrison; staff, work force	založení: founding, establishment; disposition, temperament záloha: advance (payment); ambush; reserve, supply; (mil.) reserve záložník: (mil.) reservist; half-back (in soccer)	zalog: pledge, pawn; mortgage; deposit, security zaloga: pledge, pawn; mortgage; deposit, security
[R]	[P]	[Cz]	[S-C]

NOTES

Basic meaning of root: to lie, recline

Many of the derivatives show meanings which can be traced to the two broad notions of "a place where someone or something lies, rests or is supported" (>"bed," "lair," "camp," "gun-carriage," "stock of a gun," "mechanical bearing," "placenta") and "that which lies or rests" (>"layer, stratum," "mineral deposit," "fallow land," "lager beer"). (Comparable semantic development is apparent in Eng. lair [<lie], Ger. Lager "bed; lair; camp; mechanical bearing; mineral deposit" [<liegen "to lie"], Fr. gîte "lair; mineral deposit" [ult. <Lat. jacere "to lie"].) A specialized sub-group is formed by the verb lęgnąć et al. "to hatch" and its derivatives (leglo, líheň, dziwo-ląg, wylęgarnia, wylęgarka). (Compare Fr. couver "to hatch" [<Lat. cubare "to lie"], Eng. incubate [ult. <Lat. in "on" + cubare].) The root-forms ЛОГ-ЛОЖ-ЛАГ---ŁÓG-ŁOG-ŁOŻ-ŁÓŻ---LOH-LOŽ-LŮŽ---LOG-LOŽ-LOZ-LAG are often causative, expressing the meaning "to cause to lie," i.e. "to lay, put." Polish, Czech and, in some instances, Russian perfective causative verbs form their imperfective aspect from root КЛА(Д) (etc.).

The Slavic root is cognate with Eng. lie and lay, Ger. liegen "to lie" and legen "to lay, put."

лечь: The 1 sg. form is лягу.

léći: The 1 sg. form is ležem.

łożyć: See note on Pol. nakład et al., nakładca et al.

ložiti (Cz.): a relatively recent back-formation from naložiti "to lay on, load"; the original simple verb is not attested.

ložiti (S-C): orig. "to lay, put," then "to put wood on a fire," whence ltimately the modern meanings.

ложиться: The simple causative verb is attested only in this reflexive orm, which serves as the imperfective aspect of лечь.

легáвая, лягáвая (собáка): The adjective is borrowed from Pol. legawy.

лог, ложбина: ="low-lying ground."

лóжа: ‹Pol. łoże.

cudzołożnik et al.: See łoże-lože; the first element is from cudzy-cizí alien, someone else's."

dziwoląg: ‹dziwny "strange" + the root of lęgnąć, hence = "strange offpring."

мужелóжство: See лóже; the first element is from муж "husband" in the rchaic meaning "man."

низложить: низ- = "down"; compare Eng. depose (ult. ‹Lat. de "down" + r. poser "to put").

polohopis: See poloha and note on Cz. místopis.

důležitý: Compare naléhavý.

dolegliwy: ="pressing, pushing"; compare налéчь et al.

доложить et al.: See note on S-C pridjenuti, Cz. přidělati. The meaning to report" = "to put (i.e. bring, convey) information to someone." The second meaning of the Czech word reflects the notion of supplying documentation o support an argument; compare Ger. belegen "to prove, substantiate (by eans of documentary evidence)" (‹legen "to lay, put").

изложить-izložiti, izlog: Compare Eng. expose (ult. ‹Lat. ex "out" + r. poser "to put"), Ger. aussetzen "to expose (e.g. to danger)" (‹aus "out" setzen "to set, put") and see note on Rus. выклáдывать et al., Pol. wykład, Cz. výklad.

izložba: Compare Eng. exposition (ult. ‹Lat. ex "out" + ponere "to ut"), Ger. Ausstellung "exhibition, exposition" (‹aus "out" + stellen "to ut"), Rus. выставка et al.

izložitelj: See izložiti and note on Pol. wykładnik.

należeć-náležeti, należny, należyty-náležitý: The idea of belonging rises from that of "lying near," i.e. of proximity and, hence, association; omparable semantic development is shown by Eng. belong (akin to Ger. langen to reach, extend [toward]"), Fr. appartenir "to belong" (ult. ‹Lat. ad "to, oward" + pertinere "to reach, extend"), Hung. tartozni "to belong" (="to be eld [toward]" ‹tartani "to hold"). Regarding the kindred notion of "fitess, propriety," see note on Pol. patrzeć (patrzyć) się, Cz. patřiti se.

nalegać-nalehnouti, naléhavý: Compare Ger. Anliegen "request" (‹an "on, gainst" + liegen "to lie").

naleći (se): In the second meaning, leći (a verb of motion in contrast o ležati, which denotes rest) has the force of "to move, go."

naloga: See the second meaning of naleći (se).

налóг-nalog: ="something laid (i.e. imposed) on a person as an obligation"; compare Eng. *impost* (ult. ‹Lat. *in* "on" + *ponere* "to put"), Ger. *Auflage* "tax; order, injunction" (‹*auf* "on" + *legen* "to lay, put"), S-C *namet*. The same notion of an imposed obligation underlies the use of Eng. *charge* (‹Fr. *charge* "load, burden") in the meanings "price demanded for goods or services" and "judge's instructions to the jury."

nałóg: orig. "habit" in a neutral sense; see archaic *nałożyć się* "to become accustomed (to)," literally "to put (*i.e.* apply, devote) oneself (to)."

nálož: ‹*naložiti* "to lay on, load"; compare Eng. *charge* (‹Fr. *charge* "load").

нало́жница *et al*.: See note on *souložnice*-*suložnica*.

naslaga: ‹*slagati* "to put together, pile up."

надлежа́щий: ="resting upon a person (as a duty or responsibility)"; compare Eng. *incumbent* (*upon*) (ult. ‹Lat. *in* "on" + -*cumbere* "to lie down"), Ger. *obliegend* "incumbent" (‹*ob* "above, upon" + *liegen* "to lie").

nadležan: ‹Rus. *надлежа́щий*.

niepodległy: See *podlec*.

непрело́жный: ‹obsolete *преложи́ть* "to transpose, shift; to transform."

niezależny: See *zależeć*.

obłożny: See the dialectal use of *oblec* in the meaning "to take to one's bed because of illness."

обложи́ть *et al*., *oblog*, *obłoga et al*.: Compare Ger. *belegen* "to cover; to line, face, panel; to impose (tax, fine, etc.) upon" (‹*be*- "[here =] around, over" + *legen* "to lay, put"); regarding the second meaning of *oblog* see note on S-C *kladiti se*.

odlijegati se: See note on *naleći* (*se*).

odległość-*odlehlost*: Compare Ger. *Abgelegenheit*, *Entlegenheit* "remoteness" (‹*ab*, *ent*- "away" + *liegen* "to lie").

отложи́ть (third meaning): See note on Pol. *pokład*.

polegać (first meaning): See note on Pol. *spodziewać się*.

положи́ть-*położyć*-*položiti* (Cz.): See note on Rus. *класть* *et al*.

полага́ть: ="to lay down (as true)"; compare Eng. *posit* (ult. ‹Lat. *ponere* "to put"), Cz. *pokládati*.

положи́ться: See note on Pol. *spodziewać się*; regarding the second meaning of *полага́ться*, see *полага́ть* and compare the use of Eng. *suppose* in the sentence *You are not supposed to do that*.

polog: See note on *зало́г*-*zalog*, *zaloga*, *зало́жник*.

poloha, *положе́ние* *et al*., *položaj*: The underlying meaning in most instances is "place where (or manner in which) someone or something is 'put'"; compare Eng. *position*, *posture*, *post* (all ult. ‹Lat. *ponere* "to put"), *location* (ult. ‹Lat. *locare* "to place, put") and *situation* (ult. ‹MLat. *situare* "to place, put"), Ger. *Stellung* "position (in various senses)" (‹*stellen* "to put"), Pol. *postawa*, Cz. *postavení*, S-C *stav*. Regarding the last two meanings of the Russian word, see note on Cz. *klad*.

položka: ="a position or place (on a list, in a ledger, etc.)"; see oloha and compare Fr. poste "post, place; item; entry," Ger. Position "po-ition; item" and Posten "post, place; item; entry," Pol. pozycja "position; tem; entry."

положительный: See note on Cz. kladný.

подлежать-podležati, podlec et al.: Compare Eng. succumb (ult. ⟨Lat. ub "under" + -cumbere "to lie down"), Ger. unterliegen "to be subject, iable (to); to succumb" (⟨unter "under" + liegen "to lie"); S-C podležati s borrowed from Russian.

подлежащее: modeled on Gr. ὑποκείμενον "subject" (⟨ὑπό "under" + κεῖσ-αι "to lie"); see note on Pol. podmiot et al.

подлóг: See note on Rus. подкидыш.

предложить-predložiti: Compare Eng. propose (ult. ⟨Lat. pro "forward" + r. poser "to put").

предложéние (fourth meaning): ="something put forward, proposed, stat-d"; compare modern Gr. πρότασις "proposal; (gram.) sentence, clause."

предлóг et al.: Regarding the first meaning of предлóг, see note on Cz. ředstírání. In their grammatical usage, the Russian word is a loan-transla-ion of Gr. πρόθεσις "preposition" (⟨πρό "before, in front" + τιθέναι "to ut"), Lat. praepositio (⟨prae "before, in front" + ponere "to put") and the erbo-Croatian words are borrowed from Russian.

předloha, předložka-predložak: Except as regards the second meaning of ředložka (see preceding note), these words translate Ger. Vorlage "bill; odel, pattern; bedside rug" (⟨vor "before, in front" + legen "to lay, put"); oth a legislative bill and a model or pattern represent "something put for-ard" (for approval in one case, for imitation in the other).

предположить: ="to lay down, assert in advance"; the word is modeled on er. voraussetzen "to assume, postulate" (⟨voraus "in advance" + setzen "to et, put"). Compare also Cz. předpokládati, S-C pretpostaviti.

прилéжный-priležan: ="lying close, i.e. applying oneself (to a task)"; ompare Eng. incumbent "holding office" (ult. ⟨Lat. incumbere "to apply, de-ote o.s. [to]" ⟨ in "on" + -cumbere "to lie down"), Ger. obliegen "to ap-ly, devote o.s. (to)" (⟨ob "above, upon" + liegen "to lie"). The Serbo-roatian word is borrowed from Russian.

прилегáющий et al.: Compare Eng. adjacent (ult. ⟨Lat. ad "at, near" + acere "to lie").

příležitost: ⟨obsolete příležeti "to belong; to be suitable"; see note n należeć-náležeti, należny, należyty-náležitý.

priležnica: See note on souložnice-suložnica.

приложить et al., příloha-prilog: See note on S-C pridjenuti, Cz. při-ělati and compare Ger. beilegen "to add; to append, annex, enclose; to at-ach (importance to s.th.)" and Beilage "supplement, annex, enclosure; vege-ables (with a meat course)" (both ⟨bei "by, near" + legen "to lay, put"); he last meaning of S-C prilog reflects the fact that an adverb normally accompanies another word.

(и́мя) прилага́тельное: probably modeled on Gr. ἐπίθετον "adjective" ((ἐπιτιθέναι "to add" ⟨ ἐπί "on; to" + τιθέναι "to put"), whence Eng. epithet; see the first meaning of приложи́ть and notes on Pol. przymiot, przymiotnik and on Rus. и́мя, Pol. imię, Cz. jméno.

принадлежа́ть-przynależeć-přináležeti: See note on należeć-náležeti, należny, należyty-náležitý; the Russian word is borrowed from Polish.

prinadležati: borrowed from Rus. принадлежа́ть and originally synonymou with it.

przełożony: Compare Ger. Vorgesetzte(r) "chief, superior" (⟨vor "befor in front" + setzen "to set, put"), Cz. představený, S-C pretpostavljeni.

противополо́жный: See note on Cz. protiklad.

rozlec się et al.: See note on naleći (se).

разложе́ние et al., razlog, razložan, razložit, расположе́ние et al., raspolaganje: In several of these words, the notion of "putting (i.e. taking) apart" has produced literal and figurative meanings somewhat comparabl to those discussed in the note on Rus. разбо́р et al., разбо́рчивый, разбира́тельство; semantic parallels can be found in Ger. Zersetzung "disintegration, dissolution; decomposition, decay; demoralization" (⟨zer- "apart" + setzen "to set, put"), Zerlegung "(chem.) decomposition, analysis" (⟨zer- + legen "to lay, put"), Auseinandersetzung "explanation, analysis" (⟨auseinander "apart" + setzen). In other instances, the basic idea is that of "lay ing out, arranging," whence the transferred meanings "mental arrangement, i.e. inclination, tendency, mood" and "(act of) arranging for, dealing with handling (e.g. property)"; here the semantic development closely follows that of Eng. dispose, disposal (both ult. ⟨Lat. dis- "apart" + Fr. poser "t put") and disposition (ult. ⟨Lat. dis- + ponere "to put"). See also Pol. rozkład, Cz. rozklad.

sleći se (second meaning): See note on naleći (se).

souložnice-sułożnica: Compare Eng. concubine (ult. ⟨Lat. cum "with, together" + cubare "to lie").

сложи́ться et al., слага́ться-slagati se, сложе́ние-složení, сложённый et al., слог-sloh-slog, sloha-sloga, složka, сло́жный-složan, složitý, slagar, slagalište: The semantic development of many of these words can be likened to that of Eng. compose (ult. ⟨Lat. cum "with, together" + Fr. poser "to put") and composition, composite, compositor, component, compound (all ult. ⟨Lat. cum + ponere "to put"). The meanings reflect a number of basic notio (1) "putting together" in a more or less literal sense, e.g. pooling money storing goods, adding numbers, setting (composing) type, folding; (2) "bei put together (by), made up or composed (of)," hence "having a certain form shape, structure, style, etc."; (3) "serving to put together, make up, compose" (⟩"component," "syllable," "military unit"); (4) "put together by (composed of) a number of separate elements" (⟩"complex, composite," "complicated," "compound"); (5) "things put together to form a whole" (⟩"set o millstones," "quire of paper"); (6) "getting together," *i.e*. "composing one's differences, agreeing, achieving harmony." Cz. *sloh* and (in its first two meanings) S-C *slog* are borrowed from Russian. Compare Ger. *Zusammensetzung* "composition, structure; (gram., chem.) compound" (⟨*zusammen* "together" + *setzen* "to set, put"), Rus. *скла́дываться et al*., *склад et al*., *скла́дный et al*., *склады́*, *скла́дка et al*. and *соста́в*, Pol. *składnia* and *składnik*, Cz. *skladba*, *skladník* and *skladiště*, S-C *skladba*, *skladište* and *sastav*.

złóg, *złoże*: See note on Pol. *pokład*.

složenka: ⟨*složiti* "to put down, pay."

spolehnouti (se): See note on Pol. *spodziewać się*.

сослага́тельный: ⟨*слага́ть* "to put together, join"; the Russian word is modeled on Lat. *conjunctivus* "subjunctive" (⟨*conjungere* "to join together"), so called because the subjunctive mood normally occurs in a clause which is joined (as subordinate) to another clause. (Compare Eng. *conjunctive*, a variant of *subjunctive*.)

уложе́ние-*ułożenie*: See note on Rus. *укла́д*, Pol. *układ*, *układy* and *układny*, Cz. *úklady* and *úkladný*.

úloha: See *uložiti* "to set (as a task), assign."

uloga: ⟨Cz. *úloha*.

вложе́ние-*ulaganje*, *ulog*: Compare Ger. *Einlage* "investment; enclosure; deposit (of funds); stake (in gambling)" (⟨*ein*- "in" + *legen* "to lay, put"), Rus. *вклад et al*.

vlohy: ="something put in, *i.e*. implanted (by nature)"; compare Ger. *Anlage* "talent, ability" (⟨*an* "to, on" + *legen* "to lay, put").

ulozi: ="deposits (in the joints)"; compare Pol. *złóg*.

влага́лище: orig. "scabbard, sheath"; see *вложе́ние* and compare Eng. *vagina* (⟨Lat. *vagina* "scabbard, sheath").

вы́ложить et al., *výloha*: See note on Rus. *выкла́дывать et al*., Pol. *wykład*, Cz. *výklad*.

vynaložiti: See note on Pol. *nakład et al*., *nakładca et al*.

zależeć-*záležeti*: Regarding the first meaning, compare Eng. *The matter (responsibility) rests (lies) with me*. The notion of "being important (to)" arises from that of "being close (to), hence affecting, concerning"; compare Ger. *angelegen* "important, of concern (to s.o.)" (⟨*an* "at, near" + *liegen* "to lie").

záležitost: ="something of importance, concern (to s.o.)"; see preceding note and compare Ger. *Angelegenheit* "affair, matter, business" (⟨*angelegen*), which probably served as the model for the Czech word.

zaległość: The prefix here = "back, behind."

założenie-*založení*: The first meaning reflects the inceptive action of the prefix; regarding the second meaning of the Polish word, see note on Cz. *klad*.

зало́г-*zalog*, *zaloga*, *зало́жник*: Except in the case of the last meaning of *зало́г* (the development of which is not clear), the sense of these words is "something laid down (as a guarantee)"; compare Eng. deposit (ult. ‹Lat. de "down" + ponere "to put"), Fr. hypothèque "mortgage" (ult. ‹Gr. ὑπό "under" [here = "down"] + τιθέναι "to put"), Rus. закла́д, Pol. zakład, zakładnik, zastawić and zastaw, Cz. zastaviti and zástava, S-C zaklad.

załoga: See note on Pol.-Cz.-S-C posada, Cz. posádka.

záloha, záložník: Regarding the first meaning of záloha, compare залог, zalog, zaloga, зало́жник; otherwise, zá- here = "back, behind."

ЛЕГ$_2$, ЛЬГ, ЛЬЗ	LEK, LG, LŻ	LEH, LH, LZ	LAG, LAK
лёгкий: light (in weight); slight; easy	lekki: light (in weight)	lehký: light (in weight); slight; easy	lak: light (in weight); slight; easy lagan: light (in weight); slight; easy; slow
лёгкое: lung			
льго́та: privilege, exemption		lhůta: fixed term, time-limit	
	lżyć: to insult		
		lze: it is possible	
	lekceważyć: to disregard, hold in contempt		
легкомы́сленный: frivolous	lekkomyślny: frivolous	lehkomyslný: frivolous	lakomislen: frivolous lakorječiv: loquacious lakouman: frivolous
		lehkovážný: frivolous	
легкове́рный: gullible		lehkověrný: gullible	lakovjeran: gullible
		lhostejný: indifferent, apathetic	
**испо́льзовать: to use, utilize			
нельзя́: it is impossible; it is forbidden		nelze: it is impossible; it is forbidden	
облегчи́ть, облегча́ть: to lighten; to			oblakšati, oblakšavati; olakšati,
[R]	[P]	[Cz]	[S-C]

[R]	[P]	[Cz]	[S-C]
relieve, ease; to facilitate			olakšavati: to lighten; to relieve, ease; to facilitate
	obelga: insult		
		odlehčiti, odlehčovati: to lighten; to relieve, ease	
по́льза: benefit, advantage			
по́льзовать (arch.): to treat (medically)			
по́льзоваться: to use, utilize; to enjoy (success, support, a right, etc.)			
		ulehčiti, ulehčovati: to lighten; to relieve, ease; to facilitate	
	ulga: relief, easing; privilege, exemption		
	*ulżyć: to relieve, ease		
		zlehčiti, zlehčovati: to belittle, disparage; to discredit	

NOTES

Basic meaning of root: light (in weight)

The Slavic root is related to Eng. light and Lat. levis "light" (>Eng. levity, alleviate).

lekki: for *legki.

lak: from the oblique stem *lagk- of earlier lagak (attested in dialects).

лёгкое: so called because of its lightness; compare Eng. lung (etymologically related to light) and lights "animal's lungs."

льго́та-lhůta: orig. "relief, freedom (from a burden, etc.)"; the Czech word came to mean "deferment of payment on a debt for a specified period of time," and from that meaning the present one finally developed.

lżyć: ="to make light of, take lightly"; compare Eng. slight "slur, insult" (<a. slight).

lze: See note on нельзя́-nelze.

lhostejný: literally, "light-standing," i.e. "light-living." In Old Czech, the word meant "profligate, dissolute"; the present meaning presumably evolved from the notion of "light-heartedness, carefreeness."

испо́льзовать: See по́льза.

нельзя́-nelze: from a noun which has not survived in the modern languages; the literal meaning of lze above (and of obsolete Rus. льзя) is "there is freedom, ease."

obelga: See note on lżyć.

по́льза: For the meaning, compare льго́та, облегчи́ть.

ulga: Compare льго́та.

zlehčiti: See note on lżyć.

ЛЕТ	LAT, LOT, LEC	LET, LÉT	LET
†лете́ть, лета́ть: to fly	†lecieć, latać: to fly	†letěti, létati: to fly	†letjeti, letati: to fly
лётчик: aviator	lotnik: aviator	letec: aviator	letač: aviator
лету́н (coll.): floater, drifter		letoun: airplane; chiropteran (flying mammal)	
		letadlo: airplane	
	lotnictwo: aviation; aircraft (collectively)	letectví: aviation	
		letectvo: air force	
	lotnisko: airport	letiště: airport	letilište: airport
	lotniskowiec: aircraft-carrier		
		létavice: meteor	
		leták: leaflet	letak: leaflet
лётный: flying (attr.)	lotny: flying (attr.); swift; (chem.) volatile		
		letmý: cursory, superficial; brief, fleeting	
[R]	[P]	[Cz]	[S-C]

[R]	[P]	[Cz]	[S-C]
			letimičan: cursory, superficial; brief, fleeting
летучесть: (chem.) volatility			
	górnolotny: high-flown, pompous		
мимолётный: brief, fleeting			
самолёт: airplane	samolot: airplane		
вертолёт: helicopter			
	bezlotek: penguin		
			izlet: excursion
налёт: raid, incursion; robbery; thin coating, layer	nalot: air-raid; thin coating, layer	nálet: air-raid	nalet: impact, collision; assault
			naletljiv: aggressive; importunate
			poletan: enthusiastic, spirited
			poletarac: young bird, fledgling; young girl, flapper
	podlotek: young bird, fledgling; young girl, flapper		
перелётный: migratory (bird)	przelotny: migratory (bird); brief, fleeting	přelétavý: migratory (bird); brief, fleeting	
пролётка: droshky, cab			
	ulotka: leaflet		
	ulotny: brief, fleeting		
вылет: (act of) flying away	wylot: (act of) flying away; outlet, aperture; cuff (on coat sleeve)	výlet: (act of) flying away; excursion	
			uzletište: airport

NOTES

Basic meaning of root: to fly

leták-*letak*: Compare Ger. *Flugblatt* "leaflet" (<*fliegen* "to fly" + *Blatt* "leaf; sheet of paper").

lotny (third meaning), *летýчесть*: Compare Eng. *volatile* (ult. <Lat. *volare* "to fly"), Ger. *flüchtig* "volatile" (<*fliegen* "to fly").

górnolotny: The first element is from *górny* "upper"; compare Eng. *high-flown*, Rus. *высокопáрный*, S-C *visokoparan*.

izlet: modeled on Ger. *Ausflug* "excursion" (<*aus* "out" + *fliegen* "to fly"); compare also Eng. *excursion* (ult. <Lat. *ex* "out" + *currere* "to run"), Cz. *výlet* below, Pol. *wycieczka*.

ulotka: See note on *leták*-*letak*.

výlet: See note on *izlet*.

ЛЕЗ, ЛЕС, ЛАЗ	LEŹ, ŁAZ	LEZ, LÉZ	LJES, LAZ, LAŽ
†*лезть*, *лáзить* (*лáзать*): to crawl; to climb	†*leźć*, *łazić*: to crawl; to climb	*lézti*: to crawl; to climb	*ljesti* (*laziti*): to crawl; to climb
		lezavý: piercing (cold, etc.)	
лазýтчик (arch.): scout, spy			
			ljestve (pl.): ladder
лéстница: staircase; ladder			*ljestvica*: scale (musical, etc.); small ladder
лаз: manhole			
			lazila (pl.): scaffolding
лазéйка: hole (in fence, etc.) big enough to pass through; loophole			
			bezizlazan: hopeless, desperate (situation, etc.)
			dolazak: arrival
[R]	[P]	[Cz]	[S-C]

[R]	[P]	[Cz]	[S-C]
		dolézavý: intrusive, meddlesome	
			izlaz: exit, (act of) going out; exit, egress, way out; way out, escape (from a situation); rise, rising (esp. of the sun)
			izlazište: point of departure
			iznalaziti: to invent; to discover
*налéзть (coll.): to fit (said of shoes, clothing); to swarm, collect (said of insects)		*nalézti: to find; to swarm, collect (said of insects)	*naljesti: to pass by
налезáть (coll.): to fit (said of shoes, clothing)		nalézati: to find	nalaziti: to find
		naleziště: finding place; mineral deposit; habitat	nalazište: finding place; mineral deposit; habitat
		nalezenec: foundling	
		podlézavý: fawning, servile	
			prelazan, prijelazan: transitory, temporary; transitional; (gram.) transitive; contagious
			prevazilaziti: to surpass, exceed
пролáза (coll.): sly, cunning person			
			prolazan: transient, ephemeral; passable (road)

[R]	[P]	[Cz]	[S-C]
			prolaznik: passerby
			pronalaziti: to invent; to discover
			razilaženje: separation, parting; divergence (of opinion, etc.)
	*znaleźć: to find		snalaziti: to befall (misfortune, etc.)
			snalažljiv: resourceful, clever
	właz: manhole		ulaz: entrance, entry (act of entering); entrance (place of entry)
вы́лазка: sortie, sally; excursion			
	*wynaleźć: to invent; to discover	vynalézti, vynalézati: to invent; to discover	
			zalazak: setting (of the sun)

NOTES

Basic meaning of root: to crawl; to climb

The broader meaning "to go" is apparent in a number of Russian, Polish and Czech derivatives; it has become the regular meaning in compound formations in Serbo-Croatian, where the root supplies the imperfective counterparts of compound verbs formed from root И(Д) (etc.). See the introductory notes on roots ХОД (etc.) and И(Д) (etc.).

lezavý: ="creeping (into one's bones, etc.)."

ljestvica: Compare Eng. scale (ult. <Lat. scala, usually pl. scalae "staircase; ladder").

bezizlazan: See the third meaning of izlaz.

iznalaziti: See nalaziti and note on S-C iznahoditi.

nalézti, nalézati-nalaziti: See note on Rus. находи́ть, Cz. nacházeti, S-C nahoditi.

naljesti: orig. "to come up, approach."

prelazan, prijelazan: A contagious disease "goes across," i.e. passes, from one person to another; regarding the other meanings, see note on Rus. перехóдный et al. and преходя́щий, Pol. przejściowy.

prevazilaziti: See note on Rus. превосходи́ть; the letter i before the root-syllable was inserted by analogy with the perfective form prevazići (q.v.).

прола́за: See note on Rus. пройдóха.

prolazan: See note on Rus. перехóдный et al. and преходя́щий, Pol. przejściowy.

pronalaziti: See nalaziti and note on S-C iznahoditi.

razilaženje: The letter i before the root-syllable was inserted in razilaziti se "to separate" by analogy with the perfective form razići se.

znaleźć-snalaziti: See note on Pol. znajdować, S-C snaći.

snalažljiv: <snalaziti se "to find one's way, get one's bearings"; regarding the meaning of snalaziti, see note on Pol. znajdować, S-C snaći.

вы́лазка: Compare Eng. sortie (ult. <Fr. sortir "to go out").

wynaleźć-vynalézti: See obsolete Pol. naleźć "to find," Cz. nalézti above and note on Pol. wynajdować, Cz. vynajíti.

ЛИ, ЛЕ, ЛОЙ	LA, LI, LE, ŁÓJ	LI, LÍ, LE, LÉ, LŮJ	LI, LJE, LIJE, LOJ
лить: to pour (tr. and intr.); to cast, found (metal)	lać: to pour (tr. and intr.); to cast, found (metal)	líti: to pour (tr.); to cast, found (metal)	liti (lijevati): to pour (tr. and intr.); to cast, found (metal)
	lej: funnel; bomb-crater, shell-hole		lijevak: funnel
литéйная: foundry			livnica, ljevaonica: foundry
		litina: cast iron	
		lívanec: pancake	
	łój: suet, tallow	lůj: suet, tallow	loj: suet, tallow
	jednolity: uniform, homogeneous; unitary	jednolitý: solid, compact	
кровоизлия́ние: hemorrhage			
	różnolity: heterogeneous		
Водолéй: (astr.) Aquarius			Vodolija: (astr.) Aquarius
[R]	[P]	[Cz]	[S-C]

[R]	[P]	[Cz]	[S-C]
			izliv, izljev: (kitchen) sink; outpouring (of emotion, etc.); outflow, discharge
нали́вка: fruit liqueur	nalewka: fruit liqueur	nálevka: funnel; bomb-crater, shell-hole	
		nálevna: bar, pub	
		nálevník: (zool.) infusorian	naljevnjak: (zool.) infusorian
отли́в: low tide; tint	odlew: (act of) casting, founding; casting, cast metal	odliv: low tide; outflow	odliv: low tide; (act of) casting, founding; casting, cast metal
	odlewnia: foundry		
поли́ва: glaze, enamel	polewa: glaze, enamel	poleva: glaze, enamel; icing (on cake)	
поли́вка: (act of) watering	polewka: soup; sauce, gravy	polévka, polívka: soup	polivka: soup
			poloj: marshland
подли́вка: sauce, gravy	podlewa: sauce, gravy		
перело́й (arch.): gonorrhea			
прили́в: high tide; flow, influx; surge (of energy, etc.)		příliv: high tide; flow, influx	priliv: high tide; flow, influx
проли́в: strait		průliv: strait	proliv, proljev: diarrhea
слия́ние: merger, amalgamation; confluence			slijevanje: confluence
	zlew: confluence; (kitchen) sink		sliv, slijev: river basin
	zlewisko: river basin		
	zlewka: beaker		
сли́вки (pl.): cream	zlewki (pl.): slops, leavings	slivky (pl.): slops, leavings	
		slévárna: foundry	
сли́ток: ingot		slitek: ingot	
		slitina: alloy	slitina: alloy
		úlitba: libation, drink offering	

[R]	[P]	[Cz]	[S-C]
влия́ние: influence		vliv: influence	
	wylew: flood; outflow, discharge	výlev: outpouring (of emotion, etc.); outflow, discharge	
		výlevka: (kitchen) sink	
возлия́ние: libation, drink offering			
зали́в: gulf, bay	zalew: flood	záliv: gulf, bay	zaliv: gulf, bay

NOTES

Basic meaning of root: to pour

A secondary meaning occurring in some of the derivatives is "to cast, found (metal)." (Compare Eng. found, foundry [ult. ‹Lat. fundere "to pour"].)

lej: Regarding the semantic shift from "funnel" to "funnel-like hole in the ground," compare Cz. nálevka below, Rus. воро́нка "funnel; bomb-crater, shell-hole," Ger. Trichter "funnel; bomb-crater, shell-hole."

łój et al.: The word originally referred to the process of melting down by which tallow is obtained.

jednolity-jednolitý: ="cast from a single piece"; the Czech word is borrowed from Polish. Compare różnolity.

кровоизлия́ние: The first element is from кровь "blood."

różnolity: ="cast from a number of different pieces"; the first element is from różny "different." Compare jednolity-jednolitý.

Водоле́й-Vodolija: See note under root ВОД (etc.).

nálevka: See note on lej.

nálevna: Compare Ger. Schenke "bar, pub" (‹schenken "to pour").

nálevník-naljevnjak: a loan-translation of NLat. infusorium (‹Lat. in "in" + fundere "to pour"); the class of protozoa known as "infusoria" were first observed in infusions following exposure to the air. Compare Pol. wymoczek "infusorian" (‹wy- + moczyć "to soak"), Ger. Aufgusstierchen "infusorian" (‹Aufguss "infusion" [‹auf "up, on" + giessen "to pour"] + Tierchen "small animal").

отли́в (second meaning): ="flow (i.e. play) of color."

поли́ва-polewa-poleva (first meaning): The reference is to the fusing process by which enamel is produced; compare Eng. enamel (‹the prefix en- + an earlier form of Fr. émail "enamel," which derives from a Germanic word akin to Ger. schmelzen "to melt, smelt, fuse").

перелóй: ="flow, discharge."

proliv, proljev: Compare Eng. diarrhea (ult. <Gr. διά "through" + ῥεῖν "to flow").

сли́вки: ="what is poured off."

сли́ток-slitek: Compare Eng. ingot (ult. <OEng. in "in" + gēotan "to pour").

влия́ние-vliv: The Russian word is a loan-translation of Fr. influence (ult. <Lat. in "in" + fluere "to flow"); the Czech word is borrowed, in modified form, from Russian. Compare Ger. Einfluss "influence" (<ein- "in" + fliessen "to flow"), Hung. befolyás "influence" (<be- "in" + folyni "to flow"), Pol. wpływ, S-C upliv, utjecaj and uticaj.

ЛИХ, ЛИШ	LICH	LICH, LIŠ	LIH, LIŠ
лихóй: bad, evil; bold, dashing	lichy: poor, wretched, shabby	lichý: odd (number); false, unfounded	lih: odd (number)
ли́хо: evil; misfortune	licho: odd number; evil; misfortune; (the) deuce, devil		
ли́шний: superfluous, unnecessary; spare, extra			
лишь: only (adv.)			
лиши́ть, лиша́ть: to deprive			lišiti, lišavati: to deprive
лиходе́й (arch.): scoundrel			
лихора́дка: fever			
изли́шний: superfluous, unnecessary			izlišan: superfluous, unnecessary
изли́шек: surplus, excess			
изли́шество: overindulgence (in food, drink, etc.)			
		příliš: too, excessively; too much	
сли́шком: too, excessively			
[R]	[P]	[Cz]	[S-C]

		upřílišiti, upřílišovati: to exaggerate	
			zaliha: stock, supply, reserve zališan: superfluous, unnecessary
[R]	[P]	[Cz]	[S-C]

NOTES

Basic meaning of root: left over, superfluous; bad

It is a matter of dispute whether the meaning "bad" is an outgrowth of the notion of "superfluity" or reflects what was originally a separate root.

At least insofar as the first meaning is concerned, the root is related to Eng. lend and loan, Lat. (re)linquere "to leave behind" (>Eng. relinquish) and reliquiae "remains" (>Eng. relic).

лишь: orig. "more"; the word is an old comparative form (<ли́ше) of лихо́й in the earlier sense of "excessive."

лиши́ть-lišiti: <лихо́й-lih in the earlier sense of "bereft"---an extension of the notion "left over, odd, unpaired."

лихора́дка: in all likelihood, originally a taboo-word meaning "the evil-wishing one" in which the second element is related to рад "glad."

příliš: <OCz. přieliš; pří- here = pře-.

upřílišiti: <příliš.

ЛИК, ЛИЦ, ЛИЧ	LIC, LICZ	LIC, LÍC, LIČ, LÍČ, LIŠ	LIK, LIC, LIČ
лик (arch.): face			lik: shape, form; face
лицо́: face; person	lice (lit.): cheek lica (pl., lit.): face	líce (lit.): cheek; face	lice: face; person
		líc: front side; (lit.) cheek; (lit.) face	
личи́на: mask (arch.); guise			
личи́нка: larva			ličinka: larva
[R]	[P]	[Cz]	[S-C]

[R]	[P]	[Cz]	[S-C]
		líčiti: to paint one's face, apply make-up; to describe	ličiti: to paint; to be fitting, proper; (na + acc.) to resemble
лицева́ть: to turn (a coat, dress, etc.)	licować: to conform, be in harmony (with); to be fitting, proper		
		líciti: to aim (a gun)	
		lišiti: to distinguish, differentiate	
двули́чный: two-faced, insincere	dwulicowy: two-faced, insincere		dvoličan: two-faced, insincere
			jednoličan, jednolik: monotonous; uniform
			krajolik: landscape
лицеде́й (arch.): actor			
лицеме́р: hypocrite		licoměrník: hypocrite	licemjer: hypocrite
лицеприя́тие (arch.): partiality, bias			
лицезре́ть (arch.): to contemplate, observe			
		přelíčení: trial, hearing	
безразли́чный: indifferent, apathetic; unimportant, a matter of indifference			
			doličan: fitting, proper
			izlika: excuse, pretext
изобличи́ть, изоблича́ть (lit.): to expose, unmask (an enemy, criminal, etc.)			izobličiti, izobličavati: to distort, disfigure; to expose, unmask (an enemy, criminal, etc.)

[R]	[P]	[Cz]	[S-C]
нали́чие: presence; availability			naličje: reverse (of a coin)
нали́чный: available, on hand; cash (attr.)			nalik, naličan: similar
			neprilika: trouble, distress, predicament; embarrassment
о́блик: (outward) appearance; character, nature (of a person)			oblik: shape, form; (outward) appearance
обли́чье (coll.): (outward) appearance	oblicze: face	obličej: face	obličje: shape, form; (outward) appearance; face
обличи́ть, обличáть (lit.): to expose, unmask (an enemy, criminal, etc.); (обличáть only) to show, reveal			*obličiti: to shape, form; to expose, unmask (an enemy, criminal, etc.)
			odlika: excellence, distinction; (bot., zool.) kind, variety
отличи́ть, отличáть: to distinguish, differentiate; to distinguish, honor		odlišiti, odlišovati: to distinguish, differentiate	odlikovati: to distinguish, honor
отли́чный: excellent; different		odlišný: different	odličan: excellent
	policzek: cheek	políček: slap in the face	
			prilika: opportunity; occasion; condition, circumstance; likeness; likelihood, probability
прили́чный: decent, seemly; passable, fair			priličan: fitting, proper;

[R]	[P]	[Cz]	[S-C]
			passable, fair; similar
различи́ть, различа́ть: to distinguish, differentiate; to distinguish, discern		rozlišiti, rozlišovati: to distinguish, differentiate	razlikovati: to distinguish, differentiate; to distinguish, discern
разли́чный: different; varied	rozliczny: varied	rozličný: varied	različan, različit: different; varied
			slik: rhyme
			slika: picture
			slikar: painter, artist
сличи́ть, слича́ть: to collate, compare			sličiti: to resemble
	śliczny: pretty, handsome	sličný (lit.): pretty, handsome	sličan: similar
ули́ка: evidence (of a crime)			
[R]	[P]	[Cz]	[S-C]

NOTES

Basic meaning of root: shape, form; face

The alternation between the two root-meanings (with further semantic development, in some instances, from "face" to "cheek") has parallels in Lat. facies "shape, form; face" (>Eng. face), Fr. figure "figure; face," Pol. twarz, Cz. tvář and tvar, S-C obraz.

A number of derivatives reflect the notion of similarity (i.e. likeness in form or face), whence the concept of conformity and, finally, seemliness or propriety. (See the introductory note on root ДО[Б] [etc.] and compare Rus. схо́дный, S-C shodan.) In combination with prefixes denoting separation, the root produces derivatives which express the idea of difference or distinction (i.e. contrast in form or face).

лицо́-lice (S-C): Regarding the semantic transition from "face" to "person," compare Eng. person (ult. <Lat. persona "mask worn by actors"), Gr. πρόσωπον "face; person," Hung. személy "person" (orig. "face").

личи́нка-ličinka: The Russian word (from which the Serbo-Croatian word is borrowed) is a diminutive of личи́на; the present entomological meaning arose, as a loan-translation, from the use of derivatives of Lat. larva "mask" in that sense in most European languages.

líčiti-ličiti (first meaning): The underlying sense is "to give (s.th.)

a form or appearance"; the Czech word also means "to paint or whitewash" in dialectal usage.

líciti: ="to rest a gun against one's cheek in order to take aim."

lišiti: a secondary formation resulting from loss of the prefix in *odlišiti* or *rozlišiti*.

jednoličan, *jednolik*: See note under root ОДИН (etc.).

лицедéй: See note under root ДЕ (etc.).

лицемéр et al.: generally explained as "one who measures his face (*i.e.* carefully controls his expression so as to conceal his true thoughts)"; an alternative theory is that the second element is a corrupted form of root МЕН (etc.), in which case the sense of the word would be "one who changes his face."

лицеприя́тие: a Church Slavic loan-translation of Gr. *προσωποληψία* (<*πρόσωπον* "person" + *λαμβάνειν* "to take"), which occurs in several New Testament passages and is rendered in the King James Version as "respect of persons" (*i.e.* showing of preference for one person or group of persons over another).

přelíčení: The second element is from *líčiti* in the earlier sense of "to state, maintain, assert."

безразли́чный: Underlying the two meanings are the ideas of "seeing or feeling no difference" and "making no difference"; see *разли́чный* and compare Eng. *indifferent*.

izlika: a relatively new word presumably intended to express the notion of maintaining appearances and proper form.

изобличи́ть-izobličiti (second meaning): ="to show someone's true face"; the Russian word is borrowed from Church Slavic.

нали́чие, *нали́чный*: The basic idea is "before one's face," *i.e.* before one's eyes, visible, present.

naličje: ="side opposite the face."

neprilika: orig. also "dissimilarity"; compare *prilika* and *priličan*.

обличи́ть-obličiti: See note on *изобличи́ть-izobličiti*; the Russian word is borrowed from Church Slavic.

odlišiti, *odlišný*: <**odličiti*, **odličný*.

odličan: <Rus. *отли́чный*.

prilika: The first three meanings reflect the notion of "suitability, fitness" (compare *priličan*); regarding the semantic link between "likeness" and "likelihood," compare the English sentences *It looks like rain* and *Rain is likely*.

rozlišiti: <**rozličiti*.

slik: orig. "similarity."

slika: The progression in the meaning has been "similarity" > "likeness" > "picture."

śliczny-sličný: The prefix, which has the meaning "good," is one encountered in only a few other words (see Rus. *сдóба* and *счáстье et al.*, Pol.

zboże and zdobić, Cz. zboží and zdobiti).

улика: See note on изобличить-izobličiti.

ЛОМ	ŁOM, ŁAM	LOM, LAM, LÁM	LOM, LAM
ломи́ть (coll.): to break; to charge forward, break through; to ache		lomiti: (math.) to divide; (arch.) to break	lomiti: to break
лома́ть: to break	łamać: to break	lámati: to break	lamati: to break
	łam: newspaper column		
	łamańce (pl.): acrobatics; contortions		
			brakolom, brakolomstvo: adultery
			brodolom: shipwreck
головоло́мка: puzzle, riddle		hlavolam: puzzle, riddle	
каменоло́мня: quarry, stone-pit	kamieniołom: quarry, stone-pit	kamenolom: quarry, stone-pit	kamenolom: quarry, stone-pit
	łamigłówka: puzzle, riddle		
вероло́мный: perfidious, disloyal	wiarołomny: perfidious, disloyal	věrolomný: perfidious, disloyal	vjeroloman: perfidious, disloyal
перело́м: break; (med.) fracture; crisis, turning-point	przełom: (mil.) breakthrough; crisis, turning-point	přelom: break; crisis, turning-point	prelom, prijelom: break; (med.) fracture; crisis, turning-point
проло́м: breach		průlom: breach; (mil.) break-through	prolom: breach
			razlomak: (math.) fraction
	ułamek: fragment; (math.) fraction		
	ułomny: crippled		
взло́мщик: housebreaker, burglar	włamywacz: housebreaker, burglar		
		zlomek: fragment; (math.) fraction	
[R]	[P]	[Cz]	[S-C]

	złamanie: break; (med.) fracture; breach, violation, infraction	zlomenina: (med.) fracture	
[R]	[P]	[Cz]	[S-C]

NOTES

Basic meaning of root: to break

The Slavic root is related to Eng. lame.

ломи́ть et al.: the original primary verb, supplanted in Russian, Polish and Czech by the iterative form, лома́ть et al.; Pol. łomić is obsolete.

łam: Compare Ger. Spalte "newspaper column" (<spalten "to split").

brakolom, brakolomstvo: See note under root БР (etc.).

brodolom: The first element is from brod "ship."

каменоло́мня et al.: The first element is from ка́мень-kamień-kámen-kamen "stone"; compare Ger. Steinbruch "quarry" (<Stein "stone" + brechen "to break").

вероло́мный et al.: See note under root $ВЕР_1$ (etc.).

перело́м et al., razlomak, ułamek, zlomek, zlomenina, złamanie: Compare Eng. fracture, fraction and fragment (all ult. <Lat. frangere "to break"), Rus. дробь "fraction" (<дроби́ть "to crush, splinter").

złamanie (third meaning): Compare Eng. infraction (ult. <Lat. frangere "to break"), Ger. Verbrechen "crime" (<brechen "to break"), Fin. rikos "crime" (<rikkoa "to break").

ЛЮБ	LUB	LIB, LÍB	LJUB
люби́ть: to love, like	lubić: to love, like	líbiti (arch.): to love, like líbiti se: to please líbati: to kiss	ljubiti: to love, like; to kiss
любова́ться: to admire	lubować się: to take delight (in)	libovati si: to be pleased; to take a keen interest (in) (e.g. music, sports)	
любо́й: any	luby (lit.): dear, beloved	libý (lit.): pleasant	
[R]	[P]	[Cz]	[S-C]

[R]	[P]	[Cz]	[S-C]
			ljubak: lovely, charming; pleasant
любе́зный: kind, amiable	lubieżny: lustful, lascivious	líbezný: lovely, charming; pleasant	ljubazan, ljubezan: kind, amiable
любо́вь: love			ljubav: love
	lubość: pleasure	libost: pleasure	
		libůstka: hobby; fancy, whim	
люби́тель: amateur; (sports-, book-, etc.) lover			ljubitelj: (sports-, book-, etc.) lover
люби́мец: favorite (n.)			ljubimac: favorite (n.)
			ljubica, ljubičica: violet
		líbánky (pl.): honeymoon	
	lub: or		
	lubo (arch.): although		
честолю́бие: ambition			častoljublje: ambition
			domoljublje: patriotism
			ljubomora: jealousy
любопы́тный: curious, inquisitive; curious, interesting			ljubopitan: curious, inquisitive
любостра́стие (arch.): lust, carnality			
		libovolný: optional; any; arbitrary, high-handed	
любозна́тельный: curious, inquisitive			
		libozvučný: euphonious, melodious	
прелюбоде́й (arch.): adulterer			preljubočinac: adulterer

[R]	[P]	[Cz]	[S-C]
			rodoljublje: patriotism
самолю́бие: self-esteem, pride	samolubstwo: selfishness	samolibost: smugness, complacency	samoljublje: egotism
себялю́бие: selfishness			sebeljublje: selfishness
сластолю́бие (arch.): lust, carnality			
славолю́бие (lit.): love of glory			slavoljublje: ambition
		škodolibost: gloating (n.)	
	oblubieniec (arch.): fiancé; bridegroom	oblíbenec: favorite (n., masc.)	
	oblubienica (arch.): fiancée; bride	oblíbenka: favorite (n., fem.)	
			preljubnik: adulterer
			*sljubiti se: to coalesce, blend
	ślub: vow; wedding	slib: promise	
	ulubieniec: favorite (n.)		

NOTES

Basic meaning of root: to love, like

The Russian compound formations (e.g. честолю́бие) are all of Church Slavic origin.

The Slavic root is related to Eng. love, Ger. lieben "to love," Lat. libido "desire" (>Eng. libido, libidinous).

любо́й et al.: The underlying meaning of любо́й is "whichever one you like"; compare Ger. beliebig "any" (<lieben "to love"), Cz. libovolný below, Pol. dowolny, S-C proizvoljan. A doublet form, лю́бый, and S-C ljub, both identical in meaning with Pol. luby, survive only in dialect.

libůstka: a diminutive of libost.

люби́тель (first meaning): See note on Cz. ochotník.

ljubica, ljubičica: Compare ljubak.

lub: ="if you like" (by way of introducing an alternative); compare Lat. vel "or" (<velle "to want, wish"), Port. quer ... quer "either (whether) ... or" (<querer "to want, wish"), Hung. akár ... akár "either (whether) ... or" (<akarni "to want, wish").

lubo: For the sense, see note on similarly derived Rus. хоть et al.

честолю́бие-častoljublje: See note under root ЧТ (etc.).

domoljublje: The first element is from dom "house, home."

ljubomora: The second element is from moriti "to kill; to torment" (q.v.) or mora "nightmare."

любопы́тный-ljubopitan: See note under root ПЫТ (etc.).

libovolný: See note on любо́й et al.

любозна́тельный: See note on Cz. vědychtivý.

libozvučný: The second element is from zvuk "sound"; see note on Rus. благозву́чный, S-C blagozvučan.

samoljublje: ‹Rus. самолю́бие.

сластолю́бие: The first element is from сласть "sweetness; pleasure"; the word is a Church Slavic borrowing modeled on Gr. φιληδονία "love of pleasure" (‹φίλος "loving" + ἡδονή "pleasure" ‹ ἡδύς "sweet").

slavoljublje: See note on честолю́бие-častoljublje.

škodolibost: The first element is from škoda "damage, harm"; thus, the meaning is "rejoicing at another's misfortune." The Czech word is modeled o Ger. Schadenfreude "gloating" (‹Schaden "damage, harm" + Freude "joy"). (Cz škoda was borrowed from Old High Ger. scado [=modern Ger. Schaden].) Compar Rus. злора́дство, S-C zloradost, zluradost.

sljubiti se: orig. "to become friends."

ślub-slib: The original reference was to a vow exchanged by lovers or by an engaged couple.

ЛУЧ$_1$	ŁĄCZ	LUK, LUČ, LOUČ	LUK, LUČ, LUDŽ
	łączyć: to join, unite, combine (tr.); to connect; to couple (a male animal with a female)	loučiti (lit.): to separate (tr.)	lučiti: to separate (tr.); (med.) to secrete
	łącznik: (punc.) hyphen; (gram.) copulative verb; (elec.) switch; (tech.) joint		
		lučba (arch.): chemistry	ludžba (arch.): chemistry
	dołączyć, dołączać: to add; to append, annex, enclose		
			izlučiti, izlučivati: to separate
[R]	[P]	[Cz]	[S-C]

			(tr.); (med.) to secrete
отлучи́ть, отлуча́ть: to excommunicate	odłączyć, odłączać: to separate (tr.); to disconnect; to wean (a child)	odloučiti, odlučovati: to separate (tr.)	odlučiti, odlučivati: to decide; to separate (tr.)
отлу́чка: absence		odluka: separation	odluka: decision
разлучи́ть, разлуча́ть: to separate (tr.)	rozłączyć, rozłączać: to separate (tr.); to disconnect	rozloučiti, rozlučovati: to separate (tr.)	razlučiti, razlučivati: to separate (tr.); to distinguish, differentiate
случи́ть, случа́ть: to couple (a male animal with a female)	złączyć, złączać: to join, unite, combine (tr.); to connect	sloučiti, slučovati: to join, unite, combine (tr.)	
	włączyć, włączać: to include; to switch on (current, etc.)		
	wyłączyć, wyłączać: to exclude; to switch off (current, etc.)	vyloučiti, vylučovati: to exclude; to expel; to excommunicate; (med.) to secrete	
	załączyć, załączać: to append, annex, enclose		zalučiti, zalučivati: to wean (an animal)
[R]	[P]	[Cz]	[S-C]

NOTES

Basic meaning of root: to separate; to join, unite

The original root-meaning---still apparent in Rus. лук and Cz.-S-C luk "(archer's) bow," Pol. łęk "saddle-bow"---is presumed to have been "to bend." The addition of a prefix expressing separation (e.g. in отлучи́ть et al.) produced the meaning "to separate," while the addition of one expressing the idea of junction (in случи́ть et al.) gave rise to the meaning "to join, unite." The resulting confusion as to the actual meaning of the root caused the primary verb to fluctuate between the two derived meanings; in earlier usage, Pol. łączyć, Cz. loučiti and S-C lučiti could mean either "to separate" or "to join, unite." (ORus. лучити, however, meant only "to separate.") Pol. dołączyć, włączyć and załączyć and S-C zalučiti reflect the present-day meaning of the respective primary verbs.

lučiti (second meaning): See note on Rus. вы́делить, Pol. wydzielić.

łącznik (first and second meanings): respectively a punctuation mark and a word which serve as links; compare Ger. Bindestrich "hyphen" (<binden "to bind, link" + Strich "stroke, line").

lučba-ludžba: The Czech word is formed from loučiti in the older sense of "to join, unite" (in this case, ="to mix, combine"); ludžba is borrowed from Czech.

izlučiti (second meaning): See note on lučiti.

odlučiti, odluka (S-C): The notions of separation and decision are connected in other languages as well; compare Eng. decide (ult. <Lat. de- "off + caedere "to cut"), Ger. entscheiden "to decide" (<scheiden "to separate") Fr. trancher "to cut; to decide."

ЛУЧ$_2$			LUČ
лу́чший: better, best (a.)			
благополу́чие: well-being, prosperity			
злополу́чный: unlucky, ill-fated			
получи́ть, получа́ть: to receive			polučiti, polučivati: to get, obtain; to attain, achieve
случи́ться, случа́ться: to happen			slučiti se, slučavati se: to happen
слу́чай: case, instance; accident, chance; opportunity; occurrence, event			slučaj: case, instance; accident, chance; occurrence, event
улучи́ть, улуча́ть: to seize (an opportunity, the right moment, etc.)			*ulučiti: to seize (an opportunity, the right moment, etc.)
[R]			[S-C]

NOTES

Basic meaning of root: to receive what is allotted by fate

The root-meaning is most clearly apparent in ORus. лучай and dialectal слу́ка "fate"; in modern Russian and Serbo-Croatian, it is reflected in words expressing such notions as "receiving," "happening" and "chance." (An earlir root-meaning, "to wait, watch [for s.th.]," survives in улучи́ть-ulučiti.) he links with Polish and Czech are uncertain.

лу́чший: A shift from the neutral notion of "chance, luck" to the posi- ive one of "good luck" is apparent here; see note on S-C čest.

благополу́чие: See note under root БЛАГ (etc.).

slučaj: ‹Rus. слу́чай.

ЛЮД	LUD(Z)	LID, LÍD	LJUD
люд (arch.): people taken as a group (e.g. working people)	lud: people, nation; people taken as a group (e.g. working people)	lid: people, nation; people taken as a group (e.g. working people)	
лю́ди (pl.): people (in general)	ludzie (pl.): people (in general)	lidé (pl.): people (in general)	ljudi (pl.): people (in general)
лю́дный: populous; crowded	ludny: populous; crowded	lidnatý: populous; crowded	
	ludność: population		
людско́й: human	ludzki: human; humane	lidský: human; humane	ljudski: human; humane
	ludzkość: humanity, mankind; humanity, humaneness	lidskost: humanity, humaneness	ljudskost: humanity, humaneness
		lidstvo: humanity, mankind	ljudstvo: humanity, mankind; crowd; crew; staff
			ljudeskara, ljudina: giant
	ludobójstwo: genocide		
людое́д: cannibal	ludojad: cannibal	lidojed: cannibal	
		lidumil: philanthropist, humanitarian	
	ludoznawstwo: ethnology		
	ludożerca: cannibal	lidožrout: cannibal	ljudožder: cannibal
многолю́дный: populous; crowded			mnogoljudan: populous; crowded
	wielkolud: giant		
[R]	[P]	[Cz]	[S-C]

	nadludzki: superhuman	nadlidský: superhuman	nadljudski: superhuman
нелюди́м: unsociable person, misanthrope			
	odludek: unsociable person, misanthrope		odljud: monster, inhumanly crue person
	odludny: deserted, desolate		
		vlídný: affable, friendly	uljudan: polite
[R]	[P]	[Cz]	[S-C]

NOTES

Basic meaning of root: people

The Slavic root is related to Ger. Leute "people" and probably to Lat. liber "free" (>Eng. liberty, liberal), which is thought to have referred originally to those who were "of the people" as distinct from the slave population.

ljudeskara, ljudina: an instance of derivatives which refer to an individual rather than to people collectively; the suffixes have augmentative force.

ludobójstwo: See note under root БИ (etc.).

lidumil: Compare Eng. philanthropist (ult. <Gr. φίλος "loving, friendly" + ἄνθρωπος "man, human being").

ludoznawstwo: See note under root ЗНА (etc.).

многолю́дный-mnogoljudan: The first element is from мно́го-mnogo "much, many."

wielkolud: See note on ljudeskara, ljudina.

vlídný-uljudan: ="friendly toward, easily mingling with people"; compare Ger. leutselig "affable" (<Leute "people" + selig "happy, blissful").

MAX	MACH, MASZ	MACH, MÁCH	MAH, MAŠ
махнýть, махáть: to wave, beckon; to swing, brandish	machnąć, machać: to wave, beckon; to swing, brandish	máchnouti, máchati: to wave, beckon; to swing, brandish; (máchati only) to rinse (clothing)	mahnuti, mahati: to wave, beckon; to swing, brandish
			*mahnuti se: to abandon, relinquish
			mašiti se, mašati se: to grasp (at), reach (for)
мах (coll.): movement; stroke, blow			mah: movement; stroke, blow; moment, instant
			mahalica: fan
			domašaj: range (of a gun)
			nadmašiti, nadmašivati: to surpass, exceed
			nadmašan: superior; preponderant
			omaška: mistake
			odmah: immediately
			premašiti, premašivati: to surpass, exceed
прóмах: miss (failure to hit s.th.); blunder			promašaj: miss (failure to hit s.th.); failure
размáх: swing, sweep; wingspread (of a bird), wingspan (of an airplane); scope, range	rozmach: swing, sweep; dash, élan	rozmach: swing, sweep; upsurge (economic, cultural, etc.)	
			umah: immediately
	zamach: stroke, blow; attempt (on s.o.'s life, etc.); putsch, coup		zamah: swing, sweep; impetus, momentum
	zamaszysty: brisk, vigorous		zamašan, zamašit: important, momentous
[R]	[P]	[Cz]	[S-C]

NOTES

Basic meaning of root: to wave

The secondary meaning "to grasp, reach" occurs in Serbo-Croatian.

máchati: The meaning "to rinse" is the result of relatively recent crossing with a different root; compare OCz. mákati and modern máčeti "to soak."

mahnuti se: The same notion of "waving away," i.e. giving up, is apparent in Eng. waive (related to wave).

mah: Compare Eng. movement and moment (both ult. ‹Lat. movere "to move").

nadmašiti: ="to reach beyond"; compare premašiti, Cz. přesáhnouti. A somewhat similar formation is Ger. übertreffen "to surpass" (‹über "over, beyond" + treffen "to hit, strike").

nadmašan: Compare nadmašiti.

omaška: The underlying idea is that of a false move, an unsuccessful attempt to grasp something; the prefix performs roughly the same function here as Eng. mis- in mistake. Compare Rus. оши́бка "mistake" (‹о + obs. шиб-и́ть "to hit, strike"), обмо́лвка, оговóрка (second meaning).

odmah: Compare mah.

premašiti: See note on nadmašiti.

про́мах-promašaj: The prefix conveys the idea of passing beyond or wide of the mark.

umah: Compare mah.

zamach (third meaning): Compare Eng. coup (‹Fr. coup, literally "stroke, blow").

zamah: Compare Eng. momentum (ult. ‹Lat. movere "to move").

zamašan, zamašit: ="sweeping, far-reaching"; compare Eng. momentous (ult. ‹Lat. movere "to move").

МАЛ	MAŁ, MAL	MAL, MÁL	MAO, MAL
ма́лый: small, little	mały: small, little	malý: small, little	mao: small, little
ма́ленький: small, little	maleńki: tiny	malinký: tiny	malen: small, little
ма́лость (coll.): trifle	małostka: trifle	maličkost: trifle	malenkost: trifle
ма́льчик: boy			
		málem: almost	malone, malne: almost
[R]	[P]	[Cz]	[S-C]

[R]	[P]	[Cz]	[S-C]
			malodoban: minor, under age
малоду́шный: pusillanimous, faint-hearted	małoduszny: pusillanimous, faint-hearted	maloduchý, malodušný: pusillanimous, faint-hearted	malodušan: pusillanimous, faint-hearted
малокро́вие: anemia	małokrwistość: oligemia		malokrvnost: anemia
малоле́тний: young, juvenile; minor, under age	małoletni: minor, under age		maloljetan: minor, under age
		malomocenství: leprosy	
	małomówny: taciturn	málomluvný: taciturn	
		malomyslný: despondent	
			malorijek: taciturn
малова́жный: unimportant	małoważny: unimportant		
малове́рный: skeptical		malověrný: skeptical	
	niemal, nieomal: almost		
		pomalý: slow	
умали́ть, умаля́ть: to belittle, minimize, disparage; (arch.) to diminish, lessen (tr.)			umaliti, umaljivati: to diminish, lessen (tr.)
			umalo: almost
			zamalo: almost; soon

NOTES

Basic meaning of root: small, little

The Slavic root is related to Eng. small and probably to Lat. malus "bad." (The semantic shift from "small" to "bad" is not uncommon; compare Rus. худо́й "thin; bad.")

malodoban: See note on малоле́тний et al.

малоду́шный et al.: Compare Eng. pusillanimous (ult. <Lat. pusillus "very small" + animus "mind, mood"), Ger. kleinmütig "pusillanimous, faint-hearted; despondent" (<klein "small" + Mut "[arch. or in compounds] mind,

mood; [otherwise] courage"), Cz. malomyslný below.

малокро́вие et al.: The second element is from кровь-krew-krv "blood."

малоле́тний et al.: The second element is from ле́то-lato-ljeto "summer; (in Russian and Polish, pl. only) year"; compare Ger. minderjährig "under age" (<minder "less" + Jahr "year"). See also Rus. совершенноле́тний, Pol. pełnoletni et al.

malomocenství: See note under root МО(Г) (etc.).

malomyslný: See note on малоду́шный et al.

МЯ(Т), МУТ, МУЩ	MĘT, MĄC, MUT	MAT, MÁ, MĚŤ, MUT, MOUT	ME(T), MUT, MUĆ
		másti: to confuse, muddle	mesti: to churn (butter); to interfere
мясти́сь (arch.): to be troubled, disturbed		másti se: to be confused; to be mistaken	
мути́ть: to make turbid; to trouble, disturb	mącić: to make turbid; to trouble, disturb	moutiti (arch.): to make turbid; to trouble, disturb	mutiti: to make turbid; to trouble, disturb
мяте́ж: mutiny, revolt			metež: turmoil, confusion; mutiny, revolt
муть: dregs, lees, sediment	męty (pl.): dregs, lees, sediment		mutež, mutljag: dregs, lees, sediment; turbid liquid
му́тный: turbid	mętny: turbid	mutný (lit.): turbid; sad, sorrowful	mutan: turbid
			mućak: rotten egg
безмяте́жный: tranquil, untroubled			
о́мут: whirlpool	odmęt: turbid water; whirlpool; chaos		
		pomatenec: madman	
			pometnja, pomutnja: error, oversight
		*zmásti: to confuse, muddle	smesti, smetati: to prevent, hinder; (smesti only) to disconcert, confuse,
[R]	[P]	[Cz]	[S-C]

[R]	[P]	[Cz]	[S-C]
			embarrass; (smetati only) to trouble, disturb
смяте́ние: panic, disarray		zmatek: turmoil, confusion; panic, disarray	smetenost: confusion, embarrassment, bewilderment
		změť: turmoil, confusion	
			smetnja: obstacle; disturbance
сумя́тица: turmoil, confusion			
смути́ть, смуща́ть: to disconcert, confuse, embarrass; to trouble, disturb	zmącić, zmącać: to make turbid; to trouble, disturb		smutiti, smućivati: to disconcert, confuse, embarrass; to trouble, disturb; to make turbid
сму́та (arch.): sedition; dissension, discord			smuta: snowstorm; muddle-headed person
			smutnja: intrigue, machinations; dissension, discord
сму́тный: dim, indistinct; troubled	smutny, (lit.) smętny: sad, sorrowful	smutný: sad, sorrowful	
возмути́ть, возмуща́ть: to outrage, make indignant; (arch.) to incite to rebellion			uzmutiti, uzmućivati: to make turbid; to trouble, disturb
	zamęt: turmoil, confusion		

NOTES

Basic meaning of root: to make turbid; to confuse, disturb

The original root-meaning, "to stir, mix," survives only in the first meaning of S-C mesti. The modern derivatives show the meaning "to make turbid" (more particularly, to stir a liquid and thus disturb the lees or sediment) as well as such figurative notions as "disturbance," "confusion" and, in some instances, "sorrow." The range of meanings is strikingly paralleled by that of the Latin root TURB (>turba "disturbance, tumult," turbo "whirl-pool, whirlwind" and turbidus "turbid; confused," whence ult. Eng. turbid, turbulent, trouble, disturb).

The present-day root-forms derive from two Common Slavic forms with differing vowel grades, *MĘT (>МЯТ---MAT-MĚŤ---MET) and *MǪT (>МУТ-МУЩ---MĘT-MĄC [and a doublet form MUT]---MUT-MOUT---MUT-MUĆ). The Russian form МУ is of Church Slavic origin.

mástì-mesti, мястúсь: The respective 1 sg. forms are matu, metem, мятýсь. Rus. мястú "to trouble, disturb" is obsolete; the equivalent Polish verb is unattested.

мутúть et al.: properly speaking, iterative forms of Rus. мястú and it analogues in the other languages (see preceding note).

МЕЖ, МЕЖД	MIEDZ, MIĘDZ	MEZ	MEĐ
межá: boundary	miedza: boundary	mez: boundary; limit	međa: boundary
		mezera: interval; gap	
мéжду, (arch.) меж: between, among	między: between, among	mezi: between, among	među: between, among
междуцáрствие: interregnum			
	międzyczas: interval of time	mezidobí: interval of time	
		mezihra: interlude; intermezzo	međuigra: interlude; intermezzo
междомéтие: (gram.) interjection			
	międzymorze: isthmus		
междунарóдный: international	międzynarodowy: international	mezinárodní: international	međunarodan: international
междоусóбие, (arch.) междоусóбица: civil war			međusobica: quarrel
междоусóбный: internecine			međusoban: mutual, reciprocal
		mezivládí: interregnum	međuvlada, međuvlašće: interregnum
[R]	[P]	[Cz]	[S-C]

			međuvrijeme: interval of time
			između: between, among
		obmeziti, obmezovati; omeziti, omezovati: to limit, restrict	omeđiti, omeđivati (omeđavati): to bound, border; to limit, restrict
отмежева́ться, отмежёвываться: to dissociate o.s. (from)			
	pomiędzy: between, among		
перемежа́ться: to alternate			
промежу́ток: interval			
сме́жный: adjacent, adjoining			
		vymeziti, vymezovati: to demarcate; to define	
		zameziti, zamezovati: to prevent	
[R]	[P]	[Cz]	[S-C]

NOTES

asic meaning of root: boundary

The Russian root-form МЕЖД is of Church Slavic origin.

The Slavic root is related to Eng. mid- and middle, Lat. medius "middle a.)" (>Eng. medium, median, mediate), Gr. μέσος "middle (a.)" (>Eng. mesoithic, Mesozoic).

ме́жду et al.: old locative forms whose original meaning was "on the oundary"; Pol. między is for earlier miedzy.

междуца́рствие: The second element is from the root of царь "tsar," а́рствование "reign"; see note on mezivládí et al.

mezihra-međuigra: The second element is from hra-igra "game, play"; ompare Eng. interlude (ult. <Lat. inter "between" + ludus "game, play"), er. Zwischenspiel "interlude" (<zwischen "between" + Spiel "game, play").

междоме́тие: See note under root MET (etc.).

międzymorze: The second element is from morze "sea."

междоусобие et al., междоусобный-međusoban: See note under root СЕБ (etc.).

mezivládí et al.: See note under root ВОЛО (etc.).

отмежеваться: =to draw a boundary between oneself and someone or something.

перемежаться: orig. "to occur at intervals, intermittently"; compare промежуток.

vymeziti (second meaning): See note on Rus. определить, S-C odredijeliti.

zameziti: Compare obmeziti, omeziti.

МЕН	MIAN, MIEN	MĚN, MĚŇ	MIJEN, MJEN
менять: to exchange; to change (tr.)	mieniać: to exchange	měniti: to exchange; to change (tr.)	mijenjati: to exchange; to change (tr.); (gram.) to decline; (gram.) to conjugate
мена: exchange		měna: currency (money); (lit.) change	mijena: exchange change
			mjenica: bill of exchange, draft
изменить, изменять: to change (tr.); to betray			izmijeniti, izmjenjivati: to change (tr.); to exchange
изменник: traitor			
непременный: indispensable, essential			
обменять, обменивать: to exchange		obměniti, obměňovati: to modify, change slightly	
отменить, отменять: to abolish; to revoke, repeal, cancel	odmienić, odmieniać: to change (tr.); (gram.) to decline; (gram.) to conjugate	odměniti, odměňovati: to reward; to remunerate	odmijeniti, odmjenjivati: to relieve (e.g. a sentry)
отменный (arch.): excellent	odmienny: different; changeable, variable; (gram.) declinable		otmjen: elegant, distinguished, stately
[R]	[P]	[Cz]	[S-C]

[R]	[P]	[Cz]	[S-C]
применить, применять: to apply (a method, rule, etc.)			primijeniti, primjenjivati: to apply (a method, rule, etc.)
смéна: replacement; relief (of a sentry, etc.); shift (in a factory, etc.)	zmiana: change; relief (of a sentry, etc.); shift (in a factory, etc.)	směna: exchange; shift (in a factory, etc.)	smjena: replacement; relief (of a sentry, etc.); shift (in a factory, etc.)
		směnka: bill of exchange, draft	
вы́менять, выменивать: to exchange	wymienić, wymieniać: to exchange	vyměniti, vyměňovati: to exchange	
заменить, заменять: to replace	zamienić, zamieniać: to exchange; to change (tr.)	zaměniti, zaměňovati: to replace; to mistake (for), confuse (with)	zamijeniti, zamjenjivati: to replace; to represent (act as a representative of); to mistake (for), confuse (with); to exchange
			zamjenica: (gram.) pronoun

NOTES

Basic meaning of root: to exchange

The secondary meaning "to change," apparent in many of the derivatives, is an outgrowth of the basic root-meaning. (Compare Eng. change and exchange, both ult. <Late Lat. cambiare "to exchange.")

The related notion of "reciprocity, mutuality" underlies such non-Slavic cognates as Eng. mean "base, common, vulgar" (=Ger. gemein "common, general"), Lat. communis "common, general" (>Eng. common) and munus "service; gift" (>Eng. munificent, remunerate).

изменить (second meaning), изменник: The underlying idea is that of "changeability, inconstancy, fickleness."

непременный: orig. "unchanging, immutable"; the word is borrowed from Church Slavic.

отменить: an extension of the idea of changing.

odměniti: an extension of the basic root-meaning; the idea is that of "giving in return for services rendered."

отменный et al.: The Russian word originally meant "different" (see Pol. odmienny), then "special, superior, excellent"; S-C otmjen is borrowed from Russian.

применúть-primijeniti: The underlying idea is that of modifying a thing so that it serves a given purpose; the Serbo-Croatian word is borrowed from Russian.

zamjenica: See note on Pol. zaimek, Cz. zájmeno.

МЕР$_1$, МИР	MIAR, MIER(Z)	MÍR, MÍŘ, MĚR, MĚŘ	MJER
мéра: measure (unit of measurement; action, step [urgent measure, etc.]; extent, degree; moderation)	miara: measure (unit of measurement; extent, degree; size; moderation)	míra: measure (unit of measurement; extent, degree; size; moderation)	mjera: measure (unit of measurement; action, step [urgent measure, etc.]; extent, degree size; moderation)
мéрить: to measure	mierzyć: to measure; to aim	měřiti: to measure	mjeriti: to measure
		míříti: to aim	
мéрный: slow, measured, rhythmic; measuring (attr.)	mierny: moderate; mediocre	měrný: measuring (attr.)	
мéрка: measure (of clothing); ruler (for measuring)	miarka: ruler (for measuring); measuring-glass		
мерúло (lit.): standard, criterion		měřidlo: measuring instrument	mjerilo: standard, criterion; scale, proportion
		mířidlo: sight (on a gun)	
		měřítko: ruler (for measuring); standard, criterion; scale (of a map, etc.)	
		měřictví: geometry	mjerstvo: geometry
	miernictwo: surveying		mjerništvo: surveying
			brzinomjer: speedometer
	czasomierz: chronometer	časoměr: chronometer	
		časomíra: meter (of verse)	
[R]	[P]	[Cz]	[S-C]

чрезмéрный: excessive			
	drobnomierz (arch.): micrometer		
			istosmjeran: parallel (a.)
лицемéр: hypocrite		licoměrník: hypocrite	licemjer: hypocrite
	miarodajny: authoritative, decisive		mjerodavan: authoritative, decisive
мероприя́тие: measure, action, step (urgent measure, etc.)			
		poloměr: radius	polumjer: radius
			prekomjeran: excessive
равномéрный: even, uniform	równomierny: even, uniform	rovnoměrný: even, uniform	ravnomjeran: even, uniform
		rychloměr: speedometer	
		směrodatný: authoritative, decisive	
		stejnoměrný: even, uniform	
	szybkościomierz: speedometer		
тепломéр: calorimeter	ciepłomierz: thermometer	teploměr: thermometer	toplomjer: thermometer
	współmierny: proportionate, commensurate		
высотомéр: altimeter	wysokościomierz, wysokomierz: altimeter	výškoměr: altimeter	visinomjer: altimeter
высокомéрный: haughty, arrogant			
землемéр: surveyor		zeměměřič: surveyor	zemljomjer: surveyor
безмéрный: immense, boundless	bezmierny: immense, boundless	bezměrný (lit.): immense, boundless	bezmjeran: immense, boundless
	namiar: (naut.) bearing		
намеревáться: to intend			namjeravati: to intend
[R]	[P]	[Cz]	[S-C]

[R]	[P]	[Cz]	[S-C]
	nadmierny: excessive	nadměrný: excessive	
	niezmierny: immense, boundless; extraordinary, extreme	nesmírný, nezměrný: immense, boundless	
	pomiar: measurement	poměr: relation(ship); ratio; attitude (toward s.th.)	
		poměry (pl.): conditions, circumstances	
		přiměřený: suitable, appropriate	primjeren: suitable, appropriate
приме́р: example	przymiar: ruler (for measuring)	příměr: simile, comparison	primjer: example
приме́рный: exemplary, model; approximate			primjeran: exemplary, model
			primjerak: copy (of book, etc.); sample
проме́р: measurement; error in measurement		průměr: diameter; average	promjer: diameter
разме́р: size; scope; meter (of verse); time, measure (of music)	rozmiar: size; scope	rozměr: dimension; size; scope; meter (of verse)	razmjer, razmjera: proportion; ratio; scale (of a map, etc.)
	śmierzyć (arch.): to soothe, allay		
смире́нный: humble			smjeran: humble
		směr: direction, course	smjer: direction, course; purpose, aim
		směrnice: directive, guideline	smjernica: directive, guideline
		souměrný: symmetrical	
соразме́рный: proportionate, commensurate			srazmjeran: proportionate, commensurate
уме́ренный: moderate; temperate			umjeren: moderate; temperate

[R]	[P]	[Cz]	[S-C]
	wymiar: dimension; measurement; administration (of justice)	výměr: land survey; tax assessment; judicial decision	
		výměra: area, acreage	
	zamiar: intention	záměr: intention	
		záměra: measurement	zamjera, zamjerka: objection, reproach

NOTES

Basic meaning of root: measure

In a number of derivatives with technical meanings, the root appears in combination with various words as a suffix corresponding to Eng. -meter (ult. <Gr. μέτρον "measure").

Related non-Slavic words are Eng. mete (out), Ger. messen "to measure," Lat. metiri (past part. mensus) "to measure" (>Eng. measure, dimension), Gr. μέτρον.

ме́рить et al.: denominatives formed from ме́ра et al.

mířiti: a doublet of měřiti, with differentiation of meaning.

brzinomjer: The first element is from brzina "speed."

czasomierz-časoměr: Compare Eng. chronometer (<Gr. χρόνος "time" + -meter).

чрезме́рный: The first element is from чрез (че́рез) "over, across"; see note on prekomjeran.

drobnomierz: The first element is from drobny "small"; compare Eng. micrometer (<Gr. μικρός "small" + -meter).

istosmjeran: See the first meaning of smjer.

лицеме́р et al.: See note under root ЛИК (etc.).

miarodajny-mjerodavan: ="giving the measure," i.e. setting the standard; the word is modeled on Ger. massgebend "authoritative, decisive" (<Mass "measure" + geben "to give"). Compare also Hung. mértékadó "authoritative, decisive" (<mérték "measure" + adni "to give").

мероприя́тие: Compare Ger. Massnahme "measure, action, step" (<Mass "measure" + nehmen "to take").

poloměr-polumjer: modeled on Ger. Halbmesser "radius" (<halb "half" + messen "to measure").

prekomjeran: Compare Ger. übermässig "excessive" (<über "over, across" + Mass "measure").

равноме́рный et al.: Compare Ger. gleichmässig "even, uniform" (<gleich

"equal" + Mass "measure"), Cz. stejnoměrný below.

rychloměr: The first element is from rychlý "quick, swift."

směrodatný: See směr; the word is modeled on Ger. richtunggebend "authoritative, decisive" (<Richtung "direction" + geben "to give"). Compare also Hung. irányadó "authoritative, decisive" (<irány "direction" + adni "to give").

stejnoměrný: See note on равномéрный et al.

szybkościomierz: The first element is from szybkość "speed."

тепломéр et al.: The first element is from тёплый-ciepły-teplý-topao "warm"; compare Eng. calorimeter (<Lat. calor "heat" + -meter), thermometer (<Gr. θερμός "warm" + -meter).

współmierny: Compare Eng. commensurate (ult. <Lat. cum "with" + metiri "to measure").

высотомéр et al.: Compare Eng. altimeter (<Lat. altus "high" + -meter)

высокомéрный: See note under root ВЫС (etc.).

безмéрный et al.: Compare Eng. immense (ult. <Lat. in- "un-" + metiri "to measure").

nadmierny-nadměrný: See note on prekomjeran.

niezmierny et al.: See note on безмéрный et al.

přiměřený-primjeren: ="measured (to)," i.e. adapted, suited; compare Ger. angemessen "suitable, appropriate" (<an "to" + messen "to measure").

příměr-primjer: <Rus. примéр.

průměr-promjer: Compare Eng. diameter (ult. <Gr. διά "through" + μέτρο "measure"), Ger. Durchmesser "diameter" (<durch "through" + messen "to measure"). The second meaning of the Czech word is an extension of the first; compare the figurative use of Eng. cross-section.

śmierzyć, смирéнный-smjeran: Regarding the meaning, compare умéренный-umjeren; the altered root-form in the Russian word arose through confusion with root МИР (etc.) (see, e.g., смúрный).

smjer: <Cz. směr.

souměrný: Compare Eng. symmetrical (ult. <Gr. σύν "with" + μέτρον "measure").

соразмéрный-srazmjeran: See note on współmierny; the Serbo-Croatian word is borrowed from Russian.

умéренный-umjeren: ="measured, in due measure"; compare Ger. mässig "moderate; temperate" (<Mass "measure").

wymiar-výměr: Regarding the third meaning, compare Eng. to mete (="measure") out (justice, punishment, etc.).

zamjera, zamjerka: It has been suggested that the root-meaning here is "to measure with the eyes" and the force of the prefix pejorative, whence the notion of "looking askance, disapproving."

MEC, MEШ, MEX	MIES, MIESZ	MÍS, MĚS, MĚŠ, MÍŠ, MÍCH	MIJES, MIJEŠ, MJEŠ
меси́ть: to knead	miesić: to knead	mísiti: to mix; to knead	mijesiti: to knead
меша́ть: to mix; to prevent, hinder	mieszać: to mix	míchati: to mix	miješati: to mix
	mieszaniec: hybrid; mongrel; half-breed	míšenec: hybrid; mongrel; half-breed	mješanac: hybrid; mongrel; half-breed
кровосмеше́ние: incest			
по́месь: hybrid; mongrel; mixture, jumble			
поме́шанный: madman	pomieszaniec: madman		
поме́ха: hindrance, obstacle			
		rozmíška: tiff, disagreement	
вмеша́ться, вме́шиваться: to interfere, intervene	*wmieszać się: to interfere, intervene	vměšovati se: to interfere, intervene	*umiješati se: to interfere, intervene
		výměšek, výměšek: (med.) secretion	
замеша́тельство: confusion; embarrassment	zamieszanie: confusion		
	zamieszki (pl.): rioting, disturbances		
[R]	[P]	[Cz]	[S-C]

NOTES

asic meaning of root: to mix

The secondary meanings "to hinder," "to confuse," "to disturb," etc. re apparent in many of the derivatives.

The Slavic root is related to OEng. miscian "to mix," Ger. mischen "to ix," Lat. miscere "to mix" (>Eng. mix, promiscuous).

меша́ть et al.: originally iterative forms of меси́ть et al. The form iešěti existed in Old Czech; modern Cz. míchati is paralleled by dialectal us. меха́ть.

кровосмеше́ние: The first element is from кровь "blood."

вмеша́ться et al.: Compare Fr. s'immiscer "to interfere" (<Lat. se, refl.

pron. + in "in" + miscere "to mix"), Ger. sich einmischen "to interfere" (⟨sich, refl. pron. + ein- "in" + mischen "to mix").

výměšek, výměsek: ="a mixing out," i.e. "elimination, separation"; se note on Rus. выделить, Pol. wydzielić.

замешáтельство- zamieszanie: Compare Eng. confusion, literally "a pour ing together" (ult. ⟨Lat. cum "with, together" + fundere "to pour"), and G σύγχυσις "confusion" (⟨σύν "with, together" + χεῖν "to pour").

МЕСТ, МЕЩ	MIAST, MIEST, MIEŚC, MIESZCZ, MIEJ(S)	MÍST, MĚST, MISŤ, MÍSŤ, MĚŠŤ	MJES(T), MJEŠT
мéсто: place	miasto: town, city	místo: place	mjesto: place; locality
		město: town, city	
	miejsce: place		
	mieścić: to contain, hold		
	miast (arch.), miasto (arch.): instead (of)	místo: instead (of)	mjesto: instead (of)
мéстный: local; (gram.) locative	miejscowy: local	místní: local	mjestan: local
	miejscownik: (gram.) locative case		
мéстность: locality	miejscowość: locality	místnost: premises; room, chamber	
		místný (lit.): suitable, appropriate	
	miejski: urban	městský: urban	
мещанúн: bourgeois; (fig.) Philistine	mieszczanin: city-dweller; bourgeois	měšťan: city-dweller; bourgeois	mještanin: local inhabitant
		místodržící, místodržitel: governor	
местоимéние: (gram.) pronoun			
местонахождéние: location, whereabouts			
		místopis: topography	
[R]	[P]	[Cz]	[S-C]

[R]	[P]	[Cz]	[S-C]
местопребыва́ние: residence, domicile			
месторожде́ние: mineral deposit			
местожи́тельство: residence, domicile			
	natomiast: however, on the other hand		
	natychmiast: immediately		
водоизмеще́ние: displacement (of a ship)			
			namjestiti, namještati: to put, place; to hire, employ; to furnish (a home)
			namještenik: employee
			namještaj: furniture
		náměstí: (public) square	
	namiastka: substitute	náměstka (arch.): (gram.) pronoun	
наме́стник (arch.): governor	namiestnik: governor	náměstek, (arch.) náměstník: deputy	namjesnik: governor
			nadomjestiti, nadomještati: to compensate for, make good; to replace
помести́ть, помеща́ть: to put, place; to lodge, accommodate; to invest (capital); to publish, carry (an article in a newspaper)	pomieścić, pomieszczać: to lodge, accommodate; to contain, hold		
помести́тельный: spacious, roomy; capacious			
поме́стье: estate, manor			

[R]	[P]	[Cz]	[S-C]
помéщик: land-owner, landed gentleman			
переместúть, перемещáть: to move, shift, transfer (tr.)	przemieścić, przemieszczać: to move, shift, transfer (tr.)	přemístiti, přemisťovati (přemísťovati): to move, shift, transfer (tr.)	premjestiti, premještati: to move, shift, transfer (tr.)
предмéстье: suburb	przedmieście: suburb	předměstí: suburb	
разместúть, размещáть: to distribute, arrange, dispose; to lodge, accommodate	rozmieścić, rozmieszczać: to distribute, arrange, dispose; to lodge, accommodate	rozmístiti, rozmisťovati (rozmísťovati): to distribute, arrange, dispose	razmjestiti, razmještati: to distribute, arrange, dispose
сместúть, смещáть: to remove	zmieścić, zmieszczać: to find room for, fit in		smjestiti, smještati: to lodge, accommodate; to store; to invest (capital)
			smjesta: immediately
совместúть, совмещáть: to combine			
совместúмый: compatible			
совмéстный: joint, common			
уместúть, умещáть: to find room for, fit in	umieścić, umieszczać: to put, place; to lodge, accommodate; to invest (capital); to publish, carry (an article in a newspaper)	umístiti, umisťovati (umísťovati): to put, place; to place (in a job)	umjestiti, umještati: to put, place; to distribute, arrange, dispose
умéстный: suitable, appropriate			umjestan: suitable, appropriate
вместúть, вмещáть: to insert, put in; to contain, hold	wmieścić, wmieszczać: to insert, put in		
вместúлище: receptacle, container			

[R]	[P]	[Cz]	[S-C]
вмести́мость: volume, capacity			
вмести́тельный: spacious, roomy; capacious			
вме́сте: together			
вме́сто: instead (of)			umjesto: instead (of)
	zamiast: instead (of)		
замести́ть, замеща́ть: to replace	zamieścić, zamieszczać: to publish, carry (an article in a newspaper)		
		zaměstnati, zaměstnávati: to hire, employ; to occupy (s.o. with a task, etc.)	
		zaměstnanec: employee	

NOTES

Basic meaning of root: place

A secondary meaning occurring in Polish and Czech is "town, city." (Compare the similar differentiation of meaning in Ger. Statt, Stätte "place" and the doublet form Stadt "town, city.")

A number of derivatives express the notion of "taking the place of, replacing, substituting for."

The verbal derivatives are denominatives formed from ме́сто et al.

miasto (n.): orig. "place."

město: a doublet of místo.

miejsce: orig. miestce, a diminutive of miasto.

miast et al.: Compare Eng. instead (<in + stead "place," occurring in such compounds as farmstead, homestead, bedstead).

ме́стный et al., miejscownik: Compare Eng. local, locative (both ult. <Lat. locus "place"); the locative case is so called because (in combination with a preposition) it normally expresses location.

místný: ="in its (proper) place."

miejski: orig. mieśćski.

мещани́н-mieszczanin-měšťan: A "bourgeois" was originally a freeman of a town, then---more generally---any member of the middle class; compare Fr.

bourgeois (⟨bourg "town"). Rus. мещанйн is borrowed from Polish.

místodržící, místodržitel: ="one who holds (i.e. takes) the place of another" (in this instance, his sovereign); compare Eng. lieutenant (orig. ="deputy, representative"; ult. ⟨Fr. lieu "place" + tenir "to hold"), Ger. Statthalter "governor" (⟨Statt "place" + halten "to hold").

местоимéние: See note under root ИМЯ (etc.).

místopis: See note under root ПИС (etc.).

месторождéние: See note under root РОД (etc.).

natomiast: orig. "instead"; compare miast et al. The second element is a form of ten "this."

natychmiast: Compare the use of Eng. on the spot in the sense of "immediately"; the second element is a form of ten "this."

водоизмещéние: The second element is from obsolete изместйть "to replace, displace."

namjestiti (second meaning), namještenik: Compare Ger. anstellen "to hire, employ" and Angestellter "employee" (⟨an "on, at, to" + stellen "to put, place").

namiastka-náměstka, намéстник et al.: All these words express the notion of replacement, substitution. Regarding náměstka, see note on Pol. zaimek, Cz. zájmeno; regarding намéстник et al., see note above on místodržíc místodržitel.

поместйтельный: See the first two meanings of поместйть.

помéщик: ⟨помéстье.

предмéстье et al.: Compare Ger. Vorort "suburb" (⟨vor "before, in fron of" + Ort "place; locality"); the Russian word is borrowed from Polish.

smjesta: Compare natychmiast.

совместйть, совместймый, совмéстный: Compare вмéсте.

умéстный-umjestan: See note on místný; the Serbo-Croatian word is borrowed from Russian.

вместйлище, вместймость, вместйтельный: See вместйть.

вмéсте: ="in a (i.e. one and the same) place."

вмéсто-umjesto, zamiast: See note on miast et al.

zaměstnati (first meaning), zaměstnanec: Compare the second meaning of umístiti and see note on namjestiti, namještenik.

ME(T)	MIOT, MIE(C), MIEĆ	MET, MÉ, MĚT, MIT, MÍT	ME(T), MEĆ
мести́: to sweep	mieść: to sweep	mésti: to sweep	mesti: to sweep
метну́ть, мета́ть: to throw; (мета́ть only) to baste (sew)	miotnąć, miotać: to throw	metnouti, metati: to throw	metnuti, metati: to put; to throw
	miot: throw; litter, brood (of animals)	met (arch.): throw	
			metak: bullet; projectile
метла́: broom	miotła: broom	metla: birch rod, switch; (arch.) broom	metla: broom
мете́лица, мете́ль: snowstorm		metelice: snowstorm	mećava: snowstorm
		kulomet: machine-gun	
междоме́тие: (gram.) interjection			
			nogomet: football, soccer
пулемёт: machine-gun			
			dometak: addition
			izmet, izmetina: rubbish, refuse; dung
намёт: casting-net; gallop; (arch.) shed	namiot: tent	námět: suggestion; subject, topic	namet: tax; (snow) drift
намётка: basting (sewing); basting thread		námitka: objection	
			nametljiv: intrusive, meddlesome
			nametnica: parasitic plant
			nadmetanje: competition, contest
		omítka: plaster	
опроме́тчивый: rash, hasty, precipitate			
[R]	[P]	[Cz]	[S-C]

[R]	[P]	[Cz]	[S-C]
		odmítnouti, odmítati: to reject, refuse; to refuse (to do s.th.)	odmetnuti, odmetati: to put aside; to throw away
		odmítavý: negative (reply, etc.)	
			odmetnik: renegade, apostate
помёт: dung; litter, brood (of animals)	pomiot: litter, brood (of animals)		pomet: snowstorm
			pometnuće: miscarriage
	podmiot: (gram., phil.) subject	podmět: (gram., phil.) subject	podmet: (gram.) subject
	podmiotowy: subjective	podmětový: (gram.) intransitive	
			podmeče: foundling, abandoned child
подмётка: sole (of a shoe)			
		přemítati: to meditate, reflect	premetnuti, premetati: to turn upside down; to search, ransack
перемёт: fishnet		přemet: somersault	
предмéт: object, thing; object (of affection, attention, etc.); subject, topic	przedmiot: object, thing; object (of affection, attention, etc.); (gram.) object; (mil.) objective; subject, topic	předmět: object, thing; object (of affection, attention, etc.); (gram.) object; subject, topic	predmet: object, thing; object (of affection, attention, etc.); (gram.) object; subject, topic
	przedmiotowy: objective (a.)		
			predmetak: (gram.) prefix
	przymiot: attribute, characteristic; (med., arch.) syphilis		
	przymiotnik: (gram.) adjective		

		průmět: (math.) projection	promet: traffic; (business) turnover; circulation (of currency)
		promítačka: (motion-picture) projector	
			razmetnik: spendthrift
			razmetljivac: braggart
			smet: rubbish, refuse; (snow) drift
	śmieci (pl.), śmiecie (pl.): rubbish, refuse	smetí: rubbish, refuse	smeće: rubbish, refuse
	wymioty (pl.): vomiting (n.)	výmět: excrement	
	wymieciny (pl.): rubbish, refuse		
		zamítnouti, zamítati: to reject, refuse; to repudiate, disown	zametnuti, zametati: to throw (a sack, etc. over one's shoulder); to mislay; to pick (a quarrel), start (a conversation); to set, begin to grow (said of fruit)
			zametak: embryo; fetus; germ, bud
	zamieć: snowstorm		
[R]	[P]	[Cz]	[S-C]

NOTES

Basic meaning of root: to sweep; to throw

мести́ et al.: The respective 1 sg. forms are мету́, miotę, metu, metem.

метну́ть et al.: The imperfective forms originated as iteratives of мести́ et al.; the perfectives are a more recent formation. Regarding the additional meanings of Rus. мета́ть and S-C metnuti, metati, see note on Rus. ти́снуть et al.

miot (second meaning): Compare Eng. to drop as applied to animals in the sense of "to give birth to," Cz. vrh.

kulomet: The first element is from *kule*, *kulka* "bullet."

междомéтие: modeled on Lat. *interjectio* (<*inter* "between" + *jacere* "to throw").

nogomet: The first element is from *noga* "foot."

пулемёт: The first element is from *пýля* "bullet."

dometak: See note on S-C *pridjenuti*, Cz. *přidělati*.

намёт (third meaning)-*namiot*: ="a thing thrown upon or over s.th."; compare Eng. *to pitch a tent*.

námět: See note on Cz. *návrh*.

namet (first meaning): See note on Rus. *налóг*, S-C *nalog*.

námitka: See note on Cz. *předhůzka*.

nametljiv: Compare Eng. *to be imposed* (ult. <Lat. *in* "on" + Fr. *poser* "to put") *upon*, *to be (much) put upon*.

nametnica: Compare *nametljiv*.

nadmetanje: orig. "an effort to best s.o. in throwing."

omítka: ="something thrown (*i.e*. spread) around or over"; compare Ger. *Bewurf* "plaster" (<*werfen* "to throw").

odmítnouti: Compare Eng. *reject* (ult. <Lat. *re*- "back" + *jacere* "to throw"), Rus. *отвéргнуть et al*., Pol. *odrzucić*.

odmítavý: See *odmítnouti*.

odmetnik: ="one who casts aside his faith."

помёт (second meaning)-*pomiot*: See note on *miot*.

pometnuće: See note on Rus. *вы́кидыш*.

podmiot et al.: modeled on Lat. *subjectum* (<*sub* "under" + *jacere* "to throw"); the subject, that which is spoken of, is seen as a foundation or substratum which is "thrown under," *i.e*. underlies, the various attributes ascribed to it. Compare Du. *onderwerp* "subject (gram.); subject, topic" (<*onder* "under" + *werpen* "to throw"), Rus. *подлежáщее*.

podmětový: See *podmět*; an intransitive verb, having no object, relates only to the subject of the sentence.

podmeče: <**podmetče*; see note on Rus. *подки́дыш*.

подмётка: See the second meaning of *метáть*.

přemítati: a figurative extension of the notion expressed by *přemet* and S-C *premetnuti*; compare Eng. *to turn s.th. over in one's mind*, Ger. *überlegen* "to consider, reflect upon" (orig. "to turn over"; <*über* "over" + *legen* "to lay, put").

предмéт et al.: modeled on Lat. *objectum* (<*ob* "before, in front of" + *jacere* "to throw"); an object is "that which is thrown (*i.e*. placed) before us."

przymiot (first meaning), *przymiotnik*: The semantic evolution of *przymiot* has proceeded from "that which is thrown near or against" to "that which is added, an addition" to "that which is attributed, an attribute"; *przymiotnik* is the term applied to a word which "adds" an attribute to a noun. Compare Ger. *Eigenschaftswort* "adjective" (<*Eigenschaft* "attribute" +

Wort "word") as well as Eng. adjective (ult. ⟨Lat. adjicere "to add" ⟨ ad "to, toward" + jacere "to throw"), Rus. прилагáтельное (see note), Cz. přídavné, S-C pridjev.

przymiot (second meaning): The word was originally applied to any contagious disease, the underlying notion being that the disease was "thrown" from one person to another; compare obsolete Pol. przyrzut "contagious disease" (⟨rzucić "to throw").

průmět, promítačka: Compare Eng. projection, projector (ult. ⟨Lat. pro- "forward" + jacere "to throw").

promet: Something of the semantic development of the word is suggested by Eng. turnover, Ger. Verkehr "traffic; business" (⟨kehren "to turn").

zamítnouti: See note on odmítnouti and compare Cz. zavrhnouti.

zametnuti: In the third and fourth meanings, the prefix has inceptive force; compare S-C zavrći.

zametak: See the fourth meaning of zametnuti.

МИ	MI	MI, MÍ, ME	MI
*минýть: to pass by (tr. and intr.); to pass, elapse	minąć, mijać: to pass by (tr. and intr.); to pass, elapse	minouti, míjeti: to pass by (tr. and intr.); to pass, elapse	*minuti: to pass by (tr. and intr.); to pass, elapse
**миновáть: to pass by (tr. and intr.); to escape, elude			
мúмо: past, by	mimo: past, by; despite	mimo: past, by; outside; besides; contrary to	mimo: past, by; besides; despite
		míjivý: brief, fleeting	
минýвшее: past (n.)		minulost: past (n.)	
			mimohod: march-past, military review
мимохóдом: while passing by; incidentally, en passant	mimochodem: incidentally, en passant	mimochodem: incidentally, en passant	
			mimogred: incidentally, en passant
мимолётный: brief, fleeting			
		mimořádný: extraordinary	
[R]	[P]	[Cz]	[S-C]

[R]	[P]	[Cz]	[S-C]
	mimośrodkowy: (math.) eccentric		
	mimowiedny: unconscious, unaware		
	mimowolny: involuntary, unintentional	mimovolný: involuntary, unintentional	
	ominąć, omijać: to pass by (tr.); to avoid, shun; to escape, elude; to omit		
		opomenouti (opominouti), opomíjeti: to neglect; to fail (to do s.th.)	
	pominąć, pomijać: to disregard, ignore; to omit	pominouti, pomíjeti: to pass, elapse; to disregard, ignore	
		*pominouti se: to go mad	
		pomíjející, pomíjivý: transient, ephemeral	
помимо: besides; without (s.o.'s) knowledge, participation	pomimo: despite		
			preminuće: death, decease
	przeminąć, przemijać: to pass, elapse	prominouti, promíjeti: to forgive	
	przemijający: transient, ephemeral	promíjivý: forgiving, indulgent	

NOTES

Basic meaning of root: to pass by

The Slavic root is related to Lat. meare "to go" (>Eng. permeate).

mimogred: The second element is from archaic gresti "to go."

mimośrodkowy: See note on Cz. výstředný, výstřední.

opomenouti: This form of the perfective arose alongside opominouti under the influence of unrelated zapomenouti "to forget" (q.v.).

pominouti se: The meaning originates from the expression pominouti se (s) rozumem (="to go out of one's mind, take leave of one's senses"); see rozum.

preminuće: Compare Eng. passing (="death") and to pass away (="to die").

prominouti: Compare the second meaning of pominouti.

МИЛ	MIŁ, MIL	MIL	MIO, MIL
ми́лый: dear, beloved; pleasant	miły: dear, beloved; pleasant	milý: dear, beloved; pleasant	mio: dear, beloved; pleasant
милова́ть (lit.): to caress	miłować (arch.): to love	milovati: to love	milovati: to caress; to love
ми́ловать (arch.): to pardon, grant a pardon to			
			militi se: to please
ми́лость: grace, favor; mercy, charity	miłość: love	milost: mercy, charity; pardon, amnesty; (lit.) grace, favor; (lit.) charm, loveliness	milost: grace, favor; mercy, charity; charm, loveliness
ми́лостивый (arch.): gracious, kind	miłościwy: gracious, kind	milostivý: gracious, kind	milostiv: gracious, kind
ми́лостыня: alms			milostinja: alms
			milje: joy, delight
		lidumil: philanthropist, humanitarian	
		milodar: alms; donation	milodar: alms; donation
[R]	[P]	[Cz]	[S-C]

[R]	[P]	[Cz]	[S-C]
			miloglasan: euphonious, melodious
милосéрдие: mercy, charity	miłosierdzie: mercy, charity	milosrdenství: mercy, charity	milosrđe: mercy, charity
милови́дный: pretty, attractive			milovidan: pretty, attractive
			milozvučan: euphonious, melodious
*поми́ловать: to pardon, grant a pardon to		*pomilovati: to love; to caress	*pomilovati: to pardon, grant a pardon to; to caress
	przymilić się, przymilać się: to ingratiate oneself		
*сми́ловаться (arch.): to take pity	*zmiłować się: to take pity	*smilovati se: to take pity	*smilovati se: to take pity
			samilost: compassion, sympathy
умили́ться, умиля́ться: to be moved, touched, affected (emotionally)			umiliti se, umiljavati (umiljati) se: to ingratiate oneself

NOTES

Basic meaning of root: dear, beloved

The parallel meanings "charming, pleasant" (i.e. evoking love) and "kind, charitable" (i.e. showing love) run through many of the derivatives. Compare Eng. grace (="charm, loveliness" and "mercy, charity").

lidumil: See note under root ЛЮД (etc.).

miloglasan: See note on Rus. благозву́чный, S-C blagozvučan.

милосéрдие et al.: a loan-translation of Lat. misericordia "pity, mercy" (<misereri "to pity" + cor "heart"); the Russian word is borrowed from Church Slavic.

милови́дный-milovidan: See note under root ВИД (etc.).

milozvučan: See note on Rus. благозву́чный, S-C blagozvučan.

przymilić się, umiliti se: Compare Eng. ingratiate (ult. <Lat. in "in" + gratia "grace, favor").

МИР	MIR, MIERZ	MÍR, MIŘ, MÍŘ, MĚŘ	MIR
мир: peace, quiet; peace (absence of war); world; (arch.) village community	mir: respect, esteem; (arch.) peace, quiet; (arch.) village community	mír: peace, quiet; peace (absence of war)	mir: peace, quiet; peace (absence of war); (lit.) world
мири́ть: to reconcile		míříti (arch.): to reconcile	miriti: to reconcile; to calm, pacify; to soothe, allay
			mirovina: pension
миря́нин (arch.): layman (as distinct from a clergyman)			mirjanin: layman (as distinct from a clergyman)
мирво́лить (arch.): to humor, gratify, indulge			
мировоззре́ние: ideology, Weltanschauung			
мирозда́ние (lit.): universe			
			mirozov: tattoo (bugle call)
умиротвори́ть, умиротворя́ть: to calm, pacify			
		vesmír: universe	svemir: universe
			*domiriti: to add to, complete, make up a deficiency in (s.th.)
			namiriti, namirivati: to pay; to feed
переми́рие: truce, armistice	przymierze: alliance	příměří: truce, armistice	primirje: truce, armistice
			razmirica: discord, dissension
смири́ть, смиря́ть (lit.): to subdue, humble		smířiti, smiřovati: to reconcile	smiriti, smirivati: to calm, pacify
сми́рный: quiet; meek, mild		smírný: amicable (agreement, etc.)	
[R]	[P]	[Cz]	[S-C]

усмири́ть, усмиря́ть: to calm, pacify; to quell, suppress (e.g. a revolt)		usmířiti, usmiřovati: to reconcile	smiraj: sunset umiriti, umirivati: to calm, pacify; to soothe, allay uznemiriti, uznemirivati: to disturb; to worry, perturb; to harass
[R]	[P]	[Cz]	[S-C]

NOTES

Basic meaning of root: peace

The secondary meanings "world" and "village community" both reflect th notion of a group of people living together in peace. Arising from this is the further notion of an agreement or contractual relationship, which is ap parent in the semantic development of Pol. mir (see note).

mir (Pol.): The present-day use of the word goes back to an earlier meaning, "right of citizenship" (see introductory note above), from which evolved the more general notion of "standing, status," hence "respect, esteem."

mirovina: See note on Cz. odpočivné.

миря́нин-mirjanin: one who lives "in the world"; the Serbo-Croatian wor is borrowed from Russian. Compare S-C svjetovnjak.

мировоззре́ние: a loan-translation of Ger. Weltanschauung "ideology" (<Welt "world" + Anschauung "opinion, view" < schauen "to look"); compare Pol. światopogląd.

mirozov: ="a summons to rest."

умиротвори́ть: Compare Eng. pacify (ult. <Lat. pax "peace" + facere "to make").

vesmír-svemir: See note under root ВЕС (etc.).

domiriti: The original idea was that of pacifying someone by making up the difference in something that was deficient, generally a sum of money.

namiriti: orig. "to pacify, satisfy"; regarding the first meaning, compare Eng. pacify and pay (both ult. <Lat. pax "peace") and defray (ult. <Fr frais "cost" < Middle Lat. fredum "a fine after the payment of which the vanquished obtained peace" < an earlier form of Ger. Friede "peace").

przymierze-*příměří*: for OPol. *przymirze*, OCz. *přímiřie*; the Polish word originally had the same meaning as the corresponding words in the other three languages.

smiraj: ="a going to rest."

МК, МЧ, МЫК, МОК	MK, MYK, MEK	MK, MYK, MEK	MA(K), MK, MIC
мы́кать: to harry, drive from pillar to post мчать: to rush, speed (tr.)	mknąć: to rush, dash	mykati: to card wool	maknuti (maći), micati: to move (tr.)
			izmaknuti (izmaći) (se), izmicati (se): to escape
			izmak: expiration, close; ebb, decline
			namaknuti (namaći), namicati: to put (on); to supply, provide; to raise (money)
	napomknąć, napomykać: to allude, refer; to hint		
		obemknouti, obmykati: to embrace, hug; to surround, encircle	
отомкну́ть, отмыка́ть: to unlock	odemknąć, odmykać: to open	odemknouti, odmykati: to unlock	odmaknuti (odmaći), odmicati: to move away (tr.); to get a head start
примкну́ть, примыка́ть: to fix (a bayonet); (к + dat.) to join; (к + dat.; примыка́ть only) to adjoin	przymknąć, przymykać: to half-close	přimknouti, přimykati (arch.): to half-close; to press (against)	primaknuti (primaći), primicati: to move nearer (tr.)
			razmak: interval
сомкну́ть, смыка́ть: to close (military	zemknąć, zmykać (coll.): to run away	*semknouti: to close (military ranks); to	smaknuti (smaći), smicati: to close (military
[R]	[P]	[Cz]	[S-C]

ranks); (arch.) to close (one's eyes)		press together (e.g. one's lips); to grasp	ranks); to remove, take away; to overthrow, depose; to kill
умыка́ть (arch.): to abduct	umknąć, umykać (coll.): to escape		umaknuti (umaći), umicati: to escape
		vymknouti, vymykati: to sprain, dislocate	
	wymknąć się, wymykać się: to escape	vymknouti se, vymykati se: to extricate, free oneself	
			uzmaknuti (uzmaći), uzmicati: to withdraw (intr.); (mil.) to retreat
замкну́ть, замыка́ть: to lock	zamknąć, zamykać: to shut, close	zamknouti, zamykati: to lock	zamaknuti (zamaći), zamicati: to disappear; to tie, fasten
замо́к: lock	zamek: lock; castle	zámek: lock; castle	zamak: castle
за́мок: castle			
			zamka: loop; trap
[R]	[P]	[Cz]	[S-C]

NOTES

Basic meaning of root: to make a sudden movement

The root has produced a wide range of verbal derivatives, both transitive and intransitive, in which the basic meaning undergoes such varied and extensive shifts that it is difficult to trace a consistent pattern. In general, contrasting meanings like "to close," "to open," "to press against" and "to escape" result from the action of particular prefixes on the root-meaning.

мы́кать et al.: The Polish iterative form, mykać, is obsolete; Rus. *мкнуть and Cz. *mknouti are not attested.

напомкнąć: Compare Eng. to touch upon in the sense of "to allude to."

razmak: ⟨razmaknuti "to move apart."

сомкну́ть et al.: The prefix shows the contrasting meanings "together" and "off, away."

замо́к et al., за́мок: See замкну́ть-zamknąć-zamknouti. The meaning "castle" represents semantic borrowing from Ger. Schloss "lock; castle" (<schliessen "to shut, close"); Rus. зáмок is borrowed from Polish, S-C zamak from Russian or Czech.

zamka: See the second meaning of zamaknuti.

МН, МИН, МЯ	MN, MIN, MIĘ	MN, MÍN, ME, MĚ, MA, MÁ	MN, MAN, MIN, M(E)
мнить (arch.): to think, suppose		mníti (arch.): to think, suppose	mniti: to think, suppose
мнéние: opinion			mnijenje: opinion
мни́мый: imaginary; sham, pretended			
мни́тельный: morbidly suspicious and apprehensive			
достопáмятный: memorable		pamětihodný: memorable	
самомнéние: conceit, self-opinionatedness			
	wiekopomny: memorable		
		domnívati se: to think, suppose	
		domnělý: imaginary	
	dopomnieć się, dopominać się (o + acc.): to demand		
	namiętny: passionate		
напóмнить, напоминáть: to remind	napomnieć, napominać: to admonish	napomenouti, napomínati: to admonish; to rebuke, reprimand	napomenuti, napominjati: to remark, comment upon
	niezapominajka: (bot.) forget-me-not		
незапáмятный: immemorial, ancient	niepamiętny: immemorial, ancient; unmindful	nepamětný: immemorial, ancient	
[R]	[P]	[Cz]	[S-C]

[R]	[P]	[Cz]	[S-C]
			opomenuti, opominjati: to warn; to remind; to rebuke, reprimand
*опо́мниться: to regain consciousness; to come to one's senses, collect o.s.			opomenuti se, opominjati se: to remember
по́мнить: to remember	pomnieć: to bear in mind	*pomníti (lit.): to remember	
помяну́ть, помина́ть: to mention; to pray for (s.o.)			pomenuti, pominjati: to mention
	pomny: mindful		poman, pomnjiv: careful
	pomnik: monument, memorial	pomník: monument, memorial	
поми́нки (pl.): funeral feast, wake			
		pomněnka: (bot.) forget-me-not	pomenak: (bot.) forget-me-not
па́мять: memory	pamięć: memory	paměť: memory	pamet: sense, intelligence; mind
па́мятовать (arch.): to remember	pamiętać: to remember	pamatovati (si): to remember	pamtiti (pametovati): to remember
па́мятный: memorable; memorandum (attr.)	pamiętny: memorable; mindful	památný: memorable	pametan: sensible, intelligent
па́мятник: monument, memorial	pamiętnik: diary, journal	památník: monument, memorial; album	pametnik: wiseacre, smart Alec
припо́мнить, припомина́ть: to remember	przypomnieć, przypominać: to remind	připomenouti, připomínati: to remind	pripomenuti, pripominjati: to mention
	przypomnieć sobie, przypominać sobie: to remember	připomenouti si, připomínati si: to remember	
сомне́ние: doubt	sumienie: conscience		sumnja: doubt; suspicion
			spomenuti, spominjati: to mention

			spomenik: monument, memorial
упомянýть, упоминáть: to mention	upomnieć, upominać: to admonish	upomenouti, upomínati: to remind; to dun	
	wypomnieć, wypominać: to reproach		
вспóмнить, вспоминáть: to remember	wspomnieć, wspominać: to remember; (o + loc.) to mention	vzpomenouti, vzpomínati: to remember; to commemorate	
		*vzpamatovati se: to regain consciousness; to come to one's senses, collect o.s.	
запóмнить, запоминáть: to memorize; to remember	zapomnieć, zapominać: to forget	zapomenouti, zapomínati: to forget	
	zapamiętały: frantic, frenzied; inveterate, confirmed, habitual		
[R]	[P]	[Cz]	[S-C]

NOTES

Basic meaning of root: to think

Widely represented secondary meanings are "to remember," "to remind" (whence the further meanings "to warn," "to admonish," "to reproach," "to rebuke") and "to mention."

In the Russian, Czech and Serbo-Croatian perfective verbs in -мянýть, -menouti, -menuti, the root-form is МЯ-МЕ (<Common Slavic *MĘ).

The Slavic root is akin to Eng. mind, Lat. mens "mind" (>Eng. mental, mention, comment), reminisci "to remember" (>Eng. reminisce) and monere "to remind; to warn" (>Eng. admonish, premonition, monument), Gr. μνᾶσθαι "to remember" (>Eng. mnemonic, amnesia).

мнить et al.: Pol. mnieć is obsolete but survives in numerous compounds.

достопáмятный: Regarding досто-, see note on Rus. достовéрный.

wiekopomny: The first element is from wiek "age; century."

dopomnieć się: The underlying idea is "to remind (about)."

niezapominajka: See zapomnieć.

помúнки: See the second meaning of помянýть.

pomněnka-pomenak: See pomníti and pomenuti (orig. ="to remember").

пáмять et al.: ⟨Common Slavic *pamьntь.

pamtiti: for earlier pametiti.

sumienie: for earlier sumnienie; the meaning is an extension of that o "doubt" (see Rus. сомнéние, S-C sumnja).

sumnja: Compare Ger. Verdacht "suspicion" (⟨denken "to think").

zapomnieć-zapomenouti: Here the prefix produces the meaning "to go beyond (i.e. leave) a state of mindfulness"; compare Rus. забы́ть.

zapamiętały: orig. "forgetting o.s., beside o.s."; the word is from zapamiętać się "to forget o.s."

МО(Г), МОЖ, (МОЧ), (МОЩ)	MÓ, MOG, MAG, MOŻ, (MOC), (MAC)	MO(H), MAH, MÁH, MOŽ, (MOC)	MO(G), MAG, MOŽ, (MOĆ), (MOŠT)
мочь: to be able	móc: to be able	moci: to be able	moći: to be able
мощь, (coll.) мочь: strength, power	moc: strength, power; (coll.) much, many	moc: strength, power; (coll.) much, many; (coll.) very	moć: strength, power
мóщи (pl.): relics (of a saint)			moći (pl.), mošti (pl.): relics (of a saint)
могýчий, могýщественный: powerful		mohutný: powerful; huge	moguć, mogućan: possible; powerful
мóщный: powerful	mocny: strong	mocný: powerful	moćan: powerful
мóщность: strength, power; capacity, output		mocnost: strength, power; power (i.e. sovereign state, country)	moćnost: strength, power
	mocarny: powerful		
	mocować się: to wrestle		
	mocarz: potentate; athlete	mocnář (lit.): monarch, sovereign	
	mocarstwo: power (i.e. sovereign state, country)	mocnářství (lit.): monarchy	
		mocenství: (chem.) valence	
		mocnina: (math.) power	
		mocnitel: (math.) exponent	
[R]	[P]	[Cz]	[S-C]

	możny: powerful; wealthy	možný: possible; (arch.) wealthy	
мóжно: it is possible; it is permitted		možno: it is possible; it is permitted	
	można: it is possible; it is permitted	možná: perhaps, maybe	
	możebny, możliwy: possible		
	może: perhaps, maybe		možda: perhaps, maybe
		malomocenství: leprosy	
			možebitan: possible
		svémocný (lit.): arbitrary, high-handed	
уполномóчить, уполномóчивать: to authorize, empower	upełnomocnić, upełnomocniać: to authorize, empower	zplnomocniti, zplnomocňovati: to authorize, empower	opunomoćiti, opunomoćavati: to authorize, empower
вельмóжа: magnate, dignitary	wielmoża: magnate, dignitary	velmož: magnate, dignitary	velmoža: magnate, dignitary
всемогýщий: almighty, omnipotent	wszechmogący, wszechmocny: almighty, omnipotent	všemohoucí, všemocný: almighty, omnipotent	svemoguć, svemoćan: almighty, omnipotent
		*domoci se: to achieve, attain	*domoći se: to achieve, attain
домогáться: to strive (for)	domagać się: to demand	domáhati se: to strive (for); to demand	
изнемóчь, изнемогáть: to become exhausted			iznemoći, iznemagati: to become exhausted
		námaha: effort, exertion	
			nadmoćan: superior, dominant
нéмощь, (coll.) нéмочь: weakness, impotence; illness, disease	niemoc: weakness, impotence; illness, disease	nemoc: illness, disease	nemoć: weakness, impotence; illness, disease
		nemocnice: hospital	
[R]	[P]	[Cz]	[S-C]

[R]	[P]	[Cz]	[S-C]
недомогáть: to be ailing, unwell	niedomagać: to be ailing, unwell		
			*onemoći: to become exhausted
			odmoći, odmagati: to hinder
		odmocnina: (math.) root	
помóчь, помогáть: to help	pomóc, pomagać: to help	pomoci, pomáhati: to help	pomoći, pomagati: to help
пóмочи (pl.): (children's) leading strings; suspenders			
перемóчь, перемогáть (coll.): to overcome, surmount	przemóc, przemagać: to overcome, surmount; to prevail, win out	přemoci, přemáhati: to conquer, defeat; to overcome, surmount	premoći, premagati: to conquer, defeat; to overcome, surmount; to grow stronger
	przemoc: violence, force	přemoc (arch.): predominance, supremacy	premoć: predominance, supremacy
			prenemoći se, prenemagati se: to faint, lose consciousness; (prenemagati se only) to simper, act affectedly
превозмóчь, превозмогáть: to overcome, surmount			
	przymocować, przymocowywać: to fasten, attach		
*смочь: to be able	zmóc, zmagać: to conquer, defeat	zmoci, zmáhati: to overcome, surmount; to tire, fatigue	smoći, smagati: to overcome, surmount; to raise (money); to suffice
	umocować, umocowywać: to fasten, attach; (arch.) to authorize, empower		
	*wymóc: to exact	*vymoci: to exact; to levy, collect	

вымога́ть: to extort	wymagać: to demand	vymáhati: to demand; to levy, collect vymoženost: achievement; device, contrivance	
возмо́жный: possible			
	wzmacniacz: (radio) amplifier		
		zmocniti, zmocňovati: to authorize, empower zmocniti se, zmocňovati se: to seize, take possession (of)	
	zamożny: prosperous, well-to-do	zámožný: prosperous, well-to-do	
[R]	[P]	[Cz]	[S-C]

NOTES

Basic meaning of root: to be able

Many of the derivatives reflect such notions as strength or power (and, with a negative prefix, weakness or illness), violence, compulsion, achievement (and, in imperfective verbs, striving) and help (or, with a negative prefix, hindering). In some instances, semantic parallels are provided by English words derived from Lat. posse (or potesse) "to be able" (>power, possible, potentate, impotence, omnipotent).

The forms МОЧ-МОЩ---МОС-МАС---MOC---MOĆ, except where they occur in the primary verb and its compounds, are derived from мощь et al. (See note.) The Russian form МОЩ is of Church Slavic origin.

The Slavic root is akin to Eng. may (v.) and might (v. and n.), Ger. mögen "to want, like" (orig. "to be able"), vermögen "to be able" and Macht "power, might."

мочь (v.) et al.: The respective 1 sg. forms are могу́, mogę, mohu, mogu.

мощь et al.: <Common Slavic *mogtь; regarding the colloquial meanings of Pol.-Cz. moc, see note on Rus. си́ла et al.

мо́щи et al.: The term attests to the miraculous powers attributed to the objects in question; S-C mošti is a Church Slavic borrowing.

mocenství: the degree of combining power of an element or radical; compare Eng. valence (ult. <Lat. valere "to be strong").

mocnitel: a symbol indicating the power to which a quantity is raised; see mocnina.

możny-možný: The link between the notions of power and wealth is similarly reflected in Ger. vermögen "to be able" and Vermögen "power, ability; property, wealth," Reich "empire" and reich "rich."

malomocenství: orig. "illness, disease" in general; compare nemoc.

možebitan: ⟨može biti "maybe."

svémocný: Compare Ger. eigenmächtig "arbitrary, high-handed" (⟨eigen "[one's] own" + Macht "power"), Rus. своевла́стный, S-C svojevlastan.

уполномо́чить et al.: See note under root ПОЛН (etc.).

не́мощь et al., nemocnice: Compare Eng. infirmity and infirmary (both ult. ⟨Lat. in- "un-, not" + firmus "firm, strong").

odmoći: Compare Eng. disable (⟨able).

odmocnina: Compare mocnina.

помо́чь et al.: Compare Eng. enable (⟨able).

по́мочи: ="aid, assistance"; see помо́чь.

przymocować, umocować: See note on Rus. прикрепи́ть, закрепи́ть.

zamożny-zámožný: See note on możny-možný.

МОЛВ	MÓW, MOW, MAW	MLUV, MLOUV	
*мо́лвить (arch.): to say, tell	mówić: to speak; to say, tell	mluviti: to speak	
молва́: rumor	mowa: language; speech, address; (power of) speech	mluva: language; (power of) speech	
мол: he says, they say, etc. (used for attribution of a statement)			
		mluvidla (pl.): organs of speech	
	mównica: speaker's platform	mluvnice: grammar	
	brzuchomówca: ventriloquist	břichomluvec: ventriloquist	
	krasomówstwo: eloquence; oratory	krasomluva: rhetoric, bombast	
	małomówny: taciturn	málomluvný: taciturn	
		mnohomluvný: loquacious	
[R]	[P]	[Cz]	

		samomluva: monologue, soliloquy	
		tajomluv (arch.): allegory	
	wielomówny: loquacious		
безмо́лвный: silent, speechless	bezmowny: silent, speechless		
		domluviti, domlouvati: to persuade; to rebuke, reprimand	
	namówić, namawiać: to persuade	namluviti, namlouvati: (acc. [s.th.] dat. [s.o.]) to convince (s.o. of s.th.); to arrange a match with (a girl)	
		námluvy (pl.): courtship	
	niemowlę: infant	nemluvně: infant	
недомо́лвка: reticence, omission, something left unsaid	niedomówienie: reticence, omission, something left unsaid		
		nesmlouvavý: uncompromising, intransigent	
	omówić, omawiać: to discuss	omluviti, omlouvati: to excuse; to apologize for	
обмо́лвка: slip of the tongue	obmowa: slander	omluva: excuse, apology	
	odmowa: refusal	odmluva: objection	
помо́лвка (arch.): betrothal	pomowa (arch.): slander	pomluva: slander	
	podmówić, podmawiać: to incite		
*перемо́лвить (coll.): to exchange (a word with s.o.)		přemluviti, přemlouvati: to persuade	
	przedmowa: preface, foreword	předmluva: preface, foreword	
	przymówka: taunt, gibe; allusion, hint	přímluva: intercession	
[R]	[P]	[Cz]	

	przemowa, przemówienie: speech, address	promluva: speech, address	
размолвка: tiff, disagreement	rozmowa: conversation	rozmluva: conversation	
	zmowa: conspiracy; collusion	smlouva: treaty; contract	
	umowa: agreement; treaty; contract	úmluva: agreement	
	wmówić, wmawiać (acc. [s.th.] w + acc. [s.o.]): to convince (s.o. of s.th.)		
	wymowny: eloquent	výmluvný: eloquent	
	wymowa: pronunciation; eloquence	výmluva: pretext, excuse	
	wymówka: pretext, excuse; reproach		
	zamówienie: order (for merchandise)		
	zamówić się, zamawiać się: to announce one's visit	zamlouvati se: to please, appeal (to)	
[R]	[P]	[Cz]	

NOTES

Basic meaning of root: to speak

This root, flourishing in Polish and Czech, is defunct in Serbo-Croatian and sparsely represented in Russian. See the introductory note on root ГОВОР (etc.), which has produced many comparable derivatives.

mówić, mowa: for earlier mółwić, mołwa.

мол: contracted from мо́лвил, masc. sg. past tense of мо́лвить; compare Rus. де and де́скать, Cz. prý.

brzuchomówca-břichomluvec: The first element is from brzuch-břicho "belly"; compare Eng. ventriloquist (ult. ‹Lat. venter "belly" + loqui "to speak"), Rus. чревовеща́тель.

krasomówstwo-krasomluva: The first element is from krasa-krása "beauty

mnohomluvný: The first element is from mnoho "much."

samomluva: Compare Eng. monologue (ult. ‹Gr. μόνος "sole, only" + λόγος "speech, (act of) speaking; word"), soliloquy (ult. ‹Lat. solus "sole, only" + loqui "to speak").

tajomluv: ="hidden, cryptic speech"; the first element is from tajiti "to hide."

námluvy: See the second meaning of namluviti.

niemowlę-nemluvně: ="one who cannot speak"; compare Eng. infant (ult. ‹Lat. in- "un-, not" + fari "to speak").

nesmlouvavý: ="unwilling to come to an agreement"; see smlouva and compare Eng. intransigent and transaction (both ult. ‹Lat. transigere "to come to an agreement").

обмо́лвка: See note on S-C omaška.

přemluviti: ="to talk (i.e. win) over (to one's way of thinking)"; compare Ger. überreden "to persuade" (‹über "over" + reden "to talk").

wymowny-výmluvný, wymowa-výmluva, wymówka: Compare Eng. eloquent and eloquence (ult. ‹Lat. e "out" + loqui "to speak"), Cz. výřečný and see note on S-C izgovor.

zamówienie: See note on Rus. заказа́ть, Pol. zakazać, Cz. zakázati.

zamlouvati se: Compare Eng. appeal (to) in the two meanings "to call, address oneself (to)" and "to please," Ger. ansprechen "to please, appeal (to)" (‹an "to" + sprechen "to speak") and zusagen "to please, appeal (to)" (‹zu "to" + sagen "to say, tell").

MOTP, MATP			MOTR, MATR
досмо́тр: inspection, examination надсмо́тр: supervision недосмо́тр: oversight, inadvertence несмотря́ (на + acc.): in spite (of) осмо́тр: inspection, examination осмотри́тельный: cautious, circumspect предусмотре́ть, предусма́тривать: to foresee, provide for (contin-			motriti: to look; to watch osmatrač, posmatrač: observer
[R]			[S-C]

gencies); to stipulate, provide for (by law, etc.)			
присмо́тр: supervision			prismotra: supervision
рассмотре́ть, рассма́тривать: to examine, inspect; to examine, consider (a matter); (рассма́тривать only) to consider, deem, regard (as)			razmotriti, razmatrati: to examine, inspect; to examine, consider (a matter)
смотре́ть: to look			*smotriti: to notice, perceive
			smatrati: to consider, deem, regard (as)
смотр: military review			smotra: military review; survey
			smotren: cautious, circumspect
усмотре́ние: discretion (freedom to decide)			
[R]			[S-C]

NOTES

Basic meaning of root: to look

The root occurs only in combination with the prefix с- in modern literary Russian; the word мотре́ть survives in dialect.

Many of the derivatives parallel those found under roots ГЛЯД (etc.), PATR(Z) (etc.) and ЗР (etc.).

несмотря́: See note on Cz. nehledě, nehledíc.

осмотри́тельный: See note on Pol. oględny.

предусмотре́ть: Compare Eng. provide (ult. ‹Lat. pro- "forward" + videre "to see").

smotren: See note on Pol. oględny.

МЕР$_2$, МИР, МОР	MRZ, MIER, MAR, MÓR, MORZ, MARZ	MŘ, MÍR, MR, MOR, MOŘ	MR, MIR, MOR, MAR
мере́ть (coll.): to die (in large numbers)	mrzeć: to die (in large numbers)	mříti (lit.): to die	mrijeti: to die
мор (arch.): plague	mór: plague	mor: plague	mor: death-rate
мори́ть: to exterminate (vermin, etc.); to starve (tr.); to exhaust	morzyć: to starve (tr.); to exhaust	mořiti: to starve (tr.); to harass, torment; to exhaust	moriti: to kill; to starve (tr.); to harass, torment; to exhaust
мёртвый: dead	martwy: dead	mrtvý: dead	mrtav: dead
мертви́ть (lit.): to depress, dispirit	martwić: to vex, distress		
	martwica: (med.) necrosis	mrtvice: (med.) stroke	
			mrtvilo: lethargy; stagnation
		mrtvola: corpse	
мертвечи́на: carrion			
мертве́цкая: morgue			mrtvačnica: morgue
			mrtvozornik: coroner
омертве́лость, омертве́ние: (med.) necrosis; numbness	obumarcie: (med.) necrosis; lethargy		obamrlost: (med.) necrosis; numbness; unconsciousness
			*odmoriti se: to rest (intr.)
	pomór: plague		pomor: plague; epidemic; death-rate
	*zemrzeć: to die	zemříti, zmírati: to die	*samrijeti: to die
смерть: death	śmierć: death	smrt: death	samrt, smrt: death
умере́ть, умира́ть: to die	umrzeć, umierać: to die	umříti, umírati: to die	umrijeti, umirati: to die
		úmrtí: death	
*умори́ть (coll.): to kill; to starve (tr.); to exhaust	umorzyć, umarzać: to starve (tr.); to amortize, pay off; to drop, discontinue (legal proceedings)	umořiti, umořovati: to starve (tr.); to harass, torment; to exhaust; to amortize, pay off	umoriti, umarati: to exhaust; (umoriti only) to kill
[R]	[P]	[Cz]	[S-C]

умертви́ть, умерщвля́ть: to kill; to mortify (the flesh)	umartwić, umartwiać: to mortify (the flesh) uśmiercić, uśmiercać: to kill	umrtviti, umrtvovati: to anesthetize usmrtiti, usmrcovati: to kill	umrtviti, umrtvljavati: to kill; to deaden, benumb usmrtiti, usmrćivati: to kill
[R]	[P]	[Cz]	[S-C]

NOTES

Basic meaning of root: to die

The Slavic root is related to Eng. murder and to Lat. mori "to die" (>Eng. moribund), mortuus "dead" (>Eng. mortuary) and mors "death" (>Eng. mortal, mortify).

мере́ть et al.: The simple verb has been replaced in normal usage by th prefixed forms умере́ть et al. and zemrzeć-zemříti.

мори́ть et al.: <мор et al.

мертви́ть-martwić: <мёртвый-martwy.

martwica: Compare Eng. necrosis (ult. <Gr. νεκρός "dead").

mrtvozornik: Compare Ger. Leichenbeschauer "coroner" (<Leiche "corpse" + beschauen "to inspect").

омертве́лость et al. (first meaning): See note on martwica.

odmoriti se: Compare moriti; the prefix has negative effect.

umorzyć (second meaning)-umořiti (fourth meaning): Compare Eng. amortize (ult. <Lat. mors "death").

умертви́ть et al.: <мёртвый et al.; МЕРЩВ is a Church Slavic form.

uśmiercić et al.: <śmierć et al.

МЫСЛ, МЫСЕЛ, МЫШЛ	MYSŁ, MYŚL	MYSL, MYŠL, MÝŠL	MISAO, MISL, MIŠ[L]
мы́слить: to think мысль: thought, idea	myśleć: to think myśl: thought, idea; mind; mood, spirits myśliwy, (arch.) myśliwiec: hunter	mysliti (mysleti): to think mysl: mind; mood, spirits myšlenka: thought, idea myslivec: hunter; gamekeeper	misliti: to thin[k] misao: thought, idea
[R]	[P]	[Cz]	[S-C]

[R]	[P]	[Cz]	[S-C]
	myślnik: (punc.) dash		
		dobromyslný: good-natured	
двусмы́сленный: ambiguous		dvojsmyslný: ambiguous	dvosmislen: ambiguous
	jednomyślny: unanimous	jednomyslný: unanimous	
легкомы́сленный: frivolous	lekkomyślny: frivolous	lehkomyslný: frivolous	lakomislen: frivolous
		malomyslný: despondent	
		velkomyslný: magnanimous	
бессмы́слица: nonsense			besmisao, besmislica: nonsense
до́мысел: guess, conjecture	domysł: guess, conjecture	domysl (lit.): guess, conjecture	domisao: thought, idea
	domyślny: shrewd, clever; supposed, putative	důmyslný: shrewd, clever; intricate, complicated	domišljat: shrewd, clever
		domýšlivý: conceited, arrogant	
измышле́ние: fiction, invention			izmišljotina: fiction, invention
	namysł: reflection, consideration		namisao: intention, design
		nesmysl: nonsense	nesmisao: nonsense
	obmyślić, obmyślać: to devise, contrive	obmysliti, obmýšleti: (lit.) to bestow, present; (arch.) to plan, intend	
	pomyślny: favorable	pomyslný: imaginary; abstract	
	pomysłowy: inventive, ingenious		
Про́мысл: Providence			promisao: foresight; (cap.) Providence
про́мысел: trade, business, craft	przemysł: industry (economic activity)	průmysl: industry (economic activity)	

[R]	[P]	[Cz]	[S-C]
	przemyślny: inventive, ingenious		
промы́шленность: industry (economic activity)		promyšlenost: deliberation, care	promišljenost: deliberation, care
	rozmyślny: intentional, deliberate	rozmyslný (lit.): prudent, cautious	
смысл: sense, meaning; sense, intelligence	zmysł: sense, feeling; sense (sight, hearing, etc.)	smysl: sense, meaning; sense, intelligence; sense, feeling; sense (sight, hearing, etc.)	smisao: sense, meaning; sense, intelligence; penchant, inclination
смыслово́й: semantic, pertaining to meaning	zmysłowy: sensual	smyslový: sensory	
	zmyślny: shrewd, clever; inventive, ingenious	smyslný: sensual	
	zmyślenie: fiction, invention	smýšlení: opinion	
		smyšlenka: fiction, invention	
соумы́шленник: accomplice			
у́мысел: intention, design	umysł: mind	úmysl: intention, design	umisao: idea; intention, design
умы́шленный: intentional, deliberate	umyślny: intentional, deliberate	úmyslný: intentional, deliberate	umišljen: conceited
вы́мысел: fiction, invention	wymysł: fiction, invention	výmysl: fiction, invention	
за́мысел: intention, design; (artistic) conception	zamysł: intention, design	zámysl (arch.): intention, design	zamisao: idea; intention, design
замыслова́тый: intricate, complicated			

NOTES

Basic meaning of root: to think

The Slavic root is related to Gr. μῦθος "speech; talk; story" (>Eng. myth).

мы́слить et al.: denominatives formed from мысль et al.

myśliwy et al.: The underlying idea is "clever person," i.e. one skilled in outwitting his quarry. The present meaning probably arose from the need for a taboo-word for "hunter"; compare Rus. охо́та.

myślnik: a punctuation mark often used to indicate the intrusion of a new thought; the word is modeled on Ger. Gedankenstrich "dash" (<Gedanke "thought" + Strich "stroke, line").

двусмы́сленный et al.: See смысл-smysl-smisao and note under root ДВА (etc.).

jednomyślny-jednomyslný: See myśl-mysl and note on Rus. единоду́шный, S-C jednodušan.

malomyslný: See mysl and note on Rus. малоду́шный et al.

velkomyslný: See mysl and note on Rus. великоду́шный et al.

besmisao, besmislica: for *bezsmisao, *bezsmislica.

obmysliti (first meaning): Compare the use of Eng. thoughtful in the sense of "kind, generous."

pomyślny: ="corresponding to one's thoughts and desires."

Про́мысл-promisao: The Russian word is borrowed from Church Slavic, the Serbo-Croatian word from Russian.

про́мысел et al., промы́шленность: ="that which is created by thought, ingenuity, etc."; the Czech word is borrowed from Russian.

НЕС, НОС, НОШ	NIOS, NIES, NIEŚ, NOS, NOŚ, NOSZ	NES, NÉS, NEŠ, NOS, NŮŠ, NOŠ, NAŠ, NÁŠ	NES, NIJE, NOS, NOŠ, NAŠ
нести́: to carry, bear; to lay (eggs)	nieść: to carry, bear; to lay (eggs)	nésti: to carry, bear; to lay (eggs)	nesti (arch.): to lay (eggs)
†носи́ть: to carry, bear; to wear	†nosić: to carry, bear; to wear; to lay (eggs)	†nositi: to carry, bear; to wear	nositi: to carry, bear; to wear; to lay (eggs)
но́ша: burden	nosze (pl.): stretcher, litter; bier	nůše: hamper, basket	
	nosidła (pl.): yoke (for carrying buckets)		nosila (pl.): stretcher, litter; bier
[R]	[P]	[Cz]	[S-C]

носи́лки (pl.): sedan-chair; stretcher, litter; bier		nosítka (pl.): sedan-chair; stretcher, litter; bier	nosiljka: sedan-chair; stretcher, litter
			nošnja: costume
		nosník: girder, beam	
			noseća: pregnant
			glasonoša: herald; messenger
доно́с: denunciation, informing			donos: income, proceeds
доно́счик: informer, talebearer	donosiciel: informer, talebearer	donašeč: informer, talebearer; carrier, bearer	donosilac: carrier, bearer
	donośny: sonorous		
	doniosły: important		
			doprinos: contribution; donation
			iznos: amount, sum
нано́с: alluvium; (snow) drift		nános: alluvium; sediment, deposit	nanos: alluvium; (snow) drift; sediment, deposit
недоно́сок: prematurely born child	niedonosek: prematurely born child	nedonošenec: prematurely born child	nedonošče: prematurely born child
		obnos: amount, sum	
			oponašati: to imitate
отнести́сь, относи́ться (к + dat.): to behave (toward), treat; to feel (about), regard; (относи́ться only) to relate (to), concern	odnieść się, odnosić się (do + gen.): to behave (toward), treat; to feel (about), regard; (odnosić się only) to relate (to), concern		odnositi se (na + acc.): to relate (to), concern
отноше́ние: relation(ship); ratio; attitude (toward s.th.); regard, respect (e.g.			odnos, odnošaj: relation(ship); ratio; attitude (toward s.th.)
[R]	[P]	[Cz]	[S-C]

[R]	[P]	[Cz]	[S-C]
по отноше́нию к: with regard, respect to; в э́том отноше́нии: in this regard, respect)			
поно́с: diarrhea			ponos: pride
поноше́ние: vilification, invective			ponašanje: behavior, conduct
поднести́, подноси́ть: to bring; to bestow	podnieść, podnosić: to raise		podnijeti (podnesti), podnositi: to bear, endure; to present, submit
подно́с: tray		podnos: tray	podnos: tray
			podnesak: application, petition
	podnośnik: elevator		
	podniosły: lofty, sublime		
			podnošljiv: bearable, endurable; passable, fair
перено́сный: portable; figurative, metaphorical	przenośny: portable; communicable, contagious; figurative, metaphorical	přenosný: portable; communicable, contagious	prenosan: figurative, metaphorical
		přenesený: figurative, metaphorical	prenesen: figurative, metaphorical
преподноше́ние: gift, present			
превознести́, превозноси́ть: to extol, exalt			preuznositi: to extol, exalt
		přednáška: lecture	
		přínos: contribution	prinos: contribution; donation
			prinosan: profitable
произноше́ние: pronunciation			
	zniesienie: abolition, abrogation		

[R]	[P]	[Cz]	[S-C]
сноше́ния (pl.): relations, dealings			snošaj: relation(ship); ratio
сно́ска: footnote			
сно́сный: bearable, endurable; passable, fair	znośny: bearable, endurable; passable, fair	snesitelný: bearable, endurable; passable, fair	snošljiv: bearable, endurable; passable, fair; tolerant
		snášelivý, snášenlivý: tolerant	
	uniesienie: excitement; rapture, delight	únos: abduction, kidnaping	
		usnesení: resolution; decree	
	wniosek: proposal; inference		
			unosan: profitable
вы́нос: (act of) carrying out		výnos: decree; income, proceeds; output	
выно́сливость: endurance			
вознести́, возноси́ть (lit.): to raise	wznieść, wznosić: to raise; to erect, build	vznésti, vznášeti: to raise; to present, submit	uznijeti (uznesti), uznositi: to carry up; to extol, exalt
	wzniosły: lofty, sublime	vznosný: lofty, sublime; stately	uznosit: proud
		vznešený: lofty, sublime; pompous; prominent, distinguished	uznesen: elated
взнос: payment; fee, dues			
Вознесе́ние: (rel.) Ascension	wzniesienie: hill, height; (act of) raising; (act of) erecting, building		Uznesenje: (rel.) Ascension
зано́с: (snow) drift			zanos, zanesenost: enthusiasm
зано́счивый: arrogant, insolent			

NOTES

Basic meaning of root: to carry (on foot)

Where a means of conveyance is used, the notion of carrying is expressed by verbs formed from root ВЕЗ (etc.).

A number of the derivatives of this root show the secondary meaning "to endure." (Compare the similar use of Eng. *bear* as well as Eng. *suffer* [ult. <Lat. *ferre* "to carry"], Ger. *ertragen* "to endure" [<*tragen* "to carry"].)

носи́ть et al.: The use of the verb for "to carry" in the further sense of "to wear" is not uncommon; compare Fr. *porter*, Ger. *tragen*, Lat. *gerere*, *gestare*, all of which have both meanings. In Serbo-Croatian, the iterative verb has taken over the function of archaic *nesti*.

но́ша-nosze, *nosila*, *носи́лки-nosítka*: Compare Eng. *burden* and *bier*, both related to *bear*.

nošnja: See the second meaning of *nositi* and compare Ger. *Tracht* "costume" (<*tragen* "to carry; to wear").

nosník: Compare Ger. *Träger* "girder, beam" (<*tragen* "to carry").

noseća: Compare Ger. *trächtig* "pregnant" (<*tragen* "to carry").

доно́с, *доно́счик-donosiciel-donašeč*: Compare Eng. *talebearer*, Fr. *délateur* (and rarely used Eng. *delator*) "informer" (ult. <Lat. *de* "off, away" + *latus*, past part. of *ferre* "to carry"), Eng. *relate* "to tell" (ult. <Lat. *re-* "back" + *latus*) and *report* (ult. <Lat. *re-* + *portare* "to carry"), Gr. *ἀναφέρειν* "to report" (<*ἀνά-* "back" + *φέρειν* "to carry").

donos: ="something brought in."

donośny: Compare Eng. *report* (of a gun, etc.) (ult. <Lat. *re-* "back" + *portare* "to carry") and the expression *The sound carries*.

donioslý: ="carrying far, far-reaching"; compare Eng. *important* (ult. <Lat. *in* "in" + *portare* "to carry") and *bearing* "significance, importance" (<*bear*), Fr. *portée* "significance, importance" (<*porter* "to carry").

doprinos: See note on *přínos-prinos*.

iznos: See note on *obnos*.

недоно́сок et al.: ="a child not carried all the way (by its mother)"; compare Cz. *nedochůdče*.

obnos: Compare Ger. *Betrag* "amount" (<*tragen* "to carry"), Sp. *importe* "amount" and It. *importo* "amount" (both ult. <Lat. *in* "in" + *portare* "to carry").

oponašati: orig. "to revile, abuse" (compare Rus. *поноше́ние*), then "to imitate in a derisive, disparaging manner," whence the present meaning.

отнести́сь et al., *отноше́ние et al.*: The basic notion underlying the various meanings is that of relationship; the words are loan-translations of Fr. *relation* "relation(ship)" (ult. <Lat. *re-* "back" + *latus*, past part. of *ferre* "to carry"), *rapport* "relation(ship)" (ult. <Lat. *re-* + *ad* "to" + *portare* "to carry"), *se* (refl. pron.) *rapporter* "to relate (to)." Compare

also modern Gr. ἀναφέρομαι "to relate (to)" (ult. <ancient Gr. ἀνά- "back" φέρειν "to carry").

понóс: See colloquial егó несёт "he has diarrhea" (literally, "he is carried along").

ponos: The underlying idea is that of "carrying oneself proudly."

поношéние: Compare Eng. to carry on in the sense of "to create an uproar" and invective (ult. <Lat. in "in" + vehere "to carry").

ponašanje: ="the way one carries oneself"; the word is a loan-translation of Ger. Betragen "behavior" (<tragen "to carry"). Compare also Eng. bearing "manner, behavior" (<bear), comportment and deportment (both ult. <Lat. portare "to carry").

podnieść: See note on Rus. поднять, Pol. podjąć.

поднóс et al.: See Rus. поднестú; the Czech and Serbo-Croatian words are borrowed from Russian.

podnesak: See the second meaning of podnijeti.

podnośnik, podniosły: See podnieść.

перенóсный-przenośny-prenosan, přenesený-prenesen: A metaphorical mean ing is one which has been "carried over," i.e. transferred, from the litera meaning of the word; compare Eng. metaphorical (ult. <Gr. μετά "over" + φέρειν "to carry"), Ger. übertragen "metaphorical" (<über "over" + tragen "to carry").

преподношéние: See поднестú.

превознестú-preuznositi: See вознестú-uznijeti and note on Pol. wywyższyć, Cz. vyvýšiti, S-C uzvisiti.

přednáška: modeled on Ger. Vortrag "lecture" (<vor "before, in front" tragen "to carry").

přínos-prinos: Compare Fr. apport "contribution" (ult. <Lat. ad "to" + portare "to carry"), Ger. Beitrag "contribution" (<bei "at, near" + tragen "to carry").

prinosan: See note on unosan.

произношéние: Compare Gr. προφορά "pronunciation" (<πρό "forth" + φέρειν "to carry").

zniesienie: ="(the act of) carrying or bringing down," i.e. wrecking, destroying.

сношéния-snošaj: See note on отнестúсь et al., отношéние et al.

снóска: Compare Eng. reference (ult. <Lat. re- "back" + ferre "to carry").

uniesienie: See note on Cz. uchvacující and úchvatný, Rus. восхищéние et al., Pol. zachwyt and zachwycający.

usnesení: <usnésti se "to decide, resolve; to decree"; the semantic development of the word---"mutual toleration, friendly relations" > "agreement" > "a formal, agreed decision"---is apparent from snésti "to bear, endure" (see snesitelný), snésti se "to be on good terms, get along together; (arch.) to decide, resolve." A comparable progression in meaning is evident in Ger. Vertrag "contract; treaty," vertragen "to bear, endure," sich (refl. pron.) vertragen "to be on good terms, get along together" (<tragen "to carry").

wniosek: The first meaning reflects that of wnieść "to present, submit"; regarding the second meaning, compare Eng. inference (ult. <Lat. in "in" + ferre "to carry").

unosan: Compare Ger. einträglich "profitable" (<ein- "in" + tragen "to carry").

výnos: The first meaning reflects the notion of something "brought forth" or "handed down" by an authoritative body; regarding the other two meanings, compare Ger. Ertrag "income, proceeds; output" (<er- "out" + tragen "to carry").

uznijeti: Regarding the development of the second meaning from the first, see note on Pol. wywyższyć, Cz. vyvýšiti, S-C uzvisiti.

wzniosły et al., vznešený-uznesen: See the first meaning of wznieść et al.

взнос: a thing which is "brought up, presented," i.e. paid.

Вознесéние-Uznesenje: from a Church Slavic loan-translation of Gr. 'Ανάληψις (<ἀνά- "up" + λαμβάνειν "to take").

zanos, zanesenost: See note on Cz. uchvacující and úchvatný, Rus. восхищéние et al., Pol. zachwyt and zachwycający.

занóсчивый: The basic notion is that of being "carried away" by feelings of self-importance.

НИК	NIK	NIK	NI(K), NIC
	ponik: spring (of water); underground stream	podniknouti, podnikati: to undertake podnikavý: enterprising, venturesome podnik: undertaking, venture; (business) enterprise, concern	niknuti (nići), nicati: to sprout, germinate; to arise, emerge
[R]	[P]	[Cz]	[S-C]

[R]	[P]	[Cz]	[S-C]
		podnikatel: entrepreneur, businessman	
прони́кнуть, проника́ть: to penetrate	przeniknąć, przenikać: to penetrate	proniknouti, pronikati: to penetrate	proniknuti (pronići), pronicati: to penetrate; to sprout, germinate
проникнове́нный: sincere, heartfelt			
вни́кнуть, вника́ть: to probe, inquire, go (into)	wniknąć, wnikać: to penetrate; to probe, inquire, go (into)	vniknouti, vnikati: to penetrate; to probe, inquire, go (into)	
	wyniknąć, wynikać: to result	vyniknouti, vynikati: to excel, be prominent	
возни́кнуть, возника́ть: to arise, emerge		vzniknouti, vznikati: to arise, emerge	

NOTES

Basic meaning of root: to thrust forth

A group of words with precisely the opposite root-meaning (e.g. Rus. ни́кнуть "to droop," Pol. niknąć "to disappear," Cz. zaniknouti "to lapse, expire, cease to exist," S-C poniknuti "to lower") is held by some to belong with the words listed here, the assumption being that the root-meaning "to droop, lapse, disappear" is primary and that the meanings "to emerge," "to penetrate," etc. are attributable to combination with various prefixes; S-C niknuti would then represent an instance in which the secondary meaning was retained after loss of a prefix. (The derivatives of root ЛУЧ$_1$ [etc.] "to separate; to join, unite" show similar semantic confusion.)

podniknouti, podnikavý, podnik, podnikatel: See note on Rus. предприня́ть, предприи́мчивый et al., предприя́тие and предпринима́тель et al., S-C preduzeti and preduzeće.

проникнове́нный: ‹прони́кнуть, hence = "characterized by deep feeling."

вни́кнуть, возни́кнуть: borrowed from Church Slavic.

ОБЩ	OBEC, OBC, OBCZ	OBEC, OBC, OBČ	OPĆ, OPŠT
о́бщий: general; common; total	obcy: alien, strange; foreign		opći, opšti: general; common
			općenit, opštenit: general; common
		obec: community; society (organization)	
	obecny: present, on hand; present (time)	obecný: general; common	
общи́на: community	obczyzna: foreign lands; (arch.) strange, foreign things	občina (arch.): communal land	općina, opština: community
о́бщество: society (organization); society (the company of others); society (social entity, order); company, firm		obecenstvo: (theater) audience	općinstvo, opštinstvo: the public; (theater) audience
обще́ственность: the public			
		občan: citizen	
		občanský: civil; civic; civilian	
обща́ться: to associate, consort (with)	obcować: to associate, consort (with)	obcovati: to associate, consort (with)	općiti (opštiti): to associate, consort (with)
общи́тельный: sociable			
	obcokrajowy: foreign		
общежи́тие: dormitory; social life			
			izopćiti, izopćavati: to bar, exclude; to excommunicate
сообщи́ть, сообща́ть: to communicate, report			saopćiti (saopštiti), saopćavati (saopštavati): to communicate, report
[R]	[P]	[Cz]	[S-C]

[R]	[P]	[Cz]	[S-C]
сообщник: accomplice			
	*wyobcować: to bar, exclude	*vyobcovati: to bar, exclude; to excommunicate	

NOTES

Basic meaning of root: general; common

The semantic development of the root proceeded from the original notio[n] "surrounding, situated round about" (see prefix o[б]-o[b] "around") to the more abstract concepts "general, widespread" and "common, pertaining to the community rather than the individual." The shift in the meaning of Pol. obc[y] reflects the fact that what pertains or belongs to the community as a whole is, from the individual's standpoint, "not mine, someone else's," hence foreign.

The Russian root-form and the Serbo-Croatian form OPŠT are of Church Slavic origin. (The native Russian form occurs in obsolete о́бчий.)

о́бщий et al.: The primary adjective is not attested in Czech; see obecný.

obecny-obecný: ⟨obsolete Pol. obec "community," Cz. obec; the Polish word was originally synonymous with Cz. obecný.

občan: orig. "member of a community"; see obec.

občanský: See občan and note on S-C građanin and građanski, Rus. граждани́н and гражда́нский.

izopćiti: See note on wyobcować-vyobcovati.

сообщи́ть-saopćiti: ="to make common or general," i.e. publicize; compare Eng. communicate (ult. ⟨Lat. communis "common"). The Serbo-Croatian word is borrowed from Russian.

wyobcować-vyobcovati: ="to remove from the community"; compare Eng. excommunicate (ult. ⟨Lat. ex "out" + communis "common").

OK, ОЧ	OK, OCZ	OK, OČ, ŮČ	OK, OČ, ODŽ
о́ко (arch.): eye	oko: eye	oko: eye	oko: eye
очки́ (pl.): eyeglasses			
окно́: window	okno: window	okno: window	okno: window-pane; mine-shaft
[R]	[P]	[Cz]	[S-C]

	oczkować: to ogle; (hort.) to graft	očkovati: (med.) to inoculate, vaccinate; (hort.) to graft	
		očitý (svědek): eye(-witness)	očit: obvious
			**očitovati: to declare, state; to show, display
		vůčihledě (lit.): obviously	očigledan: obvious
			očevid: inspection, examination
очевидец: eye-witness			očevidac: eye-witness
очевидный: obvious	oczywisty: obvious	očividný: obvious	očevidan: obvious
	okamgnienie: moment, instant	okamžik, (arch.) okamžení: moment, instant	
			bezočan: impudent
			naočari (pl.): eyeglasses
	naoczny: obvious; (świadek) eye(-witness)		naočit: conspicuous; imposing
			nazočan: present, on hand
		obočí (sg.): eyebrows	
			predočiti, predočavati: to demonstrate; to present; (sebi) to imagine
			predodžba: notion, idea
	przeoczenie: oversight, inadvertence		
			suočiti, suočavati: to confront
		vůči: in relation (to); in comparison (with)	uoči: on the eve (of)
			uočiti, uočavati: to see, perceive
[R]	[P]	[Cz]	[S-C]

	*zoczyć (arch.): to see, perceive	*zočiti (lit.): to see, perceive	
[R]	[P]	[Cz]	[S-C]

NOTES

Basic meaning of root: eye

The Slavic root is related to Eng. eye, Ger. Auge "eye," Lat. oculus "eye" (>Eng. ocular, binoculars).

окнó et al.: Compare Eng. window (<Old Norse vindauga "window" < vindr "wind" + auga "eye").

oczkować-očkovati: Pol. oczko, Cz. očko "little eye" have the secondary meaning "bud," whence the horticultural meaning of the verb. Compare Ger. äugeln "to graft" (<Auge "eye; bud") and Eng. eye (="bud"). Eng. inoculate (<Lat. in "in" + oculus "eye; bud") meant "to graft" in older usage; the medical application of the word, like that of Cz. očkovati, is an extension of the original meaning. Regarding the first meaning of Pol. oczkować, compare Eng. ogle, derived from a Low German word akin to Ger. äugeln "to ogle" (<Auge).

očitovati: <očit, hence = "to make obvious, manifest."

vůčihledě-očigledan: See note on очеви́дный et al.; regarding the first element in the Czech word, see note on vůči-uoči.

očevid: Compare Ger. Augenschein "inspection, examination" (<Auge "eye" + scheinen "to seem").

очеви́дный et al.: Compare Ger. augenscheinlich "obvious" (<Auge "eye" + scheinen "to seem").

okamgnienie et al.: The second element is from the root of migać-mžikati "to wink, blink"; compare Ger. Augenblick "moment" (<Auge "eye" + blicken "to look, glance").

bezočan: ="without eyes," i.e. acting heedlessly and without regard to propriety.

nazočan: ="before one's eyes"; an intrusive z appears after the prefix na-.

predočiti: ="to bring before one's eyes."

predodžba: See the third meaning of predočiti.

vůči-uoči: ="into the eyes (of)," i.e. facing; vůči is from OCz. v óči.

ПЯ, ПН, ПИН, ПОН	PIĄ, PIĘ, PIN, PON	PĚ, PJA, PN, PIN, PÍN, PON	PE(N), PIN, PN, PON
пнуть, пинáть (coll.): to kick		pnouti (lit.): to stretch, extend; to link	peti (penjati): to raise
	piąć się: to climb	pnouti se: to wind, twine (ivy, etc.); (lit.) to tower	peti (penjati) se: to climb
	napięcie: tension, strain	napětí: tension, strain	napetost: tension, strain
			napon: tension, strain
			naponi (pl.): labor pains
		napínavý: fascinating, absorbing, thrilling	
	opona: covering; tire	opona: curtain	opna: membrane
			otponac: trigger
		přepínač, přepinač: (electric light, etc.) switch	
		přepjatý: affected, artificial; exorbitant	
препинáние: punctuation			
препóна: obstacle, hindrance	przepona: (anat.) diaphragm	přepona: (math.) hypotenuse	prepona: obstacle, hindrance; (anat.) groin
перепóнка: membrane			preponka: (anat.) diaphragm
препя́тствие: obstacle, hindrance			
		předpona: (gram.) prefix	
	przypiąć, przypinać: to pin, clasp, fasten	připnouti, připínati: to pin, clasp, fasten; to couple (railroad cars)	pripeti, pripinjati: to pin, clasp, fasten; to raise
		přípona: (gram.) suffix	
распя́тие: crucifixion; crucifix	rozpiętość: wing-spread (of a bird),	rozpětí: span (of time); span (of hand);	raspeće: crucifixion; crucifix
[R]	[P]	[Cz]	[S-C]

[R]	[P]	[Cz]	[S-C]
	wing-span (of an airplane); span (of an arch, bridge); range (of prices)	wing-spread (of a bird), wing-span (of an airplane); span (of an arch, bridge); mark-up (in price)	
			raspelo: crucifix
			raspon: wing-spread (of a bird); span (of an arch, bridge)
		rozpínavý: expansionist (policy); expansible (e.g. gas); expansive (person)	
	spinka: stud, cuff-link	spínadlo: buckle, clasp	
	spona: clamp	spona: buckle, clasp; (gram.) copulative verb	spona: buckle, clasp; clamp; (gram.) copulative verb
	szpon: claw		
			upinjanje: exertion, efforts
		úponek, úponka: tendril	
		vypínač, vypinač: (electric light, etc.) switch	
		vypínavý: arrogant	
			uspinjača: funicular railway
запи́нка (coll.): stammering	zapinka: buckle, clasp		
	zapona (arch.): buckle, clasp; curtain	zápona (arch.): buckle, clasp	zapon: buckle, clasp
за́понка: stud, cuff-link	zaponka (arch.): stud, cuff-link	záponka (arch.): buckle, clasp	zaponka: buckle, clasp
			zaponac: buckle, clasp; spoke
запята́я: (punc.) comma			zapeta: (punc.) comma

NOTES

Basic meaning of root: to stretch, pull tight

The root-meaning has shifted markedly in the primary verbs, except in the case of Cz. *pnouti*, but is still apparent in most of the other derivatives.

Kindred non-Slavic words are Eng. *spin*, *span*.

пнуть et al.: Пнуть, *pnouti* are secondary infinitive formations from 1 sg. *пну*, *pnu*, replacing earlier *пять*, *píti*. Pol. *piąć* "to fasten" is obsolete.

peti, *piąć się*: The respective 1 sg. forms are *penjem*, *pnę się*.

napięcie et al., *napon*: See note on Rus. *напряжéние*, Pol. *naprężenie*.

otponac: ‹*otpinjati* "to release"; compare Fr. *détente* "trigger" (‹*détendre* "to release," ult. ‹Lat. *de* "off, down" + *tendere* "to stretch").

препинáние: from a Church Slavic verb meaning "to hinder" (compare *препóна*, *препя́тствие*), punctuation being regarded as a system whereby the reader of a text is periodically slowed or brought to a halt.

препóна: borrowed from Church Slavic.

przepona: orig. "barrier" (compare *препóна*, *prepona*); the diaphragm is a partition separating the chest cavity from the abdominal cavity.

přepona: The hypotenuse of a right-angled triangle "stretches across," *i.e.* subtends or is opposite to, the right angle; the Czech word is constructed in roughly the same manner as Eng. *hypotenuse* (ult. ‹Gr. *ὑπό* "under" + *τείνειν* "to stretch") and *subtend* (ult. ‹Lat. *sub* "under" + *tendere* "to stretch").

prepona (second meaning): ="extension, expanse," *i.e.* region extending above the genitals.

preponka: See the first meaning of *prepona* and note on *przepona*.

препя́тствие: borrowed from Church Slavic.

předpona, *přípona*: ‹*předepnouti* "to pin, clasp, fasten in front," *připnouti*; compare Eng. *prefix*, *suffix* (ult. ‹Lat. *prae* "before, in front," *sub* "under" + *figere* "to fasten, attach").

spona (Cz., S-C; last meaning): ‹*sepnouti*, *sapeti* "to link, bind"; the function of a copulative verb is to link the subject with the idea expressed by the predicate. Compare Eng. *copulative* (ult. ‹Lat. *copula* "link, bond").

szpon: ‹*spona*.

úponek, *úponka*: See the first meaning of *pnouti se*.

vypínavý: ="stretching (*i.e.* thrusting) o.s. forward."

uspinjača: ‹*uspinjati se* "to climb."

запятáя-*zapeta*: ‹obsolete *запя́ться* (=modern *запну́ться*) "to stumble; to falter in one's speech" (see *запи́нка*), *zapeti* "to get stuck, come to a standstill; to falter in one's speech"; see note on *препинáние*.

ПА(Д)	PA(D)	PA(D), PÁD	PA(D)
пасть, пáдать: to fall	paść, padać: to fall	padnouti, padati: to fall	pasti (padnuti), padati: to fall
		pád: fall, drop; downfall, ruin; (gram.) case; (arch.) cattle-plague	pad: fall, drop; downfall, ruin
падéж: (gram.) case			padež: (gram.) case
падёж: cattle-plague			
			padina: slope
пасть: trap; mouth (of an animal)	paść (arch.): trap	past: trap	
	paszcza: mouth (of an animal)		
пáдкий: fond (of), inclined (toward)		pádný: heavy; vigorous; cogent, convincing	
пáдаль: carrion	padlina: carrion		padaline (pl.): precipitation (rain, snow, etc.)
		padák: parachute	
		padouch: scoundrel	
падýчая: epilepsy	padaczka: epilepsy	padoucnice: epilepsy	padavica: epilepsy
листопáд: autumnal falling of the leaves	listopad: November	listopad: November	listopad: October
	prostopadły: perpendicular; sheer (drop, etc.)		
	spadochron: parachute		padobran: parachute
водопáд: waterfall	wodospad: waterfall	vodopád: waterfall	vodopad: waterfall
			dopasti se, dopadati se: to please
			ispad: sortie, sally; attack, assault; lunge (in fencing)
	napad: attack, assault; (med.) fit, attack;	nápad: sudden idea, notion; whim; descent,	napad, napadaj: attack, assault; (med.)
[R]	[P]	[Cz]	[S-C]

	fit (of anger, etc.)	devolution (of property to an heir)	fit, attack; fit (of anger, etc.)
нападе́ние: attack, assault		napadení: attack, assault	
напа́сть (coll.): misfortune	napaść: attack, assault		napast: temptation; misfortune
	napastliwy, napastniczy: aggressive		
		nápadný: striking, conspicuous; showy, bright; strange, odd	napadan: striking, conspicuous; showy, bright
		nápadník: pretender (to throne, etc.); suitor	
	opady (pl.): precipitation (rain, snow, etc.)		
			opadač: slanderer
	odpadki (pl.): refuse, scraps, waste materials	odpadky (pl.): refuse, scraps, waste materials	otpaci (pl.): refuse, scraps, waste materials
		odpadlík: renegade, apostate	otpadnik: renegade, apostate
		přepad: surprise attack; spillway (of dam, etc.)	prepad: surprise attack
			prepast: fear
припа́сть, припада́ть: to fall	przypaść, przypadać: to fall; to fall (on a certain day); to be (to s.o.'s liking, taste, etc.); to fall to (s.o.'s) lot	připadnouti, připadati: to fall (on a certain day); to fall to (s.o.'s) lot; to seem	pripasti, pripadati: to fall; to fall to (s.o.'s) lot; (pripadati only) to belong
припа́док: (med.) fit, attack; fit (of anger, etc.)	przypadek: chance, accident; case, instance; (gram.) case	případ: case, instance	pripadak: accessory, appurtenance
	przypadkować: (gram.) to decline		
		případný: proper, suitable; possible	pripadan: accessory, appurtenant
[R]	[P]	[Cz]	[S-C]

[R]	[P]	[Cz]	[S-C]
пропа́сть, пропада́ть: to be lost, disappear; to perish	przepaść, przepadać: to be lost, disappear; to fail; to be forfeit; (przepadać only) to be fond (of)	propadnouti, propadati (propadávati): to fall through; to fail; to be addicted (to); to be forfeit	propasti, propadati: to sink; to decay, decline; to fail; to be forfeit
			propalica: wastrel, dissolute person
про́пасть: precipice, abyss	przepaść: precipice, abyss	propast: precipice, abyss	propast: precipice, abyss; downfall, ruin
распа́д: disintegration, dissolution	rozpad: disintegration, dissolution	rozpad: disintegration, dissolution; decay, decomposition	raspad: disintegration, dissolution; decay, decomposition; downfall, ruin
	rozpadlina: crevice, fissure		
спад: drop, decline	spad: drop, decline; slope	spád: slope; course (of events, etc.); cadence	spad: drop, decline; slope
	spadek: drop, decline; slope; inheritance, legacy		
совпа́сть, совпада́ть: to coincide			
упа́док: decline, decay; decadence	upadek: fall, drop; downfall, ruin; decline, decay; decadence	úpadek: decline, decay; decadence; bankruptcy	
	upadłość: bankruptcy		
			upropastiti, upropašćivati (upropašćavati, upropaštavati): to ruin
		vpád: invasion; raid	upad: invasion; raid
впа́дина: hollow, cavity; depression (in the ground)			
			upadljiv: striking, conspicuous

[R]	[P]	[Cz]	[S-C]
выпад: attack, assault; invective; lunge (in fencing)	wypad: sortie, sally; lunge (in fencing)	výpad: sortie, sally; attack, assault; invective; lunge (in fencing)	
	wypadek: accident, mishap; incident, occurrence; case, instance		
		zpropadený: damned, accursed	
запад: west	zapad: physical collapse	západ: west; setting (of the sun); turn (of key in lock)	zapad: west; setting (of the sun)
	zapadlina: hollow, cavity; depression (in the ground)		
западня: trap	zapadnia: trap-door		
	zaprzepaścić, zaprzepaszczać: to lose; to waste, squander		
*запропаститься (coll.): to disappear	zaprzepaścić się, zaprzepaszczać się: to disappear		

NOTES

Basic meaning of root: to fall

пасть (v.) et al.: The respective 1 sg. forms of пасть and its analogues are паду́, padnę, padnu, padnem.

pád (third meaning), паде́ж-padež: modeled on Lat. casus (<cadere "to fall"), whence Eng. case, and Gr. πτῶσις (<πίπτειν "to fall"); the "oblique" cases were regarded by the ancient grammarians as "falling away" from the nominative. The Russian word is borrowed from Church Slavic, the Serbo-Croatian word from Russian. Compare Ger. Fall "(gram.) case" (<fallen "to fall"), Hung. eset "(gram.) case" (<esni "to fall").

пасть (n.) et al.: <Common Slavic *padtь. The original meaning was "hole in the ground," more particularly one used for trapping animals; the second meaning of the Russian word is a later development. Compare западня́-zapadnia.

paszcza: <paść (n.); see preceding note.

па́дкий: ="falling, i.e. leaning, inclined (toward)."

pádný: The underlying idea is "falling heavily, weighty."

пáдаль-*padlina*: Compare Eng. *cadaver* (ult. <Lat. *cadere* "to fall"), Gr *πτῶμα* "corpse" (<*πίπτειν* "to fall").

padák: See note on *spadochron*-*padobran*.

padouch: prob. = "one who has dangled from the gallows."

падýчая et al.: Compare Eng. *falling sickness* "epilepsy," Ger. *Fallsucht* "epilepsy" (<*fallen* "to fall" + *Sucht* "sickness").

листопáд et al.: The first element is from *лист*-*list* "leaf" (obsolete in Polish).

spadochron-*padobran*: Compare Eng. *parachute* (<Fr. *parachute* < It. *parare* "to protect, shield" + Fr. *chute* "fall"), Ger. *Fallschirm* "parachute" (<*fallen* "to fall" + *Schirm* "shield").

dopasti se: ="to fall out (*i.e*. turn out) well"; the word is probably loan-translation of Ger. *gefallen* "to please" (<*fallen* "to fall").

ispad: See note on *вы́пад et al*.

napad (Pol., S-C)-*napadaj*, *нападéние*-*napadení*, *napaść*: Compare Eng. *to fall upon* in the sense of "to attack," Ger. *Anfall* "attack, assault; (med.) fit, attack; fit (of anger, etc.)" (<*an* "on, to" + *fallen* "to fall"); regarding the Polish form PAŚĆ, see note on *пасть* (n.) *et al*.

nápad: Compare Ger. *Einfall* "sudden idea, notion; whim" (<*ein*- "in" + *fallen* "to fall"), *Anfall* "descent, devolution (of property to an heir)" (<*an* "on, to" + *fallen*).

напáсть-*napast*: Both misfortune and temptation are seen as something that "falls upon" a person; compare Eng. *Misfortune befell him*. Regarding the form ПАСТЬ-PAST, see note on *пасть* (n.) *et al*.

nápadný-*napadan*: modeled on Ger. *auffallend*, *auffällig* "striking, conspicuous; showy, bright; strange, odd" (<*auf* "on" + *fallen* "to fall").

nápadník: orig. "prospective heir, claimant"; see the third meaning of *nápad*.

opadač: The meaning presumably reflects the notion of "falling upon," *i.e*. attacking.

odpadki et al.: Compare Eng. *offal* (<*off* + *fall*), Ger. *Abfälle* (pl.) "refuse, scraps" (<*ab* "off, away" + *fallen* "to fall"), Fr. *déchets* (pl.) "refuse, scraps" (ult. <Lat. *de* "off, away" + *cadere* "to fall"); the singular of the Serbo-Croatian word is *otpadak*.

odpadlík-*otpadnik*: one who "falls away" from his faith or from some other allegiance; compare Ger. *Abfall* "apostasy, defection" (<*ab* "off, away + *fallen* "to fall").

přepad-*prepad*: Compare Ger. *Überfall* "surprise attack" (<*über* "over" + *fallen* "to fall").

prepast: The underlying idea is presumably that of being "fallen upon, *i.e*. suddenly overtaken, by a frightening experience; compare *prepad*. Regarding the form PAST, see note on *пасть* (n.) *et al*.

припáдок: See note on *napad*-*napadaj*, *нападéние*-*napadení*, *napaść*.

przypadek-*případ*: In many languages, the element of chance is seen as atter of how things "fall" or "fall out" (a notion strongly influenced by he game of dice); compare Eng. chance, case, accident and incident (all lt. <Lat. cadere "to fall"), Ger. Fall "case, instance," Zufall "chance, ccident" and Vorfall "incident, occurrence" (all <fallen "to fall"), Hung. set "case, instance" and esemény "incident, occurrence" (both <esni "to all"), Pol. wypadek below. Regarding the last meaning of przypadek, see ote on pád, падéж-padež.

pripadak: See the last meaning of pripadati.

przypadkować: See the last meaning of przypadek.

případný: ="suited to, or dependent upon, the given case"; see případ.

pripadan: See the last meaning of pripadati.

przepaść (v.) et al.: Compare Ger. durchfallen "to fail" (<<durch "through" + fallen "to fall") and verfallen "to decay, decline; to be ad-icted (to); to be forfeit" (<<ver-, prefix expressing the notion of loss or amage + fallen), Eng. escheat "forfeiture, reversion of land to the State" ult. <Lat. cadere "to fall"). Underlying the last meaning of Pol. przepadać s the notion of "pining away" for something. Regarding the second meaning f the Serbo-Croatian word, see also the note on упáдок et al.

propalica: See propasti; the letter d has been lost before l.

прóпасть et al.: Regarding the form ПАСТЬ-PAŚĆ-PAST, see note on пасть n.) et al.

rozpad (Cz.)-raspad: See note on упáдок et al.

spád: Compare Eng. cadence (ult. <Lat. cadere "to fall").

spadek (third meaning): that which "falls" to an heir; compare the last eaning of Cz. nápad.

совпáсть: Compare Eng. coincide (ult. <Lat. cum "with, together" + in in" + cadere "to fall"), Ger. zusammenfallen "to coincide" (<<zusammen "to-ether" + fallen "to fall").

упáдок et al.: Compare Eng. decay and decadence (both ult. <Lat. de off, away" + cadere "to fall") and see note on przepaść (v.) et al.

upropastiti: <propast.

vpád-upad: Compare Ger. Einfall "invasion; raid" (<<ein- "in" + fallen to fall").

upadljiv: See note on nápadný-napadan.

вы́пад et al.: Compare Ger. Ausfall "sortie, sally; invective; lunge (in encing)" (<<aus "out" + fallen "to fall").

wypadek: See note on przypadek-případ.

zpropadený: orig. "ruined, lost"; see propadnouti and compare Cz. za-ratiti.

зáпад-západ-zapad (S-C): See note on Pol. wschód.

западня́-zapadnia: Compare Ger. Falle "trap" (<<fallen "to fall").

zaprzepaścić, запропасти́ться-zaprzepaścić się: <przepaść (n.), прóпасть.

ПАС	PAS, PAŚ, PASZ	PAS, PÁS	PAS, PAŠ
пасти́: to tend, put out to pasture	†paść, pasać: to tend, put out to pasture	†pásti, pásati: to tend, put out to pasture	pasti: to tend, put out to pasture; to graze
	pasza: fodder		paša, pašnjak: pasture
пасту́х: shepherd, herdsman	pastuch: shepherd, herdsman	pastuch (arch.), pastucha (arch.): shepherd, herdsman	
па́стырь: pastor; (arch.) shepherd, herdsman	pasterz: shepherd, herdsman; pastor	pastýř, pastevec, pasák: shepherd, herdsman	pastir: shepherd, herdsman
па́ства: congregation, flock	pastwa: prey; (arch.) fodder	pastva: pasture	pastva: congregation, flock
	pastwić się (nad + inst.): to torment, mistreat		
па́стбище: pasture	pastwisko: pasture	pastvisko, pastviště, pastvina: pasture	pasište: pasture
		cizopasník: (biol.) parasite; parasite, sponger	
	pasożyt: (biol.) parasite; parasite, sponger		
			pustopašan: wild, unrestrained
	samopas: alone, without supervision		
спаси́бо: thank you			
безопа́сный: safe, secure			bezopasan: safe, secure
опаса́ться: to fear			
опа́сный: dangerous			opasan: dangerous
	opasły: obese		
припа́сы (pl.): supplies, provisions			
[R]	[P]	[Cz]	[S-C]

спасти́, спаса́ть: to save, rescue запа́с: stock, supply, reserve; (mil.) reserve	spaść, spasać: to fatten (in pasture) zapas: stock, supply, reserve	spásti, spásati: to consume, use up by grazing *spasiti: to save, rescue	spasti, spasavati: to save, rescue *spasiti: to save, rescue Spasovo: (rel.) Ascension
[R]	[P]	[Cz]	[S-C]

NOTES

Basic meaning of root: to tend, put out to pasture

The more general notion of "guarding, preserving, saving, etc." is apparent in many of the derivatives.

The Slavic root is related to Eng. food, fodder and foster (orig. = "to feed"), Lat. pascere "to tend, put out to pasture" (>Eng. pastor, pasture), pabulum "food" (>Eng. pabulum) and panis "bread" (>Eng. pantry).

па́стырь-pasterz, па́ства-pastva (S-C): The religious application of the words parallels that of Eng. pastor (ult. <Lat. pastor "shepherd, herdsman"), congregation (ult. <Lat. cum "with, together" + grex "herd, flock"), flock.

pastwić się: See the first meaning of pastwa.

cizopasník: The first element is from cizí "alien, foreign"; compare Rus. чужея́дный.

pasożyt: The second element is a corrupted form of the root of rzyć "buttocks"; thus, the original meaning, from which both of the present meanings developed, was "buttocks-feeder," i.e. "glutton."

pustopašan, samopas: orig. "grazing alone, untended."

спаси́бо: <*спаси́ бог "God preserve you!"; see спасти́.

безопа́сный-bezopasan: See опа́сный-opasan; the Serbo-Croatian word is borrowed from Russian.

опаса́ться: orig. "to be on one's guard"; compare опа́сный.

опа́сный-opasan: ="(which is) to be guarded against, calling for the exercise of caution"; the Serbo-Croatian word is borrowed from Russian.

спасти́-spasti: borrowed from Church Slavic.

spasiti (Cz., S-C): a denominative formed from OCz.-S-C spas "salvation," which is of Church Slavic origin.

Spasovo: <obsolete spas "savior," a Church Slavic borrowing.

	PATR(Z)	PATR, PÁTR, PATŘ	PATR
	patrzeć (patrzyć): to look	patřiti: to belong; (lit.) to look	patriti: to belong
	patrzeć (patrzyć) się: to be fitting, proper	patřiti se: to be fitting, proper	
		pátrati: to search	
		patrný: perceptible; obvious	
	niedopatrzenie: oversight, inadvertence	nedopatření: oversight, inadvertence	
	opatrzyć, opatrywać: to provide, furnish; to dress (a wound)	opatřiti, opatřovati: to provide, furnish	
	opatrunek: dressing, bandage		
	opatrzny: provident; cautious, circumspect	opatrný: cautious, circumspect	
	Opatrzność: (rel.) Providence	opatrnost: caution, circumspection	
		opatrovati: to look after, take care of	
		opatrovna (arch.): asylum, institution, home; kindergarten	
	rozpatrzyć, rozpatrywać: to examine, consider (a matter)		
		spatřiti, spatřovati (lit.): to see	
	zapatrywanie: opinion, view		
	[P]	[Cz]	[S-C]

NOTES

Basic meaning of root: to look

The only vestige of the root in Russian is dialectal пáтрать "to value esteem highly." (Compare the similar development of the meaning of Eng. regard [‹Fr. regarder "to look"], respect [ult. ‹Lat. specere "to look"].)

Many of the derivatives have semantic counterparts under roots ГЛЯД (etc.), МОТР (etc.) and ЗР (etc.).

patřiti (first meaning)-*patriti*: The semantic progression has been the following: "to look (at)" 〉 "to pay attention (to), consider" 〉 "to pertain (to), concern" 〉 "to belong (to)"; compare It. *spettare* "to belong, be owing (to)" (〈Lat. *spectare* "to look"). For similar development of the notion of listening, see Cz. *slušeti* and *příslušeti*.

patrzeć się-*patřiti se*: an extension of the idea of belonging (a meaning not, however, attested in the case of the Polish active verb); compare Ger. *gehören* "to belong" and *sich* (refl. pron.) *gehören* "to be fitting, proper," Pol. *należeć*, *należny* and *należyty*, Cz. *náležeti* and *náležitý*, Pol. *słuszny*, Cz. *slušeti* (*se*) and *slušný*, *příslušeti* and *příslušný*.

opatrzyć-*opatřiti*: ="to see to it (that something is made available)"; compare Eng. *provide* (ult. 〈Lat. *videre* "to see"), Ger. *versehen* "to provide, furnish" (〈*sehen* "to see"), Hung. *ellátni* "to provide, furnish" (〈*látni* "to see").

opatrzny-*opatrný*: See *opatrzyć* and note on Pol. *oględny*.

Opatrzność: See *opatrzyć* and note on Rus. *Провиде́ние*, S-C *Proviđenje*.

opatrovati, *opatrovna*: Compare *opatřiti*; *opatrovati* is, in origin, a doublet of *opatřovati*.

ПЕ(К), ПЕЧ	PIE(K), PIECZ	PE, PÉ, PEČ, PÉČ	PE(K), PEČ, PEC
печь: to bake, roast (tr.)	*piec*: to bake, roast (tr.)	*péci*: to bake, roast (tr.)	*peći*: to bake, roast (tr.); to distill
пе́чься: to bake, roast (intr.); (lit.) to take care (of)	*piec się*: to bake, roast (intr.)	*péci se*: to bake, roast (intr.)	*peći se*: to bake, roast (intr.)
печь: stove, oven	*piec*: stove, oven	*pec*: stove, oven	*peć*: stove, oven
	piecza: care, protection	*péče*: care, protection	
		pečlivý: careful; attentive, solicitous	
печа́ль: grief, sorrow			*pečal*: grief, sorrow
печа́льный: sad, sorrowful	*pieczołowity*: attentive, solicitous		*pečalan*: sad, sorrowful
пе́чень: liver	*pieczeń*: roast meat	*pečeně*: roast meat	
	pieczeniarz: parasite, sponger		*pečenjar*: roasting-spit
			pecara: distillery
[R]	[P]	[Cz]	[S-C]

[R]	[P]	[Cz]	[S-C]
			dvopek: biscuit
беспе́чность: heedlessness, unconcern	bezpieczeństwo: safety, security	bezpečnost: safety, security	
		bezpečiti se (lit.): to rely, depend (on)	
	niebezpieczeństwo: danger	nebezpečí, (lit.) nebezpečenství: danger	
опе́ка: guardianship, trusteeship	opieka: care, protection; guardianship, trusteeship		opeka: brick
обеспе́чить, обеспе́чивать: to provide for (one's family); to provide, supply; to guarantee, insure, assure; (arch.) to safeguard, secure			
попечи́тель: guardian, trustee			
	ubezpieczyć, ubezpieczać: to insure (against fire, theft, etc.)	ubezpečiti, ubezpečovati: to assure, give (verbal) assurance to	
	zabezpieczyć, zabezpieczać: to provide for (one's family); to safeguard, secure	zabezpečiti, zabezpečovati: to provide for (one's family); to guarantee, insure, assure; to safeguard, secure	

NOTES

Basic meaning of root: to bake, roast

A significant secondary meaning, representing a figurative extension o[f] the notion of burning or heat, is apparent in various derivatives expressin[g] both senses of the English word care, i.e. "sorrow" and "solicitude, attentiveness, protection." (Compare Rus. го́ре, Cz. hoře.) Addition of a negativ[e] prefix produced a further sub-group characterized by the meaning "freedom from care," hence "safety, security." (Lat. securus "unconcerned; secure" [>Eng. secure, sure] arose by the same process from se "without" + cura care.") See also niebezpieczeństwo et al.

The Slavic root is related to Lat. coquere "to cook" (>Eng. cook, kitch-n, concoct), Gr. πέπτειν (πέσσειν) "to cook; to digest" (>Eng. peptic, dys-eptic).

печь (v.) et al.: The respective 1 sg. forms are пеку́, piekę, peku, ečem; regarding the second meaning of peći, compare Ger. brennen "to burn; o distill" and see note on Rus. горилка et al.

печь (n.) et al.: <Common Slavic *pektь.

пе́чень: The word referred originally to the liver as an article of food see Pol. pieczeń, Cz. pečeně), then to the organ itself. Fr. foie "liver" rose in much the same way from Lat. ficatum (jecur) "the liver of an animal attened on figs" (<ficus "fig" + jecur "liver").

pieczeniarz: ="one who eats another's roast."

pecara: See the second meaning of peći and compare Ger. Brennerei "dis-illery" (<brennen "to burn; to distill"), Pol. gorzelnia.

dvopek: ="twice-baked"; compare Eng. biscuit (<Fr. biscuit < Lat. bis twice" + Fr. cuire "to cook, bake"), Ger. Zwieback "biscuit" (<zwei "two" + acken "to bake").

беспе́чность et al.: See the introductory note above.

bezpečiti se: ="to base one's security (on)"; compare bezpečnost.

niebezpieczeństwo et al.: ="non-absence of care"; two negative prefixes ombine to produce a positive meaning. Compare bezpieczeństwo-bezpečnost.

опе́ка et al.: S-C opeka "care, concern" is obsolete; the present word eflects the original meaning of the root.

обеспе́чить, ubezpieczyć-ubezpečiti, zabezpieczyć-zabezpečiti: Underly-ng the various meanings is the basic idea of "making secure, relieving of are"; compare беспе́чность et al.

ПИС	PIS	PS, PIS, PÍS	PIS
писа́ть: to write; to paint	pisać: to write	psáti: to write	pisati: to write
письмо́: writing (the ability to write); script, system of writing; letter, missive	pismo: writing (written matter); script, system of writing; (printers') type; handwriting; magazine, periodical; letter, missive	písmo: writing (the ability to write); writing (written matter); script, system of writing; (printers') type; handwriting	pismo: script, system of writing; handwriting; letter, missive
письмена́ (pl.): letters,		písmeno: letter (of alphabet)	pisme: letter (of alphabet)
[R]	[P]	[Cz]	[S-C]

characters (especially of ancient systems of writing)			
	pisownia: spelling, orthography		
		psanec: outlaw, outcast	
борзопи́сец: hack-writer			brzopisac: stenographer
	czasopismo: magazine, periodical	časopis: magazine, periodical	časopis: magazine, periodical
чистописа́ние: calligraphy			
	dalekopis: teletype, teleprinter	dálnopis: teletype, teleprinter	
	dziejopisarz: historian	dějepisec: historian	
		druhopis: copy, duplicate	
	jadłospis: menu		
		knihopis: bibliography	
		krasopis: calligraphy	krasnopis: calligraphy
ле́топись: chronicle, annals	latopis: chronicle, annals; chronicler, annalist	letopis: chronicle, annals	ljetopis: chronicle, annals
		místopis: topography	
		národopis: ethnography	narodopis (arch.): ethnography
		nerostopis: mineralogy	
		polohopis (arch.): topography	
правописа́ние: spelling, orthography		pravopis: spelling, orthography	pravopis: spelling, orthography
		přírodopis: natural science	prirodopis: natural science
	rodopis: genealogist	rodopis: genealogy	rodopis: genealogy
		rostlinopis: botany	
[R]	[P]	[Cz]	[S-C]

[R]	[P]	[Cz]	[S-C]
		rubopis: endorsement (on check, etc.)	
ру́копись: manuscript	rękopis: manuscript	rukopis: manuscript; handwriting	rukopis: manuscript; handwriting
све́топись (arch.): photography			
та́йнопись: cryptography		tajnopis: cryptography	
		těsnopis: stenography, shorthand	
		zeměpis: geography	zemljopis: geography
жи́вопись: painting, pictorial art			živopis: painting, pictorial art
		živočichopis: zoology	
жизнеописа́ние: biography		životopis: biography	životopis: biography
		dopis: letter, missive	dopis: letter, missive
на́дпись: inscription, legend	napis, nadpis: inscription, legend; title, heading	nápis, nadpis: inscription, legend; title, heading	napis, natpis: inscription, legend; title, heading
описа́ть, опи́сывать: to describe	opisać, opisywać: to describe	opsati, opisovati: to copy; to paraphrase	opisati, opisivati: to describe
	popis: show, display; (arch.) conscription; (arch.) military review, parade	popis: description	popis: list; census
подписа́ть, подпи́сывать: to sign	podpisać, podpisywać: to sign	podepsati, podpisovati: to sign	potpisati, potpisivati: to sign
пе́репись: census		přepis: (act of) copying; transcription, transliteration	prepis, prijepis: copy, duplicate
перепи́ска: (act of) copying; correspondence, exchange of letters; correspondence, letters			prepiska: correspondence, exchange of letters; correspondence, letters
предписа́ние: order, instructions		předpis: rule, regulation; order,	

[R]	[P]	[Cz]	[S-C]
		instructions; recipe; (med.) prescription	
приписа́ть, припи́сывать: to add (to a letter, etc.); to register; to ascribe, attribute	przypisać, przypisywać: to add (to a letter, etc.); to dedicate (a book); to ascribe, attribute	připsati, připisovati: to add (to a letter, etc.); to dedicate (a book); to make over, convey (property); to ascribe, attribute	pripisati, pripisivati: to add (to a letter, etc.); to ascribe, attribute
про́пись: samples of penmanship	przepis: rule, regulation; recipe; (med.) prescription	průpis: carbon copy	propis: rule, regulation
расписа́ние: schedule, time-table	rozpisanie: issuance (of bonds); writ (for an election)		
ро́спись: mural, fresco; (arch.) list		rozpis: breakdown, specification	raspis: circular (letter)
распи́ска: receipt, voucher			
	spis: list; census	spis: document; literary work, composition	spis: document; literary work, composition
спи́сок: list	spisek: conspiracy	spisek: short literary work, composition	spisak: list
		soupis: list	
вы́пись (arch.): excerpt, extract	wypis: excerpt, extract	výpis: excerpt, extract	
вы́писка: (act of) copying; excerpt, extract; subscription; discharge (from hospital, etc.)			
за́пись: entry; registration; record; recording (e.g. on tape)	zapis: bequest; registration	zápis: entry; registration; record	zapis: bequest; note; talisman
запи́ска: note; memorandum	zapisek, zapiska: note	zápisek (arch.): note	zapiska: note

NOTES

Basic meaning of root: to write

An earlier meaning, "to paint," survives only in Russian.

In a number of derivatives, the root appears in combination with various words as a suffix corresponding to Eng. -graphy (ult. <Gr. γράφειν "to write").

A related non-Slavic word is Lat. pingere "to paint" (>Eng. paint, picture).

письмена́: borrowed from Church Slavic.

psanec: a loan-translation of Lat. proscriptus "an outlaw, one whose name has been published on a list of 'proscribed' persons" (<scribere "to write").

борзопи́сец-brzopisac: The first element is from бо́рзый-brz "swift, quick."

czasopismo et al.: See note under root ЧАС (etc.).

чистописа́ние: The first element is from чи́стый "clean, neat"; see note on krasopis-krasnopis.

dalekopis-dálnopis: The first element is from daleki-dálný "distant"; Eng. tele- is from Gr. τῆλε "distant."

knihopis: The first element is from kniha "book"; compare Eng. bibliography (<Gr. βιβλίον "book" + -graphy).

krasopis-krasnopis: The first element is from krása "beauty," krasan "beautiful"; compare Eng. calligraphy (<Gr. κάλλος "beauty" + -graphy).

ле́топись et al.: The first element is from ле́то-lato-léto-ljeto "summer; (in Russian, Polish and Czech, pl. only) year"; compare Eng. annals, annalist (ult. <Lat. annus "year").

místopis: Compare Eng. topography (<Gr. τόπος "place" + -graphy).

národopis-narodopis: Compare Eng. ethnography (<Gr. ἔθνος "nation, people" + -graphy).

polohopis: See note on místopis.

правописа́ние et al.: Compare Eng. orthography (<Gr. ὀρθός "right, correct" + -graphy).

rubopis: See note under root РУБ (etc.).

ру́копись et al.: Compare Eng. manuscript (ult. <Lat. manus "hand" + scribere "to write").

све́топись: Compare Eng. photography (<Gr. φῶς "light" + -graphy).

та́йнопись-tajnopis: The first element is from та́йный-tajný "secret"; compare Eng. cryptography (<Gr. κρυπτός "secret" + -graphy).

těsnopis: Compare Eng. stenography (<Gr. στενός "narrow" + -graphy).

zeměpis-zemljopis: Compare Eng. geography (<Gr. γῆ "earth" + -graphy).

жи́вопись-živopis: See the second meaning of писа́ть; the Serbo-Croatian word is borrowed from Russian.

жизнеописáние et al.: Compare Eng. biography (<Gr. βίος "life" + -graphy).

описáть-opisać-opisati: orig. "to write about, depict in writing"; compare Eng. describe (ult. <Lat. scribere "to write"), Ger. beschreiben "to describe" (<schreiben "to write"), Hung. leírni "to describe" (<írni "to write").

popis (Pol.): The word referred originally to a general registration or census (of property, the population, military recruits, etc.), then to a presentation or muster for that purpose, finally to any sort of public display; compare Eng. conscription (ult. <Lat. scribere "to write").

popis (Cz.): See note on описáть-opisać-opisati.

подписáть et al.: Compare Eng. subscribe (ult. <Lat. sub "under" + scribere "to write").

предписáние-předpis: ="a thing written down beforehand to serve as guidance"; compare Eng. prescription (ult. <Lat. prae "before" + scribere "to write"), Ger. Vorschrift "rule, regulation; order, instructions; (med.) prescription" (<vor "before" + schreiben "to write"), Hung. előírás "rule, regulation; order, instructions; (med.) prescription" (<elő- "before" + írni "to write").

приписáть et al. (last meaning): ="to set down in the books to someone's credit or discredit"; compare Eng. ascribe (ult. <Lat. ad "to" + scribere "to write"), Ger. zuschreiben "to ascribe" (<zu "to" + schreiben "to write").

przepis-propis: See note on предписáние-předpis.

рóспись (first meaning): See the second meaning of писáть.

spisek (Pol.): orig. "list."

ПОЛН	PEŁN	PLN, PLŇ	PUN
пóлный: full	pełny: full	plný: full	pun: full
пóлнить (arch.): to fill	pełnić: to fulfil, execute, carry out	plniti: to fill; to fulfil, execute, carry out	puniti: to fill
полни́ть (coll.): to make (s.o.) look stout (said of clothing)			
		duchaplný: witty	
	pełnoletni: adult, of age	plnoletý: adult, of age	punoljetan: adult, of age
уполномóчить, уполномóчивать: to authorize, empower	upełnomocnić, upełnomocniać: to authorize, empower	zplnomocniti, zplnomocňovati: to authorize, empower	opunomoćiti, opunomoćavati: to authorize, empower
[R]	[P]	[Cz]	[S-C]

			*opunovlastiti: to authorize, empower
допо́лнить, дополня́ть: to supplement, complement	dopełnić, dopełniać: to fulfil, execute, carry out; to supplement, complement	doplniti, doplňovati: to supplement, complement	dopuniti, dopunjavati: to supplement, complement
	dopełniacz: (gram.) genitive case		
испо́лнить, исполня́ть: to fill (arch.); to fulfil, execute, carry out			ispuniti, ispunjavati: to fill; to fulfil, execute, carry out
исполни́тельный: executive (a.); industrious, painstaking			
		náplň: contents; stuffing (of meat, etc.); powder charge	
попо́лнить, пополня́ть: to replenish; (mil.) to reinforce	popełnić, popełniać: to commit, perpetrate		popuniti, popunjavati: to supplement, complement; to replenish
			potpun: complete
	spełnić, spełniać: to fulfil, execute, carry out	splniti, splňovati: to fulfil, execute, carry out	
		úplný: complete	
вы́полнить, выполня́ть: to fulfil, execute, carry out	wypełnić, wypełniać: to fill; to fulfil, execute, carry out	vyplniti, vyplňovati: to fill; to fulfil, execute, carry out	
	zupełny: complete		
[R]	[P]	[Cz]	[S-C]

NOTES

Basic meaning of root: full

Many of the verbal derivatives show development from the concrete meaning "to fill" to the abstract notion "to fulfil, execute, carry out" (or, in a pejorative sense, "to commit, perpetrate"). (See the introductory notes on roots ЧА [etc.] and ВЕРХ [etc.].)

Kindred non-Slavic words are Eng. *full*, Ger. *voll* "full," Lat. *plenus* "full" (>Eng. *plenty*, *plenary*) and (*im*)*plere* "to fill" (>Eng. *complete*, deplete, replete).

по́лнить et al.: denominative verbs formed from по́лный et al.

полни́ть: a relatively recent doublet of older по́лнить.

duchaplný: See note under root ДЫХ (etc.).

pełnoletni et al.: The second element is from lato-léto-ljeto "summer; (in Polish and Czech, pl. only) year"; compare Ger. volljährig "adult, of age" (<voll "full" + Jahr "year"), Rus. совершенноле́тний. See also Rus. малоле́тний et al.

уполномо́чить et al., opunovlastiti: ="to grant full powers to"; the words are modeled on Ger. bevollmächtigen "to authorize" (<voll "full" + Macht "power"). Compare also Eng. plenipotentiary (ult. <Lat. plenus "full" + potentia "power").

допо́лнить et al.: Compare Eng. supplement, complement (both ult. <Lat. -plere "to fill").

dopełniacz: originally so called because a primary function of the genitive is to form the complement of a noun; see the second meaning of dopełnić.

исполни́тельный: Compare испо́лнить.

попо́лнить-popuniti: Compare Eng. replenish (ult. <Lat. plenus "full") and see note on допо́лнить et al.

zupełny: formed from earlier upełny by addition of a second prefix.

ПЛЫ, ПЛАВ	PŁY, PŁAW	PLOU, PLOV, PLY, PLAV	PLU, PLOV, PLI, PLAV
плыть: to float; to swim; to sail		plouti: to float; to sail	pliti (arch.): to float; to swim
	płynąć: to flow; to float; to swim; to sail	plynouti: to flow; to elapse; to result; to follow logically (from)	*plinuti: to flood (intr.)
			ploviti: to float; to sail
†пла́вать: to float; to swim; to sail	†pływać: to float; to swim; to sail	plavati (plovati): to float; to swim	plivati: to float; to swim
пла́вить: to melt, smelt (metal)	pławić: to water (cattle); to float (timber); to melt, smelt (metal)	plaviti: to water (cattle); to float (timber)	plaviti: to flood (tr.); to float (timber)
	płyn: liquid (n.)	plyn: gas	plin: gas
[R]	[P]	[Cz]	[S-C]

[R]	[P]	[Cz]	[S-C]
	płynny: liquid (a.); smooth, flowing; fluent	plynný: gaseous; fluent	
пла́вный: smooth, flowing	pławny: navigable	plavný (lit.): smooth, flowing	plavan: subject to flooding
			plovan: navigable
			plovka: duck
			pluto: cork
		ploutev: fin	
плавни́к: fin			
		plavidlo: ship	
морепла́вание: navigation; seafaring		mořeplavba, mořeplavectví: navigation; seafaring	moreplovstvo: navigation; seafaring
воздухопла́вание: aeronautics		vzduchoplavba, vzduchoplavectví: aeronautics	vazduhoplovstvo, zrakoplovstvo: aeronautics
			zrakoplov: dirigible; balloon
наплы́в: flow, influx	napływ: flow, influx; alluvium	náplav, naplavenina: alluvium	naplava, naplavina: alluvium
	obfity: abundant		
	opływowy: streamlined		
	przepływ: flow; (act of) floating, swimming or sailing through or across	průplav: canal	
расплы́вчатый: diffuse, indistinct			
сплав: alloy; floating (of timber)	spław: floating (of timber)	splav: flood-gate; weir	splav: raft
	upływ: leak; loss (of blood); lapse (of time)	uplynutí: lapse (of time)	
		úplavice: dysentery	
	wpływ: influence; receipts, income		upliv: influence
		zaplaviti, zaplavovati: to flood (tr.)	*zaplaviti: to flood (tr.)
[R]	[P]	[Cz]	[S-C]

NOTES

Basic meaning of root: to flow; to float

The Slavic root is akin to Eng. flow, flood, float, fleet.

пла́вить et al.: the causative form of плыть et al., płynąć et al., hence = "to cause to flow, float, swim."

plin: ⟨Cz. plyn.

морепла́вание et al.: The first element is from мо́ре-moře-more "sea."

obfity: for earlier opływity ⟨ obsolete pływieć "to flow"; compare Eng. abundant (ult. ⟨Lat. abundare "to overflow; to abound" ⟨ unda "wave; water").

opływowy: Compare Rus. обтека́емый.

расплы́вчатый: Compare Eng. diffuse (ult. ⟨Lat. dis- "away, apart" + fundere "to pour").

сплав (first meaning): See пла́вить.

wpływ-upliv: See note on Rus. влия́ние, Cz. vliv.

ПОЛ	PÓŁ, POŁ, PÓL, POL, PAL	PŮL, POL	PO(L)
пол: sex	pół: half	půl, půle, půlka: half	pol: half; sex
			po: half
пола́: coat-tail; flap	poła: coat-tail; flap		pola: half; strip of cloth
	połowa: half		
	połowica: better half (wife); (arch.) half	polovice: half	polovica: half
полови́на: half		polovina: half	polovina, polutina: half
			polovan: second-hand, used
	połownik (arch.): sharecropper		polovnik (arch.): sharecropper
			polutan: mongrel; half-breed; hermaphrodite; charlatan
			polutar, polutnik: equator
	obopólny: mutual, reciprocal	obapolný (lit.): mutual, reciprocal	
[R]	[P]	[Cz]	[S-C]

[R]	[P]	[Cz]	[S-C]
по́лдень: noon; (arch.) south	południe: noon; south	poledne: noon; (arch.) south	podne, poldan: noon
по́лдник: light afternoon meal	południk: meridian	poledník: meridian	podnevak, podnevnik: meridian
		půldruhého: one and a half	podrug, poldrug: one and a half
		poloměr: radius	polumjer: radius
по́лночь: midnight; (arch.) north	północ: midnight; north	půlnoc: midnight; (arch.) north	ponoć, polnoć: midnight
полуо́стров: peninsula		poloostrov: peninsula	poluostrvo, poluotok: peninsula
			polupriječnik: radius
	półsłówko: hint		
полтора́: one and a half	półtora: one and a half		
	półwysep: peninsula		
	rzeczpospolita: republic		
	spółdzielnia: cooperative (n.)		
	spółgłoska: (phon.) consonant		
	współczesny: contemporary; modern		
	współczucie: sympathy		
	współdziałać: to cooperate		
	współdźwięk: harmony		
	współmierny: proportionate, commensurate		
	współpracować: to cooperate	spolupracovati: to cooperate	
	współrodak: fellow-countryman, compatriot		
	współrzędny: (gram.) coordinate		
	współrzędna: (math.) coordinate		

	współśrodkowy: concentric		
	współubiegać się: to compete		
	współwinowajca: accomplice	spoluviník: accomplice	
	współziomek: fellow-countryman, compatriot		
испóльщик (arch.): sharecropper			
	pospołem, pospołu: together	pospolu: together	
	pospolity: common, ordinary; vulgar	pospolitý (lit.): common, joint	
	pospólstwo: mob, rabble		
			spol: sex
	społem: together	spolu: together	
	spółka: company, firm	spolek: society (organization); club; alliance	
	społeczność: society (social entity, order)	společnost: society (social entity, order); society (the company of others); society (organization); company, firm	
	społeczeństwo: society (social entity, order)	společenstvo: society (organization)	
		společenství: companionship; society (organization); community (of interests, etc.)	
	spółkować: to have sexual intercourse		
	wspólny: common, joint	vespolný (arch.): mutual, reciprocal	
	wspólnota: community (of interests, etc.); commun-ity (urban, rural, etc.);		
[R]	[P]	[Cz]	[S-C]

[R]	[P]	[Cz]	[S-C]
	cooperation, association wspólnik: partner; accomplice zespolić, zespalać: to join, unite (tr.) zespół: machine unit; work force (of a factory, etc.); theatrical troupe		

NOTES

Basic meaning of root: half

In Polish and Czech, the notion of "going halves, i.e. sharing equally" has given rise to a wide range of derivatives reflecting the idea of "commonness, mutuality, reciprocity, partnership," etc. Pol. spół-, współ- and Cz. spolu- serve as prefixes with the meaning "with, together."

пол-pol (second meaning): Compare Eng. sex (ult. ‹Lat. sexus "sex," probably akin to secare "to cut, divide") and Pol. połowica below.

полá et al.: orig. "half," then "piece (esp. of cloth)."

połowica: Compare Hung. feleség "wife" (‹fél "half"), Fin. puoliso "spouse" (‹puoli "half").

polovan: ="half-used."

polutan (last meaning): ="one who knows, or is capable of, only half of what he claims."

obopólny-obapolný: The first element is from oba "both."

пóлдень-południe-poledne: In many languages, the word for "noon" also serves to designate the direction in which the sun is seen at noon, when it is at its highest point; comparable to the Slavic words in having the two meanings "noon" and "south" are Lat. meridies, Fr. midi, It. mezzodì, mezzogiorno, Port. meiodia, Sp. mediodía, Gr. μεσημβρία, Ger. Mittag, Hung. dél. By analogy, the word for "midnight" sometimes does double duty as "north"; see пóлночь-północ-půlnoc below and Ger. Mitternacht (and, similarly, Hung. észak "north" [‹éj "night" + szak "section"]). See also note on Pol. wschód.

południk et al.: so called because any given meridian is crossed by the sun at noon; see południe et al. and compare Eng. meridian (ult. ‹Lat. meridies "noon"), Gr. μεσημβρινός "meridian" (‹μεσημβρία "noon"), Ger. Mittagskreis "meridian" (‹Mittag "noon" + Kreis "circle"), Hung. délkör "meridian" (‹dél "noon" + kör "circle").

půldruhého et al.: ="(one plus) half of the second"; compare Ger. anderthalb "one and a half" (⟨ander "other; [arch.] second" + halb "half"), Fin. puolitoista "one and a half" (⟨puoli "half" + toinen "second; other"), полторá-półtora below.

poloměr-polumjer: See note under root $МЕР_1$ (etc.).

пóлночь et al.: The second element is from ночь-noc-noć "night"; see note on пóлдень-południe-poledne.

полуóстров et al.: The second element in the first three words is from óстров-ostrov-ostrvo "island"; compare Ger. Halbinsel "peninsula" (⟨halb "half" + Insel "island"), Hung. félsziget "peninsula" (⟨fél "half" + sziget "island") and also Eng. peninsula (ult. ⟨Lat. paene "almost" + insula "island"), Fr. presqu'île "peninsula" (⟨presque "almost" + île "island").

полторá-półtora: The second element is from вторóй-wtóry "second"; see note on půldruhého et al.

półwysep: See note on полуóстров et al.

rzeczpospolita: See pospolity, which here retains its original meaning, "common, general, public"; the word is a loan-translation of Lat. respublica (⟨res "thing; affair, matter, business" + publicus "common, general, public"), whence Eng. republic.

spółgłoska: See note on Rus. соглáсный et al.

współczesny: See note under root ЧАС (etc.).

współczucie: See note under root ЧУ (etc.).

współdźwięk: The second element is from dźwięk "sound."

współmierny: See note under root $МЕР_1$ (etc.).

współpracować-spolupracovati: The second element is from pracować-pracovati "to work."

współrzędny, współrzędna: See note under root РЯД (etc.).

współśrodkowy: See note on Cz. soustředný.

współubiegać się: See note on S-C stečaj.

współwinowajca-spoluviník: The second element is from winowajca-viník "culprit."

spol: See note on пол-pol.

ПЕР, ПИР, ПР, ПОР	PRZ, PIER, PAR, PÓR, POR	PŘ, PÍR, PĚR, PEŘ, POR, PŮR	PR, PIR, PAR, POR
перéть (coll.): to press, push	przeć: to press, push		
			preti (arch.): to accuse
		přiti se: to quarrel	preti se (arch.): to carry on litigation
[R]	[P]	[Cz]	[S-C]

[R]	[P]	[Cz]	[S-C]
перила (pl.): railing; banisters			
		pře: quarrel; lawsuit	
прения (pl.): debate; pleadings (in court)			
			parba, parnica: lawsuit
		přelíčení: trial, hearing	
напор: pressure	napór: pressure	nápor: impact; onslaught	napor: effort, exertion
опереться, опираться: to lean (against), rest (on)	oprzeć się, opierać się: to lean (against), rest (on); to resist	opříti se, opírati se: to lean (against), rest (on); to resist	oprijeti se, opirati se: to resist; to oppose
		opěra: rest, support; prop, stay	
	opór: resistance		
опора: rest, support; support, assistance	oparcie, opora: rest, support	opora: rest, support; support, assistance	oporba: opposition
отпереть, отпирать: to unlock	odeprzeć, od-pierać: to beat off, repel; to refute; to retort	odepříti, odpír-ati: to refuse, deny (s.th. to s.o.); to refuse (to do s.th.)	odaprijeti, odapirati (otpirati): to open
отпор: rebuff	odpór: resistance	odpor: resistance; revulsion, disgust	otpor: resistance
отпирательство: denial (of a fact)			
		odpůrce: opponent	
			oduprijeti se, odupirati se: to resist
	poprzeć, popierać: to support, assist	popříti, popírati: to deny (a fact)	
		podpěra: rest, support; prop, stay	
подпора, подпорка: prop, stay	podpora, podpórka: prop, stay	podpora: support, assistance; subsidy, grant	potpora: support, assistance; subsidy, grant
[R]	[P]	[Cz]	[S-C]

[R]	[P]	[Cz]	[S-C]
			potporanj, potpornjak: prop, stay
препира́ться (coll.): to quarrel			prepirati se: to quarrel
			prijepor: dispute
ра́спря (arch.): quarrel		rozepře: quarrel; dispute	raspra: quarrel; dispute
		rozpor: conflict, contradiction	
спёртый: close, stifling			
	spierać się: to quarrel		
спор: dispute	spór: dispute	spor: dispute; lawsuit	spor: dispute; lawsuit
сопе́рник: rival		soupeř: rival	suparnik: rival
	uparty: stubborn, obstinate	upřený: fixed, intent (gaze, etc.)	uprt: fixed, intent (gaze, etc.)
упо́рный: stubborn, obstinate	uporczywy, (arch.) uporny: stubborn, obstinate	úporný: stubborn, obstinate	uporan: stubborn, obstinate
	wyporność: displacement (of a ship)		
	wesprzeć, wspierać: to support, prop; to support, assist	vzepříti, vzpírati: to lift	
	wesprzeć się, wspierać się: to lean (against), rest (on)	vzepříti se, vzpírati se: to resist	
		vzpěra: prop, stay	
запере́ть, запира́ть: to lock (tr.); to lock in, up	zaprzeć, zapierać: to lock (tr.); to lock in, up	zapříti, zapírati: to deny (a fact)	zaprijeti, zapirati: to shut, close (tr.); to halt (on the road) because of exhaustion
запере́ться, запира́ться: to lock (intr.); to lock o.s. in, up; (coll.; в + prep.) to deny (a fact)	zaprzeć się, zapierać się: to lock o.s. in, up; to deny (a fact)		

запóр: lock; bolt; constipation	zaprzaniec: renegade, apostate zaparcie: constipation zapora: bolt; dam; barrier	zápor: (gram.) negation záporka: (gram.) negative particle	zapor: bolt; dam; constipation zaporka: (punc.) parenthesis, bracket
[R]	[P]	[Cz]	[S-C]

NOTES

Basic meaning of root: to press, push; to quarrel

The differentiation between concrete and abstract root-meanings goes back to Common Slavic, where it was reflected in the existence of two distinct primary verbs: *perti (whence modern Rus. перéть, Pol. przeć) and *pьrěti (surviving in Cz. příti se, S-C preti [se]). From the notion of pushing or leaning against something have arisen the meanings "to support (literally or figuratively)" and, with the addition of functional prefixes, "to open" and "to close." The idea of quarreling is apparent in such meanings as "debate," "accusation," "lawsuit" and "rival." In other instances, the lines of semantic division are less clear-cut. "Resistance," "opposition," "obstinacy," "refusal," "denial," "refutation," etc. are meanings which can be deduced as readily from the notion of pushing or thrusting away as from that of quarreling and antagonism, and, despite the evidence provided by some earlier differences in conjugational forms, not every derivative can be safely assigned to one or the other of the two primary verbs.

перéть: A second commonly listed meaning, "to trudge, plod," is actually that of an unrelated verb перéть (original meaning: "to go") which is no longer thought of as an independent word by speakers of Russian.

прéния: borrowed from Church Slavic.

přelíčení: See pře and note under root ЛИК (etc.).

nápor: <Rus. напóр or Pol. napór.

odpor: See note on Cz. odpudivý.

otpor: <Rus. отпóр or Cz. odpor.

potpora: <Rus. подпóра.

рáспря: borrowed from Church Slavic.

zaprzaniec: one who denies his faith; see zaprzeć się.

zaparcie, запóр et al., záporka-zaporka: See заперéть et al.

ПРЯ(Г), ПРЯЖ, ПРУГ, ПРУЖ	PRZĄ, PRZĘG, PRZĘŹ, PRZĄCZ, PRĘG, PRĘŻ	PŘA(H), PŘÁH, PŘE(Ž), PRUH, PROUH, PRUŽ	PRE(G), PREZ, PRUG, PRUŽ, PRUZ
			prezati: to harness
пря́жка: buckle, clasp		přezka, (arch.) přazka: buckle, clasp	
		pruh: stripe, streak; strip	
	pręga: stripe, streak	prouha: stripe, streak	pruga: stripe, streak; strip; line, route; track, rails
	prężyć: to stretch (tr.)	pružiti: to be elastic	pružiti, pružati: to stretch (tr.); to stretch out, extend (e.g. one's hand); to render, extend (assistance, etc.)
	prężny: elastic, resilient	pružný: elastic, resilient	pružan, pruživ, pružljiv: elastic, resilient
пружи́на: spring (elastic device)		pružina: spring (elastic device)	
напряже́ние: tension, strain; effort, exertion	naprężenie: tension, strain		naprezanje: effort, exertion
			opruga: spring (elastic device)
подпру́га: saddle-girth	popręg: saddle-girth	popruh: strap; saddle-girth	popruga, potpruga: saddle-girth
	rozprzężenie: unharnessing; disorganization, anarchy; licentiousness		
спряже́ние: (gram.) conjugation	sprzężenie: coupling (of railroad cars); (elec.) coupling; copulation	spřežení: team (of horses, oxen, etc.)	sprezanje: (gram.) conjugation
	sprzączka: buckle, clasp	spřežka: compound word; digraph, trigraph;	
[R]	[P]	[Cz]	[S-C]

[R]	[P]	[Cz]	[S-C]
		ligature (in printing)	
	sprężyna: spring (elastic device)		
супру́ги (pl.): man and wife			supruzi (pl.): man and wife
			suspregnuti (susprеći), susprezati: to restrain
упру́гий: elastic, resilient			
впрячь, впряга́ть; запря́чь, запряга́ть: to harness	wprząc (wprzęgnąć), wprzęgać; zaprząc (zaprzęgnąć), zaprzęgać: to harness	zapřáhnouti, zapřahati: to harness	upregnuti (upreći), uprezati; zapregnuti (zapreći), zaprezati: to harness

NOTES

Basic meaning of root: to stretch, pull tight

The modern root-forms point to the existence of two vowel grades in Common Slavic, forms ПРЯГ-ПРЯЖ---PRZĄ-PRZĘG-PRZĘŻ---PŘAH-PŘÁH-PŘEŽ---PREG-PREZ being descended from original *PRĘG and forms ПРУГ-ПРУЖ---PRĘG-PRĘŻ---PRUH-PROUH-PRUŽ---PRUG-PRUŽ-PRUZ from original *PRǪG.

přezka, přazka: ⟨*přacka ⟨ Common Slavic *pręgtьka.

pruh, pręga et al.: orig. "strap" (compare подпру́га et al.), then "anything having the form of a strap, i.e. strip, stripe, etc."; similar semantic development is apparent in Pol. wstęga et al. (q.v.).

prężyć et al.: denominative; the primary verb is represented by prezati (the only surviving unprefixed form) and впрячь, запря́чь et al.

напряже́ние-naprężenie: Compare Eng. tension (ult. ⟨Lat. tendere "to stretch") and strain (ult. ⟨Lat. stringere "to pull tight"), Ger. Spannung "tension" (⟨spannen "to stretch"), Pol. napięcie et al., S-C napon, Rus. натяже́ние, Pol. natężenie and wytężenie, S-C zateg and zategnutost.

спряже́ние et al., spřežka: The underlying notion in all these words is that of "pulling together, i.e. joining." Спряже́ние and sprezanje are modeled on Lat. conjugatio (⟨cum "with, together" + jugare "to yoke, join"); "conjugation" is the process of "joining together" the various inflectional forms of a verb.

sprzączka: for earlier sprzążka.

супру́ги-supruzi: ="two who are joined together"; the words originally had the further meaning "team of animals" (compare *впрячь*, *запря́чь* *et al*.). See note on *спряже́ние* *et al*., *spřežka* and compare Eng. *conjugal* (ult. ⟨Lat. *conjux* "spouse" ⟨ *cum* "with, together" + the root of *jugum* "yoke," *jungere* "to join"), Gr. *σύζυγος* "wife" (⟨*σύν* "with, together" + *ζυγόν* "yoke"). *Supruzi* is borrowed from the Russian word, which is itself taken from Church Slavic.

suspregnuti: Compare Eng. *restrain* (ult. ⟨Lat. *re*- "back" + *stringere* "to pull tight"), Pol. *powściągliwy*.

впрячь, *запря́чь*: The 1 sg. perfective form is -*прягу́*.

ПРАВ	PRAW	PRAV, PRÁV	PRAV, PORAV
пра́вый: right, correct; just (cause, etc.); right (opp. of left); right-wing (politically)	*prawy*: rightful, legitimate; righteous, honest; right (opp. of left)	*pravý*: real; right, correct; (math.) right (angle); right (opp. of left)	*prav*: real; true; right, correct; straight; (math.) right (angle)
	prawie: almost	*právě*: just (a moment ago); just, precisely	*pravo*: straight; directly; rightly, correctly
пра́вить: to rule, govern; to steer; to correct; to strop	*prawić*: to talk	*praviti* (lit.): to say, tell	*praviti*: to make
		prý: he says, they say, etc. (used for attribution of a statement)	
			praviti se: to pretend, feign
пра́во: law (in general); right, privilege	*prawo*: law (in general); law, statute; right, privilege	*právo*: law (in general); right, privilege	*pravo*: law (in general); right, privilege
пра́вда: truth; justice	*prawda*: truth	*pravda*: truth	*pravda*: justice
пра́вило: rule	*prawidło*: rule; shoe-tree	*pravidlo*: rule	*pravilo*: rule
пра́вильный: correct; regular	*prawidłowy*: regular	*pravidelný*: regular	*pravilan*: regular; correct
прави́ло: straightedge; shoe-tree; (arch.) helm, rudder			
[R]	[P]	[Cz]	[S-C]

[R]	[P]	[Cz]	[S-C]
		pravítko: ruler (for measuring)	
прави́тельство: government			
			pravac: direction, course
	prawica: right hand; (political) right wing	pravice: right hand; (political) right wing	pravica: justice
	prawiczka: virgin	pravička: right hand	
		hvězdopravec: astrologer	
правдоподо́бный: probable, likely	prawdopodobny: probable, likely	pravděpodobný: probable, likely	
	prawodawstwo: legislation		
			pravokutnik: rectangle
правописа́ние: spelling, orthography		pravopis: spelling, orthography	pravopis: spelling, orthography
			pravorijek: (judicial) sentence; verdict
правосла́вие: the Greek Orthodox religion	prawosławie: the Greek Orthodox religion	pravoslaví: the Greek Orthodox religion	pravoslavlje: the Greek Orthodox religion
		pravoúhelník: rectangle	pravougaonik: rectangle
правове́рный: orthodox	prawowierny: orthodox	pravověrný: orthodox	pravovjeran: orthodox
	sprawozdawca: reporter; reviewer, critic	zpravodaj: reporter	
		doprava: transportation	
испра́вить, исправля́ть: to repair; to correct; to rectify, improve; to redress			ispraviti, ispravljati: to straighten; to correct; to rectify, improve; to redress
испра́вный: in good repair; industrious, painstaking			ispravan: correct; accurate

[R]	[P]	[Cz]	[S-C]
			isprava: document, certificate
напра́вить, направля́ть: to direct (toward)	naprawić, naprawiać: to repair; to rectify, improve; to redress	napraviti, napravovati: to rectify, improve; to redress; to set (a bone)	napraviti, napravljati: to do, make; to build; to create, cause
	naprawa: repair; rectification, improvement; redress	náprava: rectification, improvement; redress; axle	naprava: device, appliance
		nadpráví (lit.): privilege	
опра́вить, оправля́ть: to set, mount; to arrange, put in order (hair, dress, etc.)	oprawić, oprawiać: to set, mount; to frame; to bind (a book); to dress, clean (fish, etc. for eating)	opraviti, opravovati: to repair; to correct	opraviti, opravljati: to repair; to attend to, dispose of
			oporaviti se, oporavljati se: to recover one's health
		oprávniti, opravňovati: to authorize; to entitle (s.o. to s.th.); to justify	
оправда́ть, опра́вдывать: to justify; to excuse; to acquit			opravdati, opravdavati: to justify; to excuse
		opravdový: real	
		ospravedlniti, ospravedlňovati: to justify; to excuse	
отпра́вить, отправля́ть: to send, ship, dispatch; (отправля́ть only) to perform (e.g. duties)	odprawić, odprawiać: to send away, rebuff; to dismiss, discharge; to celebrate (Mass)	odpraviti, odpravovati: to kill, dispatch, do away with; (arch.) to send, ship, dispatch	otpraviti, otpravljati: to send away, rebuff; to send, ship, dispatch; to perform (e.g. duties)
отпра́вка: sending, shipping, dispatch	odprawa: dismissal, discharge; severance pay; rebuke, sharp reply; briefing;		otprava: sending, shipping, dispatch

	(customs) examination		
отпра́виться, отправля́ться: to set out, depart			
попра́вить, поправля́ть: to correct; to rectify, improve; to arrange, put in order (hair, dress, etc.)	poprawić, poprawiać: to correct; to rectify, improve; to arrange, put in order (hair, dress, etc.)	popraviti, popravovati: to execute, put to death	popraviti, popravljati: to correct; to rectify, improve; to repair
	poprawny: correct		popravni: corrective; correctional; repair (attr.)
			popravilište: reformatory
припра́вить, приправля́ть: to season, flavor	przyprawić, przyprawiać: to fasten, attach; to season, flavor; (o + acc.) to cause	připraviti, připravovati: to prepare; to deprive	pripraviti, pripravljati: to prepare
распра́ва: violence, brutality	rozprawa: discussion, debate; trial, hearing; show-down, trial of strength; treatise	rozprava: discussion, debate; (arch.) treatise	rasprava: discussion, debate; trial, hearing; treatise
спра́вить, справля́ть (coll.): to celebrate; to buy	sprawić, sprawiać: to cause; to carry out, perform; to buy; to dress, clean (fish, etc. for eating)	spraviti, spravovati: to repair; to improve (tr.); (spravovati only) to rule, govern; (spravovati only) to administer, manage	spraviti, spravljati: to prepare; to store; to provide with a dowry
	sprawa: affair, matter, business; cause (e.g. cause of peace, just cause); (judicial) case; account, report	správa: repair; administration, management	sprava: device, appliance
	sprawny: skilful; efficient	správný: correct; accurate	spravan: ready
спра́виться, справля́ться: to make inquiries, seek	sprawić się, sprawiać się: to behave, conduct oneself	spraviti se, spravovati se: to improve (intr.); to	
[R]	[P]	[Cz]	[S-C]

information; (с + inst.) to cope (with), manage		recover (from an illness); to gain weight; (spravovati se only) to follow, be guided (by) (a principle, etc.)	
спра́вочник: reference book			
		souprava: set (of utensils, linen, furniture, etc.)	
	sprawdzić, sprawdzać: to check, verify		
	sprawdzian: standard, criterion; gauge		
справедли́вый: just, fair; correct	sprawiedliwy: just, fair	spravedlivý: just, fair	spravedljiv: just, fair
			upravo: straight; just, precisely; just (a moment ago)
управля́ть: to rule, govern; to administer, manage; to operate (a machine), drive (an automobile)	uprawić, uprawiać: to cultivate, till; to pursue (a profession), engage in (a sport), etc.	upraviti, upravovati: to prepare; to arrange, put in order (hair, dress, etc.); to regulate; to adjust	upraviti, upravljati: to direct (toward); (upravljati only) to rule, govern; (upravljati only) to administer, manage; (upravljati only) to operate (a machine), drive (an automobile)
	uprawny: cultivable; under cultivation	úpravný: neat, trim	upravan: direct; perpendicular; vertical
	uprawnić, uprawniać: to authorize; to entitle (s.o. to s.th.)		
	usprawiedliwić, usprawiedliwiać: to justify; to excuse		
[R]	[P]	[Cz]	[S-C]

[R]	[P]	[Cz]	[S-C]
			uspravan: erect, upright; perpendicular; vertical
	wprawa: skill, practice		
	wyprawa: campaign; expedition; trousseau; plaster; tanning (of leather)	výprava: campaign; expedition; (theatrical) sets, scenery	
вы́правка: (erect) carriage, bearing	wyprawka: layette		
		vypravování: narrative, narration	
		zpráva: news, information; account, report	
запра́вить, заправля́ть: to season, flavor; to refuel; to tuck in	zaprawić, zaprawiać: to season, flavor; to train; to wax (a floor); to stop (a hole)	zapraviti, zapravovati (lit.): to pay off (a debt)	

NOTES

Basic meaning of root: straight

In this widely ramified group of derivatives, the physical notion of straightness frequently gives rise to such transferred meanings as "right, correct" (whence "right [hand]" as distinct from "left"), "(morally) right, just," "right, privilege" (a thing to which one has a just claim) and "law" (a body of rules designed to enforce what is "right"). (Regarding the comparable semantic link between the notions of "crookedness" and "wrongness," see the introductory note on root КРИВ [etc.].)

The verbal formations tend to fall into three broad semantic groups:

(1) The idea of "causing to go in a straight line, follow a given course" is apparent in the meaning "to direct, send, dispatch" (and, reflexively, "to set out, depart"); the further notion of "fitting out, equipping (originally for a journey, but later in a more general sense)" accounts for the meanings "trousseau; layette" and "theatrical sets" (compare Eng. equip [ult. <Old Norse skipa "to fit out a ship"]).

(2) A number of derivatives reflect the notion of "directing" in the figurative sense of "ruling, governing, administering" (compare Eng. govern [ult. <Gr. κυβερνᾶν "to steer"], Du. bestuur "administration" [<sturen "to

steer"], Hung. kormány "helm, rudder; government); further elaboration of this idea has produced the meanings "rule" (="guiding, directing principle" and "regular" (="conforming to a rule").

(3) Underlying the meanings of a large group of words is the notion of "directing in some desired manner, bringing into a desired condition" (or, as a more direct outgrowth of the root-meaning, "setting straight, making right"), hence "preparing, putting in order, arranging, regulating, rectifying, repairing, redressing, adjusting, training, etc."; in a number of instances, this gives rise to the neutral meaning "to do, make" (>"to perform "to attend to," "to cause," "to create," "to build"). Many of the derivatives have come to refer to specialized activities of the most varied kind, e.g. buying, paying, celebrating, plastering, storing goods, refueling, tanning leather, setting a precious stone, binding a book, dressing fish, stropping a razor, seasoning food, cultivating the soil, waxing a floor, stopping a hole.

The distinctive verbal meaning "to say," exemplified by Pol. prawić and Cz. praviti, has been variously linked with the notions of "doing" (see the introductory note on root ДЕ [etc.]) and of "saying what is right, telling the truth" and with the earlier meaning "to try in a court of law" (attested in Old Russian and Church Slavic).

From the standpoint of vocabulary formation, this root has taken over the function performed in a number of non-Slavic languages by the Indo-European root *REĜ, whence Eng. right (which retains the original notion of straightness in right angle and the ship righted itself) and upright, Lat. regere "to direct, cause to go straight" and rectus "straight" (>Eng. rule, regular, regulate, regime, regent, rectify, rectitude, rectangle, correct, direct, [re]dress [<assumed *directiare by way of Old French], erect), Ger. recht "right (angle); right, correct; right (hand)," Recht "right, privilege, law," aufrecht "erect, upright," gerecht "just, fair," richtig "right, correct" and richten "to direct (toward); to put in order" (>anrichten "to cause," einrichten "to arrange," entrichten "to pay," verrichten "to do, perform," zurichten "to prepare"). (Fr. droit and Sp. derecho "straight; right [hand]; right, privilege; law," It. diritto "straight; right, privilege; law" are derived from Lat. directus.) Comparable processes of semantic change can be seen at work in Gr. ὀρθός "straight; right, correct" (whence various English derivatives; see notes on individual words below), Fin. oikaista "to straighten" and oikea "right, correct; right (hand); just, fair (>oikeus "right, privilege; law"), suora "straight" and suorittaa "to do, perform."

See the introductory note on root РЯД (etc.), which shows partly parallel development of the root-meaning.

prawie: orig. "correctly, precisely," then "completely," finally "all but (just less than) completely"; see next note.

právě: orig. "correctly, justly, lawfully"; regarding the semantic shift to "just, precisely," compare the various meanings of Eng. just (ult. Lat. justus "just, lawful").

prý: contracted from the 3 sg. pres. or (obsolete) 3 sg. aorist of praviti; compare Rus. де, дéскать, мол.

praviti se: See note on Rus. притвóрство, S-C pritvorstvo.

прáвило: borrowed from Church Slavic.

прáвильный-pravilan: The Russian word is borrowed from Church Slavic, the Serbo-Croatian word from Russian.

правúтельство: borrowed from Church Slavic.

prawiczka: ‹prawy in the earlier sense of "pure, virtuous."

hvězdopravec: ="one who (fore)tells from the stars." The first element is from hvězda "star"; see praviti and compare Eng. astrologer (ult. ‹Gr. ἄστρον "star" + λέγειν "to speak; to say").

правдоподóбный et al.: See прáвда-prawda-pravda and note under root ДО(Б) (etc.).

prawodawstwo: See note on Rus. законодáтельство et al.

pravokutnik: The second element is from kut "angle."

правописáние et al.: See note under root ПИС (etc.).

pravorijek: See pravo (n.) and prav; the word is probably modeled on Ger. Rechtsspruch "sentence; verdict" (‹Recht "law" + sprechen "to speak") or on Fr. verdict (ult. ‹Lat. verus "true" + dicere "to say"), Ger. Wahrspruch "verdict" (‹wahr "true" + sprechen).

правослáвие et al.: See note under root СЛЫ (etc.).

pravoúhelník-pravougaonik: The second element is from úhel-ugao "angle."

правовéрный et al.: See note under root ВЕР$_1$ (etc.).

sprawozdawca-zpravodaj: See sprawa, zpráva.

isprava: orig. "that which establishes a right or claim."

náprava (third meaning): a device which keeps a vehicle on the "right course."

naprava: Compare Ger. Vorrichtung "device, appliance" (‹richten "to direct; to put in order").

nadpráví: a "higher" right held by one person or group "over" another.

oporaviti se: for opraviti se.

oprávniti: Compare Ger. berechtigen "to authorize; to entitle; to justify" (‹Recht "right, privilege").

оправдáть-opravdati, opravdový: See прáвда-pravda.

ospravedlniti: See spravedlivý.

отпрáвить-odprawić-otpraviti, odprawa: Similar development of the basic notion of "sending on its (or one's) way, dispatching" is apparent in Ger. abfertigen "to send, ship, dispatch; to rebuff; to clear (through customs); to attend to"; compare also Cz. odbaviti.

odpraviti: Compare Ger. hinrichten "to execute, put to death" (‹hin "thither" + richten "to direct").

popraviti (Cz.): orig. "to correct," then "to take corrective measures against, punish," finally "to execute."

przyprawić: The first meaning reflects the action of the prefix.

připraviti: The construction připraviti koho o co "to deprive s.o. of s.th." arose from the archaic meaning "to bring" as a translation of Ger. jemanden um etwas bringen, in which um "around" has privative force.

распрáва et al.: See prawić-praviti (Cz.) and the discussion of them i the introductory note; the present-day meaning of the Russian word (orig. = "trial, hearing; justice") reflects the notion of "taking justice into one' own hands, wreaking vengeance."

sprawa: Underlying the first three meanings is the idea of "something done or to be done"; regarding the last meaning, see prawić.

sprava: See note on naprava.

спрáвиться (first meaning): Compare the last meaning of Pol. sprawa (⟨sprawić in the obsolete sense of "to inform").

souprava: ="arrangement (of similar things)."

sprawdzić: See prawda and compare Eng. verify (ult. ⟨Lat. verus "true"

sprawdzian: ⟨sprawdzić.

справедлúвый et al.: ⟨прáвда et al.; the Serbo-Croatian word is borrowed from Russian.

uprawnić: See note on oprávniti.

usprawiedliwić: See sprawiedliwy.

wprawa: ⟨wprawić "to train."

vypravování, zpráva: See praviti.

ПЕРЕД, ПЕРЕЖ, ПРЕД, ПРЕЖД	PRZED(Z), PRZÓD, PRZOD	PŘED, PŘÍD, PŘÍĎ	PRED, PRIJED, PREĐ
пéред(о), пред(о): before, in front of; before, prior to	przed(e): before, in front of; before, prior to; ago	před(e): before, in front of; before, prior to; ago	pred(a): before, in front of; before, prior to; ago
пред-: pre-, fore- (see compounds under various roots)	przed-: pre-, fore- (see compounds under various roots)	před(e)-: pre-, fore- (see compounds under various roots)	pred-, prijed-: pre-, fore- (see compounds under various roots)
прéжде: before, earlier			pređe: before, earlier
перёд: front	przód: front	před (arch.): front příď, (arch.) přída: bow, prow	
[R]	[P]	[Cz]	[S-C]

[R]	[P]	[Cz]	[S-C]
передо́к: front part of a carriage; limber (of a gun-carriage); vamp, upper (of a shoe)	przodek: front; limber (of a gun-carriage); ancestor	předek: front; ancestor	predak: ancestor
пре́док: ancestor			
		**předčiti: to surpass, exceed	
пере́дник: apron; pinafore			prednjak: front man (in military formation); leader, trail-blazer; limber (of a gun-carriage)
пере́дняя: anteroom			
		přednosta: chief, director	
	przodownictwo: leadership		
	przedniość: excellence	přednost: priority, precedence; advantage; virtue, merit	prednost: priority, precedence; advantage
		kupředu: forward	
преждевре́менный: premature			
		dopředu: forward	
наперёд (coll.): beforehand, in advance	naprzód: at first; first of all; forward; in front; beforehand, in advance	napřed: in front; first of all; beforehand, in advance	naprijed: forward; in front
			napredak: progress; success
опереди́ть, опережа́ть: to outstrip, outdistance			
	poprzedzić, poprzedzać: to precede		
	poprzednik: predecessor		
[R]	[P]	[Cz]	[S-C]

[R]	[P]	[Cz]	[S-C]
предупреди́ть, предупрежда́ть: to notify in advance; to warn; to prevent; to forestall, anticipate, act ahead of			preduprijediti, predupređivati: to prevent
предупреди́тельный: preventive, precautionary; obliging, attentive			
упреди́ть, упрежда́ть (arch.): to forestall, anticipate, act ahead of	uprzedzić, uprzedzać: to notify in advance; to warn; to forestall, anticipate, act ahead of; to prejudice, predispose		
	uprzedzający: obliging, attentive		
			unapredak: henceforth
			unaprijediti, unapređivati: to promote, further, advance; to promote (in rank)
вперёд: forward	wprzód, wprzódy: previously	vpřed: forward	
впереди́: in front		vpředu: in front	
впредь: henceforth			
	wyprzedzić, wyprzedzać: to outstrip, outdistance		

NOTES

Basic meaning of root: before (in space or time)

The Russian root-forms ПРЕД and ПРЕЖД are of Church Slavic origin.

přednost-prednost (second meaning): Compare Eng. advantage (⟨Fr. avantage ⟨ avant "before, prior to").

kupředu: The first element is from ku (k) "to, toward."

предупреди́ть-*preduprijediti*: The Russian word is formed from *пред-* + *упреди́ть*; *preduprijediti* is borrowed from Russian. In all four of its meanings, *предупреди́ть* renders Fr. *prévenir* (<Lat. *prae* "before" + *venire* "to come"), which has the further meaning "to prejudice" (see *uprzedzić*). Compare also Eng. *prevent* (ult. <Lat. *prae* + *venire*), *anticipate* (ult. <Lat. *ante* "before" + *capere* "to take").

предупреди́тельный (second meaning): ="anticipating another's wishes"; see *предупреди́ть* and compare Fr. *prévenant* "obliging" (<*prévenir*---see preceding note), Ger. *zuvorkommend* "obliging" (<*zuvorkommen* "to anticipate" < *zuvor* "before" + *kommen* "to come"), S-C *predusretljiv*.

упреди́ть-*uprzedzić*, *uprzedzający*: See notes on *предупреди́ть*-*preduprijediti* and *предупреди́тельный*.

unaprijediti: Compare *napredak*.

ПЕРЕК, ПЕРЕЧ, ПРЕК	PRZEK, PRZECZ	PŘÍČ	PREK, PRIJEK, PREČ, PRIJEČ
			preko, *prijeko*: over, across; more than, over; during; contrary (to)
			prijek: transverse, crosswise; urgent; sudden; harsh, severe
		příčel: rung	*prečaga*: cross-beam; rung; (anat.) diaphragm
			priječnik: diameter
пере́чить: to contradict (s.o.)	*przeczyć*: to deny (a fact)	*příčiti se*: to oppose; to be at variance (with); to disgust	*priječiti*: to prevent, hinder
	przeczący: negative (reply, etc.)		
беспрекосло́вный: absolute, unquestioning (obedience, etc.)			
			polupriječnik: radius
[R]	[P]	[Cz]	[S-C]

[R]	[P]	[Cz]	[S-C]
			prekomjeran: excessive
прекословить: to contradict (s.o.)			
		úhlopříčný: diagonal napříč: across, athwart	
			opreka: contrast conflict, contradiction
поперёк: across, athwart	(na, w) poprzek: across, athwart	popříč (arch.): across, athwart	poprijeko, poprečke: across, athwar
поперечный: transverse, crosswise	poprzeczny: transverse, crosswise		poprečan: transverse, crosswise; average
поперечина: cross-beam			
поперечник: diameter	poprzecznik: cross-beam		
попрекнуть, попрекать: to reproach			
			prepreka: obstacle, hindrance
	sprzeczka: quarrel sprzeczny: contradictory		
упрекнуть, упрекать: to reproach вопреки: despite; in defiance (of)			
			zapreka: obstacle, hindrance

NOTES

Basic meaning of root: across, athwart

From the purely physical notion expressed by the root have evolved, in many of the derivatives, such abstract meanings as "contradiction," "contrast," "opposition" and "prevention." The same semantic process is observable in Eng. athwart and to thwart and in to cross in the sense of "to thwart, oppose."

preko, prijeko: The unprefixed primary derivative survives only in Serbo-Croatian; see поперёк et al.

беспрекосло́вный: See прекосло́вить.

poluprijеčnik: See prijеčnik.

prekomjeran: See note under root $МЕР_1$ (etc.).

прекосло́вить: See note under root СЛЫ (etc.).

úhlopříčný: The first element is from úhel "angle"; compare Eng. diagonal (ult. ‹Gr. διά "through" + γωνία "angle").

poprečan (second meaning): See note on Pol. przeciętny.

вопреки́: borrowed from Church Slavic.

ПРОСТ, ПРОЩ	PROST, PROŚ	PROST, PROSŤ, PROŠŤ	PROST, PRAŠT
просто́й: simple, plain	prosty: straight; right (angle); simple, plain	prostý: simple, plain; free (of), exempt (from)	prost: simple, plain; ordinary; coarse, vulgar; free (of), exempt (from)
прости́ть, проща́ть: to forgive		prostiti (lit.): to liberate; to rid, relieve	prostiti, praštati: to forgive
прости́ться, проща́ться: to take one's leave, say good-bye			praštati se: to take one's leave, say good-bye
проста́к: simpleton	prostak: boor, lout	prosťák, prosťáček: simpleton	prostak: boor, lout
просте́йшие (pl.): protozoa			
	prostnica: rectum		
	prostokąt: rectangle		
	prostopadły: perpendicular; sheer (drop, etc.)		
		naprostý: absolute, utter	
		oprostiti, oprošťovati: to liberate; to rid, relieve; to simplify	oprostiti, opraštati: to forgive
		sprostý: coarse, vulgar	
	sprośny: obscene, bawdy	sprostný (arch.): simple, artless	
[R]	[P]	[Cz]	[S-C]

[R]	[P]	[Cz]	[S-C]
		vyprostiti, vyprošťovati: to liberate; to rid, relieve zprostiti, zprošťovati: to liberate; to rid, relieve; to dismiss, discharge	

NOTES

Basic meaning of root: straight; simple; free

The broad range of meanings of this word group is most plausibly explained by assuming the following series of semantic shifts: "straight" 〉 "simple, uncomplicated" (with further development to "common, vulgar, coars in some derivatives) 〉 "unencumbered, free"; the notion of freedom is reflected in verbal derivatives with the meanings "to liberate; to rid, relieve" and "to forgive" (="to free of guilt, debts, etc.").

простóй: in Old Russian, also "straight; free."

простúть et al.: Pol. prościć "to straighten; to liberate" is obsolete

простúться-praštati se: The original sense was "to exchange expression of forgiveness on parting."

простéйшие: ="the simplest form of life."

prostnica: modeled on NLat. rectum (intestinum) "straight intestine."

prostokąt: The second element is from kąt "angle; corner."

sprośny: 〈OPol. sprostny.

	PĘD(Z)	PUD, POUZ	PUD
	pędzić: to chase, drive; to rush, dash; to distill pęd: rush, dash; shoot, sprout napęd: gear, drive, transmission	puditi: to impel, prompt, induce pud: instinct odpudivý: repulsive, disgusting	puditi: to drive away; to frighten
	[P]	[Cz]	[S-C]

	[P]	[Cz]	[S-C]
	popęd: impulse; instinct	popud: impulse; impetus	
	popędliwy: impulsive; irascible, irritable	popudlivý: irascible, irritable	
	spędzić, spędzać: to drive together; to spend (time)		
		vzpouzeti se: to resist	
	zapęd: impetus; vehemence, violence		

NOTES

Basic meaning of root: to chase, drive

In Russian, the root survives only in dialectal пу́ди́ть "to drive away." Many of the derivatives parallel those found under root ГН (etc.).

pędzić (third meaning): See note on Rus. гнать.

puditi (Cz.): Compare Eng. impel (ult. ⟨Lat. pellere "to drive").

pęd (second meaning): Compare Cz. výhon.

pud: See note on S-C nagon.

napęd: Compare Cz. pohon.

odpudivý: Compare Eng. repulsive (ult. ⟨Lat. re- "back" + pellere "to drive"), Ger. abstossend "repulsive" (⟨ab "off, away" + stossen "to push"), Rus. отта́лкивающий "repulsive" (⟨от + the root of толка́ть "to push"), Pol. odrazić, Cz. odpor, S-C odbiti and odbojan.

popęd-popud: See note on S-C nagon.

spędzić: Compare Ger. vertreiben "to spend, kill (time)" (⟨treiben "to drive").

vzpouzeti se: The sense is, roughly, that of "pressing against"; compare Cz. vzepříti se.

ПУСТ, ПУСК, ПУЩ	PUST, PUŚC, PUSZCZ	PUST, POUST, PUŠT, POUŠT, POUŠŤ	PUS(T), PUŠT
пустóй: empty	pusty: empty	pustý: empty; desolate, deserted; dissolute	pust: empty; desolate, deserted
пусти́ть, пускáть: to let (in, out, etc.); to permit; to let go, release; to set in motion	puścić, puszczać: to let (in, out, etc.); to let go, release; to set in motion	pustiti, pouštěti: to let (in, out, etc.); to drop; to let go, release; to set in motion	pustiti, puštati: to let (in, out, etc.); to permit; to let go, release; to set in motion
пустя́к: trifle			
пýща: virgin forest	puszcza: virgin forest	poušť: desert	
пусты́ня: desert	pustynia: desert	pustina: wasteland	pustinja: desert
пусты́нник: hermit	pustelnik: hermit	poustevník: hermit	pustinjak: hermit
	pustoszyć: to devastate, lay waste	pustošiti: to devastate, lay waste	pustošiti: to devastate, lay waste
	puścizna: estate (of a deceased person)		
			pustolov: adventurer
			pustopašan: wild, unrestrained
вольноотпýщенник (arch.): freed slave or serf			
допусти́ть, допускáть: to admit, grant admittance to; to permit; to assume, take for granted	dopuścić, dopuszczać: to admit, grant admittance to; to permit	dopustiti, dopouštěti: to permit	dopustiti, dopuštati: to permit
	dopust: (divine) dispensation, visitation		dopust: leave, holiday; permission
напусти́ть, напускáть: to let in (water, smoke, etc.); to loose, set (a dog on s.o.)	napuścić, napuszczać: to admit, grant admittance to; to let in (water, smoke, etc.); to impregnate	napustiti, napouštěti: to let in (water, smoke, etc.); to fill; to impregnate	napustiti, napuštati: to leave, abandon; to loose, set (a dog on s.o.)
опусти́ть, опускáть: to lower; to drop; to omit	opuścić, opuszczać: to lower; to drop; to leave, abandon; to omit	opustiti, opouštěti: to leave, abandon	*opùstiti: to drop; to loosen, slacken
[R]	[P]	[Cz]	[S-C]

[R]	[P]	[Cz]	[S-C]
	opust: discount, rebate		
			*opústiti: to devastate, lay waste
опустоши́ть, опустоша́ть: to devastate, lay waste	*opustoszyć: to devastate, lay waste		*opustošiti: to devastate, lay waste
отпуще́ние: remission (of sins)	odpuszczenie: remission (of sins); tempering (of metal)	odpuštění: forgiveness; remission (of sins)	otpuštenje: dismissal, discharge
о́тпуск: leave, holiday; delivery, distribution; tempering (of metal)	odpust: (ecclesiastical) indulgence; kermis, village festival	odpustek: (ecclesiastical) indulgence	otpust: dismissal, discharge
отпу́щенник (arch.): freed slave or serf			otpuštenik: discharged employee
			popust: discount, rebate
попусти́тельство: connivance			
			popustljiv: indulgent, acquiescent
		přepustiti, přepouštěti: to melt down, render; to cede, yield	prepustiti, prepuštati: to leave, abandon; to cede, yield
припусти́ть, припуска́ть: to couple (a male animal with a female); to let out (a garment)	przypuścić, przypuszczać: to admit, grant admittance to; to couple (a male animal with a female); to assume, take for granted	připustiti, připouštěti: to admit, grant admittance to; to couple (a male animal with a female); to permit; to admit, acknowledge	pripustiti, pripuštati: to admit, grant admittance to
про́пуск: admission, admittance; omission; absence, non-attendance; pass, permit; (mil.) pass-word	przepust: culvert; admission, admittance	propust: culvert	propust: culvert; admission, admittance; neglect
	przepustka: pass, permit	propustka: pass, permit	

	przepustnica: (tech.) throttle		propusnica: pass, permit
		propuštěnec: discharged employee; released prisoner; (arch.) freed slave or serf	
распусти́ть, распуска́ть: to dismiss (a class), discharge (workers), disband (an army), dissolve (a parliament); to spoil, overindulge; to unfurl (a flag), let down (one's hair); to dissolve (tr.; in a liquid); to melt (tr.)	rozpuścić, rozpuszczać: to dismiss (a class), disband (an army); to spoil, overindulge; to unfurl (a flag), let down (one's hair); to dissolve (tr.; in a liquid); to melt (tr.); to spread (e.g. rumors)	rozpustiti, rozpouštěti: to dismiss (a class), discharge (workers), disband (an army), dissolve (a parliament); to let down (one's hair); to dissolve (tr.; in a liquid); to melt (tr.)	raspustiti, raspuštati: to dismiss (a class), disband (an army), dissolve (a parliament); to spoil, overindulge; to let down (one's hair)
распу́щенность: spoiled, undisciplined behavior; dissoluteness, licentiousness			raspuštenost: spoiled, undisciplined behavior; dissoluteness, licentiousness
	rozpusta: dissoluteness, licentiousness	rozpusta: naughty child	
спусти́ть, спуска́ть: to lower; to launch (a ship); to let go, release; to release (a catch, spring, etc.); to drain	spuścić, spuszczać: to lower; to drop; to launch (a ship); to let go, release; to release (a catch, spring, etc.); to drain	spustiti, spouštěti: to lower; to drop; to launch (a ship); to release (a catch, spring, etc.); to start (a motor, etc.)	spustiti, spuštati: to lower; to drop; to launch (a ship)
спуск: (act of) lowering; descent; launching (of a ship); drainage; slope; trigger	spust: drainage; drain; flood-gate; slope; trigger	spoušť: havoc, destruction; trigger	spust: descent; slope
		spousta: plenty, a lot, a great deal	
[R]	[P]	[Cz]	[S-C]

спустя́: after; afterward, later			
	spuścizna: estate (of a deceased person)		
упуще́ние: omission; neglect		upuštění: abandonment, renunciation, relinquishment	
	upust: outlet; flood-gate		
вы́пуск: issuance; output; emission; graduation; graduating class; omission; fascicle, instalment		výpust: outlet	
	wypustka: piping, edging (of dress)	výpustka: (gram.) ellipsis	
		zpustlý: neglected, abandoned, unattended; dissolute, licentious	
запу́щенный: neglected, abandoned, unattended	zapuszczony: neglected, abandoned, unattended		zapušten: neglected, abandoned, unattended
	zapust (arch.): thicket		
	zapusty (pl.): Shrovetide, carnival		
[R]	[P]	[Cz]	[S-C]

NOTES

Basic meaning of root: empty

The secondary meanings "to let (in, out, etc.), let go" and "to leave, abandon"---both extensions of the notion of "making empty, (hence) leaving free and undisturbed"---are apparent in the denominative verb пусти́ть et al. (<пусто́й et al.) and its numerous derivatives. Further meanings growing out of the idea of "letting go" are "to let fall, i.e. lower, drop" and "to loosen, dissolve."

Many of the verbal derivatives are paralleled by English words derived ultimately from Lat. mittere "to send; to let go" (see admit, dismiss, emission, omit, permit, remission).

пускать: for earlier пущать; the present form arose by analogy with other roots which show the alternation ск : щ.

пустя́к: See пусто́й.

puścizna: ="that which is left behind"; compare Ger. Nachlass "estate" (<nach "after, behind" + lassen "to let; to leave"), S-C ostavina, ostavština.

pustolov: The second element is from loviti "to hunt, chase."

pustopašan: See note under root ПАС (etc.).

dopust (Pol.): ="a thing permitted by God"; see dopuścić.

отпуще́ние-odpuszczenie-odpuštění: Compare Ger. Erlass "remission (of sins)" (<lassen "to let; to leave"); regarding the second meaning of odpuszczenie, see next note.

о́тпуск (third meaning): The underlying idea is that of "letting go, easing, relaxing," hence (in a specialized application) "making less brittle, tempering."

odpust-odpustek: Compare Ger. Ablass "(ecclesiastical) indulgence" (<ab "off" + lassen "to let; to leave"); the second meaning of the Polish word reflects the custom of holding festivals to mark the granting of indulgences.

przepust et al.: Compare Ger. Durchlass "culvert" (<durch "through" + lassen "to let; to leave").

спуск-spust (Pol.)-spoušť: Regarding the last meaning, see the next to the last meaning of спусти́ть-spuścić-spustiti (Cz.). Regarding the first meaning of spoušť, compare pustošiti.

spousta: The word referred originally to anything descending upon one suddenly in great quantities, e.g. water from a bursting dam, snow from a rooftop, rockfall from a mountain; see spustiti.

спустя́: ="having left behind (a given period of time)."

spuścizna: See note on puścizna.

вы́пуск: The various meanings reduce ultimately to "(act of) letting (putting) or leaving out" or "that which is let (put) or left out."

wypustka: Compare Eng. to let out (a dress).

zapust: Compare zapuszczony.

zapusty: ="a leaving, giving up (of meat with the onset of Lent)."

ПУТ	PĄT	PUT, POUT, POUŤ	PUT, PUĆ
путь: path, road, way; journey; way, means, method		pouť: pilgrimage; village festival; (lit.) journey	put: path, road, way; journey; way, means, method; time (jedamput, dvaput, triput, etc.: once, twice, three times, etc.)
			put: toward
пу́тный (coll.): sensible			putan: right, correct
пу́тник: traveler	pątnik: pilgrim	poutník: pilgrim; (lit.) traveler	putnik: traveler; passenger
			putanja: path; orbit; trajectory
путеше́ствие: journey			
беспу́тный: dissolute, licentious			besputan: pathless, trackless
			naputiti, napućivati: to direct, instruct
			naputnica: money-order
напу́тствие (lit.): parting words, farewell			
			otputiti se, otpućivati se: to set out, depart
			poput: like (prep.)
попу́тчик: traveling companion; (pol.) fellow-traveler			
распу́тный: dissolute, licentious			
спу́тник: traveling companion; (astr.) satellite		souputník: traveling companion; (pol.) fellow-traveler; (astr.) satellite	saputnik, suputnik: traveling companion; (astr.) satellite
[R]	[P]	[Cz]	[S-C]

сопу́тствовать: to accompany			uputiti, upućivati: to direct, send; to direct, instruct uputnica: money-order uputan: suitable; advisable, expedient
[R]	[P]	[Cz]	[S-C]

NOTES

Basic meaning of root: path, road, way

The Slavic root is related to Eng. find and (by way of borrowing from another Indo-European language) path, Lat. pons "bridge" (>Eng. pontoon), Gr. πάτος "path" (>Eng. peripatetic) and πόντος "sea" (>Eng. Hellespont).

путь et al.: The corresponding Polish word, pąć, is obsolete. The successive stages in the semantic development of the Czech word were "road" > "journey" > "religious pilgrimage" > "religious festival" > "festival." Regarding the fourth meaning of put, compare Dan.-Nor. gang, Swed. gång "time" (in the same sense), literally "a going."

пу́тный-putan: <путь-put in the meaning "(good) sense."

беспу́тный: orig. "senseless"; see preceding note.

naputiti: orig. "to send on one's way"; compare Eng. direct in its two meanings, "to send" and "to instruct," and Hung. utasítani "to direct, send; to direct, instruct" (<út "road").

naputnica: ="a sending or assignment of money"; see naputiti and compare Ger. Anweisung "money-order" (<anweisen "to direct, instruct, assign").

poput: ="in the manner (of)"; compare the third meaning of put.

распу́тный: perhaps similar to беспу́тный in its semantic development, but compare also распу́тица "season of bad roads" and Eng. (sexual) deviate (ult. <Lat. de- "off" + via "road").

uputiti, uputnica: See notes on naputiti and naputnica; regarding the formation of uputiti, compare Fr. envoyer "to send" (ult. <Lat. in "in, on" + via "road").

uputan: Compare the second meaning of uputiti.

ПЫТ	PYT	PT, PYT	PIT
пытáть: to torture	pytać: to ask		pitati: to ask
пы́тка: torture	pytki (pl.): torture		
пытáться: to try, attempt	pytać się: to ask	ptáti se: to ask	pitati se: to ask oneself, wonder
пытли́вый: curious, inquisitive; keen, searching (eyes, etc.)			pitljiv: curious, inquisitive
	pytajnik: (punc.) question mark		
		dušezpyt (arch.): psychology	
		jazykozpyt: linguistics	
любопы́тный: curious, inquisitive; curious, interesting			ljubopitan: curious, inquisitive
		národozpyt: ethnology	
		přírodozpyt (arch.): natural science	
испытáть, испы́тывать: to test; to experience		zpytovati: to search; to investigate	ispitati, ispitivati: to test; to investigate; to interrogate
		nevyzpytatelný: inscrutable, unfathomable	
óпыт: experiment; experience			opit: experiment
	popyt: (econ.) demand	poptávka: (econ.) demand	
			raspit: divorce
			upitnik: (punc.) question mark
[R]	[P]	[Cz]	[S-C]

NOTES

Basic meaning of root: to ask

See the introductory note on root КУС (etc.), many of whose derivative show semantic parallels with the words listed here.

пыта́ть, пы́тка-pytki: linguistic testimony to the use of torture as a means of extracting information; ORus. пытати meant "to ask." Compare Rus. истяза́ть.

dušezpyt: See zpytovati and compare Ger. Seelenforschung "psychology" (<Seele "soul" + Forschung "investigation, research").

jazykozpyt: The first element is from jazyk "language"; see zpytovati and compare Ger. Sprachforschung "linguistics" (<Sprache "language" + Forschung "investigation, research").

любопы́тный-ljubopitan: Like Eng. curious, the Russian word means both "showing curiosity" (the original meaning) and "arousing curiosity"; compare Pol. ciekawy. Ljubopitan is borrowed from Russian.

národozpyt, přírodozpyt: See zpytovati.

opit: <Rus. о́пыт.

raspit: See pitati djevojku "to ask a girl's hand in marriage"; the negative prefix produces the notion of an "unasking," i.e. termination of the contract originally made.

РЯД, РЯЖ	RZĄD(Z), RZĘD(Z)	ŘAD, ŘÁD, ŘAĎ, ŘAZ, ŘÍD, ŘED, ŘIZ, ŘÍZ	RED, REĐ
ряд: row; (mil.) rank, file; series; a number (of), several	rząd: row; (mil.) rank, file; harness; (biol.) order; government	řád: (set of) rules, regulations; (social, political) order, system; schedule, time-table; order, decoration, award; religious order; (biol.) class; class, category	red: row; (mil.) rank, file; line, queue; line (of print); series; turn (regular succession); rank, class, degree; order (orderly state of things); order, sequence; order, decoration, award; religious order; schedule, time-table
ряди́ть: to dress (tr.; in a masquerade costume, etc.); (arch.) to hire	rządzić: to rule, govern	řídití: to direct, conduct, manage; to drive (an automobile); to set (a watch, clock)	rediti: to tidy, put in order; to comb (flax); to ordain (a priest)
[R]	[P]	[Cz]	[S-C]

[R]	[P]	[Cz]	[S-C]
		řáditi: to rage; to cause havoc	
		řad (arch.): row; (mil.) rank, file	
		řada: row; (mil.) rank, file; series; a number (of), several; turn (regular succession)	
		řaditi: to place in a row, line up	
		řádek, řádka: row; line (of print)	redak: line (of print)
	rządny: orderly; thrifty, economical	řádný: regular; proper, suitable; decent, honorable; substantial, sizable	redni: ordinal (number)
рядовóй: ordinary; rank-and-file (a.); private (military rank)	rządowy: governmental	řadový: ordinary; rank-and-file (a.); ordinal (number)	redov: private (military rank)
			redovan, redovit: regular; ordinary
			rednja: epidemic; rotation, alternation
			redar: policeman
		ředitel: director, manager	redatelj, reditelj: stage-manager
			redovnik: monk, member of a religious order
	drugorzędny: secondary; second-rate	druhořadý: secondary; second-rate	drugoredan: secondary; second-rate
		mimořádný: extraordinary	izvanredan: extraordinary
	pierwszorzędny: first-rate, excellent	prvořadý: first-rate, excellent	
			vanredan: extraordinary
	współrzędny: (gram.) coordinate		
	współrzędna: (math.) coordinate		

[R]	[P]	[Cz]	[S-C]
беспоря́док: disorder	bezrząd: anarchy		
изря́дный: (coll.) fairly large, considerable; (arch.) excellent			izredan (arch.): excellent; extraordinary
наряди́ть, наряжа́ть: to dress, attire; to detail (soldiers); (arch.) to order, command	narządzić, narządzać: to prepare; to repair	naříditi, nařizovati: to order, command; to set (an instrument, watch, etc.)	narediti, naređivati: to order, command
наря́д: clothing, attire; order, command; detail (of soldiers)	narząd: organ (of body)		nared: agricultural equipment
наря́дный: smart, chic			naredan: next, following
	narzędzie: tool, instrument	nářadí: implements, equipment	
	narzędnik: (gram.) instrumental case		narednik: sergeant
			naporedan: parallel (a.)
	nadrzędny: higher, superior (authority, court, etc.)	nadřízený: higher, superior (authority, court, etc.)	
	nierząd: anarchy; prostitution	neřád: filth, dirt; scoundrel	nered: disorder
непоря́док: disorder	nieporządek: disorder	nepořádek: disorder	
обря́д: rite, ceremony	obrząd, obrzęd, obrządek: rite, ceremony	obřad: rite, ceremony	obred: rite, ceremony
	oporządzić, oporządzać: to tidy, put in order; to dress, clean (fish, etc. for eating); to equip		
отряди́ть, отряжа́ть: to detail (soldiers)			odrediti, određivati: to ordain, decree; to fix, set, specify; to define; to determine; to allot

отря́д: (military) detachment		odřad: (military) detachment	odred: (military) detachment
			odredište: destination
		poříditi, pořizovati: to acquire, obtain; to succeed; to draft, draw up	porediti, poređivati: to compare; (porediti only) to place in a row, line up
		pořad: program; agenda; order, sequence	
		pořadí: order, sequence; tier (of theater seats)	
		pořadač: file (of records, etc.)	
поря́док: order (orderly state of things); order, sequence; method, procedure	porządek: order (orderly state of things); order, sequence	pořádek: order (orderly state of things); order, sequence	poredak: order (orderly state of things); order, sequence
поря́дочный: decent, honorable; substantial, sizable	porządny: orderly; decent, honorable; substantial, sizable	pořádný: orderly; proper, suitable; decent, honorable; substantial, sizable	
		pořádati: to arrange, organize	*poređati (poredati): to place in a row, line up
		pořád: constantly	pored: beside, alongside; besides; despite
подряди́ть, подряжа́ть: to hire	podporządkować, podporządkowywać: to subordinate	podříditi, podřizovati; podřaditi, podřaďovati (podřazovati): to subordinate	podrediti, podređivati: to subordinate
подря́д: contract			
подря́дный: contract (attr.)	podrzędny: subordinate, secondary; second-rate; (gram.) subordinate	podřadný: subordinate, secondary; second-rate; (gram.) subordinate	
[R]	[P]	[Cz]	[S-C]

[R]	[P]	[Cz]	[S-C]
	przyrządzić, przyrządzać: to prepare (food)		prirediti, priređivati: to prepare; to arrange, organize
	przyrząd: device, appliance		
разряди́ть, разряжа́ть: to discharge (a gun, electric battery); to unload (a gun)	rozrządzić, rozrządzać: to deal (with), dispose (of); to distribute, regulate (e.g. the flow of steam with a valve)		razrediti, razređivati: to classify
разря́д: class, category; discharge (of a gun, electric battery); unloading (of a gun)	rozrząd: distribution, regulation (e.g. of the flow of steam by a valve)		razred: class, category; class (in school); section, department
распоряже́ние: order, command; disposition, (act of) disposing (of property, etc.); (в чьём-то: at s.o.'s) disposal, command	rozporządzenie: order, command; disposition, (act of) disposing (of property, etc.); (do czyjegoś: at s.o.'s) disposal, command		raspoređenje: arrangement, disposition, distribution
распоря́док: work routine			raspored: arrangement, disposition, distribution; schedule, timetable; program
	zrządzić, zrządzać: to ordain, decree (said of God, fate, etc.)	zříditi, zřizovati: to establish, set up; to institute	srediti, sređivati: to arrange, put in order; to settle, regulate
	zrzędzić: to grumble, complain		
		souřadný: (gram.) coordinate	
		souřadnice: (math.) coordinate	
снаря́д: projectile, missile, shell; instrument, appliance			

	sporządzić, sporządzać: to prepare; to draft, draw up	*spořádati: to arrange, put in order	
			sporedan: secondary, accessory, collateral
	urządzić, urządzać: to arrange, organize; to install; to furnish (a home)		urediti, uređivati: to arrange, put in order; to arrange, organize; to settle, regulate; to edit
	urząd: office, agency; official position, post	úřad: office, agency; official position, post	ured: office, agency
уря́дник (arch.): village policeman; Cossack non-commissioned officer	urzędnik: official, functionary	úředník: official, functionary	urednik: editor
			uređaj: device, appliance
			uporedan: parallel (a.)
		vřaditi, vřaďovati (vřazovati): to include; to enrol	
	wyrządzić, wyrządzać: to inflict, cause	vyříditi, vyřizovati: to execute, carry out; to transmit; to dress (ranks)	
		vyřaditi, vyřaďovati (vyřazovati): to exclude; to discard, reject	
	wyporządzić, wyporządzać: to repair; to tidy, put in order		
			usporedan: parallel (a.)
[R]	[P]	[Cz]	[S-C]

[R]	[P]	[Cz]	[S-C]
зарядить, заряжать: to load (a gun); to charge (an electric battery) заурядный: mediocre, undistinguished	zarządzić, zarządzać: to manage, administer; to order, direct	zařiditi, zařizovati: to arrange, organize; to install; to equip; to furnish (a home)	zarediti, zaređivati: to ordain (a clergyman); to do (a number of things) one after the other

NOTES

Basic meaning of root: row, straight line; order, arrangement

The semantic development of this root strikingly parallels that of Lat. ordo "row; order (in various senses)" (>Eng. order, ordain, ordinal, ordinary et al.; see notes on individual words below). The various derivatives cover a broad spectrum of meaning extending from the notion of spatial or temporal juxtaposition or succession (>"row," "line," "rank, file," "tier," "series," "sequence," "turn, alternation," "comparison," "next," "beside[s]," "parallel," "constantly") to that of orderly arrangement or procedure (>"class, category," "religious order," "[social, political] order, system," "rite, ceremony") and finally to the idea of good order, orderliness, regularity, propriety, decency, etc. in the broadest sense; somewhat specialized development of the root-meaning is reflected in the notion of "agreement arrived at in an orderly manner" (whence the meanings "contract" and "to hire") and in the meaning "order, command" (="a means of putting things in proper order"). The basic idea of "putting in order, arranging" has given rise to a wide range of largely verbal formations expressing such meanings as "to prepare," "to regulate," "to repair," "to equip" (>"harness"), "to dress (in various senses)," "to specify, define, determine," "to rule, govern," "to direct, manage," "to establish, institute," "to edit," "to comb flax" and "to load a gun"; the meanings "to execute, carry out" and "to inflict, cause" reflect the weakened notion of "doing, making."

Рядить et al. are denominative verbs derived from ряд et al. In Czech, řad and řada (variant forms of original řád) form the basis of řaditi and its compounds, a set of secondary denominatives which generally reflect the concrete root-meaning "row, line." (See also notes below on řáditi, pořádat, spořádati.)

The semantic evolution of the root shows many points of similarity with that of roots ЧИН (etc.) and ПРАВ (etc.).

řáditi: <řád; the meaning was originally ironic: "to put things in order (relentlessly and with a vengeance)."

řádný: Regarding the last meaning, see note on Cz. slušeti (se) and slušný, Pol. słuszny.

redov: ‹Rus. рядовóй.

rednja (first meaning): a disease which strikes people down "in sequence," one after another.

redar: ="one who maintains order."

ředitel: ‹OCz. řieditі (=modern říditi).

izvanredan: The first element is from izvan "outside."

pierwszorzędny-prvořadý: The first element is from pierwszy-prvý "first."

vanredan: The first element is from van "outside."

współrzędny, współrzędna: The reference is to things "of the same order or rank"; compare Eng. coordinate (ult. ‹Lat. cum "with, together" + ordo "order"), Cz. souřadný and souřadnice below.

narednik: See narediti.

obred: ‹Rus. обря́д or Cz. obřad.

odřad-odred: ‹Rus. отря́д.

pořiditi: The first two meanings are an outgrowth of the earlier meaning "to do, make, carry out"; compare Ger. verschaffen "to obtain" (‹schaffen "to do; to create").

poredak: ‹Rus. поря́док.

поря́дочный et al.: Regarding the last meaning, see note on Cz. slušeti (se) and slušný, Pol. słuszny.

pořádati: ‹OCz. pořád (=modern pořádek).

pored: See note on S-C kraj.

podporządkować et al., podrzędny-podřadný: The basic idea is that of "placing in a lower order or rank"; compare Eng. subordinate (ult. ‹Lat. sub "under" + ordo "order"), Rus. подчини́ть et al.

zrzędzić: orig. "to manage things in a scrupulous manner," then "to be peevish, fuss, complain"; the word is a doublet of zrządzić.

souřadný, souřadnice: See note on współrzędny, współrzędna.

spořádati: See note on pořádati.

sporedan: orig. "parallel," then "off to one side, of lesser importance."

ured: ‹Cz. úřad.

уря́дник: See note on redar.

vřaditi: ="to admit to the ranks"; compare Ger. einreihen "to include; to enrol" (‹ein- "in" + Reihe "row; rank, file").

vyříditi (second meaning): ="to execute, carry out" a message, etc.

vyřaditi: ="to remove from the ranks."

зауря́дный: ‹obsolete заря́д "ad interim, on an acting basis" ‹ уря́д "performance of duties on an acting basis without holding the rank appropriate to the position"; the present-day meaning of the adjective arose from such combinations as заурядписа́тель "second-rate writer."

РАЗ, РАЖ	RAZ, RAŹ, RAŻ	RAZ, RÁZ, RAŽ, RÁŽ	RAZ, RAŽ
раз: time (один раз, два ра́за, три ра́за, etc.: once, twice, three times, etc.); once	raz: stroke, blow; time (jeden raz, dwa razy, trzy razy, etc.: once, twice, three times, etc.); once; case, instance	ráz: one (used only in counting); character, nature; (arch.) stroke, blow	raz: moldboard (of a plow); strickle (leveling board for measuring grain)
рази́ть: to hit, strike; (coll.) to reek	razić: to hit, strike; to offend, shock; to dazzle, blind	raziti: to mint, coin; to clear (a path)	
рази́тельный: striking, unusual	rażący: sharp, piercing (e.g. sound); dazzling, blinding; striking, unusual; flagrant, shocking		
	raźny: brisk, lively	rázný: vigorous, energetic	
		rázovitý: characteristic, typical	
ра́зом (coll.): at one stroke; at once, immediately; at once, simultaneously	razem: together	rázem: at once, immediately; suddenly	
		razítko: (rubber-, etc.) stamp	
		ráž, ráže: caliber	
благообра́зный: handsome			
дикобра́з: porcupine		dikobraz: porcupine	dikobraz: porcupine
	iloraz: (math.) quotient		
однообра́зный: monotonous			jednoobrazan: uniform (a.)
единообра́зный: uniform (a.)			
	krajobraz: landscape		krajobraz: landscape
		obrazotvornost: imagination	
первоо́браз: prototype			
[R]	[P]	[Cz]	[S-C]

[R]	[P]	[Cz]	[S-C]
разнообра́зие: variety, diversity			
своеобра́зный: peculiar, distinctive		svérázný: peculiar, distinctive	
	teraz: now		
безобра́зный: ugly; outrageous			bezobrazan: insolent, impudent
	doraźny: immediate	důrazný: emphatic	
			izraz, izražaj: expression, term; expression (of face); expression, reflection, manifestation
			izrazit, izražajan: expressive; marked, pronounced
изразе́ц: tile			
изобрази́ть, изобража́ть: to depict, portray		zobraziti, zobrazovati: to depict, portray	izobraziti, izobražavati: to educate
	narazić, narażać: to expose, subject (to danger, etc.)	naraziti, narážeti: to knock (against); (na + acc.) to encounter; to hint, allude	
		náraz: impact, shock; gust of wind, squall	
		nárazový: urgent	
	naraz: suddenly	naráz: suddenly; at one stroke	
			naobraziti, naobražavati: to educate
	oraz: and, as well as		
	*obrazić: to offend, insult; (arch.) to injure	*obraziti: to bruise; (lit.) to reflect; (lit.) to depict, portray	

[R]	[P]	[Cz]	[S-C]
	obrażać: to offend, insult; (arch.) to injure	obrážeti: to reflect	
óбраз: shape, form; image; way, mode, manner; icon	obraz: picture, painting; image; icon	obraz: picture, painting; image; icon	obraz: cheek; face; honor
óбразный: picturesque; figurative, metaphorical		obrazný: figurative, metaphorical	obrazan: honest, honorable
	obrazowy: pictorial; picturesque; figurative, metaphorical	obrazový: pictorial	
образéц: model, pattern; sample		obrazec: graph, diagram	obrazac: model, pattern; blank form (to be filled in); formula
			obrazina: mask
образовáние: formation; education			obrazovanje: formation; education
отрази́ть, отражáть: to beat off, repel; to reflect	odrazić, odrażać: to disgust, repel	odraziti, odrážeti: to hit back (a ball); to beat off, repel; to reflect; to deduct; to cast off, shove off (from shore)	odraziti, odražavati (odrazivati): to reflect
		odrážka: (mus.) natural (n.)	
поражéние: defeat; (act of) striking; affection (by a disease)	porażenie: (med.) stroke; (med.) paralysis	poražení: slaughter (of cattle); felling (of trees)	
	porażka: defeat	porážka: defeat; slaughter (of cattle); slaughterhouse	poraz: defeat
порази́тельный: striking, unusual			porazan: crushing, annihilating
		podrážka: sole (of a shoe)	
преобрази́ть, преображáть; преобразовáть, преобразóвывать: to transform	przeobrazić, przeobrażać: to transform		preobraziti, preobražavati: to transform

[R]	[P]	[Cz]	[S-C]
		předobraz (lit.): model; prototype přirážka: surcharge; surtax	
	przerażenie: terror		
проóбраз: prototype сражéние: battle			
	zrażenie się: discouragement		
		sraz: meeting	sraz: collision
	zraz: slice of meat; graft, scion; (anat.) lobe	sráz: steep slope	
		srážka: collision; skirmish; quarrel; discount, rebate; deduction (from pay-check, etc.) srážky (pl.): precipitation (rain, snow, etc.) sraženina: sediment, deposit; clotted blood	
срáзу: at once, immediately	zrazu: at first		
соображéние: consideration, deliberation; consideration, reason, motive; understanding сообрази́тельный: shrewd, quick-witted **сообразовáть: to adapt, adjust (tr.)			saobraženje: adaptation, adjustment
	uraz: injury uraza: grudge, grievance wrażenie: (favorable, etc.) impression	úraz: injury urážka: insult	

[R]	[P]	[Cz]	[S-C]
	wrażliwy: impressionable; sensitive		
враз (coll.): at once, simultaneously; at once, immediately	wraz (z): together (with)		
воображе́ние: imagination			uobraženje, uobrazilja: imagination
			uobražen: conceited
выраже́ние: expression, term; expression (of face); expression, reflection, manifestation	wyrażenie: expression, term; expression, reflection, manifestation	vyražení: amusement, entertainment	
	wyraz: word; expression, term; expression (of face); expression, reflection, manifestation	výraz: expression, term; expression (of face); expression, reflection, manifestation	
вырази́тельный: expressive	wyraźny: express, explicit; clear, precise	výrazný: expressive; distinctive; marked, pronounced	
	wyrazisty: expressive; distinct		
		vyrážka: (med.) rash, eruption	
	wyobrazić, wyobrażać: to depict, portray	vyobraziti, vyobrazovati: to depict, portray	
	wyobraźnia: imagination		
возрази́ть, возража́ть: to object			
зарази́ть, заража́ть: to infect; to contaminate	zarazić, zarażać: to infect; to contaminate	zaraziti, zarážeti: to knock, drive (in); to stop, halt (tr.); to disconcert, nonplus	zaraziti, zaražavati: to infect; to contaminate
зара́з (coll.): at one stroke	zaraz: at once, immediately		
	zarazem: at once, simultaneously		

NOTES

Basic meaning of root: to hit, strike

The original root-meaning, "to cut," is still apparent in a number of derivatives. The meaning "stroke, blow" has given rise to that of "time" ("one stroke" = "once," "two strokes" = "twice," "three strokes" = "three times," etc.) and to such further meanings as "suddenly," "at once" (="immediately" and "simultaneously") and "together." Rus. *óбраз* *et al*. (see note below) and their derivatives form an extensive semantic sub-group.

ráz (second meaning): ="stamp, imprint, mark"; see the first meaning of *raziti* and compare Eng. *character* (ult. ⟨Gr. *χαρακτήρ* "stamp, imprint, mark").

рази́ть *et al*.: denominatives formed from *раз*-*raz*-*ráz*.

ráž, *ráže*: a reference to the stamp or mark on a gun indicating the caliber.

дикобра́з *et al*.: ="animal having a wild, strange appearance"; the first element in the Russian word, from which the other two are borrowed, is from *ди́кий* "wild, strange."

iloraz: The first element is from *ile* "how many"; see *raz*.

jednoobrazan, *единообра́зный*: See note on S-C *jednoličan*, *jednolik*.

obrazotvornost: See note on *воображе́ние* *et al*.

первообраз: The first element is from *пе́рвый* "first"; compare Eng. *prototype* (ult. ⟨Gr. *πρῶτος* "first" + *τύπος* "image; type; model"), Pol. *pierwowzór* and *prawzór et al*., Rus. *проо́браз* below.

разнообра́зие: The first element is from *ра́зный* "different, various."

своеобра́зный-*svérázný*: See the third meaning of *ráz* and compare Ger. *eigenartig* "peculiar, distinctive" (⟨*eigen* "[one's] own" + *Art* "kind; manner; character, nature").

teraz: The first element is from *ten* "this"; see *raz*.

bezobrazan: See the third meaning of *obraz*.

doraźny: ⟨obsolete *dorazu* "at once, immediately."

izraz, *izražaj*: See note on *выраже́ние*-*wyrażenie*, *wyraz*-*výraz*.

изразе́ц: ="something which has been cut out (for use as building material)."

izobraziti, *naobraziti*: See note on *образова́ние*-*obrazovanje*.

oraz: Compare *razem*, *wraz*, *zarazem*.

obraziti: In its second and third meanings, the word is a denominative formed from *obraz* and is imperfective.

obrážeti: ⟨*obraz*.

о́браз-*obraz* (Pol.-Cz.): ="something cut into wood or stone," hence "picture," hence further "image; shape, form." The origin of both drawing and writing as a process of cutting, tearing, scratching, etc. is apparent in a number of languages; see Rus. *черти́ть* and S-C *crtati* "to draw" (both ultimately from the same root as Lith. kir̃sti "to chop"), Eng. write and cognate Ger. reissen "to tear" and Riss "tear; drawing," Eng. carve and cog nate Gr. γράφειν "to write" (>Eng. graph, graphic, graphology), Gr. σκαριφᾶσθαι "to scratch" and cognate Lat. scribere "to write" (>Eng. scribe, script, scripture).

obraz (S-C): orig. "picture; shape, form" (see preceding note). Regard ing the first two meanings, see the introductory note on root ЛИК (etc.); the meaning "honor" has been attributed to the belief that a person's face reflects his moral character.

obrazac: <Rus. образе́ц or Cz. obrazec.

obrazina: See the second meaning of obraz.

образова́ние-obrazovanje: The second meaning reflects the influence of Ger. Bildung "formation; education"; the Serbo-Croatian word is borrowed from Russian.

отрази́ть et al.: Regarding the meanings "to reflect," "to disgust, repel" and "to deduct," compare Pol. odbić, S-C odbiti and see notes on Cz. odpudivý and S-C odbiti; the Serbo-Croatian word is borrowed from Russian.

odrážka: a musical character which serves to "knock off," i.e. annul, preceding sharp or flat; see odraziti and compare the use of Eng. cancel (n.) in the same sense.

преобрази́ть et al.: See note on Rus. претвори́ть et al.

předobraz: Compare Ger. Vorbild "model; prototype" (<vor "before" + Bild "picture").

přirážka: Compare Ger. Zuschlag "surcharge; surtax" (<zu "to" + schlag en "to hit, strike").

проо́браз: See note on первоо́браз.

zrażenie się: Compare odrazić.

sráz: <sraziti "to knock down; to lower."

srážka: See note on S-C odbiti.

srážky, sraženina: <sraziti "to knock together; to condense, clot, cause to precipitate."

zrazu: <raz in the earlier meaning "first time."

соображе́ние, сообрази́тельный: The underlying idea is that of forming a picture of something.

saobraženje, сообразова́ть: Compare Eng. conform (ult. <Lat. cum "with together" + formare "to form"); the Serbo-Croatian word is borrowed from Rus. соображе́ние in the earlier meaning "conformity."

uraza: orig. "injury; insult."

wrażenie: loosely modeled on Fr. impression; see note on S-C utisak.

воображе́ние et al.: Compare Eng. image and imagination, Ger. Einbildung "imagination" (<ein- "in" + Bild "picture").

uobražen: modeled on Ger. eingebildet "conceited" (<sich einbilden "to imagine"); see preceding note.

выраже́ние-wyrażenie, wyraz-výraz: loosely modeled on Fr. expression ult. ⟨Lat. *ex* "out" + *premere* "to press"), Ger. *Ausdruck* "expression" (⟨*aus* out" + *drücken* "to press").

vyražení: The underlying idea is that of "knocking a person out of" i.e. distracting him from) his troubles.

vyrážka: a loan-translation of Ger. *Ausschlag* "rash" (⟨*aus* "out" + chlagen "to hit, strike"); compare Eng. *to break out (in a rash)* and *eruption* (ult. ⟨Lat. *e* "out" + *rumpere* "to break").

wyobraźnia: See note on *воображéние et al.*

zaraziti (S-C): ⟨Rus. *заразúть*.

РЕ(К), РЕЧ, РИЦ, РОК, РОЧ	RZE(K), RZECZ, ROK, ROCZ, RACZ	ŘEK, ŘÍ(K), ŘK, ŘEČ, RČ, ROK, ROČ	RE(K), RIJEK, REČ, RJEČ, RIJEČ, RIC, RIČ, ROK, ROČ
	**rzec*: to say, tell	*říci*, *říkati*: to say, tell	**reći*: to say, tell
речь: (power of) speech; talk, conversation; speech, address	*rzecz*: thing; affair, matter, business	*řeč*: (power of) speech; language; talk, conversation; speech, address; rumor	*riječ*: word
			rječkati se: to quarrel
			rečenica: (gram.) sentence, clause; maxim, saying
		rčení: phrase, expression	
	rzecznik: advocate, spokesman; attorney	*řečník*: speaker, orator	*rječnik*: dictionary
	rzeczownik: (gram.) noun, substantive		
	rzeczywisty: real		
рок: fate	*rok*: year	*rok*: year	*rok*: date, fixed time; term, period of time
	rocznica: anniversary		
	rokować: to negotiate; to augur, hold promise of	*rokovati*: to confer, deliberate	
[R]	[P]	[Cz]	[S-C]

[R]	[P]	[Cz]	[S-C]
		blahořečiti: to be grateful (to); to praise dobrořečiti (lit.): to be grateful (to); to praise	
	grzeczny: polite		
красноречи́вый: eloquent			krasnorječiv: eloquent kratkorijek: curt, laconic lakorječiv: loquacious ljeporječiv: eloquent malorijek: taciturn
многоречи́вый (lit.): loquacious			mnogorječiv: loquacious
			pravorijek: (judicial) sentence; verdict
	rzeczpospolita: republic rzeczoznawca: expert (n.)		
велеречи́вый (arch.): pompous, bombastic			
	złorzeczyć: to curse dorzeczny: reasonable, sensible	zlořečiti: to curse	
изре́чь, изрека́ть (arch.): to utter, say изрече́ние: maxim, saying			izreći, izricati: to utter, say izreka: (gram.) sentence, clause; maxim, saying izričaj: maxim, saying izričan, izričit: explicit
*наре́чь (arch.): to name, give a name to		*nařknouti: to accuse	*nareći: to name, give a name to

[R]	[P]	[Cz]	[S-C]
нарекáть (arch.): to name, give a name to	narzekać: to complain	naříkati: to groan; to mourn, lament; to complain	naricati: to mourn, lament; to name, give a name to
нарекáние: censure, reproach	narzekanie: complaining	naříkání: groaning; lamentation; complaining	naricanje: lamentation
наречённый (masc., arch.), наречённая (fem., arch.): fiancé(e)	narzeczony (masc.), narzeczona (fem.): fiancé(e)		
нарéчие: dialect; (gram.) adverb	narzecze: dialect	nářečí: dialect	narječje: dialect
нарицáтельный: (gram.) common (noun); nominal (value---of securities, etc.)			
		nárok: claim	
нáрочный: special messenger		náročný: demanding, exacting; pretentious	
нарочи́тый: intentional			naročit: special; explicit; intentional
непререкáемый (lit.): indisputable, unchallengeable			
обрéчь, обрекáть: to doom	orzec, orzekać: to rule, decide, pronounce judgment		obreći, obricati: to promise
	orzeczenie: (judicial) sentence; opinion (medical, expert, etc.); (gram.) predicate		
обрóк (arch.): quitrent, feudal tax	obrok: fodder; (arch.) quitrent, feudal tax	obrok: fodder; (arch.) quitrent, feudal tax	obrok: meal; ration; portion, helping; dose; instalment
		obročí: ecclesiastical benefice, prebend	
			oporeći, oporicati: to recant, retract
[R]	[P]	[Cz]	[S-C]

[R]	[P]	[Cz]	[S-C]
отрица́ть: to deny (a fact)	odrzec, odrzekać: to reply	odříci (odřeknouti), odříkati: to refuse, deny (s.th. to s.o.); to cancel, revoke	odreći, odricati: to deny (a fact); to cancel, revoke
отрица́тельный: negative (reply, etc.); (math., phys.) negative; unfavorable, adverse			odrečan: negative (reply, etc.); (math., phys.) negative
отре́чься, отрека́ться (lit.): to renounce, give up; to repudiate, disown	odrzec się, odrzekać się: to renounce, give up; to repudiate, disown	odříci (odřeknouti) se, odříkati se: to renounce, give up; to repudiate, disown	odreći se, odricati se: to renounce, give up; to repudiate, disown
о́трок (arch.): boy, lad		otrok: slave	
отсро́чить, отсро́чивать: to postpone, delay	odroczyć, odraczać: to postpone, delay	odročiti, odročovati: to postpone, delay	
порица́ть: to condemn, censure			poreći (poreknuti), poricati: to recant, retract; to deny (a fact)
	porzekadło: proverb	pořekadlo: proverb	
поро́к: vice; defect			porok: vice; defect
поро́чить: to defame, discredit			
пререка́ться: to quarrel		přeříci (přeřeknouti) se, přeříkati se: to make a slip of the tongue	*prereći se: to make a slip of the tongue
предре́чь, предрека́ть (arch.): to predict			
	przyrzec, przyrzekać: to promise	*přiřknouti: to award	
			prirok: (gram.) predicate
		příročí: moratorium	
[R]	[P]	[Cz]	[S-C]

[R]	[P]	[Cz]	[S-C]
приуро́чить, приуро́чивать: to time, set for a particular time			
прорица́ть: to prophesy			proreći, proricati: to prophesy
проро́к: prophet	prorok: prophet	prorok: prophet	prorok: prophet
противоре́чить: to contradict (s.o.); to contradict, conflict (with)			protivrijećiti (protivurijećiti): to contradict (s.o.); to contradict, conflict (with)
рассро́чка: instalment plan			
			sreći, sricati: to spell
срок: date, fixed time; term, period of time			srok: rhyme
сро́чный: urgent; done at a fixed time			sročan: rhyming; harmonious, in agreement
	urzec, urzekać: to bewitch, cast a spell over	*uřknouti: to bewitch, cast a spell over	ureći (ureknuti), uricati: to bewitch, cast a spell over; to fix, set (a time)
		určiti, určovati: to determine; to fix, set, specify; to allot; to appoint	
уро́к: lesson	urok: charm, spell; charm, attractiveness	úrok: interest (on a loan)	urok: charm, spell
уро́чный: fixed, stipulated			
	uroczysty: solemn		
	urzeczywistnić, urzeczywistniać: to bring about, realize, accomplish		
	wyrzec, wyrzekać: to utter, say; (wyrzekać only) to complain	*vyřknouti: to utter, say	
		výřečný: eloquent	
[R]	[P]	[Cz]	[S-C]

[R]	[P]	[Cz]	[S-C]
	wyrok: (judicial) sentence	výrok: statement; (judicial) sentence; verdict; maxim, saying; (arch., gram.) predicate	
	wyrocznia: oracle; prophecy		
	wyrzec się, wyrzekać się: to renounce, give up; to repudiate, disown		
		výročí: anniversary	
			uzrečica: maxim, saying
			uzrok: reason, cause
	zrzec się, zrzekać się: to renounce, give up; to repudiate, disown	zříci (zřeknouti) se, zříkati se: to renounce, give up; to repudiate, disown	
заре́чься, зарека́ться (coll.): to vow, pledge (not to do s.th.)	zarzec się, zarzekać się: to renounce, give up; to repudiate, disown	zaříci (zařeknouti) se, zaříkati se: to vow, pledge (not to do s.th.)	zareći se, zaricati se: to vow, pledge; to make a slip of the tongue
заро́к: vow, pledge (to refrain from doing s.th.)			

NOTES

Basic meaning of root: to speak

Many of the derivatives reflect the notion of a stipulated time, task, amount, etc. (whence such meanings as "date, term," "year," "lesson," "special," "intentional," "interest [on a loan]," "quitrent," "prebend," "meal; ration; dose" and "instalment"). See also the introductory note on root ГОВОР (etc.).

The Czech perfective verbs in -řknouti are new formations (from the root of řku, obsolete 1 sg. of říci) which have replaced the original forms in -říci. The Russian root-form РИЦ is of Church Slavic origin.

rzec-říci-reći: The respective 1 sg. forms are rzeknę, řeknu, rečem (or reknem); Rus. речь (1 sg.: реку́) is obsolete.

rzecz: orig. "speech," then "that which is spoken of," i.e. "thing";

ompare Heb. dābhār "word; thing" (⟨dibēr "to speak").

rzeczownik: that part of speech which refers to a thing; see rzecz.

rzeczywisty: See rzecz and note on S-C stvaran.

рок: ="that which is spoken, ordained"; compare Eng. fate (ult. ⟨Lat. ari "to speak").

rokować-rokovati: ⟨rok in the former sense of "court term or session"; he second meaning of the Polish word is a figurative extension of the earier meaning "to summon to appear in court."

blahořečiti: See note under root БЛАГ (etc.).

dobrořečiti: See note under root ДОБР (etc.).

grzeczny: ⟨OPol. krzeczny ⟨ k (=modern Pol. ku) "to" + rzecz; the sucessive meanings of the word have been "to the point, relevant, suitable" ⟩ pretty, nice" ⟩ "polite."

красноречи́вый-krasnorječiv: The first element is from кра́сный "red; arch.) beautiful," krasan "beautiful"; the Serbo-Croatian word is borrowed rom Russian.

ljeporječiv: The first element is from lijep "beautiful."

многоречи́вый-mnogorječiv: The first element is from мно́го-mnogo "much"; he Serbo-Croatian word is borrowed from Russian.

pravorijek: See note under root ПРАВ (etc.).

rzeczpospolita: See rzecz and note under root ПОЛ (etc.).

rzeczoznawca: See rzecz and note under root ЗНА (etc.).

złorzeczyć-zlořečiti: See note under root ЗЛ (etc.).

dorzeczny: orig. "to the point, relevant, suitable"; see rzecz and note n grzeczny above.

изрече́ние: borrowed from Church Slavic.

izričan, izričit: Compare Eng. outspoken, Cz. výslovný.

наре́чие (second meaning): a reflection of the adverb's primary function s a verb modifier (речь being used here in its earlier meaning "word; erb"); the word is modeled on Lat. adverbium (⟨ad "at, near" + verbum word; verb"), which in turn translates Gr. ἐπίρρημα "adverb" (⟨ἐπί "on, at, ear" + ῥῆμα "word; verb"). Compare Pol. przysłówek, Cz. příslovce.

narzecze et al.: The Serbo-Croatian word is borrowed from Rus. наре́чие, s are in all probability the Polish and Czech words.

нарица́тельный: See наре́чь. The grammatical meaning reflects the fact hat a common noun (in contrast to a proper noun) "names" an entire class of hings; as used in this sense, the word is modeled on Lat. (nomen) appellaivum "common (noun)" (⟨appellare "to name"), which translates Gr. (ὄνομα) ροσηγορικόν "common (noun)" (⟨προσαγορεύειν "to name"). Regarding the second meaning, compare Eng. nominal (ult. ⟨Lat. nomen "name").

nárok: Compare Ger. Anspruch "claim" (⟨an "to" + sprechen "to speak").

náročný: See nárok.

orzeczenie (third meaning): See note on Rus. сказу́емое.

obrok (Pol.-Cz.): The first meaning arose from the common practice of making quitrent payments in kind in the form of grain for fodder.

odrzec: See note on S-C odgovoriti.

óтрок-otrok: ="one who is not permitted to speak (in public assemblie etc.)"; the prefix has negative force. See the introductory note on root P (etc.).

отсрóчить: See срок.

odroczyć-odročiti: ⟨rok in the earlier meaning "court term or session

порóк-porok: ="something deserving of censure"; see порицáть. The Russian word is borrowed from Church Slavic, the Serbo-Croatian word from Russian.

порóчить: ="to attribute a vice to someone"; see порóк.

prirok: See note on Rus. сказýемое.

příročí: ="extension of a time-limit," reflecting the earlier use of rok in the sense of "date, term."

противорéчить et al.: Compare Eng. gainsay (in which gain- = "against and contradict (ult. ⟨Lat. contra "against" + dicere "to say"), Ger. widersprechen "to contradict" (⟨wider "against" + sprechen "to speak"), S-C protusloviti and see note on Rus. прекослóвить; the Serbo-Croatian words a borrowed from Russian.

рассрóчка: See срок.

určiti: a new formation from the past participle of OCz. uřéci.

uroczysty: orig. "special" with particular reference to religious feas days, then "solemn" in both a religious and a non-religious sense.

urzeczywistnić: See rzeczywisty and note on S-C ostvariti.

výřečný: See note on Pol. wymowny, wymowa and wymówka, Cz. výmluvný a výmluva.

výrok (fourth meaning): See note on Rus. сказýемое.

uzrok: perhaps orig. "reasonable statement, reasoning, explanation"; compare Du. rede "speech" and reden "reason, cause."

PE(T), PEЧ		ŘET	RE(T), REĆ
изобрести́, изобретáть: to invent обрести́, обретáть (lit.): to find			*obresti: to discover predusresti, predusretati: to meet (tr.); to forestall, anticipate, act ahead of; to prevent
[R]		[Cz]	[S-C]

[R]		[Cz]	[S-C]
			predusretljiv: obliging, attentive
приобрести́, приобрета́ть: to gain, acquire; to purchase			
		střetnouti se, střetati se (lit.): to meet (intr.)	sresti se, sretati se: to meet (intr.)
			sreća: happiness; (good) luck
			susresti (susretnuti) se, susretati se: to meet (intr.)
встре́титься, встреча́ться: to meet (intr.)			

NOTES

Basic meaning of root: to find; to meet

The root occurs only in combination with prefixes; it is defunct in Polish except for dialectal (po)śratać "to welcome."

The Russian forms in -рести́, -рета́ть are of Church Slavic origin.

изобрести́: See обрести́ and note on S-C iznahoditi.

обрести́-obresti: The respective 1 sg. perfective forms are обрету́, obretem.

predusretljiv: See predusresti and note on Rus. предупреди́тельный.

střetnouti se: The first t is intrusive; compare the Czech forms of root СЕРД (etc.).

sresti se: The 1 sg. perfective form is sretnem se.

sreća: literally "meeting" (see sresti se), i.e. "that which befalls one, comes one's way"; regarding the shift to a positive meaning, see note on S-C čest.

встре́титься: The root is preceded by prefixes в- and с- + an intrusive т.

РОБ, РАБ, РЕБ	ROB, RÓB, RAB	ROB, RÁB, RAB	ROB, RAB
ребёнок: child		robě, robátko: baby	
раб: slave	rab (arch.): slave	rab (lit.), rob (arch.): slave	rob: slave
рабо́та: work	robota: work	robota: hard (forced) labor	rabota, robota: hard (forced) labor
	robić: to do, make; (coll.) to work	robiti (coll.): to do, make; to work	robiti: to enslave; to rob, plunde
			rabiti: to serve be of use; to use
ро́бкий: timid			
			zlorabiti: to abuse, misuse
безрабо́тица: unemployment	bezrobocie: unemployment		
	dorobek: property; achievements		
	nieróbek: idler		
	obrobić, obrabiać: to process, treat, work (metal, wood, etc.); to cultivate, till; to settle (a matter)	obrobiti, obráběti: to process, treat, work (metal, wood, etc.)	
обрабо́тать, обраба́тывать: to process, treat, work (metal, wood, etc.); to cultivate, till			
	parobczak, parobek: farmhand		
	podrobić, podrabiać: to falsify, counterfeit		
	rozrobić, rozrabiać: to dilute; to mix		
разрабо́тать, разраба́тывать: to cultivate, till; to work, exploit (a			
[R]	[P]	[Cz]	[S-C]

[R]	[P]	[Cz]	[S-C]
mine); to work out, elaborate			
	wyrobić, wyrabiać: to make, manufacture; to obtain; to knead wyrobnik: day-laborer	vyrobiti, vyráběti: to make, manufacture	
вы́работать, выраба́тывать: to make, manufacture; to work out, elaborate; (coll.) to earn			
	zarobić, zarabiać: to earn; to knead		zarobiti, zarobljavati: to take prisoner
зарабо́тать, зараба́тывать: to earn			

NOTES

asic meaning of root: child; slave; work

Since children and slaves have in common an inferior status which de-ars them from full and equal participation in the affairs of the community o which they belong, it is not surprising that a root with the original eaning "child" (see cognate Sansk. árbhas "child") should also produce a ord for "slave." (Compare Rus. о́трок and Cz. otrok, which show the same emantic relationship.) From the notion of "slavery" has evolved the more eneralized one of "work" and, in Polish and Czech, the still broader mean-ng "to do, make." In some Indo-European languages, the root-meaning "child" as given way to "orphan" (see Gr. ὀρφανός, whence Eng. orphan, and Lat. rbus) and, at one more remove semantically, "heir" (see Ger. Erbe); another on-Slavic cognate is Ger. Arbeit "work."

ребёнок et al.: The original Russian form, робёнок, survives in dia-ect. Robieniec, robionek "child" occur in Old Polish. The corresponding erbo-Croatian word is not attested.

раб et al.: The Russian and Polish words are Church Slavic borrowings see ORus. робъ, OPol. rob); Cz. rab is from Russian or Church Slavic.

рабо́та et al.: The original Russian form, робо́та, is today dialectal; -C rabota may be of Church Slavic origin.

robić et al.: S-C robiti was originally also an intransitive verb meaning "to do hard labor"; Rus. ро́бить "to work" is dialectal.

rabiti: orig. "to work," then "to serve, be of use," finally (as a transitive verb) "to use."

ро́бкий: ⟨ORus. робя "child" (see ребёнок).

podrobić: See note on Rus. подки́дыш.

rozrobić: See note on Rus. раствори́ть et al.

РОД, РОЖ, РОЖД	RÓD(Z), RÓDŹ, ROD(Z), RADZ	ROD, RŮD, ROZ	ROD, ROT, ROĐ, RAĐ, ROŽD
**роди́ть: to bear, give birth to; to produce, bring forth (crops)	rodzić: to bear, give birth to; to produce, bring forth (crops)	roditi: to bear, give birth to; to produce, bring forth (crops)	*roditi: to bear, give birth to; to produce, bring forth (crops)
рожда́ть (рожа́ть [coll.]): to bear, give birth to			rađati: to bear, give birth to; to produce, bring forth (crops)
**роди́ться: to be born; to thrive (said of crops)	rodzić się: to be born	roditi se: to be born; to thrive (said of crops)	*roditi se: to be born
рожда́ться: to be born			rađati se: to be born
род: clan, kin; birth, stock, family background; generation; kind, sort; genus; (human) race, (man)kind; (gram.) gender	ród: clan, kin; birth, stock, family background	rod: clan, kin; birth, stock, family background; genus; (arch.) sex; (gram.) gender; (gram.) voice	rod: clan, kin; birth, stock, family background; kind, sort; genus; (human) race, (man)kind; sex; (gram.) gender; harvest
	rodzaj: kind, sort; genus; (human) race, (man)kind; (gram.) gender		rođaj: birth; sunrise
	rodzajnik: (gram.) article		
родно́й: (one's) own; native; dear, darling	rodny: fertile; genital	rodný: (one's) own; native	rodan: fertile; native
		rodidla (pl.): female genitals	
ро́дина: native land	rodzina: family	rodina: family	rodina: harvest
ро́динка: birthmark			
[R]	[P]	[Cz]	[S-C]

	rodak: fellow-countryman, compatriot	rodák: native; fellow-countryman, compatriot	rođak: relative, kinsman
ро́дственник: relative, kinsman			
ро́дич (arch.): relative, kinsman	rodzice (pl.): parents	rodiče (pl.): parents	
роди́тели (pl.): parents		rodičelé (pl., arch.): parents	roditelji (pl.): parents
	rodzeństwo: siblings, brother(s) and sister(s)		
Рождество́: Christmas			Roždestvo (lit.): Christmas
родни́к: spring (of water)			
роди́тельный: (gram.) genitive			
благоро́дный: noble (a.); (arch.) of noble birth		blahorodý: honorable (title)	blagorodan: honorable (title); of noble birth
Богоро́дица: the Virgin Mary	Bogarodzica: the Virgin Mary	Bohorodička: the Virgin Mary	Bogorodica: the Virgin Mary
		činorodý: active	
детоpóдный: genital			
		domorodý: native, indigenous	domorodan: native, indigenous
двою́родный (брат), двою́родная (сестра́): (male, female) first cousin			
			istorodan: homogeneous; similar
одноро́дный: homogeneous	jednorodny: homogeneous		jednorodan: homogeneous
	kazirodztwo: incest		
кислоро́д: oxygen			
междунаро́дный: international	międzynarodowy: international	mezinárodní: international	međunarodan: international
месторожде́ние: mineral deposit			
[R]	[P]	[Cz]	[S-C]

[R]	[P]	[Cz]	[S-C]
		národopis: ethnography	narodopis (arch.): ethnography
народове́дение: ethnology		národozpyt: ethnology	
первоpóдство: primogeniture	pierworodztwo, pierworództwo: primogeniture	prvorozenství: primogeniture	prvorodstvo: primogeniture
природове́дение (arch.): natural science	przyrodoznawstwo: natural science	přírodopis, přírodověda, (arch.) přírodozpyt: natural science	prirodopis, prirodoznanstvo: natural science
разнорóдный: heterogeneous	różnorodny: heterogeneous	různorodý: heterogeneous	raznorodan: heterogeneous
			rodoljublje: patriotism
	rodopis: genealogist	rodopis: genealogy	rodopis: genealogy
			rodoskvrnjenje, rodoskvrnuće: incest
родослóвие (lit.): genealogy	rodowód: genealogy		rodoslovlje: genealogy
	słoworód: etymology		
		stejnorodý: homogeneous	
углерóд: carbon			
водорóд: hydrogen	wodoród (arch.): hydrogen		
	współrodak: fellow-countryman, compatriot		
дорóдный: portly, stout	dorodny: well-formed, handsome		
			izroditi se, izrađati se: to degenerate
нарóд: nation, people; people taken as a group (e.g. working people); (coll.) (many, few, etc.) people	naród: nation, people; (coll.) (many, few, etc.) people	národ: nation, people	narod: nation, people; people taken as a group (e.g. working people); (many, few, etc.) people
			nerotkinja: barren woman

недорóд, неурожáй: crop failure	nieurodzaj: crop failure	neúroda: crop failure	nerodica: crop failure
		obroda, obrození: regeneration, revival	
*обнарóдовать: to promulgate, publish (e.g. a law)			*obnarodovati: to promulgate, publish (e.g. a law)
	odrodzenie: regeneration, revival; (cap.) Renaissance		
		odrodilec: renegade	odrod: renegade
		odrůda: kind, variety (of fruit, etc.)	
порóда: breed, strain; mineral deposit			
			porodica: family
		porodník: obstetrician	
			preporod: regeneration, revival; (cap.) Renaissance
прирóда: nature (the physical world); nature, character	przyroda: nature (the physical world)	příroda: nature (the physical world); nature, character	priroda: nature (the physical world); nature, character
	przyrodzenie: nature, character; genitals	přirození: genitals; (arch.) nature, character	
	rozrodczy: genital		
сродствó: kinship, affinity, similarity			srodstvo: kinship, affinity, similarity; kinship, family relationship
урóд: monster; freak; ugly person			
	uroda: beauty	úroda: harvest	
урожáй: harvest; good harvest	urodzaj: harvest; good harvest		
юрóдивый: foolish, crazy			
[R]	[P]	[Cz]	[S-C]

[R]	[P]	[Cz]	[S-C]
врождённый: innate	wrodzony: innate	vrozený: innate	urođen: innate; native, indigenous
вы́родиться, вырожда́ться: to degenerate	wyrodzić się, wyradzać się: to degenerate		
возрожде́ние: regeneration, revival; (cap.) Renaissance			
		zrůda: monster; freak	
	zaródź: protoplasm		
заро́дыш: embryo; fetus; germ, bud	zarodek: embryo; fetus; germ, bud	zárodek: embryo; fetus; germ, bud	
	zarodnik: spore		

NOTES

Basic meaning of root: to give birth to, produce

The notion of "bearing, bringing forth" (living creatures as well as crops, minerals, etc.) is reflected in a semantically wide-ranging group of derivatives, many of which show the meanings (1) "group of persons who have been 'born together,' i.e. are akin," hence "family," "clan," "nation," "race," etc., and (2) "class of things or beings which have been 'created together,' i.e. are kindred, similar," hence "kind, sort" (and, with specialization of meaning, "genus," "sex," "grammatical gender or voice"). (See also note below on приро́да et al.) The idea of fertility and sound growth underlies the meanings "portly, stout," "well-formed, handsome" and "beauty," while that of unsound, aberrant development is reflected (through the action of negative prefixes) in words meaning "monster, freak."

For purposes of vocabulary formation, this root has supplanted in the Slavic languages the widely distributed Indo-European root *ĜEN, which occurs in Eng. kin, kind, kindred, etc., in Lat. gignere (and earlier genere) "to beget" (>Eng. genital[s], indigenous), nasci (for earlier gnasci) "to be born" (>Eng. nation, native, nature, Renaissance) and genus "birth, stock; kind, sort; race; sex" (>Eng. genus, gender, generation, regeneration), and in Gr. γίγνεσθαι "to be born," γένος "birth, stock; kind, sort; race; sex" and γενεά "birth, stock." (See references to other English derivatives in notes on individual words below.)

The Russian root-form РОЖД is of Church Slavic origin.

роди́ть et al.: denominatives formed from род et al.
rođaj (second meaning): ="birth of the sun."

rodzajnik: so called because an article can, among other things, indicate the gender (see rodzaj) of a noun.

rodzice-rodiče, родители et al.: Compare Eng. parents (ult. ‹Lat. parere "to bear, give birth to").

Рождество́-Roždestvo: ="birth(day) of Christ"; compare Eng. Nativity and Fr. Noël, It. Natale, Sp. Navidad "Christmas" (all ult. ‹Lat. nasci "to be born"). The Serbo-Croatian word is borrowed from Russian.

родни́к: a place where a stream of water "is born," i.e. gushes forth.

роди́тельный: modeled on Lat. genitivus (genetivus) and Gr. γενική. The latter (‹γένος "kind, sort") reflects the fact that a noun in the genitive often serves to indicate "kind," i.e. to specify the class or category to which another noun belongs; the Latin word (‹gignere [genere] "to beget") is generally thought to be a faulty loan-translation of its Greek counterpart.

благоро́дный et al.: See note under root БЛАГ (etc.).

Богоро́дица et al.: See note under root БО(Г) (etc.).

činorodý: ="giving birth to (i.e. generating, producing) action."

детоpо́дный: The first element is from the root of дитя́ "child."

domorodý-domorodan: The first element is from dům-dom "house, home."

двою́родный (брат), двою́родная (сестра́): ="(brother, sister) in the second degree of relationship."

istorodan, одноро́дный et al.: Compare Eng. homogeneous (ult. ‹Gr. ὁμός "same" + γένος "kind, sort"), Cz. stejnorodý below.

kazirodztwo: The first element is from kazić "to sully, taint."

кислоро́д: The first element is from ки́слый "sour; acid"; the word arose from the fact that oxygen is a constituent of all but a very few acids. Compare Eng. oxygen (ult. ‹Gr. ὀξύς "sharp; sour; acid" + the root of γίγνεσθαι "to be born"), Ger. Sauerstoff "oxygen" (‹sauer "sour; acid" + Stoff "matter, substance"), Cz. kyslík "oxygen" (‹kyselý "sour; acid"), S-C kisik, kiseonik "oxygen" (‹kiseo "sour; acid").

междунаро́дный et al.: See наро́д et al.

месторожде́ние: orig. "birthplace; habitat."

národopis-narodopis: See národ-narod and note under root ПИС (etc.).

народове́дение: See наро́д and note on Pol. ludoznawstwo.

národozpyt: See národ.

первоpо́дство et al.: The first element is from пе́рвый-pierwy (OPol.; =modern pierwszy)-prvý-prvi "first"; compare Eng. primogeniture (ult. ‹Lat. primus "first" + gignere [genere] "to beget").

природове́дение et al.: See приро́да et al.

разноро́дный et al.: The first element is from ра́зный-różny-různý-razan "different"; compare Eng. heterogeneous (ult. ‹Gr. ἕτερος "other; different" + γένος "kind, sort").

rodoskvrnjenje, rodoskvrnuće: The second element is from oskvrniti (oskvrnuti) "to desecrate."

родосло́вие-rodoslovlje: See note under root СЛЫ (etc.).

stejnorodý: See note on istorodan, однорóдный et al.

углерóд: an element occurring most prominently in coal (Rus. ýголь); compare Eng. carbon (ult. ‹Lat. carbo "coal").

водорóд-wodoród: See note under root ВОД (etc.).

izroditi se: See note on вы́родиться-wyrodzić się.

обнарóдовать-obnarodovati: ="to bring before the people, make public"; see нарóд-narod. The Serbo-Croatian word is borrowed from Russian.

odrodilec-odrod: ="one who disowns his kin."

природа et al.: The ideas underlying the two meanings are "sum total of all things which are 'born,' i.e. created, brought into being" and "set of 'inborn' attributes of any given thing"; see reference to Eng. nature in introductory note above and compare Hung. természet "nature (in both senses) (‹teremni "to produce; [intr.] to grow"), Fin. luonto "nature (in both senses)" (‹luoda "to create") and Gr. φύσις "nature (in both senses)" (‹φύειν "to produce" and φῦναι "to grow [intr.]"), whence Eng. physical. The Czech and Serbo-Croatian words are borrowed from Russian.

przyrodzenie-přirození: See preceding note; like the two Slavic words, Lat. natura "nature" and Gr. φύσις have the secondary meaning "genitals."

юрóдивый: a Church Slavic loan-word; compare урóд.

врождённый et al.: Compare Eng. innate (ult. ‹Lat. in "in" + natus "born" ‹ nasci "to be born").

вы́родиться-wyrodzić się: ="to depart from, become unlike, one's (or its) race or kind"; compare Eng. degenerate (ult. ‹Lat. de "off, away" + genus "race; kind"), Ger. entarten "to degenerate" (‹ent- "off, away" + Art "race; kind").

РОС(Т), РАС(Т), РОЩ, РАЩ	ROS(T), RÓŚ, ROŚ(C), ROSZCZ	ROST, RŮS(T)	RAS(T), RAŠT
растú: to grow (intr.) рост: growth, increase; stature, height; (arch.) interest (on a loan) ростовщúк: money-lender растéние: plant рóща: grove	róść (rosnąć): to grow (intr.)	růsti: to grow (intr.) růst: growth, increase	rasti: to grow (intr.) rast: growth, increase; stature, height rastenje: growth, increase rastinje: vegetation
[R]	[P]	[Cz]	[S-C]

[R]	[P]	[Cz]	[S-C]
ро́слый: tall	rosły: tall	rostlý: (well, badly, etc.) built, formed	
	roślina: plant	rostlina: plant	raslina: plant
расти́ть: to grow, raise	rościć: to advance (a claim), entertain (a hope)		
раще́ние: (act of) growing, raising	roszczenie: claim		
		nerostopis: mineralogy	
		rostlinopis: botany	
	roślinożerny: herbivorous		
	dorosły: adult (a. and n.)	dorostlý: fully grown; (lit.) adult (a. and n.)	dorastao: adult (a.); equal (to), a match (for)
	dorostek: youth, lad	dorostenec: youth, lad	
			naraštaj: (older, younger, etc.) generation
		nerost: mineral	
		odrostlý: adolescent (a.)	odrastao: adult (a.)
о́трасль: branch (of industry, science, etc.); (arch.) branch (of a tree)	odrośl: shoot, sprout		
отро́сток: shoot, sprout; (anat.) appendix	odrostek: shoot, sprout		
подро́сток: youth, lad; young girl	podrostek: youth, lad		
	przedrostek: (gram.) prefix		
	przyrostek: (gram.) suffix	přírůstek: growth, increase	prirastak: (gram.) particle
	wyrostek: shoot, sprout; youth, lad; (anat.) appendix	výrostek: youth, lad	
взро́слый: adult (a. and n.)		vzrostlý: well-built, sturdy	
во́зраст: age	wzrost: growth, increase; stature, height	vzrůst: growth, increase; stature, height	uzrast: age; stature, height; figure (shape of body)
[R]	[P]	[Cz]	[S-C]

NOTES

Basic meaning of root: to grow

растú: for ORus. рости; the modern form is probably a Church Slavic loan-word.

ростовщúк: See the third meaning of рост.

растúть: An earlier doublet form, ростúть, does not survive in the modern language.

rościć, roszczenie: The verb was originally identical in meaning with Rus. растúть but gradually became restricted to various figurative uses in the general sense of "to nurture." Its frequent occurrence in the expression rościć sobie pretensje "to lay claim" accounts for the present meaning of roszczenie (properly speaking, a verbal noun expressing the action of rościć).

rostlinopis: See rostlina.

roślinożerny: See roślina.

dorosły et al.: Compare Eng. adult (ult. ‹Lat. ad "to" + alescere "to grow"), Ger. erwachsen "adult" (‹wachsen "to grow"); the second meaning of dorastao represents semantic borrowing of Ger. gewachsen "equal (to), a match (for)" (literally "grown").

dorostek-dorostenec: Compare Eng. adolescent (ult. ‹Lat. ad "to" + alescere "to grow").

nerost: ="a substance which does not grow"; compare rostlina.

odrostlý-odrastao, подрóсток-podrostek, wyrostek-výrostek, взрóслый: See notes on dorostek-dorostenec and dorosły et al.

вóзраст: borrowed from Church Slavic.

РОВ, РАВ	RÓW	ROV	RAV
рóвный: even, level, flat	równy: even, level, flat; equal	rovný: even, level, flat; straight; equal	ravan: even, level, flat; straight; equal
рáвный: equal			
равнúна: plain (n.)	równina: plain (n.)	rovina: plain (n.); plane (surface)	ravnina: plane (surface)
			ravan: plain (n.); plane (surface)
	równik: equator	rovník: equator	
		rovnice: (math.) equation	ravnica: plain (n.)
[R]	[P]	[Cz]	[S-C]

равнéние: dressing, alignment (of troops)	równanie: dressing, alignment (of troops); (math.) equation		ravnanje: (act of) leveling, flattening; (act of) straightening; dressing, alignment (of troops); management, direction
			ravnatelj: manager, director
			ravnalo: ruler (for measuring)
	również: also, likewise	rovněž: also, likewise	
		rovnoběžný: parallel (a.)	
	równoczesny: simultaneous		
равнодéнствие: equinox		rovnodennost: equinox	ravnodnevica: equinox
равнодýшный: indifferent, apathetic			ravnodušan: indifferent, apathetic
	równoległy: parallel (a.)		
равномéрный: even, uniform	równomierny: even, uniform	rovnoměrný: even, uniform	ravnomjeran: even, uniform
	równonoc: equinox		
равноси́льный: equivalent, tantamount			
равновéсие: balance, equilibrium	równowaga: balance, equilibrium	rovnováha: balance, equilibrium	ravnoteža, ravnovjesje: balance, equilibrium
	równoważny: equivalent, tantamount	rovnovážný: balanced, of balance (e.g. position)	
		vodorovný: horizontal	vodoravan: horizontal
	porównanie: comparison	porovnání: comparison; (arch.) settlement, adjustment (of a dispute)	poravnanje: (act of) leveling, flattening; settlement, adjustment (of a dispute)
сравнéние: comparison	zrównanie: (act of) leveling,	srovnání: comparison;	sravnjenje: (act of) leveling,
[R]	[P]	[Cz]	[S-C]

	flattening; equalization	settlement, adjustment (of a dispute)	flattening; comparison
уравне́ние: equalization; (math.) equation		urovnání: (act of) leveling, flattening; settlement, adjustment (of a dispute)	
у́ровень: level (n.)		úroveň: level (n.)	
	zarówno (... jak i): both (... and)	zároveň: simultaneously; together	
[R]	[P]	[Cz]	[S-C]

NOTES

Basic meaning of root: even, level, flat

The root has acquired the secondary meaning "equal" in all four languages.

The Russian root-form РАВ is of Church Slavic origin.

równik-rovník: a line on the earth's surface equidistant from the two poles. The Polish and Czech words are modeled on Late Lat. aequator (<aequus "equal"); compare Ger. Gleicher "equator" (<gleich "equal").

rovnice, równanie (second meaning): an expression of equality between two magnitudes or operations; compare Eng. equation (ult. <Lat. aequus "equal"), Ger. Gleichung "equation" (<gleich "equal"), S-C jednačina, jednadžba.

ravnanje (fourth meaning), ravnatelj: The notion of "managing, directing" is an extension of that of "straightening, causing to go straight"; see the introductory notes on roots ПРАВ (etc.) and РЯД (etc.).

rovnoběžný: See note under root БЕГ (etc.).

równoczesny: See note under root ЧАС (etc.).

равноде́нствие et al.: See note under root ДЕН (etc.).

равноду́шный-ravnodušan: Compare Eng. equanimity (ult. <Lat. aequus "equal" + animus "mind, mood"), Ger. Gleichmut "equanimity; indifference, apathy" (<gleich "equal" + Mut "[arch. or in compounds] mind, mood; [otherwise] courage").

равноме́рный et al.: See note under root $МЕР_1$ (etc.).

równonoc: The second element is from noc "night"; see note on равноде́нствие et al.

равноси́льный: Compare Eng. equivalent (ult. <Lat. aequus "equal" + valere "to be strong").

равнове́сие et al.: Compare Eng. equilibrium (ult. <Lat. aequus "equal"

+ libra "scales"), Ger. Gleichgewicht "balance, equilibrium" (<gleich "equal" + Gewicht "weight"); ravnovjesje is borrowed from Russian.

vodorovný-vodoravan: ="even with the surface of water"; compare Ger. Wassergleich "horizontal" (<Wasser "water" + gleich "even, level").

porównanie et al., сравнéние-srovnání-sravnjenje, urovnání: To "compare" is to "make things equal," i.e. liken one thing to another; see Eng. compare (ult. <Lat. cum "with, together" + par "equal"). Underlying the notion of "settling, adjusting" is that of "flattening, smoothing, ironing out." Both of these semantic shifts are illustrated by Ger. vergleichen "to compare; to settle, adjust" (<gleich "equal; even, level").

уравнéние (second meaning): See note on rovnice, równanie.

zároveň: Compare Ger. zugleich "simultaneously; together" (<zu "to, at" + gleich "equal").

РУБ	RĄB, RĘB, RUB	RUB, ROUB	RUB
рубúть: to chop; to chop down, fell (trees); to build (of timber)		roubiti: to build (of timber)	rubiti: to chop; to hem (a garment)
	rąbać: to chop; to chop down, fell (trees)	rubati: to mine (coal); (lit.) to chop; (lit.) to chop down, fell (trees)	
	rąb, rąbek: hem	rub: back, reverse side	rub: hem; border, edging; edge; rim
		roub: graft, scion	
рубéц: scar; hem			rubac: handkerchief; kerchief
		rubáš: shroud	
рубáха, рубáшка: shirt			
	rąbanina: slaughter, carnage		rubenina, rublje: linen (underclothes, etc.)
рубéж: boundary, frontier	rubież: boundary, frontier		
рубль: ruble			
		rubopis: endorsement (on check, etc.)	
	obrąb, obręb: hem; limits, precincts, confines;	obruba: hem; border, edging; curb (of sidewalk); eyeglass frame	obrub: hem; border, edging; rim
[R]	[P]	[Cz]	[S-C]

зарубе́жный: foreign	sphere (of authority, activity, etc.) odrębny: separate, distinct wyodrębnić, wyodrębniać: to separate; to distinguish, differentiate	zevrubný: detailed	
[R]	[P]	[Cz]	[S-C]

NOTES

Basic meaning of root: to cut, chop

The specialized meaning "edge, border" appears in a number of the derivatives, while in other instances the notion of cutting has produced word for various articles of clothing. Many of the derivatives of root КРО(И) (etc.) show comparable semantic development.

rub (Cz.): orig. "underside of an animal hide, piece of material, etc.

рубе́ж-rubież: orig. a reference to the felling of trees to mark a boundary; the Polish word is borrowed from Russian.

рубль: orig. "piece (of gold or silver)."

rubopis: See rub and compare Eng. endorsement (ult. <Lat. dorsum "back").

wyodrębnić: <odrębny.

zevrubný: <vrub "notch made by an innkeeper on a piece of wood each time he extended credit"; thus, zevrubný originally meant "itemized, totaled up."

зарубе́жный: ="beyond the frontier"; see рубе́ж.

РУХ, РУШ	RUCH, RUSZ	RUCH, ROUCH, RUŠ	RUŠ
ру́шить: to knock down; to husk (grain) *ру́хнуть: to crash, tumble down	ruszyć, ruszać: to touch; to move (tr. and intr.); to set out, depart	rušiti: to disturb; to abolish, cancel, annul	rušiti: to wreck, demolish; to disturb
[R]	[P]	[Cz]	[S-C]

[R]	[P]	[Cz]	[S-C]
	ruch: movement, motion; movement (political, etc.); traffic	ruch: bustle, commotion; activity; traffic	
	ruchawka: riot, rebellion; militia, home guard		
			ruševine (pl.): ruins
нару́шить, наруша́ть: to violate, infringe; to break (a promise); to disturb	naruszyć, naruszać: to violate, infringe; to disturb	narušiti, narušovati: to violate, infringe; to disturb	narušiti, narušavati: to violate, infringe; to disturb
	nieruchomość: immobility; real estate, immovable property		
обру́шиться, обру́шиваться: to give way, collapse; (на + acc.) to attack suddenly	obruszyć się, obruszać się: to give way, collapse; to become indignant		
	odruch: reflex		
	poruszyć, poruszać: to move (tr.)	porušiti, porušovati: to spoil, ruin; to violate, infringe; to break (a promise)	*porušiti: to wreck, demolish
		porouchati, porouchávati: to damage, put out of commission	
		přerušiti, přerušovati: to interrupt; to terminate	
разру́шить, разруша́ть: to wreck, demolish	*rozruszać: to start, set in motion; to enliven, cheer up	rozrušiti, rozrušovati: to alarm, agitate; to disrupt	razrušiti, razrušavati: to wreck, demolish
	rozruch: uproar, disturbance; starting (of a motor, etc.)	rozruch: alarm, agitation	

	wyruszyć, wyruszać: to set out, depart wzruszenie: emotion	zrušiti, zrušovati: to abolish, cancel, annul; to break (a promise) vyrušiti, vyrušovati: to disturb vzrušení, vzruch: emotion; excitement	*srušiti: to knoc[k] down; to wreck demolish; to overthrow, depose
[R]	[P]	[Cz]	[S-C]

NOTES

Basic meaning of root: to move swiftly and violently

Except in Polish, where many of the derivatives reflect the meaning "t[o] move" in a neutral sense, the root-meaning tends to be expressed in words carrying some implication of violence, disturbance, destruction, etc.

The noun represented by Pol.-Cz. ruch (and dialectal Rus. рух "alarm"), is primary; the verbs are denominative in origin.

ruchawka: Present in both meanings is the notion of a general "movement" or rising of the population; compare Fr. levée en masse (literally, "mass rising"), a term applied in international law to the spontaneous action of a population in taking up arms upon the approach of an enemy.

wzruszenie et al.: See note on Cz. hnutí, S-C ganuće.

РУК, РУЧ, РУШ	RĘK, RĄK, RĘCZ, RĄCZ, RUCZ, RUSZ	RUK, RUČ, ROUČ	RUK, RUČ
рука́: hand; arm	ręka: hand; arm	ruka: hand; arm	ruka: hand; arm
ру́чка: little hand; handle, haft; (door-) knob; pen-holder; arm (of a chair)	rączka: little hand; handle, haft; pen-holder	ručka: little hand	ručka: handle, haft
рука́в: sleeve; branch (of a river); (water-) hose	rękaw: sleeve	rukáv: sleeve	rukav: sleeve; branch (of a river)
рукави́ца: mitten	rękawica, rękawiczka: glove	rukavice, rukavička: glove	rukavica: glove
[R]	[P]	[Cz]	[S-C]

[R]	[P]	[Cz]	[S-C]
ручни́к: a type of hammer used by metalworkers and carpenters	ręcznik: towel	ručník: towel	ručnik: towel
	rusznica: musket	ručnice: rifle	
	ręczyć (za + acc.): to guarantee, vouch (for)	ručiti (za + acc.): to guarantee, vouch (for)	
			ručati: to dine
руча́ться (за + acc.): to guarantee, vouch (for)			
	długorąk: gibbon		
двуру́шник: double-dealer			
рукоблу́дие: masturbation			
	rękoczyn: blow, slap; (arch.) (surgical) operation		
рукоде́лие: needlework; needlework product	rękodzieło: handicraft; handicraft product		rukodjelstvo: handicraft
рукоя́ть, рукоя́тка: handle, haft	rękojeść: handle, haft	rukojeť: handle, haft; (arch.) handbook, manual	
	rękojmia: guarantee	rukojmí: guarantor; hostage	
ру́копись: manuscript	rękopis: manuscript	rukopis: manuscript; handwriting	rukopis: manuscript; handwriting
рукоположе́ние: ordination (of a priest), laying on of hands			rukopolaganje: ordination (of a priest), laying on of hands
			rukotvorina: handicraft; handicraft product
		rukověť: handbook, manual; (arch.) handle, haft	rukovet: handful, bunch
руково́дство: leadership, guidance;			rukovodstvo: leadership, guidance;

[R]	[P]	[Cz]	[S-C]
management, direction; leadership, leaders; handbook, manual			management, direction; leadership, leaders; handbook, manual
	doręczyć, doręczać: to deliver	doručiti, doručovati: to deliver	
			doručak: breakfast
		doporučiti, doporučovati: to recommend	
			izručiti, izručivati: to deliver; to extradite
			naručiti, naručivati: to order (merchandise); to commission
			naruč: loan
			naručan: handy, convenient
			narukvica: bracelet
нару́чники (pl.): handcuffs			
			neruka: misfortune
о́бруч: hoop	obręcz: hoop; band; rim; tire	obruč: hoop; band; rim; tire	obruč: hoop; band; tire; ring
	obrączka: ring	obrouček, obroučka: hoop; eyeglass frame; (arch.) ring	
обруче́ние: betrothal			
			*oporučiti: to bequeath
		odporučiti, odporoučeti (arch.): to recommend; to commit, entrust, commend; to bequeath	otporučiti, otporučivati: to send a reply
поручи́ть, поруча́ть: to commit,	poręczyć, poręczać (za + inst.):	poručiti, poroučeti: to order,	poručiti, poručivati: to send word;
[R]	[P]	[Cz]	[S-C]

[R]	[P]	[Cz]	[S-C]
entrust, commend; to instruct, direct	to guarantee, vouch (for)	command; (arch.) to commit, entrust, commend	to order (merchandise)
	poruczyć, poruczać: to commit, entrust, commend		
по́ручень: railing	poręcz: railing; banister; arm (of a chair)		
	poręczny: handy, convenient		
пору́чик (arch.): first lieutenant		poručík: first lieutenant	
	porucznik: first lieutenant	poručník: (legal) guardian	poručnik: first lieutenant
	podręcze: arm (of a chair)	područí: dependence, subordination	područje: region; jurisdiction, sphere of competence
подру́чный: assistant			
	podręcznik: handbook, manual; textbook		
препоручи́ть, препоруча́ть (arch.): to commit, entrust, commend			preporučiti, preporučivati: to recommend
приручи́ть, приручáть: to tame			
		příručí: assistant	priručje: railing; banister
		příručka: handbook, manual	priručnik: handbook, manual; textbook
		souručenství: union, alliance; solidarity	
вручи́ть, вруча́ть: to deliver; (lit.) to commit, entrust, commend	wręczyć, wręczać: to deliver		uručiti, uručivati: to deliver

[R]	[P]	[Cz]	[S-C]
	wręcz: hand to hand, at close quarters; frankly, bluntly		
вы́ручить, выруча́ть: to rescue, help out; to gain, net (a sum of money)	wyręczyć, wyręczać: to relieve, replace (at work)		
	zręczny: skilful; clever	zručný: skilful	
	zrękowiny (pl., arch.): betrothal		
	zaręczyny (pl.): betrothal	záruka: guarantee; pledge, pawn; deposit, security; bail	zaruke (pl.): betrothal

NOTES

Basic meaning of root: hand; arm

Many of the derivatives reflect such notions as handing over ("to deliver," "to bequeath," "to lend"), placing (a task, etc.) in someone's hand ("to commit, entrust, commend," "to recommend," "to order, command"), lending a hand ("to rescue, help out," "to relieve") and giving one's hand to seal a bargain ("to pledge," "to guarantee," "to become betrothed"). (The formation of Eng. command, commend and recommend [all ult. ⟨Lat. mandare "to commit, entrust, commend; to order, command" ⟨ manus "hand" + -dere "to put"] is comparable to that of the corresponding Slavic words.)

рука́в-rukav: A comparable range of meanings is shown by Fr. manche "sleeve; strait, channel; (water-) hose" (ult. ⟨Lat. manus "hand").

rusznica-ručnice: ="hand weapon"; the Polish word (for earlier rucznica) is borrowed from Czech.

ručati: orig. "to lay hold of food with one's hands, eat greedily."

двуру́шник: one who acts "with both hands," i.e. plays both sides at once; root-form РУЧ has been altered to РУШ.

рукоблу́дие: The second element is from блуд "lechery"; compare Eng. masturbation (ult. ⟨Lat. manus "hand" + stuprare "to defile sexually," as altered under the influence of turbare "to disturb").

rękoczyn (second meaning): Compare Eng. surgery (ult. ⟨Gr. χεῖρ "hand" + ἔργον "work").

ру́копись et al.: See note under root ПИС (etc.).

руково́дство-rukovodstvo: Compare Eng. management (ult. ⟨Lat. manus "hand"); the Serbo-Croatian word is probably borrowed from Russian.

doručak: See ručati.

neruka: The meaning reflects the earlier use of ruka in the sense of "good fortune."

óбруч et al., obrączka et al.: The words referred originally to a ring (or bracelet), then to various similar objects.

обручéние: ⟨óбруч in its original meaning, "ring"; compare zrękowiny, zaręczyny-zaruke below, whose semantic development is that indicated in the introductory note.

otporučiti: The semantic relationship with poručiti (first meaning) is comparable to that between odgovoriti and govoriti (q.v.).

poruczyć: ⟨Rus. поручи́ть, Cz. poručiti.

пору́чик-poručík, porucznik et al.: ="one to whom authority has been entrusted"; the Russian, Polish and Serbo-Croatian words are all ultimately from Czech.

područí-područje: The underlying idea is that of being under someone's "hand," i.e. power or authority; regarding the first meaning of the Serbo-Croatian word, see note on Rus. вóлость et al., власть.

приручи́ть: ="to train an animal to eat out of one's hand."

součenství: ="a relationship based on reciprocal pledges."

	RZUT, RZUC	ŘÍT, ŘÍC	
	rzucić, rzucać: to throw; to leave, abandon rzucić się, rzucać się: to throw oneself (at, into s.th.) rzutki: agile; enterprising samorzutny: spontaneous narzutka: cloak, cape odrzucić, odrzucać: to throw away; to reject, refuse odrzut: recoil (of a gun) odrzutowiec: jet airplane	řítiti se: to crash, hurtle down; to rush	
	[P]	[Cz]	

	porzucić, porzucać: to leave, abandon podrzutek: foundling, abandoned child rozrzutny: extravagant, wasteful wyrzut: reproach; (med.) rash, eruption wyrzutek: refuse, trash; outcast wyrzutnia: (rocket-) launching platform; (gram.) ellipsis; (ling.) elision zarzut: reproach; objection; charge, accusation zarzutka: cloak, cape zarzutnia: fishnet	zříceniny (pl.): ruins	
	[P]	[Cz]	

NOTES

Basic meaning of root: to throw

The root is unattested in Serbo-Croatian. Rus. рютить "to throw; to push" is obsolete.

rzucić (second meaning): Compare Rus. покинуть.

narzutka: Compare Ger. Überwurf "cloak, cape" (<über "over" + werfen "to throw"), Rus. накидка, Pol. zarzutka below.

odrzucić: See note on Cz. odmítnouti, S-C odmetnuti.

odrzutowiec: The reference is to the rearward thrust of the jet stream compare odrzut and Eng. jet (<Fr. jeter "to throw").

porzucić: Compare Rus. покинуть.

podrzutek: See note on Rus. подкидыш.

wyrzut (first meaning): See note on Cz. předhůzka.

wyrzutnia (second and third meanings): ="a throwing out," i.e. an omission.

zarzut: See note on Cz. předhůzka.

zarzutka: See note on narzutka.

РВ, РЫВ	RW, RYW	RV, RYV	RV, RIV
рвать: to tear (tr.); to pick, pluck; (impers. with dir. obj.) to vomit	rwać: to tear (tr.); to pick, pluck; to rush (intr.)	rváti: to tear (tr.)	
рвáться: to tear (intr.); to explode; to long, yearn	rwać się: to tear (intr.); to long, yearn	rváti se: to fight	rvati se: to wrestle
	rwa: neuralgia		
рвань: rags; (coll.) scoundrel; (coll.) rabble, riffraff			
рвéние: zeal, ardor			
	dorywczy: occasional; fitful, desultory		
нары́в: abscess, boil			
обры́в: precipice			
оборвáнец: ragamuffin	oberwaniec: ragamuffin		
отры́вок: fragment			
отóрванный: alienated, estranged	oderwany: abstract; separate, detached		
поры́в: gust (of wind); impulse	poryw: impulse	poryv (lit.): gust (of wind)	poriv: impulse
	porywający: delightful, ravishing; fascinating		
	porwanie: abduction, kidnaping		
переры́в: interruption; intermission	przerwa: interruption; intermission		
проры́в: break; (mil.) breakthrough; breakdown (in work)			
прóрва (coll.): huge quantity; glutton		průrva: breach; ravine	
[R]	[P]	[Cz]	[S-C]

[R]	[P]	[Cz]	[S-C]
	rozrywka: amusement, entertainment		
срыв: disruption, frustration (of plans, etc.)	zryw: start (in a race); dash, sprint; flight (e.g. of fancy)		
сорване́ц: madcap			
	urywek: fragment	úryvek: fragment	
	urwisko: precipice		urvina: precipic
взрыв: explosion; burst, outburst			

NOTES

Basic meaning of root: to pull; to tear

The original root-meaning was probably "to pick, pluck (flowers, etc.) (see рвать-rwać), but the more general notion of pulling or tearing is recognizable in most of the derivatives.

S-C rvati "to pull; to attack" is obsolete.

рвать (third meaning): Compare the similar semantic development of Ger erbrechen "to vomit" (<er- "out" + brechen "to break").

рва́ться (third meaning)-rwać się (second meaning), рве́ние: The underlying notion is that of being powerfully drawn or pulled toward something; рве́ние is of Church Slavic origin.

rváti se-rvati se: ="to pull, tear at one another"; compare Rus. дра́ка

dorywczy: ="torn, fragmentary, disconnected"; compare przerwa, urywek.

нары́в: See нарва́ть "to come to a head" (said of a boil, etc.); the prefix here contributes the notion of "gathering, accumulation."

обры́в: ="a place where the ground is torn away"; compare urwisko-urvi Cz. strž.

ото́рванный-oderwany: ="pulled away"; regarding the first meaning of oderwany, see note on Rus. отвлечённый.

поры́в (second meaning)-poryw-poriv, porywający, porwanie: Common to a these words is the notion of sweeping along or carrying away; similarly co trasting figurative and literal meanings are apparent in Eng. ravishing, t ravish (orig. = "to abduct") and rapt (attention, etc.), Fr. rapt "abducti (all ult. <Lat. rapere "to seize, carry away"). See also note on Cz. uchva ující and úchvatný, Rus. восхище́ние et al., Pol. zachwyt and zachwycający. S-C poriv is borrowed from Russian.

переры́в-przerwa: See note on S-C prekinuti.

про́рва: orig. "breach in a dam; bottomless abyss"; compare průrva.

rozrywka: See note on Rus. развле́чь.

срыв: Compare Eng. disruption (ult. <Lat. dis- "off, away" + rumpere "to break, tear").

zryw: Compare rwać (third meaning), poryw.

urwisko-urvina: See note on обры́в.

СЯГ, СЯЖ, САЖ, СЯЗ, СУГ	SIĘG, SIĄG, SĄG, SIĘ(Ż), SĄŻ	SAH, SÁH, SÍ, SEŽ	SE(G), SEŽ, SEZ
	sięgnąć, sięgać: to reach out (for); to reach	sáhnouti, sahati: to touch (na + acc.); to reach out (for); to reach; to encroach, infringe (on)	segnuti, sezati: to reach out (for); to reach
	sąg: cord (of wood)	sáh: fathom; cord (of wood)	
са́же́нь: fathom; cord (of wood)	sążeń: fathom		sežanj: fathom
лжеприся́га: perjury	krzywoprzysięstwo: perjury	křivopřísežnictví: perjury	
досягну́ть, досяга́ть (arch.): to reach; to attain	dosięgnąć, dosięgać: to reach; to attain	dosáhnouti (dosíci), dosahovati: to reach; to attain	dosegnuti (doseći), dosezati: to reach; to attain
досу́г: leisure			
осяза́ть: to feel, touch	osiągnąć, osiągać: to reach; to attain; to gain, achieve	obsáhnouti, obsahovati: to span (with the fingers; obsáhnouti only); to grasp, comprehend (obsáhnouti only); to contain (obsahovati only); to embrace, comprise, include	opsegnuti (opseći), opsezati: to embrace, comprise, include
		obsah: contents, content; volume, capacity	opseg: extent, scope; circumference
посягну́ть, посяга́ть: to encroach, infringe (on)			posegnuti (poseći), posezati: to reach out (for); to encroach, infringe (on)
		přesáhnouti, přesahovati: to surpass, exceed	presegnuti, presezati: to encroach, infringe on
[R]	[P]	[Cz]	[S-C]

присяга: oath	przysięga: oath	přísaha: oath	prisega: oath
присяжный: juror	przysięgły: juror		prisežnik: juror
		rozsah: size, quantity, bulk; extent, scope; range	
		rozsáhlý: extensive	
	sprzysiężenie: conspiracy		
	zasięg, zasiąg: extent, scope; range	zásah: hit (on target); intervention; interference	
[R]	[P]	[Cz]	[S-C]

NOTES

Basic meaning of root: to reach out (for s.th.)

sięgnąć et al.: Rus. сягнýть, сягáть "to reach out" is obsolete or dialectal.

sąg-sáh, сáжéнь et al.: a unit of measure representing the distance embraced by the outstretched arms; compare Eng. fathom (<OEng. fæthm "outstretched arms"), Ger. Klafter "fathom; cord (of wood)" (akin to Eng. clasp S-C hvat. Pol. sąg, sążeń are for earlier siąg, siążeń, Rus. сáжéнь for earlier сяжéнь.

лжеприсяга et al.: See присяга et al.; the first element in the Russian word (="false") is from ложь "lie."

досýг: orig. "something achieved, attained"; compare досягнýть. The root-form СУГ (<Common Slavic *SǪG) reflects an original vowel grade different from that of all the other modern forms (<Common Slavic *SĘG).

осязáть: borrowed from Church Slavic.

obsáhnouti (second meaning): See note on Rus. понять et al. and понятие Pol. pojęcie, Cz. ponětí, pojetí and pojem, S-C pojam.

obsah-opseg: See note on Pol. objętość, Rus. объём et al.

přesáhnouti: See note on S-C nadmašiti.

присяга et al.: literally, "an act of touching"; the early Slavs, in taking an oath, generally touched some object thought to be sacred or endowed with special power.

присяжный et al.: ="one who is sworn"; see присяга et al. and compare Eng. juror (ult. <Lat. jurare "to swear"), Ger. Geschworener "juror" (<schwören "to swear").

sprzysiężenie: See przysięga and compare Fr. conjuration "conspiracy" (ult. <Lat. cum "with, together" + jurare "to swear"), Ger. Verschwörung "conspiracy" (<schwören "to swear").

САМ	SAM	SAM, SÁM	SAM
сам, сама́, само́, са́ми: myself, yourself, himself, herself, itself, oneself, ourselves, yourselves, themselves (intensive pronoun)	sam, sama, samo, sami, same: myself, yourself, himself, herself, itself, oneself, ourselves, yourselves, themselves (intensive pronoun); alone; same; the very (end, top, etc.)	sám, sama, samo, sami, samy, sama: myself, yourself, himself, herself, itself, oneself, ourselves, yourselves, themselves (intensive pronoun); alone	sam, sama, samo, sami, same, sama: myself, yourself, himself, herself, itself, oneself, ourselves, yourselves, themselves (intensive pronoun); alone; the very (end, top, etc.)
са́мый: same; the very (end, top, etc.); most (used to form the superlative of adjectives)		samý: only, nothing but; the very (end, top, etc.)	
			samo: only (adv.)
	samotnia: solitude, seclusion; secluded place	samota: solitude, seclusion; secluded place	samoća, samotinja: solitude, seclusion
саме́ц: male (n.)	samiec: male (n.)	samec: male (n.)	samac: (male) recluse; unmarried man; male bird
са́мка: female (n.)	samica: female (n.)	samice: female (n.)	samica: (female) recluse; unmarried woman; female bird; isolation cell
			samoblud, samobluđe: masturbation
самобы́тный: original, distinctive	samobytny: independent	samobytný (arch.): original, distinctive; independent	samobitan: original, distinctive
самохо́д: self-propelled machine, gun, etc.	samochód: automobile		
самочи́нный: arbitrary, high-handed	samoczynny: automatic	samočinný: automatic	
самоде́льный: home-made	samodzielny: independent		
самоде́ржец: autocrat	samodzierżca: autocrat		samodržac: autocrat
	samogłoska: (phon.) vowel	samohláska: (phon.) vowel	samoglasnik: (phon.) vowel
[R]	[P]	[Cz]	[S-C]

самого́н: home-brewed liquor	samogon: home-brewed liquor		
	samogwałt: masturbation		
	samoistny: independent		
самолёт: airplane	samolot: airplane		
самолю́бие: self-esteem, pride	samolubstwo: selfishness	samolibost: smugness, complacency	samoljublje: egotism
		samomluva: monologue, soliloquy	
самомне́ние: conceit, self-opinionatedness			
самоотве́рженность: self-denial, selflessness			
	samopas: alone, without supervision		
	samorzutny: spontaneous		
			samostan: monastery; convent
самостоя́тельный: independent		samostatný: independent	samostalan: independent
самосу́д: lynch-law, mob rule	samosąd: lynch-law, mob rule		
самоуби́йство: suicide	samobójstwo: suicide		samoubistvo: suicide
самова́р: samovar	samowar: samovar	samovar: samovar	samovar: samovar
самовла́стие (arch.): autocracy	samowładztwo: autocracy	samovláda: autocracy	samovlada, samovlast, samovlašće: autocracy
самово́льный: wilful; unauthorized	samowolny: wilful; unauthorized	samovolný: spontaneous	samovoljan: wilful
		samovražda (arch.): suicide	
самозва́нец: impostor	samozwaniec: impostor	samozvanec: impostor; usurper	samozvanac: impostor; uninvited gues
			samoživ: selfish
	tożsamość: identity (state of being identical);		
[R]	[P]	[Cz]	[S-C]

	identity (of a person) niesamowity: weird, uncanny		osama: solitude, seclusion
[R]	[P]	[Cz]	[S-C]

NOTES

Basic meaning of root: same; self; alone, only

The obvious link between the two notions "same" and "self" is attested by Eng. selfsame, Fr. même "same; self," Ger. selb "same" and selbst "self." The meaning "alone, only" arose through a semantic shift from "the same one, that very one" to "that one and no other." The use of Rus. са́мый to form the superlative of adjectives is a natural outgrowth of the meaning "the very" in, e.g., "the very top" (="the top itself").

The Slavic root is akin to Eng. same, Lat. similis "similar" (>Eng. similar), Gr. ὁμός "same" (>Eng. homogeneous, homonym, homosexual).

саме́ц et al.: orig. "solitary creature"; the meaning "male" arose from the fact that among certain animals the male lives alone much of the time, leaving the care of the young to the female.

са́мка et al.: formed from саме́ц et al. as antonyms; see preceding note.

samoblud, samobluđe: The second element is from blud "lechery."

самоде́ржец et al.: ="he who holds (power) by himself"; the words are modeled on Gr. αὐτοκράτωρ (<αὐτός "self" + κρατεῖν "to rule, govern"), whence Eng. autocrat. Compare also Ger. Selbstherrscher "autocrat" (<selbst "self" + Herrscher "ruler"). The Polish word is borrowed from Russian.

samogłoska et al.: See note under root ГОЛОС (etc.).

samogwałt: The second element is from gwałt "violence."

samoistny: See note under root ИСТ (etc.).

samomluva: See note under root МОЛВ (etc.).

samopas: See note under root ПАС (etc.).

samostan: modeled on Gr. μοναστήριον (<μόνος "alone"), whence Eng. monastery.

самостоя́тельный et al.: modeled on Ger. selbständig "independent" (<selbst "self" + stehen "to stand").

самоуби́йство et al.: See note under root БИ (etc.).

самова́р et al.: See note under root ВАР (etc.).

самовла́стие et al.: See note on самоде́ржец et al.

samovražda: The second element is from vražda "murder"; see note on самоуби́йство et al.

tożsamość: <the neuter form of tenże sam "the (very) same"; compare

СЕБ

Eng. identity (ult. ⟨Lat. idem "the same").

niesamowity: ="not itself, not having the characteristics proper to itself," i.e. unnatural; the word is borrowed from Ukrainian.

СЕБ, СЯ, СЬ, СОБ, САБ	SIEB, SIĘ, SOB, SÓB, SAB	SEB, SE, SOB	SEB, SE, SOB, SOP
себя́ (-ся, -сь): myself, yourself, himself, herself, itself, oneself, ourselves, yourselves, themselves (reflexive pronoun)	siebie (się): myself, yourself, himself, herself, itself, oneself, ourselves, yourselves, themselves; each other, one another (reflexive and reciprocal pronoun)	sebe (se): myself, yourself, himself, herself, itself, oneself, ourselves, yourselves, themselves; each other, one another (reflexive and reciprocal pronoun)	sebe (se): myself, yourself, himself, herself, itself, oneself, ourselves, yourselves, themselves; (se only) each other, one another (reflexive and reciprocal pronoun)
со́бственный: (one's) own; proper (sense of a word, etc.); (gram.) proper (noun)			sopstven: (one's) own; characteristic, distinctive; (gram.) proper (noun)
со́бственность: property (something owned); ownership			sopstvenost: property (something owned); ownership; property, characteristic
	sobek: selfish person	sobec: selfish person	sebičnjak: selfish person
междоусо́бие, (arch.) междоусо́бица: civil war			međusobica: quarrel
междоусо́бный: internecine			međusoban: mutual, reciprocal
себялю́бие: selfishness			sebeljublje: selfishness
		sebevražda: suicide	
	sobowtór: double (person perfectly resembling another)		
	(w dwój-, trój-, etc.) nasób: (two, three,	(dvoj-, troj-, etc.) násob: (two, three,	
[R]	[P]	[Cz]	[S-C]

	etc.) times as much	etc.) times as much násobiti: (math.) to multiply	
			oseban: special, particular; separate
			osebujan: peculiar, singular, odd; characteristic, distinctive
осо́ба: person	osoba: person	osoba: person	osoba: person
осо́бый: special, particular; separate			
	osobny: separate	osobní: personal	osoban: personal
осо́бенный: special, particular			osoben: special, particular; peculiar, singular, odd
	osobisty: personal	osobitý: characteristic, distinctive	osobit: special, particular; characteristic, distinctive; excellent
	osobliwy: peculiar, singular, odd	osoblivý (arch.): characteristic, distinctive	
		**osobiti si (arch.); osobovati si: to appropriate (to one's use), arrogate to o.s.	
		osobivý (arch.): presumptuous, arrogant	
обосо́бить, обособля́ть: to isolate	odosobnić, odosobniać (odosabniać): to isolate	odosobniti, odosobňovati: to depersonalize	
			osposobiti, osposobljavati: to fit, train, qualify
			poseban: special, particular; separate
посо́бие: grant, allowance; textbook, school accessory			
[R]	[P]	[Cz]	[S-C]

[R]	[P]	[Cz]	[S-C]
посо́бник: accomplice			
		působiti: to work, be active (in a profession, in public life, etc.); (na + acc.) to affect, have an effect (on); to cause	
подсо́бный: auxiliary, subsidiary			
			priseban: calm, self-possessed
приспосо́бить, приспособля́ть (приспоса́бливать): to adapt, adjust (tr.)	przysposobić, przysposabiać: to prepare; to fit, train, qualify; to adopt (a child)	přizpůsobiti, přizpůsobovati: to adapt, adjust (tr.)	
спо́соб: way, mode, manner	sposób: way, mode, manner	způsob: way, mode, manner; (gram.) mood	
спосо́бный: able, capable	sposobny: able, capable; opportune; suitable	způsobný: mannerly, well-behaved	sposoban: able, capable
		způsobilý: able, capable; suitable	
спосо́бствовать: to help, assist; to promote, further			
	usposobić, usposabiać: to incline, predispose	uzpůsobiti, uzpůsobovati: to adapt, adjust (tr.)	usposobiti, usposobljavati: to fit, train, qualify
			zaseban: special, particular; separate
	zasób: stock, supply, reserve	zásoba: stock, supply, reserve	
	zasobny: wealthy	zásobní: spare, reserve (attr.)	

NOTES

Basic meaning of root: oneself

In a number of derivatives, the root has united with prepositions to produce the general notion "by or for oneself (or itself)," whence such meanings as "separate," "special," "peculiar" and "person" (="separate entity, individual").

The Slavic root is related to Lat. se, sibi "oneself" and Ger. sich "oneself" and to root СВОЙ (etc.).

со́бственный-sopstven: See note on Pol. własny and właściwy, Cz. vlastní, S-C vlastit; the Serbo-Croatian word is borrowed from Russian.

со́бственность-sopstvenost: See со́бственный-sopstven and note on Pol. własność, Cz. vlastnost and vlastnictví, S-C vlasništvo; the Serbo-Croatian word is borrowed from Russian.

междоусобие et al., междоусо́бный-međusoban: The reference in each case is to something occurring "between (or among) themselves"; Rus. междоусо́б- is for *междусо́б-.

sebevražda: See note on Cz. samovražda.

sobowtór: The second element is from archaic wtóry "second."

nasób-násob, násobiti: Multiplication is seen as an operation in which a number is placed "on top of itself" a given number of times.

osobiti si: See note on Pol. przywłaszczyć sobie, Cz. přivlastniti si.

osobivý: See osobiti si.

обосо́бить et al.: <осо́бый, osobny-osobní.

osposobiti: See sposoban and note on приспосо́бить et al.

посо́бие, посо́бник: The basic meaning is that of assisting; the semantic development is not clear, but see following note.

působiti: orig. "to prepare" < "to put (a task, etc.) behind one."

подсо́бный: See note on посо́бие, посо́бник.

priseban: ="with or by oneself," i.e. having one's wits about one.

приспосо́бить et al.: See спо́соб et al., спосо́бный-sposobny, způsobilý and compare Eng. adapt (ult. <Lat. ad "to" + aptus "apt, suitable").

спо́соб et al., спосо́бный et al., způsobilý, спосо́бствовать: See notes on посо́бие, посо́бник and působiti. Regarding the second meaning of způsob, see note on S-C način; způsobný has a semantic parallel in Eng. mannerly (<manner).

usposobić et al.: See sposób-způsob, sposobny-sposoban, způsobilý and note on приспосо́бить et al.

zasób-zásoba: that which one has "behind one," i.e. stored up, in reserve.

СЕ(Д), СИД, САД, САЖ, САЖД	SIĄ, SIAD, SIE(D)(Z), SIO(D), SAD(Z), SED	SE(D), SÍD, SEZ, SAD, SÁD, SAZ, SÁZ	SJE(D), SE(D), SID, SI(JE), SAD, SAĐ
сидéть: to sit	siedzieć: to sit	seděti: to sit	sjedjeti (sjediti): to sit
*сесть: to sit down; (в or на + acc.) to board (a train, etc.); to land, alight; to set (said of the sun); to settle (said of dust, a building, etc.); to shrink	siąść, siadać: to sit down; (do + gen.; na + acc.) to board (a train, etc.)	sednouti (si), sedati (si): to sit down; (do + gen.) to board (a train, etc.); to land, alight	sjesti (sjednuti), sjedati: to sit down; to set (said of the sun); to settle (said of a building, etc.)
		sednouti se, sedati se: to curdle (intr.); to coagulate; to settle (said of dust, a building, etc.)	
сади́ть (coll.): to plant	sadzić: to plant; to jump	*saditi (arch.): to set, put; to plant; to bet	saditi: to plant
сажáть: to set, put; to seat; to plant	sadzać: to seat	sázeti: to set, put; to plant; to set in type; to bet	
сади́ться: to sit down; (в or на + acc.) to board (a train, etc.); to land, alight; to set (said of the sun); to settle (said of dust, a building, etc.); to shrink	sadzić się: to aim (at), strive (for)	*saditi se: to bet	
			sijelo: party, social gathering; seat (of government, etc.)
	siedziba: residence, abode; seat (of government, etc.)		sjedište: seat (place for sitting); residence, abode; seat (of government, of learning, etc.)
[R]	[P]	[Cz]	[S-C]

[R]	[P]	[Cz]	[S-C]
		sednice (arch.): sitting-room	sjednica: session, meeting
сиде́лка: (sick-)nurse			sjediljka: party, social gathering
седло́: saddle	siodło: saddle	sedlo: saddle	sedlo: saddle
седа́лище: buttocks			
		sedlina: sediment, deposit	
село́: village	sioło (lit.): village	sídlo: residence, abode; seat (of government, etc.)	selo: village
		sídliti: to reside	seliti: to move (tr.) to a new residence
сели́ться: to settle, take up residence	siedlić się (arch.): to settle, take up residence		seliti se: to move (intr.) to a new residence; to emigrate
		sedlák: farmer, peasant; pawn (in chess)	seljak: farmer, peasant
	sielanka: idyll	selanka: idyll	
сад: garden	sad: orchard	sad: orchard	sad: plantation
		sada: set (in tennis); set (of instruments, etc.)	
	sedno: sore spot; crux, main point		sadno: saddle gall (on horse)
	sadyba: residence, abode		
са́жа: soot	sadza: soot	saze (pl.): soot	
		sazba: rate; type-setting; composed type	
сельскохозя́йственный: agricultural			
досади́ть, досажда́ть: to annoy, vex		dosaditi, dosazovati: to appoint	dosaditi, dosađivati: to bore, weary; to importune, harass
доса́дный: annoying, vexatious	dosadny: forceful, vigorous; cogent, convincing		dosadan: tedious; importunate
[R]	[P]	[Cz]	[S-C]

[R]	[P]	[Cz]	[S-C]
			doseljenik: immigrant
			iseljenik: emigrant
насéдка: brood-hen	nasiadka: brood-hen		
населéние: population			naseljenje: colonization, settlement
		nadsázka: exaggeration	
непосéдливый: restless, fidgety		neposedný: restless, fidgety	
осáдок: sediment, deposit	osad: sediment, deposit		
осáдки (pl.): precipitation (rain, snow, etc.)			
осáда: siege	osada: handle, haft; setting, mounting; settlement, colony; large village; garrison; crew	osada: settlement, colony; community	
		osazenstvo: staff, personnel	
	obsada: handle, haft; garrison; crew; staff, personnel; cast (of a play)		opsada: siege
	*posiąść: to gain possession of	*posednouti: to obsess	*posjesti (posjednuti): to gain possession of
	posiadać: to own, possess; to be proficient in		posjedovati (posjedati): to own, possess
	posiedzenie: session, meeting	posezení, posedění: (act or period of) sitting	
	posada: base, foundation; job, position	posada: chicken-coop	posada: garrison; crew
посáдка: planting; boarding (of boat, train, etc.); landing (of airplane)	posadzka: inlaid floor	posádka: garrison; crew	

[R]	[P]	[Cz]	[S-C]
	przesada: exaggeration		
председатель: chairman, president		předseda: chairman, president	predsjednik, predsjedatelj: chairman, president
	przysada (arch.): admixture; defect	přísada: admixture	
	przysadkowaty, przysadzisty: thick-set, squat		
расселина: crevice, fissure (in the ground)		rozsedlina: crevice, fissure (in the ground)	rasjelina: crevice, fissure (in the ground)
ссесться, сседа́ться (coll.): to shrink (intr.); to curdle (intr.)	zsiąść się, zsiadać się: to curdle (intr.); to coagulate	ssednouti se, ssedati se: to curdle (intr.); to coagulate; to settle (said of dust, a building, etc.)	
		ssedlina: sediment, deposit	
сосед: neighbor	sąsiad: neighbor	soused: neighbor	susjed: neighbor
ссадина: scratch, abrasion			
усидчивый: assiduous, diligent			
		usedlost: farmstead; sedateness	
			usidjelica, usjedjelica: spinster, old maid
усадьба: farmstead			
		usazenina: sediment, deposit	
всадник: rider, horseman			
			useljenik: immigrant
вселенная: universe			vasiona, vaseljena: universe
		výsada: privilege	

заседа́ние: session, meeting заса́да: ambush	zasada: principle; (chem.) base zasadzka: ambush	zasedání: session, meeting zásada: principle; (chem.) base	zasjedanje: session, meeting; (act of) lying in ambush zasjeda: ambush zasada: principle
[R]	[P]	[Cz]	[S-C]

NOTES

Basic meaning of root: to sit

Many of the derivatives reflect two of the meanings of kindred Eng. settle, i.e. "to take up residence" (>"community," "village," "farmstead," "chicken-coop," "neighbor") and "to sink, subside; to precipitate" (>"crevice, fissure," "to shrink," "sediment," "soot," "to curdle, coagulate"). The root-forms САД-САЖ-САЖД---SAD(Z)---SAD-SÁD-SAZ-SÁZ---SAD-SAĐ occur chiefly in words expressing the causative meaning "to cause to sit," i.e. "to seat; to set, put; to plant" (although the meaning of some derivatives is actually reflexive or passive, hence identical with the basic root-meaning: "to seat or set oneself, be seated or set" = "to sit [down], settle").

The letter d is characteristically lost before l in Russian and Serbo-Croatian (except in седло́-sedlo, where its preservation attests to the presence of a vowel---a front or back jer---between the two consonants in Common Slavic).

The Slavic root is related to Eng. sit, seat, set, settle, saddle and soot, Ger. sitzen "to sit" and setzen "to set, put" (>Satz "sediment"), Lat. sedere "to sit" (>Eng. sedentary, sediment, session, reside, subside).

сесть-siąść: 1 sg. ся́ду-siądę goes back to a nasalized Common Slavic form; the present Polish infinitive arose from earlier sieść by analogy with the conjugational forms.

sednouti se: contracted from ssednouti se (q.v.).

sadzić: The second meaning probably reflects the influence of Ger. setzen "to set, put; to jump"; this use of the word as an intransitive verb of motion is paralleled by the use of Eng. set in such expressions as to set out on a journey and to set to work.

saditi (Cz.), sázeti: Regarding the last meaning, see note on S-C kladiti se.

сади́ться: serves as the imperfective aspect of сесть.

sadzić się: Compare Eng. to set oneself (to a task).

saditi se: See note on S-C kladiti se.

sedlina: contracted from ssedlina (q.v.).

sioło: <Rus. село́; the native Polish word siodło "residence" is obsolete.

sídliti-seliti, сели́ться et al.: denominatives formed from sídlo, selo, село́ and obsolete Pol. siodło (see preceding note).

sedlák-seljak: <*sedlo "farmstead" (an unattested variant of sídlo) and selo.

sielanka-selanka: The Polish word is formed from sioło, the Czech word borrowed from Polish.

сад et al.: ="place for planting."

sada: modeled on Ger. Satz (<setzen "to set, put"), which has both meanings of the Czech word (and is itself an instance of semantic borrowing from English in its application to tennis).

sedno: for earlier sadno; the meaning was originally the same as that of S-C sadno.

sadyba: a Ukrainian loan-word.

sazba (first meaning): ="that which is set, fixed, established"; compare Ger. Satz "rate" (<setzen "to set, put"), Rus. ста́вка, Pol. stawka.

сельскохозя́йственный: See село́; the second element is from хозя́йственный "economic."

досади́ть-dosaditi (S-C), доса́дный et al.: The underlying idea is, roughly, that of "getting at" someone, i.e. pressing someone hard; the intransitive use of the verb (which governs the dative) is comparable to that of Ger. zusetzen "to importune" (<zu "to" + setzen "to set, put"). See note on sadzić above. The Russian words are Church Slavic borrowings.

doseljenik, iseljenik, населе́ние-naseljenje: See сели́ться-seliti se; iseljenik is from *izseljenik.

nadsázka: The idea is that of putting over or beyond, i.e. carrying to excess.

оса́да et al., osazenstvo, obsada-opsada: The various meanings reflect the notion of "setting" (i.e. filling, providing, manning, occupying, surrounding) with something or someone; similar semantic development is apparent in Eng. to set (with precious stones) and to be beset (by troubles, foes, etc.) and in Ger. besetzen "to set (with precious stones); to man; to occupy" (<setzen "to set, put").

posiąść et al., posiadać-posjedovati: The notion that possession consists in "sitting upon" a piece of property is a common one; compare Eng. possess (ult. <Lat. sedere "to sit"), Ger. besitzen "to possess" (<sitzen "to sit"). The Czech word shows a figurative extension of the meaning comparable to that reflected in such English expressions as a man possessed and in Ger. besessen "obsessed, possessed" (<besitzen); Eng. obsess (ult. <Lat. obsidere "to besiege" < sedere) is etymologically related to possess but semantically quite distinct from it.

posada, posádka: ="that which is set (put, placed) somewhere or into which something or someone is set (put, placed)"; compare Pol. załoga.

posadzka: See note on *осáда et al*., *osazenstvo*, *obsada-opsada*.

przesada: See note on *nadsázka*.

председáтель et al.: Compare Eng. *president* (ult. ‹Lat. *prae* "before, in front" + *sedere* "to sit"), Ger. *Vorsitzende(r)* "chairman, president" (‹*vor* "before, in front" + *sitzen* "to sit").

przysada-přísada: Compare Ger. *Zusatz* "admixture" (‹*zu* "to" + *setzen* "to set, put").

przysadkowaty, *przysadzisty*: ="set close to the ground"; compare Ger. *untersetzt* "thick-set, squat" (‹*unter-* "down" + *setzen* "to set, put").

rasjelina: ‹**razsjelina*.

ссáдина: Compare S-C *sadno*.

усúдчивый: Compare Eng. *assiduous* (ult. ‹Lat. *ad* "at, near" + *sedere* "to sit").

usedlost (second meaning): Compare Eng. *sedate* (ult. ‹Lat. *sedare* "to calm, quiet, settle," causative of *sedere* "to sit"), Ger. *gesetzt* "sedate" (‹*setzen* "to set, put").

useljenik: See *seliti se*.

вселéнная et al.: See *селúться-seliti se*; the words are borrowed from a Church Slavic loan-translation of Gr. *οἰκουμένη* "inhabited" (sc. *γῆ* "earth") whence Eng. *ecumenical*.

výsada: The meaning arises from the notion of "putting (or taking) out, *i.e*. exempting (from some generally applicable rule).

zasjedanje, *zasjeda*, *засáда*, *zasadzka*: Compare Lat. *insidiae* "ambush" (‹*in* "in" + *sedere* "to sit"), whence Eng. *insidious*.

zasada (Pol.-S-C), *zásada*: orig. "base, foundation"; see note on Pol. *założenie*, Cz. *založení*. The Serbo-Croatian word is borrowed from Czech.

СЕ(К), СЕЧ	SIE(K), SIECZ	SEK, SÍ, SEČ	SJE(K), SIJEK, SJEČ, SJEC
сечь: to chop; to whip, flog	*siec*: to cut; to whip, flog	*síci*: to reap; to mow	*sjeći*: to cut; to chop; to chop down, fell (trees)
		**seknouti*: to chop; to cut	**sjeknuti*: to bite (said of a snake); to stab (said of a sharp pain)
	siekać: to chop	*sekati*: to chop; to cut; to reap; to mow	*sjecati*: to chop; to pull; to tease, annoy
сечéние: whipping, flogging;			*sječenje*: (act of) cutting,
[R]	[P]	[Cz]	[S-C]

(longitudinal or cross-) section; (Caesarean) section			chopping, chopping down
се́ча (arch.): battle		seč (lit.): battle	sječa: felling (of trees); slaughter, carnage
			sječivo: edge (of a knife)
секи́ра: pole-axe	siekiera: axe	sekera, sekyra: axe	sjekira: axe
секу́щая: (math.) secant	sieczna: (math.) secant	sečna: (math.) secant	sječica: (math.) secant
			kolosijek: rut; track, rails
насеко́мое: insect			
отсе́к: compartment (of a ship)			odsjek: part, section; section, department; period of time; paragraph
пересече́ние: (road) intersection; (math.) intersection			presjek: (longitudinal or cross-) section; (math.) intersection
			prosječan: average (a.)
		průsečík: (road) intersection; (math.) intersection	
		úsek: part, section; sector; period of time	
		úsečka: (math.) abscissa	
		úsečný: terse, laconic, concise	
		výsek: butcher shop	
[R]	[P]	[Cz]	[S-C]

NOTES

Basic meaning of root: to cut, chop

The Slavic root is related to Eng. saw (instrument for cutting), Lat. secare "to cut" (›Eng. section, sector, segment).

сечь et al.: The respective 1 sg. forms are секу́, siekę, seku, siječem.

секýщая et al.: a straight line which cuts a curve at two or more points; compare Eng. secant (ult. ⟨Lat. secare "to cut").

насекóмое: so called because an insect's body is "cut in" or divided into sections; the word is a loan-translation of Lat. insectum (⟨in "in" + secare "to cut"), itself modeled on Gr. ἔντομον "insect" (⟨ἐν "in" + τέμνει "to cut"), whence Eng. entomology. Compare also Ger. Kerbtier "insect" (⟨kerben "to notch" + Tier "animal"), S-C zareznik "insect" (⟨rezati "to cut").

prosječan: See note on Pol. przeciętny.

úsečka: See note on Pol. odcięta.

úsečný: Compare Eng. concise (ult. ⟨Lat. caedere "to cut").

СИЛ	SIŁ, SIL	SIL, SÍL	SIL
сúла: strength, force; (coll.) much, many	siła: strength, force; (arch.) much, many	síla: strength, force; thickness; (coll.) much, many	sila: strength, force; necessity; power (i.e. sovereign state, country); much, many
		síliti: to become strong; to become fat; to strengthen	siliti: to force, compel
сúлиться (coll.): to try, strive	silić się: to try, strive		siliti se: to try, strive
			**silovati: to rape
	silnik: motor, engine		silnik: tyrant; brutal person
	siłownia: (electric) power plant		
		silnice: highway	
равносúльный: equivalent, tantamount			
	nasilenie: intensity		
насúлие: violence, force		násilí: violence, force	nasilje: violence, force
насúльник: tyrant; brutal person		násilník: tyrant; brutal person	nasilnik: tyrant; brutal person
насúловать: to force, compel; to rape			
[R]	[P]	[Cz]	[S-C]

оси́лить, оси́ливать: to overcome, overpower			osiliti, osiljavati: to become strong
	posiłek: meal	posila: support, assistance; (mil.) reinforcements	
	posiłki (pl.): (mil.) reinforcements		
	posiłkowy: auxiliary; (gram.) auxiliary		
пересилить, пересиливать: to overcome, overpower	przesilić się, przesilać się: to subside		
	przesilenie: crisis; solstice		
			prisiliti, prisiljavati: to force, compel
уси́лие: effort		úsilí: effort	
	usiłować: to try, strive	usilovati: to try, strive	
усили́тель: (radio) amplifier			
	wysilić, wysilać: to exhaust; to strain, exert	vysíliti, vysilovati: to exhaust	
	wysiłek: effort		
		zesilovač: (radio) amplifier	
		znásilniti, znásilňovati: to rape	
	zasiłek: subsidy; allowance		
[R]	[P]	[Cz]	[S-C]

NOTES

Basic meaning of root: strength

си́ла et al.: Regarding the meaning "much, many," compare the English rustic colloquialism a power of (="much, many") and the use of Fr. force "strength, force" in such expressions as force gens "many people"; see also Pol.-Cz. moc.

си́литься et al.: Compare Fr. s'efforcer "to try" (<force "strength,

force") and see note on усилие-úsilí, wysiłek.

silovati: Compare the use of Eng. violate (related to violence and ult. ‹Lat. vis "strength") in this sense and Ger. vergewaltigen "to rape" (‹Gewalt "violence, force").

silnik (Pol.): ="source of power."

silnice: ="strong (i.e. durable, hard-surfaced) road."

равносильный: See note under root РОВ (etc.).

насиловать (second meaning): See note on silovati.

posiłek: ="that which strengthens, fortifies."

przesilić się: The underlying notion is "to decline after reaching a peak of intensity."

przesilenie: ="peak of intensity"; compare przesilić się. The summer and winter solstices are the times when the sun is farthest from the equator.

усилие-úsilí, wysiłek: Compare Eng. effort (ult. ‹Lat. fortis "strong").

usiłować-usilovati: See note on силиться et al.

znásilniti: See note on silovati.

СЛ, СЫЛ, СОЛ	SŁ, SYŁ, SEŁ	SL, SÍL, SEL	SL, ŠIL, SIL, SAO, ŠL
слать: to send	słać: to send	**sláti (arch.): to send	slati (šiljati): to send
		velvyslanec: ambassador	
			izaslanik: delegate; envoy
		obsílka: summons, subpoena	
			odaslanik: delegate; envoy
	odsyłacz: reference mark (asterisk, etc. referring reader to footnote)		odašiljač: radio transmitter
послáть, посылáть: to send	posłać, posyłać: to send	poslati, posílati: to send	poslati, pošiljati: to send
посóл: ambassador	poseł: (parliamentary) deputy; minister (diplomatic representative)	posel: messenger	posao: work; affair, matter, business
послáнник: minister (diplomatic representative)	posłannik: messenger		poslanik: (parliamentary) deputy; minister (diplomatic representative)
[R]	[P]	[Cz]	[S-C]

[R]	[P]	[Cz]	[S-C]
посла́нец: envoy	posłaniec: messenger	poslanec: (parliamentary) deputy	
посла́ние: message	posłanie: (act of) sending	poslání: mission, appointed task	poslanje: mission, appointed task
			poslanica: letter, missive
			poslovnica: office, bureau
посы́льный: messenger			posilni: officer's orderly
посы́лка: (act of) sending; parcel; (log.) premise	posyłka: (act of) sending; errand; parcel	posílka: errand	pošiljka: (act of) sending; parcel; consignment; remittance
предпосы́лка: (log.) premise; prerequisite			
	przesłanka: (log.) premise		
сосла́ть, ссыла́ть: to exile, banish	zesłać, zsyłać: to send down; to exile, banish		
сосла́ться, ссыла́ться: to refer, allude (to)			
	wysłaniec, wysłannik: messenger; envoy	vyslanec: minister (diplomatic representative)	
		vysílač, vysílačka: radio transmitter	
			zaposliti, zapošljavati: to hire, employ

NOTES

Basic meaning of root: to send

Many of the derivatives have English counterparts derived from Lat. mittere "to send" (message, messenger, mission, missive, remittance, transmitter); Eng. envoy is from Fr. envoyer "to send."

velvyslanec: See vyslanec and compare Hung. nagykövet "ambassador" (<nagy "great" + követ "minister [diplomatic representative]").

izaslanik, odaslanik: Compare Ger. Abgesandter "delegate" (<ab "off, away" + senden "to send").

odsyłacz: Compare Fr. renvoi "reference mark" (<renvoyer "to send back to refer" < re- "back" + envoyer "to send").

посóл-poseł, послáнник-poslanik: Compare Ger. Gesandter "ambassador; minister (diplomatic representative)" (<senden "to send").

posao: orig. "a thing one is sent to do," i.e. a mission or errand; see next note. A second posao, with the meaning "envoy" (compare посóл-poseł-posel), is obsolete.

poslání-poslanje: Compare posao and Eng. mission (ult. <Lat. missio "a sending").

poslovnica: ="place of business"; see posao.

posilni: <Rus. посы́льный.

посы́лка (third meaning), предпосы́лка (first meaning), przesłanka: that part of a logical proof which is "sent ahead," i.e. stated first as an assumption; the three words follow Eng. premise, Fr. prémisse (ult. <Lat. prae "before" + mittere "to send"). The second meaning of предпосы́лка is an extension of the first.

сослáться: Compare Fr. renvoyer "to refer (a matter to s.o.)" (<re- "back" + envoyer "to send").

vyslanec: See note on посóл-poseł, послáнник-poslanik.

zaposliti: ="to give work to"; see posao.

СЛЕД	ŚLAD, ŚLED(Z)	SLED, SLÍD	SLIJED, SLJED, SLJEĐ
след: track, trace	ślad: track, trace	sled: row, line; series, succession; (arch.) track, trace	slijed: track, trace; order, sequence
следи́ть: (за + inst.) to watch; to leave tracks, footprints	śledzić: to watch	slíditi: to spy	slijediti: to follow; to be owing
слéдовать: to follow; to be owing; (impers.) (one) should, ought to		sledovati: to follow	sljedovati: to follow; to be owing
слéдствие: consequence, result; investigation	śledztwo: investigation		
			sljedba: sect
[R]	[P]	[Cz]	[S-C]

[R]	[P]	[Cz]	[S-C]
		důsledek: consequence, result	
		důsledný: consistent	dosljedan: consistent
**исслéдовать: to investigate			islijediti, isljeđivati: to investigate
			naslijediti, nasljeđivati: to inherit
**наслéдовать: to inherit	naśladować: to imitate	následovati: to follow; to imitate	nasljedovati: to imitate
наслéдник: heir; successor		následník: successor	nasljednik: heir; successor
		následek: consequence, result	
послéд: (anat.) placenta	poślad: grain refuse (used for fodder)		
послéдки (pl.): remainder	pośladek: buttocks	posledek: remainder; end	posljedak: consequence, result; end
послéдний: last	pośledni: inferior, of poor quality	poslední: last	posljednji: last
послéдствие: consequence, result			posljedica: consequence, result
послéдовательный: successive, consecutive; consistent			
преслéдовать: to pursue; to persecute; to prosecute	prześladować: to persecute	pronásledovati: to pursue; to persecute	
**рассслéдовать: to investigate			
	upośledzić, upośledzać: to neglect, slight		
впослéдствии: subsequently			
		výsledek: consequence, result	

NOTES

Basic meaning of root: track, trace

The notion of "trailing behind, tracing another's steps" is apparent i: two widespread secondary meanings, "to follow" and "last (in succession)."

Many of the listed words have English counterparts derived from Lat. sequi "to follow" (past part. secutus).

slijediti, следовать-sljedovati: Underlying the meaning "to be owing" is the notion of "following naturally or logically"; something of the same idea is apparent in the English phrase He has it coming to him.

следствие (second meaning)-śledztwo: ="tracking, tracing"; compare Eng investigation (ult. ‹Lat. vestigium "track, trace"), S-C istraga "investigation" (‹trag "track, trace").

sljedba: ="a following, group of followers"; the word is modeled on Lat. secta "sect" (‹sequi "to follow").

důsledný-dosljedan: Compare Fr. conséquent "consistent" (ult. ‹Lat. sequi "to follow").

исследовать-islijediti: See note on следствие-śledztwo; the Serbo-Croatian word is from earlier izslijediti.

послед: The placenta is expelled from the womb after delivery of the fetus; see последний and compare Eng. afterbirth.

poślad: ="the last part of the grain"; see pośledni.

последки et al.: Compare последний et al.

pośledni: orig. "last, in the rear."

последовательный (second meaning): See note on důsledný-dosljedan.

преследовать et al.: Compare Eng. pursue, persecute and prosecute (all ult. ‹Lat. sequi "to follow"), Ger. verfolgen "to pursue; to persecute; to prosecute" (‹folgen "to follow"), Pol. ścigać, Cz. stíhati.

расследовать: See note on следствие-śledztwo.

upośledzić: orig. "to leave behind, outdo"; see obsolete poślad "behind, after" and compare pośledni.

СЛЫ, СЛОВ, СЛАВ, (СЛУХ), (СЛУШ), (СЛЫШ)	SŁY, SŁOW, SŁÓW, SŁAW, (SŁUCH), (SŁUSZ), (SŁYSZ)	SLOU, SLU, SLY, SLOV, SLAV, SLÁV, (SLUCH), (SLOUCH), (SLECH), (SLUŠ), (SLYŠ)	SLOV, SLIV, SI, SLAV, (SLUH), (SLUŠ), (SLIŠ)
слыть: to be reputed (to be)		slouti (lit.): to be named, called; to be renowned	
	słynąć: to be renowned	slynouti (lit.): to be renowned	
			sloviti: to be reputed (to be)
сло́во: word	słowo: word; (gram.) verb	slovo: word	slovo: letter (of alphabet); speech, address
		sloveso: (gram.) verb	
сло́вно: as if; (coll.) like			
слова́рь: dictionary; vocabulary			
сло́вник: word-list	słownik: dictionary	slovník: dictionary	
			slovnica (arch.): grammar
слове́сность (arch.): literature		slovesnost (lit.): literature	
сла́ва: glory, fame; reputation	sława: glory, fame; reputation	sláva: glory, fame; pomp, splendor; celebration	slava: glory, fame; festival
слух: (sense of) hearing; rumor	słuch: (sense of) hearing; rumor	sluch: (sense of) hearing	sluh: (sense of) hearing
		slech (arch.): (sense of) hearing; rumor	
	słuchy (pl.): ears (of a rabbit)	slechy (pl.), (arch.) sluchy (pl.): ears (of a hunting dog or game animal)	
слу́шать: to listen	słuchać: to listen; to obey	slušeti: to suit, be becoming (said of clothes); to be fitting, proper	slušati: to listen; to obey
слу́шаться: to obey	słuchać się: to obey	slušeti se: to be fitting, proper	
[R]	[P]	[Cz]	[S-C]

[R]	[P]	[Cz]	[S-C]
слы́шать: to hear	słyszeć: to hear	slyšeti: to hear	slišati, slišavati: to hear (a student) recite a lesson
	słuszny: just, fair; valid, legitimate; tall	slušný: fitting, proper; decent, seemly; passable, fair	
			slušateljstvo: audience (in a theater)
беспрекосло́вный: absolute, unquestioning (obedience, etc.)			
благослови́ть, благословля́ть: to bless	błogosławić: to bless	blahoslaviti: to praise	blagosloviti, blagosiljati (blagoslivljati): to bless
богосло́вие: theology		bohosloví: theology	bogoslovlje: theology
		citoslovce: (gram.) interjection	
	cudzysłów: quotation marks		
часосло́в: prayer-book, breviary			časoslov: prayer-book, breviary
			državoslovlje: political science
		dušesloví (arch.): psychology	
голосло́вный: unfounded, unsubstantiated	gołosłowny: unfounded, unsubstantiated		
		hláskosloví: phonetics, phonology	
	imiesłów: (gram.) participle		
			jezikoslovlje: linguistics
			krasnosloviti: to declaim, recite
многосло́вный: loquacious		mnohoslovný (lit.): loquacious	
		názvosloví: terminology, nomenclature	
	półsłówko: hint		

[R]	[P]	[Cz]	[S-C]
послесло́вие: epilogue			
правосла́вие: the Greek Orthodox religion	prawosławie: the Greek Orthodox religion	pravosláví: the Greek Orthodox religion	pravoslavlje: the Greek Orthodox religion
прекосло́вить: to contradict (s.o.)			
родосло́вие (lit.): genealogy			rodoslovlje: genealogy
славолю́бие (lit.): love of glory			slavoljublje: ambition
	słoworód: etymology		
тщесла́вный: vain, conceited, vainglorious			
		větosloví: syntax	
		významosloví: semantics, semasiology	
злосло́вие: backbiting, slander			
безусло́вный: unconditional; absolute			bezuslovan: unconditional; absolute
		doslov: epilogue; conclusion (of a speech, etc.)	
досло́вный: literal	dosłowny: literal	doslovný: literal	doslovan: literal
		doslech: hearsay	
			naslov: title, heading; address (on a letter)
		osloviti, oslovovati: to address, speak to	osloviti, oslovljavati: to address, speak to
посло́вица: proverb			poslovica: proverb
		poslechnouti, poslouchati: to listen; to obey	
послу́шный: obedient	posłuszny: obedient	poslušný: obedient	poslušan: obedient

[R]	[P]	[Cz]	[S-C]
пóслушник: (rel.) novice			poslušnik: obedient person
		posluchačstvo: audience (in a theater)	
пресловýтый: notorious			
предислóвие: preface, foreword	przedsłowie: preface, foreword		
	przysłowie: proverb	přísloví: proverb	
	przysłówek: (gram.) adverb	příslovce: (gram.) adverb	
		příslušeti: to belong	
		příslušný: belonging; appropriate; competent, authorized	
		proslulý: famous	
			protusloviti: to contradict (s.o.); to contradict, conflict (with)
сослóвие: social class, (feudal) estate			
услóвие: condition, stipulation, proviso; condition, circumstance; agreement		úsloví: phrase, locution	uslov: condition, stipulation, proviso; condition, circumstance
услóвный: conditional, contingent; agreed, stipulated; (gram.) conditional			uslovan: conditional, contingent
	wysłowić, wysławiać: to express, utter	vysloviti, vyslovovati: to express, utter; to pronounce	
		výslovný: explicit	
		výslech: interrogation	

NOTES

asic meaning of root: to be named, reputed, renowned; to hear, listen

The active meaning "to hear, listen," which is that of the original ndo-European root, survives in the Slavic languages in the expanded root-'orms СЛУХ-СЛУШ-СЛЫШ---SŁUCH-SŁUSZ-SŁYSZ---SLUCH-SLOUCH-SLECH-SLUŠ-SLYŠ---LUH-SLUŠ-SLIŠ.

Rus. *сло́во et al*. and their derivatives comprise a large sub-group in hich a number of verbal and postverbal formations reflect the basic meaning to speak." The suffix -*сло́вие*, -*sloví*, -*slovlje*, used in specialized words o express the meaning "science, theory, teaching," is modeled on the Greek-erived suffix exemplified by Eng. -*logy*, Fr.-Ger. -*logie* (ult. ‹Gr. *λόγος* word").

The Slavic root is related to Eng. *loud*, *listen*.

sloviti: a new infinitive formed from *slovem*, 1 sg. of obsolete *sluti*.

słowo, *sloveso*: Compare Eng. *verb* (ult. ‹Lat. *verbum* "word; verb").

slovo (S-C): orig. "word."

сло́вно: ‹obsolete *сло́вный* "accurate, true, similar"; compare *досло́вный*.

slovesnost: ‹Rus. *слове́сность*.

słuchać-*slušati*, *слу́шаться*-*słuchać się*: Compare Eng. *obey* (ult. ‹Lat. udire "to hear; to listen"), Ger. *gehorchen* "to obey" (akin to *hören* "to ear; to listen").

slušeti (*se*), *słuszny*-*slušný*: The Czech verb and OPol. *słuszać* (›*słuszy*) have had the successive meanings "to listen" › "to belong" (see Cz. *příslušeti* below) › "to be fitting, proper"; regarding these semantic shifts, compare Ger. *gehören* "to belong" (‹*hören* "to hear; to listen"), Fin. *kuulua* 'to belong" (‹*kuulla* "to hear") and see notes on Cz. *patřiti*, S-C *patriti* and Pol. *patrzeć* (*patrzyć*) *się*, Cz. *patřiti se*. The last meaning of Pol. *słuszny* (orig., in a wider sense, "substantial, sizable") arose in the same manner as English expressions like *a fair distance*, *a decent amount*, *a good bit*; compare Rus. *поря́дочный et al*., Cz. *hodný* and *řádný*.

беспрекосло́вный: See *прекосло́вить*.

благослови́ть et al.: modeled on Gr. *εὐλογεῖν* "to praise; to bless" (‹*εὖ* "well" + *λόγος* "word"), whence Eng. *eulogy*; see note on Cz. *blahořečiti*. The Polish word is borrowed from Cz. *blahoslaviti*, an erroneous formation from *sláva* rather than *slovo*; the Serbo-Croatian imperfectives are corruptions of an earlier form corresponding to Rus. *благословля́ть*.

богосло́вие et al.: Compare Eng. *theology* (‹Gr. *θεός* "god" + -*logy*).

citoslovce: The first element is from *cit* "feeling, emotion"; compare Ger. *Empfindungswort* "interjection" (‹*Empfindung* "feeling, emotion" + *Wort* "word").

cudzysłów: The first element is from *cudzy* "alien, someone else's."

часосло́в-*časoslov*: See note under root ЧАС (etc.).

državoslovlje: Compare Ger. Staatswissenschaft "political science" (<Staat "state" + Wissenschaft "science").

duševloví: Compare Eng. psychology (<Gr. ψυχή "soul" + -logy).

голосло́вный-gołosłowny: The first element is from го́лый-goły "naked, bare."

hláskosloví: Compare Eng. phonology (<Gr. φωνή "voice; sound" + -logy).

imiesłów: See note under root ИМЯ (etc.).

jezikoslovlje: The first element is from jezik "language"; see note on Rus. языкове́дение, Cz. jazykověda.

krasnosloviti: The first element is from krasan "beautiful."

многосло́вный-mnohoslovný: The first element is from мно́го-mnoho "much."

názvosloví: See note under root ЗВ (etc.).

послесло́вие: The first element is from по́сле "after."

правосла́вие et al.: an erroneous loan-translation of Gr. ὀρθοδοξία "orthodoxy" (<ὀρθός "right, correct" + δόξα "[sometimes] glory; [in this case, however] opinion"); the Polish, Czech and Serbo-Croatian words are borrowed from Russian.

прекосло́вить: modeled on Gr. ἀντιλέγειν "to contradict" (<ἀντί "against" + λέγειν "to speak"); see note on Rus. противоре́чить et al.

родосло́вие-rodoslovlje: Compare Eng. genealogy (<Gr. γενεά "birth, stock" + -logy).

slavoljublje: See slava and note on Rus. честолю́бие, S-C častoljublje.

тщесла́вный: See сла́ва; the first element is from the root of тще́тный "vain, futile."

větosloví: Compare Ger. Satzlehre "syntax" (<Satz "sentence, clause" + Lehre "teaching").

významosloví: Compare Eng. semasiology (<Gr. σημασία "meaning" + -logy)

безусло́вный-bezuslovan: See усло́вие-uslov.

doslovan: <Rus. досло́вный or Cz. doslovný.

osloviti (S-C): <Cz. osloviti.

посло́вица-poslovica: Compare Eng. proverb (ult. <Lat. verbum "word"); the Serbo-Croatian word is borrowed from Russian.

poslechnouti, послу́шный et al.: See note on słuchać-slušati, слу́шаться-słuchać się.

преслову́тый: orig. "famous"; the word is formed from an old present participle of слыть.

przysłowie-přísloví: See note on посло́вица-poslovica.

przysłówek-příslovce: See słowo, sloveso and note on Rus. наре́чие.

příslušeti, příslušný: The verb originally had the additional meaning "to be fitting, proper"; see note on slušeti (se), słuszny-slušný.

protusloviti: See note on Rus. противоре́чить et al.

сосло́вие: probably an erroneous loan-translation of Gr. σύλλογος "assembly" (<σύν "with, together" + -λογος "(act of) gathering" < λέγειν "to gather"), the second element in the Greek word having been mistaken for λόγος word" (<λέγειν "to speak").

условие-uslov: See the introductory note on root ГОВОР (etc.) and compare Rus. оговорка, S-C uvjet; the Serbo-Croatian word is borrowed from Russian.

uslovan: <Rus. условный.

vysloviti: See note on S-C izgovor.

výslovný: See note on S-C izričan, izričit.

СПЕ	SPIE, ŚPIE	SPĚ, SPÍ	SPJE, SPIJE, SPI
спеть: to ripen		spěti (lit.): to head (for), draw (toward)	
спешить: to hurry (intr.)	spieszyć (śpieszyć) (się): to hurry (intr.)	spěchati: to hurry (intr.)	
		spíš, spíše: rather (than)	
		dospělý: adult (a. and n.)	dospio: ripe; due, payable
доспехи (pl., arch.): armor			
приспеть, приспевать: to arrive (e.g. a certain time)		přispěti, přispívati: to assist; to contribute	prispjeti, prispijevati: to arrive; to ripen
приспешник: myrmidon, slavish follower			
		prospěch: benefit, advantage	
споспешествовать (arch.): to promote, further			
успеть, успевать: to have time, manage (to do s.th.); to be successful		*uspěti (lit.): to have time, manage (to do s.th.)	uspjeti, uspijevati: to have time, manage (to do s.th.); to be successful; to thrive (crops, etc.)
успех: success		úspěch: success	uspjeh: success
[R]	[P]	[Cz]	[S-C]

NOTES

Basic meaning of root: to advance rapidly, progress, prosper

The Slavic root is related to Eng. speed, Du. spoed "speed" and voorspoed "prosperity" (voor = "forward"), Lat. sperare "to hope" (>Eng. despair) and prosper(us) "fortunate" (>Eng. prosperous).

спеть-spěti: Śpiać "to hurry" occurs in Old Polish; the corresponding Serbo-Croatian word is not attested.

спеши́ть et al.: S-C spješiti "to hurry" is dialectal.

spíš, spíše: orig. "quickly" (see obsolete spíšiti "to hurry"), later construed as a comparative form; regarding the present meaning, compare Eng. rather (<obsolete rathe "quick; early") and the use of sooner in the sense of "rather" (e.g. I'd sooner die), Rus. скоре́е "more quickly; sooner; rather," Fr. plutôt "rather" (orig. "sooner, earlier"), Ger. eher "sooner, earlier; rather."

доспе́хи: orig. "preparations," then "gear, armor"; see dialectal доспе́т "to prepare." The word is borrowed from Church Slavic.

приспе́шник: a person who arrives promptly to do one's bidding.

споспе́шествовать: a Church Slavic loan-word.

успе́ть et al.: The Czech and Serbo-Croatian words are borrowed from Russian.

успе́х et al.: The Czech word is borrowed from Russian, the Serbo-Croatian word from Czech or Russian.

СЕРД, СЕРЕД, СРЕД	SER(D), SIERDZ, ŚROD, ŚRÓD, ŚRED	SRD, STŘED, STŘEĎ, STŘÍD	SR(D), SRĐ, SRŽ, SRIJED, SRED, SREĐ
се́рдце: heart	serce: heart	srdce: heart	srce: heart
			srž: core; marrow; essence
сердцеви́на: core			
	sercowy: heart (attr.), cardiac	srdeční: heart (attr.), cardiac	srčan: heart (attr.), cardiac; courageous
серде́чный: heart (attr.), cardiac; hearty, cordial	serdeczny: hearty, cordial	srdečný: hearty, cordial	srdačan: hearty, cordial
		srdnatý: courageous	
		srdečnice: (anat.) aorta	
[R]	[P]	[Cz]	[S-C]

серди́ться: to be angry	sierdzić się (arch.): to be angry		srditi se: to be angry
среда́: (phys.) medium; milieu, environment; Wednesday	środa: Wednesday	středa: Wednesday	srijeda: middle, center; Wednesday
		střed: middle, center	
		střída, střídka: crumb (soft part of the bread)	
	środek: middle, center; means, instrumentality; remedy		
середи́на, (arch.) среди́на: middle, center			sredina: middle, center; (phys.) medium; milieu, environment; mean, average, medium
сре́дство: means, instrumentality; remedy			sredstvo: means, instrumentality; remedy
	środowisko: (phys.) medium; milieu, environment	středisko, (arch.) střediště: center (industrial, etc.)	središte: middle, center; center (industrial, of attraction, etc.)
	średnik: semi-colon	středník: semi-colon	
	średnica: diameter		
сре́дний: middle (attr.); mean, average, medium (attr.); (gram.) neuter	średni: middle (attr.); mean, average, medium (attr.); mediocre	střední: middle (attr.); mean, average, medium (attr.); (gram.) neuter	srednji: middle (attr.); mean, average, medium (attr.); (gram.) neuter
		střídmý: temperate, moderate	
среди́, средь: among, amid; in the middle (of)	śród: among, amid; in the middle (of)		sred: among, amid; in the middle (of)
милосе́рдие: mercy, charity	miłosierdzie: mercy, charity	milosrdenství: mercy, charity	milosrđe: mercy, charity
	mimośrodkowy: (math.) eccentric		
			sredobježan: centrifugal
сердобо́лие: tender-heartedness, compassion			srdobolja: dysentery
[R]	[P]	[Cz]	[S-C]

[R]	[P]	[Cz]	[S-C]
			sredotežan: centripetal
средото́чие: center, focal point			
сосредото́чить, сосредото́чивать: to concentrate			*usredotočiti; usredsrijediti, usredsređivati: to concentrate
средневеко́вый: medieval	średniowieczny: medieval	středověký: medieval	srednjovjekovan: medieval
			vansredišni: (math.) eccentric
	współśrodkowy: concentric		
	bezpośredni: immediate, direct	bezprostřední: immediate, direct	
	dośrodkowy: centripetal	dostředivý: centripetal	
непосре́дственный: immediate, direct			neposredan: immediate, direct
	ośrodek: center (industrial, of attraction, etc.)		
			osrednji: mediocre
	odśrodkowy: centrifugal	odstředivý: centrifugal	
посре́дственный: mediocre	pośredni: middle (attr.); intermediate; indirect	prostřední: middle (attr.); intermediate; mean, average, medium (attr.); mediocre	posredan: intermediate; indirect
посре́дник: mediator, go-between; broker, middleman	pośrednik: mediator, go-between; broker, middleman	prostředník: mediator, go-between; middle finger	posrednik: mediator, go-between; broker, middleman
		prostředí: (phys.) medium; milieu, environment	
		prostředek: middle, center; means, instrumentality; remedy	
	ześrodkować, ześrodkowywać: to concentrate	soustřediti, soustřeďovati: to concentrate	

		soustředný: concentric	
усе́рдный: zealous, diligent			usrdan: zealous, diligent; hearty, cordial
	wśród: among, amid; in the middle (of)		usred: in the middle (of)
		výstředný: (math.) eccentric	
		výstřední: eccentric, odd	
	*wypośrodkować: to ascertain, find out; to conclude, infer, deduce		
		zprostředkovatel: mediator, go-between; broker, middleman	
[R]	[P]	[Cz]	[S-C]

NOTES

Basic meaning of root: heart; middle, center

The second root-meaning is an outgrowth of the first. The numerous derivatives with such meanings as "hearty," "cordial," "courageous," "zealous," "compassion" and "to be angry" reflect the common notion that the heart is the seat of human emotions.

The Russian root-form СРЕД is of Church Slavic origin. In Czech, the root-forms reflecting the meaning "middle, center" show an intrusive t.

Non-Slavic cognates are Eng. heart, Lat. cor "heart" (>Eng. cordial, courageous, accord, concord, discord), Gr. καρδία "heart" (>Eng. cardiac).

serce: <sierce <*sierdce.

srce: <srdce.

srž: <srđ; compare Eng. core (prob. <Lat. cor "heart").

сердцеви́на: See preceding note.

srčan: <srdčan.

среда́ et al.: The native Russian equivalent, середа́ "middle, center; Wednesday," is obsolete. The first and second meanings of среда́ reflect the notion that a physical medium or, by extension, a social or other environment is a "middle" (i.e. intermediate, intervening) space through which a force or an organism passes; compare Eng. medium (ult. <Lat. medius "middle [a.]"), milieu (<Fr. milieu "middle, center"). The meaning "Wednesday" prob-

ably represents early semantic borrowing from German; see modern Ger. Mitt woch "Wednesday" (<mitt- "mid-" + Woche "week").

střída, střídka: ="center of the loaf"; střída is a doublet of středa

środek: The means by which a thing is accomplished is conceived of as being in an intermediate position between the agent and the end in view; compare Eng. means and Fr. moyen "means" (both ult. <Lat. medius "middle [a.]"), Ger. Mittel "means" (<mittel "middle [a.]"), modern Gr. μέσον "mea (<μέσος "middle [a.]"), Fin. väline "means" (<väli "intervening space, interval").

sredina: See notes on среда́ et al. and сре́дний et al.

сре́дство-sredstvo: See note on środek; the Serbo-Croatian word is borrowed from Russian.

środowisko: See note on среда́ et al.

średnik-středník: so called because the semi-colon is a mark of punctuation whose effect as a "stop" lies midway between that of a comma and tha of a period or "full stop"; compare archaic Pol. medjanota "semi-colon" (<Lat. medius "middle [a.]" + nota "mark, note").

сре́дний et al.: Compare Eng. mean, medium, mediocre (all ult. <Lat. medius "middle [a.]") and middling, Fr. moyen "mean, average, medium" (ult <Lat. medius), Ger. mittelmässig "mediocre" (<mittel "middle [a.]" + Mass "measure"). As a grammatical term, the word reflects the idea of a "middle gender.

střídmý: orig. "average, medium"; see preceding note.

среди́ et al.: Compare Eng. amid (<the root of middle), Fr. parmi "amo amid" (<Lat. per "through" + medius "middle [a.]").

милосе́рдие et al.: See note under root МИЛ (etc.).

mimośrodkowy: See note on výstředný, výstřední.

sredobježan: Compare Eng. centrifugal (ult. <Gr. κέντρον "center" + L fugere "to flee"), Rus. центробе́жный, odśrodkowy-odstředivý below.

сердобо́лие-srdobolja: The second element is from боль "pain," bolja "disease." The meaning of the Serbo-Croatian word presumably arose through loose application of the same word to different internal organs; compare t use of Gr. καρδία to refer to the stomach as well as the heart.

sredotežan: Compare Eng. centripetal (ult. <Gr. κέντρον "center" + La petere "to move toward; to seek"), Rus. центростреми́тельный "centripetal" (<центр "center" + стреми́ться "to rush [toward]; to seek"), dośrodkowy-dostředivý below.

средото́чие: See note under root ТК (etc.).

сосредото́чить et al.: See средото́чие and note onześrodkować-soustředíti; usredotočiti is borrowed, in modified form, from Russian.

средневеко́вый et al.: The second element is from век-wiek-věk-vijek "age"; compare Eng. medieval (ult. <Lat. medius "middle [a.]" + aevum "age

vansredišni: The first element is from van "outside"; see note on výstředný, výstřední.

współśrodkowy: See note on soustředný.

bezpośredni-bezprostřední: The relationship between two things is an mmediate one if nothing is interposed between them (spatially, temporally r causally); compare Eng. immediate (ult. ⟨Lat. in- "un-, not" + medius middle [a.]"), Gr. ἄμεσος "immediate, direct" (⟨ἀ- "un-, not" + μέσος "middle [a.]"), Ger. unmittelbar "immediate, direct" (⟨un- "un-, not" + mittel middle [a.]"), Fin. välitön "immediate, direct" (⟨väli "intervening space, nterval" + -tön "-less, without").

dośrodkowy-dostředivý: See note on sredotežan.

непосре́дственный-neposredan: See note on bezpośredni-bezprostřední.

osrednji: See note on сре́дний et al.

odśrodkowy-odstředivý: See note on sredobježan.

посре́дственный-prostřední: See note on сре́дний et al.

pośredni-posredan: Regarding the meaning "indirect," see note on bezpo-redni-bezprostřední.

посре́дник et al.: Compare Eng. mediator (ult. ⟨Lat. medius "middle a.]"), go-between and middleman, Ger. Vermittler "mediator, go-between; roker, middleman" (⟨mittel "middle [a.]").

prostředí: See note on среда́ et al.

prostředek: See note on środek.

ześrodkować-soustředit: Compare Eng. concentrate (ult. ⟨Lat. cum "with, ogether" + Gr. κέντρον "center"), сосредото́чить et al. above.

soustředný: Compare Eng. concentric (ult. ⟨Lat. cum "with, together" + r. κέντρον "center"), współśrodkowy above.

wśród: See note on среди́ et al.

výstředný, výstřední: Compare Eng. eccentric (ult. ⟨Gr. ἐκ "out of" + έντρον "center"), mimośrodkowy and vansredišni above.

wypośrodkować: a loan-translation of Ger. ermitteln "to ascertain, find ut" (⟨er- "out" + Mittel "means"); the underlying idea is that of employing ertain means (see środek above) in order to gain a desired end.

zprostředkovatel: See note on посре́дник et al.

СТА, СТОЙ, СТО(И, -Я), СТА(И), СТАВ	STA, STOJ, STÓJ, STO(I), STAW	STA, STÁ, STE, STOJ, STAV, STÁV	STA, STOJ, STAJ, STAV
стоя́ть: to stand	stać: to stand	státi: to stand; to cost; to be worth	stajati (stojati): to stand; to cost
сто́ить: to cost; to be worth			
стать, станови́ться: to stand, take a position; to become; (стать only) to stop, halt (intr.); (стать only; + inf.) to begin (intr.)	stanąć, stawać: to stand, take a position; to stop, halt (intr.)	*stanouti (lit.): to stand, take a position; to stop, halt (intr.)	*stati: to stand, take a position; to stop, halt (intr.); (+ inf.; + da + pres.) to begin (intr.); to cost
*ста́ться: to happen	stać się, stawać się: to happen; to become	státi se, stávati se: to happen; to become	
ста́вить: to put, place	*stawić (lit.): to put, place; to build	*staviti (arch.): to stop, halt (tr.)	*staviti: to put, place
	stawiać: to put, place; to build	stavěti: to put, place; to build; to stop, halt (intr.)	stavljati: to put, place
	stanowić: to establish, institute; to be, constitute; to decide	*stanoviti: to fix, set, establish (a price, date, etc.); to ascertain, establish (a fact)	
стать: figure (shape of body)			
стан: figure (shape of body); camp; machine, mill	stan: state, condition; social class, (feudal) estate; state (political subdivision, as in United States); state, body politic; waist	stan: tent; military headquarters	stan: dwelling, living quarters; loom; military headquarters
	staw: pond; (anat.) joint	stav: state, condition; social class, (feudal) estate; head (of cattle), effective strength (of an army), stock (of	stav: position, posture; position, attitude, standpoint; paragraph; passage (in a text)
[R]	[P]	[Cz]	[S-C]

[R]	[P]	[Cz]	[S-C]
		goods) on hand; loom	
			stanje: state, condition; (gram.) voice
ста́тный: well-built, well-proportioned		statný: well-built, well-proportioned	
	statek: ship, vessel; vessel, utensil (for kitchen)	statek: estate, manor; farm; (arch.) property	
ста́точный (coll.): possible	stateczny: stable; staid, sedate	statečný: brave, courageous	
	starczyć, starczać: to suffice	**stačiti: to suffice; to keep pace; to be able (to); to cope (with)	
статья́: article (in newspaper, etc.); clause; item		stať: article (in newspaper, etc.)	
стано́к: machine-tool; loom; gun-mount		stánek: (fruit-, etc.) stand; kiosk	stanak: small dwelling
стани́ца: Cossack village		stanice: (railroad, radio) station	stanica: (railroad, radio, police) station; (anat.) cell
	stanowisko: position, standing (in society, etc.); position, post, job; position, attitude, standpoint; (mil.) position; (fruit-, cab-, etc.) stand	stanovisko: position, attitude, standpoint	
станови́ще: stopping place		stanoviště: (taxi-) stand; (mil.) (command, observation, etc.) post	stanovište: position, attitude, standpoint
			stanovništvo: population
		stanovy (pl.): statutes, articles, charter (of an organization)	

[R]	[P]	[Cz]	[S-C]
	stanowczy: decisive, resolute		
			stanovit: a certain, particular (one)
стáя: flock, flight (of birds); school (of fish); pack (of wolves)	staja, staje: unit of length (in measuring land)	stáj: stable (n.); cowshed	staja: stable (n.); cowshed
	stajnia: stable (n.)		
	stadło: married couple		
			stas: figure (shape of body)
			stalež: social class, (feudal) estate; profession
			stanka: pause; (punc.) dash
			stamen: strong; reliable
		stejný: same; equal	
стоя́ние: (act of) standing	stanie: (act of) standing	stání: (act of) standing; trial, hearing; stall (for horse or cow)	stajanje: (act of) standing; cost
стоя́нка: halt, stop; stopping place; (taxi-) stand; moorage, berth; (mil.) billet			
			stajalište: stopping place; position, attitude, standpoint
сто́йка: bar, counter; prop, support; set, point (hunting dog's position); handstand (in gymnastics)		stojka: prop, support; handstand (in gymnastics)	
сто́йло: stall (for horse or cow)			

стоя́лый: stale	stały: constant, continuous; permanent; stable; (phys.) solid	stálý: constant, continuous; permanent; stable	stalan: constant, continuous; permanent; stable
сто́йкий: steadfast, staunch; (chem., phys.) stable			
	stójkowy (arch.): policeman		
ста́вка: rate; stake (in gambling); military headquarters	stawka: rate; stake (in gambling)	stávka: strike, work stoppage	stavka: item; paragraph
ста́вень, ста́вня: shutter (of a window)			stavnja: recruitment
	stawidło: flood-gate	stavidlo: flood-gate	
	stawiennictwo: appearance in court		
ста́вленник: henchman, protégé			
благосостоя́ние: well-being, prosperity	błogostan: bliss		blagostanje: well-being, prosperity
			dobrostanje: well-being, prosperity
			gorostas: giant
	jednostajny: monotonous; uniform	jednostejný (arch.): monotonous	jednostavan: simple, plain
кста́ти: to the point, apropos; opportunely; incidentally, by the way			
		lhostejný: indifferent	
			samostan: monastery; convent
самостоя́тельный: independent		samostatný: independent	samostalan: independent
солнцестоя́ние: solstice			suncostaja: solstice
		stejnokroj: (military, etc.) uniform	
[R]	[P]	[Cz]	[S-C]

[R]	[P]	[Cz]	[S-C]
		stejnoměrný: even, uniform	
		stejnorodý: homogeneous	
светопреставлéние: doomsday, the end of the world			
	ustawodawstwo: legislation		
			vjerodostojan: trustworthy; authentic
			zlostaviti, zlostavljati: to mistreat; to torture
достáть, доставáть: (до + gen.) to reach; to get, obtain; to suffice	dostać, dostawać: (do + gen.) to reach; to get, obtain; to suffice	dostati, dostávati: to get, obtain	dostati, dostajati: to suffice
достáток: wealth, affluence	dostatek: abundance; wealth, affluence	dostatek: sufficient amount; wealth, affluence	
достáточный: sufficient; (arch.) wealthy, affluent	dostateczny: sufficient	dostatečný: sufficient	
	dostatni: wealthy, affluent; ample, abundant		dostatan: sufficient
достояние: property			
достóйный: worthy, deserving	dostojny: august, distinguished, eminent	důstojný: respectable; dignified, stately; reverend (title)	dostojan: worthy, deserving
достóинство: dignity; positive quality, merit; value, denomination (of coin, etc.); (arch.) rank, title	dostojeństwo: dignity; high rank, position	důstojenství (arch.): dignity; rank, title	dostojanstvo: dignity; rank, title
	dostojność: dignity	důstojnost: dignity	
	dostojnik: dignitary	důstojník: (military) officer	dostojanstvenik: dignitary

[R]	[P]	[Cz]	[S-C]
достáвить, доставля́ть: to supply, provide; to deliver; to cause (trouble), afford (pleasure)	dostawić, dostawiać: to supply, provide; to deliver	dostaviti se, dostavovati se: to make an appearance, present oneself	dostaviti, dostavljati: to deliver; to inform against, denounce; to notify
		dostaveníčko: rendezvous, meeting; serenade	
	dostarczyć, dostarczać: to supply, provide	dostačiti, dostačovati: to suffice	
			izostaviti, izostavljati: to omit ispostava: branch office
настáть, наставáть: to arrive (e.g. a certain time)	nastać, nastawać: to arrive (e.g. a certain time); (nastawać only) to insist	nastati, nastávati: to arrive (e.g. a certain time)	nastati (nastanuti), nastajati: to arrive (e.g. a certain time); to arise, emerge; to begin (intr.) nastavati: to dwell, reside
настоя́ть, настáивать: to insist; to draw, infuse			nastojati: to insist; to strive, exert oneself
настóйка: fruit liqueur; tincture			
настоя́тельный: insistent, persistent; urgent, vital			
настóйчивый: insistent, persistent			
настоя́щий: present (e.g. time); real			
настоя́тель: father superior (of a monastery); dean (of a cathedral)			nastojnik: manager, superintendent

[R]	[P]	[Cz]	[S-C]
		nástavek, nástavec: extension, piece added on	nastavak: continuation; extension, piece added on; (gram.) suffix; (gram.) ending
наставле́ние: precept, admonition; manual, guidebook	nastawienie: adjustment, setting (of instruments); attitude, state of mind		
наста́вник (arch.): teacher			nastavnik: teacher
			nadstojnik: manager, superintendent
			nestati, nestajati: to disappear; to run short (supplies)
			nestašica: lack, scarcity
			nestašan: roguish, frolicsome
недоста́ток: lack, scarcity; shortcoming, defect	niedostatek: lack, scarcity; poverty, need	nedostatek: lack, scarcity; poverty, need; shortcoming, defect	nedostatak: lack, scarcity; shortcoming, defect
оста́ться, остава́ться: to stay, remain		ostati, ostávati (lit.): to stay, remain	ostati (ostanuti), ostajati: to stay, remain
оста́ток: remainder	ostatek: remainder	ostatek: remainder	ostatak: remainder
оста́точный: residual	ostateczny: final, definite, conclusive; extreme		
	ostatni: last; extreme	ostatní: other, remaining	
остально́й: other, remaining			ostali: other, remaining
			*opstati: to exist; to endure
обстоя́ть: to be, stand, be getting along (matters, one's affairs, etc.)	obstawać: to insist; to persist; (za + inst.) to defend, uphold	obstáti, obstávati: to acquit o.s. well, give a good account of	opstojati: to exist

[R]	[P]	[Cz]	[S-C]
		o.s.; (obstáti only) to hold fast, stand one's ground; (obstáti only) to get along (with s.o.)	
	ostoja: support, bulwark, main-stay; refuge, shelter; (arch.) landing-place, pier		
		obstojný: fair, passable, tolerable	
обстоя́тельство: circumstance			
оста́вить, оставля́ть: to leave, abandon		ostaviti, ostav-ovati (arch.): to leave, abandon; to bequeath	ostaviti, ostavljati: to leave, abandon; to bequeath
			ostavina, ostav-ština: estate (of a deceased person)
			ostavka: resignation, retirement
		obstávka: attachment (of property, salary, etc.)	
останови́ть, остана́вливать: to stop, halt (tr.)			
обстано́вка: furniture; (theatrical) sets, scenery; situation, circumstances			
отста́лый: lagging; backward, retarded		odstálý: jutting, projecting; tepid; stale	
отсто́й: sediment, deposit			
			odstojanje: distance
	odstawa: delivery		
отста́вка: dismissal, discharge;	odstawka: dismissal, discharge;		

[R]	[P]	[Cz]	[S-C]
resignation, retirement	resignation, retirement		
		odstavec: paragraph	
			odustati, odustajati: to refrain, desist; (od + gen.) to renounce, give up
			postati (postanuti), postajati: to become; to arise, emerge
	postać: shape, form; character (in a novel, etc.); (gram.) aspect (of Slavic verb)		
			postojanje: existence
посто́й (arch.): (mil.) billeting	postój: halt, stop; (taxi-) stand; (mil.) billeting	postoj: position, posture; position, attitude, standpoint	
			postaja: (railroad) station
			postojbina: native country; habitat
постоя́лец (arch.): lodger			
постоя́нный: constant, continuous; permanent			postojan: constant, continuous; constant, steadfast, unwavering; permanent
		postavení: position, location; position, standing (in society, etc.); position, post, job; (mil.) position; construction, erection; (lit.) situation	postavljenje: appointment (to office, etc.)
	postawa: position, posture; posi-	postava: figure (shape of body);	postava: lining

	tion, attitude, standpoint; carriage, bearing	character (in a novel, etc.)	
	postawny: stately, imposing		
постáвка: delivery			postavka: premise, assumption; thesis, proposition
постановúть, постановля́ть (постанáвливать): to decide; to decree	postanowić, postanawiać: to decide; to decree		
постанóвщик: theatrical producer			
повстáнец: rebel, insurgent	powstaniec: rebel, insurgent	povstalec: rebel, insurgent	
	pozostać, pozostawać: to stay, remain	pozůstati, pozůstávati (arch.): to stay, remain	
	pozostałość: remainder; estate (of a deceased person)	pozůstalost: estate (of a deceased person)	
		pozůstatek: remainder	
	pozostawić, pozostawiać: to leave, abandon	pozůstaviti, pozůstavovati (arch.): to leave, abandon; to bequeath	
		podstata: substance, essence	
		podstatné (jméno): (gram.) noun, substantive	
подстáва (arch.): relay of horses	podstawa: base, foundation; basis	podstava, podstavec: base, foundation; rest, support	podstava: lining
подстáвка: rest, support	podstawka: rest, support; saucer		
перестáть, переставáть: to stop, cease (doing s.th.)	przestać, przestawać: to stop, cease (doing s.th.); to content oneself (with); (przestawać	přestati, přestávati: to stop, cease (doing s.th.); (lit.) to content oneself (with)	prestati, prestajati: to stop, cease (doing s.th.)
[R]	[P]	[Cz]	[S-C]

[R]	[P]	[Cz]	[S-C]
	only) to associate, consort (with)		
	przestankowanie: punctuation		
преста́виться, представля́ться (arch.): to pass away, die			prestaviti se, prestavljati se: to pass away, die
предста́ть, представа́ть: to appear (before a court, etc.)			predstati, predstajati: to appear (before a court, etc.)
предстоя́щий: forthcoming, approaching			predstojeći: forthcoming, approaching
			predstojnik: chief, director
предста́тельный: (anat.) prostate (a.)		předstojný: (anat.) prostate (a.)	
предста́вить, представля́ть: to present; (представля́ть only) to represent (act as a representative of); (себе́) to imagine; (собо́й; представля́ть only) to represent, constitute, be	przedstawić, przedstawiać: to present; (sobie) to imagine	představiti, představovati: to present; (představovati only) to represent, constitute, be; (představovati only) to represent (act as a representative of); (si) to imagine	predstaviti, predstavljati: to present; (predstavljati only) to represent, constitute, be; (sebi) to imagine
представле́ние: presentation; theatrical performance; notion, idea; request, petition	przedstawienie: presentation; theatrical performance; remonstrance, representation	představení: presentation; theatrical performance	predstavljanje: presentation
		představa: notion, idea	predstava: theatrical performance; notion, idea
			predstavka: request, petition; remonstrance, representation
представи́тель: representative (n.)	przedstawiciel: representative (n.)	představitel: representative (n.); theatrical performer	predstavnik: representative (n.)

[R]	[P]	[Cz]	[S-C]
представи́тельный: representative (a.); stately, imposing			
		představený: chief, superior (n.)	
предоста́вить, предоставля́ть: to grant, accord			
			pretpostaviti, pretpostavljati: to prefer; to assume, postulate
			pretpostavljeni: chief, superior (n.)
	przystać: to be fitting, proper		pristojati se: to be fitting, proper
			pristojba: duty, fee
присто́йный: decent, seemly	przystojny: decent, seemly; handsome		pristojan: decent, seemly; polite
приста́ть, пристава́ть: to stick, adhere; to put in (to shore); (к + dat.) to badger, importune; (приста́ть only) to be fitting, proper	przystać, przystawać: to fit tightly; (do + gen.) to join (army, etc.); to agree, accede (to)	přistati (přistáti), přistávati: to put in (to shore); to land, alight	pristati, pristajati: to fit; to agree, accede (to); (uz + acc.) to adhere (to), espouse; to put in (to shore); (pristajati only) to be fitting, proper
	przystanek: stopping place		pristanak: agreement, consent
при́стань: wharf, pier	przystań: wharf, pier		
приста́нище (coll.): refuge			pristanište: wharf, pier; harbor, port
при́стальный: fixed, intent (gaze, etc.)			
			pristalica, pristaša: adherent, supporter

[R]	[P]	[Cz]	[S-C]
при́став (arch.): police officer		přístav: harbor, port	pristav: assistant judge, assessor
		přístaviště: wharf, pier	
приста́вка: (gram.) prefix	przystawka: side-dish; extension (of a building)	přístavek: extension (of a building); (gram.) apposition	
расста́ться, расстава́ться: to part (with), take leave (of)	rozstać się, rozstawać się: to part (with), take leave (of)		rastati se, rastajati se: to part (with), take leave (of)
расстоя́ние: distance			rastojanje: distance
расста́вить, расставля́ть: to arrange, dispose, distribute; to move apart (tr.)	rozstawić, rozstawiać: to arrange, dispose, distribute; to move apart (tr.)	rozestaviti, rozestavovati: to arrange, dispose, distribute	rastaviti, rastavljati: to separate; to divide; to dismantle; (chem.) to decompose, analyze
			rastava: separation; divorce
			sastati se, sastajati se: to meet
			sustati, sustajati: to become tired
состоя́ть: to consist, reside (in); to consist, be composed (of); to be, act, serve (in some capacity)		sestávati (lit.): to consist, be composed (of)	
*состоя́ться: to take place			sastojati se: to consist, reside (in); to consist, be composed (of)
состоя́ние: state, condition; wealth, fortune			
состоя́тельный: wealthy, affluent; well-founded, valid			

[R]	[P]	[Cz]	[S-C]
составить, составлять: to put together; to put, take down; to make up (a train), compile (a dictionary), draw up (a document), form (an opinion); to be, constitute	zestawić, zestawiać: to put together; to put, take down; to make up (a train), assemble (machinery); to compare	sestaviti, sestavovati: to put together; to arrange; to make up (a train), assemble (machinery), compile (a dictionary), draw up (a document)	sastaviti, sastavljati: to put together; to assemble (machinery), compile (a dictionary), draw up (a document), compose (a letter)
состав: composition, structure, make-up; (chem.) compound; staff, personnel; (railroad) train	zestaw: machine unit	sestava: arrangement; team	sastav: composition, structure, make-up; (chem.) compound
сустав: (anat.) joint		soustava: system	sustav: system
супостат (arch.): enemy			
сопоставить, сопоставлять: to compare			
устать, уставать: to become tired	ustać, ustawać: to stop, halt (intr.); to stop, cease (doing s.th.); (arch.) to become tired	ustati, ustávati: to stop, halt (intr.); to stop, cease (doing s.th.)	
устой: abutment (of a bridge); cream			
устои (pl.): foundations (of society, etc.)			
	ustoiny (pl.): sediment, deposit		
устойчивый: steady; stable			
	ustalić, ustalać: to stabilize; to strengthen, consolidate; to fix, set, establish (a price, date, etc.); to ascer-	ustáliti, ustalovati: to stabilize; (phot.) to fix	ustaliti, ustaljivati: to stabilize; to strengthen, consolidate

	tain, establish (a fact)		
устáв: statutes, articles, charter (of an organization)		ústav: institution, establishment; institute	ustav: constitution (basic law)
	ustawa: law, statute; statutes, articles, charter (of an organization)	ústava: constitution (basic law)	ustava: dam; flood-gate
установи́ть, устанáвливать: to set, mount, install; to establish, institute; to fix, set, establish (a price, date, etc.); to ascertain, establish (a fact)	ustanowić, ustanawiać: to establish, institute; to fix, set, establish (a price, date, etc.); to appoint (to office, etc.); to enact (a law)	ustanoviti, ustanovovati: to establish, institute; to fix, set, establish (a price, date, etc.); to appoint (to office, etc.); to stipulate, provide (by law)	ustanoviti, ustanovljavati (ustanovljivati): to establish, institute; to ascertain, establish (a fact)
	wstawiennictwo: intercession		
	wystawać: to protrude		
	wystarczyć, wystarczać: to suffice	vystačiti, vystačovati: to suffice	
вы́ставка: exhibition, exposition; display-window	wystawa: exhibition, exposition; display-window; pomp, ostentation	výstava, výstavka: exhibition, exposition	
		vyvstati, vyvstávati: to arise, emerge	
встать, вставáть: to rise, get up	wstać, wstawać: to rise, get up	vstáti, vstávati: to rise, get up	ustati (ustanuti), ustajati: to rise, get up; to rise up, rebel
восстáние: uprising, rebellion			ustanak: uprising, rebellion
восстанови́ть, восстанáвливать: to restore, re-establish; to reinstate; to recall, recollect;			
[R]	[P]	[Cz]	[S-C]

to set, incite (against)			
			uspostaviti, uspostavljati: to establish, institute; to restore, re-establish
	zostać, zostawać: to stay, remain; to become; (zostać only) to be (auxiliary verb in passive constructions)	zůstati, zůstávati: to stay, remain	
		zůstatek: remainder	
	zostawić, zostawiać: to leave, abandon	zůstaviti, zůstavovati (lit.): to leave, abandon; to bequeath	
заста́ть, застава́ть: to find (s.o. at home, etc.), catch (unawares, in the act, etc.)	zastać, zastawać: to find (s.o. at home, etc.), catch (unawares, in the act, etc.)	zastati, zastávati: to find (s.o. at home, etc.); to cope with; to relieve, replace (s.o. at work); (zastávati only) to hold (an office, an opinion)	zastati, zastajati: to find (s.o. at home, etc.); to stop, halt (intr.)
		zastánce: supporter, defender, advocate	
засто́й: stagnation, inactivity	zastój: stagnation, inactivity		zastoj: stagnation, inactivity
заста́вить, заставля́ть: to force, compel; to fill, cram; to block, obstruct	zastawić, zastawiać: to fill, cram; to block, obstruct; to set (a table, a trap); to pawn; to mortgage	zastaviti, zastavovati: to stop, halt (tr.); to pawn; to mortgage	
	zastaw: pledge, pawn; mortgage; deposit, security		
заста́ва: toll-gate leading into a town; (mil.) picket, advance detachment	zastawa: barrier; flood-gate; table set, utensils	zástava: pledge, pawn; mortgage; deposit, security; (lit.) banner	zastava: flag; banner
[R]	[P]	[Cz]	[S-C]

[R]	[P]	[Cz]	[S-C]
застáвка: head-piece (in a book)	zastawka: (anat.) valve	zastávka: halt, stop; stopping place zastaveníčko: serenade	
	zastanowić, zastanawiać: to arrest (s.o.'s) attention, astonish; (arch.) to stop, halt (tr.) zastanowić się, zastanawiać się: to reflect, deliberate		
		zaostalý: backward, retarded	zaostao: lagging in arrears; backward, retarded zaustaviti, zaustavljati: to stop, halt (tr.)

NOTES

Basic meaning of root: to stand

Its vast potential for semantic elaboration has made this the most productive of all Slavic word-roots. The tendency to regard "standing" as symbolically expressive of "being" in the broadest sense is apparent in many of the meanings, e.g. "to exist," "to consist (in, of)" (="to derive one's nature or existence from"), "state, condition" (>"wealth," "social class, estate," "profession"), "(political) state." (Compare Sp. estar "to be" [<Lat. stare "to stand"], Eng. exist and consist [ult. <Lat. sistere "to stand"], state and estate [ult. <Lat. stare], Ger. bestehen "to exist; to consist" and Stand "state, condition; social class, estate" [<stehen "to stand"], Hung. állni "to stand; to consist" and [<állni] fennállni "to exist," állapot "state, condition" and állam "[political] state.") Further development of the same idea is reflected in the meanings "to stay, remain" (compare Eng. stay and Fr. rester "to stay" [both ult. <Lat. stare]) and "to dwell, reside" (>"habitat," "village," "camp," "tent," "billet," "lodger," "population"). Стать et al. and their compound formations, which are verbs of motion, often express transition or change rather than a state of being, whence such meanings as "to become," "to begin," "to happen" and (with the addition of a negative prefix) "to disappear"; in some of these words (e.g. достáть et al., настáть et al., пристáть et al., расстáться et al., sastati se), the root-meaning is in effect "to go, move." The idea of standing is

resent in a more literal sense in the meaning "to stop (intr.)" (>"to be-
me tired") and in numerous derivatives reflecting such notions as "to
tand firm" (>"to insist, persist," "to endure," "to defend, uphold," "abut-
ent, foundation," "steady, steadfast, stable," "constant"), "to stand still,
agnate, settle" (>"stale," "tepid," "sediment," "cream"), "that which
tands" (>"machine," "loom," "gun-mount"), "way of standing" (>"position,"
shape, form, figure," "unit of land measurement") and "place for standing"
>"stable, stall," "station," "bar, counter"). (Compare Eng. insist and per-
ist [ult. <Lat. sistere], stable [a. and n.], constant and station [ult.
Lat. stare], stale and stall [akin to stand], Ger. bestehen "to insist,"
eständig "constant" and stetig "constant" [<stehen], Hung. állandó "con-
tant" and állomás "station" [<állni].)

The verbs ста́вить et al., stawiać et al. (<Common Slavic *stavъ; see
ote on staw et al. below) and станови́ться, stanowić-stanoviti (<стан-stan)
re causative, expressing the meaning "to cause to stand," hence variously
to put," "to stop (tr.)," "to build." The first two of these meanings show
xtensive further development: (1) "to put" > "to supply, deliver," "to put
n place, fit" (>"joint"), "to set, fix, lay down" (>"to establish," "to de-
ide," "institution," "constitution," "law, statute") (compare Eng. statute,
nstitution and constitution [ult. <Lat. statuere "to set, put" < stare],
aw [akin to lay], Ger. Gesetz "law" [<setzen "to set, put"]); (2) "to stop"
"to block, obstruct" (>"barrier," "dam," "pond," "valve," "toll-gate,"
military picket") (compare Ger. stauen "to dam up" [<stehen]). In many of
ne causative formations the meaning is actually reflexive or passive, hence
dentical with the basic root-meaning: "to put oneself or be put (in a stand-
ng position)" = "to stand"; this sometimes results in semantic overlapping
ith words formed from the primary verbs (see станови́ться, ста́вка, postawa,
ostava [Cz.], postavení, přístav[iště]).

The two primary verbs denoting respectively rest and motion have coal-
sced as -stać in Polish compounds, which differ only in the conjugational
orms. The first of the two occurs regularly as -státi in Czech, the second
ormally as -stati. (See also note on stanąć-stanouti below.)

The Slavic root is related to Eng. stand, Ger. stehen (>stellen "to
ut"), Lat. stare and sistere, Gr. στῆναι "to stand" and ἱστάναι "to put."

státi-stajati, сто́ить: Compare Eng. cost (ult. <Lat. constare "to be
ixed, definite; to cost" < stare "to stand"); the Russian word is thought
o be based on Pol. stoi "it stands" in the earlier sense of "it costs."

stanąć-stanouti: new infinitives formed from 1 sg. stanę, stanu; com-
are stać się-státi se.

stati (last meaning): See note on státi-stajati, сто́ить.

stavěti (third meaning): originally transitive.

stan (Pol., last meaning): from the earlier meaning "figure (shape of
ody)."

staw et al.: probably postverbal (<stawić et al.) rather than primary although the meanings of the Czech word show the influence of Ger. Stand (see introductory note above) and Bestand "head (of cattle), effective strength, stock on hand" (<bestehen "to exist" < stehen "to stand"); regarding the Serbo-Croatian word, see note on Cz. poloha, Rus. положéние et al. S-C položaj and compare Cz. položka.

стáтный-statný: See стать (n.); the Czech word is borrowed from Russian.

statek (Pol.-Cz.): ="that which stands, i.e. has substance and solidity," hence "property, possessions" (with specialization of meaning in Polish).

стáточный: ="capable of happening"; compare стáться.

stateczny-statečný: <statek (see note); the original meaning of the Czech word was "strong, sturdy."

starczyć-stačiti: for earlier statczyć-statčiti < statek (see note); the basic meaning is "to be strong."

статьá-stať: ="record of an occurrence, piece of information"; see стáться. The Czech word is borrowed from Russian.

stanica (second meaning): an extension of the earlier meaning "small room, (hermit's) cell."

stanovit: ="standing firmly in place, i.e. fixed, definite."

стáя: The word referred originally to an enclosure for domestic animals (compare Cz. stáj, S-C staja), then to the animals themselves, finally to wild animals and even to birds and fish.

stadło: The successive meanings have been "state, condition" > "marital state" > "married couple."

stejný: ="standing fast, unchanging."

stání (second meaning): See the expression státi soudu "to appear before a court."

stójkowy: ="one who stands guard."

стáвка-stawka: See notes on Cz. sazba and S-C kladiti se; the third meaning of the Russian word arose from the earlier meaning "tent."

stavka: ="something which is put down (in a certain sequence)."

stavnja: ="furnishing, providing (of troops)."

stawiennictwo: Compare Cz. dostaviti se.

стáвленник: ="one who is placed"; orig. "candidate for holy orders," today "protégé, one who owes his position to his protector."

gorostas: <gora "mountain" + stas.

jednostajny et al.: ="standing (i.e. existing) in a single manner or form, unchanging and uncomplicated."

кстáти: <к "to" + стать (n.) in the earlier meaning "(suitable) manner, that which is pertinent or timely."

lhostejný: See note under root ЛЕГ$_2$ (etc.).

samostan: See note under root САМ (etc.).

самостоя́тельный et al.: See note under root САМ (etc.).

солнцестоя́ние-*suncostaja*: the time when the sun (*со́лнце*-*sunce*) appears to stand still after reaching the point farthest from the equator; compare Eng. *solstice* (ult. ‹Lat. *sol* "sun" + *stare* "to stand").

stejnokroj: See *stejný*.

stejnoměrný: See *stejný* and note on Rus. *равноме́рный* *et al*.

stejnorodý: See *stejný* and note on S-C *istorodan*, Rus. *одноро́дный* *et al*.

светопреставле́ние: See *преста́виться*.

ustawodawstwo: See *ustawa* and note on Rus. *законода́тельство* *et al*.

vjerodostojan: See *dostojan* and note on Rus. *достове́рный*.

доста́ть-*dostać*-*dostati* (S-C): See note on S-C *stignuti*, *stizati*.

досто́йный *et al*.: ="sufficient, adequate"; the original meaning was that of the Russian and Serbo-Croatian words.

досто́инство *et al*., *dostojność*-*důstojnost*: See *досто́йный* *et al*. and note on Pol. *godność*.

dostaveníčko: See *dostaviti se* and compare Eng. *rendezvous* (‹Fr. *rendez-vous* ‹ *se rendre* "to go, betake oneself" ‹ *se*, refl. pron. + *rendre* "to render, deliver"), Ger. *Stelldichein* "rendezvous" (‹*sich einstellen* "to make an appearance" ‹ *sich*, refl. pron. + *ein*- "in" + *stellen* "to put").

izostaviti: See *ostaviti*.

ispostava: so called because it is "put out" (*i.e*. sent out, detached) from the main office; the word is modeled on (Austrian) Ger. *Expositur* "branch office" (ult. ‹Lat. *ex* "out" + *ponere* "to put").

nastavati: presumed to be an irregular imperfective form of *nastati*, although with a meaning not attested for the perfective verb.

настоя́ть (second meaning): ="to put, *i.e*. pour (on something in order to extract its essence)"; -*стоя́ть* is causative here.

настоя́щий: a Church Slavic loan-word modeled on Gr. *ἐνεστώς* "(standing) close at hand, present" (‹*ἐν* "in, on" + *στῆναι* "to stand"); see also Eng. *(the 10th) instant* (ult. ‹Lat. *in* "in, on" + *stare* "to stand"). Regarding the relationship between the two meanings, compare Fr. *actuel* "actual; present."

настоя́тель: a Church Slavic loan-word modeled on Gr. *ἐπιστάτης* "overseer" (‹*ἐπί* "on, over" + *στῆναι* "to stand").

nastojnik: orig. "one who exerts himself, takes charge"; see *nastojati*.

наставле́ние, *наста́вник*-*nastavnik*: The basic idea is that of "putting (s.o.) on the right path."

nestašan: ="restless, not standing still."

obstojný: See the second meaning of *obstáti*.

обстоя́тельство: one of the set of conditions "standing around" (*i.e*. surrounding) an event; the word is modeled on Fr. *circonstance* (ult. ‹Lat. *circum* "around" + *stare* "to stand") or Ger. *Umstand* "circumstance" (‹*um* "around" + *stehen* "to stand"), which in turn translate Gr. *περίστασις* "circumstance" (‹*περί* "around" + *στῆναι* "to stand"). Compare Pol. *okoliczność* *et al*.

оста́вить et al.: ="to cause to remain"; see *оста́ться et al.*

ostavina, *ostavština*: See note on Pol. *puścizna*.

obstávka: ="stopping, detaining."

обстано́вка: ⟨obs. *обстанови́ть* "to circle, surround (with)."

odstojanje: See note on *расстоя́ние-rastojanje*.

odstavec: ="something set off (or in), indented"; compare Ger. *Absa* "paragraph" (⟨*ab* "off, away" + *setzen* "to set, put"), Pol. *ustęp*.

odustati: Compare Eng. *desist* (ult. ⟨Lat. *de* "off, away" + *sistere* stand").

postavení, *postawa*: See note on Cz. *poloha*, Rus. *положе́ние et al.*, *položaj*.

postavljenje: Compare Ger. *Bestellung* "appointment" (⟨*stellen* "to p

postawny: See the last meaning of *postawa*.

postavka: See note on Cz. *klad*.

постано́вщик: one who "puts on" (stages, arranges) a show.

повста́нец et al.: See *встать-wstać-vstáti* and note on *восста́ние-ust*

pozostać-pozůstati: See note on *zostać-zůstati*.

pozostawić-pozůstaviti: See *pozostać-pozůstati* and note on *оста́вить al.*

podstata: modeled on Lat. *substantia* (⟨*sub* "under" + *stare* "to stan which translates Gr. *ὑπόστασις* "substance, essence" (⟨*ὑποστῆναι* "to exis ⟨ *ὑπό* "under" + *στῆναι* "to stand").

podstatné (*jméno*): modeled on NLat. (*nomen*) *substantivum*; see prece note as well as note on Rus. *и́мя*, Pol. *imię*, Cz. *jméno*.

подста́ва: ⟨*подста́вить* "to put under; to substitute."

przestać-přestati: (1) "To content oneself (with)" = "to stop (at a certain point) and go no further"; (2) "to associate, consort (with)" = stay (with)."

przestankowanie: a system of "stops."

преста́виться-prestaviti se: ="to be transferred, transported (to th other world)."

predstojnik: Compare Ger. *Vorsteher* "chief, director" (⟨*vor* "before front" + *stehen* "to stand").

предста́тельный-předstojný: ="standing in front (of the bladder)"; c pare Eng. *prostate* (ult. ⟨Gr. *πρό* "before, in front" + *στῆναι* "to stand" Ger. *Vorsteherdrüse* "prostate gland" (⟨*vor* "before, in front" + *stehen* " stand" + *Drüse* "gland").

предста́вить et al., *представле́ние et al.*, *představa-predstava*, *preds ka*, *представи́тель et al.*, *представи́тельный*: The various meanings reflect notion of "putting before, presenting," either literally or in the sense "presenting to the mind" (whence the further idea of "presenting" one pe to another by acting as his representative); the second meaning of Rus. *представи́тельный* = "presenting oneself well, presentable." Compare Ger. *vorstellen* "to present; (*sich*, refl. pron.) to imagine" and *Vorstellung* theatrical performance; notion, idea; remonstrance, representation" (<*vor* before, in front" + *stellen* "to put").

představený: See note on Pol. *przełożony*.

предостáвить: See *остáвить*.

pretpostaviti: In its first meaning, the word roughly parallels Eng. *refer* (ult. <Lat. *prae* "before, in front" + *ferre* "to carry"); regarding he second meaning, see note on Rus. *предположи́ть*.

pretpostavljeni: See note on Pol. *przełożony*.

przystać-pristojati se: See note on *присто́йный et al*.

pristojba: <*pristojati se*.

присто́йный et al.: ="standing near," *i.e*. suited (to), fitting; compare er. *anständig* "decent, seemly" (<*an* "at" + *stehen* "to stand").

пристáть-pristati (last meaning): See preceding note.

при́став-pristav: ="one who is assigned or attached."

přístavek (second meaning): a grammatical relationship in which one ord is placed beside another; compare Eng. *apposition* (ult. <Lat. *ad* "at" + onere "to put").

rastati se: <*razstati se*.

расстоя́ние-rastojanje: Compare Eng. *distance* (ult. <Lat. *dis*- "away, part" + *stare* "to stand"), Ger. *Abstand* "distance" (<*ab* "off, away" + *stehn* "to stand"), Pol. *odstęp*, Cz. *odstup*; the Russian word is borrowed from hurch Slavic, the Serbo-Croatian word (<earlier *razstojanje*) from Russian.

rastaviti, *rastava*: <*razstaviti*, *razstava*.

состáв-sastav: See note on Rus. *сложи́ться et al*., *слагáться*, *сложéние*, ложённый *et al*., *слог* and *сло́жный*, Cz. *složení*, *sloh*, *sloha*, *složka* and ložitý, S-C *slagati se*, *slog*, *sloga*, *složan*, *slagar* and *slagalište*.

soustava-sustav: Compare Eng. *system* (ult. <Gr. *σύν* "with, together" + *στάναι* "to put"); the Serbo-Croatian word is borrowed from Czech.

супостáт: ="one who stands with (*i.e*. faces, confronts) another"; the ord is a Church Slavic borrowing.

ustalić et al.: <*stały et al*.

ustanoviti (S-C): <Rus. *установи́ть* or Cz. *ustanoviti*.

wstawiennictwo: Compare Ger. *sich einsetzen* "to intercede (on s.o.'s ehalf)" (<*sich*, refl. pron. + *ein*- "in" + *setzen* "to set, put").

вы́ставка et al.: See notes on S-C *izložba* and on Rus. *выклáдывать et* l., Pol. *wykład*, Cz. *výklad*.

встать et al.: <Common Slavic **vъzstati*.

восстáние-ustanak: Compare Ger. *Aufstand* "uprising, rebellion" (<*auf* 'up" + *stehen* "to stand").

zostać-zůstati: <*z*- + *ostać* (obs.) "to stay, remain," *ostati*.

zostawić-zůstaviti: See *zostać-zůstati* and note on *остáвить et al*.

застáть et al.: In the meaning "to find, catch," these verbs have the ausative force of "to stop, halt"; the other transitive meanings can be exlained as "to stand up to, stand the test of" (="to cope with"), "to stand in for" (="to relieve, replace"), "to stand in, i.e. occupy" (an office), "to stand (up) for" (a point of view, opinion).

zastawić-zastaviti, zastaw, zástava-zastava: See note on Rus. зало́г an зало́жник, S-C zalog and zaloga; the meaning "flag, banner" = "thing which i fixed, planted (in the ground)."

заста́вка: orig. "shield, screen."

zastaveníčko: ="a stop, i.e. visit (beneath a window)"; compare Ger. Ständchen "serenade" (<stehen "to stand").

zastanowić się: ="to stop, linger."

СТИ(Г)	ŚCIG	STIH, STÍH, STIŽ	STI(G), STIZ
	*ścignąć (arch.): to overtake	*stihnouti: to find (s.o. at home, etc.); to catch (a train); to befall (misfortune, etc.)	*stignuti (stići): to arrive; to overtake; to befall (misfortune, etc.); to suffice
	ścigać: to pursue; to prosecute	stíhati: to pursue; to prosecute; to befall (misfortune, etc.)	stizati: to arrive; to overtake; to befall (misfortune, etc.); to suffice
		stíhačka: fighter-plane	
дости́гнуть (дости́чь), достига́ть: to reach; to attain, achieve	doścignąć, dościgać: to overtake	dostihnouti, dostihovati: to overtake; to reach; to attain, achieve	dostignuti (dostići), dostizati: to overtake; to suffice
		dostihy (pl.): race	
насти́гнуть (насти́чь), настига́ть: to overtake			
пости́гнуть (пости́чь), постига́ть: to grasp, comprehend; to befall (misfortune, etc.)		postihnouti, postihovati: to grasp, comprehend; to befall (misfortune, etc.)	postignuti (postići), postizati: to attain, achieve
	pościgowiec: fighter-plane		
		přistihnouti, přistihovati: to catch (unawares, in the act, etc.)	pristignuti (pristići), pristizati: to arrive
[R]	[P]	[Cz]	[S-C]

[R]	[P]	[Cz]	[S-C]
	wyścignąć, wyścigać (arch.): to outstrip	vystihnouti, vystihovati: to grasp, comprehend; to depict accurately	
	wyścig: race; contest	výstižný: accurate, true to life	
застúгнуть (застúчь), застигáть: to catch (unawares, in the act, etc.)		zastihnouti, zastihovati: to find (s.o. at home, etc.); to overtake	

NOTES

asic meaning of root: to reach, overtake

All the Russian derivatives are of Church Slavic origin. ORus. стичи to overtake" does not survive in the modern language.

stignuti, stizati: Regarding the last meaning, compare Ger. langen "to each; to grasp; to suffice" and reichen "to reach; to suffice," Rus. хватгь, хватáть and достáть, Pol. dostać, S-C dostati.

ścigać-stíhati: See note on Rus. преслéдовать et al.

dostignuti (second meaning): See note on stignuti, stizati.

постúгнуть-postihnouti, vystihnouti: See note on Rus. поня́ть et al. and онятие, Pol. pojęcie, Cz. ponětí, pojetí and pojem, S-C pojam.

СТЕР, СТИР, СТОР, (СТОРОН), (СТРАН)	STRZ, ŚCIER, STWÓR, STWORZ, (STRZEN), (STRZEŃ), (STRON), (STROŃ)	STŘ, STÍR, STĚR, STOR, (STRAN), (STRÁN), (STRAŇ), (STRÁŇ)	STR, STIR, STER, STOR, (STRAN)
		stříti (arch.): to spread (tr.)	sterati: to spread (tr.); to make (a bed)
сторонá: side; party (to an agreement, in a lawsuit); land, region	strona: side; party (to an agreement, in a lawsuit); land, region; page; (gram.) voice	strana: side; party (to an agreement, in a lawsuit); political party; page	strana: side; party (to an agreement, in a lawsuit); land, region; page
[R]	[P]	[Cz]	[S-C]

[R]	[P]	[Cz]	[S-C]
страна́: country (national entity); land, region			
страни́ца: page	stronica: page		stranica: page
		stránka: page; side, aspect	stranka: party (to an agreement, in a lawsuit); political party
	stronnictwo: political party	stranictví: (political) party spirit, partisanship	
сторо́нний (arch.): outside, alien	stronny: partial, biased		stran: foreign
стра́нный: strange, odd			
сторо́нник: adherent, supporter, partisan	stronnik: adherent, supporter, partisan	straník: (political) party member	
стра́нник: wanderer			
	stronniczy: partial, biased	stranický: partial, biased; (political) party (attr.)	
		stráň: slope, hillside	
		stran: about, concerning	
	stronić (od + gen.): to shun, avoid	straniti: to side (with s.o.)	
сторони́ться: to stand aside; to shun, avoid		straniti se: to shun, avoid	
чужестра́нец (arch.): foreigner			
иностра́нец: foreigner			inostranac: foreigner
			nastran: strange, odd
отстрани́ть, отстраня́ть: to remove; to dismiss, discharge		odstraniti, odstraňovati: to remove; to eliminate	odstraniti, odstranjivati: to remove; to eliminate; to dismiss, discharge

[R]	[P]	[Cz]	[S-C]
посторо́нний: outside, alien	postronny: outside, alien; adjacent	postranní: side (attr.), lateral	postran: side (attr.), lateral
		předstírání: pretense, sham	
			pristran: partial, biased
простере́ть, простира́ть: to stretch out, extend (e.g. one's hand)		prostříti, prostírati: to spread (tr.); to set (a table)	prostrijeti (prostrti), prostirati: to spread (tr.); to make (a bed), set (a table)
	prześcieradło: bedsheet	prostěradlo: bedsheet	
просто́р: broad expanse; elbow-room, leeway	przestworze, przestwór: broad expanse	prostor, prostora: space, room	prostor: space, room
			prostorija: premises, accommodation
простра́нный: extensive, vast; verbose	przestronny: spacious, roomy	prostranný: spacious, roomy	prostran: spacious, roomy
простра́нство: space, room	przestrzeń: space, room	prostranství: space, room	prostranstvo: spaciousness, roominess
распростере́ть, распростира́ть: to spread (tr.)	rozpostrzeć, rozpościerać: to spread (tr.)	rozprostříti, rozprostírati: to spread (tr.)	rasprostrijeti (rasprostrti), rasprostirati: to spread (tr.)
распространи́ть, распространя́ть: to spread, diffuse (e.g. an odor); to disseminate, propagate (e.g. ideas); to extend, widen (e.g. the application of a law)	rozprzestrzenić, rozprzestrzeniać: to spread (tr.); to disseminate, propagate (e.g. ideas)		rasprostraniti, rasprostranjivati: to spread (tr.); to disseminate, propagate (e.g. ideas)
	ustronie, ustroń: secluded spot; seclusion	ústraní: secluded spot; seclusion	
устрани́ть, устраня́ть: to remove; to eliminate; to dismiss, discharge			
		zastříti, zastírati: to cover, veil;	zastrijeti (zastrti), zastirati:
[R]	[P]	[Cz]	[S-C]

[R]	[P]	[Cz]	[S-C]
		to conceal, disguise zástěra: apron; (arch.) pretext	to cover, veil to hang with curtains zastor: curtain zastraniti, zastranjivati: to swerve, turn aside; to deviate; to digress

NOTES

Basic meaning of root: to spread

The primary verbal derivative occurs chiefly in combination with prefixes in the modern languages.

A widely represented secondary meaning, reflected for the most part in words containing the suffixed forms СТОРОН-СТРАН---STRZEN-STRZEŃ-STRON-STRO---STRAN-STRÁN-STRAŇ-STRÁŇ---STRAN, is "space, region, country" (i.e. "that which is spread out") and, by extension, "side." An outgrowth of the meaning "side" is the further notion "alien, foreign" (i.e. "to one side, on the other side"). (See, however, notes on стра́нный and чужестра́нец, иностра́нец-inostranac.)

The Russian form СТРАН is of Church Slavic origin.

Non-Slavic cognates are Eng. strew, Lat. sternere (past part. stratus) "to spread; to pave" (>Eng. street, stratum).

stříti-sterati: The Serbo-Croatian word is the iterative form of obsolete strijeti; the simple verb is not attested in Russian or Polish.

strona et al., страни́ца et al., stránka-stranka, stronnictwo: Regarding the meaning "page," compare Ger. Seite "side; page"; regarding the meaning "political party," compare Fin. puolue "political party" (<puoli "side").

страна́: orig. also "side."

stronny, сторо́нник-stronnik, stronniczy-stranický: The idea is that of "taking someone's side or part"; compare Eng. partial, partisan (both ult. <Lat. pars "part").

стра́нный: orig. "foreign" (<страна́ in the earlier sense of "foreign country"); compare Eng. strange (ult. <Lat. extraneus "foreign").

стра́нник: <страна́.

stran: <strany < *sstrany "from the side (of)."

stronić, сторони́ться-straniti se: Compare Pol. boczyć się.

чужестра́нец, иностра́нец-inostranac: See страна́ and the third meaning of S-C strana; the first element in чужестра́нец is from чужо́й "alien, foreign."

nastran: ="off to one side," hence aberrant, abnormal; unlike стра́нный he word is not attested in an earlier meaning "foreign."

отстранить et al.: Compare Ger. beseitigen "to remove; to eliminate" ‹Seite "side").

předstírání: ="(act of) spreading s.th. before s.o., i.e. presenting it with intent to deceive)"; compare Eng. pretense (ult. ‹Lat. prae "before, n front" + tendere "to stretch out, extend").

pristran: See note on stronny, сторонник-stronnik, stronniczy-stranický.

przestworze-przestwór: ‹*przestor.

ustronie et al.: Compare Pol. ubocze.

устранить: See note on отстранить et al.

zastříti-zastrijeti, zástěra-zastor: The idea is that of "spreading across," hence covering or concealing.

zastraniti: Compare Pol. zboczyć, Cz. vybočiti and zabočiti.

СТРА(Д)	STRAD	STRÁD, STRA	STRA(D)
страдать: to suffer		strádati: to suffer; to suffer privation, be in need	stradati, stradavati: to suffer; to suffer a loss
страсть: passion		strast: suffering, affliction	strast: passion
страдательный: (gram.) passive			
любострастие (arch.): lust, carnality			
подобострастие: servility, obsequiousness			
сладострастие: lust, carnality			sladostrašće: lust, carnality
*пострадать: to suffer	*postradać: to lose	postrádati: to lack; to miss, feel the need of	*postradati: to suffer a mishap, injury
пристрастный: partial, biased			pristrastan: partial, biased
сострадание: compassion, sympathy		soustrast: compassion, sympathy	
[R]	[P]	[Cz]	[S-C]

NOTES

Basic meaning of root: to suffer

The forms СТРАСТ---STRAST---STRAST-STRAŠĆ are derived from страсть et al. (See note.)

страда́ть et al.: Pol. stradać "to lose" is obsolete.

страсть et al.: ⟨Common Slavic *stradtь. The Russian and Serbo-Croati words were originally synonymous with Cz. strast; the notion that passion essentially a form of suffering, i.e. intense feeling, is apparent also in Gr. πάθος "suffering; passion" (⟨πάσχειν "to suffer"), which influenced La passio "suffering; passion" (⟨pati "to suffer") and, ultimately, Ger. Leidenschaft "passion" (⟨leiden "to suffer").

страда́тельный: The passive voice indicates that the subject, instead acting, is "suffering" the action denoted by the verb; the Russian word is modeled on Lat. passivus "passive" (⟨pati "to suffer") and Gr. παθητικός "passive" (⟨πάσχειν "to suffer").

подобостра́стие: orig. "similarity in one's passions," later "a strivi to be similar, to please."

сладостра́стие-sladostrašće: The first element is from сла́дкий-sladak "sweet"; the Serbo-Croatian word is borrowed from Russian.

пристра́стный-pristrastan: ="passionate (in s.o.'s favor)"; compare En dispassionate. The Serbo-Croatian word is borrowed from Russian.

сострада́ние-soustrast: The Russian word is a Church Slavic borrowing modeled on Gr. συμπάθεια "sympathy" (⟨σύν "with" + πάθος "suffering"), the Czech word a loan-translation of Ger. Mitleid "sympathy" (⟨mit "with" + leiden "to suffer"); compare Eng. compassion (ult. ⟨Lat. cum "with" + pass "suffering") and condolence (ult. ⟨Lat. cum + dolere "to suffer pain"), Ru соболе́знование "condolence" (⟨с + боль "pain"). See also Rus. сочу́вствие, Pol. współczucie.

СТЕРЕ(Г), СТОРОЖ, СТОРАЖ, СТРАЖ	STRZE(G), STRZEŻ, STRÓŻ, STROŻ, STRAŻ	STŘÍ(H), STŘEH, STRAH, STRAŽ, STRÁŽ	STRAŽ
стере́чь: to guard, protect; to lie in wait for стере́чься (coll.): to beware, be careful [R]	strzec: to guard, protect strzec się: to beware, be careful [P]	stříci (lit.): to guard, protect stříci se (lit.): to beware, be careful [Cz]	 [S-C]

[R]	[P]	[Cz]	[S-C]
сто́рож: guard, watchman	stróż: guard, watchman	stráž: guard, watch (activity); guard (body of men); guard, watchman	
страж: guard, watchman	straż: guard, watch (activity); guard (body of men)		
стра́жа: guard, watch (activity); (arch.) guard (body of men)			straža: guard, watch (activity); guard (body of men)
	dostrzec, dostrzegać: to notice		
		nástraha: bait; trap, snare	
насторожи́ться, насторáживаться: to prick up one's ears		nastražiti se, nastražovati se: to prick up one's ears	
остере́чь, остерега́ть: to warn	ostrzec, ostrzegać: to warn	ostříhati (lit.): to guard, protect	
остере́чься, остерега́ться: to beware, be careful			
осторо́жный: cautious, careful	ostrożny: cautious, careful	ostražitý: vigilant	
	postrzec, postrzegać: to notice	postřehnouti, postřehovati: to notice	
предостере́чь, предостерега́ть: to warn			
	przestrzec, przestrzegać: to warn; to observe (e.g. a law)		
	spostrzec, spostrzegać: to notice		
	wystrzec się, wystrzegać się: to avoid, shun	vystříhati se: to avoid, shun	
		výstraha: warning	
	zastrzeżenie: reservation, proviso		
[R]	[P]	[Cz]	[S-C]

NOTES

Basic meaning of root: to watch, guard, be careful

The modern root-forms are descended from two Common Slavic forms with differing vowel grades, *STERG (>СТЕРЕГ---STRZEG-STRZEŻ---STŘÍH-STŘEH) and *STORG (>СТОРОЖ-СТОРАЖ-СТРАЖ---STRÓŻ-STROŻ-STRAŻ---STRAH-STRAŽ-STRÁŽ---STRA

The Russian root-form СТРАЖ is of Church Slavic origin.

стере́чь et al.: The respective 1 sg. forms are стерегу́, strzegę, stře S-C strijeći "to guard" is obsolete.

straż: prob. <Cz. stráž.

СТРОЙ, СТРО(И, -Е), СТРА(И)	STRÓJ, STROJ, STRO(I), STRAJ	STROJ	STROJ, ŠTROJ
стро́ить: to build; (mil.) to form, draw up (troops)	stroić: to array (in fine clothes); to tune (an instrument); to crack (a joke), pull (a face), play (a trick)	strojiti: to clothe, dress; to prepare; to arrange, organize	strojiti: (mil.) to form draw up (troops); to tan (leather); to geld, castrate štrojiti: to geld, castrate
		strojený: affected, mannered	
строй: (social, political) order, system; (mus.) pitch, tune; (mil.) formation; (working) order, operation, service	strój: dress, attire; (mus.) pitch, tune	stroj: machine	stroj: machine; (mil.) rank, file; tanning (of leather)
стро́йный: shapely, well-proportioned; orderly; harmonious	strojny: well dressed, chic; (arch.) harmonious		
	drobnoustrój: micro-organism		
настрое́ние: mood, frame of mind	nastrojenie: tuning (of an instrument)		
настро́йка: tuning (of an instrument)	nastrój: mood, frame of mind	nástroj: implement, tool; (musical) instrument postroj: harness	nastroj: mood, frame of mind
[R]	[P]	[Cz]	[S-C]

[R]	[P]	[Cz]	[S-C]
		přístroj: instrument, appliance	
расстро́ить, расстра́ивать: to disturb, upset, disorganize; to put (an instrument) out of tune	rozstroić, rozstrajać: to disturb, upset, disorganize; to put (an instrument) out of tune		*rastrojiti: to disturb, upset, disorganize; to put (an instrument) out of tune
	zestroić, zestrajać: to attune	sestrojiti, sestrojovati: to build	
устро́ить, устра́ивать: to arrange, organize; to suit, be convenient for	ustroić, ustrajać: to array (in fine clothes)	ustrojiti, ustrojovati: to clothe, dress	ustrojiti, ustrojavati: to arrange, organize; to tan (leather); to geld, castrate
	ustrój: organism; (social, political) order, system	ústroj: dress, attire; (arch., anat.) organ	ustroj: structure
		ústrojí: (digestive, etc.) system, organs; mechanism; (lit.) (social, political) order, system	
		výstroj: equipment, gear	

NOTES

Basic meaning of root: to arrange, put in order

строить et al.: denominatives formed from строй et al.

strojiti (S-C, third meaning), štrojiti: at first presumably a euphemistic use; compare such English expressions as to have a cat fixed.

drobnoustrój: The first element is from drobny "small"; see ustrój and compare Eng. micro-organism (micro- < Gr. μικρός "small").

rastrojiti: for *razstrojiti.

устро́ить (second meaning): Compare the use of Fr. arranger "to arrange" in the sense of "to suit."

ustrojiti (S-C, third meaning): See note on strojiti, štrojiti.

СТУП	STĄP, STĘP	STUP, STOUP	STUP
ступи́ть, ступа́ть: to step	stąpić (stąpnąć), stąpać: to step	stoupnouti, stoupati: to step; to rise	stupiti, stupati: to step; (u, na + acc.) to enter (a relationship, school, military service, etc.)
ступня́: foot; sole of the foot			
			stupica: trap
		stoupenec: adherent, supporter	
ступе́нь: step (in a staircase); stage (of development, etc.)		stupeň: step (in a staircase); degree, extent; (math., geog.) degree; stage (of development, etc.)	stupanj: step (in a staircase); degree, extent; (math., geog.) degree; stage (of development, etc.)
		stupnice: (musical, wage, thermometer, etc.) scale; (radio) dial	
клятвопреступле́ние (lit.): perjury			
	Wniebowstąpienie: (rel.) Ascension	Nanebevstoupení: (rel.) Ascension	
досту́пный: accessible	dostępny: accessible	dostupný: accessible	dostupan: accessible
			istupiti, istupati: to step out, forth; to appear, make an appearance; to withdraw (intr.)
			istup: withdrawal; offense, transgression
исступле́ние: frenzy			
наступи́ть, наступа́ть: to step (on); to arrive (e.g. a certain	nastąpić, następować: to step (on); to follow; to take place;	nastoupiti, nastupovati: to start (tr.); (do + gen.) to board (e.g. a	nastupiti, nastupati: to arrive (e.g. a certai time); to ap-
[R]	[P]	[Cz]	[S-C]

[R]	[P]	[Cz]	[S-C]
time); (наступ-áть only; mil.) to advance, be on the offensive	to arrive (e.g. a certain time)	train); to set out upon (a journey); to enter upon (duties); to line up, form ranks	pear (on the stage, etc.); to enter upon (duties)
		nástup: boarding (e.g. of a train); act of entering upon (duties); (mil.) parade, assembly	nastup: (med.) fit, attack; fit (of anger, etc.); appear-ance (on the stage, etc.); act of entering upon (duties)
	następca: successor; heir	nástupce: successor	
	następny: next	nástupní: inaugural (speech, etc.); starting (date, etc.)	nastupni: inaugural (speech, etc.); intermittent (fever)
	następstwo: consequence; succession, sequence		
		nástupiště: platform (in railroad station)	
неотсту́пный: persistent, importunate	nieodstępny: inseparable (e.g. friends)		
обступи́ть, обступа́ть: to surround	obstąpić, obstępować: to surround	obstoupiti, obstupovati: to surround	
	ostępy (pl.): dense forest		
отступи́ть, отступа́ть: to step back; to retreat; to deviate; to digress	odstąpić, odstępować: to step back; to deviate; to digress; to cede, yield; to abandon	odstoupiti, odstupovati: to step back; to withdraw (intr.); to resign; to cede, yield	odstupiti, odstupati: to withdraw (intr.); to resign; to retreat; to deviate; to cede, yield
о́тступ: indentation (at beginning of paragraph)	odstęp: interval; distance; indentation (at beginning of paragraph)	odstup: cession; interval; distance	odstup: withdrawal; resignation; retreat; cession
отсту́пник: renegade, apostate	odstępca: renegade, apostate		
поступи́ть, поступа́ть: to act, behave, proceed; (с +	postąpić, postępować: to move forward; to advance,	postoupiti, postupovati: to move forward; to advance,	postupiti, postupati: to act, behave, proceed; (s +

inst.) to treat, behave (toward); (в, на + acc.) to enter (a school, military service, etc.); to be received (e.g. contributions, applications)	progress; to act, behave, proceed; (z + inst.) to treat, behave (toward)	progress; to cede, yield; (postupovati only) to act, behave, proceed	inst.) to treat, behave (toward)
поступи́ться, поступа́ться: to renounce, give up			
по́ступь: gait, pace	postęp: progress; (math.) progression	postup: forward movement, advance; progress; process; procedure, method; cession	
посту́пок: deed, act	postępek: deed, act		postupak: procedure, method; behavior, conduct; (legal) proceedings
поступа́тельный: forward (-moving)	postępowy: progressive, forward-looking; progressive, gradual	postupný: progressive, gradual; successive	postupan: progressive, gradual
подступи́ть, подступа́ть (к + dat.): to approach	podstąpić, podstępować (pod + acc.): to approach	podstoupiti, podstupovati: to be subjected to, undergo	
по́дступ: approach; (avenue of) approach	podstęp: trick, stratagem, deceit; (arch.) approach		
престу́пник: criminal (n.)	przestępca: criminal (n.)	přestupník: violator (of a law, etc.)	prestupnik: violator (of a law, etc.)
престу́пный: criminal (a.)	przestępny: criminal (a.); bissextile, leap-(year)	přestupný: bissextile, leap-(year)	prestupni, prijestupni: criminal (a.); bissextile, leap-(year)
приступи́ть, приступа́ть (к + dat.): to set about (a task); (arch.) to approach	przystąpić, przystępować (do + gen.): to approach; to set about (a task); to join (an organization)	přistoupiti, přistupovati: (k + dat.) to approach; (do + gen.) to board (e.g. a train); (k + dat.) to set	pristupiti, pristupati: to approach; to set about (a task); to join (an organization)
[R]	[P]	[Cz]	[S-C]

[R]	[P]	[Cz]	[S-C]
		about (a task); to agree, consent; (do + gen.) to join (an organization)	
при́ступ: (mil.) assault, storm; (med.) fit, attack; fit (of anger, etc.)	przystęp: access, admittance; fit (of anger, etc.)	přístup: access, admittance; (avenue of) approach	pristup: access, admittance; (avenue of) approach; (act of) joining (an organization); introduction, prologue
проступи́ть, проступа́ть: to ooze; to show through		prostoupiti, prostupovati: to pervade	
просту́пок: offense, transgression			
уступи́ть, уступа́ть: to cede, yield; to yield, submit; to be inferior (to)	ustąpić, ustępować: to cede, yield; to yield, submit; to be inferior (to); to withdraw (intr.); to resign	ustoupiti, ustupovati: to step back; to retreat; to withdraw (intr.); to yield, submit	ustupiti, ustupati: to cede, yield; to yield, submit; to be inferior (to); to withdraw (intr.)
усту́п: ledge	ustęp: lavatory, toilet; paragraph; passage (in a book, etc.)	ústup: retreat; withdrawal	ustup: cession
вступи́ть, вступа́ть (в + acc.): to enter	wstąpić, wstępować (do + gen., w + acc.): to enter	vstoupiti, vstupovati (do + gen., v + acc.): to enter	
вступи́тельный: introductory; entrance (fee, examination, etc.)	wstępny: introductory; preliminary	vstupní: introductory	
вы́ступить, выступа́ть: to step out, forth; to depart, set out; to appear (on the stage, etc.), speak (at a meeting); to come out, take a stand (for or against s.th.); (выступа́ть only)	wystąpić, występować: to step out, forth; to appear, make an appearance; to appear (on the stage, etc.); to come out, take a stand (for or against s.th.); (występować only) to pro-	vystoupiti, vystupovati: to step out, forth; to rise; to appear (on the stage, etc.), speak (at a meeting); to come out, take a stand (for or against s.th.); (vystupovati only) to behave,	

to project, protrude	ject, protrude; to withdraw (intr.)	conduct oneself; (vystupovati only) to project, protrude; to withdraw (intr.)	
выступ: projection (from wall, etc.)	występ: projection (from wall, etc.); appearance (on the stage, etc.)	výstup: ascent; departure; scene (part of a play); (unpleasant) scene, row	
	występek: offense, transgression	výstupek: projection (from wall, etc.)	
		vzestup: rise, increase	
заступи́ть, заступа́ть (coll.): to replace	zastąpić, zastępować: to replace; to represent (act as a representative of); to block, obstruct	zastoupiti, zastupovati: to replace; to represent (act as a representative of); to block, obstruct	zastupiti, zastupati: to replace; to represent (act as a representative of); (arch.) to block, obstruct
заступи́ться, заступа́ться: to intercede (for)		zastupovati se (arch.): to intercede (for)	
за́ступ: spade	zastęp: (heavenly, etc.) host; regiment	zástup: crowd, throng	
[R]	[P]	[Cz]	[S-C]

NOTES

Basic meaning of root: to step

In many derivatives with abstract meanings, the root has the force of "to go."

A non-Slavic cognate is Eng. stamp.

stupica: ="that which is stepped into or upon"; compare Eng. trap (akin to tramp, Ger. Treppe "stairs").

stoupenec: one who keeps pace with, follows in the footsteps of, another.

ступе́нь et al.: Compare Eng. degree (ult. <Lat. gradi "to step"), Ger. Stufe "step; degree, extent; stage."

stupnice: Compare stupeň.

клятвопреступле́ние: The first element is from кля́тва "oath"; see престу́пник below.

Wniebowstąpienie-Nanebevstoupení: The second element is from niebo-nebe "sky; heaven."

достýпный et al.: Compare Eng. *accessible* (ult. ‹Lat. *ad* "to" + *cedere* "to go").

istupiti: ‹*izstupiti*; see note on *вы́ступить et al.*

istup: ‹*izstup*; see note on *występek*.

исступлéние: ="(act of) stepping or going out (of one's mind)"; compare Eng. *ecstasy* (ult. ‹Gr. *ἔκστασις* "[state of] being put out [of one's mind]" ‹ *ἐκ* "out" + *ἱστάναι* "to put") and *beside oneself* (*with rage*, etc.), Ger. *ausser sich* "beside oneself" (literally, "outside oneself"). The word is borrowed from Church Slavic.

nastoupiti-*nastupiti*: A number of the meanings reflect semantic borrowing from Ger. *antreten* "to start (tr.); to set out upon (a journey); to enter upon (duties); to line up, form ranks" (‹*an* "to, on" + *treten* "to step").

nastup: See note on *при́ступ et al.*

następca-*nástupce*, *następny*: See the second meaning of *nastąpić* and the fourth meaning of *nastoupiti*.

nastupni (second meaning): See the first meaning of *nastup*.

następstwo: See the second meaning of *nastąpić* and compare Eng. *consequence* and *sequence* (both ult. ‹Lat. *sequi* "to follow"), Ger. *Folge* "consequence; succession, sequence" (‹*folgen* "to follow").

nástupiště: See the second meaning of *nastoupiti*.

ostępy: for earlier *obstępy*, the reference being to thick growth which surrounds one on all sides; see *obstąpić*.

отступи́ть et al.: Compare Eng. *digress* (ult. ‹Lat. *dis*- "off, away" + *gradi* "to step") and *cede* (ult. ‹Lat. *cedere* "to go; to yield"), Ger. *abtreten* "to cede" (‹*ab* "off, away" + *treten* "to step").

odstęp-*odstup* (Cz.): See note on Rus. *расстоя́ние*, S-C *rastojanje*.

отстýпник-*odstępca*: Compare Eng. *apostate* (ult. ‹Gr. *ἀπό* "off, away" + *στῆναι* "to stand").

поступи́ть et al., *поступи́ться*, *postęp*-*postup*, *postupak*, *postępowy et al.*: Compare Eng. *proceed*, *process* and *procedure* (all ult. ‹Lat. *pro*- "forward" + *cedere* "to go"), *progress*, *progression* and *progressive* (all ult. ‹Lat. *pro*- + *gradi* "to step"), *gradual* (ult. ‹Lat. *gradi*), Ger. *Vorgang* "process" (‹*vor* "before, in front" + *Gang* "[act of] going"), *Verfahren* "process; procedure; (legal) proceedings" (‹*fahren* "to go"), *Fortschritt* "progress" (‹*fort* "forward; away" + *schreiten* "to step"); regarding the meanings "to cede, yield," "cession" and "to renounce, give up," see note on *отступи́ть et al.*

podstoupiti: Compare Eng. *undergo*.

престýпник et al., *престýпный et al.*: Compare Eng. *transgression* (ult. ‹Lat. *trans* "over, across" + *gradi* "to step"), Ger. *Übertretung* "offense, transgression" (‹*über* "over, across" + *treten* "to step"), and see note on *występek*. The English and Slavic words for "leap-year" reflect the fact that, in a leap-year, any given date after February 29 "leaps (or steps) over" the day of the week on which it would have fallen in an ordinary year

přistoupiti (fourth meaning): Compare Eng. *accede* (ult. <Lat. *ad* "to" *cedere* "to go"), Ger. *beitreten* "to agree" (<*bei* "near, by" + *treten* "to step"), Hung. *hozzájárulni* "to agree" (<*hozzá*- "to" + *járulni* "to approach" < *járni* "to go").

при́ступ et al.: Compare Eng. *access* (ult. <Lat. *ad* "to" + *cedere* "to go"), which can also mean "fit (of disease, anger, etc.)."

prostoupiti: Compare Eng. *pervade* (ult. <Lat. *per* "through" + *vadere* "to go").

просту́пок: See note on *престу́пник et al.*, *престу́пный et al.*

уступи́ть et al.: See note on *отступи́ть et al.*

усту́п: Compare Eng. *recess* (ult. <Lat. *re*- "back" + *cedere* "to go").

ustęp: A comparable notion of a lavatory as a place to which one withdraws is reflected in Ger. *Abtritt* "lavatory" (<*ab* "off, away" + *treten* "to step"), Pol. *wychodek*, Cz. *záchod*, S-C *zahod*; regarding the meaning "paragraph" (and, by extension, "passage"), see note on Cz. *odstavec*.

вы́ступить et al.: The basic notion of stepping out has given rise to the contrasting meanings "to come forward, appear" and "to withdraw"; regaring the meaning "to project, protrude," compare Eng. *to stand out* and *process* (ult. <Lat. *pro*- "forward" + *cedere* "to go") in the anatomical sense o "projecting part, protuberance."

výstup: Compare Ger. *Auftritt* "scene (part of a play); scene, row" (<*a* "up" + *treten* "to step").

występek: Compare Eng. *excess* (ult. <Lat. *ex* "out" + *cedere* "to go") i the sense of "outrageous act," Ger. *Ausschreitung* "outrage, excess" (<*aus* "out" + *schreiten* "to step"), and see note on *престу́пник et al.*, *престу́пный et al.*

заступи́ть et al.: ="to step into (=take) the place of (*i.e.* replace, represent)" and "to step in the way of (*i.e.* block, obstruct)"; the words reflect semantic borrowing from Ger. *vertreten* "to replace; to represent; t block, obstruct" (<*treten* "to step").

заступи́ться–zastupovati se: Compare Eng. *intercede* (ult. <Lat. *inter* "between" + *cedere* "to go").

zastęp–zástup: orig. "act of stepping or going," then "people who are stepping or going, *i.e.* a crowd"; comparable semantic development is shown by Eng. *gang*, which originally meant "act of going."

СЫП, СП, СОП	SU, SYP, SP, SEP	SOU, SU, SYP, SP, SEP, SOP	SU, SIP, SP, SAP
	suć (arch.): to pour, strew (a dry substance)	souti (arch.): to pour, strew (a dry substance)	
сы́пать: to pour, strew (a dry substance)	sypać: to pour, strew (a dry substance)	sypati: to pour, strew (a dry substance)	sipati: to pour, strew (a dry substance); to pour (a liquid)
	suty: plentiful, abundant		
		sutiny (pl.): ruins	
сыпь: (med.) rash, eruption			sip: embankment
			sipina: sand-dune
со́пка: hill, knoll; volcano		sopka: volcano	
	półwysep: peninsula		
на́сыпь: embankment	nasyp: embankment	násep, násyp: embankment	nasip: embankment
	osutka: (med.) rash, eruption	osutiny (pl., arch.): (med.) rash, eruption	
о́сыпь: fallen rock, talus			osip: (med.) rash, eruption
	osypka: mash (fodder for livestock)	osypky (pl.): measles	
	osypisko: landslide; fallen rock, talus		
о́спа: smallpox	ospa: smallpox		ospe (pl.): (med.) rash, eruption
			ospice (pl.): measles
	odsep, odsepisko: alluvium		
		přesyp: sand-dune	
	przysep, przysypisko: alluvium		
			prosutost: rupture, hernia
			rasulo: ruin, downfall
[R]	[P]	[Cz]	[S-C]

россыпь: mineral deposit		rozsyp: mineral deposit	rasap: ruin, downfall; waste, squandering rasipač, rasipnik: spendthrift
		ssutiny (pl.): ruins	
	wysypka: (med.) rash, eruption		
	wyspa: island	výspa: sandbar; promontory; (lit.) island	
	zaspa: snowdrift; sand-dune		
[R]	[P]	[Cz]	[S-C]

NOTES

Basic meaning of root: to pour, strew

Except in Serbo-Croatian, the root expresses solely the pouring or strewing of a dry substance (compare root ЛИ [etc.]). The notion of piling up or accumulating earth, sand, etc. is apparent in such meanings as "embankment," "island," "alluvium," "sand-dune" and "volcano." The derivatives referring to various types of skin eruptions reflect the notion of strewing or scattering.

A non-Slavic cognate is Lat. (dis)sipare "to scatter" (>Eng. dissipate).

suć-souti, сыпать et al.: The words currently in use in the four languages were originally iterative forms of the primary verb represented by archaic suć and souti; ORus. сути does not survive in the modern language, while S-C suti is obsolete.

sopka: <Rus. сопка.

półwysep: See wyspa and note on Rus. полуостров et al.

rasulo, rasap, rasipač, rasipnik: <*razsulo, razsap, razsipač, razsipnik.

výspa: <Pol. wyspa.

СУД, СУЖД	SĄD(Z), SĘDZ	SOUD, SUD, SUZ	SUD, SUĐ
судить: to judge; to try (in court); to predestine, foreordain	sądzić: to judge; to think, believe; to try (in court); to predestine, foreordain	souditi: to judge; to think, believe; to try (in court); to predestine, foreordain	suditi: to judge; to think, believe; to try (in court); to predestine, foreordain
суд: (law-) court; trial, adjudication; judgment, opinion	sąd: (law-) court; trial, adjudication; judgment, opinion	soud: (law-) court; trial, adjudication; judgment, opinion; (arch.) sentence, verdict, decision	sud: (law-) court; sentence, verdict, decision; judgment, opinion
судья́: judge	sędzia: judge	soudce, (arch.) sudí: judge	sudija, sudac: judge
судьба́, (lit.) судьби́на: fate, destiny		sudba (lit.): fate, destiny	sudba, sudbina: fate, destiny
самосу́д: lynch-law, mob rule	samosąd: lynch-law, mob rule		
			dosuditi, dosuđivati: to award
осуди́ть, осужда́ть: to condemn, sentence; to condemn, censure	osądzić, osądzać: to judge, deem; to condemn, sentence		osuditi, osuđivati: to condemn, sentence; to condemn, censure
	osąd: judgment, opinion	osud: fate, destiny	
обсуди́ть, обсужда́ть: to discuss			
	odsądzić, odsądzać: to deprive (of one's rights, good name, etc.)	odsouditi, odsuzovati: to condemn, sentence; to condemn, censure	odsuditi, odsuđivati: to condemn, sentence; to condemn, censure
	posądzić, posądzać: to suspect	posouditi, posuzovati: to judge, evaluate	posuditi, posuđivati: to lend; to borrow
подсуди́мый: defendant	podsądny: defendant		
			presuda: sentence, verdict, decision
			presudan: decisive
[R]	[P]	[Cz]	[S-C]

[R]	[P]	[Cz]	[S-C]
предрассу́док: prejudice		předsudek: prejudice	predrasuda: prejudice
присуди́ть, присужда́ть: to condemn, sentence; to impose (a penalty); to award	przysądzić, przysądzać: to award	přisouditi, přisuzovati: to impose (a penalty); to award; to ascribe, attribute	
		přísudek: (gram.) predicate	
	przesąd: prejudice; superstition		
рассу́док: reason, intelligence	rozsądek: reason, intelligence	rozsudek: sentence, verdict, decision	rasuda: judgment, opinion
ссу́да: loan			
			usuditi se, usudivati se: to dare, venture
		úsudek: judgment, opinion	usud: fate, destiny
	zasądzić, zasądzać: to condemn, sentence; to award		

NOTES

Basic meaning of root: to judge

The verbal derivatives are denominatives from суд et al.

The Russian root-form СУЖД is of Church Slavic origin.

posuditi: The meaning was presumably first "to award by judicial decision" (see dosuditi), then "to lend," finally also "to borrow." The use of a single verb to express the two reciprocal operations of lending and borrowing is not uncommon; compare Ger. borgen (cognate with Eng. borrow) "to lend, to borrow," Pol. pożyczyć, S-C zajmiti.

presudan: Compare presuda.

предрассу́док et al.: The Russian word is modeled on Fr. préjugé "prejudice" (<pré- "before" + juger "to judge"), the Czech and Serbo-Croatian words on Ger. Vorurteil "prejudice" (<vor "before" + Urteil "judgment"); compare also Eng. prejudice (ult. <Lat. prae "before" + judicium "judgment").

přísudek: ="that which is ascribed (to the subject of a sentence)"; see the third meaning of přisouditi.

przesąd: See note on предрассу́док et al.

rasuda: ⟨razsuda.

ссу́да: See note on posuditi.

usuditi se: perhaps orig. "to tempt fate, try one's luck"; see usud.

СВЕТ, СВЕЧ, СВЕЩ	ŚWIAT, ŚWIET, ŚWIT, ŚWIEC, ŚWIECZ	SVĚT, SVÍT, SVIT, SVĚC, SVÍC, SVÍČ	SVIJET, SVJET, SVIT, SVIJEĆ, SVJEĆ
свет: light (n.); world	świat: world	svět: world	svijet: world; people
	światło: light (n.)	světlo: light (n.)	svijetlo: light (n.)
	świt: dawn	svit: shine, gleam	
			svjetina: crowd, throng; rabble, riffraff
свеча́: candle; spark-plug; suppository	świeca: candle; spark-plug	svíce: candle	svijeća: candle
све́чка: candle; suppository	świeczka: candle	svíčka: candle; spark-plug	svjećica: candle; spark-plug
свети́ло: luminary, heavenly body; luminary, prominent person	świecidło, świecidełko: spangle; trinket, bauble	svítidlo: lamp	
		svítilna: lamp; lantern	svjetiljka: lamp; lantern
свети́льник: lamp			svjetionik: lighthouse
		světnice: room, chamber	
	światowiec: man of the world	světák: man of the world	svjetovnjak: layman (as distinct from a clergyman)
	świetny: brilliant, splendid, excellent		
	obieżyświat: globetrotter		
			probisvijet: vagabond
		světoběžník: globetrotter	
све́топись (arch.): photography			
[R]	[P]	[Cz]	[S-C]

[R]	[P]	[Cz]	[S-C]
	światopogląd: ideology, Weltanschauung		
светопреставле́ние: doomsday, the end of the world			
	wszechświat: universe		
	naświetlić, naświetlać: to expose (film); (med.) to irradiate		
	oświata: public education; enlightenment	osvěta: public education; enlightenment	
			osvit, osvitak: dawn
просвеще́ние: public education; enlightenment			prosvjećenje: enlightenment
просве́чивание: translucence; (med.) radioscopy	przeświecanie: translucence	prosvěcování: illumination; (med.) radioscopy	prosvjećivanje: teaching, instruction; enlightenment
			prosvjeta: public education; enlightenment
		průsvitný: translucent	prosvjetan: educational
просветле́ние: brightening; (mental) lucidity	prześwietlenie: (med.) radioscopy	prosvětlení: illumination	prosvjetljenje: illumination; enlightenment
рассве́т: dawn	rozświt (lit.): dawn		rasvit, rasvitak: dawn
		úsvit: dawn	
		vysvitnouti, vysvítati: to follow, be evident (from s.th.)	
	wyświetlić, wyświetlać: to elucidate; to show, project (a motion picture)	vysvětliti, vysvětlovati: to explain	

NOTES

Basic meaning of root: light, illumination

The secondary meaning "world" occurs in all four languages. In Polish, Czech and Serbo-Croatian, it has pre-empted the primary noun derivative, świat et al., and the original root-meaning has been taken over by a secondary form, światło et al. Semantic borrowing from the Slavic languages is apparent in Hung. világ "light; world" and in Rum. lumină "light" and lume "world" (both <Lat. lumen "light").

The Russian root-form СВЕЩ is of Church Slavic origin.

The Slavic root is related to Eng. white.

svijet: The semantic shift from "world" to "people" (as in mnogo svijeta "many people, a crowd") has parallels in other languages; compare Fr. monde, modern Gr. κόσμος, Rum. lume, all of which mean both "world" and "people" (see, e.g., Fr. beaucoup de monde "many people").

svjetina: See the second meaning of svijet.

světnice: orig. "a brightly lighted room," e.g. sitting-room, as distinct from the kitchen, hallway, etc.

svjetovnjak: See note on Rus. миря́нин, S-C mirjanin.

probisvijet: See note under root БИ (etc.).

свéтопись: See note under root ПИС (etc.).

światopogląd: See note on Rus. мировоззре́ние.

wszechświat: See note under root ВЕС (etc.).

rasvit, rasvitak: <razsvit, *razsvitak.

СВОЙ, СВО(И,-Е, -Я), СВА(И)	SWÓJ, SWOJ, SWO(I), SWAJ, SW(A)	SVŮJ, SVOJ, SV(É,-A)	SVOJ, SVAJ, SV(A)
свой: my, your, his, her, its, one's, our, their (reflexive possessive adjective) своя́к: brother-in-law свойство́: relationship by marriage [R]	swój: my, your, his, her, its, one's, our, their (reflexive possessive adjective) swojak: compatriot; relative, kinsman [P]	svůj: my, your, his, her, its, one's, our, their (reflexive possessive adjective) svak (arch.): brother-in-law [Cz]	svoj: my, your, his, her, its, one's, our, their (reflexive possessive adjective) svak, svojak: brother-in-law svojta: relatives, kinfolk [S-C]

свóйство: property, characteristic	swoistość: peculiarity		svojstvo: property, characteristic
			svojina: property (something owned); ownership
		svéhlavý: obstinate; wilful	svojeglav: obstinate; wilful
		svémocný (lit.): arbitrary, high-handed	
своеобрáзный: peculiar, distinctive		svérázný: peculiar, distinctive	
своевлáстный: wilful			svojevlastan: wilful
своевóльный: wilful	swawolny: licentious; frolicsome, prankish	svévolný: arbitrary, high-handed	svojevoljan: arbitrary, high-handed; voluntary
освóить, освáивать: to master (new methods), assimilate (experience), develop (land, resources, etc.)	oswoić, oswajać: to familiarize (s.o. with s.th.); to tame	osvojiti si, osvojovati si: to appropriate (to one's use), arrogate to o.s.; to master (new methods), acquire (a habit); to adopt (a child)	osvojiti, osvajati: to conquer
			*odsvojiti: to expropriate
			posvojiti, posvajati: to appropriate (to one's use), arrogate to o.s.; to adopt (a child)
			posvojan: (gram.) possessive
присвóить, присвáивать: to appropriate (to one's use), arrogate to o.s.; to confer, award	przyswoić, przyswajać: to adopt, take over; to assimilate (food); to tame; to adopt (a child)	přisvojiti si, přisvojovati si (lit.): to appropriate (to one's use), arrogate to o.s.	prisvojiti, prisvajati: to appropriate (to one's use), arrogate to o.s.
		přisvojovací (arch.): (gram.) possessive	prisvojan: (gram.) possessive
[R]	[P]	[Cz]	[S-C]

усво́ить, усва́ивать: to master (a subject), acquire (a habit); to assimilate (food) [R]	[P]	[Cz]	usvojiti, usvajati: to adopt, take over; to adopt, approve (a proposal); to adopt (a child) [S-C]

NOTES

Basic meaning of root: one's own

The Slavic root is related to Lat. suus "one's own," sui "of oneself" (>Eng. suicide) and Ger. sein "his" and to root СЕБ (etc.).

сво́йство-svojstvo, svojina: See note on Pol. własność, Cz. vlastnost and vlastnictví, S-C vlasništvo; S-C svojstvo is borrowed from Russian.

svéhlavý-svojeglav: See note under root ГОЛОВ (etc.).

svémocný: See note under root МО(Г) (etc.).

своеобра́зный-svérázný: See note under root РАЗ (etc.).

своевла́стный-svojevlastan: See note on svémocný.

osvojiti si (first meaning): See note on Pol. przywłaszczyć sobie, Cz. přivlastniti si.

odsvojiti: See note on S-C izvlastiti.

posvojiti (first meaning), присво́ить (first meaning)-přisvojiti si-prisvojiti: See note on Pol. przywłaszczyć sobie, Cz. přivlastniti si.

	CIĄ, CIĘ, CIN	TÍ, ŤA, TN, TÍN, TON	
	**ciąć: to cut docinek: taunt, gibe odcięta: (math.) abscissa odcinek: part, section; (mil.) sector; (math.) segment; coupon przycinek: taunt, gibe przeciętny: average (a.) [P]	*títi (tnouti): to cut [Cz]	

	przecinek: (punc.) comma		
	ściąć się, ścinać się: to coagulate; to freeze; to fail (in an examination)		
		stínadlo: guillotine	
		stonek: stem, stalk	
	zacięty: stubborn, tenacious	zaťatý: clenched (teeth, fists)	
	⌊P⌋	⌊Cz⌋	

NOTES

Basic meaning of root: to cut

ORus. тяти "to cut" failed to survive into the modern language. The root is not attested in Serbo-Croatian.

ciąć: The 1 sg. form is tnę.

tnouti: a secondary infinitive formation from 1 sg. tnu.

odcięta: "the segment cut off from the axis of X by a line drawn throu it and parallel to the axis of Y from a given point"; compare Eng. abscissa (ult. ⟨Lat. ab "off, away" + scindere "to cut"), Cz. úsečka.

odcinek: Compare Eng. section, sector, segment (all ult. ⟨Lat. secare "to cut") and coupon (ult. ⟨Fr. couper "to cut"), Cz. úsek, S-C odsjek.

przeciętny: The basic idea is that of making a cross-section; compare Ger. durchschnittlich "average (a.)" (⟨durch "through" + schneiden "to cut" S-C prosječan, poprečan.

przecinek: modeled on the Greek-derived word used in English and other languages. Gr. κόμμα (⟨κόπτειν "to cut") denoted a short clause, i.e. a "cu or "slice" of a sentence; its modern derivatives also refer to the mark of punctuation used to set off parts of a sentence. Compare also S-C zarez "comma" (⟨rezati "to cut").

ściąć się: The active verb has the meanings "to cut off" and "to behea kill"; from the latter of these the meaning "to coagulate, freeze" is thoug to have evolved as an outgrowth of the idea of "making lifeless, motionless

stonek: orig. "stump of a tree," i.e. "something cut off."

zacięty: Cz. zaťatý suggests the meaning; compare Ger. verbissen "stub-born, tenacious" (⟨beissen "to bite").

ТЯ(Г), ТЯЖ, ТЯЗ, ТУГ, ТУЖ	CIĄG, CIĘG, CIĄŻ, CIĘŻ, TĘG, TĘŻ, TĄŻ	TAH, TÁH, TĚH, TÍH, TAŽ, TĚŽ, TÍŽ, TÁZ, TUH, TOUH, TUŽ, TOUŽ	TEG, TEŽ, TEŠ, TEZ, TUG, TUŽ
тянýть: to pull, draw; (coll.) to weigh (intr.)	ciągnąć: to pull, draw; to move, proceed	táhnouti: to pull, draw; to move, proceed; to march	*tegnuti: to weigh (intr.)
тягáть (coll.): to pull, draw	ciągać (coll.): to pull, draw	†tahati: to pull, draw	
		tázati se: to ask	
	ciąg: course (of time, events); series, succession; draft, current of air; migration of birds	tah: traction; drawing (in a lottery); draft, current of air; migration of birds; move (e.g. in chess); draught, gulp; stroke (of the pen); line; (facial) feature; (arch.) march, procession	teg: weight
тя́га: traction; draft, current of air; control-rod; migration of birds; inclination, penchant	cięgi (pl.): beating, drubbing	tíha: weight; burden	
		tažení: traction; campaign	
	ciągły: continuous	táhlý: long-drawn-out (sound); gentle (slope)	
тягýчий: viscous; ductile, malleable; slow, leisurely			tegljiv: viscous
	ciągnik: tractor		
тя́гло: draft animals; (arch.) tax	cięgło: coupling rod	táhlo: rod (in a machine)	teglo: tow-line
		tíhlo (arch.): yoke	
			teglić: tugboat
			teglica: siphon
тя́жба (arch.): lawsuit			
[R]	[P]	[Cz]	[S-C]

[R]	[P]	[Cz]	[S-C]
		těžiti: to mine, extract; to benefit, profit (from)	težiti: to till, cultivate
тя́гость, тягота́: burden			tegoba, tegota: hardship, toil
	ciąża: pregnancy	tíže: heaviness; weight; burden; difficulty; (phys.) gravity	teža: weight; (phys.) grav-ity; (phys.) gravitation
	ciężar: weight; load; burden		
тя́жкий (lit.): heavy; serious, grave (illness, etc.); severe (punishment, etc.); painful, distressing	ciężki: heavy; difficult; serious, grave (illness, etc.); severe (punishment, etc.); painful, distressing	těžký: heavy; difficult; serious, grave (illness, etc.); severe (punishment, etc.); painful, distressing	težak: heavy; difficult; serious, grave (illness, etc.); painful, distressing; pregnant
тяжёлый: heavy; difficult; serious, grave (illness, etc.); severe (punishment, etc.); painful, distressing			
тя́жесть: heaviness; weight; burden; difficulty; (phys.) gravity	ciężkość: heaviness; (phys.) gravity	těžkost: heaviness; difficulty	teškoća: difficulty
тяготе́ние: (phys.) gravitation; inclination, penchant			
	ciążenie: (phys.) gravitation; inclination, penchant		teženje, težnja: inclination, penchant
	ciężarna: pregnant	těhotná: pregnant	
	ciężarówka: truck		
туго́й: tight, taut	tęgi: strong, vigorous; fat, corpulent	tuhý: stiff, rigid; tough; severe	
		touha: longing, yearning	tuga: sorrow, grief
тужи́ть (coll.): to grieve (intr.)		toužiti: to long, yearn; (arch.) to complain	tužiti: to grieve (intr.); to accuse; to sue bring suit against

[R]	[P]	[Cz]	[S-C]
тýжиться (coll.): to exert oneself		tužiti se: to exert oneself	
	tężec: tetanus		
			ravnoteža: balance, equilibrium
			sredotežan: centripetal
	wodociąg: water-pipe, conduit; aqueduct; water supply		
истязáть: to torture			
натяжéние: tension, strain	natężenie: tension, strain; effort, exertion; intensity		
натýга: effort, exertion			natega: effort, exertion
	niedociągnięcie: deficiency		
	ociągnąć się, ociągać się: to hesitate; to delay		
		obtah: (printer's) proof	
		otěže (pl.): reins	
		otázka: question	
		obtíž: trouble, difficulty	
	ociężały: cumbersome; sluggish		
		odtažitý (lit.): abstract (a.)	
	pociąg: (railroad) train; attraction	potah: team (of horses, oxen, etc.); upholstery	poteg: blow, stroke; crank lever
			potez: stroke (of the pen); line; move (e.g. in chess)
	pociągły: oblong, elongated		
		potíž: trouble, difficulty	
потýги (pl.): labor pains	potęga: power; (math.) power		

[R]	[P]	[Cz]	[S-C]
	powściągliwy: restrained, moderate		
подтя́жки (pl.): suspenders			
			preteżnost: preponderance; predominance, supremacy
притяга́тельный (lit.): attractive, appealing		přitažlivý: attractive, appealing; (phys.) attractive, exercising attraction	
притяжа́тельный: (gram.) possessive			
			pritežalac: owner
притяза́ние: claim			
		přítěž: ballast	
протяже́ние: stretch, distance; period, space of time	przeciąg: draft, current of air; period, space of time	průtah: delay	
протя́жный: long-drawn-out (sound); drawling	przeciągły: protracted; long-drawn-out (sound); drawling	protáhlý: oblong, elongated; long-drawn-out (sound)	
			stega: discipline; clamp
			steznik: corset
стяжа́тель: money-grubber			
		soutěž, soutěžení: competition, contest	
		stěží: hardly, scarcely; with difficulty	
		stěžovati si: to complain	
состяза́ние: competition, contest			
			utega: corset; truss (for hernia)
	uciążliwy: burdensome, onerous		

	wyciąg: extract, excerpt; (chem.) extract; elevator	*výtah*: extract, excerpt; elevator	
вытяжка: (act of) drawing out; escape (of gas, etc.); (chem.) extract		*výtažek*: (chem.) extract	
		výtěžek: profit, gain; output	
	wytężenie: tension, strain; effort, exertion		
		vztah: relation(ship); attitude	
	wstęga, *wstążka*: ribbon, band; tape	*stuha*, *stužka*: ribbon, band	
	zaciąg: recruitment, enlistment	*zátah*: casting (of a fishnet); police raid	*zateg*, *zategnutost*: tension, strain
затяжной: protracted	*zaciężny*: mercenary, hired (soldier)		
[R]	[P]	[Cz]	[S-C]

NOTES

Basic meaning of root: to pull, draw; weight, heaviness

The notion of weight or gravity as a "pulling" exerted upon a body is one which arises logically from the primary verbal meaning of the root. The root-meaning "to pull" is also reflected in derivatives with such meanings as "tight, stiff" (whence, by extension, "tough, strong"), "effort, tension, strain," "lawsuit, competition" (a "pulling" or "tugging" between parties) and "long-drawn-out, protracted," while the idea of weight underlies the meanings "burden" (whence "pregnancy"), "toil," "difficulty," "seriousness, severity," "distress" and "grief." The various meanings of Eng. *draw* and of the corresponding noun *draft* (*draught*) are apparent in a number of the derivatives, and there is considerable semantic overlapping with words listed under root ВОЛОК (etc.).

The modern root-forms are assignable to two Common Slavic forms with differing vowel grades: ТУГ-ТУЖ---TĘG-TĘŻ-TĄŻ---TUH-TOUH-TUŽ-TOUŽ---TUG-TUŽ to Common Slavic *TǪG and the remaining forms to an original *TĘG.

The Slavic root is related to Swed. *tung* "heavy" (>Eng. *tungsten*, literally "heavy stone").

ciągnąć-*táhnouti*: Regarding the intransitive meaning "to move, proceed," compare Eng. the troops pulled out, he drew near, etc.; the last mea ing of the Czech word represents semantic borrowing from Ger. ziehen "to pull; to march."

tegnuti: orig. "to pull."

тягáть-ciągać: originally iterative forms of тянýть-ciągnąć.

tázati se: ="to draw out, extract (information)"; the word is a double of tahati.

ciąg-tah, тя́га, tažení: A number of the meanings of these noun formations reflect the intransitive meanings of ciągnąć-táhnouti; the words show extensive semantic parallelism with (and, particularly in Czech, direct influence by) Ger. Zug (<ziehen "to pull, draw"). In the meaning "feature" (<"line," i.e. "that which is drawn"), Cz. tah tallies both with Zug and with Eng. trait (ult. <Lat. trahere "to pull, draw"). Compare also Eng. traction (ult. <Lat. trahere), Hung. vonal "line" (<vonni "to pull, draw").

cięgi: <archaic sg. cięga "lash, stroke of the whip"; compare the firs meaning of S-C poteg.

ciągnik: Compare Eng. tractor (ult. <Lat. trahere "to pull").

тя́гло (second meaning): <тянýть in the earlier sense "to pull (i.e. bear, be subject to) a tax."

těžiti: variously explained as "to pull out," hence "to extract (coal, profit, etc.)," and as "to exert oneself, work" (compare tužiti se).

težiti: <teg in the earlier meaning "labor."

tíže-teža, тя́жкий et al., тяжёлый, тя́жесть-ciężkość, тяготéние, ciążenie: Compare Eng. grave, gravity, gravitation (all ult. <Lat. gravis "heavy").

ciężarówka: <ciężar; compare Rus. грузови́к "truck" (<груз "load").

tuga, тужи́ть et al.: Compare Eng. grief and grieve (both ult. <Lat. gravis "heavy"), Ger. sich beschweren "to complain" (<schwer "heavy").

tężec: Compare Eng. tetanus (ult. <Gr. τείνειν "to stretch, pull tight").

ravnoteža: See note on Rus. равновéсие et al.

sredotežan: See teženje, težnja and note under root СЕРД (etc.).

истязáть: orig. "to ask"; see notes on tázati se above and on Rus. пытáть and пы́тка, Pol. pytki. The word is borrowed from Church Slavic.

натяжéние-natężenie: See note on Rus. напряжéние, Pol. naprężenie.

niedociągnięcie: =failure to reach a given point, to achieve a goal; see the second meaning of ciągnąć.

ociągnąć się: See note on Pol. odwlec.

obtah: Compare Eng. to pull a proof.

otěže: Compare Ger. Zügel "reins" (<ziehen "to pull").

otázka: See tázati se.

odtažitý: See note on Rus. отвлечённый.

pociąg: See note on Cz.-S-C vlak, Cz. vlečka.

potah: Regarding the first meaning, compare Ger. Zug "team (of horses, xen, etc.)" (<ziehen "to pull"). The second meaning reflects the notion of 'pulling over, covering"; see note on Rus. наволока et al., обволочь, облечь t al., облачить et al. and оболочка, Pol. obłóczyny.

potez (second meaning): See note on ciąg-tah, тяга, tažení.

потуги-potęga: See тугой-tęgi.

powściągliwy: See note on S-C suspregnuti.

pretežnost: See note on Pol. przewaga et al.

притягательный-přitažlivý: See note on Rus. привлекательный et al.

притяжательный, pritežalac, притязание: Underlying the various meanings s the notion of "pulling something to oneself," i.e. appropriating or acquiring it; Rus. притязание is a Church Slavic loan-word.

průtah: See note on Pol. odwlec.

przeciągły: Compare Eng. protracted (ult. <Lat. pro- "forward" + trahere 'to pull, draw"), Cz. vleklý.

stega, steznik: The underlying idea is that of pulling together, tightening.

стяжатель: one who "pulls together," i.e. amasses, accumulates; the word is borrowed from Church Slavic.

stěžovati si: See note on tuga, тужить et al.

utega: See note on stega, steznik.

wyciąg-výtah, вытяжка-výtažek: Compare Eng. extract (ult. <Lat. ex "out" + trahere "to pull, draw"), Ger. Auszug "extract, excerpt; (chem.) extract" (<aus "out" + ziehen "to pull, draw"), Hung. kivonat "extract, excerpt; (chem.) extract" (<ki "out" + vonni "to pull, draw").

výtěžek: See těžiti.

wytężenie: See note on Rus. напряжение, Pol. naprężenie.

vztah: A similar notion of "pulling" (hence relating) one thing or person to another is apparent in Ger. Beziehung "relation(ship)" (<ziehen "to pull"), Hung. vonatkozás "relation(ship)" (<vonni "to pull").

wstęga et al.: Regarding the semantic development, see note on Cz. pruh, Pol. pręga et al.; the Czech prefix is from earlier vz-.

zaciąg, zaciężny: Compare Eng. draft "conscription," Ger. Einziehung "conscription" (<ein- "in" + ziehen "to pull").

zateg, zategnutost: See note on Rus. напряжение, Pol. naprężenie.

затяжной: See note on przeciągły.

ТЕ(К), ТЕЧ, ТОК, ТОЧ	CIE(K), CIECZ, TOK, TAK, TOCZ, TACZ	TEK, TÉ, TĚK, TEČ, TOK, TOČ, TÁČ, TÁC	TE(K), TIJEK, TEČ, TJEC, TIC, TOK, TAK, TOČ
течь: to flow; to leak	ciec (cieknąć): to flow; to leak	téci: to flow; to leak	teći: to flow; to leak; to acquire
точи́ть: to grind, sharpen; to turn (on a lathe); to eat away, corrode; (arch.) to shed (tears)	[1]toczyć, taczać: to roll (tr.); (toczyć only) to draw (wine from a barrel), shed (tears); (toczyć only) to grind, sharpen; (toczyć only) to turn (on a lathe); (toczyć only) to eat away, corrode; (toczyć only) to wage (war), conduct (negotiations)	točiti: to draw (wine from a barrel); to turn (tr.); to turn (on a lathe); to wind, twist (tr.)	točiti: to pour out (a drink); to sell (liquor) in a tavern; to grind, sharpen; to turn (on a lathe); to eat away, corrode
			takati: to roll (dough)
течь: leak	ciecz: liquid (n.)		
		tekutina: liquid (n.)	tekućina: liquid (n.)
ток: (electric) current; threshing-floor	tok: course (of events); threshing-floor	tok: flow; (river, electric) current	tijek, tok: flow; (river) current; course (of time, events)
тече́ние: flow; (air, river) current; course (of time, events)	cieczenie: flow	tečení: flow	tečenje: flow; acquisition, (act of) acquiring
			tečaj: course (of time, events); circulation (of currency); exchange rate (of currency); course (in school)
теку́щий: flowing; current (a.)	ciekący: flowing	tekoucí: flowing	tekući: flowing; current (a.)
те́чка: sexual heat, rut			
			teklić: messenger
	ciekawy: curious, inquisitive;	těkavý: fickle, inconstant;	
[R]	[P]	[Cz]	[S-C]

	curious, interesting	wandering (eyes, gaze); (chem.) volatile	
	toczek: disk		točak: wheel
тóкарь: turner, lathe-operator	tokarz: turner, lathe-operator		tokar: turner, lathe-operator
		točna: swivel; (railroad) turntable; (geog.) pole	
			kolotečina: rut, track
кровотечéние: hemorrhage	krwotok: hemorrhage	krvotok: hemorrhage	krvotok: hemorrhage; circulation of the blood
			poluotok: peninsula
	dociekanie: investigation; research		
истéчь, истекáть: to elapse, expire; to bleed profusely			isteći, isticati: to elapse, expire; to flow out; to rise (said of the sun)
истóк: source (of a river); source, origin			istok: east; sunrise; outflow
истóчник: spring (of water); source, origin			istočnik: spring (of water); source, origin; east wind
	naciek: stalagmite, stalactite		
			natjecanje: contest, competition
отёк: edema		oteklina: swelling (n.)	oteklina: swelling (n.)
	otok: rim; (med.) pus	otok: swelling (n.); edema	otok: island; swelling (n.); edema
			optjecaj, opticaj: circulation (of blood, currency, etc.)
			optok: circulation (of blood); mounting (of
[R]	[P]	[Cz]	[S-C]

[R]	[P]	[Cz]	[S-C]
			a precious stone); border, edging
обтекáемый: streamlined			
	otoczyć, otaczać: to surround	otočiti, otáčeti: to turn (tr.)	
пáтока: molasses, treacle	patoka: virgin honey	patoky (pl.): weak beer	patoka: weak brandy
потóк: swift stream; flood (of tears, etc.); mass-production system	potok: swift stream; flood (of tears, etc.); mass-production system	potok: brook; flood (of tears, etc.)	potok: brook
потóчный: mass-production (attr.)	potoczny: everyday, commonplace; colloquial	potoční: brook (attr.)	potočni: brook (attr.)
	potoczysty: smooth; fluent		
		potáceti se: to stagger, reel	
			pretek: excess, superfluity
предтéча (arch.): forerunner, precursor			preteča: forerunner, precursor
притóк: tributary (of a river); flow, influx		přítok: tributary (of a river); flow, influx	pritok, pritoka tributary (of a river)
	przytoczyć, przytaczać: to roll up (tr.); to quote, cite	přitočiti, přitáčeti: to pour (more of s.th.)	
протóк: channel; (anat.) duct	przetoka: (med.) fistula	průtok: flow; canal	
	przetak: sieve		protak: sieve
проистéчь, проистекáть: to result, spring (from)			proisteći, proisticati: to result, spring (from)
		roztok: (chem.) solution	rastok: (chem.) antimony
	roztoka: mountain stream; (arch.) watershed		rastočje, rastoka: river delta
расточи́тель: spendthrift			
стечéние: confluence; crowd, throng;			sticanje, stjecanje: acquisition,

[R]	[P]	[Cz]	[S-C]
concurrence, coincidence			(act of) acquiring; confluence; concurrence, coincidence
			stečaj: bankruptcy; contest, competition
	ściek: drain; sewer		
сток: drainage; drain; sewer	stok: spring (of water); slope	stok: confluence	
	stocznia: shipyard		
		stoka: drain; sewer	stoka: cattle
	uciekinier: refugee; deserter	utečenec: fugitive; refugee	
		útok: attack	utok: mouth (of a river); appeal (from a judicial decision)
		útočiště: refuge; recourse, resort	utočište: refuge; recourse, resort
			utjecaj, uticaj: influence
		vtok: mouth (of a river)	
	wycieczka: excursion; sortie, sally		
		vytáčka: subterfuge, evasion	
	wściekłość: rage, fury	vzteklost: irascibility	
		vztek: rage, fury	
	wścieklizna: rabies, hydrophobia	vzteklina: rabies, hydrophobia	
восто́к: east			
		zteč: assault, storming (of fortress, etc.)	
	zaciekły: fierce, relentless		
	zatoka: gulf, bay; (anat.) sinus	zátoka: gulf, bay	
[R]	[P]	[Cz]	[S-C]

заточéние: imprisonment, incarceration; seclusion			zatočenje: banishment, exile; imprisonment, incarceration
[R]	[P]	[Cz]	[S-C]

NOTES

Basic meaning of root: to flow

Many of the derivatives reflect the secondary root-meaning "to run" ar show semantic development comparable to that of words listed under root БЕI (etc.).

A number of causative formations (точи́ть et al. and compounds derived from them, takati, тóкарь et al., toczek-točak, točna, potáceti se, przetak protak) express the notion of "causing to flow" (i.e. pouring, shedding) or "causing to run" (hence rolling or turning); two specialized meanings are "to grind, sharpen" (=to "turn" or rub against a stone) and "to eat away, corrode" (originally a reference to the "turning" or boring of a worm or termite). In Serbo-Croatian, the primary verb is itself causative in the meaning "to acquire" (="to cause something to flow, i.e. accrue, to one-self").

течь et al.: The respective 1 sg. forms are теку́, ciekę, teku, tečem.

toczyć (last meaning): ="to roll," i.e. to keep in motion.

ток et al., течéние, tečaj, теку́щий-tekući: Compare Eng. current and course (both ult. <Lat. currere "to run"), Ger. laufend "current (a.)" and Verlauf "course (of time, events)" (both <laufen "to run"), Pol. bieg, bieżący and przebieg, Cz. běh, běžný and průběh; the present meanings of S-tečaj (orig. = "flow") are the result of semantic borrowing from Fr. cours and Ger. Kurs (both ult. <Lat. currere). The meaning "threshing-floor" hark back to the ancient practice of threshing grain by having horses "run," i.e trample, on it.

тéчка: orig. "a running (after the female)."

ciekawy: orig. "running, swift" and (as applied to a hunting dog) "following a scent"; compare dociekanie and see note on Rus. любопы́тный, S-C ljubopitan.

těkavý: ="running," hence "wandering, changing."

točna: orig. also "pivot"; see note on Pol. biegun.

kolotečina: See note under root КОЛ (etc.).

кровотечéние et al.: The first element is from кровь-krew-krev-krv "blood."

poluotok: See otok and note on Rus. полуóстров et al.

dociekanie: The sense of the word is that of running (i.e. going) afte or pursuing a matter; compare Pol. dochodzenie.

исто́к, исто́чник-izvor: The figurative meaning "source" is not uncommonly acquired by words which refer to a spring or other source of water; compare Eng. source in its literal and figurative senses, Ger. Quelle "spring; source," Hung. forrás "spring; source," Gr. πηγή "spring; source," Cz. pramen "spring; source," Pol. źródło, S-C vrelo and izvor.

istok: See note on Pol. wschód.

natjecanje: ⟨nadtjecanje; the original idea was that of striving to surpass another in running.

otok (S-C, first meaning): ="land around which water flows"; compare Rus. о́стров, Pol. ostrów, Cz. ostrov, S-C ostrvo "island" (⟨o + a root akin to Eng. stream).

обтека́емый: Compare Pol. opływowy.

па́тока et al.: literally "after-flow," the Russian word referring to a by-product of sugar manufacturing and the Czech and Serbo-Croatian words denoting inferior beverages obtained in the last stages of the brewing or distillation process; Pol. patoka originally meant "dregs, sediment."

potoczny: orig. "rolling"; the present meanings represent semantic borrowing from Fr. courant "current; common, ordinary, usual" (⟨courir "to run"). Compare Cz. běžný.

pretek: Compare Eng. superfluity (ult. ⟨Lat. super "over" + fluere "to flow"), Ger. Überfluss "superfluity" (⟨über "over" + fliessen "to flow").

предте́ча-preteča: a Church Slavic loan-word modeled on Gr. πρόδρομος "forerunner" (⟨πρό "before" + δραμεῖν "to run"); compare Eng. forerunner, precursor (ult. ⟨Lat. prae "before" + currere "to run"). The Serbo-Croatian word is from earlier predteča.

pritok, pritoka: ⟨Rus. прито́к.

rastok: perhaps so called because antimony readily combines with various metals to form alloys.

расточи́тель: a Church Slavic borrowing; regarding the meaning, see точи́ть in the earlier sense of "to pour."

стече́ние et al.: See note on Cz. sběh, Pol. zbieg and zbiegowisko.

stečaj: modeled on Ger. Konkurs "bankruptcy; contest, competition," Fr. concours "contest, competition" (both ult. ⟨Lat. cum "with, together" + currere "to run"). The meaning "bankruptcy" arose from what was originally a reference to the meeting at which the creditors agreed upon the apportionment of the bankrupt's assets; regarding the second meaning, compare Pol. współubiegać się.

stocznia: See the second meaning of stok; the reference is to the ways, or inclined structure, on which a ship is built and from which it is launched upon completion.

stoka (S-C): orig. "something acquired, property"; see sticanje, stjecanje and note on S-C blago.

útok: See note on Rus. набе́г et al.

utok: In the first meaning, u- = "in"; the meaning "appeal" represents semantic borrowing from Ger. Rekurs "appeal" (ult. ‹Lat. re- "back" + currere "to run").

útočiště-utočište: See note on Rus. прибе́жище.

utjecaj, uticaj: See note on Rus. влия́ние, Cz. vliv.

wycieczka: See note on S-C izlet.

vytáčka: See the last meaning of točiti.

wściekłość-vzteklost, vztek, wścieklizna-vzteklina: Compare Eng. rage and rabies (both ult. ‹Lat. rabies "rage"); the meaning has been variously linked with that of zteč (q.v.) and with the notion of a rushing, turbulent stream.

восто́к: borrowed from Church Slavic; see note on Pol. wschód.

zteč: z- ‹ vz-; see note on Rus. набе́г et al.

zaciekły: See note on wściekłość-vzteklost, vztek, wściekliznavzteklina.

zatoka-zátoka: ="a turning, bend, curve"; see toczyć-točiti and compare Eng. gulf (ult. ‹Gr. κόλπος "bosom; gulf, bay; sinus"), sinus (‹Lat. sinus "bend, curve; bosom; gulf, bay; sinus"), bight "bay" (akin to the verb bow "to bend").

заточе́ние-zatočenje: See ORus. точити "to drive" (="to cause to run or go"); the Serbo-Croatian word is borrowed from Russian.

ТИС(К), ТЕС	CIS(K), CIŻ, CIAS, CIEŚ	TISK, TĚS(K), TÍS	TIS(K), TISAK, TIŠ(T), TIJES, TJES(K), TIJEŠ
ти́снуть, ти́скать: to print; (coll.) to squeeze, press	cisnąć, ciskać: to throw; (cisnąć only) to squeeze, press	tisknouti: to squeeze, press; to print	tisnuti, tiskati: to squeeze, press; (tiskati only) to print
			tištati: to squeeze, press; to afflict, oppress
тиски́ (pl.): vise			
	ciżba: crowd, throng		tiska, tišma: crowd, throng
те́сный: narrow; tight	ciasny: narrow; tight	těsný: narrow; tight	tijesan: narrow; tight
тесни́ть: to squeeze, press		tísniti: to squeeze, press; to depress, dishearten	tijesniti: to narrow, tighten (tr.)
[R]	[P]	[Cz]	[S-C]

тесни́на: ravine, pass	cieśnina: strait; ravine, pass	těsnina: ravine, pass	tjesnac: strait; ravine, pass
		těsnopis: stenography, shorthand	
на́тиск: onslaught, assault	nacisk: pressure; emphasis		
о́ттиск: print, impression; print, proof, copy	odcisk: print, impression; corn (on foot)	otisk: print, impression; print, proof, copy	otisak: print, impression; print, proof, copy
	pocisk: projectile, missile, shell	potisk: textile pattern	
	przycisk: accent, stress; paper-weight; push-button		pritisak: pressure
			stiska: crowd, throng; difficult position, straits
	ścisły: compact; close (friendship, etc.); exact, precise, accurate; strict (diet, orders, etc.)		
		soutěska: ravine, pass	sutjeska: ravine, pass
стеснённый: straitened, difficult (circumstances, etc.)		stísněný: narrow; tight; depressed, dejected; straitened, difficult (circumstances, etc.)	stiješnjen: squeezed, pressed
стесни́тельный: shy, diffident; inconvenient			
	ucisk: oppression; pressure	útisk: oppression	
	uścisk: embrace; grip		
			utisak: (favorable, etc.) impression
[R]	[P]	[Cz]	[S-C]

NOTES

Basic meaning of root: to squeeze, press

ти́снуть et al.: Compare Eng. press and print (both ult. ‹Lat. premere "to press"), Ger. drücken "to press" and drucken "to print." The striking shift in meaning in cisnąć, ciskać is characteristic of verbs of motion, which tend to be semantically unstable in most languages; compare Eng. heave and cognate Ger. heben "to lift," Eng. leap and Ger. laufen "to run," Eng. smite and Ger. schmeissen "to throw," Eng. throw and Ger. drehen "to turn," Eng. warp and Ger. werfen "to throw," Fr. mettre "to put" (‹Lat. mittere "to send"), It. salire "to rise" and Sp. salir "to go out" (‹Lat. salire "to jump"), Pol. chwycić et al., Rus. дви́нуть et al., Rus. гнуть et al., Rus. ки́нуть et al., Rus. метну́ть et al., Pol. wierzgnąć et al. Cisnąć is imperfective in the meaning "to squeeze, press."

cizba: for earlier ciszczba (from a palatalized form of CISK corresponding to S-C TIŠT).

тесни́ть et al., тесни́на et al.: ‹те́сный et al.

těsnopis: See těsný and note under root ПИС (etc.).

nacisk: Compare Ger. Nachdruck "emphasis" (‹nach "after" + drücken "to press").

otisak: for *odtisak.

pocisk: See the first meaning of cisnąć, ciskać.

soutěska-sutjeska: from the root of те́сный et al.

uścisk: uś- is a double prefix (u- + ś-).

utisak: Compare Eng. impression (ult. ‹Lat. in "in" + premere "to press"), Ger. Eindruck "impression" (‹ein- "in" + drücken "to press"), Rus. впечатле́ние "impression" (‹в + the root of печа́тать "to print"), Pol. wrażenie.

ТК, ТЧ, ТЫК, ТЫЧ, ТОЧ	TK, TYK, TYCZ, TECZ	TK, TČ, TYK, TÝK, TYČ, TEČ	TA(K), TIK, TIC, TAČ, TOČ
ткнуть, ты́кать (coll.): to stick, poke, jab	tknąć, tykać: to touch		taknuti (taći), ticati: to touch
ткну́ться, ты́каться: to bump (into); to fuss, bustle about		tknouti se, týkati se: to touch (tknouti se only); to relate (to), concern	ticati se: to relate (to), concern; to adjoin
	tkać: to stuff, cram		
[R]	[P]	[Cz]	[S-C]

[R]	[P]	[Cz]	[S-C]
		tykadlo: feeler, antenna	ticalo: feeler, antenna
	tkliwy: tender, affectionate	tklivý: touching, moving, pathetic	
			tik: alongside, adjoining
	tyczka, tyka: pole	tyč, tyčka: pole; rod	
	tyczyć się: to relate (to), concern	tyčiti se: to tower, loom up	
то́чка: point, dot; point (of view, of contact, etc.); (punc.) period		tečka: point, dot; (punc.) period	tačka, točka: point, dot; point (of contact, etc.); point, item; (punc.) period
то́чный: exact, precise, accurate, punctual			tačan, točan: exact, precise, accurate, punctual
		tečna: (math.) tangent	
двоето́чие: (punc.) colon		dvojtečka: (punc.) colon	dvotočka: (punc.) colon
средото́чие: center, focal point			
сосредото́чить, сосредото́чивать: to concentrate			*usredotočiti: to concentrate
	wszeteczny (arch.): lewd, dissolute	všetečný: inquisitive, nosy	
	dotknąć, dotykać: to touch; to offend; to afflict, befall; to touch (upon), allude (to)		dotaknuti (dotaći), doticati: to touch
	dotknąć się, dotykać się: to touch	dotknouti se, dotýkati se: to touch; to offend; to touch (upon), allude (to)	dotaknuti (dotaći) se, doticati se: to touch; to touch (upon), allude (to)
		důtka: reprimand	
		důtky (pl.): cat-o'-nine-tails	
	dotkliwy: keen, sharp, painful	důtklivý: earnest, insistent	
	dotykalny: tangible		

[R]	[P]	[Cz]	[S-C]
	dotyczyć: to relate (to), concern		
			istaknuti (istaći), isticati: to emphasize
		netečný: indifferent, apathetic	
	nietykalny: inviolable	nedotknutelný: inviolable	
		nedůtklivý: touchy, irritable; fussy	
	potknąć się, potykać się: to stumble	potýkati se: to fight	
		potkati, potkávati: to meet (tr.)	
		půtka: skirmish; quarrel	
	potyczka: skirmish	potyčka: skirmish	
			poticaj: motive; stimulus
	przytykający: adjacent		
	przytyk: taunt, gibe		
при́тча: parable			priča: story
стык: joint (n.); junction	styk: junction; (elec.) contact	styk: contact, relations, dealings	
сты́чка: skirmish; quarrel			
	styczna: (math.) tangent		
су́тки (pl.): day (twenty-four hours)	sutki (pl.): narrow alleyway		
споткну́ться, спотыка́ться: to stumble	spotkać się, spotykać się: to meet (intr.)		spotaknuti (spotaći) se, spoticati se: to stumble
		utkání: military engagement; athletic contest, match	
	wtyczka: (electric) plug		utikač: (electric) plug
		výtka: reproach	
		výtečný: excellent, outstanding	

	wytyczyć, wytyczać: to stake out, trace, mark wytyczna: directive, guideline	vytyčiti, vytyčovati: to stake out, trace, mark zatčení: arrest, detention	
затычка (coll.): plug, stopper	zatyczka: plug, stopper	zátka: plug, stopper	
[R]	[P]	[Cz]	[S-C]

NOTES

Basic meaning of root: to stick, poke, jab

A widely represented secondary meaning is "to touch" (from which have evolved such further meanings as "to adjoin," "to meet," "to clash," "to offend," "to afflict," "to relate [to], concern," "to touch [upon], allude [to]").

ткнуть et al.: Cz. tknouti, týkati "to touch" is obsolete.
tklivý: ‹Pol. tkliwy.
tyczka et al.: ="a thing stuck into the ground."
tyčiti se: orig. "to stand upright"; see tyč, tyčka.
тóчка et al.: Compare Eng. point (ult. ‹Lat. pungere "to stick, prick"); the Czech and Serbo-Croatian words are borrowed from Russian.
тóчный et al.: See тóчка et al. and compare Eng. punctual (ult. ‹Lat. punctum "point"); the Serbo-Croatian words are borrowed from Russian.
tečna: "a straight line which touches a curve"; compare Eng. tangent (ult. ‹Lat. tangere "to touch").
двоетóчие et al.: See тóчка et al.
средотóчие: ="mid-point"; see тóчка.
сосредотóчить-usredotočiti: See note under root СЕРД (etc.).
wszeteczny-všetečný: ="touching everything"; the original meaning of the Polish word was "meddlesome, intrusive."
důtka: orig. "allusion, comment, remark"; see dotknouti se.
důtklivý: orig. "offensive"; see dotknouti se.
dotykalny: Compare Eng. tangible (ult. ‹Lat. tangere "to touch").
istaknuti: ="to thrust out or forth."
netečný: ="not touched (i.e. affected) by anything."
nietykalny-nedotknutelný, nedůtklivý: ="not to be touched"; regarding the first two words, compare Fr. intangible "inviolable; (more commonly) intangible" (ult. ‹Lat. in- "un-, not" + tangere "to touch").
poticaj: Compare Eng. stimulus (‹Lat. stimulus "goad; sharp stake").

притча-priča: orig. "happening, occurrence" (from the idea of striking against, meeting up with); the Serbo-Croatian word is from earlier pritča.

стык et al.: Compare Eng. contact (ult. <Lat. cum "with, together" + tangere "to touch").

styczna: See note on tečna.

сутки: ="a meeting or joining of night and day."

sutki: ="passageway between buildings which nearly meet"; the word is borrowed from Ukrainian.

výtka: ="something thrust forth, i.e. forcefully pointed out."

výtečný: Compare Eng. outstanding.

wytyczyć-vytyčiti, wytyczna: See tyczka et al.; the figurative meaning of wytyczna has a parallel in Du. bepalen "to fix, determine, decide" (<paal "pole, stake").

zatčení: presumably "a thrusting, pushing" (into prison).

ТРАТ, ТРАЧ	TRAC	TRAT, TRAC, TRÁC	TRAT, TRAĆ
тратить: to spend (money, time), expend (energy)	tracić: to lose; to waste, squander; to execute, put to death	tratiti: to lose	tratiti (traćiti): to waste, squander
		potrat: miscarriage	
растратчик: embezzler			
			stratište: scaffold, place of execution
утратить, утрачивать: to lose	utracić, utracać: to lose	utratiti, utráceti: to spend (money), expend (energy); to kill	
	wytracić, wytracać: to exterminate		
затратить, затрачивать: to spend (money), expend (energy)	zatracić, zatracać: to lose; to destroy	zatratiti, zatracovati: to curse, damn	
	zatraceniec: scoundrel, reprobate	zatracenec: scoundrel, reprobate	
[R]	[P]	[Cz]	[S-C]

NOTES

Basic meaning of root: to use up, waste, destroy

The secondary meaning "to lose" appears in many of the derivatives. A similar range of meanings can be seen in Rus. губи́ть et al., Lat. perdere "to waste; to destroy; to lose" (>Eng. perdition).

zatratiti: a back-formation from zatracení "perdition, damnation," which is modeled on Lat. perditio (see introductory note above); compare Cz. zpropadený.

zatraceniec-zatracenec: ="one who is lost, consigned to perdition"; see preceding note.

ТОРГ, ТОРЖ	TARG	TRH, TRŽ	TRG, TRZ
	targnąć, targać: to pull (s.o.'s ears, hair, etc.); to tear	trhnouti, trhati: to pull; (trhati only) to tear; (trhati only) to pick, pluck; (trhati only) to pull out, extract; (trhati only) to blast, blow up	trgnuti, trzati (trgati): to pull; to tear; (trgati only) to pick, pluck; (trgnuti only) to withdraw, retract; (trgnuti only) to decline, subside; (trgnuti only) to spurt
		trhan: ragamuffin	
		trhlina: crevice, fissure	
		trhavina: explosive (n.)	
исто́ргнуть, исторга́ть: to expel, eject; (arch.) to pull out, extract; (arch.) to extort, exact			istrgnuti (istrgati), istrzati: to pull out, extract
		otrhanec, otrhánek: ragamuffin	
расторже́ние: cancellation, annulment, abrogation	roztargnienie: absent-mindedness, distraction	roztržitost: absent-mindedness, distraction	
		roztržka: disagreement, falling out	
[R]	[P]	[Cz]	[S-C]

[R]	[P]	[Cz]	[S-C]
		strž: ravine	
		utrhač: slanderer	
втóргнуться, вторгáться (в + acc.): to invade; to encroach (upon)	wtargnąć, wtargać (do + gen.): to invade	*vtrhnouti (do + gen.): to invade	
		vytržení: rapture, delight; extraction (e.g. of a tooth)	
		výtržník: rioter, rowdy	
востóрг: rapture, delight			
	zatarg: quarrel, dispute		

NOTES

Basic meaning of root: to pull; to tear

With the exception of втóргнуться, the modern Russian derivatives are of Church Slavic origin. The Russian primary verb тóргнуть, торгáть is obsolete.

trgnuti: The seemingly contradictory fifth and sixth meanings (both extensions of the notion of "pulling") are clear in context, e.g. Groznica je trgla "The fever has subsided," Krv mu je trgla na nos "The blood spurted from his nose."

roztargnienie-roztržitost: The underlying idea is that of being "drawn away" from reality, from the matter at hand, etc.; compare Eng. distraction (ult. ⟨Lat. dis- "away" + trahere "to pull, draw").

roztržka: ="a pulling apart," i.e. separation, estrangement.

strž: See note on Rus. обрыв.

utrhač: See note on Pol. uwłaczanie.

vytržení (first meaning), востóрг: See note on Cz. uchvacující and úchvatný, Rus. восхищéние et al., Pol. zachwyt and zachwycający.

zatarg: ="a pulling, tugging."

	TRZYM	TŘÍM	
	trzymać: to hold trzymadło: handle; vise otrzymać, otrzymywać: to get, obtain; to receive podtrzymać, podtrzymywać: to support, uphold, sustain; to maintain, keep up utrzymać, utrzymywać: to maintain, keep up; to maintain, support (as a financial dependent); to maintain, contend, assert wytrzymać, wytrzymywać: to bear, endure wstrzymać, wstrzymywać: to stop, halt (tr.) zatrzymać, zatrzymywać: to stop, halt (tr.); to detain; to arrest, apprehend; to keep, retain [P]	třímati (lit.): to grasp, grip [Cz]	

NOTES

Basic meaning of root: to hold

See the introductory note on root ДЕРЖ (etc.).

The root is not attested in Russian or Serbo-Croatian.

wytrzymać: See note on S-C izdržati, Pol. zdzierżyć.

ТВОР, ТВАР	TWOR(Z), TWÓR, TWARZ	TVOR, TVŮR, TVOŘ, TVAR, TVÁR, TVÁŘ	TVOR, TVAR
твори́ть: to create; to slake (lime); to knead	tworzyć: to create; to form	tvořiti: to create; to form	tvoriti: to create; to manufacture, produce; to form
	twór: creature; work (of art, etc.)	tvor: creature	
тварь: (coll.) scoundrel; (arch.) creature (or creatures, collectively)	twarz: face	tvář: face; cheek	tvar: material, substance
		tvar: shape, form	
		tvářnost: (outward) appearance	
	tworzywo: material, substance; subject matter		tvorivo: material, substance
			tvornica: factory
твори́тельный: (gram.) instrumental			
благотво́рный (lit.): beneficial			blagotvoran: beneficial
благотвори́тельный: charitable, philanthropic			
боготвори́ть: to idolize, adore			
			djelotvoran: active; efficient
			dobrotvoran: charitable, philanthropic
	drobnotwór: micro-organism		
	dziwotwór: monster		
		jednotvárný: monotonous	
			**krivotvoriti: to falsify, counterfeit
[R]	[P]	[Cz]	[S-C]

	nowotwór: neologism; tumor, growth, neoplasm	novotvar: neologism; tumor, growth, neoplasm	novotvorina: neologism; novelty
		obrazotvornost: imagination	
			*oživotvoriti: to bring about, realize, accomplish rukotvorina: handicraft; handicraft product
удовлетвори́ть, удовлетворя́ть: to satisfy; to supply (with) умиротвори́ть, умиротворя́ть: to calm, pacify			
		netvor, nestvůra: monster	
			ostvariti, ostvarivati: to bring about, realize, accomplish patvoriti: to falsify, counterfeit
	potwora, potwór: monster	potvora: scoundrel; (arch.) monster	potvora: slander
	potwarz: slander		
потво́рство: connivance			
претвори́ть, претворя́ть: to transform	przetworzyć, przetwarzać: to transform; to process	přetvořiti, přetvářeti: to transform	pretvoriti, pretvarati: to transform
		přetvářka: pretense, sham pitvořiti se: to grimace	pretvorstvo: pretense, sham
притво́рство: pretense, sham			pritvorstvo: pretense, sham
раствори́ть, растворя́ть: to dissolve (tr.; in a liquid); to knead	roztworzyć, roztwarzać: to dissolve (tr.; in a liquid); to dilute		rastvoriti, rastvarati: to dissolve (tr.; in a liquid); (chem.) to
[R]	[P]	[Cz]	[S-C]

			decompose, analyze
	stwór (arch.): creature		stvor: creature
	stwora: monster	stvůra: monster	
			stvar: thing; affair, matter, business; cause (e.g. cause of peace, just cause); (judicial) case
			stvaran: real
у́тварь: utensils		útvar: (social, etc.) structure; (geol.) formation; (mil.) unit	utvari (pl.): church-plate
			utvara: specter, apparition
вытворя́ть (coll.): to do (something foolish or objectionable)	wytworzyć, wytwarzać: to manufacture, produce; to create	vytvořiti, vytvářeti: to create	
	wytwórnia: factory		
	wytworny: elegant		
		výtvarník: artist	
		znetvořiti, znetvořovati: to disfigure	
[R]	[P]	[Cz]	[S-C]

NOTES

Basic meaning of root: to make, create, form

twarz-tvář: orig. also "shape, form"; see introductory note on root ЛИК (etc.).

благотво́рный-blagotvoran: See note on Rus. благодея́ние, благоде́тель and благоде́тельный, S-C blagodejanje and blagodjetan.

боготвори́ть: See note under root БО(Г) (etc.).

drobnotwór: The first element is from drobny "small"; compare Eng. micro- (<Gr. μικρός "small").

dziwotwór: The first element is from dziwo "wonder, marvel."

jednotvárný: See tvar and note under root ОДИН (etc.).

nowotwór et al.: The first element is from nowy-nový-nov "new"; compare Eng. neoplasm (ult. <Gr. νέος "new" + πλάσσειν "to form").

obrazotvornost: See note on Rus. воображе́ние et al.

удовлетвори́ть: See note under root ВЕЛ$_2$ (etc.).

умиротворить: See note under root МИР (etc.).

nestvůra: ‹ne- + stvůra (see note).

ostvariti: ="to make real"; see stvaran and compare Eng. real and realize, Pol. urzeczywistnić.

patvoriti, potwora et al., potwarz: The force of the prefixes here is pejorative; regarding the meaning of patvoriti, compare Cz. padělati, S-C pačiniti.

потворство: The development of the meaning is not clear.

претворить et al.: Compare Eng. transform (ult. ‹Lat. trans "over, across" + formare "to form"), Rus. преобразить et al.

přetvářka: ="change of face"; see tvář.

pretvorstvo: ="change, transformation"; see pretvoriti.

pitvořiti se: in origin, a doublet of obsolete přitvořiti se "to pretend, feign" (see притворство-pritvorstvo below); the prefix was altered by dissimilation.

притворство-pritvorstvo: The underlying idea, apparent in Rus. притвориться "to pretend, feign," is that of "making oneself" (i.e. causing oneself to appear) a certain way; the Serbo-Croatian word is borrowed from Russian. Compare S-C činiti se, pričiniti se, praviti se.

растворить et al.: See the second and third meanings of творить and the dialectal use of tworzyć in the sense of "to dilute." However, the general notion of loosening or breaking up, hence dissolving, diluting or decomposing, seems also to reflect the meaning of the prefix; compare Rus. разбавить, Pol. rozczynić and rozrobić, S-C raščiniti.

stwora-stvůra: orig. "creature" and "creation," respectively.

stvaran: ="of the nature of a thing"; see stvar and compare Eng. real (ult. ‹Lat. res "thing"), Pol. rzeczywisty.

утварь-utvari: orig. "adornment."

utvara: ‹utvarati se "to appear (as an apparition)"; see note on притворство-pritvorstvo.

wytworny: ="resulting from creative effort"; compare Cz. výtvarník.

znetvořiti: ‹netvor.

УК, УЧ, (В)ЫК, (В)ЫЧ	UK, UCZ, WYK, (W)YCZ	UK, UČ, VYK, YČ	UK, UČ, (V)I(K), (V)IČ
учить: to teach; to learn; to study учиться: to learn; to study [R]	uczyć: to teach uczyć się: to learn; to study [P]	učiti: to teach učiti se: to learn; to study [Cz]	učiti: to teach; to learn; to study učiti se: to learn; to study; to become accustomed (to) [S-C]

учи́тель: teacher		učitel: teacher	učitelj: teacher
	uczeń: pupil, student; apprentice; disciple	učeň: apprentice	
учени́к: pupil, student; apprentice; disciple		učedník: apprentice; (arch.) disciple	učenik: pupil, student; apprentice; disciple
учёный: scientist; scholar	uczony: scientist; scholar	učenec: scholar	učenjak: scientist; scholar
учи́лище: school	uczelnia: school	učiliště: school	učilište: school
			učan: accustomed (to); versed, skilled (in)
			vičan: accustomed (to); versed, skilled (in)
чрезвыча́йный: extraordinary			
		kromobyčejný (arch.): extraordinary	
			sveučilište: university
			nauk: precept, admonition, moral; apprenticeship
нау́ка: science	nauka: science; knowledge, learning; doctrine; teaching, instruction; study	nauka: doctrine; branch of science	nauka: science; knowledge, learning; doctrine; study; habit
	nauczyciel: teacher		
			naučenjak: scientist; scholar
			naučnik: apprentice; scientist; scholar
на́вык: habit; skill, practice, experience	nawyk, nawyczka: habit	návyk: habit	navika: habit
	nadzwyczajny: extraordinary	nadobyčejný (arch.): extraordinary	
[R]	[P]	[Cz]	[S-C]

[R]	[P]	[Cz]	[S-C]
не́уч: ignoramus	nieuk: ignoramus		neuk: ignorant, illiterate
обы́чай: custom	obyczaj: custom	obyčej: custom; habit	običaj: custom; habit
	obyczajny: moral, decent; polite, civil	obyčejný: usual, customary; common, ordinary	običajan: usual, customary
обы́чный: usual, customary			običan: usual, customary; common, ordinary
обыкнове́нный: usual, customary; common, ordinary		obvyklý: usual, customary	obikao: accustomed (to)
		poučka: thesis, proposition; (math.) theorem	poučak: thesis, proposition; (math.) theorem
привы́кнуть, привыка́ть: to become accustomed (to)	przywyknąć, przywykać: to become accustomed (to)	přivyknouti (si), přivykati (si): to become accustomed (to)	priviknuti (privići), privikavati: to accustom (to); to become accustomed (to)
привы́чка: habit			
	zwyczaj: custom; habit	zvyk: custom; habit	
	zwyczajny: common, ordinary		
	zwykły: usual, customary; common, ordinary	zvyklý: accustomed (to)	
			zavičaj: native country; domicile

NOTES

Basic meaning of root: to teach; to become accustomed (to s.th.)

The root-forms show two vowel grades, which are also differentiated in meaning. The Russian forms УК, УЧ and their analogues in the other languages normally express the transitive meaning "to teach" (see, however, the second and third meanings of Rus. учи́ть, S-C učiti). Russian ВЫК, ВЫЧ and their analogues (with a prothetic v which is usually lost after the prefix ob) normally express the intransitive meaning "to become accustomed" (an exception is the first meaning of S-C priviknuti). There is some overlapping of the two basic meanings in Serbo-Croatian (see učiti se, učan, nauka).

The primary verb with the meaning "to become accustomed" has not survived in the modern languages, which show only prefixed forms. (Rus. вы́кнут Pol. wyknąć, Cz. vyknouti, S-C viknuti are obsolete.)

чрезвыча́йный: The first element is from чрез (че́рез) "over, across."

kromobyčejný: The first element is from krom (kromě) "except; besides" (orig. "outside, beyond").

obyczajny: ="acting in accordance with accepted customs"; compare Eng. moral (ult. ‹Lat. mos "custom"), Ger. sittlich "moral" (‹Sitte "custom").

zavičaj: ="a place to which one is accustomed"; for further instances of the semantic link between the notions of "habit" and "place of abode," see Eng. habit, habitat and inhabit, Ger. wohnen "to dwell" and Gewohnheit "habit."

УМ	UM	UM	UM
ум: mind		um (lit.): mind; skill	um: mind
у́мный: intelligent		umný (lit.): skilful	uman: intelligent; mental
уме́ть: to be able, know how	umieć: to be able, know how	uměti: to be able, know how	umjeti: to be able, know how
уме́ние: skill		umění: art	umjenje: skill
	umiejętność: skill; knowledge; science		umjetnost: art
уме́лый: skilful		umělý: artificial	
	umiejętny: skilful; knowledgeable		umjetan: artificial; artistic
			umješan: skilful
			dvoumica: doubt
			lakouman: frivolous
сумасбро́д: madcap			
сумасше́дший: mad, insane; madman			
умозре́ние: speculation, theorizing			
			veleum: genius
безу́мный: reckless; (arch.) mad, insane			bezuman: mad, insane; senseless, absurd
[R]	[P]	[Cz]	[S-C]

	dorozumieć się, dorozumiewać się: to guess	dorozuměti se, dorozumívati se: to come to an understanding	
изуми́ть, изумля́ть: to amaze			*izumiti: to deceive, delude
			izumjeti, izumijevati: to invent
			naum: intention
наобу́м: at random, haphazardly			
недоуме́ние: perplexity			nedoumica, nedoumlje: perplexity; indecision
ра́зум: reason, intelligence	rozum: reason, intelligence	rozum: mind; reason, intelligence	razum: reason, intelligence
разуме́ть: to mean, have in mind; (arch.) to understand	rozumieć: to understand; to mean, have in mind	rozuměti: to understand; to mean, have in mind	razumjeti, razumijevati: to understand
			sporazum: agreement
вразуми́тельный: intelligible; convincing, persuasive			
		vyumělkovaný: affected, mannered	
	wyrozumiały: lenient, indulgent		
	zarozumiały: conceited, arrogant		
[R]	[P]	[Cz]	[S-C]

NOTES

Basic meaning of root: mind

ум et al.: Pol. um "mind; reason, intelligence" is obsolete.

уме́ть et al.: denominatives formed from ум et al.

umění: ⟨uměti; an "art" is a skill or ability as distinct from a "science," which is a body of knowledge (note, however, the contrasting semantic development of Pol. umiejętność); compare Ger. Kunst "art" (⟨können "to be able").

umiejętność-umjetnost: See preceding note.

umělý, umjetan (first meaning): Compare umění and umjetnost and see note on Rus. искýсственный.

dvoumica: See note on S-C dvojba.

сумасбрóд: ="one who wanders (see бродúть 'to wander') from his mind (умá)"; compare сумасшéдший.

сумасшéдший: past act. part. of сойтú с умá "to go out of one's mind"; compare сумасбрóд.

умозрéние: See note under root ЗР (etc.).

dorozumieć się-dorozuměti se: See rozumieć-rozuměti.

изумúть-izumiti: ="to drive out of one's mind, deprive of one's reason the Russian word is borrowed from Church Slavic.

izumjeti: ="to create from one's mind."

наобýм: ="however a thing strikes one's mind."

nedoumica, nedoumlje: modeled on Rus. недоумéние.

рáзум: borrowed from Church Slavic.

sporazum: ="an understanding"; see razumjeti.

vyumělkovaný: Compare umělý.

wyrozumiały: ="understanding," i.e. sympathetic, willing to make allowances; see rozumieć and compare S-C uviđavan.

zarozumiały: ="having too exalted a conception of oneself"; see rozumi and compare Eng. conceit (orig. = "conception, understanding").

ВАГ, ВАЖ	WAG, WAH, WAŻ	VAH, VÁH, VAŽ, VÁŽ	VAG, VAŽ
вáга (arch.): large scales; lever	waga: weight; scales; importance	váha: weight; importance	vaga: weight; scales
		váhy (pl.): scales	
	wahać się: to swing; to hesitate; to fluctuate	váhati: to hesitate	vagnuti, vagati: to weigh (tr. and intr.)
	wahadło: pendulum; scale-beam	vahadlo: scale-beam	
	ważyć: to weigh (tr. and intr.)	vážiti: to weigh (tr. and intr.)	važiti: to matter, be of importance; to be regarded (as), reputed (to be); to be valid (e.g. a ticket, a law)
		vážiti si: to respect	
[R]	[P]	[Cz]	[S-C]

[R]	[P]	[Cz]	[S-C]
ва́жный: important; pompous	ważny: important; valid (ticket, law, etc.)	vážný: serious, earnest; serious, grave (illness, etc.); important	važan: important
		lehkovážný: frivolous	
	lekceważyć: to disregard, hold in contempt		
малова́жный: unimportant	małoważny: unimportant		
	równowaga: balance, equilibrium	rovnováha: balance, equilibrium	
	równoważny: equivalent, tantamount	rovnovážný: balanced, of balance (e.g. position)	
		opovážlivý: audacious; presumptuous	
отва́жный: courageous	odważny: courageous	odvážný, (arch.) odvážlivý: courageous	odvažan: courageous
	powaga: seriousness, earnestness; seriousness, gravity (of an illness, etc.); authority, prestige	povaha: nature, character	
	poważny: serious, earnest; serious, grave (illness, etc.); substantial, considerable	povážlivý: serious, grave (illness, etc.)	
	poważać: to respect	považovati (za + acc.): to consider, deem, regard (as)	
	przewaga: preponderance; predominance, supremacy	převaha: preponderance; predominance, supremacy	prevaga: preponderance; predominance, supremacy
	rozwaga: discretion, prudence; consideration, reflection	rozvaha: discretion, prudence; balance-sheet	
		svah: slope	
	uwaga: attention; remark, observation	úvaha: consideration, reflection; essay	

[R]	[P]	[Cz]	[S-C]
*уважить: to grant, comply with (a request); (coll.) to humor, indulge (s.o.)		*uvážiti: to consider, reflect upon; to consider, take into account	*uvažiti: to consider, take into account; to grant, comply with (a request)
уважать: to respect	uważać: to pay attention; (za + acc.) to consider, deem, regard (as)	uvažovati: to consider, reflect (upon); to consider, take into account	uvažavati: to appreciate, hold in esteem to consider, take into account; to grant, comply with (a request)
	upoważnić, upoważniać: to authorize, empower		
	znieważyć, znieważać: to insult		
		závažný: important	

NOTES

Basic meaning of root: to weigh

The notion of weight has given rise, in a number of derivatives, to such figurative meanings as "importance" and "seriousness." (Compare the similar development of Ger. wichtig "important" < wiegen "to weigh.") Similarly, many of the verbal derivatives reflect the notion of "weighing" in a figurative sense; hence the meanings "to reflect upon, consider, pay attention to" (compare Eng. ponder [ult. <Lat. ponderare "to weigh"] and deliberate [v.] [ult. <Lat. libra "scales"]) and, by extension, "to respect, esteem."

The Slavic root is an early Germanic borrowing. (See modern Ger. Waage "scales" and wiegen "to weigh," Eng. weigh and the introductory note on root ВЕЗ [etc.].)

wahać się-váhati: orig. "to swing to and fro like a pair of scales"; the Polish word is borrowed from Czech.

wahadło: <Cz. vahadlo.

równowaga-rovnováha: See note on Rus. равновесие et al.

opovážlivý: See next note.

отважный et al.: The underlying idea is that of resolving upon a course of action after first weighing the consequences; the Russian and possibly the Czech words are borrowed from Polish, the Serbo-Croatian word from Russian.

povaha: orig. "inclination, leaning, liking"; see note on *svah*.

przewaga et al.: Compare Ger. *Übergewicht* "preponderance" (<*über* "over" + *Gewicht* "weight"), Eng. *preponderance* (ult. <Lat. *prae* "before, in front" + *ponderare* "to weigh"), Rus. *перевéс*, S-C *pretežnost*.

svah: The notion of inclining comes from that of shifting weight.

увáжить et al., *уважáть et al*.: The Russian words are borrowed from Polish, the Serbo-Croatian words from Russian.

upoważnić: See the third meaning of *powaga*.

znieważyć: ="to lack regard, respect for"; compare *poważać*.

ВАЛ	WAL, WAŁ	VAL, VÁL	VAL
валить: to knock down; to pile up (intr.)	*walić*: to beat; to knock down; to pile up (tr.)	*valiti*: to roll (tr.)	
валять: to drag (tr.); to knead; to felt, full	*walać*: to soil	*váleti*: to roll (tr.); to drag (tr.); to knead	*valjati*: to roll (tr.); to drag (tr.); to felt, full
вал: high wave, billow; shaft (in machinery)	*wał*: shaft (in machinery); (arch.) high wave, billow		*val*: wave
валýн: boulder		*valoun*: boulder	
	walny: general; (arch.) excellent	*valný*: general; large	
валовóй: gross (income, etc.)			
	nawał: huge quantity; (med.) congestion	*nával*: crowd, throng; huge quantity; fit (of anger, etc.); (med.) congestion	
	nawała: flood; crowd, throng		*navala*: attack, assault; crowd, throng; (med.) congestion
	nawałnica: rainstorm		
обвáл: collapse; landslide			
повáльный: general (a.)			
		povaleč: idler	
			podvala: trickery, deception
[R]	[P]	[Cz]	[S-C]

[R]	[P]	[Cz]	[S-C]
перевáл: mountain pass			prevala: mountain pass
привáл: stop, halt; stopping place		přival: torrent	
провáл: collapse; gap, hole; failure	przewał: spillway (of a dam)		provala: burglary, housebreaking; outburst; raid, incursion; collapse
			provalija: precipice, abyss
развáлины (pl.): ruins	rozwaliny (pl.), rozwalisko: ruins	rozvaliny (pl.): ruins	razvaline (pl.): ruins
	zwał: heap, pile; mass	sval: muscle	
	zwaliska (pl.): ruins		
		úval: valley; depression (in the ground)	uvala: valley; depression (in the ground)
завáл: obstruction	zawał: heart failure		
		zavalitý: thickset, stocky	

NOTES

Basic meaning of root: to roll

The secondary meanings "to beat, knock down, move suddenly and violently" and "to amass, pile up" are apparent in many of the derivatives.

The Slavic root is related to Eng. well (source of water) and to well (up), Lat. volvere "to roll" (>Eng. evolve, involve, revolve).

вали́ть et al.: The Serbo-Croatian primary verb is not attested.

валя́ть et al.: orig. an iterative form of вали́ть et al.

вал et al.: Obsolete Cz. val "stream; crowd, throng" survives in the adverb valem "gushing, in a stream; swiftly." (Rus. вал [>подвáл "basement"], Pol. wał, Cz. val "embankment" are an unrelated borrowing from Ger. Wall "embankment" [=Eng. wall].)

walny-valný, валовóй: <вал et al. The basic notion is that of mass, accumulation; a further semantic extension is seen in the second meaning of Pol. walny.

повáльный: <obsolete повáл "anything universal or far-reaching in its impact, e.g. a plague or epidemic"; see preceding note.

podvala: See note on Rus. подки́дыш.

привáл: <привали́ть "to lean, prop; (hence) to berth, put in to harbor."

sval: ="a gathering together (of tissue)."

úval-uvala: The prefix here = "in"; the meaning is thus "indentation, place where the ground has caved in."

(В)ЯЗ, УЗ, ЮЗ, ВЕНЗ	WIĄZ, WIĘZ, WIĘŹ, WĘZ, JUSZ	VAZ, VÁZ, VÍZ, VĚZ, UZ, BUZ	VEZ, VES, VEŽ, UZ, UŽ
			vesti: to embroider
вязáть: to tie, bind; to knit	wiązać: to tie, bind	vázati: to tie, bind	vezati: to tie, bind
вя́знуть: to get stuck, caught	więznąć: to get stuck, caught	váznouti: to get stuck, caught	
вязь: ligature (in printing)	więź: connection, link; cluster, bunch	vaz: (anat.) ligament; back of the neck	vez: embroidery
			veza: connection, link; tie, bond; relation(ship); liaison, love affair
	więzy (pl.): fetters; ties, bonds		
вязáнка: bundle (of wood)	wiązanka: cluster, bunch; bouquet	vázanka: necktie	
	wiązadło: (anat.) ligament		
	wiązar: rafter, girder		
			veznik: (gram.) conjunction
	więzień: prisoner	vězeň: prisoner	
		vazba: arrest, detention; binding (of a book); grammatical construction; rafters, roof frame	
у́зы (pl.): ties, bonds; (arch.) fetters			uze (pl.): prison
у́зел: knot; knot (nautical mile); bundle;	węzeł: knot; knot (nautical mile); tie,	uzel: knot; knot (nautical mile); bundle;	uzao: knot
[R]	[P]	[Cz]	[S-C]

junction (rail-road, etc.)	bond; bundle; junction (rail-road, etc.)	junction (rail-road, etc.)	
			uzica: string
			uže: rope
у́зник: prisoner			uznik: prisoner
ве́нзель: monogram			
навя́зчивый: importunate, obtrusive			
неотвя́зный: importunate, obtrusive			
		obvaz: bandage	
		obvaziště: (military) aid station	
обяза́тельство: obligation	obowiązek: duty; obligation		obaveza, obveza: duty; obligation
обя́занность: duty			obavezanost, obvezanost: duty; obligation
			obveznica: bond (certificate of indebtedness); promissory note
обу́за: burdensome obligation			
повя́зка: bandage			povez: bandage; binding (of a book)
			povezača: kerchief
подвя́зка: garter	podwiązka: garter	podvazek: garter	podveza, podvezica: garter
при́вязь: leash; tether	przywięź: mooring rope		
привя́занность: attachment, affection	przywiązanie: attachment, affection; loyalty, devotion		
		příbuzný: related, kindred; relative, kinsman	
развяза́ть, развя́зывать: to untie; to loosen (s.o.'s tongue)	rozwiązać, rozwiązywać: to untie; to solve; to dissolve (a	rozvázati, rozvazovati: to untie; to dissolve (a marriage),	razvezati, razvezivati: to untie; to loosen (s.o.'s tongue)
[R]	[P]	[Cz]	[S-C]

	marriage), abrogate (an agreement); to loosen (s.o.'s tongue)	abrogate (an agreement); to loosen (s.o.'s tongue)	
развя́зный: forward, overly familiar	rozwiązły: dissolute, profligate		
развя́зка: dénouement, outcome			
		rozuzlení: dénouement, outcome	
связь: connection, link; relation(ship); communications; (mil.) liaison; liaison, love affair		svaz: union, association	svez: junction; (anat.) suture, seam
			savez: union, association; alliance; federation
			sveza: connection, link; (gram.) conjunction
свя́зка: sheaf (of papers), bunch (of keys); (anat.) ligament; (gram.) copulative verb	związek: connection, link; relation(ship); liaison, love affair; union, association; (chem.) compound	svazek: tie, bond; sheaf (of papers), bunch (of keys, carrots); volume (part of a book)	sveska, svezak: volume (part of a book)
			svezica: (gram.) conjunction
			svežanj: bundle; package; bunch (of keys); bouquet
	zwięzły: terse, concise		
		svízel: trouble, distress	
			sužanj: prisoner; slave
сою́з: union, association; alliance; (gram.) conjunction	sojusz: alliance		
	uwięź: leash		
⌊R⌋	⌊P⌋	⌊Cz⌋	⌊S-C⌋

[R]	[P]	[Cz]	[S-C]
	wywiązać się, wywiązywać się: to arise, emerge; (z + gen.) to discharge (an obligation) zobowiązanie: obligation		
zа́вязь: (bot.) ovary	zawiązek: germ, bud	zа́vazek: obligation	zavezak, zavežljaj: bundle

NOTES

Basic meaning of root: to tie, bind

The modern root-forms are descended from two Common Slavic forms with differing vowel grades, *(V)ĘZ (>[B]ЯЗ---WIĄZ-WIĘZ-WIĘŹ---VAZ-VÁZ-VÍZ-VĚZ---VEZ-VES-VEŽ) and *(V)ǪZ (>УЗ-ЮЗ---WĘZ---UZ---UZ-UŽ).

A number of the derivatives have English equivalents which are related to bind (bandage, bond, bundle) or derived from Lat. ligare "to tie, bind" (>ligament, ligature, liaison, alliance, obligation). Other parallels are to be found in German derivatives of binden "to tie, bind" (>Band "ligament; volume [part of a book]," Bund "federation," bündig "terse, concise," Bündnis "alliance," Verband "bandage; union, association").

Rus. у́зкий, Pol. wąski, Cz. úzký, S-C uzak "narrow, tight" are thought by some to form part of this group.

vesti, вяза́ть et al.: The primary verb survives only in vesti; вяза́ть et al. were originally iteratives.

vaz (second meaning): ="link" (between the head and the spinal column).

ве́нзель: <Pol. węzeł.

навя́зчивый: <навяза́ть "to tie, fasten (on); to foist, impose."

неотвя́зный: <не + отвяза́ться "to come untied; to detach oneself (from s.o.), leave (s.o.) alone."

obvaziště: <obvaz.

obveznica: ="obligation"; see obveza.

příbuzný: <OCz. přívuzný.

rozwiązać-rozvázati: Compare Eng. solve and dissolve (both ult. <Lat. solvere "to loosen, untie"), Ger. lösen "to loosen, untie; to solve; to dissolve (a marriage), abrogate (an agreement)."

развя́зный-rozwiązły: ="loose" (in behavior); see развяза́ть-rozwiązać and compare Eng. dissolute (ult. <Lat. solvere "to loosen, untie").

развя́зка, rozuzlení: ="untying, unknotting" (of the plot of a drama); see развяза́ть and uzel and compare Fr. (>Eng.) dénouement (<dénouer "to

untie, unknot").

svízel: orig. "fetter, manacle."

союз-sojusz: The Russian word is borrowed from Church Slavic, the Polish word from Russian.

wywiązać się: In its first meaning, the word applied originally to budding fruit (see note on завязь-zawiązek); underlying the second meaning is the notion of "unbinding" oneself.

zobowiązanie: zobo- is a double prefix (z- + obo-); compare obowiązek.

завязь-zawiązek: See завязаться-zawiązać się "to set, begin to grow (said of fruit)" and compare Fr. nouer "to tie, knot; to set, begin to grow."

ВЕД$_1$, ВИД, ВЕЖ, ВЕЖД, (ВЕСТ), (ВЕЩ)	WIAD, WIED(Z), WIEDŹ, (WIEŚĆ), (WIEŚC), (WIESZCZ), (WIAST)	VĚD, VÍD, VĚĎ, (VĚST), (VĚŠT)	VIJED, VIJET, VJED, VID, VIĐ, VJEŽ, (VIJES[T]), (VJES[T]), (VJEŠT), (VJEŠĆ)
ведать: to manage, be in charge (of); (arch.) to know	wiedzieć: to know	věděti: to know	
	wiedza: knowledge	věda: science	
	wiadomy: known	vědomý: aware, conscious	
ведомость: list, register	wiadomość: news; information; knowledge	vědomost: information; knowledge	
ведомство: (governmental) department			
ведьма: witch	wiedźma: witch	vědma: witch	
вежливый: polite			
весть: news	wieść: news; rumor		vijest: news; rumor
вестник: journal; (lit.) herald, messenger		věstník: journal	vijesnik: journal; herald, messenger
вестовой: officer's orderly			
вещий (lit.): prophetic	wieszczy: prophetic		vješt: skilled; experienced
вещун (arch.): prophet	wieszcz: prophet; poet, bard	věštec: prophet	vještac: sorcerer, wizard
[R]	[P]	[Cz]	[S-C]

[R]	[P]	[Cz]	[S-C]
			vještak: expert (n.)
			vještački: artificial; masterly; pertaining to an expert
	wieszczba: prophecy	věštba: prophecy	vježba: practice exercise, training
бла́говест (arch.): ringing of church bells			Blagovijest: (rel.) Annunciation
Благове́щение: (rel.) Annunciation			
			blagovjesnik: apostle; evangelist, preacher of the gospel
		duševěda (arch.): psychology	
языкове́дение: linguistics		jazykověda: linguistics	
естествове́дение (arch.): natural science			
		krasověda (arch.): esthetics	
лжесвиде́тельство: perjury			
	mimowiedny: unconscious, unaware		
народове́дение: ethnology			
природове́дение (arch.): natural science		přírodověda: natural science	
		vědychtivý: curious, inquisitive	
злове́щий: ominous	złowieszczy: ominous	zlověstný: ominous	
	dowiedzieć się, dowiadywać się: to find out; (dowiadywać się only) to inquire	dověděti se, dovídati se: to find out	

	doświadczenie: experience; experiment	dosvědčení: testimony; certification, attestation	
изве́дать, изве́дывать: to experience	zwiedzić, zwiedzać: to visit	zvěděti, zvídati: to find out	izvidjeti, izviđati: to reconnoiter; to investigate
	zwiady (pl.): reconnaissance	zvědy (pl.): reconnaissance	izvid, izviđaj: investigation
		zvědavý: curious, inquisitive	izvjedljiv: curious, inquisitive
изве́стие: news		zvěst (lit.): news	izvješće, izvještaj: information; report
извести́ть, извеща́ть: to inform			izvijestiti, izvješćivati (izvještavati): to inform; to report
	Zwiastowanie: (rel.) Annunciation	Zvěstování: (rel.) Annunciation	
	zwiastun: herald, messenger; harbinger		
изве́стный: known; well-known, noted; a certain, particular (one)			izvjestan: certain, sure; a certain, particular (one)
			izvještačen: artificial, affected
**испове́доваться: to confess	spowiadać się: to confess	zpovídati se: to confess	ispovjediti se, ispovijedati se: to confess
наве́даться, наве́дываться (coll.; к + dat.): to visit	nawiedzić, nawiedzać: to afflict, visit evil upon; (arch.) to visit		
навести́ть, навеща́ть: to visit			navijestiti, navješćivati (navještavati); nagovijestiti, nagovješćivati (nagovještavati): to announce; to predict; to presage, portend
[R]	[P]	[Cz]	[S-C]

[R]	[P]	[Cz]	[S-C]
		návěst: signal; (log.) premise	
		návěští: signal; placard, poster	navještaj: announcement
		napověděti, napovídati: to prompt; to hint	napovjediti, napovijedati: to publish the marriage banns
невéжа: ill-mannered person, boor			nevježa: inexperienced person, novice; ignoramus
невéжда: ignoramus		nevědomec: ignoramus	
неисповеди́мый (arch.): inscrutable			
	obwieścić, obwieszczać: to announce		obavijestiti, obavješćivati (obavještavati): to inform
			onesvijestiti se, onesvješćivati se: to faint, lose consciousness
	opowiedzieć, opowiadać (o + loc.): to tell (about), recount	opověděti, opovídati (arch.): to announce	
	opowiadanie, opowieść: story		
оповести́ть, оповеща́ть: to inform			
осве́домить, осведомля́ть: to inform			
	oświadczyć, oświadczać: to declare, state	osvědčiti, osvědčovati: to prove; to show, display, manifest	osvjedočiti, osvjedočavati: to convince
	oświadczyny (pl.): proposal of marriage		
отве́дать, отве́дывать (arch.): to taste (tr.)	odwiedzić, odwiedzać: to visit		
	odpowiedzieć, odpowiadać: to answer;	odpověděti, odpovídati: to answer;	otpovijedati: to give notice (to
[R]	[P]	[Cz]	[S-C]

	to correspond, conform	(odpovídati only) to correspond, conform	employee, landlord, etc.)
óтповедь: rebuke	odpowiedź: answer	odpověď: answer	otpovijed: notice (to employee, landlord, etc.)
	odpowiedzialny: responsible		
	odpowiedni: corresponding; suitable, appropriate	odpovědný: responsible	
*поведáть (arch.): to impart, disclose	powiedzieć, powiadać: to say, tell	pověděti, povídati: to say, tell	povijedati: to say, tell
		povídka: story	
	powiadomić, powiadamiać: to inform		
пóвесть: story	powieść: novel; story	pověst: legend; reputation; rumor	povijest, povjesnica: history
повéстка: summons, subpoena; agenda	powiastka: (short) story		
	poświadczyć, poświadczać: to certify, attest		posvjedočiti, posvjedočavati: to testify; to certify, attest
	podpowiedzieć, podpowiadać: to prompt		
	przeświadczyć, przeświadczać (arch.): to convince	přesvědčiti, přesvědčovati: to convince	
предвéстие: omen, portent		předzvěst: omen, portent	
		předpověď: prediction	
	przypowieść: parable	přípověď (arch.): promise	pripovijetka, pripovijest: story
	przyświadczyć, przyświadczać: to certify, attest; to confirm; to agree, assent	přisvědčiti, přisvědčovati: to confirm; to agree, assent	
прóповедь: sermon; preaching	przepowiednia: prediction	průpověď, průpovídka: maxim, saying	propovijed: sermon; preaching
[R]	[P]	[Cz]	[S-C]

ВЕД$_1$

[R]	[P]	[Cz]	[S-C]
			prosvjedovati: to protest
разве́дка: intelligence, secret service; reconnaissance; prospecting		rozvědka: intelligence, secret service; reconnaissance	
све́дения (pl.): information			
свиде́тель: witness	świadek: witness	svědek: witness	svjedok: witness
свиде́тельство: testimony; certificate	świadectwo: testimony; certificate	svědectví: testimony	svjedočanstvo: testimony; certificate
	świadomość: consciousness, awareness; consciousness, waking state	svědomí: conscience	
со́весть: conscience			savjest: conscience
			svijest: consciousness, awareness; consciousness, waking state
			uviđavan: sensible, intelligent; lenient, indulgent
уве́домить, уведомля́ть: to inform	uwiadomić, uwiadamiać: to inform	uvědomiti, uvědomovati: to inform; to make (s.o.) conscious, aware (of s.th.)	
	wywiad: interview; intelligence, secret service; reconnaissance	výzvědy (pl.): reconnaissance	
		vyzvědačství: espionage	
	wypowiedzieć, wypowiadać: to express, utter; to declare (war); to give notice (to employee, landlord, etc.); to denounce (a treaty)	vypověděti, vypovídati: to tell (everything); to declare (war); to give notice (to employee, landlord, etc.); to denounce (a treaty); to exile; to testify	

[R]	[P]	[Cz]	[S-C]
	wyświadczyć, wyświadczać: to render (a service, etc.)		
		vysvědčení: certificate	
возвестить, возвещать: to announce			
заве́довать: to manage, be in charge (of)	zawiadywać: to manage, be in charge (of)		
	zawiadomić, zawiadamiać: to inform		
за́поведь: precept; commandment (esp. one of the Ten Commandments)	zapowiedź: announcement; augury	zápověď: ban, prohibition	zapovijed: order, command; commandment (esp. one of the Ten Commandments)
	zapowiedzi (pl.): marriage banns		
запове́дник: (forest, game, etc.) preserve			zapovjednik: commander
запове́дный: maintained as a (forest, game, etc.) preserve; secret, intimate (thoughts, etc.)			zapovjedni: compulsory, by command; (gram.) imperative

NOTES

Basic meaning of root: to know

The semantic development of many of the words is comparable to that described in the introductory note on root ЗНА (etc.).

Rus. свиде́тель et al. have produced a set of derivatives (including, in Polish, Czech and Serbo-Croatian, numerous verbal formations with the stem świadcz-, svědč-, svjedoč-) which reflect the notion of "bearing witness to" or "being a witness of," whence such meanings as "to experience," "to experiment," "to testify," "to certify, attest" (>"to confirm," "to agree"), "to state" and "to show, manifest" (>"to render [a service]"). (Compare Eng. testify and attest [ult. <Lat. testis "witness"], Ger. bezeugen "to certify, attest" [<Zeuge "witness"].) Another significant sub-group is formed by Rus. пове́дать et al. and their derivatives, which show the basic meaning "to say, tell" (i.e. "to let s.o. know").

The forms ВЕСТ-ВЕЩ---WIEŚĆ-WIEŚC-WIESZCZ-WIAST---VĚST-VĚŠT---VIJES(T)-

ВЕД$_1$

VJES(T)-VJEŠT-VJEŠĆ are derived from весть et al. (See note.) The vowel in Russian root-form ВИД and in the Serbo-Croatian forms VID and VIĐ is the result of contamination by ви́деть-vidjeti "to see" (q.v.).

The root is related to root ВИД (etc.) ("to have seen" = "to know"). Non-Slavic cognates are archaic Eng. wit "to know" (as in to wit, unwitting and wit (n.), Ger. wissen "to know," Gr. εἰδέναι "to know" and ἱστορία "inquiry; knowledge; story; history" (>Eng. story, history).

ве́дать et al.: The primary verb is not attested in Serbo-Croatian.

věda: Compare Eng. science (ult. <Lat. scire "to know"), Ger. Wissenschaft "science" (<wissen "to know"), Hung. tudomány "science" (<tudni "to know"), Fin. tiede "science" (<tietää "to know"), S-C znanost.

ве́домость: orig. "information."

ве́домство: See the first meaning of ве́дать.

ве́дьма et al.: orig. "one who is knowing, wise"; compare Rus. зна́харь, Pol. znachor, S-C vještac below. The Polish and Czech words are borrowed from Russian.

ве́жливый: orig. "knowledgeable," then, more narrowly, "knowledgeable about social forms, proper behavior, etc."; compare неве́жа.

весть et al.: <Common Slavic *vědtь; Cz. věst "news" is obsolete.

věstník: <Rus. ве́стник.

вестово́й: so called because one of an orderly's duties is to carry dispatches.

vještac: See note on ве́дьма et al.

vještački: <vještak; regarding the first meaning, compare Hung. mesterséges "artificial" (<mesterség "craft, trade" < mester "master craftsman") and see note on Rus. иску́сственный.

vježba: <*vještba.

бла́говест-Blagovijest, Благове́щение, blagovjesnik: See note under root БЛАГ (etc.).

duševěda: Compare Ger. Seelenkunde "psychology" (<Seele "soul" + Kunde "knowledge").

языкове́дение-jazykověda: The first element is from язы́к-jazyk "language"; compare Ger. Sprachkunde and Sprachwissenschaft "linguistics" (<Sprache "language" + Kunde "knowledge," Wissenschaft "science"), Rus. языкозна́ние, Pol. językoznawstwo, S-C jezikoslovlje.

krasověda: The first element is from krása "beauty"; compare Ger. Schönheitslehre "esthetics" (<Schönheit "beauty" + Lehre "teaching, science").

лжесвиде́тельство: The first element is an invariable combining form with the meaning "false"; see свиде́тельство.

народове́дение: See note on Pol. ludoznawstwo.

vědychtivý: Compare Ger. wissbegierig "curious, inquisitive" (<wissen "to know" + begierig "eager, greedy"), Rus. любозна́тельный, S-C radoznao and znatiželjan.

doświadczenie: See introductory note on root КУС (etc.).

izvješće: ⟨Rus. изве́стие.

изве́стный-izvjestan: Compare Ger. gewiss "certain" (⟨wissen "to know").

izvještačen: See vještački.

nagovijestiti: The intrusive syllable go has not been explained.

návěst (second meaning): prob. = "that which is known (i.e. given, postulated)."

неве́жа: orig. "ignoramus"; see note on ве́жливый.

nevježa: ⟨Rus. неве́жа.

неве́жда: a Church Slavic doublet of неве́жа.

неисповеди́мый: orig. "inexpressible, unutterable."

onesvijestiti se: See svijest.

osvjedočiti: See note on przeświadczyć-přesvědčiti.

odpowiedzieć-odpověděti, о́тповедь-odpowiedź-odpověď, odpowiedzialny, odpowiedni-odpovědný: See notes on S-C odgovoriti, odgovoran and odgovarajući; Rus. о́тповедь was originally synonymous with its Polish and Czech counterparts.

пове́стка: ⟨obsolete повести́ть "to inform, announce."

przeświadczyć-přesvědčiti: ="to win over to one's opinion by the testimony of witnesses"; the words are modeled on Ger. überzeugen "to convince" (⟨über "over, across" + Zeuge "witness").

prosvjedovati: a somewhat anomalous loan-translation of Fr. protester, Ger. protestieren, etc. (ult. ⟨Lat. pro "before, in front" + testari "to testify" ⟨ testis "witness"); pro- here is the Latin rather than the Slavic prefix, while -svjedovati is used in place of the customary -svjedočavati as a denominative formation from svjedok.

rozvědka: ⟨Rus. разве́дка.

свиде́тель et al.: ="one who has knowledge of a thing"; compare Eng. witness (⟨wit "to know").

svědomí, со́весть-savjest: modeled on Lat. conscientia "consciousness, awareness; conscience" (⟨scire "to know"), Gr. συνείδησις "consciousness, awareness; conscience" (⟨εἰδέναι "to know"); compare also Ger. Gewissen "conscience" (⟨wissen "to know"). The Russian word is borrowed from Church Slavic, the Serbo-Croatian word from Russian.

uviđavan: Regarding the second meaning, see note on Pol. wyrozumiały.

vypověděti: The fifth meaning reflects, roughly, the idea of "ordering (s.o.) out, telling (s.o.) to go"; regarding the last meaning, see note on S-C iskazati.

заве́довать-zawiadywać: Compare Rus. ве́дать.

за́поведь-zápověď-zapovijed: See note on Rus. заказа́ть, Pol. zakazać, Cz. zakázati.

запове́дник: ⟨запове́дать "to order, command" in its earlier meaning "to forbid"; see note on S-C branjevina.

zapovjedni: See note on Pol. rozkazujący, Cz. rozkazovací.

ВЕ(Д)$_2$, (В)ОД, ВОЖД	WIE(DZ), WOD(Z), WÓD(Z), WADZ	VÉ, VED, VOD, VŮD, VAD, VÁD, VOZ	VED, (V)OD, VOĐ
†вести́, води́ть: to lead	†wieść, wodzić: to lead	†vésti, voditi: to lead	voditi: to lead
			vod: platoon; (elec.) wire, lead
вождь: leader	wódz: leader; commander	vůdce: leader	vođ, vođa: leader; guide
		vodič: (phys.) conductor	vodič: guide; guidebook; (phys.) conductor
			vođice (pl.): reins
		knihvedoucí (arch.): accountant, bookkeeper	knjigovođa: accountant, bookkeeper
пищево́д: esophagus			
			računovođa: accountant, bookkeeper
	rodowód: genealogy		
руково́дство: leadership, guidance; management, direction; leadership, leaders; handbook, manual			rukovodstvo: leadership, guidance; management, direction; leadership, leaders; handbook, manual
счетово́д: accountant, bookkeeper			
водопрово́д: water-pipe, conduit; aqueduct; water supply		vodovod: water-pipe, conduit; aqueduct; water supply	vodovod: water-pipe, conduit; aqueduct; water supply
воево́да (arch.): voivode (military commander and provincial governor)	wojewoda (arch.): voivode (military commander and provincial governor)	vévoda: duke; (arch.) voivode (military commander and provincial governor)	vojvoda: duke; (arch.) voivode (military commander and provincial governor); (arch.) field marshal
		vévoditi: to dominate	
времяпрепровожде́ние: pastime			
[R]	[P]	[Cz]	[S-C]

до́вод: reason, ground, argument	dowód: proof; document, certificate; reason, ground, argument	důvod: reason, ground, argument	
		dovedný: skilful	
			izvod: deduction, inference, conclusion; extract, excerpt; derivation
			izvedba: performance; execution, carrying out
		návod: instructions, directions; incitement, instigation	navod: quotation; statement, assertion
			navodnik: quotation marks
обво́д: (act of) encircling; (act of) outlining	obwód: circumference, periphery; girth; district; (elec.) circuit	obvod: circumference, periphery; girth; district; (elec.) circuit	
о́бод: rim			obod: rim; edge; hat-brim
			obodac: earring
			obodnica: circumference, periphery
отво́д: challenge (of a juror, witness); allotting (of land)	odwód: (mil.) reserve; (arch.) retreat	odvod: conscription	odvod: drainage
		odvozenina: (ling.) derivative (n.)	
по́вод: cause, occasion, reason; rein	powód: cause, occasion, reason; plaintiff; rein	původ: origin	povod: cause, occasion, reason; rein; leash
		původní: original, initial; original (not derivative or copied)	
поведе́ние: behavior, conduct	powodzenie: success		povođenje: imitation
[R]	[P]	[Cz]	[S-C]

ВЕД$_2$

[R]	[P]	[Cz]	[S-C]
			povodljiv: compliant, tractable
		povedený: successful	
подвóда: cart	podwoda: cart		
		podvodník: swindler, cheat	podvodač, podvodnik: procurer
перевóд: translation; transfer; draft, money-order		převod: transfer; gear, drive, transmission	prevod, prijevod: translation
привóд: gear, drive, transmission		přívod: supply	
прóвод: (elec.) wire, lead	przewód: leadership, command; legal proceedings, trial; (anat.) canal, duct; (elec.) wire, lead	průvod: procession; suite, retinue; escort	provod: accompaniment; pastime
		provoz: operation, functioning; traffic; workshop	
			provodadžija: matchmaker
проводни́к: guide; conductor (on train); (phys.) conductor	przewodnik: guide; guidebook; (phys.) conductor	průvodce: guide; guidebook	provodnik: guide; conductor (on train)
		průvodčí: conductor (on train)	
	przewodniczący: chairman, president		
	prowadzenie się: behavior, conduct		
произвóдство: production, manufacture; promotion (in rank); execution, carrying out			proizvodnja, proizvodstvo: production, manufacture
произведéние: work (of art, etc.); (math.) product			proizvod: product; (math.) product

развóд: divorce; changing of the guard	rozwód: divorce	rozvod: divorce; (tech.) distributor, regulator	razvod: divorce
			razvodnica: watershed; usher; (anat.) aorta
		rozváděč: switchboard	
свод: arch, vault; code (of laws, etc.)	zwód (arch.): drawbridge	svod: seduction; code (of laws, etc.)	svod: arch, vault
	zwodzenie: deception		
свóдка: summary			
свóдник: procurer			svodnik: procurer
			sprovod: funeral procession
			sprovodnik: guide; (phys.) conductor
	uwiedzenie, uwodzenie: seduction; abduction, kidnaping		
	uprowadzenie: abduction, kidnaping		
ввóдный: introductory, prefatory; (gram.) parenthetical		úvodní: introductory, prefatory	uvodan: introductory, prefatory
		uvozovky (pl.): quotation marks	
		uvaděč, uváděč: usher	
вы́вод: deduction, inference, conclusion; withdrawal; outlet	wywód: deduction, inference, conclusion; argumentation, reasoning; derivation	vývod: deduction, inference, conclusion; outlet; (anat.) duct	
вы́водок: brood, hatch			
		zvednouti, zvedati: to raise, lift	
взвод: platoon; cocking recess (in a gun)			
заведéние: institution, establishment;		zavedení: installation (of equipment);	
[R]	[P]	[Cz]	[S-C]

(arch.) habit, custom		introduction (of new methods, etc.)	
завóд: factory; winding mechanism; (act of) winding	zawód: profession, occupation; disappointment	závod: factory; (business) enterprise, concern; competition, contest	zavod: institution, establishment
	zawody (pl.): competition, contest		
	zawodny: deceptive		zavodljiv: seductive
[R]	[P]	[Cz]	[S-C]

NOTES

Basic meaning of root: to lead

In many of the derivatives, the root has the force of "to bring, take, carry, put, etc."

The Russian root-form ВОЖД is of Church Slavic origin.

вести́ et al.: The respective 1 sg. forms of вести́-wieść-vésti are веду́, wiodę, vedu; the Serbo-Croatian iterative verb has taken over the function of obsolete vesti (1 sg.: vedem), which appears today only in compounds.

vod (first meaning): See note on взвод below.

vodič (Cz.-S-C): Compare Eng. conductor (ult. ‹Lat. ducere "to lead").

knihvedoucí-knjigovođa: The first element is from kniha-knjiga "book."

пищевóд: The first element is from пи́ща "food."

računovođa: The first element is from račun "account."

rodowód: For the sense of -wód here, see the last meaning of wywód.

руковóдство-rukovodstvo: See note under root РУК (etc.).

водопровóд et al.: Compare Eng. aqueduct (ult. ‹Lat. aqua "water" + ducere "to lead") and conduit (ult. ‹Lat. ducere), Ger. Wasserleitung "water pipe, conduit; aqueduct; water supply" (‹Wasser "water" + leiten "to lead").

воевóда et al.: The first element is from the root of вóйско-wojsko-vojsko-vojska "army"; compare Eng. duke (ult. ‹Lat. ducere "to lead"), Ger. Herzog "duke" (‹Heer "army" + ziehen "to pull" [here = "to lead"]).

времяпрепровождéние: See проводи́ть "to pass, spend (time)."

дóвод et al.: that which leads one to a certain conclusion or inference.

dovedný: prob. = "able to lead or carry a thing to a successful conclusion."

izvod: See note on вы́вод et al.

izvedba: Compare Ger. Ausführung "execution, carrying out" (‹aus "out" + führen "to lead").

návod: Compare Ger. Anleitung "instructions, directions" (<an "to, on" + leiten "to lead").

navod: Compare Eng. adduce (ult. <Lat. ad "to" + ducere "to lead"), Ger. Anführung "quotation; statement, assertion" (<an "to, on" + führen "to lead").

обво́д et al., о́бод-obod, obodac, obodnica: Underlying the various meanings is the notion of "leading" (i.e. drawing) a line around something, hence encircling or circumscribing it; similar semantic development is shown by Eng. circumference (ult. <Lat. circum "around" + ferre "to carry") and periphery (ult. <Gr. περί "around" + φέρειν "to carry").

отво́д et al.: The first meaning of the Russian word reflects the idea of "leading away" (i.e. removing) the challenged juror or witness. The notion of allotting or holding in reserve arose in much the same way as the comparable meaning of Eng. to set aside. Implicit in the last three meanings is, again, the idea of "leading away" (troops, recruits, waste water).

odvozenina: See note on вы́вод et al.

по́вод et al.: In the meaning "cause, occasion, reason," the underlying sense is "that which leads to a given action or result"; compare Eng. induce and conduce (both ult. <Lat. ducere "to lead"). The second meaning of the Polish word reflects the fact that the plaintiff is the one who "causes," i.e. institutes, a legal action. In the case of Cz. původ, the meaning may be an outgrowth of the notion of "cause" or, it has been suggested, may bespeak the view that to originate is to be "led," i.e. derived, from a source; see note on вы́вод et al.

поведе́ние: the manner in which a person "leads himself"; compare Eng. conduct (ult. <Lat. ducere "to lead").

powodzenie: The idea is probably that of leading or carrying a thing to a favorable conclusion; compare dovedný above.

povođenje: the behavior of one who is "led" or guided by another.

povodljiv: ="easily led."

povedený: See note on powodzenie.

подво́да-podwoda: the means by which someone or something is "led" (i.e. brought) to a place.

podvodník: See note on uwiedzenie-uwodzenie, uprowadzenie.

podvodač-podvodnik: Compare Gr. προαγωγός "procurer" (<πρό "forth, forward" + ἄγειν "to lead").

перево́д-prevod-prijevod: Compare Eng. translation (ult. <Lat. trans "over, across" + latus, past part. of ferre "to carry"), Fr. traduction "translation" (ult. <Lat. trans + ducere "to lead") and see note on Pol. przekład, Cz. překlad.

przewód: Compare Eng. duct (ult. <Lat. ducere "to lead").

provod (second meaning): See provoditi "to pass, spend (time)."

provoz: The basic idea is that of carrying on an activity; compare Ger. durchführen "to execute, carry out" (<durch "through" + führen "to lead").

provodadžija: See note on podvodač-podvodnik.

проводни́к-przewodnik-provodnik, průvodčí: See note on vodič; the Serbo-Croatian word is borrowed from Russian.

prowadzenie się: See note on поведе́ние.

произво́дство et al., произведе́ние-proizvod: The notion of "leading" (or bringing) forth is similarly reflected in Eng. product(ion) (ult. <Lat. pro- "forth, forward" + ducere "to lead"), Du. voortbrengsel "product" (<voort "forth, forward" + brengen "to bring"); underlying the meaning "promotion" is the idea of leading (s.o.) forward. Regarding the third meaning of произво́дство, see note on izvedba. The Serbo-Croatian words are borrowed or adapted from their Russian equivalents.

разво́д et al., razvodnica, rozváděč: The different meanings reflect the basic notion of "leading in various directions," hence separating or distributing.

свод et al., zwodzenie, сво́дка, сво́дник-svodnik: The contrasting meanings of the prefix give rise to the notions of leading or bringing together (>"arch, vault," "code," "summary," "procurer") and leading or bringing off, away or down (>"drawbridge," "seduction," "deception"). Pol. zwód is from zwodzić "to lower." (Compare earlier wzwód "drawbridge" < obs. wzwodzić "to raise.") Regarding the meanings "seduction," "deception" and "procurer," see notes on uwiedzenie-uwodzenie, uprowadzenie and on podvodač-podvodnik. S-C svod is borrowed from Russian.

sprovodnik: See note on vodič.

uwiedzenie-uwodzenie, uprowadzenie: Compare Eng. seduction and abduction (ult. <Lat. se- "aside," ab "off, away" + ducere "to lead"), Ger. Verführung "seduction" and Entführung "abduction" (<ver- "mis-," ent- "off, away" + führen "to lead").

вво́дный et al.: Compare Eng. introductory (ult. <Lat. intro "within" + ducere "to lead"), Ger. einleitend "introductory" (<ein- "in" + leiten "to lead"); the second meaning of the Russian word arises from the notion of bringing in or inserting.

uvozovky: See note on navod.

вы́вод et al.: Compare Eng. deduction (ult. <Lat. de "off, away" + ducere "to lead"), Ger. Ableitung and Herleitung "deduction, inference, conclusion; derivation" (<ab "off, away," her "hither" + leiten "to lead") and see note on przewód.

вы́водок: ="that which is led or brought forth"; compare произво́дство, произведе́ние.

zvednouti: reconstructed (with loss of the initial consonant) from OCz. vzvésti, vzvoditi.

взвод (first meaning): ="that which is led (brought, marched) up"; compare Ger. Zug "platoon" (<ziehen "to pull; to move, march").

заведе́ние-zavedení, заво́д et al., zawody, zawodny-zavodljiv: The basic notion of starting, setting in motion, introducing, establishing (in which the prefix has inceptive force) is apparent in many of the meanings; the meaning "competition, contest" arose from the idea of getting a quick (or running) start, engaging in a race. Regarding the meanings "deceptive" and "seductive," see note on uwiedzenie-uwodzenie, uprowadzenie; the semantic link between the notions of deception and disappointment is further illustrated by Fr. déception "disappointment."

ВЕЛ$_1$	WIEL	VEL	VEL, VEO
			velji: big, large
	wiele: much, many		
вели́кий: great	wielki: big, large; great	velký, veliký: big, large; great	velik: big, large; great
		velmi: very	veoma: very
	wielce: very	velice: very	
	wielbić: to extol, glorify; to worship	velebiti: to extol, glorify	
	wielebny: reverend (title)	velebný: majestic; reverend (title)	veleban: majestic
велича́ть: to honor in peasant ceremonies (e.g. bride and bridegroom); (arch.) to name, call			veličati: to extol, glorify
велича́вый, вели́чественный: majestic			veličajan, veličanstven: majestic
Вели́чество: Majesty (form of address)		Veličenstvo: Majesty (form of address)	veličanstvo: majesty, grandeur; (cap.) Majesty (form of address)
велика́н: giant		velikán: giant	velikan: giant; great man
		velikáš (lit.): megalomaniac	velikaš: magnate, dignitary
	wielobok: polygon		
	wielobóstwo: polytheism		
		veledílo: masterpiece	
		veleduch: genius	
великоду́шный: magnanimous	wielkoduszny: magnanimous	velkodušný: magnanimous	veledušan, velikodušan: magnanimous
[R]	[P]	[Cz]	[S-C]

[R]	[P]	[Cz]	[S-C]
	wielokąt: polygon		
великоле́пный: magnificent		velkolepý: magnificent	velelijepan: magnificent
	wielkolud: giant		
	wielomęstwo: polyandry		
	wielomówny: loquacious		
вельмо́жа: magnate, dignitary	wielmoża: magnate, dignitary	velmož: magnate, dignitary	velmoža: magnate, dignitary
		velkomyslný: magnanimous	
	Wielkanoc: Easter; Passover	Velikonoce (pl.): Easter; Passover	
велере́чивый (arch.): pompous, bombastic			
	wieloryb: whale	velryba: whale	
			veleum: genius
		velvyslanec: ambassador	
	wielożeństwo: polygamy		
преувели́чить, преувели́чивать: to exaggerate			preuveličati, preuveličavati: to exaggerate
увели́чить, увели́чивать: to increase, enlarge; to enlarge (a photograph); to magnify (with a microscope, etc.)			uveličati, uveličavati: to exaggerate; to enlarge (a photograph); to magnify (with a microscope, etc.)
возвели́чить, возвели́чивать: to extol, glorify			uzveličati, uzveličavati: to extol, glorify
		zvelebiti, zvelebovati: to improve (tr.)	
		zveličiti, zveličovati: to exaggerate	

NOTES

Basic meaning of root: big, large; much, many

A number of the derivatives have English counterparts derived from Lat. magnus "big, large; great" (>magnate, magnify, magnificent) and its comparative form (>majesty, majestic). (See also note on великоду́шный et al. below.)

velji: The unsuffixed adjective (compare вели́кий et al.) is also represented by ORus. велии, OPol. wieli, OCz. velí.

вели́кий: The meaning "big, large" survives only in the short predicative form вели́к.

wielki: for OPol. wieliki.

veleban: <Cz. velebný.

велича́ть: The second meaning reflects the notion of honoring or dignifying; compare Pol. godność.

velikán: <Rus. велика́н.

velikáš: one suffering from delusions of grandeur or greatness; Eng. megalo- is from Gr. μέγας "big, large; great."

wielobóstwo: See note on Rus. многобо́жие et al.

великоду́шный et al.: Compare Eng. magnanimous (ult. <Lat. magnus "big, large; great" + animus "mind, mood"), Ger. grossmütig "magnanimous" (<gross "big, large; great" + Mut "[arch. or in compounds] mind, mood; [otherwise] courage"), Cz. velkomyslný below.

wielokąt: The second element is from kąt "angle"; compare Eng. polygon (ult. <Gr. πολύς "much, many" + γωνία "angle").

великоле́пный et al.: The second element is from ле́пый (obs.)-lepý-lijep "beautiful"; the Czech word is borrowed from Russian.

wielomęstwo: The second element is from mąż "man; husband"; compare Eng. polyandry (ult. <Gr. πολύς "much, many" + ἀνήρ "man; husband."

velkomyslný: See note on великоду́шный et al.

Wielkanoc-Velikonoce: The second element is from noc "night."

wieloryb-velryba: The second element is from ryba "fish."

velvyslanec: See note under root СЛ (etc.).

wielożeństwo: The second element is from żona "wife."

ВЕЛ$_2$, ВОЛ, ВЛ	WOL, WAL	VEL, VŮL, VOL	VEL, VOL
**веле́ть: to order, command		veleti: to order, command	velim (velju): I say
во́ля: will, desire; freedom	wola: will, desire	vůle: will, desire	volja: will, desire
	woleć: to prefer	voliti: to choose; to elect	voljeti: to like
во́льный: free	wolny: free; slow; loose	volný: free; slow; loose	voljan: willing
благоволи́ть (arch.): to show benevolence, good will; to deign, condescend			blagovoljeti: to show benevolence, good will; to deign, condescend
		blahovolný: benevolent	
доброво́льный: voluntary	dobrowolny: voluntary	dobrovolný: voluntary	dobrovoljan: voluntary; good-humored
			dragovoljan: voluntary
	gwoli: for the sake (of); because (of)	kvůli: for the sake (of); because (of)	
		libovolný: optional; any; arbitrary, high-handed	
	mimowolny: involuntary, unintentional	mimovolný: involuntary, unintentional	
мирво́лить (arch.): to humor, gratify, indulge			
самово́льный: wilful; unauthorized	samowolny: wilful; unauthorized	samovolný: spontaneous	samovoljan: wilful
своево́льный: wilful	swawolny: licentious; frolicsome, prankish	svévolný: arbitrary, high-handed	svojevoljan: arbitrary, high-handed; voluntary
удовлетвори́ть, удовлетворя́ть: to satisfy; to supply (with)			
вольноотпу́щенник (arch.): freed slave or serf			
[R]	[P]	[Cz]	[S-C]

[R]	[P]	[Cz]	[S-C]
		zlovolný: malevolent	zlovoljan: ill-humored
довле́ть: (над + inst.) to weigh heavily (upon), oppress; (arch.) to suffice			
дово́льный: satisfied, content	dowolny: optional; any; arbitrary, high-handed		dovoljan: sufficient
дово́льно: enough; rather, fairly; contentedly	dowolnie: at one's discretion, as one pleases		dovoljno: enough
дово́льство: prosperity, easy circumstances; contentment			
дово́льствие: military ration, allowance			
дозво́лить, дозволя́ть (arch.): to permit	dozwolić, dozwalać: to permit	dovoliti, dovolovati: to permit	dozvoliti, dozvoljavati: to permit
изво́лить (arch.): to deign, condescend			izvoljeti, izvolijevati: to deign, condescend
нево́ля: slavery; captivity; compulsion, necessity	niewola: slavery; captivity; compulsion, necessity	nevůle: unwillingness; disagreement, discord; displeasure, indignation	nevolja: misfortune, trouble; poverty, need
		nevole: displeasure, indignation	
нево́лить: to force, compel	niewolić: to force, compel		
нево́льный: involuntary, unintentional	niewolny (arch.): unfree	nevolný: unfree; uncomfortable, uneasy	nevoljan: wretched, miserable; involuntary, unintentional
		nevolnost: indisposition, malaise; nausea	
нево́льник: (lit.) slave; (arch.) prisoner	niewolnik: slave; prisoner	nevolník: slave; serf	nevoljnik: poor wretch
[R]	[P]	[Cz]	[S-C]

[R]	[P]	[Cz]	[S-C]
			povelja: charter; legal instrument, deed
повели́тельный: imperious, peremptory; (gram.) imperative			
	powolny: slow; compliant, tractable	povolný: compliant, tractable	povoljan: favorable, propitious
позво́лить, позволя́ть: to permit	pozwolić, pozwalać: to permit	povoliti, povolovati: to permit; to yield, submit; to relax, slacken (tr. and intr.)	*povoljiti: to humor, gratify, indulge
		pozvolný: slow	
		podvoliti se, podvolovati se: to yield, submit	
приво́лье: broad expanse; free, untrammeled life			
	przyzwolić, przyzwalać: to agree, consent	přivoliti, přivolovati: to agree, consent	*privoljeti: to agree, consent; to persuade
продово́льствие: food			
произво́льный: arbitrary, high-handed; voluntary (movement of a limb, etc.)			proizvoljan: arbitrary, high-handed; any
	rozwolnienie: diarrhea; looseness (of morals)		
		svoliti, svolovati: to agree, consent	
соизво́лить, соизволя́ть (arch.): to deign, condescend	zezwolić, zezwalać: to permit		
уво́лить, увольня́ть: to dismiss, discharge; (уво́лить only)	uwolnić, uwalniać: to liberate; to release; to free, re-	uvolniti, uvolňovati: to loosen; to release; to vacate;	
[R]	[P]	[Cz]	[S-C]

to free, re-lieve (of an obligation, etc.)	lieve (of an obligation, etc.)	to relax, slacken (tr.)	
		uvoliti se, uvolovati se: to agree, consent	
удово́льствие: pleasure			
вы́зволить, вызволя́ть (coll.): to rescue, help out	wyzwolić, wyzwalać: to liberate		
		zvůle: arbitrary, high-handed action	
	zwolennik: adherent, supporter	zvolenec (arch.): delegate, deputy	
	zwolnić, zwalniać: to slow (tr.); to loosen; to release; to dismiss, discharge; to free, re-lieve (of an obligation, etc.); to exempt	zvolniti, zvolňovati: to slow (tr.)	
	zadowolić, zadowalać: to satisfy		zadovoljiti, zadovoljavati: to satisfy
[R]	[P]	[Cz]	[S-C]

NOTES

Basic meaning of root: to want, wish

Most of the word-formation in this root-group is based on the noun во́ля et al.; the primary verb веле́ть et al. (see note below) shows little development. The various derivatives tend (with some overlapping) to fall into three broad semantic groupings:

(1) Those reflecting the presence or assertion of will or desire, whence such meanings as "to command," "to prefer," "to choose," "to deign," "voluntary," "spontaneous," "arbitrary" and "licentious";

(2) Those reflecting the fulfilment or granting of a desire, whence such meanings as "to permit," "to consent," "favorable," "optional; any" (="at will, as one pleases"), "free" (and, by extension, "slow," "loose") and "sufficient" (>"satisfied," "pleasure," "prosperity," "food," "ration, allowance");

(3) Negative formations reflecting the absence of desire or its nonfulfilment, whence such meanings as "involuntary," "slavery," "compulsion," "displeasure," "uncomfortable," "misfortune" and "poverty."

The Russian verbs containing the form ЗВОЛ are borrowed from the Polish equivalents.

Non-Slavic cognates are Eng. *will* (v. and n.), Ger. *wollen* "to want, wish," *Wille* "will, desire" and *wählen* "to choose; to elect," Lat. *velle* "to want, wish" (>Eng. *volition*) and *voluntas* "will, desire" (>Eng. *voluntary*).

велéть et al.: The corresponding Polish word is not attested; S-C *velim* (*velju*) is a defective verb with only present and imperfect forms.

woleć et al.: Rus. *вóлить* "to want, wish" is obsolete.

blahovolný: Compare Eng. *benevolent* (ult. <Lat. *bene* "well" + *velle* "to want, wish"), Rus. *благожелáтельный* and *доброжелáтельный*, S-C *dobrohotan*.

dragovoljan: The first element is from *drag* "dear; glad."

gwoli-*kvůli*: The first element is from OPol. *k* (=modern *ku*), Cz. *k* "to"; the original form of the Polish word was *kwoli*. Compare Ger. *um* ... *willen* "for the sake (of)" (<*um* "around; for" + *Wille* "will, desire").

libovolný: See note on Rus. *любóй et al*.

удовлетворúть: See the second meaning of *довлéть* and compare Eng. *satisfy* (ult. <Lat. *satis* "enough" + *facere* "to do, make"), Ger. *Genugtuung* "satisfaction" (<*genug* "enough" + *tun* "to do, make"), Pol. *zadośćuczynienie et al*.

zlovolný: Compare Eng. *malevolent* (ult. <Lat. *male* "badly, ill" + *velle* "to want, wish"), Rus. *зложелáтельный*.

довлéть: a Church Slavic loan-word showing the zero grade of the root; the first meaning resulted from confusion with the unrelated word *давúть* "to press, weigh (upon)."

dowolny: See note on Rus. *любóй et al*.

dozvoliti: <Rus. *дозвóлить*.

изволить: borrowed from Church Slavic.

nevůle, *nevole*: Compare Ger. *Unwille* "unwillingness; displeasure, indignation" (<*un-* "un-" + *Wille* "will, desire").

povelja: <obsolete *poveljeti* "to order, command."

повелúтельный: See *велéть* and note on Pol. *rozkazujący*, Cz. *rozkazovací*.

privoljeti: The second meaning is, in effect, the causative equivalent of the first.

продовóльствие: borrowed from Church Slavic.

proizvoljan: <Rus. *произвóльный*; see note on Rus. *любóй et al*.

удовóльствие: See introductory note above and compare Ger. *Vergnügen* "pleasure" (<*genug* "enough").

zwolennik: <obsolete *zwolić* "to choose"; the word was originally applied to the twelve apostles, *i.e*. those chosen by Christ to be his companions and preach the gospel.

zvolenec: <*zvoliti*, the perfective form of *voliti*.

BEP_1	WIAR, WIER(Z)	VÍR, VĚR, VĚŘ	VJER
ве́ра: faith, belief, trust; faith, religion	wiara: faith, belief, trust; faith, religion	víra: faith, belief, trust; faith, religion	vjera: faith, belief, trust; faith, religion
ве́рить: to believe; to trust	wierzyć: to believe; to trust	věřiti: to believe; to trust	*vjeriti: to plight one's troth to
ве́ровать (lit.): to believe			vjerovati: to believe; to trust
ве́рный: true, loyal, faithful; true (opp. of false); accurate; certain	wierny: true, loyal, faithful; accurate	věrný: true, loyal, faithful; accurate	vjeran: true, loyal, faithful; accurate
	wierzyciel: creditor	věřitel: creditor	vjerovnik: creditor
	wiarus: old soldier		
достове́рный: trustworthy; authentic			
		hodnověrný: trustworthy; authentic	
			krivovjerac: heretic
легкове́рный: gullible	łatwowierny: gullible	lehkověrný: gullible	lakovjeran: gullible
малове́рный: skeptical		malověrný: skeptical	
неимове́рный: incredible, extraordinary, very great			
правове́рный: orthodox	prawowierny: orthodox	pravověrný: orthodox	pravovjeran: orthodox
			praznovjerje: superstition
суеве́рие: superstition			sujevjerje: superstition
удостове́рить, удостоверя́ть: to certify, attest			
			vjerodajnica: credentials
	wiarogodny: trustworthy; authentic	věrohodný: trustworthy; authentic	vjerodostojan: trustworthy; authentic
[R]	[P]	[Cz]	[S-C]

[R]	[P]	[Cz]	[S-C]
вероя́тный: probable, likely			vjerojatan, vjerovatan: probable, likely
вероло́мный: perfidious, disloyal	wiarołomny: perfidious, disloyal	věrolomný: perfidious, disloyal	vjeroloman: perfidious, disloyal
		bezvěrec: atheist	bezvjerac, bezvjernik: atheist
дове́рить, доверя́ть: to commit, entrust; (доверя́ть only) to trust; (доверя́ть only) to confide	dowierzać: to trust	důvěřovati: to trust	
довери́тельный: confidential		důvěrný: intimate; confidential	
		důvěrník: confidant	
дове́ренность: power of attorney, proxy			
			iznevjeriti, iznevjeravati: to betray, forsake
изуве́р: cruel fanatic			
		nevěrec: atheist; infidel	
		nevěrník: disloyal, unfaithful person	nevjernik: atheist; infidel; traitor
	niedowiarek: skeptic		
		ověřiti, ověřovati: to check, verify; to certify, attest	ovjeriti (ovjeroviti), ovjeravati: to certify, attest
пове́рье: popular belief, superstitious idea		pověra: superstition	
пове́рить, поверя́ть: to confide; to check, verify	powierzyć, powierzać: to commit, entrust; to confide	pověřiti, pověřovati: to entrust, charge (s.o. with s.th.)	povjeriti, povjeravati: to confide; to commit, entrust
пове́ренный: agent	powiernik: confidant; trustee	pověřenec: agent	povjerenik: confidant; commissioner

[R]	[P]	[Cz]	[S-C]
			povjerilac: creditor
			prevjera: apostasy
прове́рить, проверя́ть: to check, verify		prověřiti, prověřovati: to check, verify	provjeriti, provjeravati: to check, verify
	przeniewierstwo: perfidy		pronevjera: embezzlement
све́рить, сверя́ть: to collate, compare	zwierzyć, zwierzać: to confide	svěřiti, svěřovati: to commit, entrust; to confide	
	sprzeniewierzenie: embezzlement	zpronevěra: embezzlement; perfidy	
уве́рить, уверя́ть: to assure; to convince	*uwierzyć: to believe; to trust	*uvěřiti: to believe; to trust	uvjeriti, uvjeravati: to assure; to convince
		úvěr: (comm.) credit	
	uwierzytelnić, uwierzytelniać: to certify, attest; to accredit (a diplomat)		
вве́рить, вверя́ть: to commit, entrust; to confide			
заве́рить, заверя́ть: to assure; to certify, attest	zawierzyć, zawierzać: to trust; to confide		zavjeriti se, zavjeravati se: to pledge, vow; to plot, conspire

NOTES

Basic meaning of root: truth; faith, belief, trust

Regarding the relationship between the two root-meanings, compare Eng. true and the related words trust and archaic trow "to believe."

The Slavic root is cognate with Ger. wahr "true," Lat. verus "true" (>Eng. very, verity, veracity, verify, aver).

ве́рить et al.: denominatives formed from ве́ра et al.

vjeriti: Compare Eng. troth (in origin, a doublet of truth), Ger. trauen "to trust; to join in marriage" and see introductory note above.

wierzyciel et al.: ="one who believes or trusts"; the words are modele on Lat. *creditor* (<*credere* "to believe"), Ger. *Gläubiger* "creditor" (<*glaub* "to believe").

достове́рный: a Church Slavic loan-word modeled on Gr. *ἀξιόπιστος* "trus worthy" (<*ἄξιος* "worthy" + *πίστις* "faith, belief, trust"); the first elemen is probably related to S-C *dosta* "enough," its use here being influenced by Church Slavic *достоинъ* "worthy" (see Rus. *досто́йный*). Compare Eng. *trustworthy*, Ger. *glaubwürdig* "trustworthy; authentic" (<*Glaube* "faith, belief, trust" + *würdig* "worthy").

hodnověrný: See preceding note.

łatwowierny: The first element is from *łatwy* "easy."

неимове́рный: See note under root Я (etc.).

правове́рный et al.: Compare Ger. *rechtgläubig* "orthodox" (<*recht* "righ correct" + *Glaube* "faith, belief, trust").

praznovjerje: The first element is from *prazan* "empty."

суеве́рие-sujevjerje: The first element is from the root of *суета́-sujet* "vanity" (orig. "emptiness"); the Russian word is borrowed from Church Slavic, the Serbo-Croatian word from Russian or Church Slavic.

удостове́рить: See *достове́рный*.

vjerodajnica: ="that which gives faith"; compare Eng. *credentials* (ult <Lat. *credere* "to believe").

wiarogodny et al.: See note on *достове́рный*.

вероя́тный et al.: See note under root Я (etc.).

вероло́мный et al.: Compare Ger. *treubrüchig* "perfidious, disloyal" (<*Treue* "loyalty, faithfulness" + *brechen* "to break").

изуве́р: orig. "one who tries to convince another"; compare *уве́рить*. The word is borrowed from Church Slavic.

ověřiti-ovjeriti: See note on *uwierzytelnić*, *заве́рить*.

пове́рье-pověra: The prefix is pejorative here.

пове́ренный et al.: ="someone to whom a thing has been committed, entrusted or confided."

povjerilac: See note on *wierzyciel et al.*

prevjera: ="a change of faith."

prověřiti: <Rus. *прове́рить*.

pronevjera: <obsolete Cz. *proněvěra*; see note on *sprzeniewierzenie-zpronevěra*.

све́рить: Compare *пове́рить* (second meaning), *прове́рить*.

sprzeniewierzenie-zpronevěra: Compare Ger. *Veruntreuung* "embezzlement" (<*un-* "un-, not" + *treu* "true, loyal, faithful").

úvěr: ="the giving of goods or money on the strength of the giver's faith that he will be paid at some future time"; compare Eng. *credit* (ult. <Lat. *credere* "to believe").

uwierzytelnić, *заве́рить*: Compare Eng. *accredit* (ult. <Lat. *credere* "to

believe"), Ger. beglaubigen "to certify, attest; to accredit (a diplomat)" (<Glaube "faith, belief, trust").

zavjeriti se: Regarding the first meaning, compare vjeriti; the second meaning is an outgrowth of the first.

BEC, BE3, BC	WSZ	VEŠ, VŠ, VŽ, VES	SAV, SV, VAS, VAZ
весь: all, entire	wszystek: all, entire	všechen, všecek, (lit.) veškeren, (lit.) veškerý: all, entire	sav, vas: all, entire
вся́кий: every; any; every kind of			svak: every; any
	wszelki: every; any	všeliký: every kind of	
	wszelaki: every kind of	všelijaký: every kind of	
везде́, всю́ду: everywhere	wszędzie, (arch.) wszędy: everywhere	všude, všade: everywhere	svuda, svugdje, svagdje: everywhere
всегда́: always		vždy, vždycky: always	svagda, svakad, vazda: always
	wszak, wszakże: however; after all	však: however; surely	
	wszelako: however		
весьма́: very			
	wszechnica: university		
повседне́вный: daily, every-day; everyday, commonplace	powszedni: daily, every-day; everyday, commonplace; venial	všední: daily, every-day; everyday, commonplace	
всея́дный: omnivorous			
		vesmír: universe	svemir: universe
всемогу́щий: almighty, omnipotent	wszechmogący, wszechmocny: almighty, omnipotent	všemohoucí, všemocný: almighty, omnipotent	svemoguć, svemoćan: almighty, omnipotent
	wszechświat: universe		
	wszeteczny (arch.): lewd, dissolute	všetečný: inquisitive, nosy	
			sveučilište: university.
[R]	[P]	[Cz]	[S-C]

[R]	[P]	[Cz]	[S-C]
	wszystkożerny: omnivorous		svežder, svaštožder: omnivorous
	owszem: yes, indeed	ovšem, ovšemže: of course	
повсю́ду: everywhere			posvuda: everywhere
	powszechny: general (a.)	povšechný: general (a.)	
	rozpowszechnić, rozpowszechniać: to disseminate, propagate (e.g. ideas)		
совсе́м: completely, altogether			sasvim: completely, altogether
	zawsze: always		

NOTES

Basic meaning of root: all

весь et al.: In Polish and Czech, suffixed forms have replaced OPol. wszy and OCz. veš (although the older oblique forms---všeho, všemu, etc.--- continue to be used in Czech). In Serbo-Croatian, a transposed form of the root appears in sav alongside older vas (and in all the derivatives with the exception of vazda).

vesmír-svemir, wszechświat: Compare Ger. Weltall "universe" (⟨Welt "world" + all "all"); the Czech and Serbo-Croatian words are probably adapted from Rus. всеми́рный "universal."

wszeteczny-všetečný: See note under root ТК (etc.).

svaštožder: The first element is from svašta "all kinds of things" (⟨s + šta, što "what").

rozpowszechnić: ⟨powszechny.

(В)ЕТ, ВИТ, ВЕЧ, (В)ЕЩ	IAT, (W)IEC	VĚT, (V)ĚŤ	VJET, VIJEĆ, EĆ, VJEŠT
веща́ть: to broadcast (on the radio); (arch.) to prophesy			vijećati: to confer, deliberate
ве́че (arch.): meeting, gathering	wiec: meeting, gathering		vijeće: council
вити́я (arch.): orator			
		věta: (gram.) sentence, clause; (math.) theorem; (log.) proposition	
чревовеща́тель: ventriloquist			
		větosloví: syntax	
			bezuvjetan: unconditional; absolute
беззаве́тный: utter, wholehearted (devotion, etc.)			
		dovětek: codicil; postscript	
наве́т (arch.): slander			
**обеща́ть: to promise	obiecać, obiecywać: to promise		obećati, obećavati: to promise
обе́т: vow	obiata (arch.): vow; sacrificial offering	oběť: sacrifice; victim	
отве́тить, отвеча́ть: to answer		*odvětiti (lit.): to answer	
отве́тственный: responsible			
отве́тчик: defendant, respondent (in a lawsuit)			odvjetnik: lawyer
приве́т: greeting			
приве́тливый: affable, friendly		přívětivý: affable, friendly	
[R]	[P]	[Cz]	[S-C]

[R]	[P]	[Cz]	[S-C]
совещáние: conference			
совéт: council; soviet; advice, counsel			savjet: council; advice, counsel
соответствовать: to correspond, conform			
соответствующий: corresponding; suitable, appropriate			
увещевáть (увещáть): to admonish, remonstrate with			
			uvjet: condition, stipulation, proviso
			uvjetan: conditional, contingent
завещáние: will, testament			zavještanje: will, testament
завéт: precept, advice (to posterity); testament (of the Bible)		závěť: will, testament	zavjet: vow; testament (of the Bible)
завéтный: intimate; cherished; hidden			zavjetan: votive

NOTES

Basic meaning of root: to speak

See the introductory note on root ГОВОР (etc.).

The Russian root-form ВЕЩ is of Church Slavic origin.

вещáть-vijećati: The primary verb also occurs in ORus. вѣтити and dialectal Cz. větiti (both of which show the original root-meaning) but is unattested in Polish. The Church Slavic loan-word вещáть originally meant "to speak"; the meaning "to prophesy" probably reflects the influence of the unrelated words вéщий and вещýн (q.v.).

витúя: for ORus. вѣтия, which is a Church Slavic borrowing.

чревовещáтель: The first element is from чрéво "belly"; see note on Pol. brzuchomówca, Cz. břichomluvec.

větosloví: See věta and note under root СЛЫ (etc.).

bezuvjetan: See uvjet.

беззаве́тный: ="unconditional"; see note on заве́т.

наве́т: borrowed from Church Slavic.

отве́тить-odvětiti, отве́тственный: See notes on S-C odgovoriti and odgovoran.

odvjetnik: ‹obsolete odvjet "answer; defense."

приве́тливый-přívětivý: ="speaking to or greeting others"; see приве́т and compare Eng. affable (ult. ‹Lat. affabilis "easy to speak to" ‹ ad "to" + fari "to speak").

сове́т: borrowed from Church Slavic.

соотве́тствовать, соотве́тствующий: See notes on S-C odgovoriti and odgovarajući.

uvjet: Compare Rus. огово́рка and усло́вие, S-C uslov.

zavještanje: borrowed from Church Slavic.

заве́т: orig. also "will, testament; vow; condition."

заве́тный: orig. "preserved or transmitted in accordance with a testament or a solemn vow"; see preceding note.

ВЕЗ, (В)ОЗ	WIEŹ, WOZ, (W)ÓZ, WOŹ	VÉZ, VOZ, VŮZ	VOZ
[1]везти́, вози́ть: to carry (in a vehicle)	[1]wieźć, wozić: to carry (in a vehicle)	[1]vézti, voziti: to carry (in a vehicle)	voziti: to carry (in a vehicle); to drive (a vehicle)
воз: cartload	wóz: wagon; automobile; railroad car	vůz: wagon; automobile; railroad car	voz: cartload; (railroad) train
		vozidlo: vehicle	vozilo: vehicle
	woźny: bailiff; messenger		
возня́: fuss, bustle; trouble, bother			
			kolovoz: August; rut
парово́з: locomotive	parowóz: locomotive		
	dowóz: delivery, transportation	dovoz: import(ation); delivery, transportation	dovoz: delivery, transportation
изво́з (arch.): carrier's trade			izvoz: export(ation)
[R]	[P]	[Cz]	[S-C]

извóзчик: cabman; drayman, wagoner			
навóз: manure	nawóz: manure; fertilizer	návoz: embankment	
обóз: baggage train (of an army); wagon train	obóz: camp		
ввоз: import(ation)	wwóz: import(ation)		uvoz: import(ation)
	wąwóz: ravine, pass	úvoz: road leading through a hollow or depression	
вы́воз: export(ation)	wywóz: export(ation)	vývoz: export(ation)	
[R]	[P]	[Cz]	[S-C]

NOTES

Basic meaning of root: to carry (in a vehicle)

The verbs formed from this root serve to translate Eng. carry in all cases where some means of conveyance is used; compare root НЕС (etc.).

The Slavic root is related to Eng. weigh (see the introductory note on root ВАГ [etc.]), wagon (<Du. wagen) and way, Lat. vehere "to carry" (>Eng. vehicle, vector).

voziti (S-C): The iterative verb has taken over the function of unattested *vesti, which appears only in compounds.

kolovoz: See note under root КОЛ (etc.).

паровóз-parowóz: The first element is from пар-para "steam."

dowóz et al., izvoz: Compare Eng. transportation (ult. <Lat. trans "across" + portare "to carry"), import(ation) (ult. <Lat. in "in" + portare, export(ation) (ult. <Lat. ex "out" + portare).

навóз-nawóz: ="s.th. carried up (to be strewn in the field)."

návoz: ="s.th. carried up, i.e. heaped up, accumulated."

обóз-obóz: The Russian word originally referred to a group of wagons drawn up in a circle around a camp (note the prefix); hence the meaning of Pol. obóz, which is probably borrowed from Russian.

ввоз et al., вы́воз et al.: See note on dowóz et al., izvoz.

wąwóz-úvoz: The underlying meaning is probably "ground worn down by the constant passage of vehicles."

ВИ(Д)	WI(D)(Z)	VI(D)	VI(D), VIĐ
ви́деть: to see	widzieć: to see	viděti: to see	**vidjeti: to see
вид: (outward) appearance; form, shape; view, sight; view, vista; kind; species; (gram.) aspect (of Slavic verb)		vid: (gram.) aspect (of Slavic verb)	vid: eyesight; view, sight; pretext; (gram.) aspect (of Slavic verb)
	widz: spectator		
	widok: view, sight; view, vista; prospect, outlook		vidik: view, sight; view, vista; horizon
	widmo: specter, apparition; spectrum	vidmo (arch.): spectrum	
		vidina: specter, apparition	
	widziadło: specter, apparition		
	widowisko: sight, spectacle; show, theatrical performance		
	widownia: auditorium; scene; stage		
ви́дный: visible; eminent, distinguished	widny: light, bright		vidan: light, bright; visible; eminent, distinguished; visual; (anat.) optic
ви́димый: visible; obvious	widomy: visible; obvious; seeing (not blind)	vidomý: seeing (not blind)	
	widzialny: visible		vidljiv: visible
	widoczny: visible; obvious		
		viditelný: visible	
благови́дный: seemly; specious			
	czarnowidz: pessimist		
[R]	[P]	[Cz]	[S-C]

[R]	[P]	[Cz]	[S-C]
	dalekowidz: (med.) far-sighted person; (arch.) telescope		
	drobnowidz (arch.): microscope		
яснови́дец: clairvoyant (n.)	jasnowidz: clairvoyant (n.)	jasnovidec: clairvoyant (n.)	
милови́дный: pretty, attractive			milovidan: pretty, attractive
			očevid: inspection, examination
очеви́дец: eye-witness			očevidac: eye-witness
очеви́дный: obvious	oczywisty: obvious	očividný: obvious	očevidan: obvious
	ostrowidz (arch.): lynx		
разнови́дность: kind, variety (of fruit, etc.)			
	skorowidz: index		
сновиде́ние: dream			snoviđenje: dream
телеви́дение: television			
	widnokrąg: horizon		vidokrug: horizon
			zemljovid: map
ненави́деть: to hate	nienawidzić (nienawidzieć): to hate	nenáviděti: to hate	nenavidjeti: to envy; to hate
привиде́ние: specter, apparition	przywidzenie: hallucination		priviđenje: hallucination; specter, apparition
			prividan: seeming, illusory
прови́дение (arch.): prevision, prescience	przewidywanie: prevision, prescience; anticipation; forecast		
Провиде́ние: (rel.) Providence			Providenje: (rel.) Providence
			providan: transparent
[R]	[P]	[Cz]	[S-C]

свида́ние: meeting, appointment, rendezvous за́висть: envy [R]	zawiść: envy [P]	závist: envy [Cz]	sviđanje: liking, fondness; pleasure zavist: envy [S-C]

NOTES

Basic meaning of root: to see

Many of the derivatives are paralleled by English words derived from Lat. videre "to see" (>view, visible, vista, visual, prevision, television) and specere "to look" (>spectacle, spectator, specter, spectrum, prospect). (See also notes on individual words below.) A number of comparable formations are to be found under roots ГЛЯД (etc.) and ЗР (etc.).

The root is related to root ВЕД$_1$ (etc.). Non-Slavic cognates are Lat. videre, Gr. ἰδεῖν "to see" (>Eng. idea).

вид et al.: The meanings "appearance," "form, shape," "kind," "species," "aspect" all reflect the notion of how a thing is seen or looked at; compare Eng. species, aspect (both ult. <Lat. specere "to look"). The Czech word is borrowed from Russian.

vidmo: <Pol. widmo.

благови́дный: ="having a good appearance"; see вид and compare Eng. specious (ult. <Lat. species "appearance" < specere "to look").

czarnowidz: The first element is from czarny "black"; compare Ger. Schwarzseher "pessimist" (<schwarz "black" + sehen "to see").

dalekowidz: The first element is from daleki "distant"; see note on Cz. dalekohled.

drobnowidz: The first element is from drobny "small"; see note on Cz. drobnohled.

ясновидец et al.: The first element is from я́сный-jasny-jasný "clear"; compare Eng. clairvoyant (ult. <Fr. clair "clear" + voir "to see"), Ger. Hellseher "clairvoyant" (<hell "clear" + sehen "to see").

милови́дный-milovidan: See вид; the Serbo-Croatian word is borrowed from Russian.

očevid: See note under root ОК (etc.).

очеви́дный et al.: The Polish form WIST is from Common Slavic *VIDT; see note under root ОК (etc.).

ostrowidz: The first element is from ostry "sharp."

разнови́дность: See вид; the first element is from ра́зный "different."

skorowidz: The first element is from skory "quick."

сновиде́ние-snoviđenje: The first element is from сон-san "sleep"; the Serbo-Croatian word is borrowed from Russian.

телеви́дение: The first element is from Gr. τῆλε "distant," whence Eng. tele-.

widnokrąg-vidokrug: See note on Rus. кругозо́р.

ненави́деть et al.: in origin, a negation of an obsolete verb meaning "to look upon with pleasure or fondness."

Провиде́ние-Providenje: a reference to the foresight with which God is presumed to guide men and shape their ends; compare Eng. Providence (ult. ‹Lat. pro- "before" + videre "to see"), Ger. Vorsehung "Providence" (‹vor "before" + sehen "to see"), Pol. Opatrzność, Cz. prozřetelnost.

providan: See note on Pol. przejrzysty, S-C proziran, Rus. прозра́чный et al.

sviđanje: ‹sviđati se "to please" (orig. "to be seen," hence "to seem"; see the introductory note on root ДОБ (etc.).

за́висть et al.: ‹Common Slavic *zavidtь. The underlying idea is that of looking askance at someone; compare Eng. envy (ult. ‹Lat. in "in, on, at" + videre "to see"), Pol. zazdrość.

ВИС, ВЕС, ВЕШ	WIS, WIAS, WIES, WIEŚ, WIESZ	VIS, VĚS, (V)ĚŠ	VIS, VJES, (V)JEŠ
висе́ть: to hang (intr.)	wisieć: to hang (intr.)	viseti: to hang (intr.)	visjeti (visiti): to hang (intr.)
ве́сить: to weigh (intr.); (coll.) to weigh (tr.)		věsiti: to hang (tr.)	
ве́шать: to hang (tr.); to weigh (tr.)	wieszać: to hang (tr.)	věšeti: to hang (tr.)	vješati: to hang (tr.)
вес: weight			
весы́ (pl.): scales			
висо́к: (anat.) temple			visak: plumb, plummet
ви́селица: gallows			vješala: gallows
равнове́сие: balance, equilibrium			ravnovjesje: balance, equilibrium
наве́с: shed; awning	nawias: (punc.) parentheses, brackets		
незави́симый: independent	niezawisły: independent	nezávislý: independent	nezavisan: independent
	obwieś: gallows-bird, reprobate	oběšenec: hanged man	obješenjak: gallows-bird, reprobate
[R]	[P]	[Cz]	[S-C]

[R]	[P]	[Cz]	[S-C]
отвéс: plumb, plummet; sheer drop			
повéса: gallows-bird, reprobate			
перевéс: preponderance			
	zwisły: drooping, sagging	svislý: perpendicular; vertical	
		souvislý: coherent; continuous	suvisao: coherent
зави́сеть: to depend		záviseti: to depend	zavisiti: to depend
	zawiesina: (phys.) suspension		
завéса: (fig.) screen, veil; (arch.) curtain	zawias, zawiasa: hinge	závěs: curtain; hinge	zavjesa: curtain
зáнавес, занавéска: curtain			

NOTES

Basic meaning of root: to hang

The secondary meaning "to weigh" occurs in Russian. A comparable semantic relationship is apparent in Lat. pendĕre "to hang (tr.); to weigh," pondus "weight" (>Eng. pound, ponderous), ponderare "to weigh" (>Eng. ponder).

вéсить-věsiti: These two words and obsolete Pol. wiesić (S-C *vjesiti is not attested) represent the original causative form of висéть et al., although only Cz. věsiti continues to perform that function in the modern language; see next note.

вéшать et al.: orig. an iterative form of вéсить and its analogues in the other languages.

висóк: orig. "hanging strand of hair."

равновéсие-ravnovjesje: See note under root РОВ (etc.).

nawias: The reference was originally to "something hanging, projecting, curved" (compare Rus. навéс), then to the mark of punctuation; the present use of the word presumably also reflects the meaning of the adverb nawiasem "incidentally" (orig. "askance, to one side, curving rather than straight").

незави́симый et al.: See note on зави́сеть et al. and compare Eng. independent, Ger. unabhängig "independent" (<un- "un-" + abhängen); Pol. niezawisły is from zawisnąć "to hang, remain suspended" (orig. also "to depend").

перевéс: See note on Pol. przewaga et al.

svislý: Compare Eng. *perpendicular* (ult. <Lat. *pendĕre* "to hang [tr.]"); Hung. *függőleges* "perpendicular; vertical" (<*függni* "to hang").

souvislý-suvisao: Compare Ger. *zusammenhängend* "coherent" (<*zusammen* "together" + *hängen* "to hang").

зави́сеть et al.: Compare Eng. *depend* (ult. <Lat. *de-* "off" + *pendēre* "to hang [intr.]"), Ger. *abhängen* "to depend" (<*ab* "off" + *hängen* "to hang").

zawiesina: Compare Eng. *suspension* (ult. <Lat. *pendĕre* "to hang [tr.]").

заве́са et al., *за́навес*, *занаве́ска*: Compare Eng. *hinge* (akin to *hang*), Ger. *Vorhang* "curtain" (<*vor* "before, in front" + *hängen* "to hang"), Hung. *függöny* "curtain" (<*függni* "to hang").

ВОЛО, (В)ЛАД, ([В]ЛАСТ)	WŁOD, WŁA(D)(Z), (WŁOŚĆ), (WŁOŚC), (WŁAŚC), (WŁASZCZ), (WŁAS)	VLAD, VLÁ(D), ([V]LAST)	(V)LAD, (V)LAĐ, ([V]LAS[T]), (VLAŠĆ)
владе́ть: to own, possess; to wield, handle; to control; to be proficient (in)	*władać*: to wield, handle; to control; to be proficient (in)	*vládnouti*: to rule, govern; to wield, handle; to control; to prevail, be prevalent	*vladati*: to rule, govern; to control; to be proficient (in); to prevail, be prevalent
			vladati se: to behave, conduct oneself
	władza: power; rule, sway; authority; control	*vláda*: government; rule, sway; reign; control	*vlada*: government; rule, sway; reign
	włodarz (arch.): steward, overseer	*vladař*: ruler, sovereign	*vladar*: ruler, sovereign
	władca: ruler, sovereign	*vládce*: ruler, sovereign	
владе́лец: owner			*vladalac*: ruler, sovereign
влады́ка: ruler, sovereign; (arch.) Orthodox bishop	*władyka*: Orthodox bishop; ruler, sovereign	*vladyka* (arch.): nobleman of low rank	*vladika*: Orthodox bishop
во́лость (arch.): district	*włość* (arch.): estate, manor	*vlast*: fatherland	*vlast*: power; rule, sway; authority; control
власть: power; rule, sway; authority; control			
[R]	[P]	[Cz]	[S-C]

[R]	[P]	[Cz]	[S-C]
	włościanin: peasant	vlastenec: patriot	
власти́тель (arch.): ruler, sovereign	właściciel: owner	vlastník: owner	vlasnik: owner
властели́н (arch.): ruler, sovereign			vlastelin: landed proprietor, squire
вла́стный: imperious, peremptory; (вла́стен, pred.) having the power (to do s.th.)	własny: (one's) own; (gram.) proper (noun)	vlastní: (one's) own; peculiar (to); proper (sense of a word, etc.); real, actual; (gram.) proper (noun)	vlastan: authorized, empowered
	właściwy: peculiar (to); proper, suitable, appropriate; proper (sense of a word, etc.); real, actual; competent, authorized		vlastit: (one's) own; (gram.) proper (noun)
	własność: ownership; property (something owned); property, characteristic	vlastnost: property, characteristic	
		vlastnictví: ownership; property (something owned)	vlasništvo: ownership; property (something owned)
		bohovláda: theocracy	
единовла́стие: autocracy	jednowładztwo, jedynowładztwo: autocracy		
		krutovláda: tyranny	
		mezivládí: interregnum	međuvlada, međuvlašće: interregnum
			*opunovlastiti: to authorize, empower
самовла́стие (arch.): autocracy	samowładztwo: autocracy	samovláda: autocracy	samovlada, samovlast, samovlašće: autocracy
своевла́стный: wilful			svojevlastan: wilful

безвла́стие: anarchy	bezwład: (med.) paralysis; inactivity	bezvládí: anarchy	bezvlađe: anarchy
	bezwładność: (phys.) inertia	bezvládnost: (med.) paralysis	
			izvlastiti, izvlašćivati: to expropriate
		(státní) návladní: public prosecutor	
			nadvladati, nadvlađivati: to conquer, defeat; to overcome, surmount
		nadvláda: supremacy, hegemony	
	niedowład: (med.) paresis		
*овладе́ть: to seize, take possession (of); to master, gain proficiency (in)	*owładnąć: to seize, take possession of	*ovládnouti: to gain control of; to master, gain proficiency in	
овладева́ть: to seize, take possession (of); to master, gain proficiency (in)	owładać: to seize, take possession of	ovládati: to rule, govern; to control; to be proficient in	*ovladati: to seize, take possession (of); to conquer, defeat
			ovlastiti, ovlašćivati: to authorize, empower
облада́ть: to own, possess			*obladati: to seize, take possession (of); to conquer, defeat
о́бласть: region; sphere, field (of knowledge, activity, etc.)		oblast: region; sphere, field (of knowledge, activity, etc.)	oblast: (governmental) authority, organ; region
			povladiti, povlađivati: to acclaim, applaud
			povlastica: privilege; license, permit
[R]	[P]	[Cz]	[S-C]

[R]	[P]	[Cz]	[S-C]
преобладáть: to predominate, prevail		převládnouti, převládati: to predominate, prevail	prevladati, prevlađivati; preovladati, preovlađivati; preobladati, preoblađivati: to predominate, prevail
	przywłaszczyć sobie, przywłaszczać sobie: to appropriate (to one's use), arrogate to o.s.	přivlastniti si, přivlastňovati si: to appropriate (to one's use), arrogate to o.s.	
		přivlastňovací: (gram.) possessive	
*совладáть (coll.; с + inst.): to control; to cope (with)		zvládnouti, zvládati: to overcome, surmount; to cope with	savladati, savlađivati; svladati, svladavati: to conquer, defeat; to overcome, surmount; to cope with
	wywłaszczyć, wywłaszczać: to expropriate	vyvlastniti, vyvlastňovati: to expropriate	
	zwłaszcza: especially, particularly	zvlášť, zvláště: especially, particularly; separately	
завладéть, завладевáть: to seize, take possession (of)	*zawładnąć: to seize, take possession (of)	*zavládnouti: to set in (silence, calm, etc.)	*zavladati: to take power, begin to rule; to seize, take possession (of); to become prevalent

NOTES

Basic meaning of root: to wield power

Many of the derivatives reflect the secondary notion of ownership, i.e. power over a thing.

The forms ВЛАСТ---WŁOŚC-WŁAŚC-WŁASZCZ-WŁAS---VLAST---VLAST-VLAŠĆ are, except in the case of Pol. zwłaszcza, derived from власть, włość et al. (See note.) All the Russian forms with the exception of that reflected in вóлость are of Church Slavic origin; the Polish forms in a probably show Russian or Czech influence.

Kindred non-Slavic words are Eng. wield, Ger. walten "to rule, govern,"

Lat. valere "to be strong" (>Eng. valid, valiant, value, avail, prevail, convalesce).

владе́ть et al.: The Polish and Serbo-Croatian words are iterative forms of a primary verb reflected in ORus. власти, OPol. włość, OCz. vlásti (1 sg. владу, włodę, vladu). Modern Cz. vládnouti is a reconstructed form of vlásti while Rus. владе́ть is a denominative from Ch. Sl. влада "power." The Russian and Czech iteratives влада́ть and vládati are obsolete.

vladati se: ="to govern, control oneself."

władyka: <Rus. влады́ка.

во́лость et al., власть: <Common Slavic *voldtь. The first three words show the semantic progression "power" > "area over which power is exercised" > "area (in general)"; see note on Cz. područí, S-C područje and compare Ger. Gebiet "region" (<gebieten "to command; to rule, govern").

włościanin-vlastenec: See włość-vlast.

własny-vlastní, właściwy-vlastit: Underlying the various meanings is the notion "(one's) own," i.e. belonging to, characteristic of or suited to a particular person or thing; compare Eng. proper and appropriate (both ult. <Lat. proprius "[one's] own"), Ger. eigentlich "real, actual" and geeignet "proper, suitable, appropriate" (both <eigen "[one's] own"), Rus. со́бственный, S-C sopstven.

własność-vlastnost, vlastnictví-vlasništvo: A possession and a characteristic are alike in being "one's own"; see własny-vlastní, vlastník-vlasnik and compare Eng. property (ult. <Lat. proprius "[one's] own"), Ger. Eigentum "property (something owned)" and Eigenschaft "property, characteristic" (both <eigen "[one's] own"), Rus. со́бственность and сво́йство, S-C sopstvenost, svojstvo and svojina.

bohovláda: Compare Eng. theocracy (ult. <Gr. θεός "god" + κρατεῖν "to rule, govern").

единовла́стие et al.: See note under root ОДИН (etc.).

mezivládí et al.: Compare Eng. interregnum (ult. <Lat. inter "between" + regnum "rule, reign"), Rus. междуца́рствие.

opunovlastiti: See note under root ПОЛН (etc.).

самовла́стие et al.: See note on Rus. самоде́ржец et al.

своевла́стный-svojevlastan: See note on Cz. svémocný.

безвла́стие-bezvládí-bezvlađe: See note on Rus. безнача́лие.

izvlastiti: See vlastit and compare Eng. expropriate (ult. <Lat. ex "out of" + proprius "[one's] own"), Ger. enteignen "to expropriate" (<ent- "un-, dis-" + eigen "[one's] own"), S-C odsvojiti.

(státní) návladní: ="state's attorney"; the term is modeled on Ger. Staatsanwalt "public prosecutor" (<Staat "state" + Anwalt "attorney" < an "to" + walten "to rule, govern; to administer").

о́бласть et al.: Regarding the meaning "region," see note on во́лость et al., власть; the Czech word is borrowed from Russian.

povladiti: orig. apparently "to strengthen, encourage."

przywłaszczyć sobie-přivlastniti si: See własny-vlastní and compare Eng. appropriate (ult. ⟨Lat. ad "to" + proprius "[one's] own"), Ger. aneignen "to appropriate (to one's use), arrogate to o.s." (⟨an "to" + eigen "[one's] own"), Rus. присво́ить, Cz. osobiti si, osvojiti si and přisvojiti si, S-C posvojiti and prisvojiti.

wywłaszczyć-vyvlastniti: See własny-vlastní and note on izvlastiti.

zwłaszcza et al.: from adjectival forms ultimately derived from Common Slavic *voldtjь; regarding the meaning, see note on własny-vlastní, właściwy-vlastit.

ВОЛО(К), ВОЛАК, (В)ОЛОЧ, (В)ЛЕ(К), ВЛЕЧ, ЛАК, (В)ЛАЧ	(W)LE(K), WŁÓK, (W)ŁOK, (W)ŁÓCZ, WŁOCZ, WŁACZ	(V)LÉ(K), VLEK, VLEČ, (V)LAK, VLÁČ	(V)U(Č), (V)LAK, (V)LAČ
воло́чь (coll.): to drag	wlec: to drag	vléci: to drag	vući: to pull; to drag
волочи́ть: to draw (wire); (coll.) to drag	[1]włóczyć: to drag; to harrow (a field)	[1]vláčeti: to drag; to harrow (a field)	vlačiti: to harrow (a field); to card (wool)
влечь: to attract; (за собо́й) to involve, entail; (arch.) to drag			
влачи́ть (arch.): to drag			
во́лок: (place of) portage; fishnet	włók: fishnet	vlak: (railroad) train	vlak: (railroad) train; fishnet
		vlečka: train (of a dress); (railroad) siding	
		vleklý: chronic, lingering; slow, long-drawn-out; protracted	
волоки́та: (bureaucratic) red tape; (coll.) ladies' man			
	włóczęga: tramp, vagabond; vagabondage		
			oblakoder: skyscraper
[R]	[P]	[Cz]	[S-C]

[R]	[P]	[Cz]	[S-C]
			odugovlačiti: to delay
на́волока, на́волочка: pillow-case	nawłóczka: pillow-case		navlaka: pillow-case
обволо́чь, обвола́кивать: to envelop			
обле́чь, облека́ть (lit.): to clothe, dress; to invest (with authority, an air of mystery, etc.)	oblec, oblekać (lit.): to clothe, dress; to don, put on; to cover	obléci (obléknouti), oblékati: to clothe, dress; to don, put on	*obući: to clothe, dress; to don, put on
облачи́ть, облача́ть: to clothe (in priestly robes)	obłóczyć (arch.): to clothe, dress; to don, put on; to cover		oblačiti: to clothe, dress; to don, put on
	obłóczyny (pl.): (nun's) taking of the veil		
оболо́чка: cover, casing; membrane			
о́блако: cloud	obłok: cloud	oblak: cloud	oblak: cloud
отволо́чь, отвола́кивать (coll.): to drag away	odwlec, odwlekać (odwłóczyć): to drag away; to delay	odvléci (odvléknouti), odvlékati: to drag away	odvući, odvlačiti: to pull away; to drag away
отвле́чь, отвлека́ть: to distract, divert			
отвлечённый: abstract (a.)			
			pavlaka: cream
	powłoka: cover, casing; coating, film	povlak: cover, casing; pillow-case; coating, film	povlaka: cream; train (of a dress)
	powłoczka: pillow-case		
			povučenost: seclusion
		podvlékačky (pl.): underpants, drawers	
			prevlaka: cover, casing; pillow-case; coating, film; isthmus

привлекáтельный: attractive, appealing			privlačan, privlačiv: attractive, appealing
	przewlekły: chronic, lingering		
прóволока: wire	przewłoka: delay		
развлéчь, развлекáть: to amuse, entertain, divert			
	rozwlekły: verbose, long-winded	rozvleklý: slow, long-drawn-out	
		rozvláčný: verbose, long-winded; slow, long-drawn-out	
разоблачи́ть, разоблачáть: to expose, unmask; (arch.) to undress, disrobe (tr.)			
свóлочь: scoundrel; rabble, riffraff			
	zwłoka: delay		
	zwłoki (pl.): corpse, mortal remains		
увлечéние: enthusiasm, passion			
	uwłaczanie: disparagement, detraction		
	wywłoka: strumpet; nag, broken-down horse; unfrocked priest		
заволóчь, заволáкивать: to becloud	zawlec, zawlekać (zawłóczyć): to drag (off, away); to bring in, introduce (an infection, disease)	zavléci (zavléknouti), zavlékati: to drag (off, away); to abduct; to involve (s.o. in s.th.); to bring in, introduce (an infection, disease)	zavući, zavlačiti: to put (in); to delay
[R]	[P]	[Cz]	[S-C]

завлéчь, завлекáть: to lure, entice [R]	[P]	[Cz]	[S-C]

NOTES

Basic meaning of root: to pull, drag

The meanings "to drag or draw out, delay, protract" and "to pull on or over, cover, clothe" are apparent in many of the derivatives. Comparable semantic development is shown by a number of the words listed under root ТЯ(Г) (etc.).

The Russian root-forms ВЛЕК, ВЛЕЧ, ЛАК and ВЛАЧ are of Church Slavic origin.

волóчь et al., влечь: The respective 1 sg. forms are волокý, wlokę, vleku, vučem, влекý; regarding the third meaning of влечь, compare Fr. entraîner "to involve, entail" (⟨traîner "to pull, drag").

вóлок (first meaning): a place where boats are "dragged" overland between two navigable waters.

vlak (Cz.-S-C), vlečka: Compare Eng. train (ult. from an earlier form of Fr. traîner "to pull, drag"), Ger. Zug "(railroad) train" (⟨ziehen "to pull") and Schleppe "train (of a dress)" (⟨schleppen "to drag"), Hung. vonat "(railroad) train" (⟨vonni "to pull"), Pol. pociąg.

vleklý: See note on Pol. przeciągły.

волокúта (second meaning): See волочúться "to chase (after women)."

oblakoder: See oblak and compare Ger. Wolkenkratzer "skyscraper" (⟨Wolke "cloud" + kratzen "to scratch"), Cz. mrakodrap "skyscraper" (⟨mrak "[dark] cloud" + drápati "to scratch").

odugovlačiti: See note on odwlec.

нáволока et al., обволóчь, облéчь et al., облачúть et al., obłóczyny, оболóчка: Compare Ger. beziehen "to cover," Bezug "cover, casing" and anziehen "to clothe, dress; to don, put on" (all ⟨ziehen "to pull"), Cz. potah; regarding the figurative use of облéчь, compare Eng. invest (ult. ⟨Lat. vestire "to clothe, dress").

óблако et al.: ="covering."

odwlec: Compare Ger. (ver)zögern "to delay" (related to ziehen "to pull"), Pol. ociągnąć się, Cz. průtah.

отвлéчь: Compare Eng. distract (ult. ⟨Lat. dis- "away" + trahere "to pull, draw").

отвлечённый: ="drawn away" from concrete, specific things; compare Eng. abstract (ult. ⟨Lat. ab[s] "away" + trahere "to pull, draw"), Hung. elvont "abstract" (⟨el- "away" + vonni "to pull, draw"), Pol. oderwany, Cz. odtažitý.

pavlaka: ="covering, coating"; compare Pol. powłoka, Cz. povlak.

powłoka et al., powłoczka: See notes on на́волока et al., обволо́чь, обле́чь et al., облачи́ть et al., obłóczyny, оболо́чка, on pavlaka and on vlak, vlečka.

povučenost: Compare Eng. withdrawal (⟨with- "back" + draw), retirement (ult. ⟨Lat. re- "back" + Fr. tirer "to pull").

podvlékačky: Compare Eng. drawers (⟨draw).

prevlaka: Compare Ger. Überzug "cover, casing; coating, film" (⟨über "over" + ziehen "to pull"); the meaning "isthmus" is an outgrowth of the earlier meaning "portage" (see note on во́лок).

привлека́тельный et al.: Compare Eng. attractive (ult. ⟨Lat. ad "to" + trahere "to pull"), Ger. anziehend "attractive" (⟨an "to" + ziehen "to pull"), Rus. притяга́тельный, Cz. přitažlivý.

про́волока: See the second meaning of волочи́ть.

przewłoka: See note on odwlec.

развле́чь: Compare отвле́чь and Pol. rozrywka.

разоблачи́ть: See облачи́ть.

сво́лочь: The successive meanings of the word have been "things dragged together, collected" ⟩ "rubbish" ⟩ "rabble, riffraff" ⟩ "scoundrel"; see note on Cz. sběř, sebranka.

zwłoka: See note on odwlec.

zwłoki: orig. "skin of a flayed carcass"; see zwlec "to pull, strip off."

увлече́ние: See note on Cz. uchvacující and úchvatný, Rus. восхище́ние et al., Pol. zachwyt and zachwycający.

uwłaczanie: The underlying idea is that of "drawing (i.e. taking) away" from someone's reputation; compare Eng. detraction (ult. ⟨Lat. de "away" + trahere "to pull, draw"), Cz. utrhač.

wywłoka: Regarding the various meanings, see wywłóczyć "to drag about, bedraggle; to undress, disrobe."

заволо́чь: See note on о́блако et al.

zavući: See note on odwlec.

ВОД	WOD(Z), WÓD, WÓDŹ, WAD	VOD	VOD, VOT, VOĐ
вода́: water во́дка: vodka водя́нка: dropsy [R]	woda: water wódka: vodka wodzianka: soup made of bread and water wodnica: dropsy; water-nymph [P]	voda: water vodka: vodka vodnice: turnip [Cz]	voda: water votka: vodka [S-C]

		vodnatelnost: dropsy	
	Wodnik: (astr.) Aquarius	Vodnář: (astr.) Aquarius	
	wodór: hydrogen	vodík: hydrogen	vodik, vodonik: hydrogen
	wodan, wodzian: hydrate		
углево́д: carbohydrate	węglowodan: carbohydrate	uhlovodan: carbohydrate	
водобоя́знь: hydrophobia	wodowstręt: hydrophobia		
водохрани́лище: reservoir			
	wodociąg: water-pipe, conduit; aqueduct; water supply		
водоизмеще́ние: displacement (of a ship)			
водоём: reservoir		vodojem: reservoir	
Водоле́й: (astr.) Aquarius			Vodolija: (astr.) Aquarius
водопа́д: waterfall	wodospad: waterfall	vodopád: waterfall	vodopad: waterfall
водопрово́д: water-pipe, conduit; aqueduct; water supply		vodovod: water-pipe, conduit; aqueduct; water supply	vodovod: water-pipe, conduit; aqueduct; water supply
водоразде́л: watershed			vododijelnica: watershed
водоро́д: hydrogen	wodoród (arch.): hydrogen		
		vodorovný: horizontal	vodoravan: horizontal
водоворо́т: whirlpool			
	wodozbiór: reservoir		
земново́дный: amphibious	wodnoziemny, ziemnowodny: amphibious		vodozeman: amphibious
наводни́ть, наводня́ть: to flood	nawodnić, nawadniać: to irrigate		navodniti, navodnjavati: to irrigate
па́водок: flood	powódź: flood	povodeň: flood	povodanj, povodnja: flood
[R]	[P]	[Cz]	[S-C]

		rozvodí: watershed zavodniti, zavodňovati: to irrigate	razvođe: watershed
[R]	[P]	[Cz]	[S-C]

NOTES

Basic meaning of root: water

The Slavic root is cognate with Eng. water, Lat. unda "wave" (>Eng. undulate, abundant, inundate), Gr. ὕδωρ "water" (>Eng. hydraulic, hydrology, hydrate).

во́дка et al.: ="little water"; the Czech and Serbo-Croatian words are borrowed from Russian.

водя́нка, wodnica (first meaning), vodnatelnost: a pathological condition characterized by abnormal accumulation of water in the body; compare Eng. dropsy (a shortened form of hydropsy, ult. <Gr. ὕδωρ "water"), Ger. Wassersucht "dropsy" (<Wasser "water" + Sucht "disease").

Wodnik-Vodnář: See note on Водоле́й-Vodolija.

wodór et al.: See note on водоро́д-wodoród.

углево́д et al.: The first element is from у́голь-węgiel-uhlí "coal."

водобоя́знь-wodowstręt: so called because one symptom of the disease in humans is an inability to swallow liquids and a sensation of extreme fear and revulsion at even the sight of water; the second elements in the two words are from, respectively, боя́знь "fear" and wstręt "disgust." Compare Eng. hydrophobia (ult. <Gr. ὕδωρ "water" + φόβος "fear").

водоизмеще́ние: See note under root МЕСТ (etc.).

Водоле́й-Vodolija: a constellation also known as the Water Bearer; compare Eng. Aquarius (<Lat. aquarius "water-bearer" < aqua "water").

водопрово́д et al.: See note under root ВЕД$_2$ (etc.).

водоразде́л-vododijelnica: a dividing line between the drainage areas of two rivers; compare Eng. watershed (in which shed = "separation"), Ger. Wasserscheide "watershed" (<Wasser "water" + scheiden "to separate").

водоро́д-wodoród: so called because water is generated by the combustion of hydrogen. The words are constructed like Eng. hydrogen (ult. <Gr. ὕδωρ "water" + the root of γίγνεσθαι "to be born"); compare also Ger. Wasserstoff "hydrogen" (<Wasser "water" + Stoff "matter, substance").

vodorovný-vodoravan: See note under root РОВ (etc.).

rozvodí-razvođe: See note on водоразде́л-vododijelnica.

	WOŁ	VOL	
	wołać: to call	volati: to call	
	wołacz: (gram.) vocative case		
	obwołać, obwoływać: to proclaim		
	odwołać, odwoływać: to revoke, repeal, cancel; to recall (e.g. an ambassador); to retract, recant	odvolati, odvolávati: to revoke, repeal, cancel; to recall (e.g. an ambassador); to dismiss, discharge; to retract, recant	
	odwołać się, odwoływać się: to appeal	odvolati se, odvolávati se: (proti + dat.) to appeal (a judicial decision); (na + acc.) to refer (to), cite	
	powołać się, powoływać się (na + acc.): to refer (to), cite		
	powołanie: vocation, calling; (mil.) call-up	povolání: occupation, profession; vocation, calling; (mil.) call-up	
		předvolání: summons, subpoena	
		provolati, provolávati: to proclaim	
	wywołać, wywoływać: to call (s.o.) out, up; to proclaim; to evoke; to cause, provoke; (phot.) to develop	vyvolati, vyvolávati: to call (s.o.) out, up; to evoke; to cause, provoke; (phot.) to develop	
		zvolání: exclamation	
	[P]	[Cz]	

NOTES

Basic meaning of root: to call

The root is found only in Polish and Czech. Many of the derivatives have semantic counterparts among those listed under root ЗВ (etc.).

wołacz: See note on Rus. зва́тельный.

odwołać-odvolati: See note on S-C opozvati.

odwołać się-odvolati se, powołać się: Compare Ger. sich berufen "to appeal; to refer (to), cite" (‹sich, refl. pron. + [be]rufen "to call").

powołanie-povolání: See note on S-C poziv, Rus. призва́ние.

wywołać-vyvolati: Compare Eng. to call forth (a response, etc.), evoke (ult. ‹Lat. e "out" + vocare "to call"), provoke (ult. ‹Lat. pro- "forth, forward" + vocare).

BEP_2, (B)OP, BP	WRZ, WIER(Z), WAR, WR, WÓR, (W)OR(Z), FOR	VŘ, VÍR, VĚR, VEŘ, VR, (V)OR	VR, VER, VIR, (V)OR, VAR
			verati (arch.): to push (in); to hide
			verati se: to climb
воро́та (pl.), врата́ (pl., arch.): gate	wrota (pl.): gate	vrata (pl.): gate	vrata (pl.): door; gate
	wierzeje (pl., arch.): door; gate	veřej: doorpost	
		veřejný: public (a.)	
верёвка: rope; string			vrpca, vrvca: string; ribbon
вери́ги (pl., arch.): chains, fetters (worn by ascetics as an act of penance)			verige (pl.): chain; chains, fetters
верени́ца: file, row, line			
			vreća: bag
	wór, worek: bag	vor: raft	
	workowate (pl.): marsupials		
[R]	[P]	[Cz]	[S-C]

	obora: cowshed; cattle	obora: (forest, game, etc.) preserve	obor: enclosure, pen, fold (for livestock)
	obornik: manure		
обо́рка: frill (on a dress)			
отвори́ть, отворя́ть: to open (tr.)	otworzyć (odewrzeć), otwierać: to open (tr.)	otevříti, otvírati (otevírati): to open (tr.)	otvoriti, otvarati: to open (tr.)
	zwarcie: compression; (elec.) short circuit		
	zwieracz: (anat.) sphincter	svěrák: vise; clamp	
		svíravý: astringent	
		svorný: harmonious, concordant	
		svor: clamp	svor: bolt, pin
сво́ра: leash; pack (of dogs)	sfora: leash; pack (of dogs)	svora, svorka: clamp	
шво́рень, шкво́рень: bolt, pin	sworzeń: bolt, pin		
	sworznik: front axle	svorník: bolt, pin	svornik: bolt, pin
	zwornik: keystone		
		uveřejniti, uveřejňovati: to publish	
		uzavříti, uzavírati: to shut, close (tr.); to enclose; to conclude, end (tr.); to conclude, infer, deduce; to conclude (an agreement, etc.)	
	wywrzeć, wywierać: to exert (influence), make (an impression)		
	zawrzeć, zawierać: to shut, close (tr.); to conclude (an agreement, etc.); to contain	zavříti, zavírati: to shut, close (tr.); to confine, imprison	zavrijeti, zavirati: to hide; to brake
[R]	[P]	[Cz]	[S-C]

[R]	[P]	[Cz]	[S-C]
затвори́ть, затворя́ть: to shut, close (tr.)			zatvoriti, zatvarati: to shut, close (tr.); to arrest; to confine, imprison
		závěr: conclusion, end; conclusion, inference, deduction; bolt (of a gun) závěrka: balance-sheet; shutter (on a camera)	
	zawór: valve zawora: bolt (on a door)	závora: bolt (on a door) závorka: (punc.) parenthesis, bracket	zavor: brake
затво́р: bolt (on a door, gun, etc.); shutter (on a camera); flood-gate; seclusion затво́рник: hermit, recluse	zatwór: bolt (on a door)		zatvor: arrest; confinement, imprisonment; prison; constipation zatvorenik: prisoner

NOTES

Basic meaning of root: to close

A number of the derivatives show the secondary meanings "to enclose" and "to link, bind." Combination of the root with the negative prefix от-ot (od) produces the meaning "to open."

The primary verb has vanished in modern literary Russian (see, however, dialectal вера́ть "to close; to put [in]; to hide" and заверéть "to tie together; to lace up") and survives only in compounds in Polish and Czech (see obsolete Pol. wrzeć "to push, press"). Отвори́ть-otworzyć-otvoriti is denominative (compare the various noun formations in ВОР-WÓR-VOR); corresponding imperfectives have been formed in Russian and Serbo-Croatian, while in Polish the original imperfective form survives (together with the original perfective odewrzeć, now an archaic alternative form). The verb затвори́ть-zatvoriti arose as a back-formation from отвори́ть-otvoriti, in which o- was mistakenly regarded as the prefix and ТВОР-TVOR as the root.

The Slavic root is related to Eng. weir "dam," Ger. wehren "to defend," Lat. *verire in aperire "to open; to uncover" (>Eng. aperture, overt, overture) and operire "to close; to cover" (>cooperire "to cover entirely" > Eng. cover, covert).

verati se: orig. "to push, get (in)," then "to climb (in)."

вра́та: borrowed from Church Slavic.

veřejný: ⟨veřej; the meaning has been variously explained as "open (to all)," as "out of doors (hence public rather than private)" and as reflecting the custom of posting public notices on the town gate.

vor: so called because a raft is made of logs lashed or bound together

workowate: ⟨worek.

обо́рка: ⟨obs. обо́ра "string, lace."

svorný: ="bound together."

sfora: for earlier swora.

шво́рень, шкво́рень: ⟨*сворень; the form шкво́рень has been attributed to the influence of сквозь "through."

uveřejniti: ⟨veřejný.

uzavříti: See note on Rus. заключи́ть, S-C zaključiti.

wywrzeć: orig. "to open; to release."

zawrzeć, závěr: See note on Rus. заключи́ть, S-C zaključiti.

závěrka (first meaning): ="closing of the books."

затво́р, затво́рник: Compare Eng. seclusion, recluse (both ult. ⟨Lat. claudere "to close").

ВАР	WRZ, WAR(Z)	VŘ, VAR, VAŘ, VÁŘ	VR, VOR, VAR
	wrzeć: to boil (intr.)	vříti: to boil (intr.)	vreti: to boil (intr.); to ferment; to gush, well up
		vřídlo: hot spring, geyser	vrelo: spring (of water); source, origin
			vrućica: fever
			vrućina: heat
вари́ть: to boil (tr.); to cook (tr.); to brew (tr.); to digest (tr.); to cast, found	warzyć: to boil (tr.); to cook (tr.); to brew (tr.); to blight, nip	vařiti: to boil (tr.); to cook (tr.); to brew (tr.)	variti: to boil (tr.); to cook (tr.); to brew (tr.); to digest (tr.); to weld
ва́рево (coll.): soup	warzywo: vegetable	vařivo: cooking ingredients	varivo: vegetables (as a dish)
варе́нье: jam, preserves			
самова́р: samovar	samowar: samovar	samovar: samovar	samovar: samovar
			izvor: spring (of water); source, origin
[R]	[P]	[Cz]	[S-C]

			izvoran: original
пóвар: cook сварúть, свáривать: to weld; (сварúть only) to boil (tr.); (сварúть only) to cook (tr.); (сварúть only) to brew (tr.)	zwarzyć, zwarzać: to boil (tr.); to cook (tr.); to curdle (tr.); to blight, nip; (arch.) to weld	svařiti, svařovati (svářeti): to boil (tr.); to weld zavařenina: jam, preserves	svariti, svarivati: to boil (tr.); to cook (tr.); to digest (tr.); to weld
[R]	[P]	[Cz]	[S-C]

NOTES

Basic meaning of root: to boil

wrzeć et al.: The Russian primary verb survives in dialectal вреть "to sweat profusely."

vrelo: See note on Rus. истóк and истóчник, S-C izvor.

варúть et al.: the causative form of wrzeć et al. The meaning "to digest" reflects the notion that food is "cooked" or "melted down" in the stomach; compare Gr. πέπτειν (πέσσειν) "to cook; to digest," Ger. verdauen "to digest" (probably related to Eng. thaw), Swed. smälta "to melt; to digest," modern Gr. χωνεύω "to cast, found (metal); to digest." In the meaning "to blight, nip (fruit, etc.)," Pol. warzyć shows a semantic shift to the notion of damaging by extreme cold rather than heat.

самовáр et al.: ="self-heater," i.e. a vessel which heats without the need of a stove; the Polish, Czech and Serbo-Croatian words are borrowed from Russian.

izvor: See note on Rus. истóк and истóчник, S-C izvor.

zwarzyć-svariti: See note on варúть et al.

ВЕРХ, ВЕРШ	WIERZCH	VRCH, VRŠ	VRH, VRŠ
верх: top вершúть: to manage, direct вéрхний: upper верхóвный: supreme	wierzch: top wierzchni: upper	vrch: top; hill vršiti: to pile up (tr.) vrchní: upper; supreme	vrh: top vršiti: to execute, carry out vrhovni: supreme
[R]	[P]	[Cz]	[S-C]

[R]	[P]	[Cz]	[S-C]
			vrhnje: cream
		vrchnost: the authorities, powers-that-be	
	wierzchowiec: saddle-horse		
совершенноле́тний: adult, of age			
доверши́ть, доверша́ть: to complete		dovršiti, dovršovati: to complete	dovršiti, dovršivati (dovršavati): to complete; to end, terminate
			izvršiti, izvršivati (izvršavati): to execute, carry out; to commit, perpetrate
			izvršan: executive (a.); enforceable (judicial order, etc.)
			ovrha: distraint, execution
	powierzchnia: surface	povrch: surface	površina, površje: surface
	powierzchowny: outward, external; superficial (knowledge, wound, etc.)	povrchní: superficial (knowledge, wound, etc.)	površan: superficial (knowledge, wound, etc.)
пове́рхность: surface	powierzchowność: (outward) appearance; superficiality	povrchnost: superficiality	površnost: superficiality
пове́рхностный: superficial (knowledge, wound, etc.); surface (attr.)			
			*prevršiti: to overstep, exceed (the bounds of s.th.)
			svrha: purpose, aim, end
	zwierzchnik: chief, superior (n.)	svrchník: overcoat	

[R]	[P]	[Cz]	[S-C]
		svrchovanost: sovereignty	
соверши́ть, соверша́ть; (lit.) сверши́ть, сверша́ть: to perform, accomplish; (соверши́ть, соверша́ть only) to commit, perpetrate			savršiti, savršivati; svršiti, svršivati (svršavati): to complete; to end, terminate
соверше́нный: perfect; absolute, utter; (gram.) perfective (aspect of Slavic verb)			savršen: perfect; completed
			svršen: completed; (gram.) perfective (aspect of Slavic verb)
заверши́ть, заверша́ть: to complete			završiti, završivati (završavati): to complete; to end, terminate
[R]	[P]	[Cz]	[S-C]

NOTES

Basic meaning of root: top

The top of a thing can readily be conceived of as its end---hence the numerous verbal derivatives with such meanings as "to end, complete" and, by extension, "to execute, carry out, accomplish, manage" (or, in a pejorative sense, "to commit, perpetrate"). (See the introductory notes on roots ЧА [etc.] and ПОЛН [etc.].)

Several of the listed words have English counterparts derived from Lat. super "above" (>superior, supreme, sovereignty).

vrhnje: Compare Ger. Obers "cream" (<ober "upper").

vrchnost: Compare Ger. Obrigkeit "(the) authorities, powers-that-be" (<ober "upper").

совершенноле́тний: The second element is from ле́то "summer; (pl. only) year"; see note on Pol. pełnoletni et al.

prevršiti: ="to go over or beyond the top."

svrha: orig. "end" in the literal sense.

соверши́ть: borrowed from Church Slavic.

соверше́нный-savršen, svršen: See note on Pol. dokonany and doskonały, Cz. dokonavý and dokonalý.

ВРЕМЯ, ВРЕМЕН			VRIJEME, VREME(N)
вре́мя: time; (gram.) tense			vrijeme: time; weather; (gram.) tense
вре́менный: temporary			vremenit: temporary; elderly
			vremešan: elderly
			istovremen: simultaneous; contemporary
одновре́ме́нный: simultaneous			jednovremen: simultaneous; contemporary
			međuvrijeme: interval of time
преждевре́менный: premature			prijevremen: premature
времяпрепровожде́ние: pastime			
безвре́менье (arch.): hard times; period of social stagnation			
			nevrijeme: bad weather; inopportuneness
			privremen: temporary
совреме́нный: contemporary; modern			savremen, suvremen: contemporary; modern
[R]			[S-C]

NOTES

Basic meaning of root: time

Вре́мя-vrijeme is generally thought to be a suffixed derivative of root ВЕРТ (etc.), time being conceived of as an unending process of rotation. Wrzemię existed in Old Polish; there is no trace of the word in Czech. (Compare root ЧАС [etc.].)

The Russian root-forms are of Church Slavic origin; the native form веремя existed in Old Russian.

врéмя-*vrijeme*: Like the Serbo-Croatian word, Rus. *врéмя* originally meant "weather" as well as "time"; see note on Pol. *czas*, Cz. *čas*.

врéменный-*vremenit*: See note on Pol. *czasowy*, Cz. *časový* and *časný*.

istovremen: See note on Pol. *równoczesny*.

prijevremen: The first element is from *prije* "before, earlier."

privremen: See note on Pol. *czasowy*, Cz. *časový* and *časný*.

современный *et al.*: The Serbo-Croatian words are borrowed from Russian; see note on Pol. *współczesny*.

ВЕРГ, ВЕРЖ	WIERZG	VRH, VRŽ	VR(G), VRŽ
	wierzgnąć, *wierzgać*: to kick	*vrhnouti*, *vrhati*: to throw	**vrći* (*vrgnuti*): to put; to throw
		vrh: throw; litter, brood (of animals)	
ниспровéргнуть, *ниспровергáть*: to overthrow, depose			
самоотвéрженность: self-denial, selflessness			
извéргнуть, *извергáть* (lit.): to expel, exclude; to vomit, disgorge; to excrete			*izvrći* (*izvrgnuti*), *izvrgavati*: to expose, subject (to)
и́зверг: monster, inhumanly cruel person			
		návrh: proposal; draft, sketch; plan, project	
опровéргнуть, *опровергáть*: to refute		*opovrhnouti*, *opovrhovati*: to despise, scorn	*opovrći* (*opovrgnuti*), *opovrgavati*; *oprovrći* (*oprovrgnuti*), *oprovrgavati*: to refute
отвéргнуть, *отвергáть*: to reject, refuse		*odvrhnouti*, *odvrhovati*: to cast off (e.g. a burden); (lit.) to reject, refuse	**odvrći* (*odvrgnuti*): to reject, refuse
[R]	[P]	[Cz]	[S-C]

[R]	[P]	[Cz]	[S-C]
отве́рженный, (arch.) отве́рженец: outcast			
			*odvrći (odvrgnuti) se: to desert, defect
подве́ргнуть, подверга́ть: to expose, subject (to)		podvrhnouti, podvrhovati: to falsify, forge; to foist, palm off	podvrći (podvrgnuti), podvrgavati: to subjugate, subject; to expose, subject (to)
приве́рженец: adherent, supporter		přívrženec: adherent, supporter	privrženik: adherent, supporter
		rozvrhnouti, rozvrhovati: to distribute; to plan, schedule	*razvrći (razvrgnuti): to annul, cancel, abrogate
све́ргнуть, сверга́ть: to overthrow, depose		svrhnouti, svrhovati: to throw down; to overthrow, depose	svrći (svrgnuti), svrgavati: to overthrow, depose; to dismiss, discharge
вве́ргнуть, вверга́ть: to throw (into jail), plunge (into despair, poverty, etc.)		uvrhnouti, uvrhovati: to throw (into jail), plunge (into despair, poverty, etc.)	
		vyvrhel: monster, inhumanly cruel person	
		vyvrženec: outcast	
		zvrhlík: degenerate, pervert	
		zavrhnouti, zavrhovati: to reject, refuse; to repudiate, disown	*zavrći (zavrgnuti): to throw (a sack, etc. over one's shoulder); to mislay; to pick (a quarrel)

NOTES

Basic meaning of root: to throw

wierzgnąć et al.: Rus. ве́ргнуть, верга́ть "to throw" is obsolete; regarding the shift in the meaning of the Polish and Serbo-Croatian words, see note on Rus. ти́снуть et al.

vrh (second meaning): See note on Pol. miot.

ниспрове́ргнуть: нис- = "down."

самоотве́рженность: See отве́ргнуть.

изве́ргнуть: borrowed from Church Slavic.

izvrći: Compare Eng. expose (ult. ‹Lat. ex "out" + Fr. poser "to put"), Ger. aussetzen "to expose, subject" (‹aus "out" + setzen "to set, put").

и́зверг: orig. "outcast"; the word is borrowed from Church Slavic.

návrh: The underlying sense is that of "throwing out" or putting forward an idea; compare Eng. project (ult. ‹Lat. pro- "forward" + jacere "to throw"), Dan. udkast and Nor.-Swed. utkast "draft, sketch" (‹ud, ut "out" + Dan.-Nor. kaste, Swed. kasta "to throw, cast"), Rus. набро́сок "draft, sketch" (‹на + бро́сить "to throw"), Cz. námět.

опрове́ргнуть-opovrći, oprovrći: ="to throw over, overturn"; S-C oprovrći is borrowed from Russian.

opovrhnouti: Compare odvrhnouti.

отве́ргнуть et al.: See note on Cz. odmítnouti.

подве́ргнуть-podvrći: Compare Eng. subject (ult. ‹Lat. sub "under" + jacere "to throw"), Ger. unterwerfen "to subjugate, subject; to expose, subject" (‹unter "under" + werfen "to throw").

podvrhnouti: See note on Rus. подки́дыш.

приве́рженец et al.: one who "throws himself" (i.e. adheres, attaches himself) to another; the Russian word is borrowed from Church Slavic, the Czech and Serbo-Croatian words from Russian.

rozvrhnouti: orig. "to throw around, scatter," then "to allocate, distribute."

razvrći: The progression in the meaning has been "to throw around" › "to scatter, dissipate" › "to destroy" › "to annul."

vyvrhel: orig. "outcast."

zvrhlík: ‹zvrhnouti se "to be thrown over, overturned; to change for the worse, degenerate."

zavrhnouti: See note on Cz. odmítnouti and compare Cz. zamítnouti.

zavrći: In the third meaning, the prefix has inceptive force; compare S-C zametnuti.

(В)ЕР(Т), ВЕРЕТ, (В)ОРОТ, ВОРОЧ, (В)ОРАЧ, (В)РАТ, (В)РАЩ	WART, WIERC, WRZEC, (W)ROT, (W)RÓT, (W)RÓC, (W)RAC	VRT, VŘET, (V)RAT, (V)RÁT, (V)RAC, VRÁC	(V)R(T), VRET, (V)RAT, (V)RAĆ
верте́ть: to whirl (tr.)	wiercić: to drill, bore; to whirl (tr.); to wag (an animal's tail)	vrtěti: to shake (one's head), wag (an animal's tail); to churn	vrtjeti: to drill, bore; to whirl (tr.)
		vrtati: to drill, bore	vrtati: to drill, bore
*верну́ть: to return, give back; to recover, get back			*vrnuti: to return, give back
*верну́ться: to return, go back		*vrtnouti se: to move, stir (intr.); to go	*vrnuti se: to return, go back
**вороти́ть (coll.): to turn (tr.); to control; to recover, get back	*wrócić: to return, go back; to return, give back	*vrátiti: to return, give back	*vratiti: to return, give back
воро́чать (coll.): to turn (tr.); to control; to move (tr.)	wracać: to return, go back; to return, give back	vraceti: to return, give back	vraćati: to return, give back
*вороти́ться (coll.): to return, go back		*vrátiti se: to return, go back	*vratiti se: to return, go back
воро́чаться (coll.): to turn (intr.); to move (intr.)		vraceti se: to return, go back	vraćati se: to return, go back
враща́ть: to revolve (tr.)			
во́рот: collar; windlass			vrat: neck
воротни́к: collar			
		vratidlo: windlass	vratilo: weaver's beam; shaft (in machinery); horizontal bar (in a gymnasium)
			vrtlog: whirlpool
		vrtoch: whim, caprice	
[R]	[P]	[Cz]	[S-C]

		vrtule: propeller	
		vrtulník: helicopter	
вёрткий (coll.): nimble, agile	wartki: swift	vratký: unstable, unsteady	
		vrtkavý: fickle	
веретено́: spindle	wrzeciono: spindle	vřeteno: spindle	vreteno: spindle
круговоро́т: rotation (of the seasons), succession (of events)			
			okovratnik: collar; necktie
		slunovrat: solstice	
водоворо́т: whirlpool			
			vrtoglavica: dizziness, giddiness
вертолёт: helicopter			
изврати́ть, извраща́ть: to distort, pervert			izvrnuti, izvrtati; izvratiti, izvraćati: to overturn, upset; to distort, pervert
изворо́тливый: resourceful, clever			
навороти́ть, навора́чивать (coll.): to heap up	nawrócić, nawracać: to turn back, retrace one's steps; to convert (to a religion) (tr.)	navrátiti, navraceti: to return, give back	navratiti, navraćati: to divert (a stream)
наоборо́т: on the contrary; backwards, the wrong way			
оберну́ть, обёртывать: to wrap; to turn (tr.)			obrnuti, obrtati: to turn (tr.); to turn away (tr.)
обороти́ть, обора́чивать (coll.): to turn (tr.)	obrócić, obracać: to turn (tr.); to revolve (tr.); to turn, convert (into)	obrátiti, obraceti: to turn (tr.); to turn, direct (attention, etc.); to turn, convert (into);	obratiti, obraćati: to turn (tr.); to revolve (tr.); to turn, direct (attention, etc.);
[R]	[P]	[Cz]	[S-C]

		to convert (to a religion) (tr.)	to turn, convert (into); to convert (to a religion) (tr.)
оборoти́ться, обора́чиваться (coll.): to turn (intr.)	obrócić się, obracać się: to turn (intr.); to revolve (intr.); to turn (into) (intr.)	obrátiti se, obraceti se: to turn (intr.); to turn (into) (intr.); to convert (to a religion) (intr.); to address o.s., apply, appeal (to)	obratiti se, obraćati se: to turn (intr.); to revolve (intr.); to convert (to a religion) (intr.); to address o.s., apply, appeal (to)
обрати́ть, обраща́ть: to turn, direct (attention, etc.); to turn, convert (into); to convert (to a religion) (tr.)			
обрати́ться, обраща́ться: to turn (intr.); to turn (into) (intr.); to convert (to a religion) (intr.); to address o.s., apply, appeal (to); (обращ-áться only) to circulate (said of blood, currency, etc.); (обращ-áться only; с + inst.) to treat, behave (toward); (об-ращáться only; с + inst.) to handle (e.g. a tool)			
			obrt: turn, revolution; (business) turnover; trade, handicraft; turning-point, crisis
оборо́т: turn, revolution; (business) turnover; turn	obrót: turn, movement; turn, revolution; (business)	obrat: turn, movement; (business) turnover; turn	obrat: turning-point, crisis
[R]	[P]	[Cz]	[S-C]

(of events); phrase, turn of speech; back, reverse side	turnover; turn (of events)	(of events); phrase, turn of speech	
оборо́тный: reverse (side, etc.); working, circulating (capital)	obrotny: resourceful, clever	obratný: skilful, adroit	obratan: reverse (side, etc.); opposite, contrary
обра́тный: opposite, contrary; reverse (side, etc.); inverse; retroactive; return (trip), round-trip (ticket)			
		obrátka: turn, revolution	
о́боротень: werewolf			
		obratel: vertebra	
	obrotnica: (railroad) turntable	obratník: tropic	obratnik, obratnica: tropic
			ovratnik: collar; necktie
отверну́ть, отвёртывать: to turn away (tr.); to unscrew; to turn on (e.g. a faucet)			odvrnuti, odvrtati: to turn away (tr.); to unscrew; to turn on (e.g. a faucet)
отвороти́ть, отвора́чивать (coll.): to turn away (tr.)	odwrócić, odwracać: to turn away (tr.); to reverse; to avert, prevent; to divert, distract	odvrátiti, odvraceti: to turn away (tr.); to avert, prevent; to divert, distract	odvratiti, odvraćati: to turn away (tr.); to avert, prevent; to divert, distract; to dissuade
отврати́ть, отвраща́ть: to avert, prevent			
отворо́т: lapel	odwrót: retreat; reverse, converse	odvrat: (act of) turning away	
отврати́тельный, (coll.) отвра́тный: repulsive, disgusting	odwrotny: opposite, contrary; reverse (side, etc.); inverse		odvratan: repulsive, disgusting
[R]	[P]	[Cz]	[S-C]

[R]	[P]	[Cz]	[S-C]
поверну́ть, повёртывать: to turn (tr. and intr.)			povrnuti, povrtati: to turn (tr.); to return, give back
повороти́ть (coll.), повора́чивать: to turn (tr. and intr.)	powrócić, powracać: to return, go back		povratiti, povraćati: to return, give back; to vomit
поворо́тный: rotary; turning-(point), decisive (moment)	powrotny: return (trip), round-trip (ticket); relapsing, recurrent (fever)		povratan: round-trip (ticket); retroactive; relapsing, recurrent (fever); (gram.) reflexive
поворо́тливый: nimble, agile			povratljiv: forgiving, easily appeased
			povratnik: tropic
		podvratný: subversive (a.)	
преврати́ть, превраща́ть: to turn, convert (into)			
			prevrtljiv: fickle
переворо́т: revolution, upheaval	przewrót: revolution, upheaval	převrat: revolution, upheaval	prevrat: revolution, upheaval
превра́тный: wrong, false; (arch.) changing, inconstant	przewrotny: perverse, wrongheaded	převratný: revolutionary	prevratan: revolutionary
			preobratiti, preobraćati: to turn, convert (into); to convert (to a religion) (tr.)
предотврати́ть, предотвраща́ть: to avert, prevent			
	przywrócić, przywracać: to restore, re-establish		
			provrtan: busy, active

развра́т: debauchery, licentiousness		rozvrat: disorganization, disorder	razvrat: debauchery, licentiousness
соврати́ть, совраща́ть: to seduce, lead astray			
свёрток: package			
			svratište: hotel, inn
			saobraćaj: traffic; communication; circulation (of currency)
увёртка: subterfuge, evasion			
	wywracanie: (act of) overturning, upsetting	vyvrácení: refutation	
	wywrotowy: subversive (a.)		
		*vyzvraceti (vyzvrátiti): to vomit	
возврати́ть, возвраща́ть: to return, give back			uzvratiti, uzvraćati: to return, give back; to return (a favor, visit, etc.); to retort
возврати́ться, возвраща́ться: to return, go back			
возвра́тный: relapsing, recurrent (fever); (gram.) reflexive			uzvratan: given in exchange
	zwrot: turn, movement; return, (act of) giving back; reimbursement; phrase, turn of speech	zvrat: turning-point, crisis	
	zwrotny: returnable; turning-	zvratný: relapsing, recurrent	
[R]	[P]	[Cz]	[S-C]

	(point), decisive (moment); (gram.) reflexive zwrotka: stanza zwrotnik: tropic zwrotnica: railroad switch zawrotny: dizzy, giddy	(fever); (gram.) reflexive závratný: dizzy, giddy	zavrtanj: screw zavratak: cuff; lapel
[R]	[P]	[Cz]	[S-C]

NOTES

Basic meaning of root: to turn

Many of the derivatives are paralleled by English words derived from Lat. vertere "to turn," i.e. vertebra, vertigo, avert and aversion (a- = "off, away"), convert, converse, divert (di- = "aside"), inverse, pervert and perverse (<pervertere "to overturn, overthrow, ruin"), reverse (re- = "back"), subversive (<subvertere "to overturn, overthrow, ruin"). Similar semantic correspondences are shown by German derivatives of kehren "to turn": bekehren "to convert (to a religion)," umgekehrt "opposite, contrary; reverse; inverse" (um- = "around"), Verkehr "traffic; communication," verkehrt "wrong, false; perverse, wrongheaded" (ver- here = "mis-, astray"), wiederkehren "to return, go back" (wieder- = "back, again"). (See also notes on individual words below.)

The Russian root-forms ВРАТ and ВРАЩ are of Church Slavic origin.

Non-Slavic cognates are Eng. (back-, down-, for-)ward(s), Ger. werden "to become" (="to turn [into]"), Lat. vertere.

vrtnouti se (second meaning): Compare Eng. went < wend (one's way) (=Ger. wenden "to turn").

воротить et al., ворочать et al., вращать: causative forms of the primary verb вертеть et al., which was originally intransitive; воротить is imperfective in the first two meanings, perfective in the third.

ворот-vrat, воротник: The original meaning of both ворот and vrat was "neck" (i.e. "that which turns"); regarding the meaning "collar," compare Eng. collar (ult. <Lat. collum "neck"), Ger. Kragen "collar" (orig. "neck").

вёрткий-wartki: See note on obrotny-obratný.

okovratnik: ="that which is around the neck"; see vrat and note on ворот-vrat, воротник.

slunovrat: the time when the sun (slunce) "turns" after reaching the point farthest from the equator; the word is modeled on Ger. Sonnenwende "solstice" (<Sonne "sun" + wenden "to turn"). See note on obratník et al.

vrtoglavica: See reference to Eng. vertigo in the introductory note.

изворо́тливый: See note on obrotny-obratný.

наоборо́т: See the last meaning of оборо́т.

обрати́ться: Regarding the last two meanings of the imperfective verb, see note on Rus. обходи́ться et al. and обходи́тельный, S-C ophodljiv.

obrt: The third meaning developed in fairly recent times from dialectal obrtan "busy, active"; see provrtan.

obrotny-obratný: Compare Ger. gewandt "agile, clever, skilful" (<wenden "to turn").

о́боротень: ="one who turns (into a wolf)."

obratník et al.: either of the two parallels at which the sun "turns" after reaching the point farthest from the equator; compare Eng. tropic (ult. <Gr. τροπικός "of or like a turn" [sc. κύκλος "circle"]), Ger. Wendekreis "tropic" (<wenden "to turn" + Kreis "circle") and see note on slunovrat.

ovratnik: See note on okovratnik.

отврати́тельный, отвра́тный-odvratan: See reference to Eng. aversion in the introductory note; the Serbo-Croatian word is borrowed from Russian.

povratan (last meaning): ="turning back (upon the subject)"; compare Eng. reflexive (ult. <Lat. re- "back" + flectere "to bend, turn").

поворо́тливый: See note on obrotny-obratný.

povratljiv: ="quickly returning (i.e. recovering) from anger."

povratnik: See note on obratník et al.

развра́т-razvrat: Compare изврати́ть et al.

свёрток: See the first meaning of оберну́ть.

svratište: <svratiti se "to put up (at a hotel)"; compare Ger. einkehren "to put up (at a hotel)" (<ein- "in" + kehren "to turn").

возвра́тный, zwrotny-zvratný: See note on povratan.

zwrotka: prob. a loan-translation of Gr. στροφή "turning of the chorus; hence, the strain sung during that movement, strophe, stanza" (<στρέφειν "to turn"), whence Eng. strophe.

zwrotnik: See note on obratník et al.

zawrotny-závratný: See reference to Eng. vertigo in the introductory note.

ВЫС, ВЫШ	WYS, WYŚ, WYŻ(SZ)	VYS, VÝS, VYŠ, VÝŠ	VIS, VIŠ
высо́кий: high	wysoki: high	vysoký: high	visok: high
вы́ше: higher (adv. and pred. a.); above (adv. and prep.)	wyżej: higher (adv.); above (adv.)	výš, výše: higher (adv.); above (adv.)	više: more; several; higher (adv.); above (adv. and prep.)
вы́шка: tower		výška: height	
			višak: surplus, excess
	wyższość: superiority		
Высо́чество: Highness (title)	wysokość: height; (cap.) Highness (title)	Výsost: Highness (title)	Visočanstvo, Visost: Highness (title)
	wyśmienity: excellent		
высотоме́р: altimeter	wysokościomierz, wysokomierz: altimeter	výškoměr: altimeter	visinomjer: altimeter
высокоме́рный: haughty, arrogant			
высокопа́рный: high-flown, pompous			visokoparan: high-flown, pompous
			nadvisiti, nadvisivati (nadvišavati, nadvišivati): to surpass, exceed
	nadwyżka: surplus, excess		
			odviše: too, excessively; too much
повы́сить, повыша́ть: to raise; to heighten; to increase; to promote (in rank)		povýšiti, povyšovati: to promote (in rank); to be promoted (in rank)	povisiti, povisivati (povišavati, povišivati): to heighten; to increase
		povýšenec: upstart, parvenu	
	podwyższyć, podwyższać: to heighten; to increase		
[R]	[P]	[Cz]	[S-C]

[R]	[P]	[Cz]	[S-C]
превы́ше: (over and) above			previše: too, excessively; too much
превы́сить, превыша́ть: to surpass, exceed	przewyższyć, przewyższać: to surpass, exceed	převýšiti, převyšovati: to surpass, exceed; (převyšovati only) to be higher than	previsiti, previšavati: to surpass, exceed
			Preuzvišenost: Excellency (title)
			suviše: too, excessively; too much
			suvišak: surplus, excess
	wywyższyć, wywyższać: to raise; to extol, exalt	vyvýšiti, vyvyšovati: to raise; to extol, exalt	
возвы́сить, возвыша́ть: to raise			uzvisiti, uzvisivati (uzvišavati, uzvišivati): to raise; to extol, exalt

NOTES

Basic meaning of root: high

In the primary adjective, the root appears in combination with a suffix. The Polish form WYŻ(SZ) is for earlier WYSZ.

высотоме́р et al.: See note under root MEP_1 (etc.).

высокоме́рный: Compare Eng. haughty (‹Fr. haut "high").

высокопа́рный-visokoparan: The second element is from пари́ть-pariti "to soar"; compare Eng. high-flown, Pol. górnolotny.

wywyższyć-vyvýšiti, uzvisiti: Compare Eng. extol (ult. ‹Lat. tollere "to raise") and exalt (ult. ‹Lat. altus "high"), Rus. превознести́, S-C preuznositi and uznijeti.

ЗД, ЗИД, ЗИЖД, ЗОД	ZD	ZED, ZEĎ	ZD, ZID
			zidati: to build
зи́ждиться: to be based (on)			
зда́ние: building, edifice			zdanje (arch.): building, edifice
зо́дчий: architect			
		zeď: wall	zid: wall
		zedník: mason, bricklayer	
		zednář: (free) mason	zidar: mason, bricklayer; (free) mason
	zdun: potter; stove-fitter		
мироздание (lit.): universe			
назида́тельный (lit.): edifying			
созда́ть, создава́ть (созида́ть): to create			sazdati (sazidati), sazdavati: to build; (sazdati, sazdavati only) to create
[R]	[P]	[Cz]	[S-C]

NOTES

Basic meaning of root: to build

Verbal derivatives of the root survive only in Russian and Serbo-Croatian. With the possible exception of зо́дчий, the Russian words are of Church Slavic origin.

зи́ждиться: a new infinitive formed from зижду, зиждешь, etc., the present tense of ORus. зьдати.

назида́тельный: ="building" (i.e. uplifting, improving) morally; compare Eng. edify and edifice (both ult. ⟨Lat. aedificare "to build"), instruct and construct (both ult. ⟨Lat. struere "to build"), Ger. erbaulich "edifying" (⟨bauen "to build"), Pol. budujący "edifying" (⟨budować "to build").

ЗЕМ	ZIEM, ZIOM	ZEM	ZEM
земля́: earth (the planet); earth, soil; land, ground; (lit.) country (national entity)	ziemia: earth (the planet); earth, soil; land, ground; (lit.) country (national entity)	země: earth (the planet); earth, soil; land, ground; country (national entity)	zemlja: earth (the planet); earth, soil; land, ground; country (national entity)
земля́к: fellow-countryman, compatriot	ziomek: fellow-countryman, compatriot		zemljak: fellow-countryman, compatriot
земляни́ка: strawberry			
	ziemniak: potato		
зе́мство (arch.): zemstvo (elective district council)	ziemstwo (arch.): county court; local landed gentry		
чужезе́мец (arch.): foreigner	cudzoziemiec: foreigner	cizozemec: foreigner	tuđozemac: foreigner
инозе́мец (arch.): foreigner	innoziemiec: foreigner	jinozemec (arch.): foreigner	inozemac: foreigner
тузе́мец: native (n.)	tuziemiec: native (n.)	tuzemec: native (n.)	tuzemac: native (n.)
	współziomek: fellow-countryman, compatriot		
		zeměbrana (arch.): militia, home guard	
земледе́лие: agriculture		zemědělství: agriculture	zemljodjelstvo: agriculture
землеме́р: surveyor		zeměměřič: surveyor	zemljomjer: surveyor
		zeměpis: geography	zemljopis: geography
			zemljoradnja: agriculture
			zemljouz: isthmus
			zemljovid: map
земново́дный: amphibious	wodnoziemny, ziemnowodny: amphibious		vodozeman: amphibious
назём: manure			
		odzemí: (astr.) apogee	
позём: manure	poziom: level (n.); horizon		
[R]	[P]	[Cz]	[S-C]

	poziomy: horizontal; base, vulgar		
	poziomka: strawberry		
	przyziemie: ground floor	přízemí: ground floor; pit, orchestra (in theater); (astr.) perigee	prizemlje: ground floor
приземистый: low; thick-set, squat			prizemljast: low
		území: territory	
		zázemí: hinterland; (mil.) rear	
[R]	[P]	[Cz]	[S-C]

NOTES

Basic meaning of root: earth, land, ground

The Slavic root is related to Lat. humus "earth, land, ground" (>Eng. humus, exhume), humilis "low" (>Eng. humble, humility, humiliate).

земляника: so called because the ripe berries often lie on the ground; compare Ger. Erdbeere "strawberry" (<Erde "earth, ground" + Beere "berry").

ziemniak: Compare Fr. pomme de terre, Ger. Erdapfel "potato" (both literally "earth-apple").

чужеземец et al.: The first element is from чужой-cudzy-cizí-tuđ "alien, foreign."

туземец et al.: The first element is from ту (ORus.; =modern Rus. тут)-tu "here."

zeměpis-zemljopis: See note under root ПИС (etc.).

zemljoradnja: The second element is from radnja "work."

zemljouz: The second element is from uzak "narrow"; compare Ger. Landenge "isthmus" (<Land "land" + eng "narrow").

odzemí: modeled on Gr. ἀπόγειον (<ἀπό "off, away from" + γῆ "earth"), whence Eng. apogee.

poziom: a line running parallel to, or formed by, the earth's surface.

poziomy: Regarding the first meaning, see poziom and compare Eng. horizontal (<horizon). The second meaning is an outgrowth of the earlier meaning "low"; compare Lat. humilis (referred to in the introductory note above) and Eng. base (a.) (<Fr. bas "low").

poziomka: See note on земляника.

přízemí: In its third meaning, the word translates Gr. περίγειον (<περί "near, around" + γῆ "earth"), whence Eng. perigee.

призéмистый-*prizemljast*: Compare Lat. *humilis* (referred to in the introductory note above).

zázemí: modeled on Ger. *Hinterland* (<*hinter* "behind" + *Land* "land").

ЗЛ	ZŁ	ZL	ZAO, ZL
злой: malicious; angry	*zły*: bad; angry	*zlý*: bad; malicious	*zao*: bad; malicious
зло: evil, wrong, harm; malice	*złe*, *zło*: evil, wrong, harm	*zlé*, *zlo*: evil, wrong, harm	*zlo*: evil, wrong, harm
злить: to anger			
		zlobiti: to anger	*zlobiti*: to wish (s.o.) harm; to do (s.o.) harm
	złościć: to anger		
злóстный: malicious	*złośliwy*: malicious; (med.) malignant	*zlostný*: angry	
	złoczyństwo (arch.): crime	*zločin*: crime	*zločin*, *zločinstvo*: crime
злодея́ние (lit.), *злодéйство* (lit.): crime	*złodziejstwo*: theft, thievery	*zlodějství*: theft, thievery	*zlodjelo*: misdeed
злободнéвный: topical, burning (issue, etc.)			
			zloglasnost: disrepute
злокáчественный: (med.) malignant			
злоключéние (arch.): mishap			
злополýчный: unlucky, ill-fated			
			zlorabiti: to abuse, misuse
злорáдство: gloating (n.)			*zloradost*, *zluradost*: gloating (n.)
	złorzeczyć: to curse	*zlořečiti*: to curse	
злослóвие: backbiting, slander			
[R]	[P]	[Cz]	[S-C]

			zloslutan: ominous
			zlostaviti, zlostavljati: to mistreat; to torture
		zlosyn: scoundrel	
злоупотребить, злоупотреблять: to abuse, misuse			zloupotrebiti, zloupotrebljavati: to abuse, misuse
зловещий: ominous	złowieszczy: ominous	zlověstný: ominous	
		zlovolný: malevolent	zlovoljan: ill-humored
зложелательный (arch.): malevolent			
[R]	[P]	[Cz]	[S-C]

NOTES

Basic meaning of root: bad

Many of the derivatives show the secondary meaning "angry, malicious." (Compare Eng. malicious [ult. ‹Lat. malus "bad"], Ger. böse "bad; angry" and see note on Pol. gorszyć.) The root is frequently used as a prefix meaning "bad" or "badly" in the formation of abstract compounds. (See the numerous antonyms under roots БЛАГ [etc.] and ДОБР [etc.].)

złoczyństwo et al., злодеяние et al.: Compare Eng. malefaction (ult. ‹Lat. male "badly, ill" + facere "to do").

злободневный: See note under root ДЕН (etc.).

злокачественный: The second element is from качество "quality."

злоключение: See note under root КЛЮК (etc.).

злорадство et al.: The second element is from рад-rad "glad"; see note on Cz. škodolibost.

złorzeczyć-zlořečiti: modeled on Lat. maledicere "to slander; to curse" (‹male "badly, ill" + dicere "to say"), whence Eng. malediction.

zloslutan: The second element is from slutiti "to portend."

zlosyn: The second element is from syn "son."

злоупотребить-zloupotrebiti: The second element is from употребить-upotrebiti "to use."

zlovolný: See note under root $ВЕЛ_2$ (etc.).

зложелательный: The second element is from желать "to wish"; see preceding note.

ЗНА	ZNA	ZNA, ZNÁ	ZNA
знать: to know	znać: to know	znáti: to know	znati: to know
	znajomy: familiar, well known; acquaintance (person with whom one is acquainted)	známý: famous; familiar, well known; familiar, acquainted (with); acquaintance (person with whom one is acquainted)	
			znanac: acquaintance (person with whom one is acquainted)
			znanost: science
знать (arch.): (the) nobility, aristocracy			
зна́тный: distinguished, outstanding; (arch.) noble, aristocratic			znatan: distinguished, outstanding; important; substantial, considerable
		znatelný: perceptible, appreciable	
зна́харь: quack doctor	znachor: quack doctor		
знато́к: expert; connoisseur	znawca: expert; connoisseur	znalec, znatel: expert; connoisseur	znalac: expert; connoisseur
знак: sign; mark	znak: sign; signal; mark	znak: sign; mark; coat-of-arms	znak: sign; signal; mark; symptom
значо́к: mark; badge	znaczek: sign; mark; badge; (postage) stamp	značka: sign; mark; (chem.) formula	značka: badge
знако́мый: familiar, well known; familiar, acquainted (with); acquaintance (person with whom one is acquainted)	znakomity: distinguished, outstanding; excellent		
зна́чить: to mean, signify	znaczyć: to mean, signify; to mark	značiti: to mean, signify; to mark	značiti: to mean, signify; to be significant, important
[R]	[P]	[Cz]	[S-C]

[R]	[P]	[Cz]	[S-C]
значи́тельный: significant, meaningful; significant, important; substantial, considerable	znaczny: substantial, considerable	značný: substantial, considerable	značajan: significant, meaningful; significant, important; characteristic
зна́мя: banner	znamię: characteristic; birthmark; (arch.) banner		znamen: symbol; birthmark
зна́мение (arch.): sign		znamení: sign; signal; mark	znamenje: omen, portent; holy water
		známka: (postage) stamp; sign; mark	
знамени́тый: famous	znamienity: distinguished, outstanding	znamenitý: excellent	znamenit: famous
знамена́тельный: significant, important	znamienny: significant, important; characteristic		
знаменова́ть (lit.): to mark, signify (e.g. the beginning of a new era)	znamionować: to characterize	znamenati: to mean, signify; to mark	**znamenovati: to mark; to sprinkle with holy water
знамена́тель: (math.) denominator			
	bliskoznaczny: synonymous		
двузна́чный: (math.) consisting of two digits	dwuznaczny: ambiguous	dvojznačný: ambiguous	
однозна́чный: synonymous; (math.) simple (consisting of one digit)	jednoznaczny: synonymous	jednoznačný: synonymous; unambiguous	
естествозна́ние: natural science			
языкозна́ние: linguistics	językoznawstwo: linguistics		
любозна́тельный: curious, inquisitive			
	ludoznawstwo: ethnology		
[R]	[P]	[Cz]	[S-C]

[R]	[P]	[Cz]	[S-C]
		předznamenati, předznamenávati: to presage, portend	
предзнамено́вание: omen, portent			
предназна́чить, предназнача́ть: to destine, intend (for)			
призна́ть, признава́ть: to recognize (a government); to admit, acknowledge; to consider, deem, regard (as)	przyznać, przyznawać: to admit, acknowledge; to award	přiznati, přiznávati: to admit, acknowledge; to award	priznati, priznavati: to admit, acknowledge
призна́тельный: grateful, appreciative			
при́знак: sign; symptom		příznak: sign; symptom	
	przeznaczyć, przeznaczać: to destine, intend (for)		
	rozeznać, rozeznawać: to distinguish, differentiate; to distinguish, discern	rozeznati, rozeznávati: to distinguish, differentiate; to distinguish, discern	razaznati, razaznavati: to distinguish, differentiate; to distinguish, discern; to understand
распозна́ть, распознава́ть: to distinguish, differentiate; to distinguish, discern; to diagnose	rozpoznać, rozpoznawać: to recognize (a voice, etc.); to distinguish, discern; to diagnose	rozpoznati, rozpoznávati: to distinguish, discern; to diagnose	raspoznati, raspoznavati: to distinguish, differentiate; to distinguish, discern
созна́ние: consciousness, awareness; consciousness, waking state; confession	zeznanie: testimony, deposition; (tax, etc.) statement, declaration		saznanje: knowledge
		seznam: list	
		souznačný: synonymous	
узна́ть, узнава́ть: to recognize (a voice, etc.); to find out	uznać, uznawać: to recognize (a government); to admit, acknowledge;	uznati, uznávati: to recognize (a government); to admit, acknowledge;	*uznati: to find out

	(za + acc.) to consider, deem, regard (as)	to appreciate, think highly of; (za + acc.) to consider, deem, regard (as)	
	wyznać, wyznawać: to confess; to profess (a religion)	vyznati, vyznávati: to confess; to profess (a religion)	
	wyznaczyć, wyznaczać: to fix, set, specify; to appoint (to office, etc.); to mark	vyznačiti, vyznačovati: to mark	
		význačný: distinguished, outstanding; characteristic	
		vyznamenati, vyznamenávati: to distinguish, honor; to decorate (with a medal, etc.)	
		význam: meaning	
		významný: significant, meaningful; significant, important; distinguished, outstanding	
	zaznać, zaznawać: to experience		*zaznati: to find out; to become aware
		zaznamenati, zaznamenávati: to note, record	
[R]	[P]	[Cz]	[S-C]

NOTES

Basic meaning of root: to know

Many of the derivatives reflect such notions as gaining knowledge or awareness ("to experience," "to find out," "to identify," "to realize," "to recognize," "to distinguish"), causing or permitting a thing to be known ("to announce," "to testify," "to acknowledge," "to confess," "to profess"), etc.

A significant sub-group (identifiable by the expanded root-forms ЗНАК-ZNAK, ЗНАЧ-ZNACZ-ZNAČ) derives from Rus. знак et al. "sign; mark" (="that b which a thing is known"; compare Eng. note, ult. <Lat. nota "sign; mark; note" < [g]noscere "to know"). From the notions of marking, marking (or pointing) out and giving a sign have evolved such meanings as "to mean, signify" (see note on зна́чить et al. below), "to characterize," "to assign," "to appoint," "to designate," "to specify," "to distinguish" and "to destine, intend (for)." A second group of derivatives formed from the stem of Rus. зна́мя et al. and зна́мение et al. "(orig. =) sign; mark" shows much the same range of meanings. (Comparable semantic development is apparent in Eng. assign and designate [both ult. <Lat. signum "sign; mark"], Ger. bezeichnen "to characterize; to designate" and auszeichnen "to distinguish" [both <Zeichen "sign; mark"]; see also the notes on individual words below.)

A number of the derivatives have semantic parallels among the words listed under root $ВЕД_1$ (etc.).

The Slavic root is related to Eng. know, Ger. kennen "to know" (>sich bekennen "to confess; to profess," erkennen "to recognize"), Lat. (g)noscere (>Eng. notice, notion, cognizant, recognize, ignoramus, acquaintance), Gr. γιγνώσκειν "to know" (>Eng. gnostic, agnostic, diagnosis, prognosis).

znanost: See note on Cz. věda.

знать (n.), зна́тный: The same view of the nobility as comprising a group of well-known, prominent persons is reflected in Eng. noble (ult. <Lat. [g]noscere "to know").

зна́харь-znachor: orig. "wise man, magician"; compare Rus. ве́дьма et al., S-C vještac.

знато́к et al.: Compare Eng. connoisseur (ult. <Lat. [g]noscere "to know"), Ger. Kenner "expert; connoisseur" (<kennen "to know").

зна́чить et al.: See the introductory note above and compare Eng. signify (ult. <Lat. signum "sign; mark"), denote (ult. <Lat. nota "sign; mark; note") and betoken (<token), Du. betekenen "to mean" (<teken "sign; mark"), Hung. jelenteni "to mean" (<jel "sign; mark"), Fin. merkitä "to mean" (<merkki "sign; mark") and Gr. σημαίνειν "to mean" (<σῆμα "sign; mark"), whence Eng. semantics.

знамена́тель: The denominator "marks," i.e. indicates, the parts into which the unit is divided; see note on Cz. jmenovatel et al.

bliskoznaczny: The first element is from bliski "near."

dwuznaczny-dvojznačný: See note on Rus. двусмы́сленный et al.

языкозна́ние-językoznawstwo: The first element is from язы́к-język "language"; see note on Rus. языкове́дение, Cz. jazykověda.

любозна́тельный: See note on Cz. vědychtivý.

ludoznawstwo: Compare Ger. Völkerkunde "ethnology" (<Volk "people, nation" + Kunde "knowledge" < kennen "to know"), Rus. народове́дение.

radoznao: The first element is from rad "glad"; see note on Cz. vědychtivý.

rzeczoznawca: Compare Ger. Sachkenner "expert" (<Sache "thing; affair,

matter, business" + kennen "to know").

významosloví: See význam and note under root СЛЫ (etc.).

znatiželjan: The second element is from željeti "to wish"; see note on Cz. vědychtivý.

zvjezdoznanstvo: The first element is from zvijezda "star"; compare Ger. Sternkunde "astronomy" (⟨Stern "star" + Kunde "knowledge" ⟨ kennen "to know").

obneznaniti (obeznaniti) se: In the second of the two forms, the first n has been lost through dissimilation.

poznámka: Compare Eng. mark and remark, Ger. Bemerkung "remark" (⟨Marke "mark"), Rus. замечáние "remark" (⟨мéтить "to mark").

przyznać-přiznati: The second meaning reflects the notion of acknowledging or recognizing a person's entitlement to a thing; compare Ger. zuerkennen "to award" (⟨zu "to" + erkennen "to recognize").

признáтельный: ="acknowledging, recognizing (someone's kindness, etc.)" compare Fr. reconnaissant "grateful" (⟨reconnaître "to recognize"), Ger. erkenntlich "grateful" (⟨erkennen "to recognize").

seznam: Compare Ger. Verzeichnis "list" (⟨Zeichen "sign; mark").

ЗР, ЗИР, ЗЕР, ЗОР	JRZ, ZR, ZDR, ZIER, ZER, ZWIER, ZÓR, ZOR(Z)	ZŘ, ZR, ZÍR, ZOR	ZR, ZIR, ZOR
зреть (arch.): to see		zříti (lit.): to see	zreti (arch.): to see
		zírati (lit.): to stare	zirati: to squint
	zerknąć, zerkać: to peep, glance		zirnuti, zirkati: to peep, glance
			zrikati: to squint
зря (coll.): to no purpose, for nothing, aimlessly; in vain			
зрéние: eyesight; view, vision			
		zor (lit.): look, glance	zor: opinion, view; intuition
зрéлище: sight, spectacle; show, theatrical performance			
[R]	[P]	[Cz]	[S-C]

[R]	[P]	[Cz]	[S-C]
зри́тель: spectator		zřetel: consideration, regard (for s.o. or s.th.)	
		zřítelnice: pupil (of the eye)	
зо́ркий: sharp-sighted; vigilant			
		zřejmý: obvious	
зри́тельный: visual; (anat.) optic	rzetelny: honest, honorable	zřetelný: clear, distinct; obvious	
зе́ркало, (arch.) зерца́ло: mirror	zwierciadło: mirror	zrcadlo: mirror	zrcalo: mirror
		zrak: eyesight; look, glance	zrak: air; ray
			zraka: ray
зрачо́к: pupil (of the eye)			zračak: small ray
			dalekozor: telescope
кругозо́р: field of vision; mental horizon, outlook			
лицезре́ть (arch.): to contemplate			
мировоззре́ние: ideology, Weltanschauung			
			mrtvozornik: coroner
	pierwowzór: prototype		
		pozoruhodnosti (pl.): sights (e.g. of a city)	
			sitnozor: microscope
умозре́ние: speculation, theorizing			
			zrakoplov: dirigible; balloon
			zrakoplovstvo: aeronautics
беспризо́рник: homeless child, waif			

дозо́р: patrol	dozór: supervision	dozor: supervision	
		názor: opinion, view	nazor: opinion, view
		názorný: graphic, clear	
надзо́р: supervision	nadzór: supervision		nadzor: supervision
	niedozór: oversight, inadvertence		
необозри́мый: vast, boundless	nieprzejrzany: vast, boundless; pitch-dark, impenetrable	nedozírný: vast, boundless	
невзира́я (на + acc.): in spite (of)			
невзра́чный: unsightly, unattractive			
обзо́р: survey; field of vision		obzor: horizon	obzor, obzorje: field of vision
			obzir: consideration, regard (for s.o. or s.th.); regard, respect (e.g. s obzirom na: with regard, respect to)
		obezřelý, obezřetný: cautious, circumspect; provident	obazriv, obziran: cautious, circumspect; considerate, thoughtful (of others)
озорно́й: mischievous, naughty			
позо́р: shame, disgrace	pozór: (outward) appearance; pretext	pozor: attention	pozor: attention
			pozorište: theater
			pozornica: stage (in a theater)
подозрева́ть: to suspect	podejrzewać: to suspect	podezírati (podezřívati): to suspect	podozrijevati: to suspect
	prawzór: prototype	pravzor: prototype	prauzor: prototype
[R]	[P]	[Cz]	[S-C]

[R]	[P]	[Cz]	[S-C]
презре́ть, презира́ть: to despise, scorn		přezírati: to despise, scorn	prezreti, prezirati: to despise, scorn
призре́ние (arch.): charitable care			prizrenje: obligingness, attentiveness
			prizor: sight, spectacle; scene (part of a play)
при́зрак: specter, apparition		přízrak: specter, apparition	
		průzor: peephole	prozor: window
прозорли́вый: perspicacious, sagacious	przezorny: cautious, circumspect; provident		
	przejrzysty: transparent	prozíravý, prozřetelný: provident	proziran: transparent
		prozřetelnost: providence; (rel., cap.) Providence	
прозра́чный: transparent	przezroczysty: transparent	průzračný: transparent	prozračan: transparent
созерца́ть: to contemplate			
	spojrzeć, spozierać: to look		
узо́р: pattern, design			
	*upozorować: to try to justify, give a pretext for (s.th.)	upozorniti, upozorňovati: to draw s.o.'s attention (to s.th.); to warn	upozoriti, upozoravati: to draw s.o.'s attention (to s.th.); to warn
взор: look, glance	wzór: model; pattern, design; example; sample, specimen; formula	vzor: model; pattern, design; example	uzor: model; example
	wzorowy: exemplary, model	vzorný: exemplary, model	uzoran, uzorit: exemplary, model
	wzorzec: standard	vzorec: formula	
	wzrok: look, glance; eyesight		
	wzrokowy: visual; (anat.) optic		

[R]	[P]	[Cz]	[S-C]
воззре́ние (lit.): opinion, view		vzezření: (outward) appearance	
зазо́р: clearance (in machinery); (coll.) shame, disgrace			zazor: aversion, repugnance; shame, disgrace
	zazdrość: envy; jealousy		
		zázrak: miracle	

NOTES

Basic meaning of root: to see

Many of the derivatives have semantic counterparts among the words listed under roots ГЛЯД (etc.), МОТР (etc.), PATR(Z) (etc.) and ВИД (etc.). (See the introductory note on root ВИД [etc.].)

The expanded Russian forms ЗРАК and ЗРАЧ are of Church Slavic origin. The Polish form JRZ is a corruption of earlier ŹRZ. (See note on зреть et al. below.)

зреть et al.: Pol. źrzeć is obsolete.

zírati-zirati: iterative forms of zříti-zreti; Rus. зира́ть and Pol. zierać are obsolete.

зря: orig. the present adverbial participle of зреть; the sense of the word has been variously explained as "looking on but doing nothing" and "at a glance, i.e. by guesswork, without reflection."

rzetelny: borrowed (in the earlier form źrzetelny) from Cz. zřetelný; the present meaning reflects the notion of moral "clarity," i.e. candor, sincerity, honesty.

зе́ркало et al.: Compare Eng. mirror (ult. <VLat. mirare "to look"), Ger. Spiegel "mirror" (ult. <Lat. specere "to look"), S-C ogledalo. Rus. зерца́ло is a Church Slavic borrowing; the present spelling of the Polish word (for earlier zierciadło) shows the influence of wiercić "to turn, twirl."

zrak (S-C), zraka: The original meaning of zrak was "brightness, light," whence the present meanings of the two words.

dalekozor: The first element is from dalek "distant"; see note on Cz. dalekohled.

кругозо́р: See note under root КРУГ (etc.).

мировоззре́ние: See воззре́ние and note under root МИР (etc.).

mrtvozornik: See note under root $МЕР_2$ (etc.).

pierwowzór: The first element is from the root of pierwszy "first"; see wzór and note on Rus. первоо́браз.

pozoruhodnosti: See pozor and compare Ger. Sehenswürdigkeiten "sights"

(<*sehen* "to see" + *würdig* "worthy").

sitnozor: The first element is from *sitan* "small"; see note on Cz. *drobnohled*.

умозрéние: Compare Eng. *speculation* (ult. <Lat. *specere* "to look"), *theory* (ult. from the root of Gr. *θεᾶσθαι* "to see").

zrakoplov, *zrakoplovstvo*: See the first meaning of *zrak*.

беспризóрник: Compare *призрéние*.

nazor: <Cz. *názor*.

názorný: See note on Rus. *нагля́дный*.

необозри́мый et al.: See note on Cz. *nedohledný* and *nepřehledný*, S-C *nedogledan* and *nepregledan*, Rus. *неогля́дный*.

невзирáя: See note on Cz. *nehledě*, *nehledíc*.

obzor (S-C): <Rus. *обзóр* or Cz. *obzor*.

obzir: See note on Cz. *ohled*.

obezřelý et al.: See note on Pol. *oględny*.

озорнóй: The underlying notion is that of shameful behavior; see next note.

позóр: orig. "spectacle," then "shameful spectacle."

pozorište: Compare Eng. *theater* (ult. from the root of Gr. *θεᾶσθαι* "to see"), Cz. *divadlo* "theater" (<*dívati se* "to look").

подозревáть et al.: ="to look (at s.o.) stealthily or askance"; compare Eng. *suspect* (ult. <Lat. *sub* "under" + *specere* "to look"), Gr. *ὑποπτεύειν* "to suspect" (<*ὑπό* "under" + *ὀπτεύειν* "to see"). The Serbo-Croatian word is borrowed from Russian.

prawzór et al.: See *wzór et al.* and note on Rus. *первоóбраз*.

презрéть et al.: ="to look down upon"; compare Eng. *despise* (ult. <Lat. *de* "down" + *specere* "to look"). The Russian words are borrowed from Church Slavic.

призрéние-prizrenje: The underlying idea is that of looking after someone, seeing to someone's wants; the Russian word is a Church Slavic borrowing.

прозорли́вый: Compare Eng. *perspicacious* (ult. <Lat. *per* "through" + *specere* "to look").

przezorny, *prozíravý*, *prozřetelný*: Compare Eng. *provident* (ult. <Lat. *pro* "before" + *videre* "to see"), Ger. *vorsichtig* "cautious" (<*vor* "before" + *Sicht* "sight").

przejrzysty-proziran, *прозрáчный et al.*: Compare Ger. *durchsichtig* "transparent" (<*durch* "through" + *Sicht* "sight"), Cz. *průhledný*, S-C *providan*.

prozřetelnost: See *prozřetelný* and note on Rus. *Провидéние*, S-C *Providenje*.

созерцáть: borrowed from Church Slavic.

узóр: See note on *wzór et al.*, *wzorzec-vzorec*.

upozorować et al.: See *pozór et al.*

wzór et al., wzorzec-vzorec: ="a thing to be looked at"; compare Eng. specimen (ult. ⟨Lat. specere "to look"), S-C ogled, ugled. Cz. vzor is borrowed from Polish, S-C uzor from Czech.

зазóр-zazor: Regarding the meanings "shame" and "aversion," see note on позóр; the first meaning of the Russian word reflects the notion of "a space through which one can see."

zazdrość: for earlier zazrość; see note on Rus. зáвисть et al.

zázrak: variously explained as referring to a thing which is "out of sight" (za zrakem), i.e. beyond one's ken, supernatural, or to something "which is seen, which manifests itself"; the second explanation suggests semantic development similar to that of Gr. θαῦμα "miracle" (from the root of θεᾶσθαι "to see"), whence Eng. thaumaturgy.

ЗВ, ЗЫВ, ЗОВ	ZW, ZEW, ZOW	ZV, ZEV	ZV, ZIV, ZOV
звать: to call, summon; to call, name; to invite	zwać: to call, name; (arch.) to call, summon	zváti: to invite; (lit.) to call, name	zvati: to call, summon; to call, name; to invite
звáние: rank, title		zvaní: invitation	zvanje: (act of) calling; occupation, profession; official position, post
			zvaničan: official (a.)
звáтельный: (gram.) vocative			
			mirozov: tattoo (bugle call)
		názvosloví: terminology, nomenclature	
самозвáнец: impostor	samozwaniec: impostor	samozvanec: impostor; usurper	samozvanac: impostor; uninvited guest
			dozivalo: megaphone
			izazov: challenge; provocation
			izazivanje: challenge; provocation; (phot.) development
[R]	[P]	[Cz]	[S-C]

[R]	[P]	[Cz]	[S-C]
назва́ние: name, designation	nazwa, nazwanie: name, designation	název: name, designation; term	naziv: name, designation; term
	nazwisko: surname	názvisko (arch.): nickname	
			nazivlje: terminology, nomenclature
			nazivnik: (math.) denominator
	nieodzowny: inevitable; essential, indispensable		
			ozivi (pl.): marriage banns
			opozvati, opozivati: to revoke, repeal, cancel; to recall (e.g. an ambassador); to retract, recant
отзы́в: recall (e.g. of an ambassador)			
о́тзыв: response; reference, testimonial; review (of a book)	odzew: response		odziv: response; echo
	odezwa: proclamation; appeal	odezva: response	
отзы́вчивый: responsive, sympathetic			
позы́в: urge, inclination	pozew: summons, subpoena		poziv: call, summons; invitation; summons, subpoena; vocation, calling; occupation, profession
	przezwisko: nickname	přízvisko: nickname	
призы́в: appeal; (mil.) call-up			priziv: appeal (against a judicial decision)
призва́ние: vocation, calling; mission, appointed task			

3B

прозва́ние, про́звище: nickname			
	wezwanie: call, summons; summons, subpoena		
вызов: call, summons; challenge; provocation; summons, subpoena		výzva: call, summons; challenge; provocation; proclamation; appeal; (mil.) call-up	
	wyzwanie: challenge; provocation	vyzvání: challenge; provocation; appeal	
	wyzwisko: term of abuse		
воззва́ние: proclamation; appeal			
[R]	[P]	[Cz]	[S-C]

NOTES

Basic meaning of root: to call

Many of the derivatives show semantic parallels with those listed under root WOŁ-VOL.

зва́ние: Compare назва́ние.

zvanje, zvaničan: See note on poziv, призва́ние and compare Hung. hivatal "official position, post" and hivatalos "official" (both <hívni "to call").

зва́тельный: modeled on Lat. vocativus (<vocare "to call") and Gr. κλητική (<καλεῖν "to call"); the vocative case denotes that which is called or addressed. Compare Pol. wołacz.

mirozov: See note under root МИР (etc.).

názvosloví: See název and compare Eng. terminology (<Middle Lat. terminus "term" + Eng. -logy, referred to in the introductory note on root СЛЫ [etc.]), nomenclature (ult. <Lat. nomen "name" + calare "to call").

izazov, izazivanje: Compare Eng. provocation (ult. <Lat. pro- "forth, forward" + vocare "to call").

nazivlje: See naziv and note on názvosloví.

nazivnik: See naziv and note on Cz. jmenovatel et al.

nieodzowny: orig. "irrevocable"; compare Eng. irrevocable (ult. <Lat. in- "un-, not" + re- "back" + vocare "to call").

opozvati: Compare Eng. revoke (ult. <Lat. re- "back" + vocare "to

call") and repeal (<OFr. rapeler "to call back"), Pol. odwołać, Cz. odvolati.

о́тзыв et al., odezva, отзы́вчивый: The prefix gives rise to the notion of "calling back (to s.o.)," hence responding; see note on S-C odgovoriti.

позы́в: orig. "call, summons."

poziv (fourth and fifth meanings), призва́ние: The notion of being "called" and hence having a "calling" is an originally religious concept which ultimately came to be applied to any pursuit or occupation to which an individual felt himself drawn; compare Eng. vocation (ult. <Lat. vocare "to call"), Ger. Beruf "vocation, calling; occupation, profession" (<rufen "to call"), Hung. hivatás "vocation, calling; occupation, profession" (<hívni "to call"), Pol. powołanie, Cz. povolání and see note on zvanje, zvaničan above.

přízvisko: pří- <OCz. přie- (=pře-).

вы́зов-výzva, wyzwanie-vyzvání: See note on izazov, izazivanje.

ЖИ(В)	ŻY(W), GO(I), HOJ	ŽI(V), ŽÍ, HOJ	ŽI(V), GOJ
жить: to live	żyć: to live	žíti: to live	živjeti: to live
живо́й: living, live, alive; lively	żywy: living, live, alive; lively	živý: living, live, alive; lively	živ: living, live, alive; lively
живи́ть (lit.): to enliven	żywić: to feed; to cherish (a hope), nurse (a grievance)	živiti: to feed; to support (one's family); to cherish (a hope), nurse (a grievance)	
	goić: to heal (tr.)	hojiti: to heal (tr.)	gojiti: to grow (crops), breed (cattle), rear (children); to fatten (tr.); to cherish (a hope), nurse (a grievance)
	hojny: generous	hojný: abundant, plentiful	gojan, gojazan: fat, stout
живо́т: belly, abdomen; (arch.) life	żywot (arch.): life; womb	život: life; (coll.) belly, abdomen	život: life
живо́тик (coll.): little belly, tummy		živůtek: bodice; vest	
житьё (coll.), житие́ (arch.): life	życie: life	žití: life	žiće: life
жизнь: life			
жили́ще: dwelling, living quarters			
[R]	[P]	[Cz]	[S-C]

жи́тель: inhabitant, resident			žitelj: inhabitant, resident
жи́то: grain	żyto: rye	žito: rye	žito: grain
	żyzny: fertile		
живо́тное: animal			životinja: animal
		živočich: animal	
		živina: nutriment	živina: animal; cattle; poultry
			živad: poultry
			živež: food
жи́вность (coll.): poultry	żywność: food	živnost: trade, business, occupation	
			živica: hedge
живе́ц: live bait	żywiec: live bait; lively person	živec: feldspar	živac: nerve
			živa: mercury, quicksilver
	żywioł: element	živel: element	
	życzyć: to wish		
	życzliwy: benevolent, kindly disposed		
			dvoživac: amphibian (n.)
местожи́тельство: residence, domicile			
	nowożytny: modern		
		obojživelník: amphibian (n.)	
общежи́тие: dormitory; social life			
			*oživotvoriti: to bring about, effect, accomplish
			samoživ: selfish
жи́вопись: painting, pictorial art			živopis: painting, pictorial art
		živočichopis: zoology	
жизнеописа́ние: biography		životopis: biography	životopis: biography
	żywopłot: hedge		
[R]	[P]	[Cz]	[S-C]

[R]	[P]	[Cz]	[S-C]
	życiorys: biography		
			doživljaj: adventure
	dożywocie: life annuity		
изжи́ть, изжива́ть: to get rid of, overcome (defects, shortcomings, etc.)			
иждиве́ние: maintenance, support (of a financial dependent)			
нажи́ва: gain, profit			
нажи́вка: bait			
	nadużyć, nadużywać: to abuse, misuse	nadužíti, nadužívati: to abuse, misuse	
	nieżyt: catarrh	nežit: abscess, boil	
		neštovice (pl.): smallpox	
			ožiljak: scar
			odgoj: education
па́жить (arch.): pasture		pažit: lawn	
пожило́й: elderly			
			požiljak: scar
		poživatiny (pl.): foodstuffs	
	pożytek: benefit, advantage	požitek: enjoyment	
пожи́тки (pl.): belongings		požitky (pl.): income	
	pożyczyć, pożyczać: to lend; to borrow	půjčiti, půjčovati: to lend	
	podżyły: elderly		
			praživotinja: protozoan (n.)
пережива́ние: (an) experience	przeżycie: (an) experience; survival		
пережи́ток: relic, vestige, survival	przeżytek: relic, vestige, survival	přežitek: relic, vestige, survival	

приживáльщик: parasite, sponger		příživník: parasite (biol.); parasite, sponger	
		prožitek: (an) experience	
	spożyć, spożywać: to consume (goods); to eat, consume		
	użyć, używać: to use; to enjoy	užíti, užívati: to use; to enjoy	uživati: to use; (u + loc.) to enjoy
	użytek: use	užitek: benefit, advantage	užitak: enjoyment
	użyczyć, użyczać: to grant, accord, bestow		
		vžitý: deep-rooted	
		vyžilý: worn out by dissipation; blasé	
		výživné: alimony	
		zneužíti, zneužívati: to abuse, misuse	
	zużyć, zużywać: to consume (fuel, energy, time, etc.); to use; to use up, wear out		
зажи́ть, заживáть: to heal (intr.)	zażyć, zażywać: to take (medicine, snuff, etc.); to enjoy; to experience	zažíti, zažívati: to digest; to experience	
	zażyły: intimate, familiar		
зажи́точный: prosperous, well-to-do	zażywny: fat, stout	záživný: digestible	
[R]	[P]	[Cz]	[S-C]

NOTES

Basic meaning of root: to live

Many of the derivatives reflect the notion of health and physical well-being (whence the meanings "to heal," "scar" [="place where a wound has healed"], "fat, stout" and "fertile") or the logically related idea of material advantage and prosperity (apparent in such meanings as "to use" [>further "to consume," "to eat," "to digest," "pasture"], "to enjoy," "gain, profit" and "abundant"). The view of food as a means of sustaining life is reflected in a number of words (with semantic specialization evident in the meanings "grain" and "bait"), as it is in Eng. victuals and viand (both ult. <Lat. vivere "to live"), Ger. Lebensmittel "food" (<Leben "life" + Mittel "means"), Hung. élelem "food" (<élni "to live").

Живи́ть et al. and goić et al. (the latter retaining an unpalatalized initial consonant before a back vowel) are causative formations with the basic meaning "to cause or enable to live."

The Slavic root is akin to Eng. quick (the original meaning of which survives chiefly in a few phrases like the quick and the dead), Lat. vivere "to live" (>Eng. vivid, vivacious, revive, survive) and vita "life" (>Eng. vital), Gr. ζῆν "to live," ζῷον "animal" (>Eng. zoology) and βίος "life" (>Eng. biology).

živjeti: for earlier žiti.

goić et al.: Rus. го́ить "to shelter, tend, take care of" survives only in dialect.

hojny: <Cz. hojný.

живо́т-żywot-život (Cz.): The original meaning in all three cases was "life"; compare Ger. Leib "body; belly, abdomen; womb" (orig. "life").

živůtek: a diminutive of život in the second sense of the word; compare Eng. bodice (<body), Ger. Leibchen "bodice; vest" (dim. of Leib "body; belly, abdomen").

житие́, жили́ще: borrowed from Church Slavic.

живо́тное-životinja, živočich, živina (S-C), živad: Regarding the meaning, see reference to Gr. ζῷον in the introductory note above and compare Fin. eläin "animal" (<elää "to live"); the Russian word is a Church Slavic borrowing.

жи́вность: orig. "food."

živnost: Compare Eng. livelihood and (to earn one's) living.

živica: Compare żywopłot.

živec: The meaning has been attributed to the mineral's property of readily breaking apart and its variable appearance as well as to the fact that it provides sustenance for plants.

živa: so called because of its fluidity; compare Eng. quicksilver, in which quick = "living, live" (see the introductory note above).

żywioł-živel: The "elements" (fire, air, water and earth) were conceived of by the early philosophers as the basic substances or principles to which all forms of life or existence could be reduced.

życzyć: orig. "to wish (s.o.) well"; the word arose from pożyczyć through loss of the prefix at a time when the latter word meant "to bestow."

życzliwy: <życzyć; see preceding note.

dvoživac: See note on obojživelník.

nowożytny: The first element is from nowy "new."

obojživelník: The first element is from oba "both"; compare Eng. amphibian (ult. <Gr. ἀμφί- "both" + βίος "life"), S-C dvoživac above.

жи́вопись-živopis: See note under root ПИС (etc.).

živočichopis: See živočich.

жизнеописа́ние-životopis (Cz.-S-C): See жизнь, život (Cz.-S-C) and note under root ПИС (etc.).

żywopłot: The second element is from płot "fence."

życiorys: See życie; the second element is from rysować "to draw, sketch."

иждиве́ние: ult. <Ch. Sl. иждити "to spend" (="to live through," i.e. go through, a sum of money) < earlier изжити; compare Rus. изжи́ть.

nieżyt-nežit: ="something inimical to life and health."

neštovice: <earlier nežitovice < nežit.

odgoj: <gojiti.

pożyczyć-půjčiti: <*pożytczyć-požitčiti < pożytek-požitek; the original idea was that of "giving s.o. the use or benefit of s.th." without any obligation to return the thing given---a meaning still apparent in Pol. użyczyć. Regarding the contrasting meanings of pożyczyć, see note on S-C posuditi.

praživotinja: See životinja and compare Eng. protozoan (ult. <Gr. πρῶτος "first" + ζῷον "animal"), Ger. Urtierchen "protozoan" (<ur- "first, original" + Tier "animal").

пережива́ние-przeżycie: Compare Ger. Erlebnis "(an) experience" (<leben "to live").

прижива́льщик-příživník: A parasite "lives with" and feeds upon another organism (or person).

prožitek: See note on пережива́ние-przeżycie.

użyczyć: <*użytczyć < użytek.

výživné: See živiti and note on S-C prehrambina.

zażyć-zažíti: See note on пережива́ние-przeżycie.

zażyły: <obs. zażyć się "to be intimate, familiar (with)," which reflects the notion of "living oneself" into a close relationship with someone.

ЖР, ЖЕР, ЖОР, ГОР	ŻR, ŹR, ŻER, ŻAR, GAR	ŽR, ZŘ, ŽÍR, ŽER, HR	ŽDR, ŽDER, GR
жрать (coll.): to devour	żreć: to devour; to corrode, eat away	žráti: to devour; to corrode, eat away	žderati (ždrijeti): to devour
	żarłoczny: gluttonous	žravý: gluttonous	žderav: gluttonous
	żarłacz: shark	žralok: shark	
го́рло: throat	gardło: throat	hrdlo: throat	grlo: throat; gorge, ravine;
[R]	[P]	[Cz]	[S-C]

[R]	[P]	[Cz]	[S-C]
			muzzle (of a gun)
жерло́: crater (of a volcano); muzzle (of a gun)	źródło: spring (of water); source, origin	zřídlo: spring (of water)	ždrijelo, ždrlo: throat; chasm, abyss; gorge, ravine; crater (of a volcano); muzzle (of a gun)
		býložravý: herbivorous	biljožder: herbivorous
		darmožrout: parasite, sponger	
		kostižer: (med.) caries	kostožder: vulture
	ludożerca: cannibal	lidožrout: cannibal	ljudožder: cannibal
	mięsożerny: carnivorous	masožravý: carnivorous	mesožder: carnivorous
	roślinożerny: herbivorous		
	trawożerny: herbivorous		travožder: herbivorous
	wszystkożerny: omnivorous		svežder, svaštožder: omnivorous
		náhrdelník: necklace	
			ogrlica: necklace; collar
ожере́лье: necklace			oždrijelje: collar
обжо́рство: gluttony	obżarstwo: gluttony	obžerství: gluttony; drunkenness	
прожо́рливый: gluttonous			proždrljiv: gluttonous
		rozežrati, rozežírati (rozžírati): to corrode, eat away	
	wyżreć, wyżerać: to corrode, eat away; to erode; to devour	vyžrati, vyžírati: to corrode, eat away; to erode; to devour	
	zażarty: fierce, bitter	zažraný: inveterate, confirmed, habitual	

NOTES

Basic meaning of root: to devour

Many of the derivatives show semantic parallels with those listed under root Е(Д) (etc.).

The two groups го́рло et al. and жерло́ et al. are doublets, originally identical in meaning; in the first of the two, the initial consonant has remained unpalatalized before an original back vowel. The palatalized root-forms in Serbo-Croatian show an intrusive d throughout.

The Slavic root is cognate with Lat. vorare "to devour" (>Eng. voracious, devour, omnivorous, etc.).

żreć-žráti: See note on Rus. разъе́сть, S-C razjesti.

grlo, ždrijelo, ždrlo: Compare Eng. gorge (<Fr. gorge "throat").

źródło-zřídlo: for OPol. żrzódło, żródło, OCz. žřiedlo; regarding the second meaning of źródło, see note on Rus. исто́к and исто́чник, S-C istočnik.

kostižer-kostožder: The first element is from kost "bone."

mięsożerny et al.: The first element is from mięso-maso-meso "flesh; meat."

trawożerny-travožder: The first element is from trawa-trava "grass."

náhrdelník, ogrlica: <hrdlo, grlo.

ожере́лье-oždrijelje: <ORus. жерело "throat" (=жерло́) and ždrijelo.

rozežrati, wyżreć-vyžrati: See note on Rus. разъе́сть, S-C razjesti.

zażarty-zažraný: <zażreć się, orig. "to eat heartily, with abandon," and zažrati se "to eat in(to s.th.); to become absorbed (in s.th.)"; compare Rus. зая́длый, Pol. zajadły.

SELECTED BIBLIOGRAPHY

Russian

A. I. Smirnitsky. Russian-English Dictionary. New York, 1959.

V. K. Müller. Russian-English Dictionary. New York, 1944.

С. И. Ожегов. Словарь русского языка. Москва, 1960.

В. Даль. Толковый словарь живого великорусского языка. Петербург-Москва, 1903-09.

И. И. Срезневский. Материалы для словаря древне-русского языка. Петербург, 1893-1912.

M. Vasmer. Russisches etymologisches Wörterbuch. Heidelberg, 1953-58.

А. Преображенский. Этимологический словарь русского языка. Москва, 1910-14.

Н. М. Шанский, В. В. Иванов, Т. В. Шанская. Краткий этимологический словарь русского языка. Москва, 1961.

Н. М. Шанский. Этимологический словарь русского языка (А-В). Москва, 1963-68.

Н. Горяев. Сравнительный этимологический словарь литературного русского языка. Тбилиси, 1896.

Polish

K. Bulas, L. L. Thomas, F. J. Whitfield. The Kościuszko Foundation Dictionary, vol. II: Polish-English. The Hague, 1961.

J. Stanisławski. English-Polish and Polish-English Dictionary. New York.

D. Hessen, R. Stypuła. Wielki słownik polsko-rosyjski. Warszawa-Moskwa, 1967.

М. Ф. Розвадовская. Польско-русский словарь. Москва, 1958.

P. Kalina. Słownik podręczny niemiecko-polski i polsko-niemiecki. Warszawa, 1956.

P. Kalina. Słownik francusko-polski i polsko-francuski. Warszawa, 1956.

S. Szober. Słownik poprawnej polszczyzny. Warszawa, 1958.

J. Karłowicz, A. Kryński, W. Niedźwiedzki. Słownik języka polskiego. Warszawa, 1900-27.

A. Brückner. Słownik etymologiczny języka polskiego. Kraków, 1927.

F. Sławski. Słownik etymologiczny języka polskiego (A-łabędź). Kraków, 1952-73.

Czech

I. Poldauf. Czech-English Dictionary. Prague, 1959.

J. Procházka. English-Czech and Czech-English Dictionary. London, 1952.

А. И. Павлович. Чешско-русский словарь. Москва, 1959.

E. Melnikov, Z. Šromová, M. Martinková. Česko-ruský slovník. Praha, 1958.

F. Trávníček. Slovník jazyka českého. Praha, 1952.

Československá akademie věd. Slovník spisovného jazyka českého. Praha, 1960-71.

J. Gebauer. Slovník staročeský (A-netbalivost). Praha, 1903.

V. Machek. Etymologický slovník jazyka českého a slovenského. Praha, 1957.

J. Holub, F. Kopečný. Etymologický slovník jazyka českého. Praha, 1952.

N. Reiter. Die deutschen Lehnübersetzungen im Tschechischen. Berlin, 1953.

Serbo-Croatian

M. Drvodelić. Croato-Serbian-English Dictionary. Zagreb, 1961.

И. И. Толстой. Сербско-хорватско-русский словарь. Москва, 1958.

V. Frančić. Słownik serbochorwacko-polski. Warszawa, 1956.

A. Hurm. Hrvatskosrpsko-njemački rječnik. Zagreb, 1958.

A. P. Perić. Rečnik srpskohrvatsko-francuski. Beograd, 1959.

Jugoslavenska akademija znanosti i umjetnosti. Rječnik hrvatskoga ili srpskoga jezika (A-visokorođe). Zagreb, 1880-1972.

T. Maretić. "Ruske i češke riječi u književnom hrvatskom jeziku." Rad Jugoslavenske Akademije Znanosti i Umjetnosti (Zagreb), CVIII, 1892.

Other

F. Miklosich. Lexicon palaeoslovenico-graeco-latinum. Vienna, 1862-65.

E. Berneker. Slavisches etymologisches Wörterbuch (A-mor). Heidelberg, 1908-13.

F. Miklosich. Etymologisches Wörterbuch der slavischen Sprachen. Wien, 1886.

K. Sandfeld Jensen. "Notes sur les calques linguistiques." Festschrift Vilhelm Thomsen. Leipzig, 1912.

B. Unbegaun. "Le calque dans les langues slaves littéraires." Revue des études slaves (Paris), 12, 1932.

INDEX OF ROOT-FORMS

Listed below, together with page references, are the various forms assumed by the roots in the four languages. A limited number of expanded root-forms (e.g. Rus. БОРОН, ВЕСТ, ДЕЛ) which have taken on a more or less independent existence for purposes of word-formation are given in parentheses along with the primary forms.

Russian

Polish

Czech

Serbo-Croatian

PARTIAL INDEX OF WORDS

Listed below, together with page references, are words containing root-forms which are not readily recognizable (either because of distortion or because of their position in relation to other elements in the word) and are in some instances not included in the index of root-forms.

Russian

Polish

Czech

Serbo-Croatian

DEMCO

FOR REFERENCE

Do Not Take From This Room

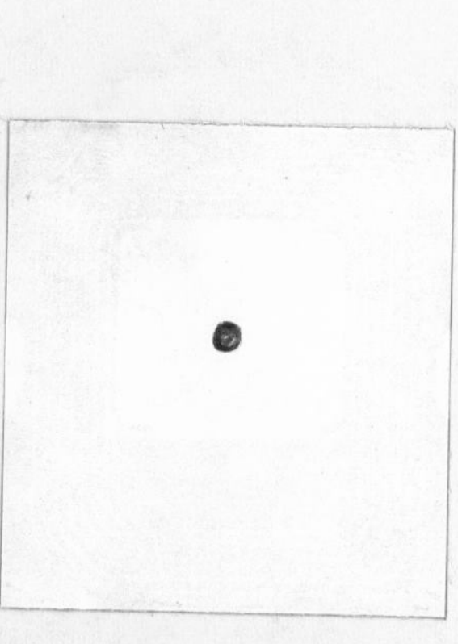